Windows® 11

ALL-IN-ONE

2nd Edition

by Ciprian Adrian Rusen

Windows® 11 All-in-One For Dummies®, 2nd Edition

Published by: **John Wiley & Sons, Inc.,** 111 River Street, Hoboken, NJ 07030-5774, www.wiley.com

Published simultaneously in Canada

For general information on our other products and services, please contact our Customer Care Department within the U.S. at 877-762-2974, outside the U.S. at 317-572-3993, or fax 317-572-4002. For technical support, please visit https://hub.wiley.com/community/support/dummies.

Wiley publishes in a variety of print and electronic formats and by print-on-demand. Some material included with standard print versions of this book may not be included in e-books or in print-on-demand. If this book refers to media that is not included in the version you purchased, you may download this material at http://booksupport.wiley.com. For more information about Wiley products, visit www.wiley.com.

Library of Congress Control Number is available from the publisher.

ISBN 978-1-394-27688-2 (pbk); ISBN 978-1-394-27690-5 (ebk); ISBN 978-1-394-27689-9 (ebk)

SKY10094742_123024

Table of Contents

Introduction

Welcome to *Windows 11 All-in-One For Dummies*, 2nd Edition, a comprehensive guide to the latest version of Windows. This book stands out for its detailed yet friendly approach, making it the perfect companion for your transition from Windows 10 to Windows 11. It's not just a heavy book; it's a source of knowledge that will equip you with a deep understanding of Windows 11 and its many apps, tools, and features.

If you're new to Windows, this book is a great guide to understanding Windows 11 and how its most important features work. If you read this book in its entirety, you'll learn everything you need to know about this operating system — and quite a bit more than most people. You won't become a tech support expert by the end of it, but you'll surely know enough to help others as well, especially when they're puzzled about the things Windows 11 can and can't do.

About This Book

Windows 11 All-in-One For Dummies starts with the basics about navigating Windows 11: turning your PC on and off, signing in to Windows, handling notifications, user accounts, and permissions. Then I dig into the desktop and the Start menu and take you through all the important features, one by one, in detail.

Using simple language as much as possible, I provide in-depth information to make you a proficient Windows 11 user. Additionally, I address common issues, highlight important technical aspects, and provide assistance where you need it the most.

Whether you want to get two or more email accounts set up to work simultaneously, personalize your Start menu, or learn the best way to protect your PC from viruses, this is your book. Or should I say ten books? The topics are divided into ten minibooks so you can easily navigate to a topic. The book wasn't designed to be read from front to back. It's a reference. Each chapter and section focuses on solving a particular problem or describing a specific Windows feature. However, I recommend reading the introductory chapters in Book 1 before skipping to those you find interesting.

Foolish Assumptions

I don't make many assumptions about you, dear reader, except to acknowledge that you're intelligent, well-informed, and of impeccable taste. That's why you chose this book, right?

On a more serious note, this book is suitable for both beginners and experienced users who want to learn about Windows 11 in more depth. I assume you already know how to use a mouse and keyboard and are familiar with navigating the web, launching apps, and using copy-and-paste operations.

I don't assume you're a hardware enthusiast, a hardcore gamer, or a software developer, even though I include content that may also be useful for such audiences. *Windows 11 All-in-One For Dummies* was written to be accessible to everyone dealing with Windows 11 computers and devices. Basically, anyone with a minimal knowledge of computers, smartphones, and other gadgets should be able to read, understand, and follow the instructions I provide.

Icons Used in This Book

Some of the points in *Windows 11 All-in-One For Dummies* merit your special attention. I set off these points with icons as follows.

TIP

This icon signals information that makes using Windows 11 easier. When browsing through the chapters of this book, I highly recommend reading the tips. I'm sure you'll appreciate most of them.

REMEMBER

It's a good idea to carefully read the text marked with this icon and remember it while using Windows 11. You can also dog-ear the pages in this book where they appear to have an easier time finding them later when needed.

WARNING

Anywhere you see a warning icon, you can be sure it's important. Please pay attention, and most of all, don't do the opposite of what I recommend unless you want to get into trouble.

TECHNICAL STUFF

This is where the technical stuff comes in. Most people won't need this information, but more knowledgeable users will appreciate it, especially if those who want to delve deeper into Windows.

Beyond the Book

When I wrote the first edition of this book, I covered the initial release of Windows 11, dated October 5, 2021. For *Windows 11 All-in-One For Dummies,* 2nd Edition, I used Windows 11 version 24H2, dated September 2024. At the time of writing, 24H2 is the latest major update for Windows 11, introducing significant changes to the original Windows 11. To keep things interesting, Microsoft promises to keep Windows 11 updated for a few more years. Therefore, for details about significant updates or changes that occur between editions of this book, go to `www.dummies.com`, search for *Windows 11 All-in-One For Dummies,* and view this book's dedicated page.

In addition, the cheat sheet for this book has handy Windows shortcuts and tips on other cool features worth checking out. To get to the cheat sheet, go to `www.dummies.com`, and type *Windows 11 All-in-One For Dummies Cheat Sheet* in the Search box.

Where to Go from Here

That's about it. It's time for you to turn the page and start reading. Begin with the first minibook for an overview of what you can expect from Windows 11, details about Microsoft's design philosophy for Windows 11, and information about the various editions and versions of Windows 11. This is a great starting point. After that, look at the table of contents and decide where to go next.

REMEMBER

Don't forget to bookmark `www.digitalcitizen.life`. I'm the chief editor of this website. My team and I keep you updated on all the Windows 11 stuff you need to know — tutorials about the latest features and updates, fixes to annoying problems, reviews about the latest gadgets, and much more.

And if you want to contact me for advice about all things Windows, you'll find me at `ciprianrusen@digitalcitizen.ro`. Sometimes, it's worth reading the Introduction, isn't it?

1 Getting Started with Windows 11

Contents at a Glance

IN THIS CHAPTER

» Understanding what counts as hardware and what is software

» Seeing Windows's place in the grand scheme of things

» Defining important technical terms

» Buying a Windows 11 computer

» Checking whether your old computer can run Windows 11

» Learning about the most important Windows 11 annoyances

Chapter 1 Introducing Windows 11

We all started as newbies who did not know much about technology. If you've never used an earlier version of Windows, you're in luck because you won't have to force your brain to forget so much of what you've learned! Windows 11 is a mix of Windows 10 and macOS, tossed into a blender, speed turned up to full, and poured out on your screen.

Although Windows 10 was a major improvement over Windows 8 and 8.1, some people still had problems understanding and using features such as tiles, Microsoft Store apps, Cortana, or the Settings app. Windows 11 makes the experience a bit gentler for everyone. It also further optimizes the touchscreen approach so that it works well with a mouse, too. The user interface is more consistent — it doesn't look like the old desktop — and the new touchscreen approach is designed a lot better than in older versions of Windows.

Some of you are reading this book because you chose to run Windows 11. Others are here because Windows 11 came preinstalled on a new computer or because your company forced you to upgrade to Windows 11. Whatever the reason, you've ended up with a solid operating system that should serve you well, as long as you understand and respect its limitations. However, you should know that other choices are available, and I present them in this chapter. Who knows, maybe you're considering returning your new Windows 11 PC already.

Before I get technical, I want you to take a quick look at Windows 11. Then, I explain some important technical terminology and give an overview of what you need to keep in mind when buying your first Windows 11 PC, laptop, or tablet. And for those considering upgrading an old PC to Windows 11, I share how to check for compatibility. Lastly, I describe what you might not like about Windows 11. It's better to know all that sooner rather than later. Right?

Taking Your First Look at Windows 11

First things first. Position yourself in front of your computer and press the power button to turn it on. This thing called Windows 11 will load and then be staring at you, as shown in Figure 1-1. Microsoft named this the lock screen, and it doesn't say *Windows,* much less *Windows 11.* The lock screen displays a picture (Microsoft sets one for you automatically, but you can change it, as described in Book 2 Chapter 2), the current date and time, with a tiny icon or two to indicate whether your Wi-Fi or wired connection is working and how much battery you have left. At the bottom of the lock screen, you may also see widgets displaying things like weather forecasts, sports, or stock market data.

FIGURE 1-1: The Windows 11 lock screen.

You may be tempted to sit and admire the gorgeous picture, whatever it may be, but if you swipe up from the bottom, click or tap anywhere on the picture, or press any key on your keyboard, you see the sign-in screen, resembling the one in Figure 1-2.

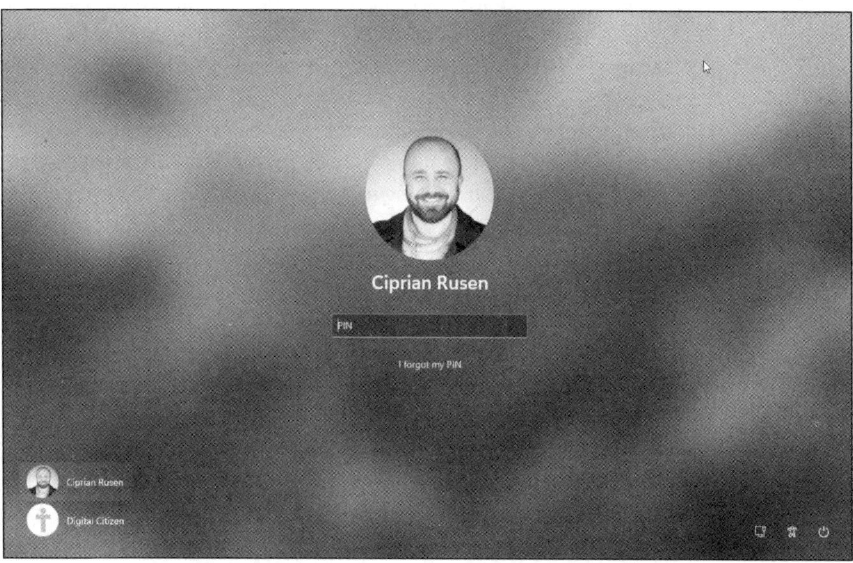

FIGURE 1-2: The Windows 11 sign-in screen.

The sign-in screen doesn't say *Login, Welcome to Windows 11,* or *Howdy.* If more than one person is set up to use your computer, you'll see more than one name listed in the bottom-left corner. In the bottom-right corner, additional icons show up for enabling accessibility tools (like the onscreen keyboard, narrator, magnifier, and voice access) and opening the power menu.

Hardware versus Software

At the most fundamental level, computers are about two things: hardware and software. *Hardware* is anything you can touch — a computer screen, a mouse, a hard drive, a keyboard, a USB flash drive, and so on. *Software* is everything else: your Microsoft Edge browser, the movies you stream on Netflix, the digital pictures of your last vacation, and programs such as Office or Teams. If you shoot a bunch of pictures, the pictures themselves are just bits — software. But they're probably sitting on a memory card inside your smartphone or digital camera. That memory card is hardware. Get the difference?

Windows 11 is software. You can't touch it in a physical sense, even if you interact with it using the keyboard and a mouse or a touchscreen. Your PC, on the other hand, is hardware. Kick the computer screen, and your toe hurts. Drop the big box on the floor, and it smashes into pieces. That's hardware.

Chances are that one of the major PC manufacturers — such as Lenovo, HP, Dell, Acer, or ASUS — Microsoft, with its Surface line, or even Apple made your hardware. However, Microsoft, and Microsoft alone, makes Windows 11.

When you bought your computer, you paid for a license to use one copy of Windows on that PC. Its manufacturer paid Microsoft a royalty to sell Windows and the PC to you. (That royalty may have been close to zero dollars, but it's a royalty nonetheless.) You may think that you got Windows from, say, Lenovo — indeed, you may have to contact Lenovo for technical support on Windows questions — but Windows came from Microsoft.

If you upgraded from Windows 10 to Windows 11, you might have received a free upgrade license — but it's still a license, whether you paid for it or not. You can't give it away to someone else.

REMEMBER

Most software, including Windows 11, requires you to agree to an End User License Agreement (EULA). When you first set up your PC, Windows asks you to click or tap the Accept button to accept a licensing agreement that's long enough to reach the top of the Empire State Building. If you're curious about what agreement you accepted, take a look at the official EULA repository at `www.microsoft.com/en-us/Useterms/Retail/Windows/11/UseTerms_Retail_Windows_11_English.htm`.

Must You Run Windows?

Are you wondering if you must run Windows? The short answer is that you don't have to run Windows on your PC.

The PC you have is a dumb box. (You needed me to tell you that, eh?) To get that box to do anything worthwhile, you need a computer program that takes control of the PC and makes it do things, such as show apps on the screen, respond to mouse clicks, and print resumes. An *operating system* controls the dumb box and makes it do worthwhile things in ways people can understand.

Without an operating system, the computer can sit in a corner and display profound messages on the screen, such as *Operating System not found* or *BootDevice Not Found.* You need an operating system if you want your computer to do more than that.

REMEMBER

Windows is not the only operating system in town. The other big contenders in the PC-like operating system market are the following:

- **Chrome OS:** Created by Google, Chrome OS is the operating system used on Chromebooks. Affordable Chromebooks have long dominated the best-seller lists at many computer retailers —for good reason. If you want to surf the web, work on email, compose simple documents, or do anything in a browser — which covers a lot of ground these days — a Chromebook and Chrome OS are all you need. Chromebooks can't run Windows programs such as Office or Photoshop (although they *can* run web-based versions of them, such as Office Web Apps or Photoshop on the Web). Despite this limitation, they don't get infected by traditional viruses and have few maintenance problems. You can't say the same about Windows: That's why you need a large book to keep it going. Yes, it would be best to have a reliable internet connection to get the most out of Chrome OS. However, some parts of Chrome OS and Google's apps, including Gmail, can work even if you don't have an active internet connection.

  Chrome OS is built on Linux and looks and feels much like the Google Chrome web browser. There are a few minor differences, but generally, you feel like you're working in the Chrome browser.

- **ChromeOS Flex:** This different flavor of Chrome OS is designed to run on older PCs that can't run Windows 11. Google makes it easy to create a bootable USB drive with the ChromeOS Flex setup and get your PC up and running with this operating system in about 5 minutes. This operating system is also designed to work on devices without a Trusted Platform Module (TPM) chip, which is required for Windows 11 to encrypt your data and keep it safe from hackers. Another significant difference between Chrome OS and ChromeOS Flex is that the latter can't run Android apps. Visit `https://chromeos.google/products/chromeos-flex/` for more details about this operating system.

- **macOS:** If you don't know how to use Windows or own a Windows computer, consider buying a MacBook Air or a MacBook Pro. The latest models powered by Apple's M3 chips deliver excellent performance and energy efficiency, as well as support for workloads related to artificial intelligence (AI). However, they can natively run only macOS, not Windows. If you want Windows on the latest MacBooks, you must purchase Parallels Desktop for Mac from `www.parallels.com`. And, if you're a PC fan, you'll be happy to know that you can build a custom computer and run macOS on it. Check out `www.hackintosh.com`. But, no, it isn't legal — the macOS End User License Agreement explicitly forbids installation on a non-Apple-branded computer. Also, installing it is certainly not for the faint of heart.

» **Linux:** The big up-and-coming operating system, which has been up-and-coming for a couple of decades now, is Linux (pronounced "LIN-uchs"). If you are not an IT professional and use your PC only to get on the internet — to surf the web and send emails — Linux can handle that, with few of the headaches that remain as the hallmark of Windows. By using free programs such as LibreOffice (`www.libreoffice.org`) and online services such as Google Workspace and Google Drive (`www.drive.google.com`), you can even cover the basics in word processing, spreadsheets, presentations, contact managers, calendars, and more. Even though Linux doesn't support Windows's vast array of consumer hardware, it's popular with many software developers and power users.

In the tablet sphere, iPadOS and Android rule. Windows 11 doesn't compete with any of them, even though it works on Qualcomm chips designed for mobile devices and is available on tablets and convertible devices such as the Surface line.

WARNING

Windows 11 in S mode is a confusing development with an unclear future. Designed to compete with Chrome OS, *S mode* refers to a set of restrictions on "real" Windows. Supposedly in an attempt to improve battery life, reduce the chance of the PC getting infected, and simplify your life, the S mode in Windows 11 doesn't run most regular Windows programs. S mode limits users only to apps found in the Microsoft Store. You get Spotify and Apple Music as well as Firefox, Opera, and Microsoft Edge but not Google Chrome. Fortunately, you can go to the Microsoft Store and buy an upgrade for getting out of S mode.

What do other people choose? Measuring the percentage of PCs running Windows versus Mac versus Linux is hard. StatCounter (`www.statcounter.com`) specializes in analyzing the traffic of millions of sites globally and provides useful statistics based on the data they collect. One stat tallies how many Windows computers hit those sites compared to macOS and Linux. While their data may not be 100 percent representative of real-world market share, it does an excellent job of giving us an idea of operating system penetration. If you look at only desktop operating systems — Windows (on desktops, laptops, 2-in-1s) and macOS — the numbers in May 2024 (according to StatCounter) tell the story from Figure 1-3.

In May 2024, Windows had a market share of 73.9 percent of all desktop operating systems, and macOS had 14.91 percent. Linux's share is around 3.77 percent, while ChromeOS's is just 2.55 percent.

Windows 10 is king in Microsoft's world, with a 68 percent market share. Windows 11 is a distant second, with 27.64 percent, a value growing much slower than Microsoft would like. Windows 7 is still used in 2.87 percent of computers, even though it reached its end of life on January 14, 2020, and Microsoft no longer offers updates for it.

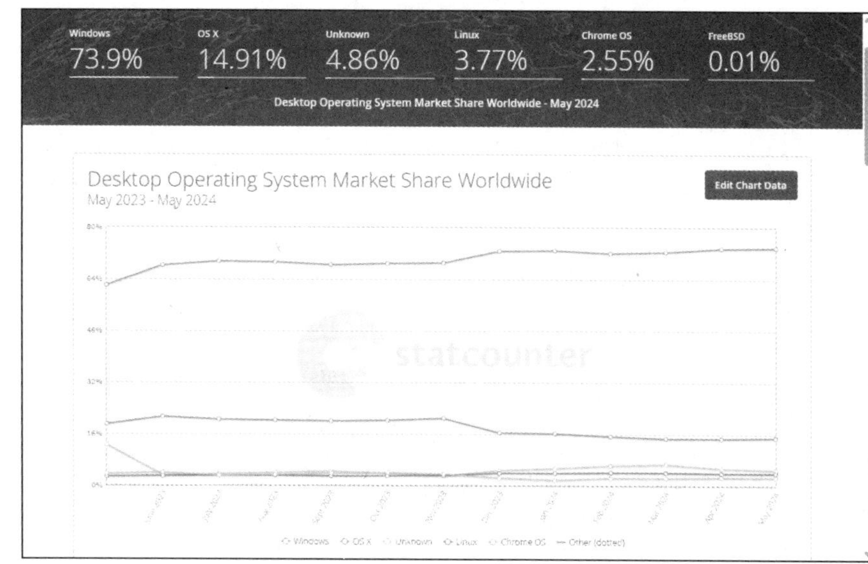

FIGURE 1-3: Worldwide market share of desktop operating systems from May 2023 to May 2024.

REMEMBER

The numbers change dramatically if you look at the bigger picture, including tablets and smartphones. As of May 2024, StatCounter says that 43.86 percent of all devices on the internet use Android, while just 27.97 percent use Windows, and 17.8 percent use iOS (read iPhone). Mobile operating systems are swallowing the world — and the trend has been in favor of mobile, not Windows, for many years. The number of smartphones sold every year exceeds the number of PCs sold. And according to Statista, in the last quarter of 2023, 58.67 percent of all internet traffic was from mobile devices. Things are pretty clear, aren't they?

Which Windows Version Is Best?

As you have seen, Windows 10 commands the biggest market share in the PC world. However, this doesn't mean that it's a better operating system. And after October 14, 2025, Windows 10 won't be the better operating system for one simple yet important reason: Microsoft will end its support for it. After that date, you'll have to pay Microsoft for security updates, which will be available until 2028. However, this option is only for business customers, who will pay around $61 for one PC during the first year, double for the second year, and double again for year three. The only institutions that will get an affordable fee are those that use the Windows 10 Education edition. They'll pay $1 per PC for the first year, $2 for the second year, and $4 for the third and final year.

After October 14, 2025, non-business users will be exposed to an increasing number of security problems that will make their Windows 10 computer an easy target for malware creators, hackers, and other malicious entities lurking on the internet. Another problem is that Microsoft is no longer actively developing new features for Windows 10. Version 22H2, released on October 18, 2022, is the last version of Windows 10.

Therefore, the best version of Windows today is Windows 11 for the following reasons:

- Microsoft actively maintains it, and it receives security updates and new features regularly.
- Each year, we get a major update for Windows 11, which introduces new features to the operating system and increases its support window by another two years.

Microsoft has not said when it intends to end its support for Windows 11. However, I expect that their approach to be similar to the one for Windows 10: They will retire Windows 11 a few years after they launch Windows 12 but continue developing both operating systems in parallel for another year. Then, they will slowly phase out Windows 11 in favor of Windows 12.

Understanding Important Terminology

Some terms pop up so frequently that you'll find it worthwhile to memorize them or at least understand where they come from. That way, you won't be caught off-guard when your first grader comes home and asks to install TikTok on your computer.

TIP

If you want to drive your technical friends nuts the next time you have a problem with your Windows 11 computer, tell them that the hassles occur when you're "running Microsoft." They won't know whether you mean Windows, Word, Outlook, OneNote, or any dozen other programs. Also, they won't know if you're talking about a Microsoft program on Windows, the Mac, iPad, iPhone, Android, or even Linux.

Windows 11, the *operating system,* is a sophisticated computer program. So are computer games, Office, Microsoft Word (the word processor part of Office), Google Chrome (the web browser made by Google), those nasty viruses you've heard about, and the Instagram app on your teenager's smartphone.

An *app*, *program*, or *desktop app* is software that works on a computer (see the earlier "Hardware versus Software" section in this chapter). An app is modern and cool, while a program is old and boring. A *desktop app* or *application* manages to hit both gongs, but they all mean the same thing.

A *Windows app* is a program that runs on any edition of Windows 11. By design, *apps* should run on Windows 11 and Windows 10 on a desktop, a laptop, and a tablet— and even on an Xbox game console, a giant wall-mounted Surface Hub, a HoloLens augmented reality headset, and possibly Internet of Things tiny computers. They also run on Windows 11 in S mode (read Chapter 3 in this minibook).

WARNING

Although they might look the same, apps and desktop apps or programs have some significant differences. Initially, Windows apps were distributed only through the Microsoft Store. Nowadays, some desktop apps or programs, such as Mozilla Firefox and Adobe Photoshop, are also distributed through the Microsoft Store. Desktop apps can also be distributed separately from the Microsoft Store. However, if you don't download them from the Microsoft Store, they aren't updated automatically — you'll need to handle this process on your own. Another difference is that apps can run on Windows 11 in S mode, while desktop apps that aren't delivered through the Microsoft Store can't.

REMEMBER

A special kind of program called a *driver* makes specific pieces of hardware work with the operating system. The driver acts like a translator that enables Windows to ask your hardware to do what the operating system wants. Imagine that you have a document that you want to print. You edit the document in Word, click or tap the Print button, and wait for the document to be printed. Word is an application that asks the operating system to print the document. The operating system takes the document and asks the printer driver to print the document. The driver takes the document and translates it into a language that the printer understands. Finally, the printer prints the document and delivers it to you. Everything inside your computer and all that is connected to it has a driver: The hard disk inside the PC has a driver, the printer has a driver, your mouse has a driver, and Tiger Woods has a driver (several, actually, and he makes a living with them). I wish that everyone was so talented.

Windows includes many drivers, some created by Microsoft and others created by third parties. The hardware manufacturer is responsible for making its hardware work with your Windows PC, and that includes building and fixing the drivers. However, if Microsoft makes your computer, Microsoft is responsible for the drivers too. Sometimes, you can get a driver from the manufacturer that works better than the one that ships with Windows.

When you stick an app or a program or a driver on your computer — and set it up so that you can use it — you can say that you *installed* the app or program or driver.

When you crank up a program — that is, get it going on your computer — you can say you *started* it, *launched* it, *ran* it, or *executed* it. They all mean the same thing.

If the program quits the way it's supposed to, you can say it *stopped, finished, ended, exited,* or *terminated.* Again, all these terms mean the same thing. If the app stops with some weird error message, you can say it *crashed, died, cratered, went belly up, jumped in the bit bucket,* or *GPFed* (techspeak for "generated a General Protection Fault" — don't ask), or employ any of a dozen colorful but unprintable epithets. If the app just sits there and you can't get it to do anything, no matter how you click your mouse or poke the touchscreen, you can say that it *froze, hung,* or *stopped responding.*

A *bug* is something that doesn't work right. A bug is not a virus! If you ask me, viruses work as intended far too often. Speaking of bugs, did you know that the term *bug* comes from a real-life insect? US Navy Rear Admiral Grace Hopper — the intellectual guiding force behind the COBOL programming language and one of the pioneers in the history of computing — is credited with popularizing the term. It turns out that she found a moth inside the relay of an ancient Mark II Aiken Relay Calculator. The moth was taped into the technician's logbook on September 9, 1947. (See Figure 1-4.)

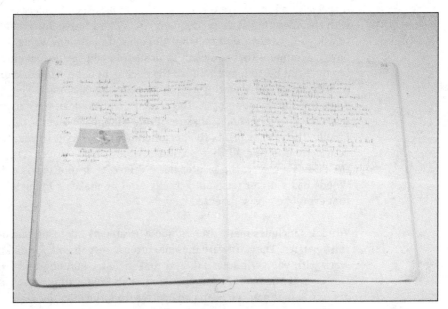

FIGURE 1-4: Admiral Grace Hopper's log of the first actual case of a bug being found.

Source: US Navy

The people who invented all this terminology think of the internet as being some great blob in the sky — it's *up,* as in "up in the sky." So, if you send something from your computer to the internet, you're *uploading.* If you take something off the internet and put it on your computer, you're *downloading.*

The *cloud* is just a marketing term for the internet. Saying that you put your data "in the cloud" sounds so much cooler than saying you copied it to storage on the internet. Programs can run in the cloud — which is to say that they run on the internet. Just about everything that has anything to do with computers can be done in the cloud.

REMEMBER

If you use *cloud storage,* you're just sticking your data on some company's computers. Put a file in Microsoft OneDrive, and it goes onto one of Microsoft's computers. Put it in Google Drive, and it goes to Google's storage in the sky. Move it to Dropbox, and it's sitting on a Dropbox server.

When you connect computers and devices to each other, you *network* them. The network can be wired, using cables; wireless, often called *Wi-Fi,* the name for the main body of wireless networking standards; or a combination of wired and wireless. At the heart of a network sits a box, called a *router* or an *access point,* that computers and devices connect to via cables or Wi-Fi. If the router has "rabbit ears" on top, for wireless connections, it's usually called a *Wi-Fi router.* Do keep in mind that some Wi-Fi routers have antennae hidden inside their box.

You can hook up to the internet in two basic ways: wired and wireless. *Wired* is easy: You plug one end of a network cable into a router or some other box that connects to the internet and the other end into your computer. *Wireless* networks fall into two categories: Wi-Fi connections, as you'll find in many homes, coffee shops, airports, and all kinds of public places, and cellular (mobile phone–style) wireless connections. Cellular wireless internet connections are identified with one of the G levels: 3G, 4G, or 5G. Each G level is faster than its predecessor.

This part gets a little tricky. If your smartphone can connect to a 4G or 5G network, you can set it up to behave like a Wi-Fi router: Your laptop talks to the smartphone, and the smartphone talks to the internet over its 4G (or 5G) connection. That's called *tethering* — your laptop is tethered to your smartphone. Not all smartphones can tether, and not all manufacturers and mobile carriers allow it.

Special boxes called *mobile hotspot* units work much the same way: The mobile hotspot connects to the 4G or 5G connection, and your laptop gets tethered to the mobile hotspot box. Most smartphones these days can be configured as mobile hotspots.

If you plug your internet connection into the wall, you have *broadband,* which may run via *fiber* (a cable that uses light waves), *DSL* or *ADSL* (which uses regular old phone lines), *cable* (as in cable TV), or *satellite.* The fiber, DSL, cable, or satellite box is often called a *modem*, although it's really a *router*. Although fiber-optic lines are inherently much faster than DSL or cable, individual results can vary. Ask your neighbors what they're using, and then pick the best. If you don't like your current service, vote with your wallet.

TECHNICAL STUFF

Turning to the dark side of the force, the distinctions among *viruses*, *worms*, and *trojans* grow blurrier every day. That's why most journalists and tech specialists use the generic term *malware* to describe anything that can harm a computer, smartphone, or any other gadget. In general, they're programs that replicate and can be harmful, and the worst ones blend different approaches. *Spyware* gathers information about you and then phones home with all the juicy details. *Adware* gets in your face with dodgy ads, all too frequently installing itself on your computer without your knowledge or consent. *Ransomware* scrambles (or threatens to scramble) your data and demands a payment to unscramble it.

If a bad guy manages to take over your computer without your knowledge, turning it into a zombie that spews spam by remote control, you're in a *botnet*. (And yes, the term *spam* comes from the immortal *Monty Python* routine that's set in a cafe serving Hormel's Spam luncheon meat, the chorus bellowing "lovely Spam, wonderful Spam.") Check out Book 9 for details about preventing malware from messing with your Windows computer.

The most successful botnets employ *rootkits* — programs that run underneath Windows, evading detection because regular antivirus programs can't see them. Even though rootkits are less of a threat than they used to be, they can still inflict severe damage, especially when used to infiltrate business networks or government infrastructure.

TIP

This section covers about 80 percent of the buzzwords you hear in common tech talk. If you get stuck at a party where people are simply too geeky for your own sensibilities, do not hesitate to invent your own words. Nobody will ever know the difference.

Buying a Windows 11 Computer

Here is how it usually goes: You decide that you need to buy a new PC, and then spend a couple weeks brushing up on the details — price, storage, size, processor, memory — and doing some comparison shopping. You then end up at your local Best Buy shop, and the guy behind the counter convinces you that the best bargain you'll ever see is sitting right here, right now, and you better take it quick before somebody else nabs it.

YOU MAY NOT NEED TO PAY MORE TO GET A CLEAN PC

I don't like it when the computer I want comes loaded with all that "free" bloatware. I would seriously consider paying more to get a clean computer. You do not need an antivirus and internet security program preinstalled on your new PC. It's going to open and beg for money next month. Windows 11 comes with Windows Security (formerly known as Windows Defender), and it works great — for free.

Trialware? Whether it's Quicken, Adobe Photoshop Elements, or any of a dozen other programs, if you must pay for a preinstalled app in one month or three months, you don't want it.

Unfortunately, it's difficult to find a new computer without all the unwanted extras. All companies are trying to increase their profit margins by bundling bloatware on our PCs. The only vendor that sells computers with less bloatware is Microsoft: Its Surface tablets and laptops are elegant and slim with preinstalled software. However, they're quite costly too. On the upside, the online Microsoft Store sells new, clean(er) computers from major manufacturers. Before you spend money on a computer, check to see whether it's available at the Microsoft Store. Go to `www.microsoft.com/en-us/store/b/sale` and choose any PC. The ones on offer usually ship without much junk preinstalled on them.

If you bought a new computer with bloatware on it, you can get rid of it by using some specialized tools. See Book 10, Chapter 4 for details.

Your eyes glaze over as you look at yet another spec sheet and try to figure out one last time whether DDR5 is better than DDR4 memory, whether a solid-state drive is worth the effort, and whether you need a SATA drive, or NVMe, or USB 3 or USB C. In the end, you figure that the person behind the counter must know more than you, so you plunk down your credit card and hope that you got a good deal.

The next Sunday morning, you look at the ads on Newegg (`www.newegg.com`) or Amazon (`www.amazon.com`) and discover that you could have bought the same PC for 20 percent less. The only thing you know for sure is that your PC is hopelessly becoming out of date, and the next time you'll be smarter about the entire process.

If that describes your experiences, relax. It happens to everybody. Take solace in the fact that technology evolves at an incredible pace, and many people can't keep up with it. As always, I'm here to help and share everything you need to know about buying a Windows 11 PC:

- **Decide if you're going to use a touchscreen.** Although a touch-sensitive screen is not a prerequisite for using apps on Windows 11, you'll probably find it easier to use apps with your fingers than with your mouse. Swiping with a finger is easy; swiping with a trackpad works well, depending on the trackpad; swiping with a mouse is a disaster. However, if you know that you won't be using Windows 11 apps optimized for touch from the Microsoft Store, a touchscreen won't hurt but probably is not worth the additional expense.

TIP

There is no substitute for physically trying the hardware on a touch-sensitive Windows 11 computer. Hands come in all shapes and sizes, and fingers, too. What works for size XXL hands with ten thumbs (present company included) may not cut the mustard for svelte hands and fingers experienced at taking cotton balls out of medicine bottles.

- **Get a screen that's at least 1920 x 1080 pixels — the minimum resolution to play high-definition (1080p) movies.** You probably want to stream movies from Netflix and watch videos on YouTube. For a pleasant experience, don't get stingy when purchasing a monitor. Make sure that it's at least full HD — meaning that it has 1920 x 1080 pixels in resolution. Going higher makes for an even better experience. Therefore, if you have the cash, you won't be sorry if you buy a 1440p (2560 x 1440 pixels) or a 4K (3840 x 2160 pixels) display.
- **Get a solid keyboard and a mouse that feels comfortable.** If you are upgrading your computer and love your keyboard and mouse, you may want to keep them. Corollary: Don't buy a computer online unless you know that your fingers are going to like the keyboard, your wrist will tolerate the mouse, and your eyes will fall in love with the monitor.
- **Go overboard with hard drives.** In the best of all worlds, get a computer with a solid-state drive (SSD) for the system drive (the C: drive) plus a large hard drive for storage. For the low-down on SSDs, hard drives, backups, and putting them all together, see the upcoming section "Managing disks and drives."

TIP

How much hard drive space do you need? Unless you have an enormous collection of videos, or computer games, 1TB (1,024GB or 1,048,576MB) should suffice. That's big enough to handle about 500 hours of TV shows in standard definition. Interestingly, the Hubble Space Telescope produces approximately 10 TB of data per year. Imagine having a year's worth of cosmic images and discoveries on your computer's SSD drive?

If you're getting a laptop or an ultrabook with an SSD, consider buying an external 1TB or larger drive at the same time. You will use it. External hard drives are cheap and work with a simple plug-and-play.

Or you can just stick all that extra data in the cloud, with OneDrive, Dropbox, Google Drive, or some other competitor. For what it's worth, I used Dropbox in every phase of writing this book, as well as OneDrive to back up my home computers.

REMEMBER

If you want to spend more money, go for a faster internet connection, a better sit/stand desk and an ergonomic chair. You need these items much more than you need a marginally faster or bigger computer.

Looking inside your PC

It's time to share some information about the inner workings of a desktop or laptop PC. The big box that is your computer is named *PC* or *Personal Computer* (see Figure 1-5). The main computer chip inside is called *CPU,* or *central processing unit.* Less knowledgeable people often confuse the big box with the CPU because the computer is the one doing the calculations in their view.

FIGURE 1-5: The enduring, traditional desktop PC.

Courtesy of Dell Inc.

However, the computer contains many parts and pieces (and no small amount of dust and dirt), but the crucial, central element inside every PC is the motherboard, not the CPU. (You can see a picture of a motherboard here: `www.asus.com/motherboards-components/motherboards/csm/z790-ayw-wifi-w-csm/`). That's because the motherboard is the component tying together all the others and helping them communicate and work with one another. Inside each computer, many items are attached to the motherboard:

- **The processor or CPU:** This gizmo does the main computing. It's probably from Intel or AMD. Different manufacturers rate their processors in different ways, and it's impossible to compare performance by just looking at the part number. Yes, Intel Core i9 CPUs usually run faster than Core i7s and Core i5s, while Core i3s are the slowest of the lineup. The same goes for AMD's Ryzen 9, Ryzen 7, Ryzen 5, and Ryzen 3 line-up of processors.

  Unless you tackle intensive video games, create and edit audio or video files, or recalculate spreadsheets with the national debt, the processor doesn't count for much. You don't need a fancy processor if you're streaming audio and video (say, with YouTube or Netflix). If in doubt, check out the reviews at `www.tomshardware.com` and `gamersnexus.net`. Windows 11 requires an Intel Core processor from at least 2017, an AMD Ryzen processor from 2019 onward, or a processor from the Qualcomm Snapdragon lineup that was designed for this operating system.

- **Memory chips and places to put them:** Memory is measured in megabytes (1MB = 1,024KB = 1,048,576 characters), gigabytes (1GB = 1,024MB), and terabytes (1TB = 1,024GB). Microsoft recommends a minimum of 4GB of RAM. Unless you have an exciting cornfield that you want to watch grow while using Windows 11, aim for 8GB or more. Most desktop computers allow you to add more memory, while many laptops don't.

  Boosting your computer's memory to 8GB from 4GB makes the machine snappier, especially if you run memory hogs such as Microsoft Office, Photoshop, or Google Chrome. If you leave Outlook open and work with it all day and run almost any other major program at the same time, 16GB is a wise choice. If you're going to do some video editing, gaming, or software development, you probably need more. But for most people, 8GB or 16GB will run everything well.

- **Video card:** Most motherboards include remarkably good built-in video. If you want more video oomph, you must buy a video card and put it in a card slot. Advanced motherboards have multiple PCI-Express card slots, to allow you to strap together two video cards and speed up video even more. If you're not a gamer, any graphics card released in the last four years will do just fine. If you are a gamer or are interested in using AI-based features and tools, you'll need a newer graphics card from NVIDIA's GeForce RTX40 series or AMD's Radeon RX 7000 series, or newer.

- **SSD:** Solid-state drives, or SSDs, are fast and cheap storage. You don't have to buy an expensive drive to benefit from tangible speed improvements. If you don't want to wait a lot for your programs to load, and you don't want Windows 11 to take minutes to boot, buying an SSD is a must. In comparison, hard disk drives (HDDs) are slow and dated. You should use an HDD for storing your personal files and backing up your data, not for running Windows 11, games, and apps. Remember, Windows 11 alone requires 64GB of storage, so don't be stingy with your SSD: Choose one with at least 256GB of storage space. 512 GB or 1 TB of storage is ideal for most people.

- **Card slots (also known as expansion slots):** Laptops have limited (if any) expansion slots on the motherboard. Desktops contain several expansion slots. Modern slots come in two flavors: PCI and PCI-Express (also known as PCIe or PCI-E). Many expansion cards require PCIe slots: video cards, sound cards, network cards, and so on. PCI cards don't fit in PCIe slots and vice versa. To make things more confusing, PCIe slots come in four sizes — literally, the size of the bracket and the number of bumps on the bottom of the card is different. The PCIe 1x is smallest, the relatively uncommon PCIe 4x is considerably larger, and PCIe 8x is a bit bigger still. PCIe 16x is just a little bit bigger than an old-fashioned PCI slot. Most video cards these days require a PCIe 16x slot, sometimes two, depending on how big they are.

  If you're buying a monitor separately from the rest of the system, make sure the monitor takes video input in a form that your PC can produce. See the upcoming section "Displays" for details.

- **USB (Universal Serial Bus) connections:** The USB cable has a flat connector that plugs into your USB ports. Keep in mind that USB 3 is considerably faster than USB 2, and any kind of USB device can plug into a USB 3 slot, regardless of whether the device itself supports USB 3 level speeds.

  USB Type-C (often called USB-C) is a different kind of cable that requires a different kind of slot. It has two big advantages: The plug is reversible, making it impossible to plug in upside down, and you can run a considerable amount of power through a USB-C, making it a good choice for power supplies. Many laptops these days get charged through a USB C connection.

  Make sure you get plenty of USB slots — at least two and preferably four or more. Pay extra for a USB C slot or two. More details are in the section "Managing disks and drives," later in this chapter.

Here are a few upgrade dos and don'ts:

- **Do not** let a salesperson talk you into eviscerating your PC and upgrading the CPU: Intel Core i7 isn't that much faster than Intel Core i5; a 3.0-GHz PC doesn't run a whole lot faster than a 2.8-GHz PC. The same is true for AMD's Ryzen 7 versus Ryzen 5. If you're not doing high-performance computing, you won't need an Intel Core i9 or AMD Ryzen 9 processor. Those processors cost a lot more, require more electrical energy to work, and won't deliver a tangible enough performance improvement to be worth the cost.

» **Do not** expect big performance improvements by adding more memory when you hit 16GB of RAM, unless you're running Google Chrome all day with 42 open tabs or editing videos.

» **Do** consider upgrading to a faster video card or one with more memory if you have an older one installed. Windows 11 will take good advantage of an upgraded video card.

» **Do** wait until you can afford a new PC, and then give away your old one, rather than nickel-and-dime yourself to death on little upgrades.

» **Do** buy a new SSD if you can't afford to buy a new PC and you want more performance. Install Windows 11 and all your apps and games on the SSD. No other hardware component delivers bigger performance improvements than the switch from HDD to SSD.

TIP

If you decide to add memory, have the company that sells you the memory install it. The process is simple, quick, and easy — if you know what you're doing. However, having the dealer install the memory also puts the monkey on the dealer's back if a memory chip doesn't work or is not compatible with your computer's motherboard or CPU.

Secure boot, TPM, and Windows 11

Windows 11 is a big deal when it comes to the security requirements it has for running on PCs and devices. Microsoft wants it to be the most secure Windows version ever and decided to enforce some stringent restrictions. As a result, for Windows 11 to work, your PC must have a processor with an embedded Trusted Platform Module (TPM) 2.0 and Secure Boot support. The TPM 2.0 chip has been a requirement for Windows devices since 2016, and Secure Boot has been around since the days of Windows 8. Because of that, you may think that these security features aren't a big deal and that most computers should be able to handle Windows 11. However, many computers with a TPM 2.0 chip don't have it enabled by default, and you have to fiddle with your computer's UEFI (read Book 8, Chapter 3 for more details) to enable it — a task many users have no idea how to perform. To cope with this issue, motherboard manufacturers like ASUS have released new BIOS updates that enable this chip for you. However, if your PC runs Windows 10, and you want to upgrade to Windows 11, you can't do that without enabling TPM and Secure Boot first.

TECHNICAL STUFF

What is a TPM chip, you ask? It's a device used to generate and store secure and unique cryptographic keys. The cryptographic keys are encrypted and can be decrypted only by the TPM chip that created and encrypted them. Encryption software such as BitLocker (read Book 9, Chapter 3) in Windows 11 uses the TPM chip to protect the keys used to encrypt your files. Since the key stored in each

TPM chip is unique to that device, encryption software can quickly verify that the system seeking access to the encrypted data is the expected system and not a different one.

Secure Boot, on the other hand, detects tampering attempts that may compromise your PC's boot process (which spans when you press the power button on your PC to when Windows starts) and key files of the operating system. When Secure Boot detects something fishy, it rejects the code and makes sure only good code is executed. Both security features are a big deal when it comes to protecting your data and your computer from all kinds of nasty cyberthreats.

These requirements significantly reduce the list of processors that work with Windows 11. To run this operating system, PCs and devices must have an Intel Core processor from at least 2017 or an AMD Ryzen processor from 2019 onward. They also need at least 4GB of RAM and 64GB of storage on their hard drives. Although Windows 11 places high demands on the computers on which it can be used, remember that this operating system has been around for some years now, and new computers sold today in computer shops worldwide are capable of running Windows 11, unless they come with another operating system preinstalled, such as Linux.

Tablets and 2-in-1s

Although tablets have been on the market for decades, they didn't really take off until Apple introduced the iPad in 2010. The old Windows 7 tablets required a *stylus* (a special kind of pen) and had truly little software that took advantage of touch input. Since the iPad took off, every Windows hardware manufacturer has been clamoring to join the game. Even Microsoft has entered the computer-manufacturing fray with its line of innovative tablets known as Surface.

The result is a confusing mix of Windows tablets, many kinds of 2-in-1s (some of which have a removable keyboard, as shown in Figure 1-6, and thus transform to a genuine tablet), and laptops and ultrabooks with all sorts of weird hinges, including some that flip around like an orangutan on a swing.

The choice has never been broader. All major PC manufacturers offer traditional laptops as well as some variant on the 2-in-1, many still have desktops, and more than a few even make Chromebooks!

I did most of the touch-sensitive work in this book on an ASUS Zenbook S 16 laptop (see Figure 1-7). It's a new Copilot+ PC device, with a cutting-edge AMD Ryzen AI 9 365 processor and a dedicated neural processor for running artificial intelligence tasks. It's a good-looking, capable, and versatile laptop.

FIGURE 1-6: Surface Pro tablets have attachable/removable keyboards.

Courtesy of Microsoft

FIGURE 1-7: The ASUS Zenbook S 16 laptop that I used for writing parts of the book.

Courtesy of ASUS

It has fast Wi-Fi 7 connectivity, two USB 4.0 Gen 3 type-C ports with support for power delivery, one USB 3.2 type-A port, an HDMI output for high-definition monitors (or TVs!), and a microSD card reader. Another cool feature is the webcam with facial-recognition support, which makes it easy to sign into Windows 11 using your face instead of your password. Don't worry, your photo isn't sent to Microsoft; it's stored locally, on your PC.

Of course, this oomph came at a price, around $1,699. However, you don't need to spend as much. If you just want a laptop, you can find respectable, traditional Windows 11 laptops, with or without touchscreens, for a few hundred dollars.

Microsoft's Surface Pro (refer to Figure 1-6) starts at $999. A more affordable option is the Surface Laptop Go, which starts at $699. The Surface Laptop Studio, which is both a laptop and a tablet, starts at $1,852.

If you're thinking about buying a Windows 11 tablet or 2-in-1, keep these points in mind:

REMEMBER

- **Focus on weight, heat, and battery life.** Touch-sensitive tablets or 2-in-1s are meant to be carried, not lugged around like a suitcase. The last thing you need is a box so hot that it burns a hole in your pants, or a fan so noisy you can't carry on a conversation during an online meeting.
- **Make sure you get multi-touch.** Some manufacturers like to skimp and make tablets or touchscreens that respond only to one or two touch points. You need at least four just to run Windows 11, and ten wouldn't be overkill.
- **The screen should have 1920 x 1080 or more pixels.** Anything with a lower resolution will have you squinting to look at the desktop.
- **Get a solid-state drive.** In addition to making the machine much, much faster, a solid-state drive (SSD) also saves on weight, heat, and battery life. Don't be overly concerned about the amount of storage on a tablet. Many people with Windows 11 tablets end up putting all their data in the cloud using OneDrive, Google Drive, Dropbox, or Box. (For more info on cloud storage solutions, see Book 10, Chapter 4.)
- **Try before you buy.** The screen must be sensitive to your big fingers and look good, too. Not an easy combination. You might have specific issues; for example, I dislike keyboards with a very low-profile design because they don't provide tactile feedback. Better to know the limitations before you fork over the cash.
- **Make sure you can return it.** If you try the device and it doesn't provide the productivity benefits you were expecting or if you don't like using the touchscreen, it's best if you can return the product, get your money back, and invest in a traditional laptop instead.

Laptops, Ultrabooks, Gaming laptops

Netbooks, a popular concept in the days of Windows 7, were small laptops designed to provide the basics people needed from a laptop at an affordable price. Think of them as the precursor to today's Chromebooks.

Then along came the iPad, and at least 80 percent of the reason for using a netbook disappeared. Sales of netbooks have not fared well and this entire segment died. Tablets blew the doors off netbooks, and 2-in-1s mopped up the remains.

Ultrabooks are a slightly different story. Intel coined (and trademarked) the term *Ultrabook* and set the specs. For a manufacturer to call its piece of iron an Ultrabook, it must be less than 21mm thick, run for 5 hours on a battery charge, and resume from hibernation in 7 seconds or less. In other words, it must work a lot like an iPad, even though it is a laptop.

Intel invested a $300 million marketing budget on Ultrabooks, but they fizzled. Now the specs seem positively ancient, and the term *Ultrabook* doesn't have the wow factor it once enjoyed. However, Ultrabooks remain the best choice for most people, even though they're more expensive than a traditional laptop. Therefore, if you're on a modest budget, buy a cheap laptop instead of an Ultrabook.

Another family of portable devices that you might consider is gaming laptops. They started becoming popular in the 2010s due to their sheer power, and their capability to replace desktop computers in terms of performance. However, for many years, they were heavy, clunky devices, difficult to carry, and with unsatisfactory battery life. In recent years, manufacturers have brought several innovative approaches to cooling gaming laptops, improving their charging speeds and battery life. As a result, you can now buy gaming laptops that are not only powerful enough to run the latest games and serve professionals for video editing, graphic design, and game development, but are also slim and easy to carry. If you're on the lookout for a slim gaming laptop, consider the ASUS Zephyrus G14, Dell XPS 17, or Lenovo Legion 5 Slim 14. They're good and beautiful but also expensive.

OLED VERSUS LED

OLED (organic light-emitting diode) screens are found on TVs, computer monitors, laptop screens, tablets, and even smartphones. Their prices have lowered over the years. Can or should they supplant LED screens, which have led the computer charge since the turn of the century? That's a tough question with no easy answer.

First, understand that an LED screen is an LCD (liquid crystal display) screen — an older technology — augmented by backlighting or edge lighting, typically from LEDs or fluorescent lamps. A wide variety of LED screens are available, but most of the screens you see nowadays incorporate IPS (in-plane switching) technology, which boosts color fidelity and viewing angles.

OLED is a horse of a different color. IPS LED pixels rely on the backlight or sidelight to push the color to your eyes. OLED (pronounced "oh-led") pixels make their own light. If you take an LED screen into a dark room and bring up a black screen, you can see variations in the screen brightness because the backlight intensity changes, if only a little bit. OLED blacks, by contrast, are uniform and thus deeper.

All sorts of new techniques are being tried with LED, and LED screens are getting better and better. HDR (high dynamic range) improvements, for example, make LED pictures stand out in ways they never could before. Quantum dots improve lighting and color. Many people feel that OLEDs have blacker blacks, but the best LEDs produce better bright colors.

The huge difference is in price: OLED screens are still more expensive than LED, although the price of OLED has dropped in recent years. In addition, OLEDs don't last as long as LEDs — say, a decade with normal use. There is also some concern that OLEDs draw more power and will burn through a laptop battery faster than LCDs, but some contest that statement. Much depends on the particular LED and OLED you compare.

Displays

The computer monitor or screen — and LED, LCD, OLED, and plasma TVs — use technology that's quite different from old-fashioned television circuitry of your parents' childhood. A traditional TV scans lines across the screen from left to right, with hundreds of lines stacked on top of each other. Colors on each individual line vary. The almost infinitely variable color on an old-fashioned TV combined with a comparatively small number of lines makes for pleasant but fuzzy pictures.

By contrast (pun intended, of course), computer monitors, touch-sensitive tablet screens, and plasma, LED, OLED, and LCD TVs work with dots of light called *pixels.* Each pixel can have a different color, created by tiny, colored gizmos sitting next to each other.

REMEMBER

The more pixels you can cram on a screen — that is, the higher the screen resolution — the more information you can pack on the screen. That's important if you tend to have more than one word-processing document open at a time, for example. At a resolution of 1024 x 768, two open Word documents placed side by side look big and fuzzy, like caterpillars viewed through a dirty magnifying glass. At 1280 x 1024, those same two documents look sharp, but the text may be so small that you must squint to read it. If you move up to wide-screen territory — 1920 x 1080 (full HD), or even 2560 x 1440 (also called 1440p) — with a good monitor, two documents side-by-side look stunning. Run up to 4K technology, at 3840 x 2160 or better — the resolution available on many premium Ultrabooks — and you need a magnifying glass (preferably a clean one this time) to see the pixels.

A special-purpose computer called a *graphics processing unit (GPU)*, stuck on your video card or integrated into the CPU, creates everything displayed on your computer's screen. The GPU has to juggle all the pixels and all the colors, so if you're a gaming fan, the speed of the video card (and to a lesser extent, the speed of the monitor) can make the difference between a zapped alien and a lost energy shield. If you want to experience Windows 11 in all its glory, play the latest games in maxed-out graphical detail, or do video editing, 3D modeling, virtual reality, and the like, you need a fast GPU with at least 8 GB (preferably 12 GB or more) of its own memory.

Computer monitors and tablets are sold by size, measured diagonally (glass only, not the bezel or frame), like TV sets. And just like with TV sets, the only way to pick a good computer screen over a run-of-the-mill one is to compare them side-by-side or to follow the recommendation of someone who has the knowledge to test them in detail and make a thorough review. Luckily, plenty of hardware review websites and YouTube channels do a fantastic job testing all the latest computer hardware.

Managing disks and drives

Your PC's memory chips hold information only temporarily: Turn off the electricity, and the content of RAM disappears. If you want to re-use your work, keeping it around after the plug has been pulled, you must save it, typically on a hard drive or possibly in the *cloud* (which means you copy it to a location on the internet).

The following list describes the most common types of disks and drives:

- **Hard drive:** Traditional hard disk drives (HDDs) have been replaced by *solid-state drives* (SSDs), which have no moving parts and, to a lesser extent, *hybrid drives,* which bolt together a rotating drive with an SSD. Each technology has benefits and drawbacks. Yes, you can run a regular HDD drive as your C: drive, and it will work fine. But tablets, laptops, or desktops with SSD drives run like lightning. The SSD wins as speed king. After you use an SSD as your main system (C:) drive, you'll never go back to a spinning platter, I guarantee.

  SSDs feature low power consumption and give off less heat than HDDs. SSDs have no moving parts, so they don't wear out like hard drives. And, if you drop a hard drive and a solid-state drive off the Leaning Tower of Pisa, one of them may survive. Or maybe not.

  SSDs are great for the main drive, but they may be too expensive for storing pictures, movies, and photos. Price and technical considerations (see the sidebar "Solid-state drives have problems, too") assure that hard drives will still be around.

Hybrid drives combine the benefits and problems of both HDDs and SSDs. Although HDDs have long had *caches* — chunks of memory that hold data before being written to the drive and after it's read from the drive — hybrid drives have an entire SSD to act as a buffer.

If your budget stretches that far, start with an SSD for the system drive and a big hard drive (one that attaches with a USB cable) for storing photos, movies, and music, and then get another drive (which can be inside your PC, outside attached with a USB cable, or even on a different PC on your network) to run File History (see Book 8, Chapter 1).

TECHNICAL STUFF

If you want full on-the-fly protection against dying hard drives, get three hard drives — one SSD and two hard drives, either inside the PC or outside attached with USB or eSATA cables — and run Storage Spaces (see Book 7, Chapter 5).

Many people opt for a fast SSD for files needed immediately, coupled with cloud storage for the big stuff. If you opt for a Microsoft 365 subscription, which gives you 1 TB of cloud storage space, your need for hard drives will be reduced considerably.

A three-tier system, with SSDs storing data you need all the time, intermediate backup in the cloud, and multi-terabyte data repositories hanging off your PC, is the way to go for enthusiasts. Privacy concerns (and the intervention of various governments) have people worried about cloud storage, and rightfully so.

- **SD card memory:** Many Windows laptops, mini PCs, and some tablets have built-in SD card readers. You probably know Secure Digital (SD) cards best as the kind of memory used in digital cameras and smartphones (see Figure 1-8). A microSD card can be plugged into an SD card adapter to have it function like an SD card.

TIP

Many desktop computer cases have drive bays. Why not use one of them for a multifunction card reader? That way, you can slip a memory card from your digital camera and transfer files at will. A multifunction reader costs a pittance and can read them all: SD card, microSD card, CompactFlash, memory stick, whatever you have.

- **CD, DVD, or Blu-ray drive:** Of course, these types of drives work with CDs, DVDs, and Sony Blu-ray discs, respectively, which can be filled with data or contain music or movies. CDs hold about 700MB of data; DVDs hold 4GB, or six times as much as CDs. Dual-layer DVDs (which use two separate layers on top of the disc) hold about 8GB, and Blu-ray discs hold 50GB, or six times as much as a dual-layer DVD.

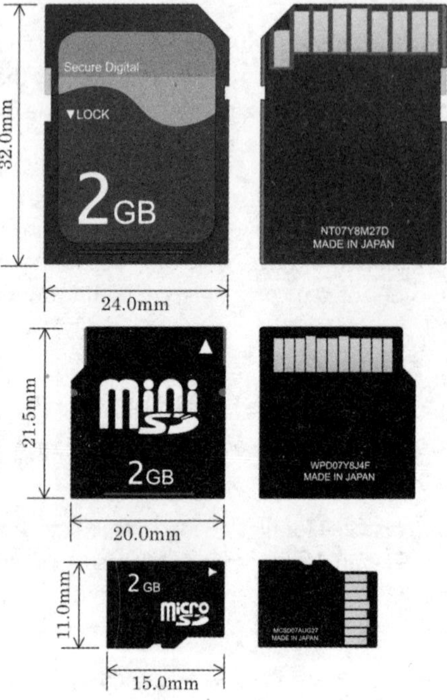

FIGURE 1-8: Comparative sizes of an SD, a miniSD, and a microSD card.

Source: tweezers / Wikimedia Commons / CC BY-SA 3.0.

Fewer and fewer machines these days come with built-in DVD drives: If you want to move data from one place to another, a USB drive works fine — and going through the cloud is even easier. For most storage requirements, big, cheap USB drives are hard to beat.

- **USB drive or key drive:** It's half the size of a pack of gum and can hold an entire PowerPoint presentation or two or six, plus a few full-length movies. Flash memory (also known as a jump drive, thumb drive, or memory stick) should be your first choice for external storage space or for copying files between computers. (See Figure 1-9.) You can even use USB drives on many DVD players and TV set-top boxes.

  Pop one of these guys in a USB slot, and suddenly Windows knows it has another drive — except that this one's fast, portable, and incredibly easy to use. It's okay to go for the cheapest flash drive you can find as long as it belongs to a recognized manufacturer.

TIP

What about USB 3? If you have a hard drive that sits outside your computer — an *external drive* — or a USB drive, it'll run faster if it's designed for USB 3 and attached to a USB 3 connector. Expect performance with USB 3 that's three to five times as fast as USB 2. For most other outside devices, USB 3 is overkill, and USB 2 works just as well.

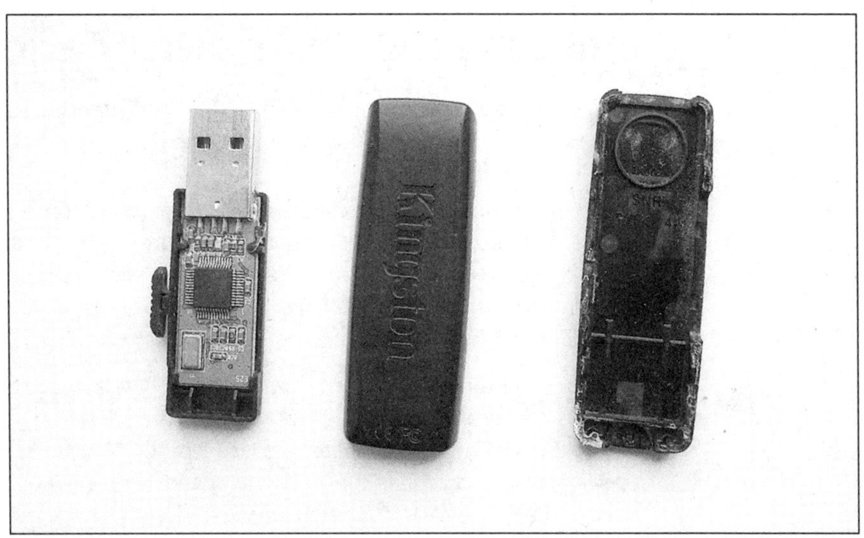

FIGURE 1-9: The inside of a USB drive.

Source: Ravenperch / Wikimedia Commons / CC BY-SA 3.0.

This list is by no means definitive: New storage options come out every year.

SOLID-STATE DRIVES HAVE PROBLEMS, TOO

Although I love my SSD system drives and would never go back to rotating hard disk drives (HDDs), SSDs aren't perfect. First, they don't have any moving parts, and it looks like they're more reliable than HDDs. But when an HDD starts to go belly up, you can usually tell because of its unusual slowness, the sounds it makes (usually a repetitive clicking sound), and the errors you start encountering. Expiring SSDs don't give off advanced warning signals or sounds. When trying to open a file, you may encounter a sudden system freeze, followed by tons of read and write errors. When an HDD dies, you can frequently get the data back, although it can be expensive and time-consuming. When an SSD goes, you rarely get a second chance.

SSDs must take care of lots of internal bookkeeping for trimming unused space and load balancing to guarantee uniform wear patterns. *Trimming* is the process in which the operating system tells the SSD which data blocks are no longer needed and can be deleted or are marked as free for rewriting. SSDs slow down after you've used them for a few years. The speed decrease is usually associated with the bookkeeping programs kicking in over time.

Connecting your PC to other devices

Your PC connects to the outside world by using a bewildering variety of cables and connectors. I describe the most common in this list:

- **USB (Universal Serial Bus) cable:** This cable has a flat connector (known as *USB A*) that plugs into your PC, as shown in Figure 1-10. The other end is sometimes shaped like a D (called *USB B*), but smaller devices have tiny terminators (usually called *USB mini* and *USB micro,* each of which can have two different shapes).

  USB 2 connectors work with any device, but hardware — such as a hard drive — that uses USB 3 will be much faster if you use a USB 3 cable and plug it into the back of your computer in a USB 3 port. USB 2 works with USB 3 devices, but you won't get the additional speed. Note that not all PCs, especially older PCs, have USB 3 ports.

  USB-C is a special kind of USB connector that supports amazingly fast data transmission and high power levels depending on which USB standard you're using. You know when you have USB-C because it's impossible to insert the plug upside down — both sides work equally well. It's becoming the go-to choice for connecting peripherals and, in some cases, power supplies.

  USB is the connector of choice for just about any hardware — printer, scanner, smartphone, digital camera, portable hard drive, and even the mouse. After many years of using a proprietary Lighting port, Apple's new iPhones and iPads finally use USB-C, just like the rest of the technology world. If you run out of USB connections on the back of your PC, get a USB hub with a separate power supply and plug away.

- **LAN cable:** Also known as a CAT-5e, CAT-6, or Ethernet cable, a LAN cable is a common type of network connector. Each end of the cable has an RJ-45 connector, which resembles an overweight telephone plug (see Figure 1-11). One end plugs in to your PC, typically into a *network interface card* (or *NIC,* pronounced "nick") or a network connector on the motherboard. The other end plugs in to your wireless router (see Figure 1-12) or switch or into a cable modem, DSL box, router, or other internet connection-sharing device.
- **Keyboard and mouse cable:** Most mice and keyboards (even wireless mice and keyboards) come with USB connectors.
- **Bluetooth** is a short-distance wireless connection. Once upon a time, Bluetooth was finicky and hard to set up. In recent years, it has become quite useful and is now used to connect all kinds of accessories: speakers, headsets, mice, and keyboards.

» **DisplayPort and HDMI connectors:** Modern computer monitors and smart TVs use HDMI (see Figure 1-13), mini HDMI, or micro HDMI, DisplayPort (see Figure 1-14), or mini DisplayPort connectors, which transmit both audio and video over one cable.

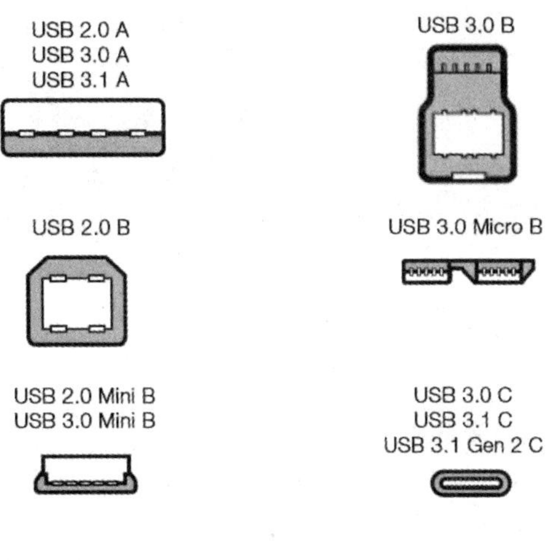

FIGURE 1-10: The most common USB A, B, C, Mini, and Micro USB connectors.

Source: Wikimedia

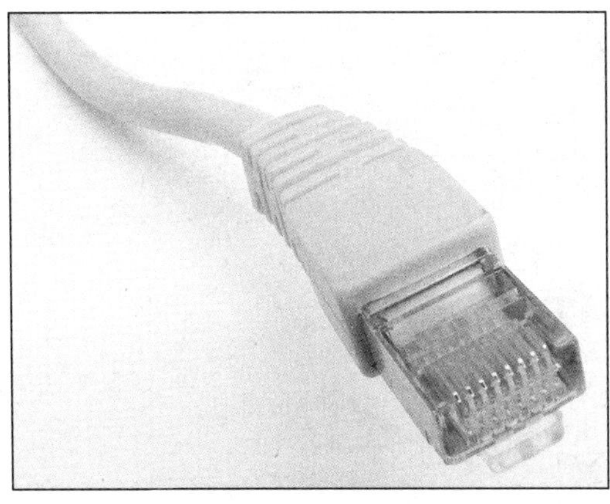

FIGURE 1-11: An Ethernet cable with an RJ-45 connector.

Source: David Monniaux / Wikimedia Commons / CC BY-SA 3.0.

FIGURE 1-12: The back of a wireless router.

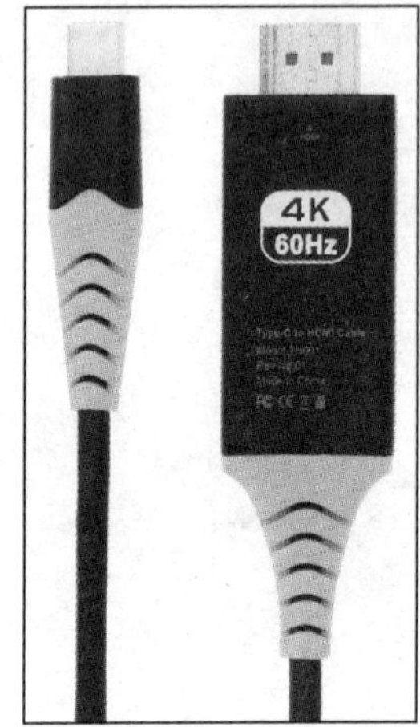

FIGURE 1-13: HDMI replaced the old VGA and DVI-D video adapters.

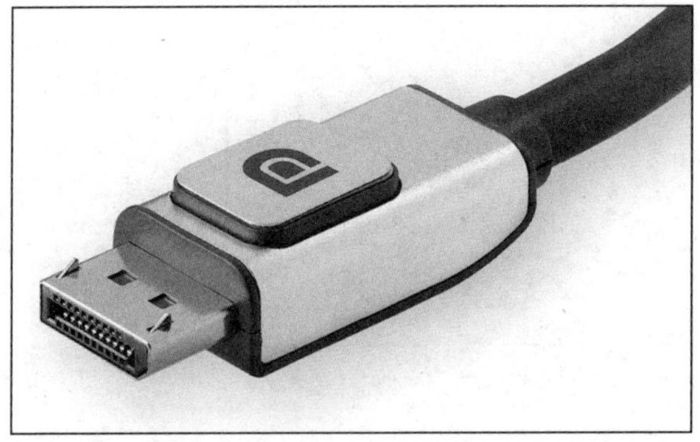

FIGURE 1-14: DisplayPort is the modern alternative to HDMI.

Source: Belkin / Wikimedia Commons / CC BY-SA 3.0.

Video, sound, and multimedia

When it comes to connecting your speakers to a desktop PC or a microphone to your laptop, you must be concerned about the five specific sound jacks, as each one serves a different function. Here's how the five key jacks are usually marked, although sometimes you must read the documentation of your PC or laptop to find the details (see Figure 1-15):

- **Line In:** This stereo input jack is usually blue. It feeds a stereo audio signal — generally from an amplified source — into the PC. Use this jack to receive audio output into your computer from your iPad, cable box, TV set, radio, electric guitar, or other audio-generating box.

FIGURE 1-15: The audio jacks on the back of a desktop computer.

- **Mic In:** This jack is usually pink. It's for unamplified sources, like most microphones or some electric guitars. If you use a cheap microphone for Skype, Teams, or another VoIP service that lets you talk long distances for free, and the mic doesn't have a USB connector, plug in the microphone here. In a pinch, you can plug any of the Line In devices into the Mic In jack — but you may hear only mono sound, not stereo, and you may have to turn the volume way down to avoid some ugly distortion when the amplifier inside your PC increases the strength of an already amplified signal.
- **Line Out:** This stereo output jack is usually lime green. In many cases, it can be used for headphones or patched into powered speakers. Line Out is the source for the highest-quality sound your computer can produce. If you go for a multi-speaker setup, Line Out is for the front speaker.

- **SPDIF Out:** SPDIF stands for Sony/Philips Digital Interface, from the names of the companies which developed this interface. You can plug an optical audio cable into this jack, which allows the transfer of digital audio signals. This interface was popular for transferring digital audio from CD and DVD players to amplifiers, TVs, or computers. It's rarely used these days.
- **Rear Surround Out:** Usually black, this jack isn't used often. It's intended to be used if you have independent powered rear speakers. Most people with rear speakers use the Line Out connector and plug it into their home theater system, which then drives the rear speakers, or they use the HDMI cable (see the preceding section) to hook up to their TVs. If your computer can produce full surround sound output, and you have the amplifier to handle it, you'll get much better results using the black audio jack.

Many desktop computers have two more jacks: The orange one is a direct feed for your subwoofer, and the gray (or brown) one is for your side speakers. Again, it would be best to put an amplifier between the jacks and your speakers.

Laptops typically have just two jacks, pink for Mic In and lime for Line Out. If your headphones have a microphone, that's the right combination. It's also common to plug powered external speakers into the lime jack.

Some tablets and smartphones have a headphone jack, which works just like a lime green Line Out jack on your desktop PC.

High-end audio systems may support optical connections. Check the alignment of both the computer end of the connection and the speaker/receiver end.

TIP

PC manufacturers love to extol the virtues of their advanced sound systems, but the simple fact is that you can hook up a plain-vanilla PC to a home stereo and get good enough sound. Just connect the Line Out jack on the back of your PC to the Aux In jack on your home stereo or entertainment center. *Voilà!*

Is your old PC or laptop compatible with Windows 11?

Before upgrading a Windows 10 laptop or PC to Windows 11, it's a good idea to download and install the PC Health Check app from Microsoft. The app is free and does all the background checks for you, sharing a simple message on whether your computer can run Windows 11. Most importantly, if it can't run Windows 11, the app will tell you why. Sometimes, the problem is easy to fix, such as insufficient free storage space on your SSD or the TPM chip being available but not enabled.

Here's how to use the PC Health Check on your Windows 10 PC:

1. **Open your favorite web browser in Windows 10 and navigate to this address:** `https://aka.ms/GetPCHealthCheckApp`.

   A file named WindowsPCHealthCheckSetup gets downloaded onto your computer.

2. **Double-click or tap WindowsPCHealthCheckSetup to install the app.**

   You are first shown the license agreement.

3. **Select the I Accept the Terms in the License Agreement box and press Install.**

   The app gets installed in a couple of seconds.

4. **Click or tap Finish.**

   The PC Health Check app opens, as shown in Figure 1-16.

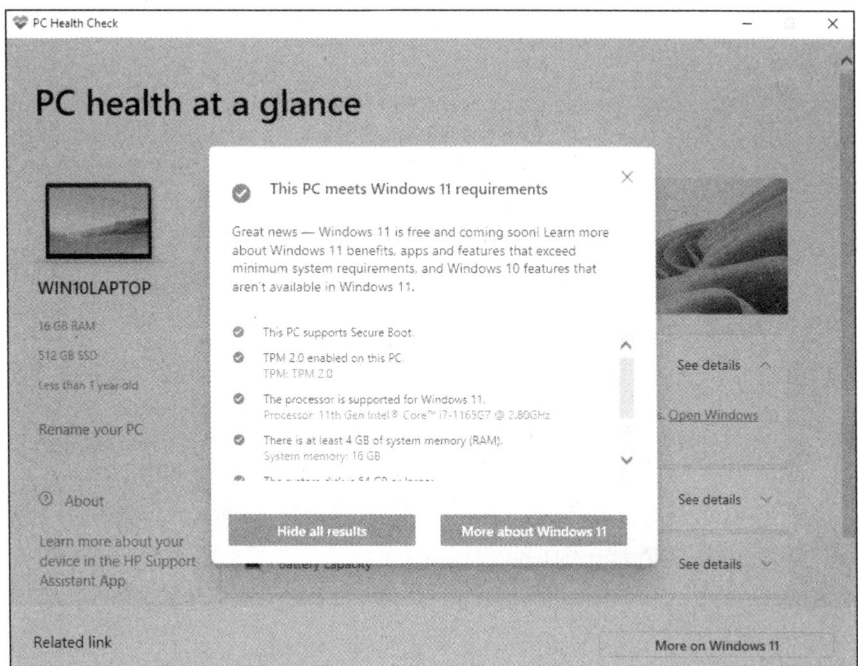

FIGURE 1-16: The PC Health Check app tells you whether you can upgrade to Windows 11.

5. **Click or tap Check Now.**

   The app summarizes its findings and tells whether your PC meets the Windows 11 system requirements.

6. **To see more information, click or tap See All Results.**

   You see the technical aspects that the PC Health Check app checks and its findings.

7. **When you're finished using the app, close it.**

What You Might Not Like about Windows 11

Windows 11 is not all greatness. There are frustrating bits, as in any operating system. Here are the negative aspects that I think every Windows 11 customer should know before using it:

- **Forced updates:** Windows 11 users do not have any choice about updates. When Microsoft releases a patch, it gets applied. Considering the troublesome update history of Windows 10, this is not a great policy on Microsoft's part. Unfortunately, you can only pause Windows 11 updates for up to five weeks. How annoying is that? Well, you'll soon find out.
- **Inflexible hardware requirements:** As mentioned earlier in this chapter, you must have an Intel Core processor from at least 2017 or an AMD Ryzen processor from 2019 onward. As a result, only people with a new PC can run Windows 11, and they must also enable security features like the TPM chip and Secure Boot. These restrictions lowered the adoption rate for Windows 11 to a level below Microsoft's expectations. While Windows 11 is better than Windows 10 in some ways, that doesn't justify the cost of replacing a not-so-old computer with a new one.
- **Privacy concerns:** Microsoft follows the same path blazed by Google, Facebook, and many other tech companies. They're all scraping information about you, snooping on your actions to sell you things. I don't think Microsoft is worse than the others, and Windows 11 has lots of privacy controls built in. However, things could be better in this regard. In Book 2, Chapter 7, I talk about reducing the amount of data that Microsoft collects about you.

- **Enforced Microsoft account:** Another annoyance is that Microsoft doesn't allow Windows 11 users to install the operating system using a local account. You have to jump through many complicated technical hoops to do that. The company insists that you sign up with a Microsoft account, which allows it to track you and badger you to buy a Microsoft 365 subscription, a Copilot subscription, an Xbox Game Pass, and other services on top of Windows 11.
- **Lots of preinstalled apps:** Many people rely on apps to get their work done. The problem is that most Windows 11 PCs come with lots of preinstalled bloatware: free apps and games you don't need, trialware antivirus software that eventually asks you for money, and so on.

I've learned how to block or at least postpone some of Microsoft's forced updates and have come to peace with the knowledge that Windows 11 is snooping on me. Hey, I've used Google's Chrome browser and Android operating system for years, and both have been harvesting data the entire time. Windows 11 may or may not give you more headaches than the alternatives, but it also gives you more opportunities.

Welcome to Windows 11!

IN THIS CHAPTER

» Knowing the story of Windows 11

» Understanding the types of apps available in Windows 11

» Checking what's new in Windows 11

» Learning what was removed from Windows

Chapter 2

Seeing What's New in Windows 11

Windows 11 is available as a free upgrade for Windows 10 users. You can get it through Windows Update if Microsoft sends you a message to upgrade, or you can manually upgrade using the Windows 11 Installation Assistant at `www.microsoft.com/en-us/software-download/windows11`. Additionally, you can purchase Windows 11 from retailers such as Amazon and install it yourself, or get it preinstalled on a new laptop, tablet, PC, or hybrid device.

Now that you have Windows 11 on your computer or device, it's time to learn how Windows 11 came to be, how it was designed, and what's new about this version. As you'll see for yourself, this operating system not only looks different from Windows 10 but also works differently in some ways. You'll probably appreciate some of the new stuff and won't like some of its limitations.

Windows 11 can work with more apps than older versions of Windows. This is why I also talk about the kinds of apps that can run on Windows 11 and how they differ. Although Windows 11 apps may look similar, the way they're programmed is not, and it's important to know the differences.

Lastly, I list the most important features that no longer exist in Windows 11 but that you may have come to appreciate in Windows 10 or earlier versions.

Microsoft's Design Philosophy behind Windows 11

Initially, Microsoft planned to make Windows 10X (code-named Santorini), not Windows 11. Windows 10X was going to be a simplified version of Windows 10 that would compete with Chrome OS and be released on foldable mobile devices such as Surface Neo (another product that didn't make it to the market).

Windows 10X was expected to be released sometime in 2020, and it featured some significant changes compared to Windows 10:

- A new taskbar with icons aligned to the center rather than to the left
- The removal of legacy operating system components and legacy desktop apps from Windows 10 that were designed for PCs, not mobile devices with touchscreens
- A redesigned Start menu without tiles and a friendlier user interface with an easier to use right-click menu

In May 2021, Microsoft announced that Windows 10X was cancelled, but many of its features would be used in future products. In Windows 11, Microsoft didn't remove the legacy desktop apps and components from Windows 10, but it did adopt many of the user interface features that were developed for Windows 10X. The new operating system features a more pleasant-looking user interface, with lots of translucency effects, shadows, a new color palette, new icons, round corners for app windows, and sleek desktop backgrounds. Simply look at Figure 2-1 to see what I mean or give yourself a tour by opening the Start menu, File Explorer, Settings, and other Windows 11 apps.

Microsoft aimed at making Windows 11 a bit more intuitive than Windows 10 and, in some regards, they succeeded. For example, I like the new Settings app more than its predecessor from Windows 10. It's not only friendlier but also organized a little bit better, and it includes more settings for you to configure. However, some tasks require more clicks in Windows 11, such as connecting to Wi-Fi (read Book 3, Chapter 5), which may frustrate some users.

Microsoft did succeed in creating a more coherent user experience across platforms and devices. For all its strengths, Windows 10 can be jarring in its mix of user interfaces from the old desktop PC world and the newer touchscreen-oriented apps and features. Microsoft has gradually improved its apps and user interface, and many Windows 11 apps have a modern, cohesive interface and more system features, as does the Settings app.

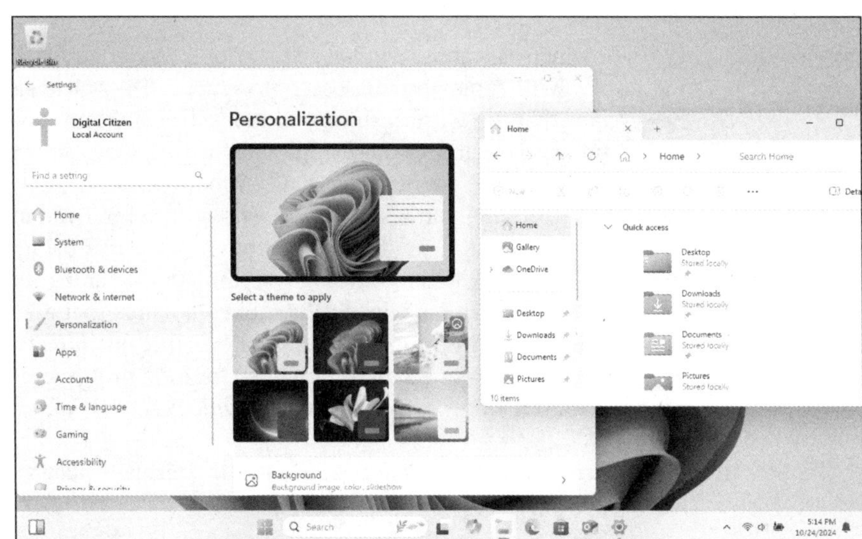

FIGURE 2-1: Windows 11 is the most beautiful Windows version yet.

Visually, Windows 11 is the most beautiful Windows ever. However, as you will discover while reading this book and familiarizing yourself with Windows 11, it can also be one of the most frustrating.

Understanding the Types of Windows 11 Apps

Windows 11 can run several different kinds of programs. Computer programs (you can also call them applications or desktop apps if you want) work by interacting with the operating system. Since the dawn of Windows, programs have communicated with the operating system through a specific set of routines (application programming interfaces, or APIs) known colloquially and collectively as Win32. With rare exceptions, Windows desktop apps — the kind you use daily — use Win32 APIs to work with Windows.

In early June 2011, at the D: All Things Digital conference in California, Steven Sinofsky and Julie Larson-Green gave their first demo of Windows 8. As part of the demo, they showed off new Metro apps, as they called them back then, which interacted with Windows in a different way. They used the newly minted application programming interface (API) set known as Windows Runtime or, more commonly, the WinRT API. Microsoft started calling the WinRT based apps *immersive* and *full screen*, but most of the world settled on Microsoft's internal code name, Metro apps. Microsoft, however, has since changed the name to Modern

UI, then Windows 8 apps, Windows Store Apps, Modern apps, Universal Windows Platform (UWP) apps, and Microsoft Store apps. They all mean the same thing: newer apps that run with this new API instead of the traditional Win32 APIs. One important aspect that sets these apps apart is that they can run natively on ARM processors such as those made by Qualcomm for Windows, not just on traditional computers with Intel and AMD processors. Because Intel and AMD use a different architecture than ARM, traditional computer programs using Win32 APIs can't run natively on ARM, and they need to be emulated, meaning that Windows translates the code written for Win32 APIs into commands that are understood by the ARM architecture. This process lowers performance and affects battery life. When using apps, they don't need to be emulated for ARM processors because their code runs just fine on all processors, no matter who makes them.

In this book, to minimize confusion, I use the terms *Windows 11 app* and just *app* when referring to apps that use the new API.

Windows 11 apps have several characteristics that make them different from desktop apps:

- They're sandboxed — stuck inside a software cocoon that isolates the apps from the operating system and from each other so that it's hard to spread infections through them. These apps can't modify system files and settings, which makes them safer to use.
- They can be easily interrupted, so their power consumption can be minimized. If a Windows 11 app hangs, it's almost impossible for it to freeze the entire machine.
- They're designed to work both with touchscreens and a mouse and keyboard. In contrast, desktop apps were optimized for mouse and keyboard.
- You can't run multiple instances of the same app in parallel like you do with many desktop apps or programs. You can open Microsoft Edge in two or more different windows because it's a desktop app, but you can't do the same with Photos because it's a Windows app.
- Apps are distributed only through the Microsoft Store. In contrast, desktop apps can be downloaded from anywhere on the internet, even though some are distributed also through the Microsoft Store. One upside is that Windows 11 apps are updated automatically by the Microsoft Store app. Often, desktop apps need to be updated manually, or they have a separate updater that runs in the background.
- When you buy an app from the Microsoft Store, Microsoft gets a commission. In contrast, you can buy a desktop app anywhere, and the company doesn't get a commission unless you buy it from the Microsoft Store or the app is made by Microsoft.

Although it does not include as many apps, games, and other types of content as Google Play or Apple's App Store, the Microsoft Store is slowly growing to include more apps, desktop apps, and games. To top things off, it also includes movies that can be bought or rented and apps powered by artificial intelligence (see Figure 2-2).

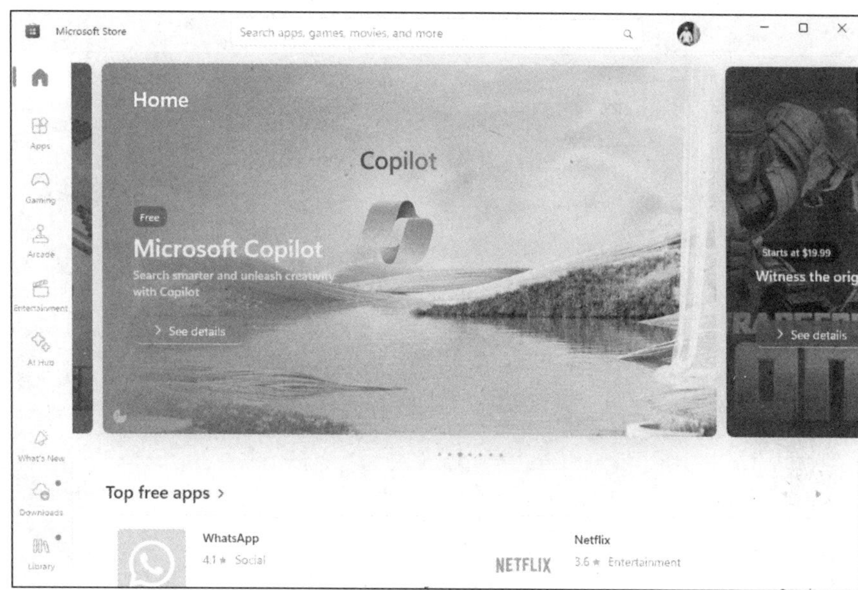

FIGURE 2-2: The Microsoft Store includes apps, desktop apps, games, movies, and AI apps.

One aspect I appreciate about the Microsoft Store is that it started to include an increasing number of useful apps such as VLC Media Player, GIMP, Discord, Reddit, Mozilla Firefox, Instagram, and Zoom Workplace, to name just a few. After the appalling app store for Windows 8 and the mediocre store for Windows 10, this seems a bit too good to be true, doesn't it?

Read Book 5, Chapter 1 to learn about the Microsoft Store and how to use it to find and install apps.

Seeing What's New for the Windows Crowd

Depending on which version of Windows you're coming from, Windows 11 may be a bit different or a lot different. In the sections that follow, I present the most significant changes that you're likely to notice.

A new Start menu and taskbar

Windows 11 has a new Start menu and taskbar. Inspired by the world of macOS, they're more beautiful than previous incarnations but also less customizable. They're both centered on the screen, as shown in Figure 2-3.

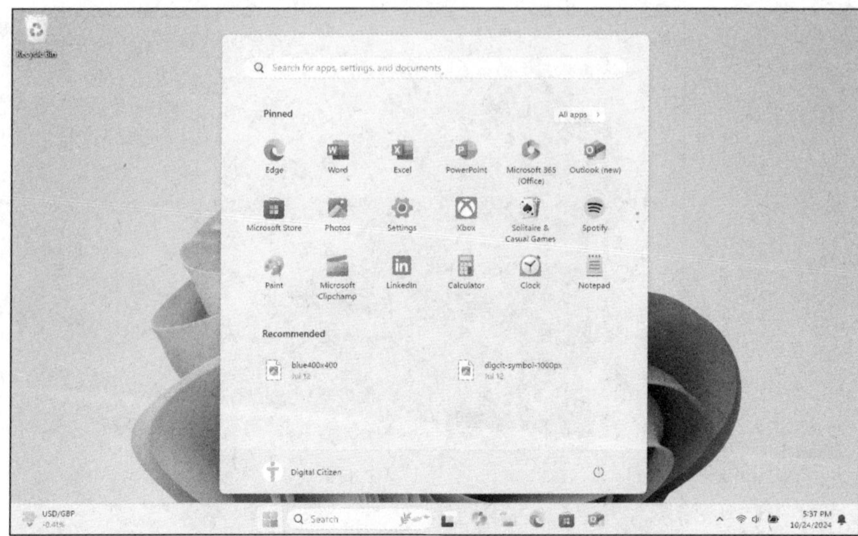

FIGURE 2-3: Windows 11 has a new taskbar and Start menu.

Unlike in Windows 10, the new Start menu doesn't have *tiles* (dynamic shortcuts that display live data from the apps they point to). The classic shortcuts from Windows 7 are back. (For details on personalizing the Start menu, see Book 3, Chapter 2.) Also, you can no longer resize the Start menu, and the way it is organized permits little in the way of customization.

The taskbar looks good and works well with not only the mouse and keyboard but also touchscreen devices. However, you can't place the taskbar at the side of the screen, add toolbars to it, or change its size. (For more on working with the taskbar, read Book 3, Chapter 3.) What you can do is change the taskbar's alignment to the left side of the screen, so that it's positioned like the one in Windows 10.

Increased role for Settings

One of the things I love about Windows 11 is the new Settings app. First, it is better organized than it was in Windows 10 and a lot better than it was in Windows 8.

You can get where you need to faster because the categories in Settings appear in a column on the left, with the relevant settings alongside on the right, as shown in Figure 2-4. There's no intermediary step as there was in Windows 10. In addition, a Search box enables you to find any setting quickly.

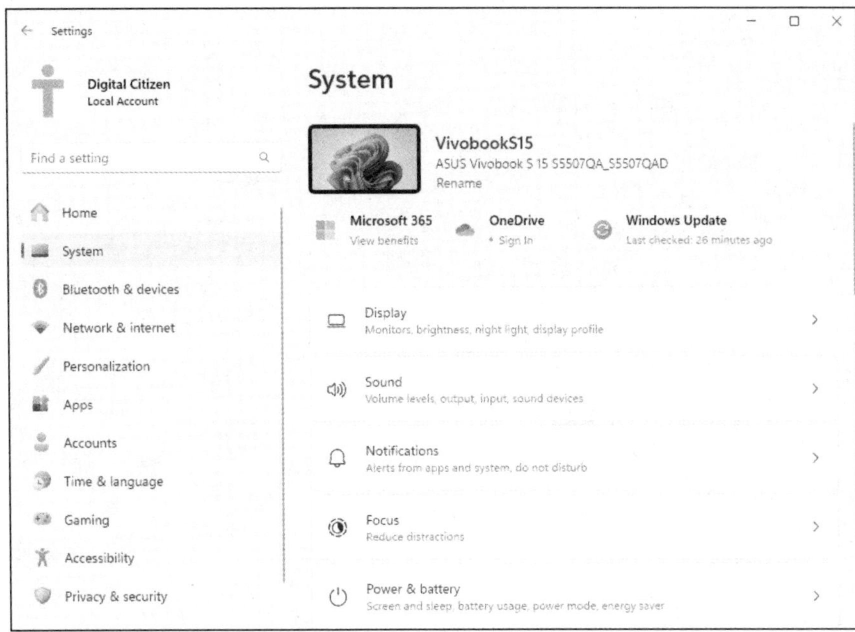

FIGURE 2-4: The Settings app has received a major redesign in Windows 11.

Unfortunately, not everything is great about the Settings app. One downside is the Home page, which, in theory, recommends links to settings that are shown based on how you use your computer. However, this page is also used to recommend a Microsoft account instead of a local account and manage your Microsoft 365 subscription and OneDrive storage space. If you don't want a Microsoft account and Microsoft's services, the Home page becomes an annoyance instead of a useful section. Luckily, you can ignore it and move on to the sections that contain the settings you want to change.

On the upside, even more settings have migrated from the old Control Panel, making Settings a lot more useful than its Windows 10 version. If only Microsoft had finished this journey so that I could completely stop using the dated Control Panel, which works well only with a mouse, not with touch.

The Control Panel has shrunk

The Control Panel continues to coexist alongside the Settings app, and it retains the same traditional user interface that was designed for keyboard and mouse users, as shown in Figure 2-5.

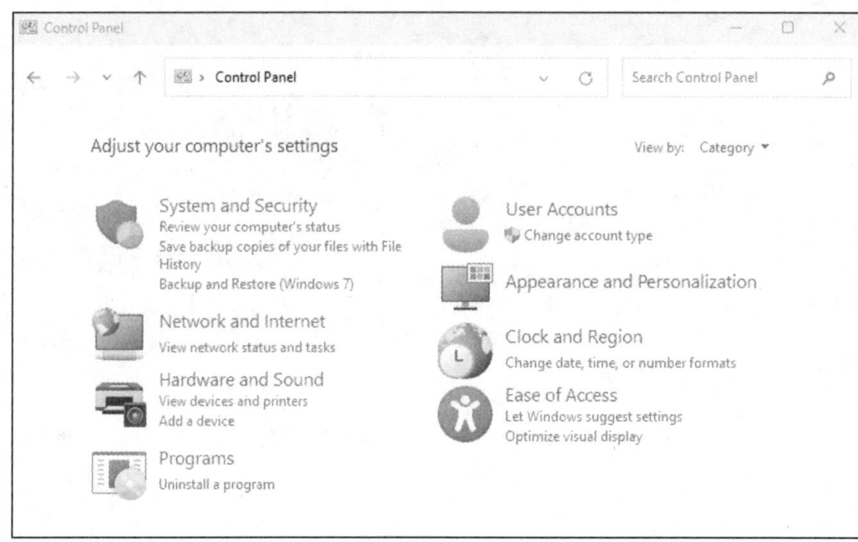

FIGURE 2-5: The Control Panel has shrunk but is not dead yet.

However, an increasing number of settings have been moved from Control Panel to Settings, which is great. The problem is that plenty of stuff is left in the Control Panel, that can only be accessed from there. For example, BitLocker Drive Encryption has not been upgraded to be accessible from the Settings app. It remains inside the Control Panel.

To make things confusing, some Windows 11 features can be set both from the Settings app and the Control Panel. For example, you'll find AutoPlay settings in both, alongside a list of programs and features installed on your PC and the options to manage user accounts. The confusion doesn't end here, however, because in the Control Panel, you'll find links that take you to the Settings app. For example, if you go to Control Panel ⇨ Appearance and Personalization and click Taskbar and Navigation, you'll see that it opens the personalization settings for the taskbar in the Settings app. I wish Microsoft had made things simpler and removed from the Control Panel the links to the stuff configured in the Settings app. They should also have also removed from the Control Panel the settings that are found in both places. It would have made for a more cohesive user experience.

Improved performance

According to Microsoft, Windows 11 should offer better performance than Windows 10. Although the company would have you believe that the differences in performance are significant, my experience proved that they're mostly incremental and not always easy to notice.

Among all the improvements, one that caught my attention is that Windows 11 can prioritize apps in the foreground. Apps you're opening or using receive more hardware resources than the ones in the background. That alone should make apps feel a little bit faster in Windows 11.

Battery life is another important focus area in Windows 11. Optimizations for laptop and tablet users mean the operating system uses less power than previous versions of Windows. For example, in Microsoft Edge, the Sleeping Tabs feature is on by default, putting open browser tabs in sleep mode after they haven't been used for a certain amount of time. According to Microsoft, this feature can lead to a huge decrease in processor and memory usage — about 30 percent less. To confirm Microsoft's promises, my team at Digital Citizen (the publication I lead) ran several benchmarks on two laptops and compared Microsoft Edge to Google Chrome, Mozilla Firefox, and Opera. Our aim was to see whether Microsoft Edge does indeed deliver better battery life. We were happy to see that it does, and by a huge margin, at least when compared to Google Chrome. If you're curious to see the results yourself, check out this web page: `https://bit.ly/40AIubN`.

Other improvements were introduced to the sleep process, and Windows 11 delivers 25 percent faster wake times than Windows 10. A small but welcome improvement for laptop users.

WARNING

Unfortunately, the Windows 11 launch was plagued by bugs and driver issues that impaired performance, especially on powerful AMD Ryzen processors. Luckily, they got fixed over time, even though some Ryzen 9 processors we're using for our work at Digital Citizen still have issues occasionally.

Gaming was supposed to be an area where Windows 11 delivered major performance increases. Unfortunately, Microsoft hasn't delivered on this promise, and gamers and tech bloggers alike have shown that Windows 10 and Windows 11 are mostly on par when it comes to how fast they run games.

Better gaming

While the gaming performance isn't much improved in Windows 11, gaming is a big deal in this operating system. For example, one important aspect that's changed is the High Dynamic Range (HDR) support offered by Windows 11.

HDR is a technology designed to make images on the screen resemble the real world as closely as possible. To make images look authentic, devices with HDR use wider ranges of colors, brighter light areas, and darker blacks for shades.

If you have a monitor with HDR support, you can take advantage of a cool aspect of Windows 11: the auto HDR feature (see Figure 2-6), which intelligently expands the color and brightness range up to HDR in games. This seamless feature gives you a new gaming experience that takes full advantage of your HDR monitor's capabilities.

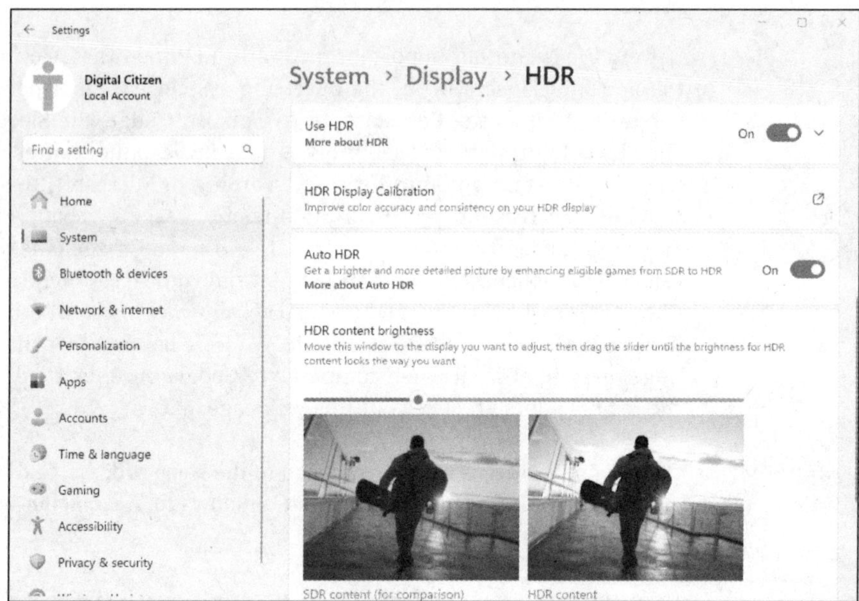

FIGURE 2-6: Auto HDR makes non-HDR games more beautiful in Windows 11.

There's also *dynamic refresh rate functionality*, which automatically helps you switch between different refresh rates. For example, Windows 11 might use 60 Hz when reading your email or a Word document on your laptop, which lowers battery consumption, but it then switches to 120 Hz automatically when gaming to give you the most fluid gaming experience.

A more interesting technical feature of Windows 11 that will affect the gaming of the future is *direct storage*, which allows your computer to bypass the processor when it needs to load data from an NVMe solid-state drive to the graphics card.

TECHNICAL STUFF

NVMe, or Non-Volatile Memory Express, is a standard software interface that enables SSDs and other components to run directly through the PCI Express (PCIe) physical interface directly attached to a computer's processor.

Direct storage decreases the amount of processor power required by games when loading textures (the graphics you see on the screen), which means that games should load faster, too. However, games must implement specific support for direct storage, and so far few titles have implemented it. One of the most popular games that benefits from using direct storage is Forspoken, a game that offers users an amazing 2-second load time.

To cater to the needs of gamers, Windows 11, just like Windows 10, has a game mode that starts automatically when it detects that you're playing something. You can also start it manually. *Game mode* prioritizes the processor and graphics card resources to your game. It also stops Windows Update from installing driver updates or showing update notifications during your play. Another useful feature is that it stops all notifications from all apps so that they don't interfere with your game.

One last feature is the *game bar*. With it, you can take screenshots while you play and record videos of your gameplay. You can also use it to quickly adjust the audio and voice settings — useful when you play online with others and must coordinate with them. The game bar also shows you the performance of your computer (processor, RAM, and graphics card resource consumption) and allows you to chat and interact with your friends on Xbox, as shown in Figure 2-7.

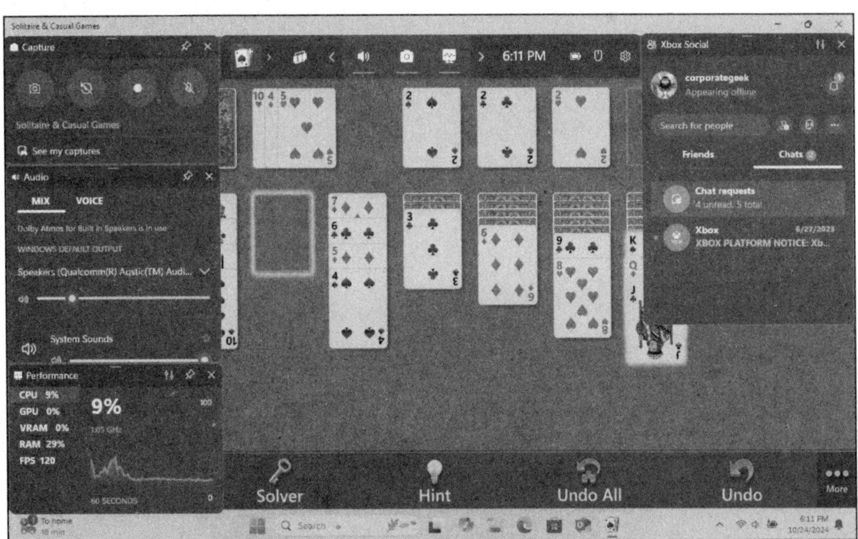

FIGURE 2-7: The game bar has many features useful to gamers.

TIP

Press Windows+G to display the game bar at any time, including when you're not playing. Familiarize yourself with all the buttons and features to use them productively while playing games.

I discuss Windows 11 gaming more in Book 4, Chapter 9.

RGB lighting

In the world of modern gaming, RGB accessories are all the rage. RGB refers to the three colors red, green, and blue. These primary colors can be combined in various amounts to get any other color from the color spectrum that the human eye can see.

Mice, keyboards, microphones, headsets, gaming chairs, computer motherboards, RAM, graphic cards, sound cards, and cooling systems have RGB lighting on them. We even have computer cases with RGB lighting systems. This technology allows users to personalize their computers, but no industry-wide standard existed for managing RGB lighting.

Luckily, Microsoft stepped in. In September 2023, Windows 11 introduced *dynamic lighting* to eliminate the fragmentation between vendors of systems, components, and accessories utilizing RGB lighting. You can see it in action in Figure 2-8.

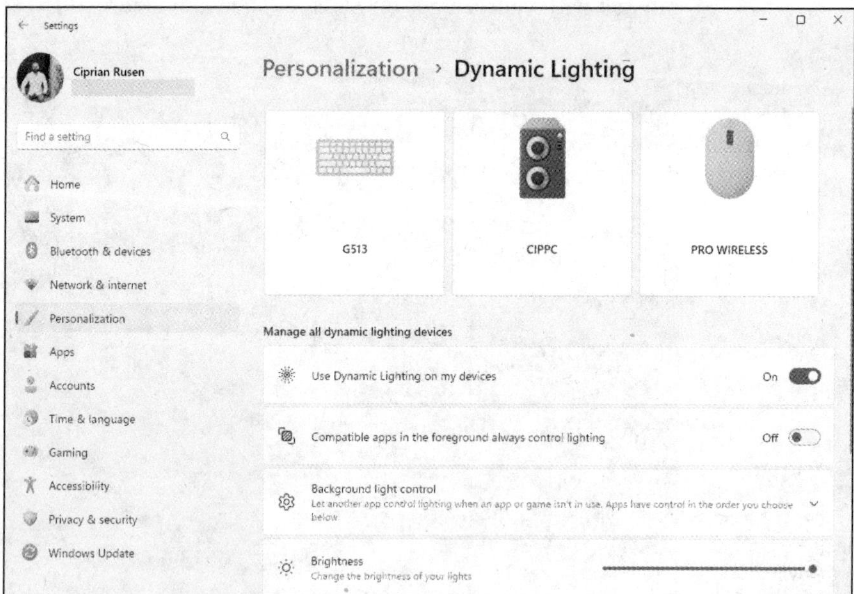

FIGURE 2-8: Dynamic lighting simplifies your management of RGB accessories.

In the past, if you bought a keyboard from ASUS, a mouse from Logitech, and a headset from Razer, each used its own standard for RGB lighting as well as specific drivers and personalization apps. As a result, you couldn't use the same lighting, colors, and effects on all of them without installing different personalization apps. To avoid this issue, you had to buy all your accessories with RGB lighting from the same vendor.

Dynamic lighting fixes this problem by using the HID LamArray standard, which was created by a group of companies including Logitech, Google, Apple, Intel, NVIDIA, and Synaptics. The standard's name comes from high-intensity discharge lamps, which produce light by means of an electric arc. LamArray makes RGB lighting handling easier for all hardware, regardless of the manufacturer. It applies to keyboards, mice, game controllers, headsets, microphones, computer cases, and other devices. Companies can choose to support dynamic lighting and, if they do, RGB accessories from multiple vendors become compatible, and you can configure how they light up straight from Windows 11.

Vendors such as Razer, ASUS, HyperX, MSI, and Microsoft announced their support and are slowly rolling out driver updates to make their accessories compatible with dynamic lighting.

Microsoft Edge

Microsoft Edge has replaced Internet Explorer from older Windows versions and is now based on the same Chromium open-source project found in Google Chrome, Opera, and other web browsers.

The new Edge from Windows 11 (shown in Figure 2-9) is a fast browser, ready to take on any website anywhere. It has a well-designed user interface and plenty of useful features (some of you will enjoy its vertical tabs or Workspaces feature), and it benefits from aggressive promotion by Microsoft. Laptop users will love the fact that it's the most energy-efficient web browser, allowing you to use your laptop for more time on a single charge.

Microsoft's advances with Edge have paid off; its share of the desktop browser market increased in May 2024 to 11.23 percent. Although this is still lower than Google Chrome's commanding 65.12 percent share, Microsoft Edge has enjoyed a positive evolution, which I hope continues. To learn about using Microsoft Edge, see Book 4, Chapter 1.

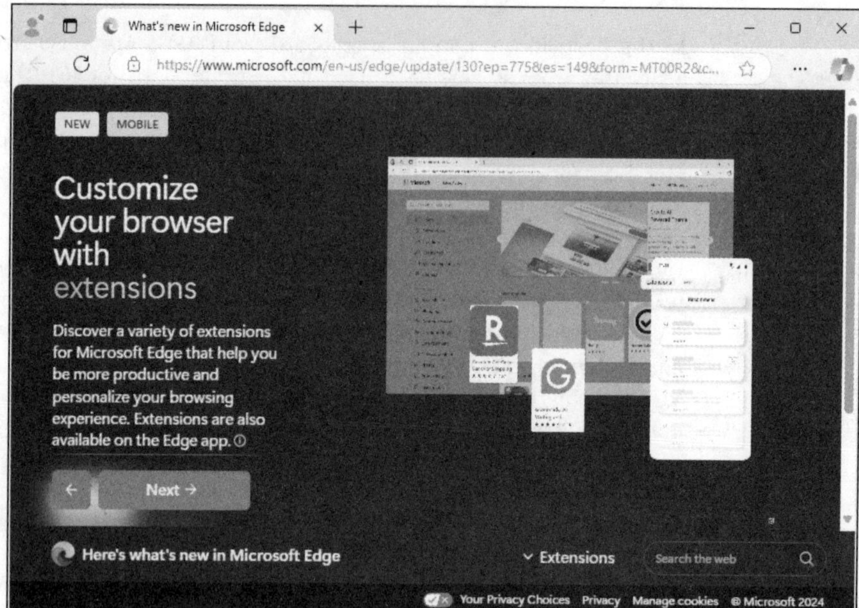

FIGURE 2-9: Microsoft Edge is a great web browser. You should try it!

Copilot

Microsoft had Cortana as its AI-based virtual assistant for many years. Due to the advances in artificial intelligence and large language models, the company replaced Cortana with Copilot in September 2023. Copilot is a much more advanced virtual assistant that is based on ChatGPT and integrated with Microsoft's Bing search engine. This integration allows it to provide you answers and references taken straight from the web, making it a useful companion for many tasks.

Copilot is everywhere in Windows 11: It has its own shortcut on the taskbar and its own app, and it's embedded in Microsoft Edge, Paint, Photos, Clipchamp, and other places.

Since Copilot (shown in Figure 2-10) was launched, its capabilities have expanded dramatically, and it was integrated with all the ChatGPT models that became available over time. By the time this book is published, we will most probably have GPT-5, with Copilot using it together with Bing. You learn about Copilot and what it can do in Book 4, Chapter 2.

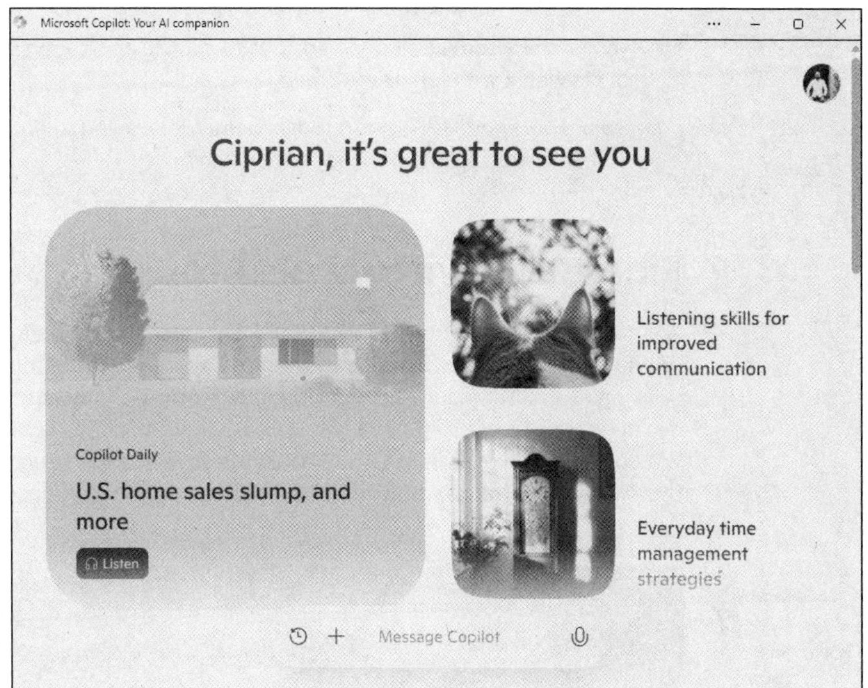

FIGURE 2-10: Copilot is a powerful AI assistant.

Improved security

Due to its strict security hardware requirements (supported processors, UEFI, Secure Boot, TPM), Windows 11 is a safer choice for business organizations. Because of this hardline approach, you get the following benefits:

- Encryption is turned on by default, which means that lost or stolen Windows 11 devices are harder to crack.
- Chip-to-cloud protection (or virtualization-based security) is built-in, meaning that many cloud-based security solutions and services can be operated more securely, including in remote or hybrid work scenarios.
- Container isolation for apps that are frequent targets for cyberattacks, such as Office or Microsoft Edge, means that a compromised app can't mess with the operating system, because it has no access to it, and can't cause even more damage. Container isolation in Windows 11 keeps apps separate from each other, like having different rooms for different activities. This helps protect

your system from attacks and ensures that if one application is compromised or crashes, it won't affect the others.

- Secure passwordless logins through biometric authentication, USB keys, or authentication apps provide for faster logins.

Fine-tuned virtual desktops

Windows has had virtual (or multiple) desktops since Windows XP, but before Windows 10, you had to install a third-party app — or something like Sysinternals Desktops from Microsoft — to get them to work. Windows 11 implements virtual desktops (see Figure 2-11) in a way that is useful and a bit less confusing than in Windows 10. For example, virtual desktops in Windows 11 no longer include the timeline from Windows 10. You can also name virtual desktops any way you want.

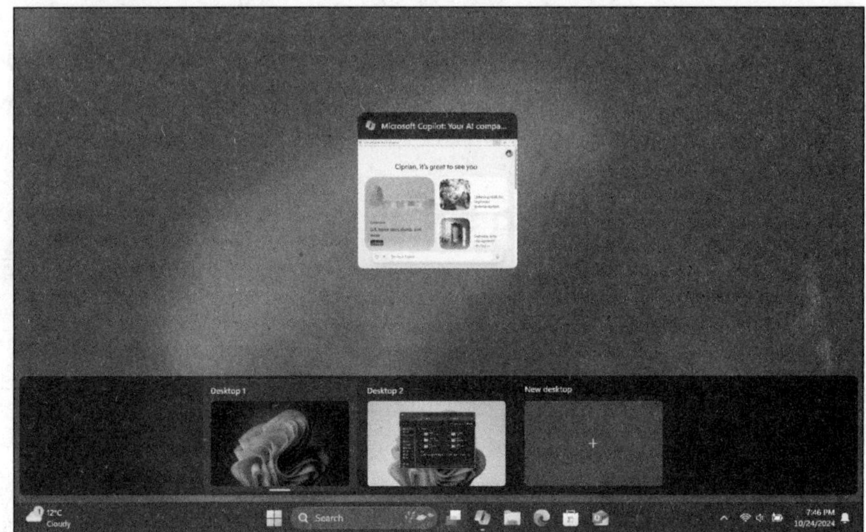

FIGURE 2-11: Task view displays all the multiple desktops you've set up.

Multiple desktops are handy if you tend to multitask. You can set up one desktop to handle your mail, calendar, and day-to-day stuff and another desktop for your latest project. Got a crunch project? Fire up a new desktop.

TIP

To start a new desktop, press Windows+Ctrl+D. To see all available desktops, click or tap the task view icon on the taskbar (to the right of the Search box) or press Windows+Tab. App windows can be moved between desktops by right-clicking and choosing Move To. Alt+Tab still rotates among all running windows. Clicking or tapping an icon in the taskbar brings up the associated program, regardless of which desktop it's on.

You learn how to use virtual desktops in Book 3, Chapter 1.

Improved window snapping and grouping

You use multiple windows and apps on your computer, and one of the easiest ways to organize them on the desktop is with the *snap feature.* It lets you quickly position your app windows on the screen by dragging them to the sides or corners. You can split the screen into two, three, or four areas. In Windows 11, snap is even better and easier to use: Hover your cursor on the square icon next to the close icon (X) in the top-right corner of any window, and you see a list of up to six snap layouts to choose from (Figure 2-12).

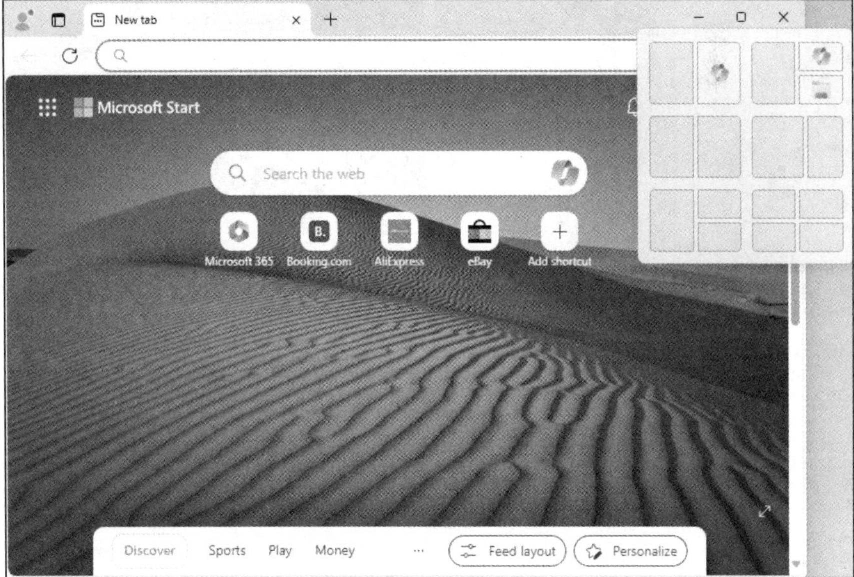

FIGURE 2-12: Windows 11 has many more useful snap layouts.

TECHNICAL STUFF

The number of layouts depends on the resolution of your screen. Displays that are full HD or higher have six snap layouts. On older monitors or on resolutions lower than full HD (or 1080p), you get four snap layouts.

Open windows are also organized into snap groups that remember the positions of windows on the screen, and as of February 2024, Windows 11 suggests quick app arrangements based on the apps you're using most frequently.

Widgets are back

Widgets are a group of small apps designed to provide at-a-glance information about news, weather, sports results, stocks, traffic, and the like, as shown in Figure 2-13. They are accessible straight from the taskbar and can be customized to show only the widgets you want.

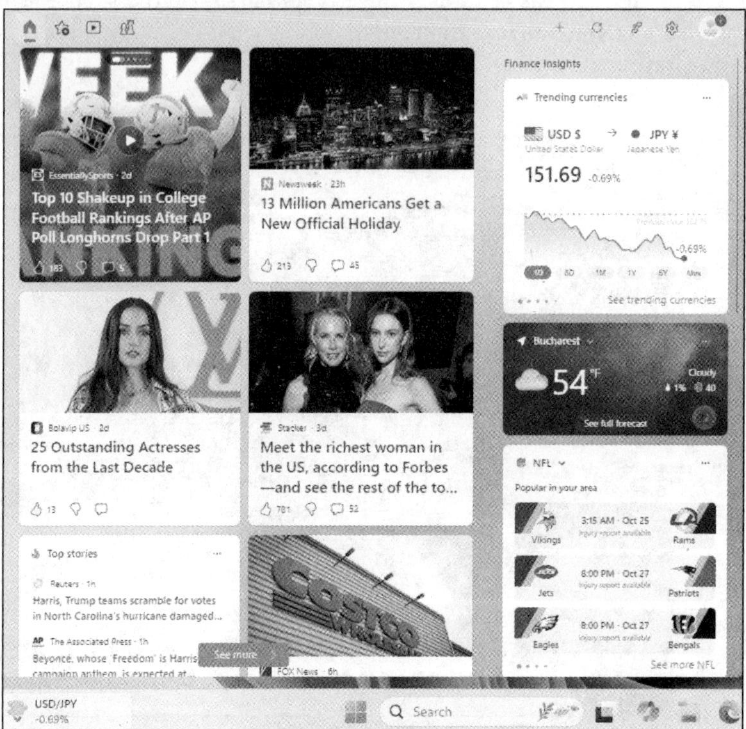

FIGURE 2-13: Widgets present live news and information.

The look and content delivery style of Windows 11's widgets are similar to the News and Interests widget in Windows 10. And just like News and Interests, when you click a link for a piece of news shown by the widgets, it's opened in Microsoft Edge, even if you've set your default web browser to Chrome, Opera, Firefox, or something else. I find this behavior a bit annoying, and you may too.

Read more about widgets in Book 4, Chapter 7.

Other apps and improvements

Microsoft has given to some built-in apps a much-needed makeover:

- **Windows Terminal** is now built into Windows 11 instead of a separate app you download from the Microsoft Store. With it, you can use a single command-line shell for executing commands in PowerShell, Command Prompt, and Azure Cloud Shell.
- **File Explorer** has changed dramatically from Windows 10. It has a new user interface, tighter integration with OneDrive, and new features like the Gallery, which shows you all your recent pictures.
- **Paint** has received a fresh look, with sleek menus and visuals and useful tools for basic image editing. It also uses AI for generating images or doing things like removing the background from an existing image.
- **Photos** has a better user interface, a new photo-viewing experience, and an updated photo-editing toolbar. Book 4, Chapter 4 shares what you need to know about using this app.
- **Snipping Tool** combines the Snipping Tool and Snip & Sketch apps from Windows 10 into one screenshot-taking app. The new app from Windows 11 is better and simpler to use than its predecessors. I present this app in Book 4, Chapter 10.
- **Xbox** from Windows 11 is better than it was in Windows 10. If you have an Xbox Game Pass Ultimate subscription, the Xbox app lets you play through Xbox Cloud Gaming directly, with no browser required.
- **Clock** now includes focus sessions, which help you improve productivity by implementing time-management methodologies such as the Pomodoro technique.
- **Calculator** is even more advanced than it was in Windows 10 and can plot equations in graphing mode.
- **Microsoft Teams** has its own Windows 11 app, which can be added to the taskbar. Like it or not, Teams is widely used in the corporate world and is an important productivity tool. Read Book 6, Chapter 2 for more on Teams.

There are also some general improvements at a user interface level, which come in handy:

- Quick settings are now separate from notifications and offer more things you can toggle on and off. Windows 11 apps can add their own quick settings (for example, Spotify), and they're easily accessible with a mouse, keyboard, and touch. To see them in action, press Windows+A on your keyboard.

» Microsoft has improved the touch experience, with more space between icons on the taskbar. Windows 11 also adds haptics to your digital pen, so you can hear and feel vibrations while taking notes or drawing on the screen.
» Windows 11 introduces voice typing, voice commands, and some new accessibility apps, which I cover in Book 2, Chapter 8.

Discovering What Was Removed from Windows

Windows 11 is not only about new features, apps, and a new user interface. Microsoft also decided to remove some apps from this operating system. Here's what we no longer have in Windows 11:

» **Cortana** never hit it out with users. It was discontinued and has now been removed from the operating system.
» **WordPad** was useful for basic word processing. The app wasn't improved for many years, and Microsoft decided to retire it and promote its Microsoft 365 subscription instead.
» **Steps Recorder** was used by some people for troubleshooting and getting help from others. This app, too, hasn't been updated in years, and both Microsoft and Windows users have lost interest in it.
» **Microsoft Support Diagnostic Tool** was useful in repairing Windows problems. Now these tools are getting axed.
» **Windows Mixed Reality** never took off and is being retired.

I hope you enjoyed this tour of Windows 11 and my summary of what's new, what has changed, and what has been removed. Before you dive in to using Windows 11, I recommend reading the next chapter in this minibook to learn about the differences between the various versions and editions of Windows 11.

IN THIS CHAPTER

» **Discovering the various versions and editions of Windows 11**

» **Finding your version and edition of Windows 11**

» **Upgrading from Windows 11 Home to Pro**

» **Summing up Microsoft 365**

Chapter 3
Windows 11 Versions

In 2015, Microsoft announced that Windows 10 would be the last version of Windows. However, in October 2021, they reversed their decision and introduced Windows 11. Since then, new versions of Windows 11 have been released annually. Rumor has it that Windows 12 is also in the works. To make things even more confusing, Windows 11 has several editions, most of which you can ignore, and a Windows 11 Home in S mode edition that's troublesome if you run it when you don't know what it is. In this chapter, I explain how Windows 11 versions and editions differ and advise you on which one to buy.

Also, contrary to what you might expect, Windows 11 isn't free, even though you get it preinstalled on a new laptop, PC, Microsoft Surface, or all-in-one device or as a free upgrade to Windows 10.

REMEMBER

Here are some facts about purchasing Windows 11:

- You can upgrade from a genuine copy of Windows 10 to Windows 11 for free, if your PC meets the minimum system requirements that I detail in Chapter 1 of this minibook.
- If you're building a new PC, you must buy Windows 11. And if you buy a new PC with Windows 11 preinstalled, the PC manufacturer most likely paid for Windows 11 and passed along this cost in the price of the PC.

If you haven't yet bought a copy of Windows, you can save yourself some headaches and more than a few bucks by buying the right edition the first time.

I explain all the many versions and editions of Windows in simple terms, so that you can understand which is best for you.

Finally, you may already have Windows 11 on your computer, but you don't know the edition and version. This information is helpful in understanding what you can and can't do with Windows 11, as well as when you need tech support. Continue reading this chapter for steps on finding the exact edition and version you're using.

EDITION VERSUS VERSION

Microsoft makes a distinction between *versions* and *editions* of Windows. *Windows versions* started with Windows 1.0 back in 1985, continued through Windows XP and Windows 7, and all the versions up to Windows 11. Microsoft is supporting and improving Windows 11 while also working on Windows 12, which is rumored to be released sometime in 2025.

In the past, there were big version changes, such as from Windows 7 to Windows 8, and then to Windows 10. However, after the release of Windows 10, Microsoft introduced a new way of updating Windows by releasing new versions of the same operating system twice a year. Each new Windows 10 version came with new features, bug fixes, and improvements. The version numbers changed to correspond roughly to when they were released. As a result, we had Windows 10 versions 21H1, 21H2, and 22H2. Version 22H2 is the last Windows 10 version, released in the second half (H2) of 2022 (22).

Getting back to Windows 11, Microsoft releases one new version each year, each with its own version bump, similar to Windows 10: Windows 11 version 21H2, 22H2, 23H2, and so on. The most recent version and the one I use is 24H2.

Although Windows 8 differed a lot from Windows 7, a modern-day Windows 11 version represents a minor upgrade over the previous one, with just a few new features and improvements, as well as several bug fixes. A significant difference between Windows 11 versions is that each has its own support window, which lasts about two years. For example, Windows 11 version 23H2 (released in the second half of 2023) is supported by Microsoft with updates and security patches until November 11, 2025. After that date, if you want to continue using Windows 11, you must upgrade to a newer version such as 24H2 if you want official support from Microsoft.

Windows editions are different from *Windows versions* because they refer strictly to the capabilities and features of an individual copy of Windows. You probably know about Windows Home and Windows Pro. And if you're working in a corporate office, you surely know about Windows Enterprise, too.

Windows 11 Editions

Windows 11 is available in eight major editions. Fortunately, most people must concern themselves with only two editions, and you can quickly narrow the list to one. In a nutshell, the Windows 11 editions (and targeted customer bases) are these:

REMEMBER

- **Windows 11 Home** is the edition you probably want for your personal computers. It includes most of the core features covered in this book. A big bonus for many is that Windows 11 Home can be used in over 100 languages at no extra cost. Its biggest downside is that it doesn't include BitLocker encryption and forces you to use a Microsoft account when installing it. If you're a business user, you should know that you can't use the Home edition to join Active Directory, and this may be an important downside for you.
- **Windows 11 Pro** includes everything in Windows 11 Home plus BitLocker for encrypting and protecting your data, Hyper-V for running virtual machines, and Windows Sandbox for making programming or software testing experiments in a safe environment. Another plus is that it can use more RAM than the Home edition (up to 2TB instead of 128GB for Home), two processors instead of one, and many more cores for higher-performance computers.
- **Windows 11 Enterprise** is available only to companies that buy Microsoft's Volume Licensing program. Compared to the Pro edition, Enterprise offers useful tools for large organizations, such as additional Microsoft Defender security features that allow networking administrators to enforce security policies, universal print, Active Directory support, and integrations with Microsoft's Azure cloud services. This edition is also sold via Windows 11 Enterprise E3 and E5 subscriptions, which are licensed on a per-user basis and tied to an Azure Active Directory account.
- **Windows 11 Education** looks and works just like Windows 11 Enterprise but is available only to schools and similar institutions through a program called Academic Volume Licensing. This edition is designed to provide education-specific default settings and tools.
- **Windows 11 Pro Education** is a special edition of Windows 11 for the educational sector, similar to Windows 11 Pro. It includes a Set Up School PCs app that allows administrators to set up computers using only a USB flash drive. You can consider it a Pro edition tailored to use default settings that are useful only for the education sector.
- **Windows 11 SE for Education** is designed with cloud-first tools, which enable educational institutions to create centrally controlled environments that are affordable and easy to manage. It bundles only apps that are considered essential for the academic sector. This edition is usually installed on very affordable

computers with modest hardware configurations. Think of them as Microsoft's alternative to the Chromebooks that are increasingly popular in schools.

- **Windows 11 Pro for Workstations** is designed for high-end hardware that costs a lot, as well as intensive computing tasks and the latest server processors and file systems. Unlike other editions of Windows 11, Pro for Workstations works on PCs with four processors (instead of a maximum of two) and a maximum of 6TB of RAM (instead of a maximum of 2TB). If you are a data scientist, CAD professional, researcher, or media producer, this edition is probably the best for you.
- **Windows 11 IoT Enterprise** is designed for low-cost computers such as the Raspberry Pi and specialized machines, such as robots, ATMs, POS terminals, and barcode scanners. (IoT means Internet of Things.)

In markets such as the European Union and Korea, you'll find single language, N, and KN variation of these Windows 11 Editions. For example, a Windows 11 Home Single Language edition doesn't allow you to install an additional language or change its base language unless you purchase the full, language-neutral version. N versions are available in the European Union, while KN versions are sold in Korea. They both have several media playback features removed because of legal restrictions.

TECHNICAL STUFF

Windows 11 Home can run in S mode. While this mode can work on Intel and AMD processors, Microsoft promotes it mostly for laptops equipped with Qualcomm Snapdragon processors, which offer high-energy efficiency but use a different processor architecture. When using Windows 11 Home in S mode, you can install and run apps only from the Microsoft Store. In the past, this meant you were stuck using only Microsoft Edge as your web browser. Luckily, in recent years, browsers like Opera, Firefox, and Brave have shown up in the Microsoft Store, so you can change your default web browser if you want.

WARNING

Windows 11 Home in S mode doesn't run old-fashioned Windows programs. It's restricted to running only Windows 11 apps from the Microsoft Store. Luckily, only Windows 11 Home can run in S mode.

Narrowing your choices

If you're a regular home user, you should decide between Windows 11 Home and Pro. Your choice is simple. Get Windows 11 Home, unless you need to do one of the following:

- **Connect to a corporate network.** If your company doesn't give you a copy of Windows 11 Enterprise, you need to spend the extra bucks and buy Windows 11 Pro.

» **Play the role of the host in a Remote Desktop interaction.** If you're need Remote Desktop, you must buy Windows 11 Pro.

TIP

Many business users find that TeamViewer or AnyDesk, two free alternatives to Remote Desktop, do everything they need and that Remote Desktop amounts to overkill. Both TeamViewer and AnyDesk let you access and control your home or office PC from anywhere with an internet connection. For details, visit `www.teamviewer.com` and `anydesk.com`.

» **Provide added security to protect your data from prying eyes or to keep your data safe even if your laptop is stolen.** Start by determining whether you need Encrypting File System (EFS), BitLocker, or both (see the "BitLocker and Encrypting File System" sidebar). Windows 11 Pro has EFS and BitLocker — with BitLocker To Go tossed in for even more protection.

» **Run Hyper-V.** Some people can benefit from running virtual machines inside Windows 11. If, for instance, you must get an old Windows 7 program to cooperate, running Hyper-V with a licensed copy of Windows 7 may be the best choice. For most people, virtual machines are an interesting toy but not much more. Luckily, there are many alternatives to Hyper-V, including free products such as VirtualBox, which can be used even on Windows 11 Home.

BITLOCKER AND ENCRYPTING FILE SYSTEM

BitLocker runs *underneath* Windows and starts before the operating system starts. The Windows partition on a BitLocker-protected drive is completely encrypted, so malicious third parties who try to access the file system can't read it.

Encrypting File System (EFS) is a method for encrypting individual files or groups of files on a hard drive. EFS starts after Windows boots: It runs as a program under Windows, which means it can leave traces of itself and the data that's being encrypted in temporary Windows places that may be sniffed by malicious programs. The Windows directory isn't encrypted by EFS, so malicious third parties who can get access to the directory can hammer it with brute-force password attacks. Widely available tools can hack EFS if they can reboot the computer they are trying to hack. Thus, for example, EFS can't protect the hard drive on a stolen laptop.

However, EFS and BitLocker are complementary technologies: BitLocker provides coarse all-or-nothing protection for an entire drive, while EFS lets you encrypt specific files or groups of files. Used together, they can be hard to crack.

There's also BitLocker To Go, which provides BitLocker-style protection to removable drives, including USB drives. You should use it when storing important data on your USB drives.

64-bit is the new normal

If you've settled on Windows 11 as your operating system of choice, there's no more stressing about whether you want the 32-bit or the 64-bit flavor of the Home edition, as was the case with Windows 10 and older versions. That's because Windows 11 is the first consumer operating system from Microsoft to support only 64-bit processors. It doesn't work on older 32-bit processors and accepts only modern hardware that meets its strict security requirements. This is one of the biggest reasons why, in April 2024, according to StatCounter, Windows 11's market share was just 26.19 percent, while Windows 10 remained the most popular version, commanding a market share of 69.89 percent.

Not being able to use Windows 11 on old hardware can be annoying, but this enforcement on Microsoft's part has important benefits:

- **Performance:** The 32-bit flavor of Windows, which everyone was using more than a decade ago, has a limit on the amount of memory that it can use. Give or take a nip here and a tuck there, 32-bit machines can see, at most, 3.4 or 3.5 gigabytes (GB) of memory. You can stick 4GB of RAM into your computer, but in the 32-bit world, anything beyond 3.5GB is simply out of reach. With many desktop apps such as the Google Chrome browser acting like resource hogs, you want 4GB or more on any PC.
- **Security:** Security is one more good reason for running a 64-bit variant of Windows. Microsoft enforced strict security constraints on drivers that support hardware in 64-bit machines — constraints that just couldn't be enforced in the older, laxer 32-bit environment.

There's only one problem with 64-bit Windows: drivers. Some people have older hardware that isn't supported if the manufacturer decides against building a solid 64-bit savvy driver that would allow the old hardware to work with the new operating system. You, as a customer, get the short end of the stick and are forced to buy new hardware. And many users decide to postpone doing it for as long as possible.

Applications, however, are a different story. All 32-bit apps work on 64-bit Windows and shouldn't be an issue. You can install and use 32-bit versions of Microsoft Office and even run 32-bit browsers such as Google Chrome. However, your apps also benefit from running their 64-bit versions because they can address a lot more memory, process larger amounts of data, and run more complex calculations. If you want to work with large spreadsheets in Excel or huge databases in Access, install a 64-bit version of Microsoft Office on your Windows 11 computer.

Which Version and Edition of Windows 11 Are You Running?

You may be curious to know which version and edition of Windows 11 your current machine is running. Here's how to see your specific edition and version:

1. **Click or tap the Search box on the taskbar and type** about.

   Search results appear. At the top of the stack, you should see something like *About Your PC.*

2. **Press Enter or click or tap About Your PC.**

   You see an About window with lots of technical details.

3. **On the right, look for Device Specifications, and click or tap it to expand it, if necessary.**

   In Figure 3-1, next to System Type, you can see that I'm using a 64-bit version of Windows 11.

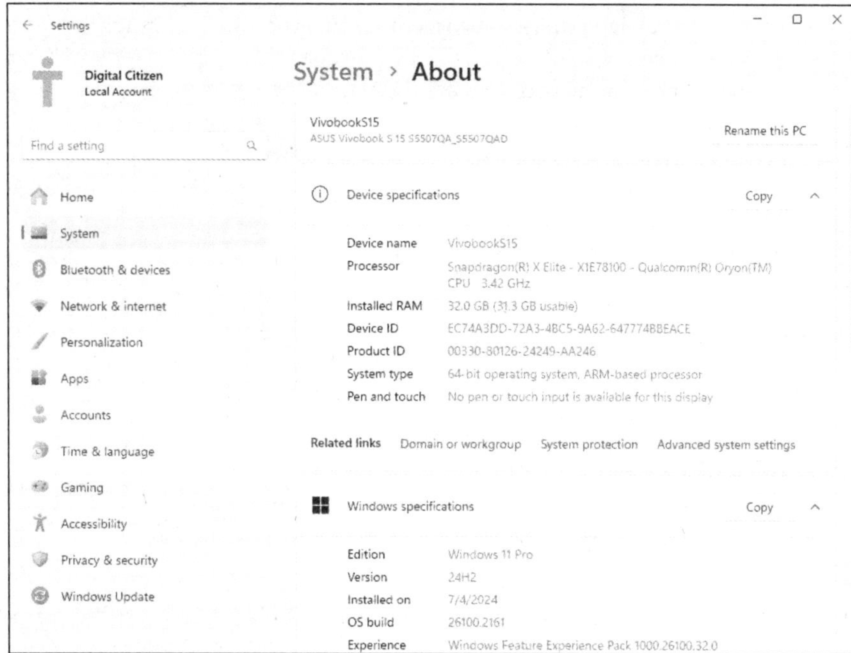

FIGURE 3-1: The About page tells you the Windows 11 edition, version, and much more.

4. **Scroll down to Windows Specifications, and click or tap this section to expand it if it isn't already open.**

   This section shows the edition of Windows 11, the version, the date it was installed, and the OS build number.

TIP

The OS build number is useful if you need to contact Microsoft's tech support service. It helps the support engineer figure out the exact build of Windows 11 and the appropriate patches or steps required to troubleshoot problems with your specific version.

Upgrading from Windows 11 Home to Pro

What if you aim too low and buy Windows 11 Home and decide later that you really want Windows 11 Pro? Don't worry! Switching editions is not as tough as you think.

If you want to move from Windows 11 Home to Windows 11 Pro (the only upgrade available to individuals), you need to buy an upgrade key, which is available through retailers such as Amazon or Best Buy, or purchase a Windows 11 Pro product key. The upgrade key is cheaper than a full Windows 11 Pro product key, but buying the correct edition the first time is even cheaper.

After you purchase the necessary upgrade or product key, here's how to upgrade from Windows 11 Home to Pro:

1. **Press Windows+I.**

   The Settings window appears on the screen.

2. **Click or tap System.**

   An extensive list of system settings appears.

3. **Scroll down and click or tap the Activation entry.**

   The Windows 11 edition you're using and its activation state are displayed.

4. **Click or tap Upgrade Your Edition of Windows.**

   The options shown in Figure 3-2 appear, which allow you to enter the key that you purchased or open the Microsoft Store and purchase the upgrade from there.

5. **Click or tap the Change button.**

   The Enter Product Key window shown in Figure 3-3 pops up.

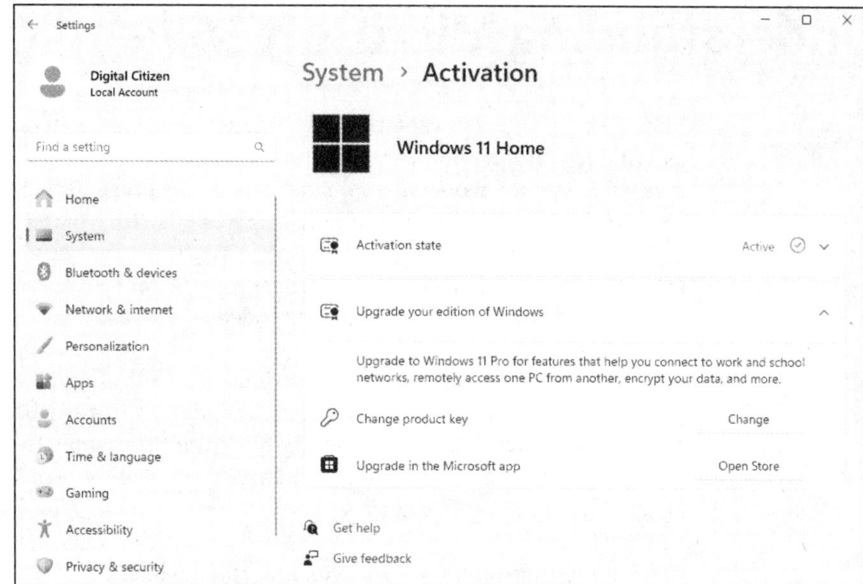

FIGURE 3-2: See your Windows 11 edition and activation state.

6. **Type the key you purchased or simply copy and paste it, and then press Next.**

   Windows shows a succession of progress screens, and your system restarts. After completing the upgrade, you receive a notification informing you that it was a success.

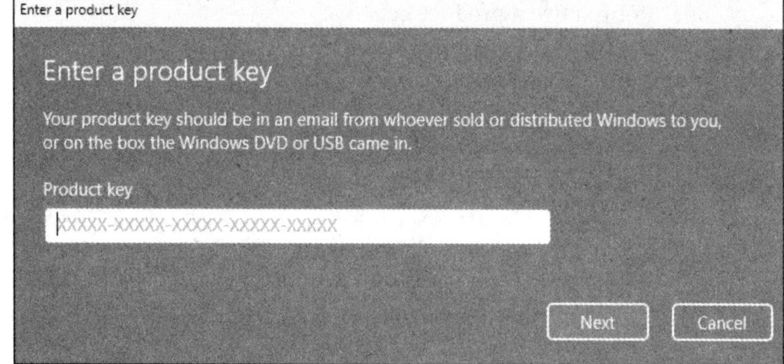

FIGURE 3-3: Enter the key for upgrading to Windows 11 Pro.

TIP

Moving from Windows 11 Home in S mode to plain Windows 11 Home can be done only from the Microsoft Store by accessing the Switch Out of S Mode page.

Understanding Microsoft 365 and Office

Microsoft Office, also called simply Office, is just as well-known and popular as Windows. It's a suite of useful productivity applications that enable users to create documents, work with spreadsheets, make presentations, send emails, and more. Before 2013, users would purchase a license for Microsoft Office and could use it indefinitely. Since 2013, however, Microsoft has promoted Office 365, a subscription-based model, as the primary way to access Microsoft Office. To add to the complexity, Office 365 was rebranded as Microsoft 365 in 2020.

Microsoft 365 is available as a subscription for both individuals and businesses, providing access to Office applications. Individuals can opt between a Microsoft 365 Personal plan, which gives access to all the Office apps for one user on up to five computers and devices, and a Microsoft 365 Family plan, which can be used by up to six users on five devices each.

In addition, there are Microsoft 365 Enterprise plans that offer Windows licenses along with Office access. These plans also include features such as device and app management through Intune (a cloud-based management service provided by Microsoft), advanced identity and access management, threat protection, information protection, and compliance management.

TIP

If users in an organization have a Microsoft 365 Enterprise subscription that includes a Windows license, they can automatically upgrade a computer with Windows 11 Pro to Windows 11 Enterprise by joining the device to Azure Active Directory with the credentials associated with that subscription. This upgrade does not require a product key.

If all this isn't complicated enough, you will also find an app named Microsoft 365 (Office) when you check the apps preinstalled with Windows 11. This app is free and acts as a gateway to your Microsoft 365 subscription if you have one. You can see it in action in Figure 3-4.

From this app, you can install all the Office apps available with your subscription, access your Office files, and create ones using Office. If you don't have a paid Microsoft 365 subscription, the app allows you to use the free versions of Word, Excel, and PowerPoint.

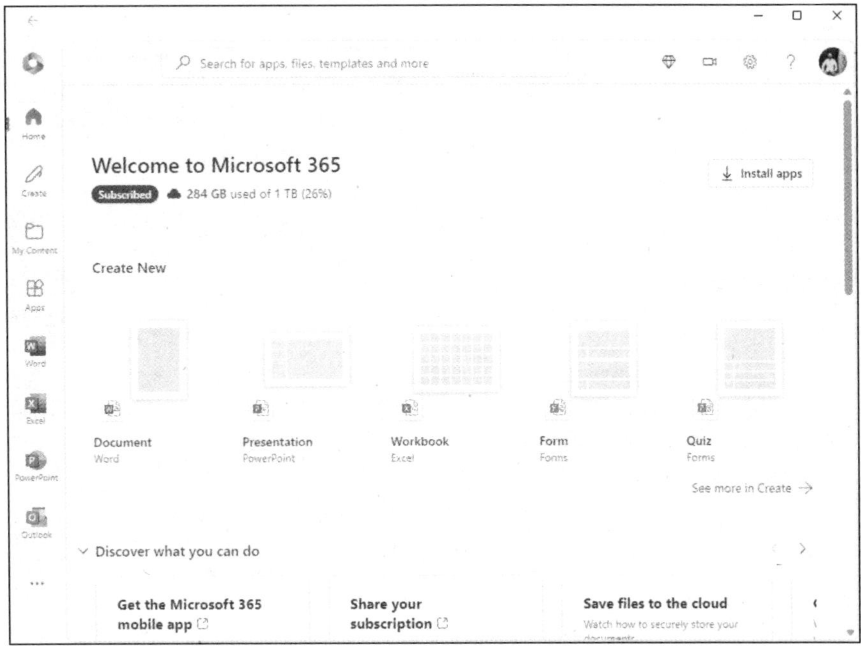

FIGURE 3-4: The Microsoft 365 (Office) app.

Windows 11 Versions

2 Personalizing Windows

Contents at a Glance

IN THIS CHAPTER

» Navigating the basics of the desktop

» Working with Windows 11 on a touchscreen

» Knowing when to shut down, restart, sleep, lock, or sign out

» Learning useful keyboard shortcuts

» Using the mouse and touchpad gestures

Chapter 1 Getting Around in Windows

Are you ready to familiarize yourself with Windows 11 but not quite ready to dive in fully? No worries, you're in the right place for a gentle introduction. This chapter won't be too challenging — just a bit of navigating around Windows. If you're an experienced Windows 7 user, you may notice some familiar elements in Windows 11 and some features that resemble those found on a Mac or an iPhone. If you're currently using Windows 10, you'll feel mostly at home and appreciate the more seamless user experience, especially if your device has a touchscreen.

Navigating the Windows 11 desktop is not difficult, but I give you a quick tour in this chapter. Also, I discuss how Microsoft approaches touchscreens in this version of Windows. It's a bit different and better than in Windows 10.

But what about turning Windows 11 off and on again? This question has become a popular meme among people who provide tech support to their friends and co-workers. In this chapter, I show you how to power off your machine and explain the best way to do it, depending on how long you'll be away from it.

Toward the end, I show you a few useful keyboard shortcuts alongside the classic Ctrl+C and Ctrl+V that many know. Using shortcuts will make you more productive and help you find your way around Windows 11 more quickly. Finally, you learn some tricks about using the mouse and the trackpad on a Windows 11 laptop.

Navigating Around the Desktop

Whether you use a mouse, a trackpad, or your finger, the desktop is where you'll spend most of your time in Windows. Here's a guided tour of your PC, which you can perform with a mouse, a finger, or even a stylus, your choice:

1. **Click or tap the Start icon (Windows logo), shown in the margin.**

   You see the Start menu (see Figure 1-1). Note the Search box at the top, the list of pinned apps, and the Recommended section populated with recent files and recently installed apps.

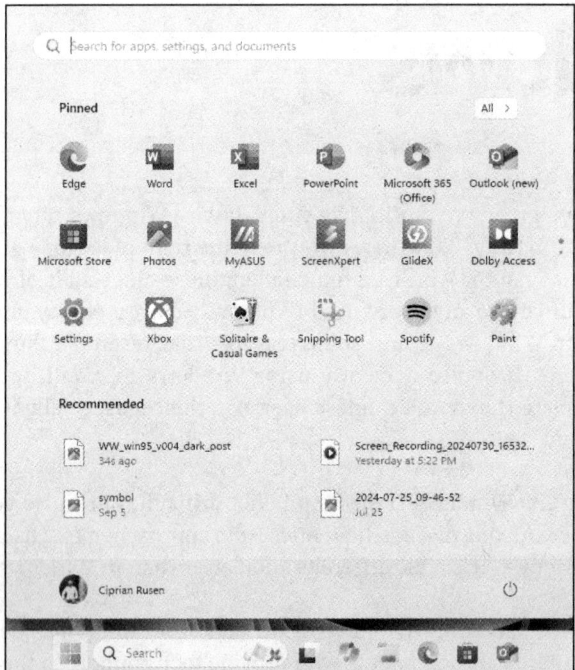

FIGURE 1-1: The Start menu is simpler than the one in Windows 10.

2. **In the Pinned section, click or tap the Photos icon. If it doesn't appear there, choose All and then Photos.**

   Microsoft's Photos app starts, as shown in Figure 1-2. Before you can use it, it may try to convince you to buy a subscription to OneDrive.

FIGURE 1-2: The Photos app is a solid Windows 11 app.

3. **Close the messages about OneDrive and look closely at the Photos app window.**

   Like other app windows, the Photos window can be resized by moving your mouse cursor over to an edge and then clicking (or pressing) and dragging it. You can move the entire window by clicking (or tapping) the title bar and dragging. You can minimize the window — make it shrink down to an icon on the taskbar — by clicking or tapping the horizontal line in the upper-right corner. And finally, you can close the app by clicking or tapping the X in the upper right.

4. **On the taskbar, next to the Start icon, click or tap in the Search box (shown in the margin).**

   The Windows 11 search menu appears, where you can type the names of apps, files, folders, settings, or websites to find what you need.

5. **In the search field (at the bottom), type the word** photos.

   The first result is the Photos app, as shown in Figure 1-3. The results will also include settings, web results, and folders and files on your computer that contain the word *photos* in their name.

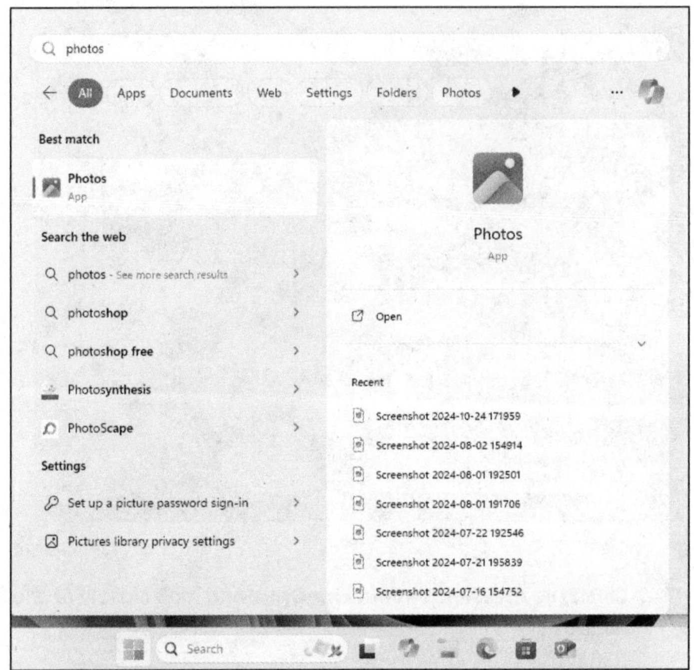

FIGURE 1-3: Search is a useful feature of Windows 11.

6. **Click or tap the task view icon (shown in the margin), which is to the right of the Search box.**

   Windows 11 can have multiple virtual desktops, each displaying a separate set of app windows. The first desktop is named Desktop 1, and you see it displayed at the bottom of the screen (see Figure 1-4).

7. **Click or tap the New Desktop button (above the taskbar).**

   Desktop 2 is created and added to the list of virtual desktops. Any app that you open from now on will be assigned to this virtual desktop.

8. **Move the mouse pointer over Desktop 1, right-click (or press and hold) the Photos app, and choose Move To ➪ Desktop 2.**

   You've successfully moved the Photos app from Desktop 1 (the default) to Desktop 2, which you created in Step 7.

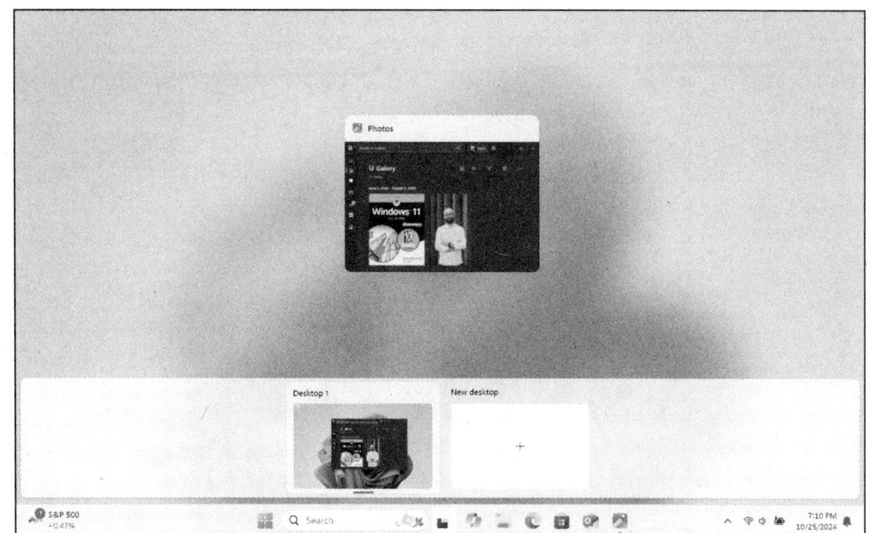

FIGURE 1-4: Your virtual desktops are found in task view.

9. **Click or tap Desktop 2.**

   Note how the Photos app is now on Desktop 2.

10. **In the Photos app window, click or tap the X in the top-right corner to close it.**

    Desktop 2 now has zero running apps.

73°F Sunny

11. **On the left side of the taskbar, click or tap the widgets icon (shown in the margin).**

    This icon usually looks like a weather forecast, but it can also display a stock market graph or a traffic alert.

    The Windows 11 widgets appear, as shown in Figure 1-5. They display information such as the weather forecast, the latest news, sports updates, stock market data, and traffic data.

12. **Click or tap somewhere on the desktop outside the widgets.**

    You return to the Windows 11 desktop. Take a breather.

This was a quick tour of some of the highlights of the desktop. There's much more to discover — you only scratched the surface.

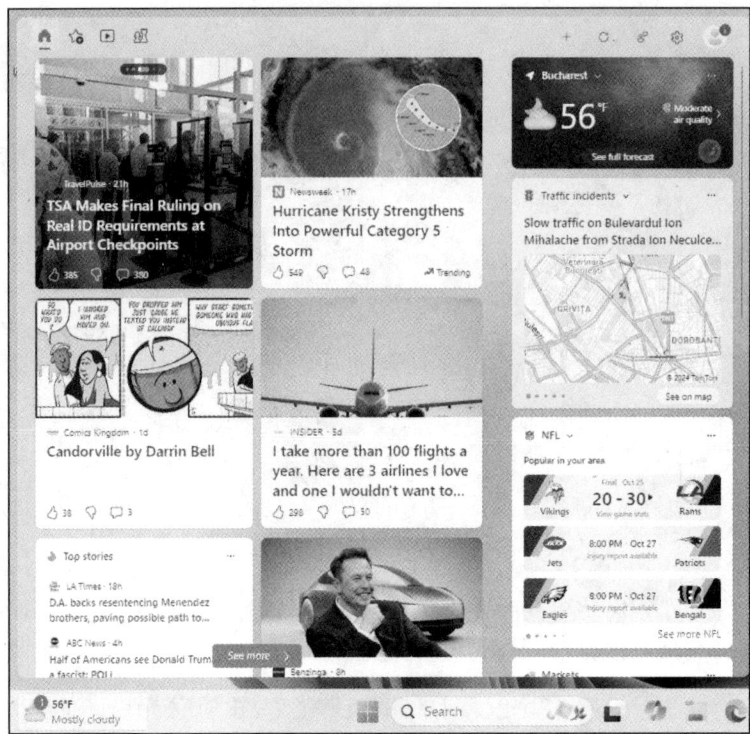

FIGURE 1-5: The widgets display tons of information.

Using Windows 11 on Tablets and Touchscreens

Windows 10 had a special tablet mode optimized for touchscreens. While it wasn't perfect, it was easy to turn on and enabled you to use touch instead of the mouse and keyboard. Windows 11 has ditched tablet mode but handles touch better than Windows 10. How is that possible?

Microsoft decided to stop offering two environments in parallel (one for the mouse and keyboard and another for touch) and redesigned the user interface to work equally well for both. As a result, when Windows 11 detects that you're using touch, it automatically increases the spacing between icons and other interface elements, so they're more touch-friendly. Most people can't tell the difference between Windows 11 on a desktop PC and a laptop with a touchscreen. You must have a PC and a device with touch next to each other to notice the subtle differences.

To use Windows 11 on a touchscreen, you need to know a few basic gestures that are performed with just one finger:

- **Tap** to select an item, such as a file or a shortcut. This gesture is the equivalent of a click.
- **Press and hold** to right-click an item.
- **Double-tap** to open a file or an app. This gesture is the equivalent of a double-click.
- **Tap and drag** to move an item across the screen. This action is the equivalent of drag-and-drop with the mouse.

Learning how to swipe with your fingers on the screen helps too:

- **Swipe right to left** (from the right side of your screen to the left) to open notifications and the calendar.
- **Swipe left** (from the left side of the screen to the right) to view the widgets.

As you browse around Windows 11, notice how almost everything is more touch-friendly than it was in Windows 10. I appreciate the new Settings app in Windows 11. It's simpler and better for both touch and mouse than the Settings in Windows 10. Also, the highly improved File Explorer (see Figure 1-6) makes navigating files and folders much easier on a tablet because it ditches the ribbon interface from Windows 10.

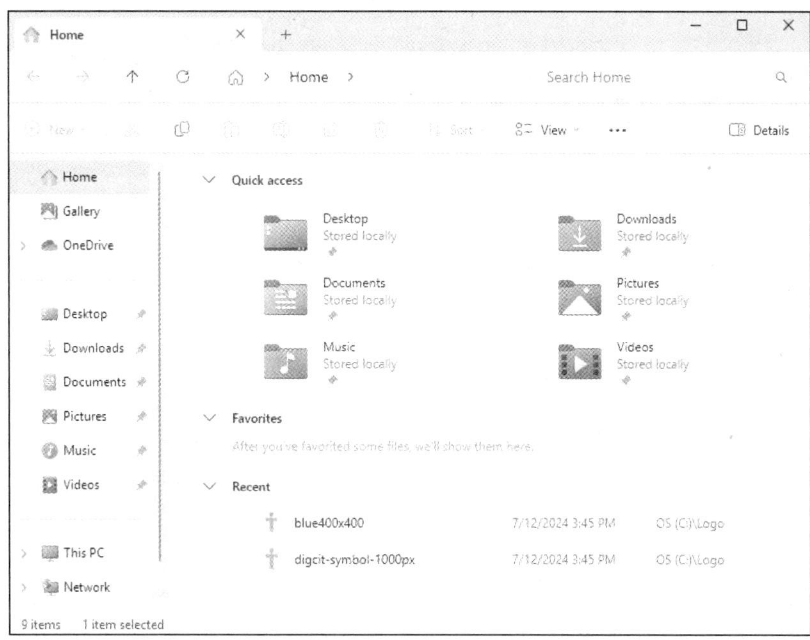

FIGURE 1-6: File Explorer in Windows 11 works much better on touchscreens.

Shut Down, Sleep, Restart, Sign Out, Lock, Sleep

If you plan to not use your Windows 11 device for a long time, shut it down. This means turning it off completely. You restart it by simply pressing the device's power button.

If you're taking a break for an hour or so, put your device to sleep. This mode turns off the display but keeps your computer awake and uses little energy. Also, your work is kept as you left it, and your PC will resume faster. To resume from sleep mode, move the mouse around, press any key, or press the power button.

Another option is to lock your Windows 11 computer so others don't see your work and can't access your account.

If you have a family or work computer that you share with others, you should know how to sign out of your account so that other people can sign in with theirs. Knowing how to restart your computer is helpful, too, especially after a Windows 11 update is installed or when you encounter problems.

Here's how to do all those tasks:

1. **Click or tap the Start icon (shown in the margin).**

   The Start menu is displayed. (Refer to Figure 1-1.)

2. **Click or tap the power icon in the Start menu's bottom-right corner (and shown in the margin).**

   You see all the options from the Power menu, as shown in Figure 1-7. You can choose Lock, Sleep, Shut Down, or Restart.

WARNING

   Clicking or tapping one of these options starts the specified action immediately.

3. **Click or tap your user account name in the bottom-left corner of the Start menu.**

   A menu opens with options related to your user account, as shown in Figure 1-8, including Sign Out. You can also see your account name, the associated email address (if you're using a Microsoft account), whether or not you have an active Microsoft 365 subscription, and how much cloud storage you have available in your account.

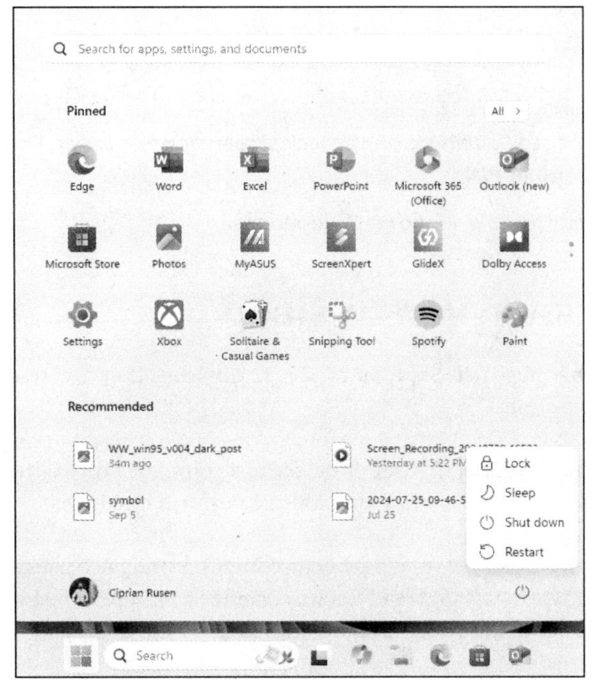

FIGURE 1-7: Use the Power menu to lock, sleep, shut down, or restart your device.

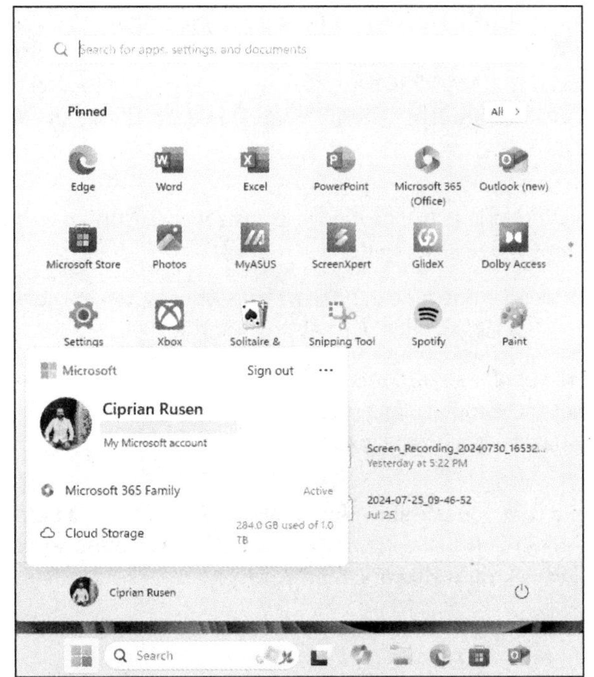

FIGURE 1-8: You can lock your computer or sign out from your user menu.

4. **Choose Sign Out.**

   The Windows 11 lock screen is shown, where you see the time and date.

5. **Click or tap anywhere on the lock screen or press Enter. Enter your user password or PIN.**

   You return to the Windows 11 desktop.

Shut down versus sleep

Many people put their laptops to sleep, thinking they're completely turned off when they're not.

REMEMBER

Shutting down your computer or device is a complete stop. When shut down, your device no longer uses energy and doesn't perform any tasks.

REMEMBER

Sleep is a low-power state where your computer or device uses a bit of energy and stores your work in RAM (read Book 1, Chapter 1 for all the technical terminology). It turns off some hardware components such as the processor and the hard disk.

When you shut down a computer, all your work is closed. When you put your Windows 11 laptop to sleep, your work is saved as-is. Powering your computer back on takes longer after it's shut down because it must start and load Windows again. Doing the same when resuming from sleep takes less time because your apps and work are saved in RAM. This benefit may entice people to always put their devices to sleep instead of shutting them down. However, doing so causes the following problems:

- Devices continue to use power while in sleep mode (this may be problematic on laptops with weaker batteries).
- If left in sleep mode for extended periods, your laptop may overheat and face performance issues when you resume using it.
- Some drivers for some components have poor resume-from-sleep support, and they may stop working properly, forcing you to restart Windows 11 so that you can use it normally again.

TIP

I recommend that you use sleep for short periods of time, a half hour to an hour or two. If you plan to stay away from your Windows 11 computer for a couple of hours or more, always shut it down.

Using the Keyboard and Keyboard Shortcuts

One thing I didn't expect to change anytime soon was the keyboard we use on our desktop computers and laptops. It turns out that as of January 2024, keyboards won't be the same because Microsoft introduced a new Copilot key for Windows 11 computers and devices. On most laptops, it will be placed next to the right-side Alt key, as shown on the Surface Laptop 6 in Figure 1-9. It will replace the menu key that was introduced alongside the Windows key, more than 30 years ago, and the Office-dedicated key that Microsoft added to its keyboards back in 2019.

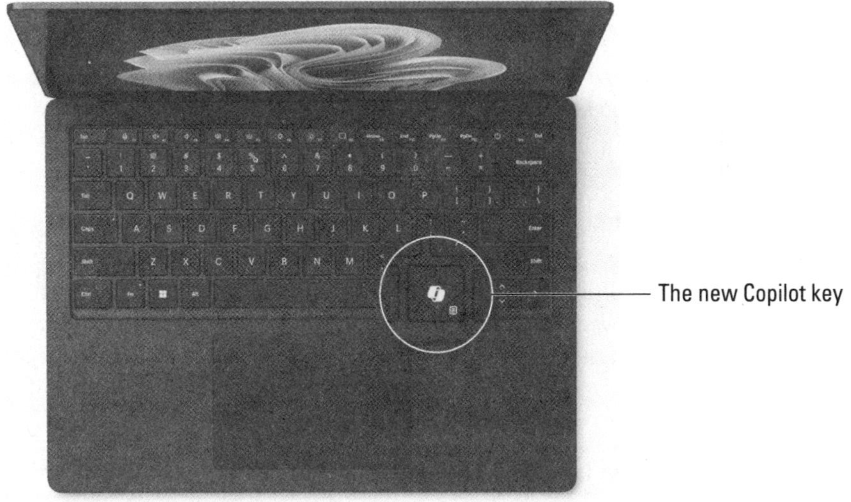

FIGURE 1-9: The Copilot key on a Surface Laptop 6.

Source: Microsoft

The Copilot key launches Copilot, which is built into Windows 11 (see Book 4, Chapter 2), and allows you to interface with it as quickly as possible. If Copilot isn't available in your country, the Copilot key will launch the Search window instead. At the time of writing, this key can't be personalized to do something other than start Copilot. However, Microsoft announced that it's working on adding such personalization options.

Until we get more clarity on Microsoft's approach with this new key, we can use hundreds of keyboard shortcuts to work faster. I don't use many of them because they're difficult to remember. However, some are easy to remember and will make your work with Windows 11 a lot easier.

REMEMBER

Here are the keyboard shortcuts that everyone should know. They've been around for a long, long time:

- **Ctrl+C** copies whatever you've selected and puts it on the clipboard. On a touchscreen, you can do the same thing in most applications by pressing and holding your selection and then choosing Copy.
- **Ctrl+X** cuts whatever you've selected and puts it on the clipboard. Again, you can press and hold your selection, and Cut should appear on the menu.
- **Ctrl+V** pastes whatever is in the clipboard to the current cursor location. Tap and hold usually works the same.
- **Ctrl+A** selects everything, although sometimes it's hard to tell what *everything* means — different applications handle Ctrl+A differently. Press and hold usually works here, too.
- **Ctrl+Z** usually undoes whatever you just did. Few touch-enabled apps have a press-and-hold alternative; you usually must find Undo on a ribbon or menu.
- When you're typing, **Ctrl+B, Ctrl+I,** and **Ctrl+U** usually change your text to bold, italic, or underlined, respectively. Press the same key combination again, and the text returns to normal.

REMEMBER

In addition to all the key combinations you may have encountered in previous Windows versions, there's a healthy crop of new combinations. These are the important ones:

- The **Windows key** brings up the Start menu and closes it if you press it again.
- **Windows+A** opens Quick Settings.
- **Windows+E** launches File Explorer.
- **Windows+I** opens the Settings app.
- **Windows+C** opens Copilot. If you don't have a computer with the Copilot key, this is what you should use instead.
- **Windows+M** minimizes all open apps and windows on the current desktop.
- **Windows+Tab** opens task view, with the virtual desktops listed at the bottom. In the middle is a preview of the open apps in each virtual desktop.
- **Alt+Tab** cycles through all running apps on the current desktop, one by one. See Figure 1-10.

FIGURE 1-10: Alt+Tab cycles through all running apps.

- **Windows+D** shows you the desktop. Press it again, and it returns to the desktop's initial state.
- **Windows+K** opens the *Cast* pane, where you can connect to wireless displays and audio devices. For example, you can use the shortcut to connect to a Smart TV and hold a presentation on it, or to view on your TV a movie from your laptop.
- **Windows+P** opens the *Project* pane, where you can search for projectors and external displays to connect to.
- **Ctrl+Alt+Del** brings up a screen that lets you choose to lock your PC, switch the user, sign out, or run Task Manager (see Book 8, Chapter 5).

You can also right-click (or press and hold) the Start icon or press Windows+X to display a special menu, which is shown in Figure 1-11. Some call it the WinX menu, others the Power User Menu, others a hidden Start menu. The name you give it doesn't matter; what matters is that you use it.

And finally, the trick I know you'll use over and over: When you want to type an emoji in a document, press Windows+. (period) or Windows+; (semicolon). The screen shown in Figure 1-12 appears, and you can add emoji, animated GIFs, Kaomoji (a series of characters that resemble drawings), symbols, and much more. Try it out and see for yourself.

Who says Windows 11 isn't as cool as your smartphone?

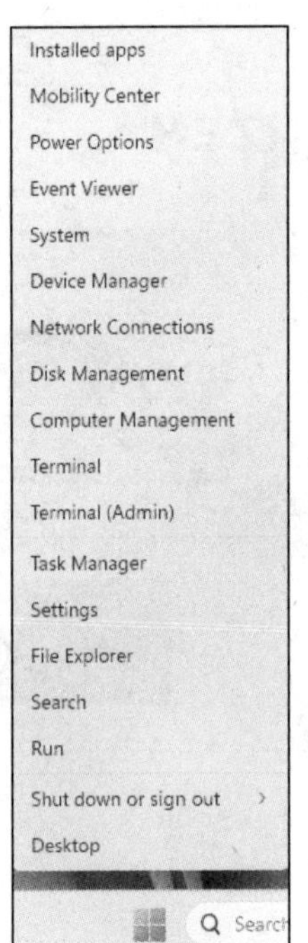

FIGURE 1-11: The WinX menu can get you into the innards of Windows 11.

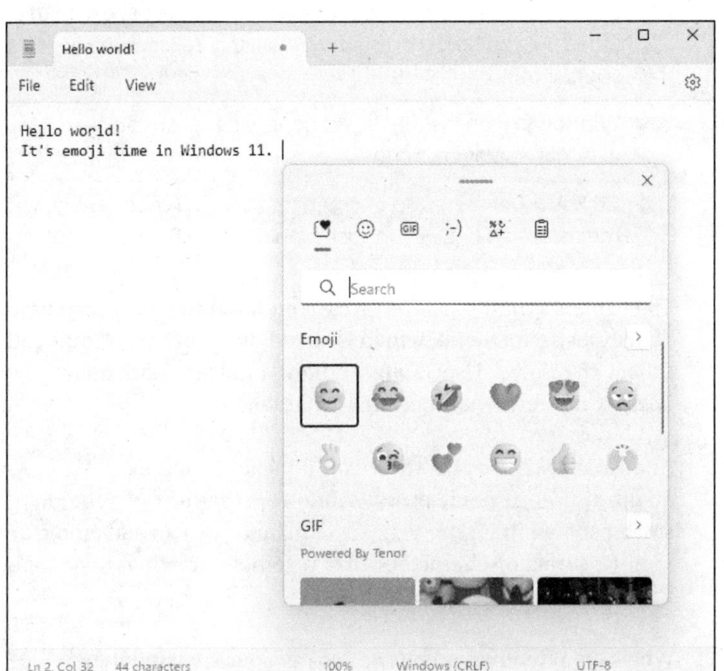

FIGURE 1-12: Emojis are just a keyboard command away.

Using the Mouse and Touchpad

Luckily, the way we use the mouse hasn't changed with Windows 11:

- **Click:** Selects an item, such as a file, folder, or shortcut.
- **Right-click:** Accesses a contextual menu with options relevant to the item you've selected.
- **Double-click:** Opens a file, a folder, or an app.
- **Click and hold:** Enables you to use the mouse to drag the item to a new location. When you complete the move, release the left click button.

Laptop users often don't have a mouse, so they use the built-in touchpad instead. Windows 11 requires laptop manufacturer to offer precision touchpads with touch-sensitive surfaces that can detect multiple fingers and allow the use of more sophisticated gestures than a mere click and right-click. On precision touchpads, you can make gestures with one, two, three, or even four fingers. Here's what these gestures do:

- **One-finger tap:** Tap the touchpad with one finger to select an item or open a link on a web page.
- **One-finger double-tap:** Tap the touchpad twice with one finger to open an item or launch an app. This is the equivalent of a double-click when using the mouse.
- **One-finger drag:** Tap and hold on the touchpad with one finger and then move it to drag an item, select multiple items, or select text.
- **One-finger right-click:** Tap the lower-right corner of the touchpad to right-click an item and open its context menu.
- **Two-finger right-click:** Tap the touchpad with two fingers to right-click an item and open its context menu.
- **Two-finger scroll:** Put two fingers on the touchpad and slide them up or down to scroll vertically, or slide them left or right to scroll horizontally.
- **Two-finger zoom:** Place two fingers on the touchpad and pinch them together or apart to zoom in or out, respectively.
- **Two-finger rotation:** Put two fingers on the touchpad and rotate them clockwise or counterclockwise to rotate an object, such as an image.
- **Three-finger tap:** Tap the touchpad with three fingers to open Search. You can then use it to look for files, apps, settings, web pages, and more.

- **Three-finger swipe up:** Swipe up with three fingers on the touchpad to open task view.
- **Three-finger swipe down:** Swipe down with three fingers on the touchpad to show the desktop and minimize all open windows.
- **Three-finger swipe left or right:** Swipe left or right with three fingers on the touchpad to switch between open windows or apps.
- **Four-finger tap:** Tap the touchpad with four fingers to open notifications and the calendar.
- **Four-finger swipe up:** Swipe up with four fingers on the touchpad to open task view.
- **Four-finger swipe down:** Swipe down with four fingers on the touchpad to minimize everything on the screen and display the desktop.
- **Four-finger swipe left or right:** Swipe left or right with four fingers on the touchpad to switch between your virtual desktops.

You don't have to remember all these gestures now. See which ones are easiest to perform and seem useful, and then integrate them into how you use your Windows 11 laptop. And if you need to configure how your mouse or trackpad works, read Book 3, Chapter 1.

IN THIS CHAPTER

» **Signing in**

» **Setting PIN, facial or fingerprint recognition**

» **Personalizing the lock screen**

Chapter 2
Logging into Windows 11

After you push the power button on your computer, Windows 11 starts to load, and then it takes you through the following steps:

» First, it displays the *lock screen,* and you have to get past it. To do that, simply click with the mouse or press any key on your keyboard.

» You then see the *sign-in screen*. If more than one account is set up on the computer, you must choose which will log in. I go into detail about setting up user accounts in Book 2, Chapters 4, 5, and 6.

» If a password is associated with the account, you must type it into the computer. However, Windows allows various ways of logging in, which are all designed to confirm your identity. Therefore, you can replace the password with a shorter PIN that's easier to type and remember, as well as facial recognition or fingerprint recognition. Corporate users may also use smart cards or security keys set up by their company to log in without entering a password.

Only after clearing these three hurdles are you granted access to the desktop and, from there, to everything Windows 11 has to offer. In this chapter, you find out how to sign into Windows 11, how to replace a password with other ways of signing in and confirming your identity, and how to personalize the lock screen.

Signing into Windows 11

When you start Windows 11 and anytime you shut it down, restart it, or let the machine go idle for long enough, you're greeted with the lock screen, as shown in Figure 2-1. The lock screen sports a beautiful image, with the date and time in the middle and small battery and network icons at the bottom-right corner. You don't see the battery icon in Figure 2-1 because I made the screenshot on a virtual machine on a desktop PC, which doesn't have a battery. The icon is there on laptops and tablets — I promise.

FIGURE 2-1: The Windows 11 lock screen.

You can get rid of the lock screen by doing any of the following:

- » Swipe up with your finger if you have a touch-sensitive display.
- » Click with your mouse.
- » Press any key on the keyboard.

You aren't stuck with the default lock screen Microsoft gives you. You can customize the picture and what is shown on it. I show you how to do that at the end of the chapter.

To sign in, first make the lock screen go away by using any of the three methods just presented. You see the *sign-in screen*, with the name and picture for the last account that was used. Other accounts (if any) are listed in the bottom-left corner, as shown in Figure 2-2. Select the account you want to use, and the sign-in screen asks for your password, PIN, or biometric authentication (if it was set up). Choose the authentication method you want and enter the required information. As soon as you comply, you're signed into Windows 11.

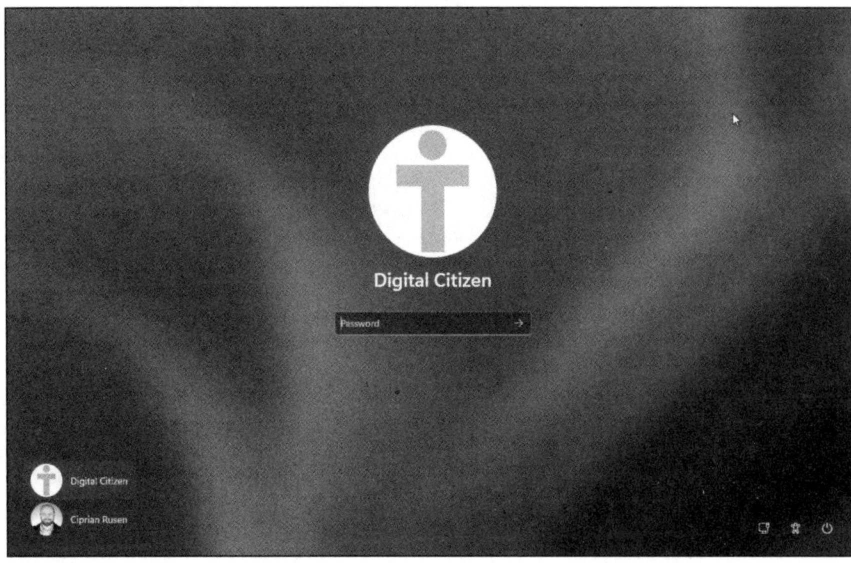

FIGURE 2-2: The Windows 11 sign-in screen.

In the bottom-right corner of the sign-in screen are icons for your Ethernet or Wi-Fi connection, accessibility tools that can make your login easier, and the power icon, so you can shut down, restart, or put your machine to sleep. If several languages or keyboard layouts are installed in Windows 11, you'll also see an icon for switching between them.

TIP

When you have finished using Windows 11 and want to sign out (or log off) so that you can switch to another user account, click or tap the Windows icon, click or tap your user icon, and then choose Sign Out in the menu that appears.

Changing the Sign-In Password

If you're using a local user account, you can change your password straight from Windows 11. You can even set your password as a blank one and log in without typing anything. However, I don't recommend doing that unless you live alone, without regular visitors.

Let's see how to change the password for a local user account:

1. **Click or tap the Start icon (shown in the margin), the Settings icon, and then Accounts.**
2. **On the right, scroll down and choose Sign-In Options.**

   The sign-in settings for your account appear, as shown in Figure 2-3.

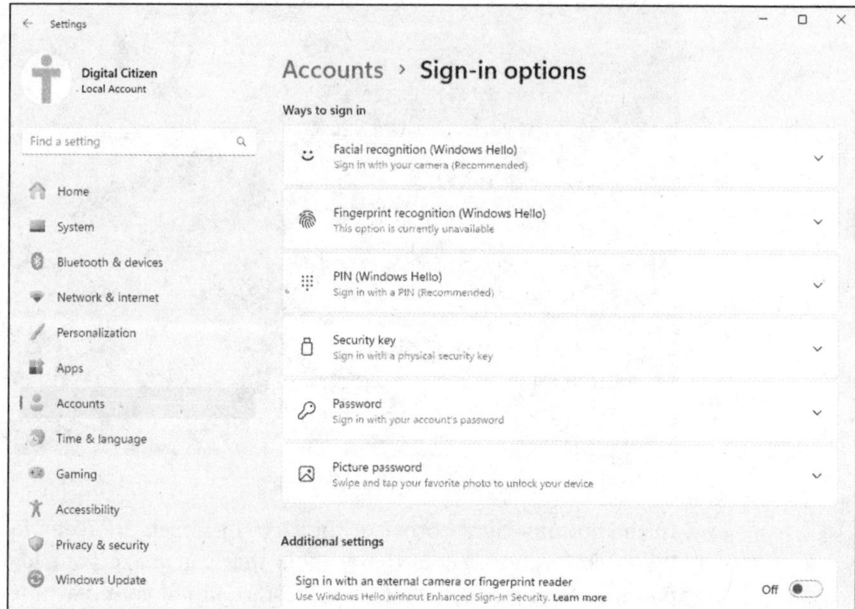

FIGURE 2-3: The sign-in options available in Windows 11.

3. **Click or tap Password, followed by Change.**

   A Change Your Password wizard appears on the screen, asking you to enter the current password.

4. **Type the current password and then click or tap Next.**
5. **Type all the requested information and click or tap Next.**

   Type the new password, confirm it, and then type a password hint to help you remember it when you forget it, as shown in Figure 2-4.

   You are informed that the next time you sign in, you should use the new password that you just set.

6. **Click or tap Finish.**

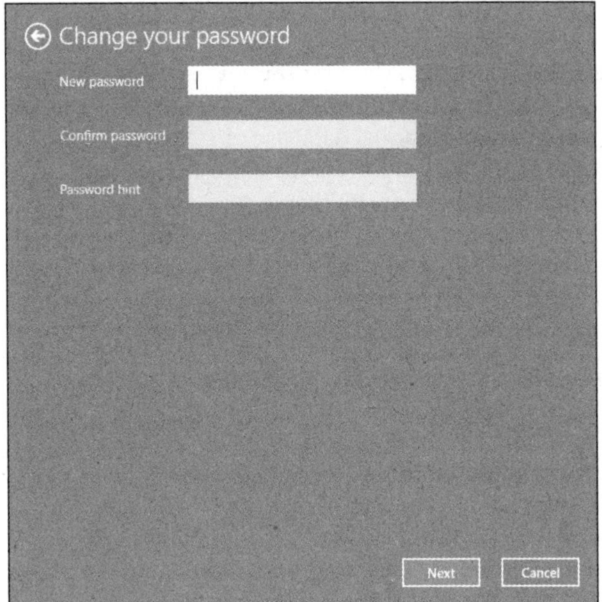

FIGURE 2-4: Changing the password for a local account.

WARNING

If you're changing the password for a Microsoft or work or school account using this method, you'll notice that the Password option shown in Figure 2-3 is missing during Step 3. That's because the password for a Microsoft account is changed online (read Book 2, Chapter 4 for details) but the password for a work or school account is changed using specialized tools implemented by your company. Speak to your organization's IT support department for details.

Logging in Without a Password

In this section, I guide you step by step through setting up a PIN and tell you how to show your face to Windows Hello.

Creating a PIN

We have PIN codes for debit cards, credit cards, smartphones, tablets, and just about everything.

WARNING

Using the same PIN code for multiple devices and credit cards can be risky. Imagine someone looking over your shoulder, observing you enter your Windows 11 PIN, and then taking your wallet. Protect yourself by using a different PIN for each device and card.

PINs have some advantages over passwords. They're short and easy to remember. Fast. Technically, though, the best thing about a PIN is that it's stored on your computer — it's tied to that one computer, and you don't have to worry about it getting stored in some hacked database or stolen with your credit card numbers. In Windows 11, the PIN is part of Windows Hello, Microsoft's service for secure authentication options. More on that in the next section.

For now, remember that creating a PIN is easy. Here's how to do it:

1. **Click or tap the Start icon, followed by Settings and then Accounts.**
2. **On the right, scroll down and choose Sign-In Options.**

   The sign-in settings for your account appear (refer to Figure 2-3).
3. **Click or tap PIN (Windows Hello) and then Set Up.**

   Windows 11 asks you to verify your user account password.
4. **Type your password and then click or tap OK.**

   Windows 11 prompts you to type your PIN, as shown in Figure 2-5, and then retype it to confirm it. ***Note:*** Most PINs for credit and debit cards are four digits, but you can have a longer PIN in Windows 11. You can also use letters and symbols for your PIN, not just digits.
5. **Type your PIN, confirm it, and click or tap OK.**

   The PIN is set, and you can log in with it.

FIGURE 2-5: Creating a PIN is easy.

Changing a PIN

If someone else has seen you typing your PIN, it's a good idea to change it so that they don't use it to access your account. Luckily, changing a PIN is easy:

1. **Click or tap the Start icon, followed by Settings and then Accounts.**
2. **On the right, scroll down and choose Sign-In Options.**

   The sign-in settings for your account appear, as shown in Figure 2-3.
3. **Click or tap PIN (Windows Hello) and then Change PIN.**

   Windows 11 asks you to enter the existing PIN and then set the new one, as shown in Figure 2-6.

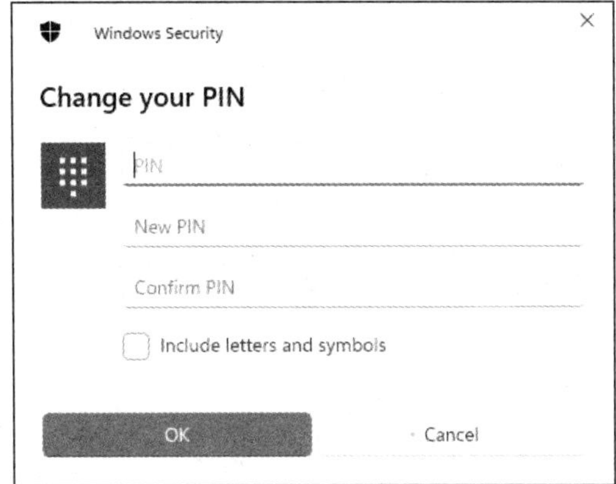

FIGURE 2-6: Changing the PIN is as easy as creating one.

4. **Type your PIN, enter the new PIN, and then confirm it.**

   Don't forget that you can also use letters and symbols, not just digits.
5. **Click or tap OK.**

   The PIN is changed, and you can use it the next time you sign in with your account.

TIP

If you want to stop using a PIN, you can remove it by following the same procedure. During Step 3, click or tap Remove instead of Change PIN, and enter your password to confirm your choice.

Setting up facial recognition to sign in (Windows Hello)

Windows Hello provides biometric authentication, which is much faster than using a password or a PIN. This technology includes fingerprint recognition, face recognition, or both. Some Windows 11 laptops offer only one of these authentication methods, while others offer both. Cheaper laptops may not offer either of these options.

To log in using your face, the camera on your Windows 11 device must feature infrared sensors, which are more expensive. On a desktop computer, you can also use a USB webcam that has this technology, such as the Logitech Brio Ultra HD webcam and the Lenovo 500 FHD webcam. However, they're harder to find and, with few exceptions, more expensive than normal webcams.

WARNING

I'm a fan of Windows Hello face recognition because it's fast, precise, and convenient. I can unlock my Windows 11 laptop just by looking at it. However, there are some downsides too: Sometimes I sit in front of the laptop and don't want to log in. If I put my face anywhere near the laptop when it's turned on, bang, I'm logged in. Then, if I want to log in to a different account, I have to manually sign out first, which is annoying.

If your computer's webcam supports Hello face recognition, try it and see if you like it. Here's how:

1. **Click or tap the Start icon, followed by Settings and then Accounts.**
2. **On the right, scroll down and choose Sign-In Options.**

   The sign-in settings for your account appear (refer to Figure 2-3).
3. **Click or tap Facial Recognition (Windows Hello) and then Set Up.**

   The Welcome to Windows Hello window appears, as shown in Figure 2-7.

   If you see This Option Is Currently Unavailable, your Windows 11 computer doesn't support Windows Hello facial recognition.
4. **Click or tap Get Started.**

   Windows 11 asks you to verify your user account password or PIN.
5. **Type your PIN or password, depending on what's asked of you.**
6. **When asked to look directly at your camera, as shown in Figure 2-8, do as instructed until you see a message that you're all set.**
7. **Click or tap Close.**

   Face recognition is set, and you can log in just by looking at your Windows 11 laptop, tablet, or 2-in-1 device.

Windows Hello setup

Welcome to Windows Hello

Your device just got more personal. Start using your face to unlock your device, verify your identity, and buy things in the Store.

Learn more

Get started

Cancel

FIGURE 2-7: Setting up facial recognition.

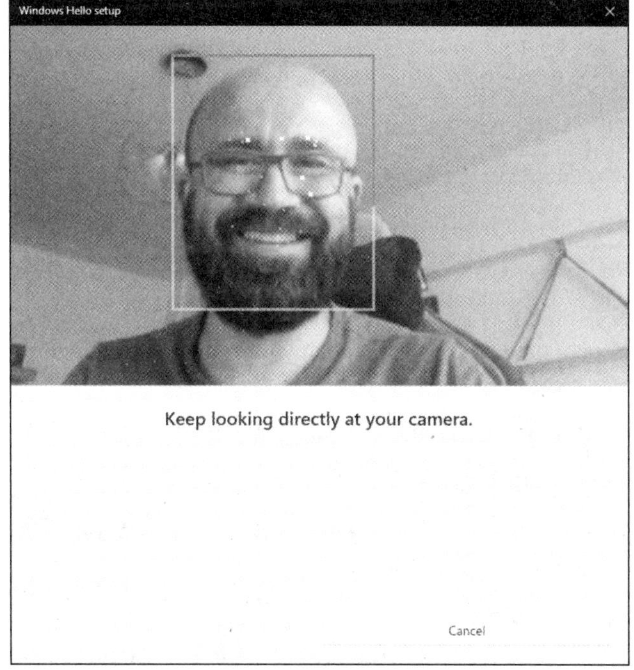

FIGURE 2-8: Look at your camera as instructed.

TIP

If you want to stop using facial recognition in Windows 11, you can remove it by following the same procedure. In Step 3, click or tap Remove after you choose Facial Recognition (Windows Hello). The data about your face is deleted immediately, without any need for confirmation.

Setting up fingerprint recognition to sign in (Windows Hello)

If your Windows 11 laptop has a fingerprint reader, you can use it to authenticate. I like this method too because it's fast, efficient, and secure. Remember that your fingerprint is stored locally and not sent to Microsoft's cloud.

To set up fingerprint recognition on your Windows 11 machine, follow these steps:

1. **Click or tap the Start icon, followed by Settings and then Accounts.**
2. **On the right, scroll down and choose Sign-In Options.**

   The sign-in settings for your account appear (refer to Figure 2-3).
3. **Click or tap Fingerprint Recognition (Windows Hello), and then click or tap Set Up.**

   The Welcome to Windows Hello window appears, as shown in Figure 2-9, left. If you see This Option Is Currently Unavailable, your Windows 11 computer doesn't support Windows Hello fingerprint recognition.
4. **Click or tap Get Started.**

   Windows 11 asks you to verify your user account password or PIN.
5. **Type your PIN or password, depending on what's asked of you.**

   You're asked to touch the fingerprint sensor on your laptop, as shown in Figure 2-9, right
6. **Touch, then lift, move, and rest your finger on the fingerprint sensor as instructed.**

   When your fingerprint is recorded, you see a message that you're all set.
7. **Click or tap Close.**

   Finger recognition is set, and you can log in by placing your finger on the sensor.

TIP

You can use more than one finger to log in. For example, I always record one finger from each hand, to make sure I can sign in fast, no matter how I'm holding my laptop. To add another fingerprint, follow the same procedure and at Step 3, click or tap Fingerprint Recognition (Windows Hello) and then Add a Finger. Then follow the remaining steps.

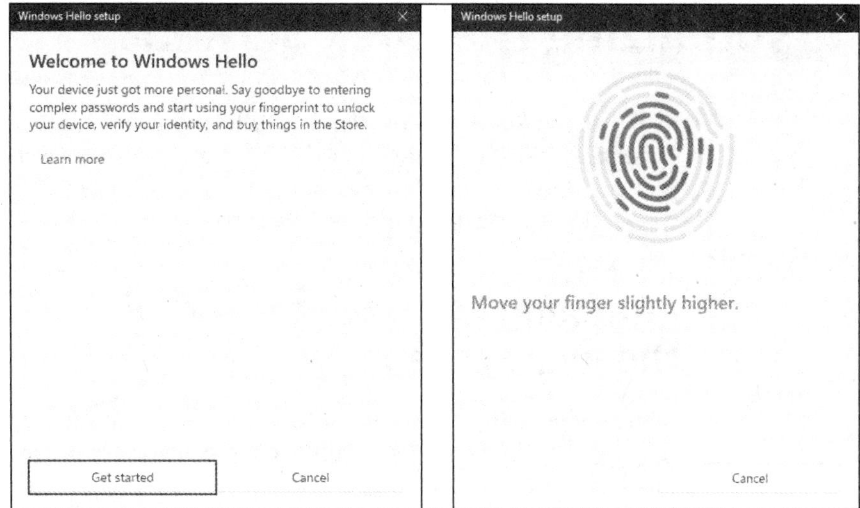

FIGURE 2-9: Setting up fingerprint recognition.

Bypassing passwords

So now you have four convenient ways to tell Windows 11 your password: You can type it, just like a normal password; you can pretend it's a smartphone and enter a PIN; or you can simply look at your webcam or scan your fingerprint.

But what if you don't want a password? What if your computer is secure enough — it's sitting in your house, it's in your safe deposit box — and you just don't want to be bothered with typing or tapping a password?

TIP

If you have a local account, you can just remove your password. Follow the steps in the "Changing the Sign-In Password" section to change your password but leave the New Password field blank.

Microsoft accounts can't have blank passwords, but local accounts can. If you have a blank password, when you click or tap your username on the sign-in screen, Windows 11 ushers you to the desktop. If only one user is on the PC and that user has a blank password, just getting past the lock screen takes you to the desktop.

If you have a Microsoft account, you must use a method to authenticate yourself: a PIN, a password, or Windows Hello each time you sign in.

TIP

Some large business organizations that use Microsoft's Active Directory can use smart cards to authenticate their employees on all their computers. Smart cards require personal identification numbers (PINs) and provide two-factor authentication: The user who attempts to sign in must possess the smart card and know its PIN.

Personalizing the Lock Screen

Now that you know how to sign into Windows 11 and all the ways you can skip using passwords, it's time to share how to personalize the lock screen, the screen you see before you can choose to sign in. You can change two thing about the lock screen: the wallpaper and the displayed widgets.

Changing the background of the lock screen

Changing the wallpaper of your lock screen is easy. (See the nearby sidebar "Individualized lock screens" for details about the difference between your lock screen and the system's lock screen.) Just do the following:

1. **Click or tap the Start icon, followed by Settings and then Personalization.**
2. **On the right, choose Lock Screen.**

   The lock screen's settings window appears.

3. **Click or tap the Personalize Your Lock Screen drop-down list and choose Windows Spotlight, as shown in Figure 2-10.**

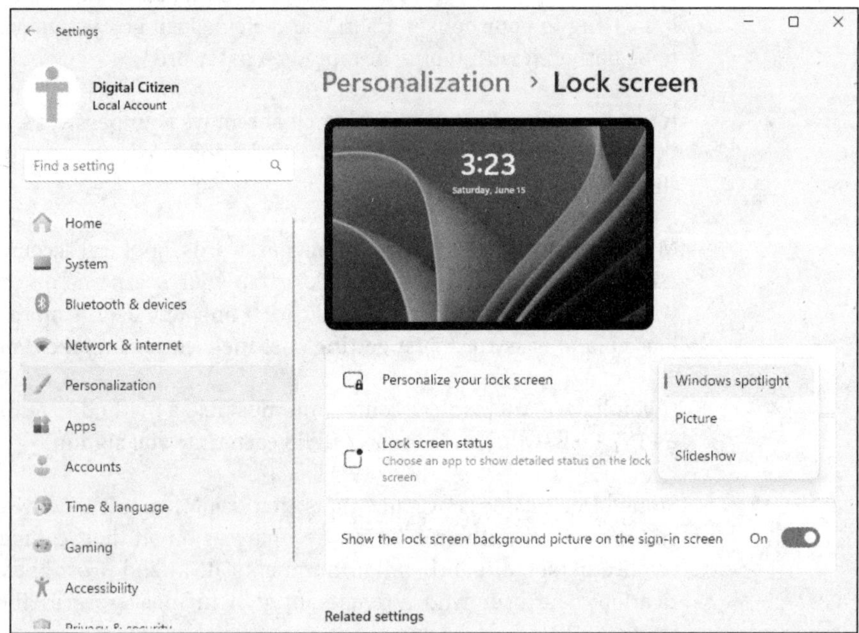

FIGURE 2-10: Change your lock screen here.

Windows Spotlight images come directly from Microsoft — more specifically, from Bing — and change frequently. Microsoft reserves the right to put advertising on Windows Spotlight screens to tell you about features in Windows 11 that you might not have used yet.

4. **If you want to have a single photo for the lock screen, do the following:**

   (a) *In the Personalize Your Lock Screen drop-down list, choose Picture, and expand the Personalize Your Lock Screen section.*

   (b) *Choose a picture.* If you like one of the pictures on offer, click or tap it. If you'd rather find your own picture, click or tap Browse Photos, select a picture of your own, and click or tap Choose Picture, as shown in Figure 2-11.

   (c) *Decide whether you want your chosen picture to be overlaid with "fun facts, tips, tricks, and more on your lock screen,"* and enable or disable the appropriate check box.

FIGURE 2-11: Choose your own picture, with or without Microsoft advertising.

5. **If you would rather have a slideshow for the lock screen, do the following:**

   (a) *Choose Slideshow in the Personalize Your Lock Screen drop-down list.*

   (b) *Click or tap Browse.*

   (c) *Choose a folder containing pictures.*

   (d) *Scroll down to the Advanced Slideshow Settings section and set the rules for your slideshow.* As shown in Figure 2-12, you can set whether the slideshow should be pulled from your camera roll, whether the chosen pictures must be large enough to fit your screen, and more.

6. **Close Settings.**

   There's no Apply or OK button to click or tap.

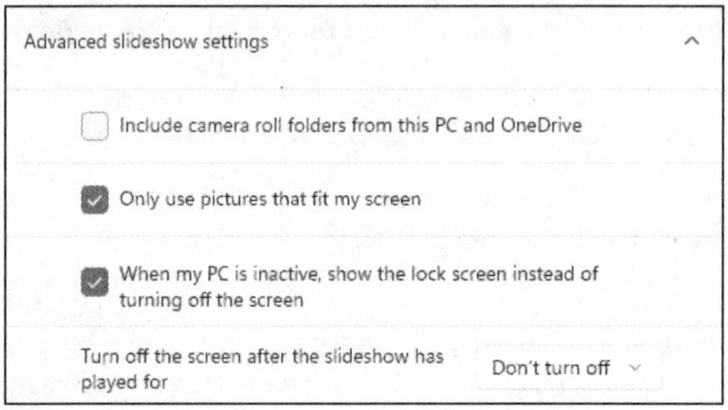

Advanced slideshow settings

Include camera roll folders from this PC and OneDrive

Only use pictures that fit my screen

When my PC is inactive, show the lock screen instead of turning off the screen

Turn off the screen after the slideshow has played for

Don't turn off

FIGURE 2-12: Setting the slideshow for the lock screen.

INDIVIDUALIZED LOCK SCREENS

If you read the Microsoft help documentation, you may think that Windows 11 keeps one lock screen for all users, but it doesn't. Instead, it has a lock screen for each individual user and another lock screen for the system as a whole.

If you're using the system and you lock it — say, tap your picture on the Start menu and choose Lock — Windows 11 shows your personal lock screen with the settings and data you've chosen. If you swipe up or click, you're asked to provide your PIN or password, or other authentication information. There's no intermediary step to ask which user should log in.

If, instead of locking the system when you leave it, you tap your picture and choose Sign Out, Windows 11 behaves differently. It shows the system's lock screen with the system's settings. Your lock screen and data are nowhere to be seen. If you drag or swipe to go through the lock screen, you're asked to choose which user will log in.

Bottom line: If you change your lock screen using the techniques in this chapter, you change only *your* lock screen. Windows's idea of a lock screen stays the same.

Test to make sure that your personal lock screen has been updated. The easiest way is to go to the Start menu, click or tap your picture in the bottom-left corner, and choose Lock or Sign Out.

Adding or removing widgets on the lock screen

At the end of March 2024, Microsoft deployed an update that added a feature to the lock screen: widgets. Yes, they're the same as the widgets you find on the taskbar (see Book 4, Chapter 7) but adjusted to display their data on the bottom of the lock screen.

The widgets on the lock screen display the weather forecast, stock market information, and sports updates. I am interested only in the weather forecast. I don't follow the NBA and don't want stock market updates on the lock screen. Unfortunately, Microsoft didn't provide a way to personalize which widgets get displayed. You can choose to display all the data Microsoft wants or disable the widgets. I find it frustrating that Microsoft released this feature without considering that users might want to enable specific widgets and not have unwanted data displayed on their computers. It's spammy and annoying!

If you don't like them either, here's how to remove the widgets from the Windows 11 lock screen:

1. **Click or tap the Start icon, followed by Settings.**
2. **On the left, choose Personalization.**
3. **On the right side of the Settings window, choose Lock Screen.**
4. **Click or tap the Lock Screen Status drop-down list and choose None (see Figure 2-13).**

   Choosing None means that no widgets can display data on the lock screen. Your changes are applied immediately. Keep in mind that the number options you see in this drop-down list vary based on which apps you've installed on your Windows 11 computer or device. Some apps can add widgets to the lock screen.

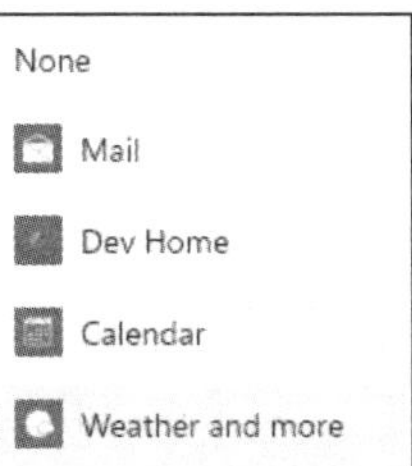

FIGURE 2-13: Choose whether you want widgets on the lock screen.

Go back out to the lock screen — click or tap the Start icon, your picture, and then Lock — and see whether you like the changes. If you don't like what you see, start over.

TIP

If you want to enable the widgets and have them display their data on the lock screen, repeat the same steps but choose Weather and More instead of None in Step 4.

IN THIS CHAPTER

» Understanding Windows 11 notifications

» Using and configuring notifications

» Limiting distractions with Do Not Disturb and Focus sessions

» Browsing the calendar from your taskbar

» Using Quick Settings

Chapter 3 Handling Notifications and Quick Settings

Windows 11 keeps you updated with notifications from apps, services, and features, alerting you about everything from incoming emails and messages on Teams to alarms and website notifications. Thankfully, managing these notifications is straightforward, as you discover in this chapter.

In this chapter, you learn how to manage notifications effectively, boost your productivity with focus sessions, and utilize the calendar for all your scheduling needs. Finally, you explore Quick Settings, which provide easy access to some of the most used features of Windows, and find out how to make the most of them.

What Exactly Is a Notification?

A *notification* is a message accompanied by a brief sound that you receive from Windows 11 or an app, informing you when something happens. The notification can be about anything: Windows telling you that you just plugged in a USB memory stick and asking you to choose what to do with it; a new email message in the Outlook app; the snipping tool sharing that a screenshot was copied to the clipboard and saved; or Microsoft Store telling you that it has updated an app on your PC. You may even see promotions for Microsoft products you don't need and requests for feedback. Even websites can send you notifications when new content is posted if you allow them to do so in your web browser. The message that you receive is called a *notification banner*, which appears in the lower-right corner of your screen (see Figure 3-1) and is collected in the notification center, much like on smartphones.

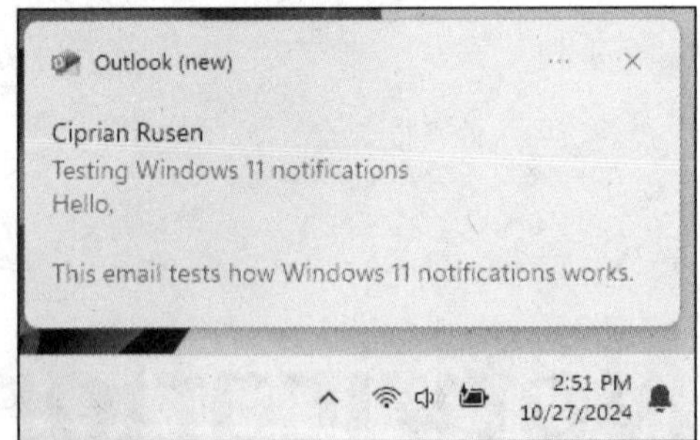

FIGURE 3-1: A new email notification in Windows 11.

Notifications contain the name and icon of the app or Windows feature sending the notification in the top-left corner as well as the contents of the notification. If it's an email, you see who sent the email, the subject (if any), and a portion of the message. Other app notifications briefly state what just happened and allow you to click the notification. When you click or tap a notification, it takes you to the app or Windows feature that sent it to you. For example, if you click or tap an email notification, the Outlook app opens the email you received so you can read and reply to it. Other notifications, like the one you see when you plug in an external USB drive, might ask you to decide what to do next. Make your choice, and the notification is gone.

Using the Notification Center

The place where notifications are stored is called the notification center. In the bottom-right corner of the taskbar is a bell icon for opening the notification center. When it has new notifications for you to see, the bell icon is lit up. When there are no new notifications, the bell icon is no longer lit, but remains visible.

If you didn't click or tap a notification when it was displayed in the bottom-right corner, you can view it later, alongside all the other notifications you ignored, like this:

1. **In the bottom-right corner of the screen, click or tap the bell icon next to the time and date.**

   You see the current date on the bottom and a list of notifications on top. You might also see a calendar for the current month under today's date.

2. **If the calendar for the current month is visible, click or tap the downward-pointing arrow to the right of the current date.**

   You now see only the notification center, as shown in Figure 3-2.

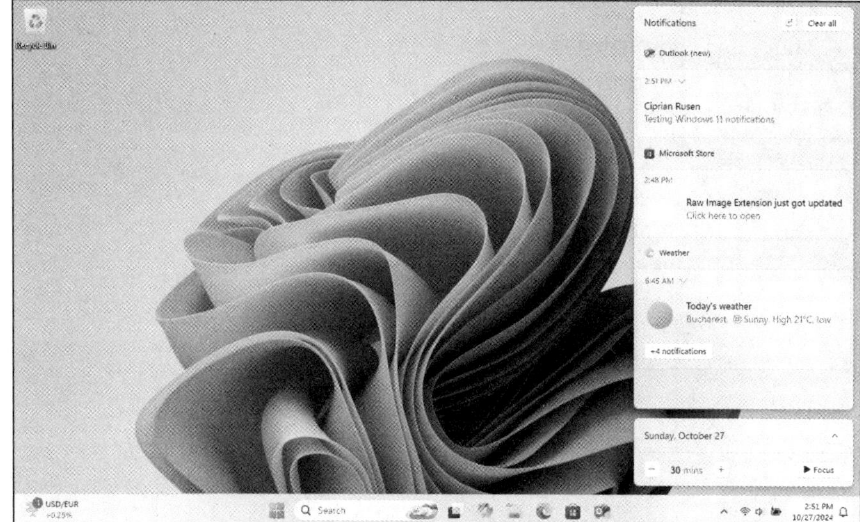

FIGURE 3-2: The notification center in Windows 11.

3. **Hover the mouse cursor over a notification to see additional options for interacting with it.**

   For example, in Figure 3-3, the ellipsis icon (Settings) and the X appear to the right of the notification.

4. **To remove a notification, click or tap the X to its right.**

5. **To expand a notification, click or tap the downward-pointing arrow under the name of the app displaying the notification.**

   Note the additional information displayed for the expanded notification, as shown in Figure 3-4. Some notifications may even display buttons for actions you can take.

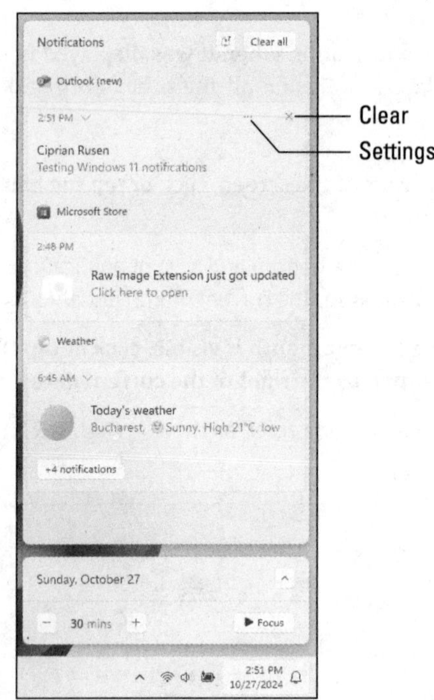

FIGURE 3-3: These options appear when you hover your cursor over a notification.

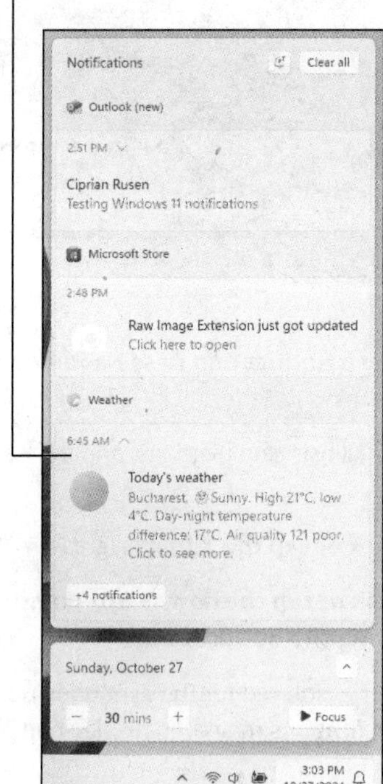

FIGURE 3-4: An expanded notification offers more information or interaction options.

6. **When you no longer want to see the notifications, click or tap the Clear All button in the top right of the notification center.**

   This action clears all notifications from Windows 11 and leaves room for new ones.

TIP

A quick way to access the notification center is to press Windows+N.

Mastering Notifications

If you find notifications distracting, you can easily clear them, disable them permanently, or temporarily silence them with Do Not Disturb. For people who prefer to keep notifications but still want to maintain focus, Windows 11 offers the focus session feature, which works great alongside productivity techniques like the Pomodoro Technique. I've found this combination incredibly effective for staying productive while ensuring I take regular breaks.

Read on to learn how to disable notifications from specific apps or all apps, enable or disable Do Not Disturb, and use Focus sessions to enhance your productivity.

Disabling notifications

If a particular program is generating notifications that you don't want to see, you can stop it from doing so. And if you consider all notifications annoying, you can disable them all easily. Here's how to disable notifications from a specific app or all notifications:

1. **Right-click (or press and hold) the time and date or the bell icon on the taskbar.**

   The menu shown in Figure 3-5 appears.

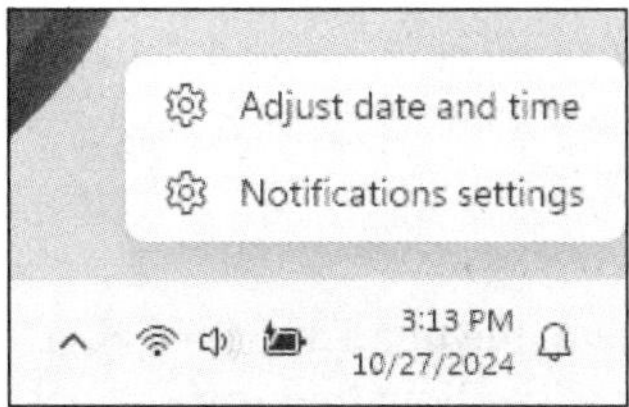

FIGURE 3-5: Accessing the notifications settings.

2. **Choose Notifications Settings.**

   The Notifications section of the Settings app appears, as shown in Figure 3-6. In the top half of the window, you see settings for how notifications work in Windows 11; in the bottom half, you see the most recent apps that have sent notifications.

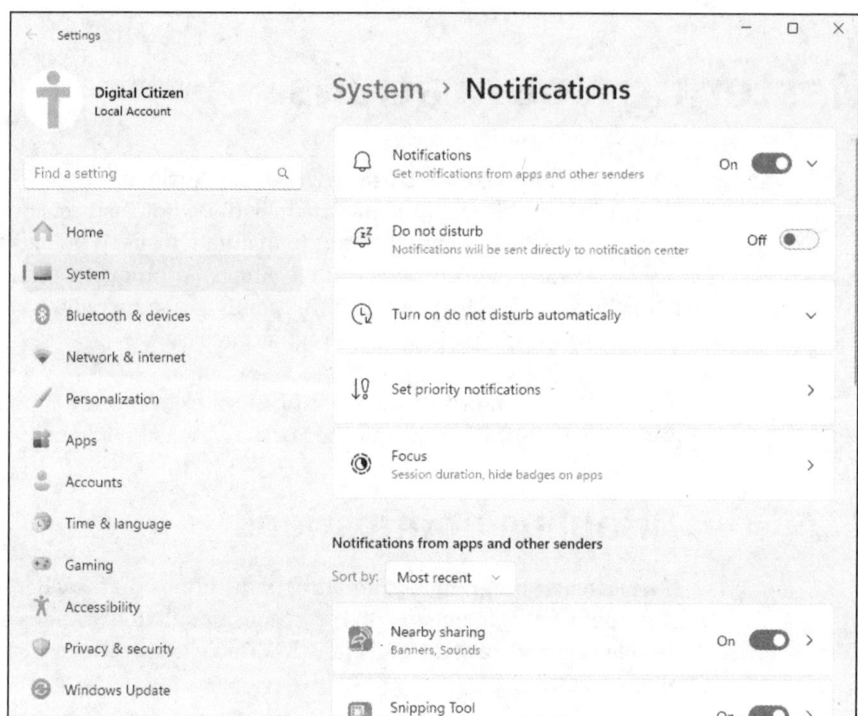

FIGURE 3-6: Silence notifications from individual apps.

3. **Do one of the following:**

   - *To silence just one app:* Scroll down, find the app in the list, and turn its switch off.
   - *To disable all notifications from all apps, including Windows 11:* Click or tap the Notifications switch on the top and set it off.

   You're finished. You can close Settings or minimize it and do something else.

TIP

During Step 3, if you click or tap the name of an app instead of moving its switch, you get access to options for controlling how its notifications are displayed. For example, you can disable the sound played for each notification and set its priority in the notification center. If you want to ensure that an app's notifications are prioritized, such as your Outlook emails or conversations on Teams, set its priority to Top or High.

Muting notifications with Do Not Disturb

While turning off notifications in Windows 11 is easy, you may not want to opt for such a hardline approach because some notifications are useful. If you don't want to be disturbed for a set period of time, you can enable Do Not Disturb and disable it later when you're okay with being interrupted. Here's how it works:

1. **Right-click (or press and hold) the time and date or the bell icon on the taskbar.**

   The menu shown previously in Figure 3-5 appears.

2. **Choose Notifications Settings.**

   The Notifications section of the Settings app appears (refer to Figure 3-6).

3. **Click or tap the Do Not Disturb switch to turn it on.**

   Note how the bell icon on the taskbar has some z letters next to it, signaling that your notifications are "sleeping." They are now sent directly to the notifications center without interrupting you. You can review them in the notifications center anytime.

   When you want to stop using Do Not Disturb, repeat the same steps, but set the switch off in Step 3.

TIP

You can set a schedule and rules for Do Not Disturb. For example, if you work from home, you can set Windows 11 so that it displays notifications only during work hours and have it stop bothering you outside that interval. You can also enable rules for not displaying notifications when you're playing a game or when you're duplicating your display to ensure that they don't bother you when you deliver a presentation.

Follow these steps:

1. **Right-click (or press and hold) the time and date or the bell icon on the taskbar.**

   The menu shown previously in Figure 3-5 appears.

2. **Choose Notifications Settings.**

   The Notifications section of the Settings app appears (refer to Figure 3-6).

3. **Click or tap Turn on Do Not Disturb Automatically to expand this section.**

   You see the settings shown in Figure 3-7.

4. **Select During These Times and then set when you want to turn on and off Do Not Disturb.**

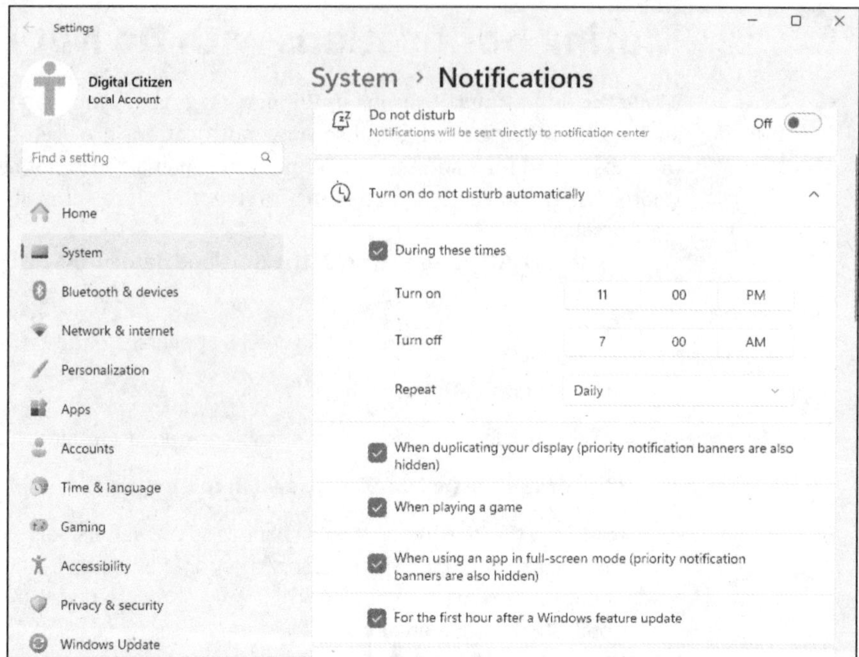

FIGURE 3-7: Configuring how you want Do Not Disturb to work.

5. **Click or tap the Repeat drop-down list and choose whether you want this schedule repeated daily, on weekends, or on weekdays.**
6. **Select the boxes next to the other times when you want Do Not Disturb turned on automatically:**
   - When duplicating your display (priority notification banners are also hidden)
   - When playing a game
   - When using an app in full-screen mode (priority notification banners are also hidden)
   - For the first hour after a Windows feature update
7. **When you're finished setting Do Not Disturb, close Settings.**

Enhancing productivity with focus sessions

Focus session is a Windows 11 feature that helps you remain focused by censoring the display of notifications for a time interval that you set, usually 20 minutes followed by a 5-minute break. It's inspired by a time management method developed by Francesco Cirillo in the late 1980s named the Pomodoro Technique. This technique is simple and efficient because it utilizes fixed time intervals for focused work, usually somewhere between 20 and 30 minutes, followed by short breaks. This structured approach keeps your mind alert and engaged, significantly reducing the inclination to procrastinate and enabling a deeper focus on tasks.

When enabling a focus session, Windows 11 shows a timer with how much time you have left until the next break or work session, hides badges on taskbar apps, hides flashing on taskbar apps, and enables Do Not Disturb so that you can focus solely on what you are doing, without interruptions.

If you're willing to give focus session a try, follow these steps:

1. **Right-click (or press and hold) the time and date or the bell icon on the taskbar.**

   The menu shown previously in Figure 3-5 appears.

2. **Choose Notifications Settings.**

   The Notifications section of the Settings app appears (refer to Figure 3-6).

3. **Click or tap Focus.**

   The focus settings shown in Figure 3-8 appear.

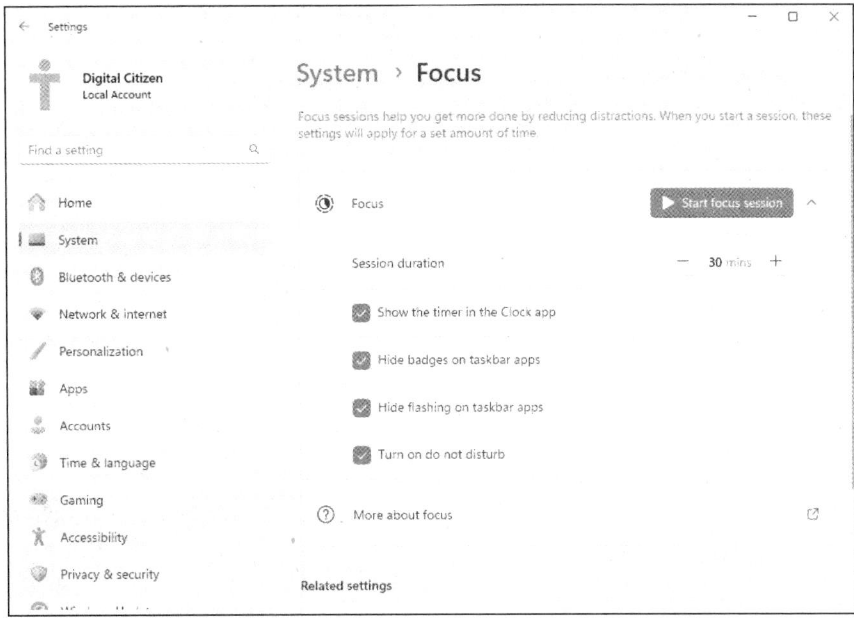

FIGURE 3-8: Configuring a focus session.

4. **Click or tap the minus and plus signs to explore the durations available for a focus session and choose the value you want.**

   I recommend short periods between 20 and 30 minutes.

5. **Select the boxes next to the things you want the focus session to do:**
   - Show the timer in the Clock app. You see the time remaining from the current sessions and what's up next.
   - Hide badges on taskbar apps.
   - Hide flashing on taskbar apps.
   - Turn on Do Not Disturb.

6. **Click or tap Start Focus Session.**

   If you selected the Show the Timer in the Clock App setting, you'll see the time in the Clock app, similar to Figure 3-9. When the time is up and it's time for a break, you receive a notification from the Clock app. The same happens when it's time to get back to your task. During this time, you can do your work without being bothered by notifications.

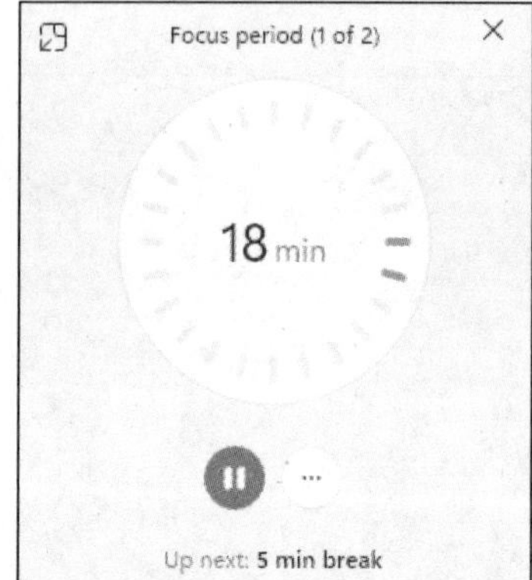

FIGURE 3-9: The remaining time in the current focus session.

To end the focus session, repeat the same steps, but click or tap Stop Focus Session in Step 6.

TIP

A quick way to start a focus session is to click or tap the bell icon on the taskbar. Below the current date (and the calendar, if expanded), choose the minutes you want the session to last, and click or tap Focus. To stop the session, click or tap the bell icon again and then click or tap End Session.

Using the Calendar

Under the notification center, Windows 11 also displays the current date, which can be expanded into a calendar of the current month. The data displayed by the calendar is useful when you want to plan anything from the next conference call with your team to your family vacation. Here are the basics of using the calendar available from the Windows 11 taskbar:

1. **In the bottom-right corner of the screen, click or tap the bell icon next to the time and date.**

   You see the current date on the bottom and a list of notifications on top (refer to Figure 3-2).

2. **Click or tap the upward-pointing arrow to the right of the current date.**

   The calendar for the current month is displayed, as shown in Figure 3-10.

FIGURE 3-10: Viewing the calendar.

3. **Click or tap the up or down arrow (next to the month and year) to navigate to the previous or next month, respectively.**

4. **To skip to another month, click or tap the name of the month that you're currently viewing, and then click or tap the month you want to view.**

5. **To skip to another year:**

   a. Click or tap the name of the month you're currently viewing.

   b. Click or tap the year you're viewing. A list appears with the years you can select.

   c. Click or tap the year and then choose the month you want to view.

Using Quick Settings

If you click or tap the network, volume, or battery icon in the bottom-right corner of the Windows 11 desktop, you'll see a readily accessible pane with quick settings, as shown in Figure 3-11. This pane includes quickly adjustable settings, such as the screen's brightness, sound volume, Bluetooth, and Wi-Fi. They also mimic what you would find on a smartphone — airplane mode is an obvious example but so too is energy saver. In some cases, a quick setting displays a Settings page or a pane with more options or toggles for a specific feature, such as studio effects, which is exclusive to Copilot+ PC devices with a Windows 11 equipped with a neural processing unit (NPU).

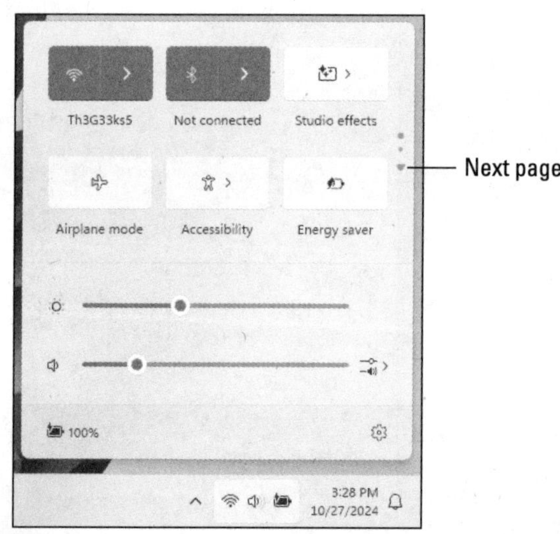

FIGURE 3-11: The quick settings available on an ASUS Vivobook S 15 Copilot+ PC.

The quick settings available vary depending on whether you're using a desktop PC, laptop, tablet, or 2-in-1; the device's hardware configuration; and the apps installed. For example, if Spotify is installed, you might also see some controls for the music you play, allowing you to pause the current song or skip to the next one.

Unfortunately, you can't add your own quick settings, but you can drag them to change their order. Before Windows 11 version 24H2, you could edit the quick settings and keep only those you wanted to use. However, this functionality has been removed from Windows 11.

Leaving this frustrating limitation aside, you should familiarize yourself with quick settings and what they do. Let's take a brief tour of the settings available on a Windows 11 computer or device:

1. **Click or tap the network, volume, or battery icon.**

   It doesn't matter which one you choose. The quick settings appear on the right side of the screen.

2. **Click or tap the Wi-Fi icon to disable the wireless network connectivity. Click or tap it again to enable it.**

3. **If you have an entry named Studio Effects, click or tap it.**

   You see a pane with effects that you can apply to your webcam.

4. **Click or tap the back arrow in the top left to see your quick settings again.**

5. **To scroll down the list of quick settings, click or tap the downward-facing arrow.**

   If you hover your mouse cursor over the arrow, it says Next Page. Browse the quick settings available on this section page.

6. **To move an icon for a quick action, just click and drag it where you want (or press and hold the icon while dragging).**

   Unfortunately, you can't drag a quick action off the grid.

7. **When you've finished checking the quick settings, click or tap somewhere on the desktop to close them.**

TIP

One useful thing you can do is right-click a quick setting and select Go to Settings. This action takes you to the Settings page relevant to the quick setting you chose. For example, right-clicking the Wi-Fi quick setting takes you to the Wi-Fi Settings page, where you can configure the wireless networking settings.

Table 3-1 explains what each configurable Quick Settings icon does when you click or tap it. They're listed in alphabetical order.

TABLE 3-1 Quick Actions and What They Do

Click or Tap This Icon	And This Happens
Accessibility	Turns on or off different accessibility tools such as magnifier, color filters, narrator, mono audio, live captions, and sticky keys.
Airplane mode	Turns all wireless communication on and off. See the Settings app's Network & Internet, Airplane Mode setting.
Bluetooth	Turns Bluetooth on or off.
Brightness	Adjusts the screen brightness to the level you want. Available on portable devices but not on desktop PCs.
Cast	Searches for wireless display and audio devices to project to — Miracast in particular.
Energy saver	Enables energy saver, dims the display, and reduces power consumption. Doesn't work if the laptop or tablet is plugged in.
Live captions	Provides audio and video captions in real-time and translated into the language you select.
Mobile hotspot	Turns your Windows 11 laptop, tablet, or 2-in-1 device into a wireless hotspot.
Nearby sharing	Enables you to share files with other Windows computers and devices found nearby.
Night light	Uses warmer colors on your display to help you sleep.
Project	Projects the image on your screen to an external display or a projector.
Rotation lock	Prevents the screen from rotating from portrait to landscape and vice versa. Available only on devices with touchscreens that can be rotated.
Studio effects	Allows you to select which visual effects to apply to your camera.
Volume	Adjusts the sound volume to the level you want.
Wi-Fi	Enables Wi-Fi connectivity and allows you to discover and connect to wireless networks.

IN THIS CHAPTER

» Figuring out Microsoft accounts

» Deciding whether you even want a Microsoft account

» Setting up and managing a Microsoft account

» Limiting the settings synced with your Microsoft account

» Closing a Microsoft account

Chapter 4

Understanding Microsoft Accounts

Microsoft has been trying to get people to sign up for company-branded accounts for a long time and has become increasingly successful. One way they achieved this was by suggesting that people use Microsoft accounts in Windows. Now, with the latest iterations of this operating system, they're forcing people to create such accounts. While I don't like this approach, Microsoft accounts have become an integral part of the Windows experience, and they're just as important as our Google accounts or Apple IDs. Therefore, understanding Microsoft accounts is crucial for getting the most out of your operating system and enjoying a positive user experience with all that this company has to offer in terms of products and services.

I start this chapter by exploring what constitutes a Microsoft account and how to recognize one. You learn about the differences between Microsoft and local accounts and why Microsoft forcefully encourages their use. I weigh the pros and cons of using a Microsoft account, discussing its conveniences and the privacy considerations that come with it.

If you decide a Microsoft account is right for you, I walk you through setting one up. Whether you want to use an existing email address not registered with

Microsoft or create a new Outlook.com account, I've got you covered. I also show you how to manage your Microsoft account, from changing personal details to implementing two-factor authentication for added security.

For those who prefer more control over their data, I explain how to fine-tune what gets synced with your Microsoft account in Windows 11. And if you ever decide you no longer need your Microsoft account, I guide you through the process of closing it for good.

By the end of this chapter, you'll have a comprehensive understanding of Microsoft accounts in Windows 11, empowering you to make informed decisions about using and managing your digital identity in the Microsoft ecosystem. So, let's get started and demystify the world of Microsoft accounts!

Realizing Which Accounts Are Microsoft Accounts

Over the years, Microsoft has used many names and IDs for its accounts. Luckily, the company finally settled on the name *Microsoft account.* But what is a Microsoft account, you ask?

An email address that ends with @outlook.com, @hotmail.com, @msn.com, or @live.com is a Microsoft account. You don't have to use your Microsoft account, but you probably have one, especially if you use Microsoft products such as Windows, Office, Xbox, LinkedIn, or Skype.

REMEMBER

Many people don't know that *any* email address can be a Microsoft account. It doesn't matter if that email address is from Gmail, Yahoo!, and so on. You need only register that email address with Microsoft; I show you how in the "Setting Up a Microsoft Account" section, later in the chapter.

In the context of Windows 11, the Microsoft account takes on a new dimension. When you set up an account to log in to Windows, it can be either a Microsoft account or a *local account* (also called an *offline account*). The key differences between them follow:

- **Microsoft accounts** are always email addresses and must be registered with Microsoft. When you log in to Windows 11 with a Microsoft account, the operating system automatically synchronizes some settings — such as your apps, passwords, and language preferences — so if you change something on one machine and log in with the same Microsoft account on another one, the changes go with you.

In addition, a Microsoft account gives you a one-stop login to internet-based Microsoft services. For example, if you have a OneDrive account, logging in to Windows 11 with a Microsoft account automatically connects you to your OneDrive files. Also, you can sign in with the same Microsoft account on your Windows 11 laptop, Windows 10 computer, Microsoft 365 subscription, and your Xbox, or buy Xbox games from Windows 11 and have them available on your console right away.

- **Local (offline) accounts** can be just about any name or combination of characters. If you sign in with a local account, Microsoft can't sync anything on different machines. Sign in to Windows 11 with a local account, and you must sign in to OneDrive, Microsoft Store, and other Microsoft apps and services separately, providing your Microsoft account. When you're using a local account, Windows 11 remembers your settings — your backgrounds, passwords, favorites, and the like — but they won't be moved to other PCs. They remain local and are lost when you remove your user account.

For example, `happywindowsuser@hotmail.com` is a Microsoft account. Since it's an `@hotmail.com` email address, it's already associated with Microsoft. I can create a user on a Windows 11 device with the email `happywindowsuser@hotmail.com`, and Windows will recognize it as a Microsoft account. On the other hand, I can set up an account called Ciprian Rusen on a Windows 11 PC. Because Microsoft accounts must be email addresses (you see why in the section "Setting Up a Microsoft Account"), the Ciprian Rusen account is a local (offline) account.

When setting up a new Windows 11 PC, you must enter a Microsoft account. Unfortunately, installing Windows 11 (even the Pro edition) without one requires quite a bit of manual hacking (read Book 8, Chapter 2). To make things worse, Windows 11 makes it surprisingly difficult to create a local account even after you first sign in with a Microsoft account. Still, it will begrudgingly let you (see Book 2, Chapter 5).

Deciding Whether You Want a Microsoft Account

If Microsoft has access to all Microsoft accounts, you may ask, why would I want to sign in to Windows 11 with a Microsoft account? Good question!

Signing in to Windows 11 with a Microsoft account brings several benefits. In particular:

- **Some of your Windows 11 settings will travel with you.** Your user picture, apps, Microsoft Edge favorites, and other settings will find you no matter which PC you log into. I find this helpful in some ways and annoying in others.

  For example, your Windows 11 apps — the ones that came with Windows 11 or that you downloaded from the Microsoft Store — carry your settings and user content from one device to the next. For example, your open tabs in Microsoft Edge can be accessed from other PCs when you use the same Microsoft account. The settings for the Weather app travel from one device to the next. Even Windows 11 apps *that Microsoft doesn't make* may have their settings moved from machine to machine. However, Microsoft uses this information to display ads and recommend apps to install on your Windows 11 computer(s).
- **Sign-in credentials for apps and websites travel with you.** If you rely on Microsoft Edge to keep sites' login credentials, those will find you if you switch machines.
- **You are automatically signed in to Windows 11 apps and services that use the Microsoft account.** Outlook, the Office apps from Microsoft 365, OneDrive, Teams, Skype, and the Microsoft website are all in this category.

Microsoft offers these benefits to encourage the use of a Microsoft account. However, it's worth noting that these features require a centralized system to work. Without a unique identifier managed by Microsoft, it wouldn't be possible to provide these interconnected services across different devices and platforms.

WARNING

Using a Microsoft account to sign in to Windows comes with some privacy considerations. For starters, Microsoft keeps a record of when you log in to any PC with your account. When you use Microsoft Edge, you're automatically signed in with your Microsoft account, allowing the company to collect data about your browsing habits (except when using InPrivate mode). Your Bing searches are also linked to your account. Microsoft gathers information about the apps you access through their Store, and if you use Copilot, all your queries and interactions are stored as well. Microsoft then builds a comprehensive user profile linked to your account, compiling data from various services and interactions. It's important to be aware of the extent of personal information the company can potentially collect through regular use of its integrated services.

TIP

Perhaps it's true that you have no privacy and should get over it, and most people don't care about this subject. But if you do care, you should read Book 2, Chapter 7, where I talk about Windows 11's privacy settings.

WHAT IF MY HOTMAIL OR OUTLOOK.COM ACCOUNT IS HIJACKED?

Maybe you have set up a Hotmail account or Outlook.com to log in to your Windows PC, and suddenly the account gets hijacked. Someone else gets into your account and changes the password. What happens next time you try to log in to your Windows 11 PC?

Windows 11 doesn't let you log in and gives you a link to reset your password and another for a Forgot Password? wizard. If you've enabled two-factor authentication, where Microsoft sends you a code on your smartphone or recovery email address (different from your Microsoft account email), you can proceed and change your password. Unfortunately, many people don't use two-factor authentication, even though they should.

To get your account back, you need to contact the people at Microsoft and convince them that you're the rightful owner. Go to `https://account.live.com/resetpassword.aspx`, and complete as much information as possible. Depending on how you have set up your Microsoft account and how correctly you answer all the questions, you may be able to recover your account.

Setting Up a Microsoft Account

If you don't have a Microsoft account, the way I see it, you have three choices for setting one up:

- **You can use an existing email address not registered with Microsoft.** But if you do that, Microsoft will put that email address in its database. It can cross-reference the address to many things you do with Windows 11.
- **You can use (or set up) an Outlook.com, Hotmail, Xbox, or Skype account.** If you already have one of these accounts, Microsoft tracks it and knows when you receive and send emails, for example. But that's true of any online email service, including Gmail and Yahoo! Mail. Using an Outlook.com account to log in to Windows 11 means that Microsoft can track additional information and associate it with your Outlook.com account — the times you log in to Windows 11, your locations, and so on. You may be okay with that, or you may not want Microsoft to be able to track that kind of additional information.

» **You can create an additional Outlook.com account and use it ONLY to log in to Windows 11.** The Outlook.com account is free and easy to make, and if you use it wisely, nobody will ever know the difference. The downsides: If you use Outlook.com, you have to tell the Outlook app to look in your other inbox; your existing Outlook.com contacts won't get carried over into the Outlook app automatically; and Skype will want to work with your new ID instead of your old one — the same with OneDrive, Microsoft 365, and other services.

Although none of these options seem ideal to me, think things through and choose the one you prefer.

Creating an Outlook.com account

Here's how to set up a new Outlook.com account to use in Windows 11 and Microsoft's other products and services:

1. **Using your favorite web browser, go to** `www.outlook.com`**.**

   The main screen lets you sign in or create a free account.

2. **Click or tap Create Free Account.**

   You see the Create Account form, as shown in Figure 4-1.

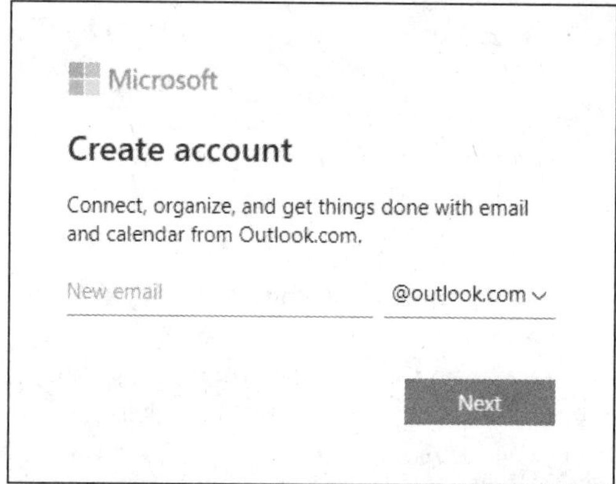

FIGURE 4-1: Sign up for a Microsoft account.

3. **Type an account name and click or tap Next.**

   If someone already has the email address you entered, type another and click or tap Next again.

4. **Type the password you want to use, deselect the box that tells Microsoft to send you information (another word for spam), and then click or tap Next.**
5. **Fill out your first and last name, and then click or tap Next.**
6. **Give Microsoft your country (which they can find anyway by looking at your IP address) and fill out a birthdate. Click or tap Next.**

   If your birthdate indicates that you're less than 18 years old, you may have problems using the account.
7. **Type the CAPTCHA code or solve the puzzle that Microsoft displays to verify that you are human, and then click or tap Next.**
8. **If Microsoft asks if you want to stay signed in, click or tap Yes.**

   Outlook.com asks you to choose the Outlook layout.
9. **Make your choice and then click or tap OK.**

   You see your inbox and Microsoft's welcome message, as shown in Figure 4-2. That's it.

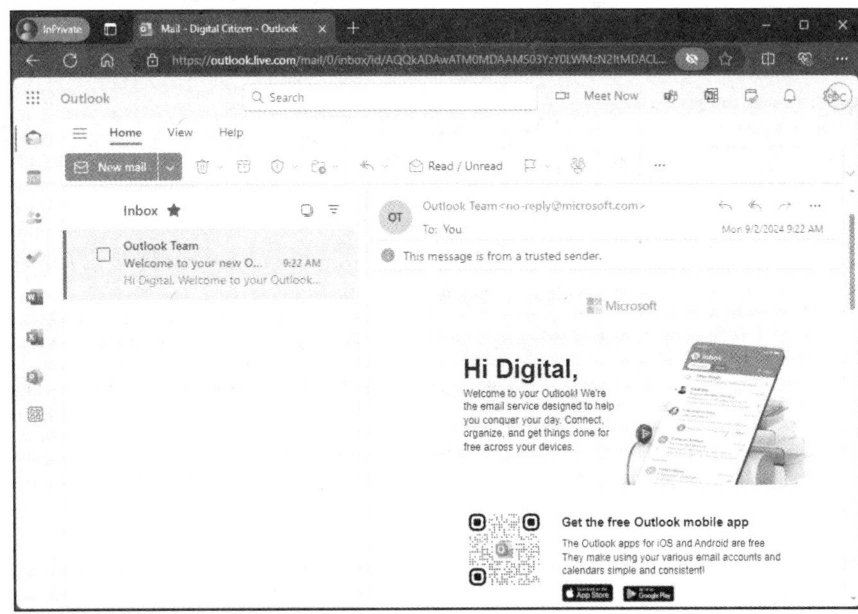

FIGURE 4-2: Your new Microsoft account is live and working.

You can now use your new Outlook.com account as a Windows 11 login ID. You can also use it for email, Copilot, Bing, Skype, Xbox, OneNote, OneDrive, and everything else from Microsoft. However, before you can log in to Windows 11 with this new Outlook.com account, you must add it as a user. Read Chapter 5 in this minibook to learn how.

Making any email address a Microsoft account

You must follow a different procedure to turn any email address into a Microsoft account. The steps are simple as long as you can retrieve the email sent to the address:

1. **Using your favorite web browser, go to** `https://signup.live.com`.

   You see the Create Account wizard, as shown in Figure 4-3, where you can create a Microsoft account without a Microsoft email address.

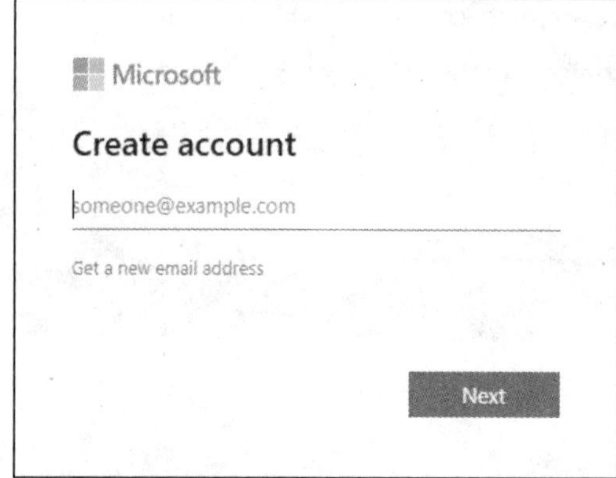

FIGURE 4-3: Creating a Microsoft account with an email address from another company.

2. **Type your email address from Gmail, Yahoo! Mail, or some other place. Then click or tap Next.**
3. **Enter the password you want to use and click or tap Next.**

REMEMBER

   Note that the password you provide here is for your Microsoft account. It is *not* your email password. The password you enter here will be the password you need to use to log in to Windows 11 or any website that requires a Microsoft account. I advise you not to re-use your email password as your Microsoft account password.

4. **Fill out your first and last name, and then click or tap Next.**
5. **Give Microsoft your country and fill out a birthdate. Click or tap Next.**

   Microsoft sends a 6-digit verification code to your email address. If you do not see the email, check your Spam/Junk folder.

6. **Type the verification code, deselect the box that allows Microsoft to send you emails, and click or tap Next.**

7. **Type the CAPTCHA code or solve the puzzle that Microsoft displays to verify that you are human, and then click or tap Next.**

   Microsoft displays a note about your new account.

8. **Click or tap OK, and if Microsoft asks if you want to stay signed in, choose Yes.**

   Microsoft may ask you to add a backup phone number.

9. **Click or tap Add Now, follow the wizard's prompts to verify your identity, and enter your phone number. You may also need to solve another puzzle or type a CAPTCHA code.**

   Your Microsoft account page is finally loaded, as shown in Figure 4-4.

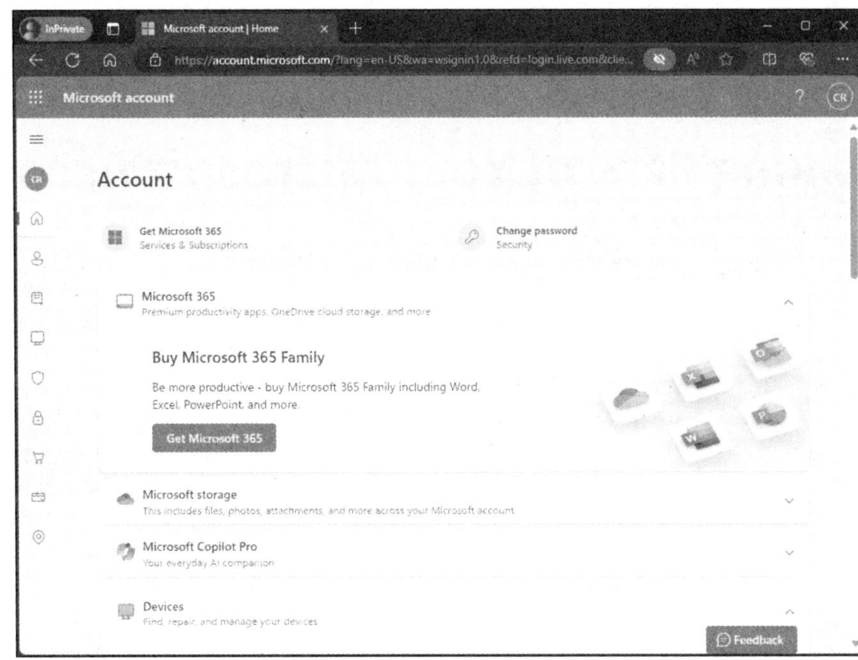

FIGURE 4-4: Your new Microsoft account is created with an email from a provider other than Microsoft.

TWO-FACTOR AUTHENTICATION

Microsoft has a security feature called *two-factor authentication,* or *two-step verification,* and it's a great choice to enable and configure it. Usually, when you log in with your Microsoft account using a machine that hasn't been explicitly identified (by you) as being a trusted device, Microsoft issues a challenge to verify that you are who you say you are. The authentication usually comes in the form of an SMS sent to your phone, a code displayed in a mobile authentication app, or an email sent to another email address. The benefits are obvious: People may be able to steal your password, but it's rare that they get both your password and your computer (which bypasses two-factor authentication entirely), and it's even more difficult to get both your password and your smartphone — or access to your other email address.

Most people are leery about giving their phone numbers to Microsoft. However, Microsoft doesn't use your phone number for nefarious purposes. And smartphone-based two-factor authentication works great. You should try apps such as Microsoft Authenticator or Google Authenticator, which are available for Android and iPhone. I prefer the Microsoft app, but Google's is okay too.

Taking Care of Your Microsoft Account

Modifying your Microsoft account details is straightforward once you know where to look. To manage your account, visit `https://account.microsoft.com` and sign in. This page displays your account information (refer to Figure 4-4).

You'll find options for updating various aspects of your account. The relevant options are here, whether you want to edit your personal information, change the account picture, set up two-factor authentication for added security, or change your password. Simply click or tap the appropriate link for the item you want to modify. You can also add family members and set up parental controls, as you learn in Chapter 6 of this minibook, manage your subscriptions (Xbox Game Pass, Microsoft 365, and so on), add payment options, and review recent orders you've made.

Controlling What Is Synchronized with Your Microsoft Account

If you don't explicitly change anything, logging in to Windows 11 with a Microsoft account synchronizes some settings across all the PCs you use. You can tell Microsoft that you don't want to sync specific items. Here's how:

1. **Click or tap the Start icon, followed by Settings and then Accounts. You can also press Window+I and choose Accounts.**

2. **On the right, scroll down and click or tap Windows Backup.**

   The screen shown in Figure 4-5 appears.

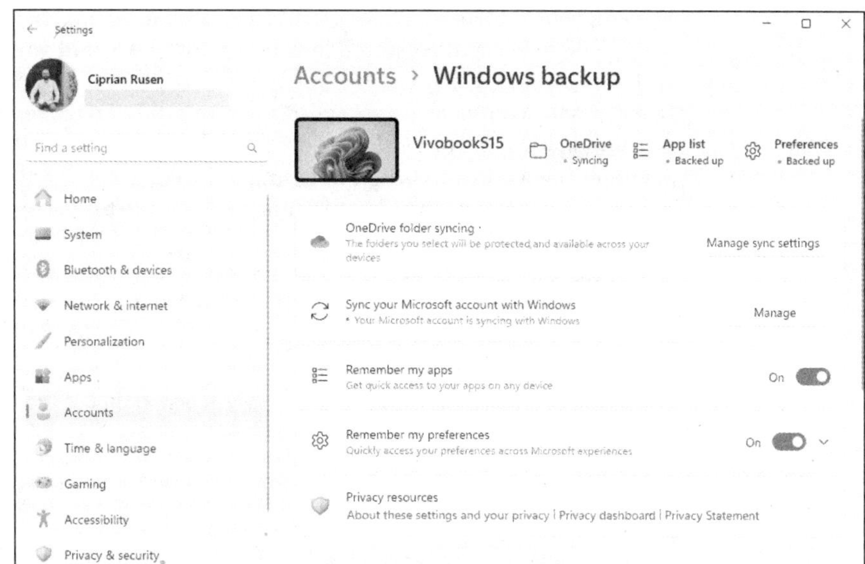

FIGURE 4-5: Controlling what gets synchronized using your Microsoft account.

3. **If you don't want Windows 11 to remember your apps and synchronize them across devices, turn off the switch for Remember My Apps.**

4. **If you don't want Windows 11 to sync your settings across devices, turn off the switch for Remember My Preferences.**

5. **If you don't want to sync your Microsoft account with Windows, click or tap Manage and then choose No, Don't Sync.**

6. **Click or tap Done to finish.**

   The changes take effect with your next login.

REMEMBER

Sync happens only when you log in with the same Microsoft account on two or more PCs.

Closing Your Microsoft Account

If you decide that you no longer need a Microsoft account and want to remove it, you can request its closure, which will be processed automatically in up to 60 days. When you cancel a Microsoft account, you cancel any current subscriptions (like those for Microsoft 365 or Xbox), your balances (Microsoft or Xbox gift card balance), your remaining Skype credit (if any), and so on. Basically, at the end of those 60 days, everything stored in your Microsoft account will get deleted.

If you're sure you want to go ahead with this task, remove your user account from Windows 11 and other devices where you're using it (see the next chapter in this minibook for details), sign in with a different account (maybe a local offline account or a different Microsoft account), and do the following:

1. **Using your favorite web browser, go to `www.outlook.com` and sign in with the Microsoft account you want to delete.**

   You see the Outlook inbox.

2. **In the same browser tab, go to `https://account.live.com/closeaccount.aspx` and click or tap Next.**

   You're asked to mark your account for closure and to confirm that you're okay with losing all kinds of data and access.

3. **Select all the boxes as well as why you want to close your account. Then click or tap Mark Account for Closure.**

   Microsoft shares the date when the account will be closed and what you can do to prevent this from happening.

4. **Click or tap Done.**

   You're signed out from your Microsoft account. Remember not to sign in again, or the closure procedure will be canceled.

Note that your old Microsoft account is no longer valid for signing into any computer or device. You must sign in using other user accounts, local or Microsoft ones.

IN THIS CHAPTER

» Choosing an account type

» Adding or removing a user (local or Microsoft account)

» Adding a child account

» Modifying the settings of other accounts

» Switching between users

Chapter 5

Managing User Accounts

Many Windows PCs have just one user account, even when multiple people use them. This often happens because users feel intimidated by the process of setting up multiple user accounts. If this is the case for you, don't worry — I guide you through the process step by step. Even if you're the sole user of your PC, creating a second account can be beneficial. This chapter explores why you might want to do this and why you might not. It's all about finding what works best for your situation.

Note that your user account control options are limited if you're using Windows 11 Enterprise or Pro on a corporate network (a domain). In these cases, your IT department typically manages user account security and permissions. While this can sometimes be frustrating, it's generally a good thing for the overall security of the company's network, its users, and devices. However, this chapter focuses on PCs connected to small networks like those at homes or small businesses without a complicated network setup or stand-alone machines.

First, I present the types of Windows 11 accounts: standard and administrator accounts, and how they can be local offline or Microsoft accounts. You see how they differ and how they mix with each other.

I also show you how to add any account you want, including a special type called the child account, which is useful for families. Lastly, you see how to edit other user accounts from an administrator account and how to switch between accounts. When you no longer need to use an account, I show you how to remove it from Windows 11 and clear some storage space.

Don't let this range of topics intimidate you. I describe each one clearly and concisely, ensuring that you understand how to manage user accounts effectively in Windows 11.

Understanding Why You Need Separate User Accounts

All sorts of problems appear when several people share a PC. You may have set up your desktop just right, with all your shortcuts right where you can find them, and then your significant other comes along and changes the wallpaper, accidentally deletes some files you may need, and adds their own apps and shortcuts on the desktop. It's worse than sharing a TV remote.

Also, I'm sure you don't want others to open Microsoft Edge and peek into your Facebook account or see all the recent videos you've played on your computer. To get around this issue, it's a good idea to create a separate user account for each individual using your computer.

WARNING

If someone else can get their hands on your computer, it isn't your computer anymore. This can be a real problem if the cleaning staff uses your PC after hours or a snoop breaks into your study. Unless you use BitLocker (in Windows 11 Pro), anybody who can restart your PC can also look at, modify, and delete your files or stick a virus on your PC. How? It's surprisingly easy to bypass Windows 11 directly and start your PC with another operating system, running it from a USB flash drive. With BitLocker out of the picture, compromising a PC doesn't take much work.

Windows 11 helps keep peace in the family — and in the office — by requiring people to log in. The process of *logging in* (also called *signing in*) lets the operating system keep track of each person's settings: You tell Windows 11 who you are, and it lets you play in your own sandbox without affecting others.

Choosing Account Types

When dealing with user accounts, you bump into one essential fact of Windows life: The type of account you use may limit what you can do. Unless your PC is hooked up to a big corporate network, user accounts can be divided into administrator accounts and standard accounts.

Administrator accounts can do almost anything on the computer, such as installing apps and changing important Windows settings. Standard accounts are more limited and are good for everyday tasks, but they can't make big changes.

What's a standard account?

If you're running Windows 11 with a *standard account*, you can do only standard tasks:

- Run programs already installed on your computer, including programs on USB drives.
- Use hardware already installed on your computer.
- Create, view, save, modify, and use documents, pictures, and sounds in the Documents, Pictures, or Music folders as well as in the PC's Public folders.
- Change your password or switch back and forth between requiring and not requiring a password for your account. You can also add a PIN. If your computer has the necessary hardware, you can use Windows Hello to set up a face scan or a fingerprint reader — just like in the movies.
- Switch between a local offline account and a Microsoft account. I talk about both in the previous chapter of this minibook.
- Change the picture that appears next to your name, on the left side of the Start menu, change the desktop wallpaper, add items to the taskbar and Start menu, and make other small changes that don't affect other user accounts.

If you're using a standard account, you can't even change the time on the clock. The account is quite limited regarding the system settings it can configure.

On the upside, if you start Windows 11 with a standard account and accidentally run a virus or some other piece of malware, the damage is usually limited: The malware can delete or scramble files in your Documents folder and probably in the Public folders, but that's about the extent of the damage. Usually. Unless it's exceedingly clever, the virus can't install itself into the computer, so it can't run repeatedly, and it may not be able to replicate.

When a person with a standard account tries to make changes to system-wide settings such as changing the system time or installing new programs or drivers, they're requested to provide an administrator account's username and password (or PIN). If they enter the necessary details, the change is performed. If they don't, nothing happens.

A special limited version of the standard account is called a child account, which is useful for families with children. Child accounts can be controlled and monitored by those with standard and administrator accounts.

What's an administrator account?

People using *administrator accounts* can change almost anything, anywhere, at any time. However, certain Windows folders (such as the folders where the operating system is installed) remain off-limits, and you must jump through some difficult hoops to work around the restrictions. People with administrator accounts can even change the passwords of other local accounts — a good thing to remember if you ever forget your password.

Someone with an administrator account can get into all the files owned by other users: If you thought that attaching a password to your account and putting a top-secret spreadsheet in your Documents folder would keep it away from prying eyes, you're in for a surprise. Anybody who can get into your machine with an administrator account can look at it. On the other hand, standard users are limited to looking at only their own files.

Choosing between standard and administrator accounts

REMEMBER

The first account on a new PC is always an administrator account. If you bought your PC with Windows 11 preinstalled, the account that you have — the one you probably set up shortly after you took the computer out of the box — is an administrator account. Or if you installed Windows 11 on a PC, the account you set up during installation is an administrator account. It doesn't matter whether that account is a Microsoft one (with an email address attached to it) or a local (offline) one.

After you install Windows and set up your first account, any other accounts you create start as standard accounts. If you ask me, that's how it should be. However, administrator accounts and standard accounts aren't set in concrete. In fact, Windows 11 helps you shift between the two as circumstances dictate:

» If you're using a standard account and trying to do something that requires an administrator account, Windows 11 prompts you to provide the administrator account's name and password or PIN, as shown in Figure 5-1.

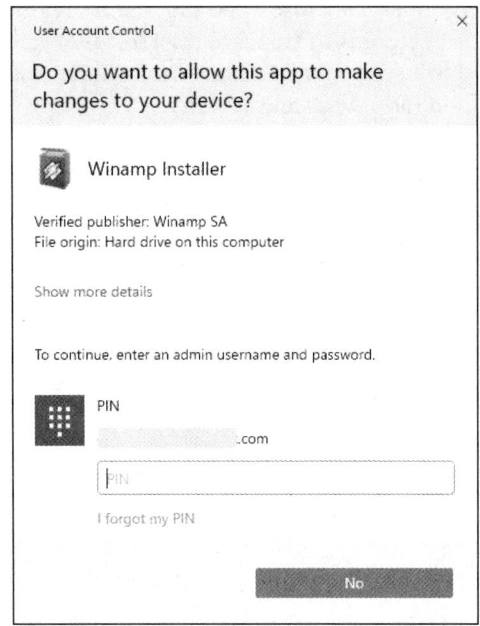

FIGURE 5-1: User Account Control (UAC) asks for permission before performing administrative actions.

» Even if you're using an administrator account, Windows 11 normally runs as though you had a standard account, in some cases adding an extra hurdle (usually in the form of an additional confirmation dialog) when you try to run a program that can make substantial changes to your PC. You must clear the same kind of hurdle if you try to access folders that aren't explicitly shared (see Figure 5-2). That extra hurdle helps prevent destructive programs from sneaking into your computer and running with your administrator account, doing their damage without your knowledge or permission.

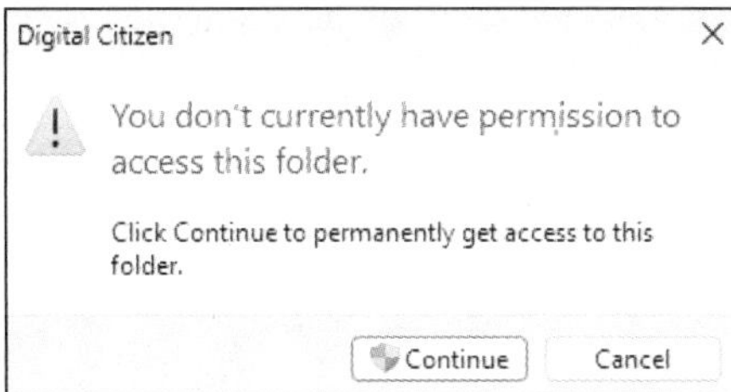

FIGURE 5-2: Windows 11 challenges you before diving into another user's folder.

TIP

Because you can add new users only if you're using an administrator account, I recommend that you save that one administrator account for a rainy day and set up standard accounts for yourself and anyone else who uses the PC. Use Windows 11 with a standard account, and I bet you'll seldom notice the difference. If you dislike using a Microsoft account that logs data about you, you can set that one administrator account as a Microsoft account, use it only when you must, and then set up all the other accounts as standard local (offline) accounts. This practical compromise may just be the solution that balances Microsoft's push for online accounts with your need for privacy and security.

Adding Accounts in Windows 11

In Windows 11, you can add three types of accounts: Microsoft accounts, local accounts, and child accounts. In this section, I discuss them one by one. Each type of account can be set as an administrator or as a standard user.

Adding a user with a Microsoft account

After you log in to an administrator account, you can add more users easily. Here's how to add another user who has a Microsoft account:

1. **Click or tap the Start icon, followed by Settings.**

   You see the Home tab of the Settings app.

2. **On the left, choose Accounts. On the right, scroll down until you see Other Users and click or tap it.**

   The screen shown in Figure 5-3 appears.

3. **Click or tap Add Account.**

   You see the challenging How Will This Person Sign In? dialog box, as shown in Figure 5-4.

4. **If the new user already has a Microsoft account (or a `@hotmail.com` or `@outlook.com` email address — which are automatically Microsoft accounts), type the email address in the box and then click or tap Next.**

5. **Click or tap Finish.**

   Windows 11 sets up your account and you see it in the list of users. You'll be asked to enter this account's password when you first sign in. Remember that the user is set by default as having a standard account, not an administrator account.

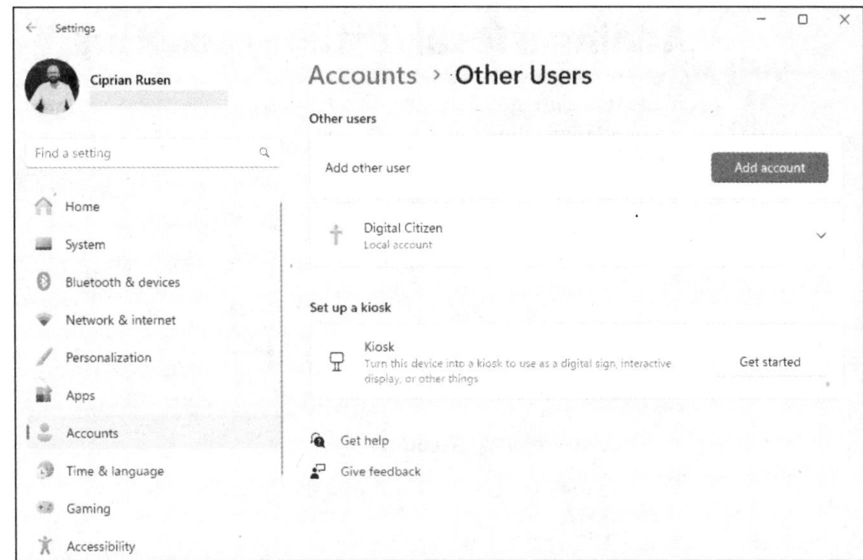

FIGURE 5-3: Add other users to Windows 11.

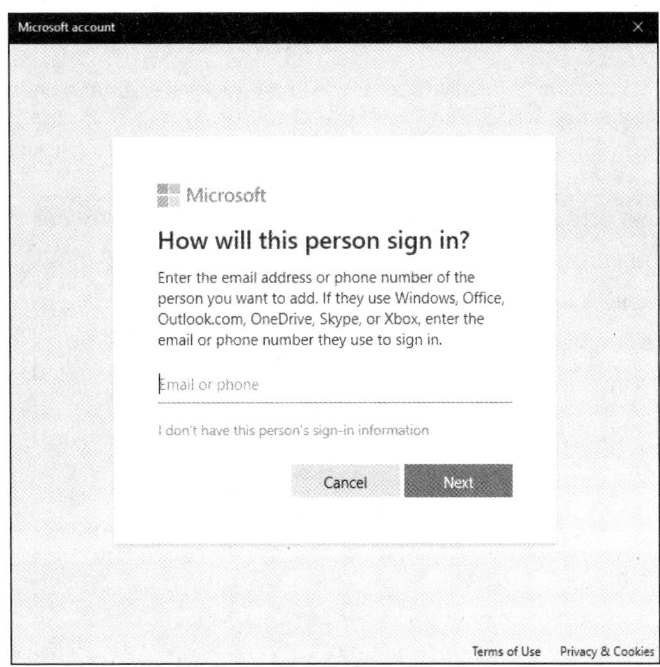

FIGURE 5-4: Microsoft wants you to set up a Microsoft account.

TECHNICAL STUFF

If you have a Microsoft account, don't imagine that you can log in on any Windows 11 computer from anywhere. Before you can do that, a user who is an administrator needs to add your Microsoft account first, using the steps I just shared.

Adding a local (offline) account

While there are good reasons for using a Microsoft account, adding a local account is a good idea when you don't want Microsoft to know much about what you do on your Windows 11 PC, or when you want to log in without a password. Here's how to add a local account in Windows 11:

1. **Click or tap the Start icon, and then Settings.**

   The Settings app appears on your desktop.

2. **On the left, select Accounts. On the right, select Other Users.**

   The Other Users screen appears (refer to Figure 5-3).

3. **Click or tap Add Account.**

   You see the dialog box shown previously in Figure 5-4.

4. **In the How Will This Person Sign In? dialog box, click or tap the link at the bottom that says I Don't Have This Person's Sign-in Information.**

   Windows 11 gives you yet another opportunity to set up a Microsoft account.

5. **Click or tap Add a User without a Microsoft Account.**

   Windows 11 (finally!) asks you to enter the local account name and password. See Figure 5-5.

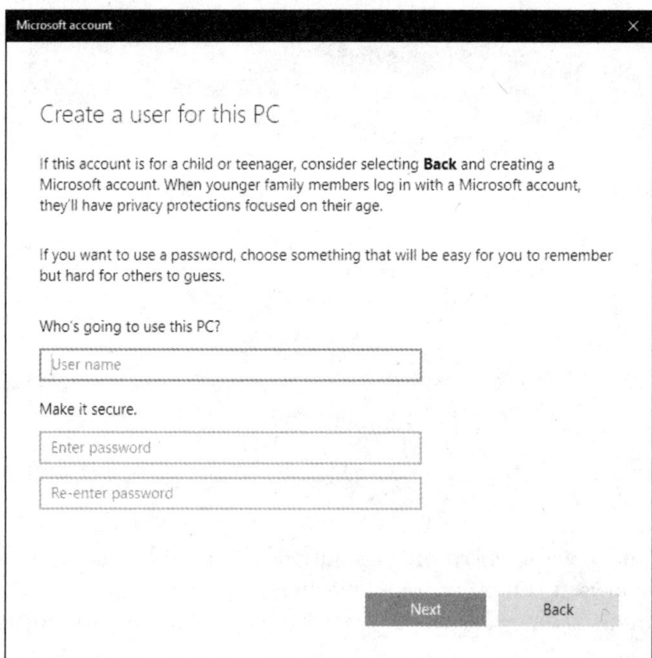

FIGURE 5-5: You finally get to create a local account.

6. **In the Who's Going to Use This PC? field, type a name for the new account.**

   You can give a new account just about any name you like: first name, last name, nickname, titles, abbreviations . . . no sweat, as long as you don't use the characters / \ [ ]"; : | < > + = , ? or *.

7. **(Optional) Type a password twice, select three security questions and write answers for them.**

   These questions and answers can be used later to reset the password you've just set, if you forget it. If you leave the password fields blank, the user can log in directly by simply clicking or tapping the account name on the sign-in screen.

8. **Click or tap Next.**

   You have a new standard local account, and its name now appears in the list of Other Users.

If you want to turn the new account into an administrator account, follow the steps in the "Changing Other Users' Settings" section, later down in the chapter.

TIP

If you created a local account without a password, you can add a password later, after you sign in with that account and go to Settings ➪ Accounts ➪ Sign-In Options ➪ Password.

TECHNICAL STUFF

You aren't allowed to create a new account that's named Administrator. There's a good reason why Windows 11 prevents you from making a new account with that name: You already have one. Even though Windows 11 goes to great lengths to hide the account named Administrator, it's there, and you may encounter it by accident. For now, don't worry about the ambiguous name and the ghostly apparition. Just refrain from trying to create a new account named Administrator. You can create any account with any other name, with or without administrator permissions.

Adding a child account

A child account is a standard Microsoft account that can be managed by parents. To manage a child account, you must have a Microsoft account on your Windows 11 PC that is set as administrator. From it, you can add your child's Microsoft account and set it as a member of your family using Microsoft's Family Safety. For more details, visit `www.microsoft.com/en-us/microsoft-365/family-safety`.

If you have created a Microsoft account for your child, and are logged in with your own Microsoft account, here's how to add your child's account to Windows 11:

1. **Click or tap the Start icon, followed by Settings.**
2. **In the Settings window, click or tap Accounts, followed by Family.**

   The Family screen appears, as shown in Figure 5-6.

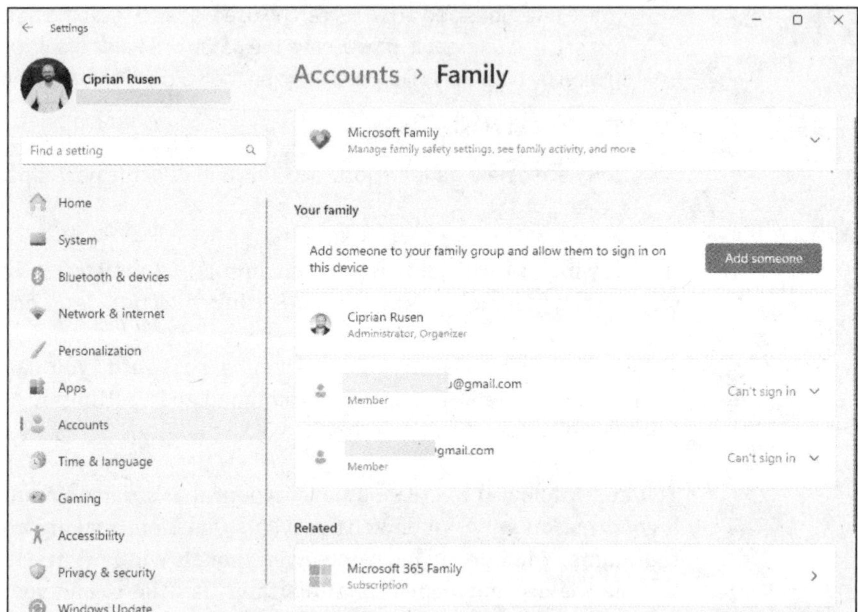

FIGURE 5-6: Setting up the members of your Microsoft Family.

3. **Click or tap Add Someone.**

   A dialog named Microsoft Account appears.

4. **Type the email address of your child's Microsoft account, and then click or tap Next.**

   You're asked about the role of this account, as shown in Figure 5-7.

5. **Choose Member and then click or tap Invite.**

   The account is added to Windows 11, and your child receives an email with an invitation to join your family. If your child accepts, you can set up Family Safety rules.

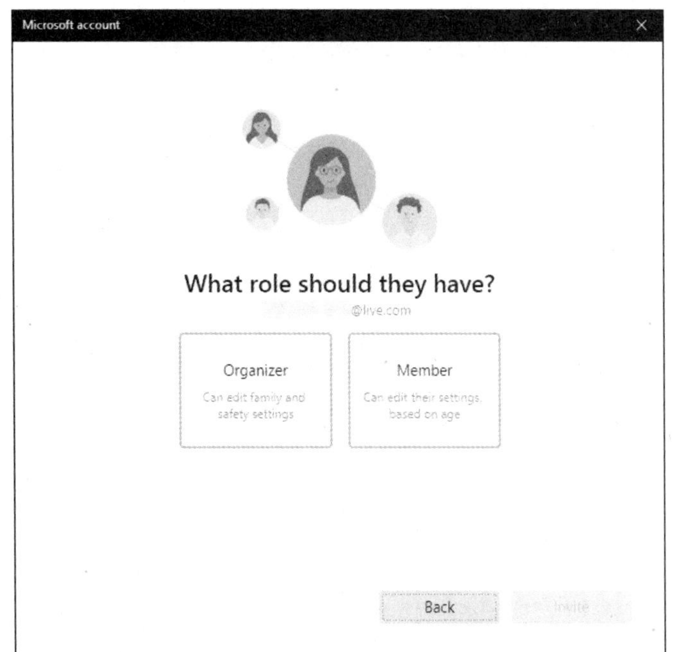

FIGURE 5-7: Choosing the role for your child's account.

With Microsoft Family Safety, you can set screen time, app, and game limits, get access to reports about your child's activities, and have Microsoft Edge and Bing automatically filter inappropriate content online. You can learn more about using Microsoft Family Safety in the next chapter of this minibook.

Changing Other Users' Settings

If you have an administrator account, you can change many aspects of other user accounts on your computer. In this section, I cover the most important things you can do.

Setting a standard account as administrator

To change another account from a standard account to an administrator account, do the following:

1. **Click or tap the Start icon, followed by Settings.**

   The Home tab of the Settings app appears.

2. **On the left, choose Accounts. On the right, select Other Users.**

   A list of all the accounts on the computer appears (refer to Figure 5-3).

3. **Click or tap on the account you want to change.**

   For example, in Figure 5-8, I chose to change my local account called Digital Citizen.

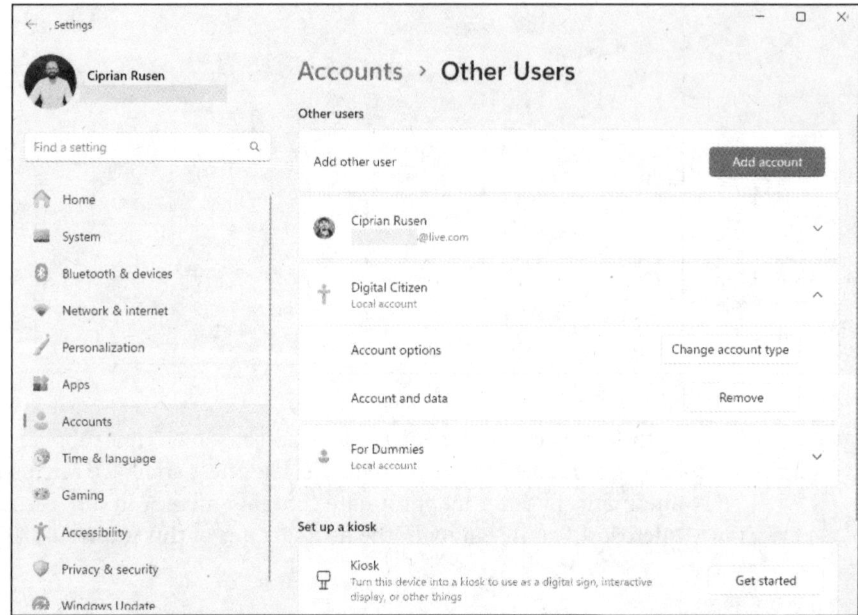

FIGURE 5-8: Choose the account you want to change from standard to administrator or vice versa.

4. **Click or tap the Change Account Type button under the selected account.**

   Windows 11 responds with the option to change from a standard user account to an administrator account and back.

5. **Select the new account type and click or tap OK.**

   The account's type changes immediately.

Modifying the settings of other accounts

You need to venture into the old-fashioned Control Panel for other kinds of account changes. Here's how to get to the options related to managing user accounts in the Control Panel:

1. **Click or tap inside the Search box on the taskbar and type** Control Panel**.**
2. **In the list of search results, choose Control Panel.**

   The Control Panel appears.

3. **Choose User Accounts, and then choose User Accounts again. Click or tap Manage Another Account.**

   A list of all accounts on the computer appears.

4. **Click or tap the account you want to change.**

   Windows 11 presents you with several options, as shown in Figure 5-9.

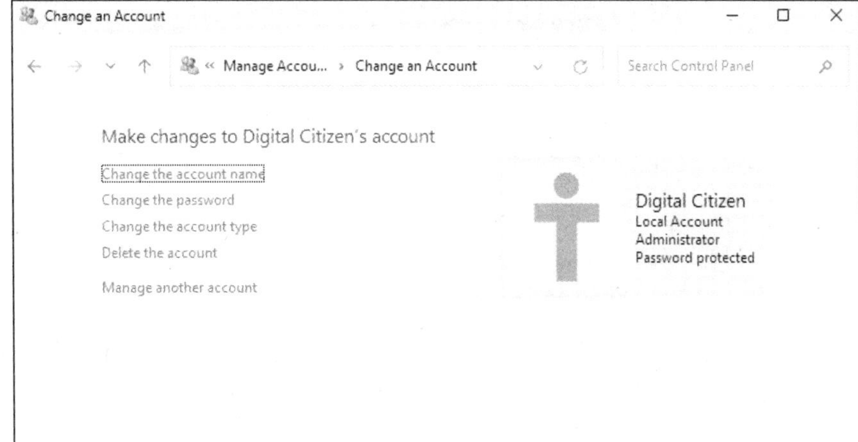

FIGURE 5-9: Maintain another user's account.

Here's what the available options entail:

- **Change the Account Name:** This option appears only for local accounts. (It'd be problematic if Windows 11 let you change someone else's Microsoft account.) Selecting this option modifies the name displayed on the sign-in screen and the Start menu while leaving all other settings intact. Use this option if you want to change only the name on the account — for example, if Little Bill wants to be called Sir William.
- **Create a Password/Change the Password:** Again, this option appears only for local accounts. (*Create* appears if the account doesn't have a password; *Change* appears if the account already has a password.) If you create a password for the chosen user, Windows 11 requires a password to log in with that user account. You can't get past the sign-in screen (using that account)

without it. This setting is weird because you can change it for other people. You can force Bill to use a password when none was required before, you can change Bill's password, or you can even make it blank.

Passwords are cAse SenSitive — you must enter the password, with uppercase and lowercase letters, precisely the way it was originally typed. If you can't get the computer to recognize your password, make sure that the Caps Lock setting is off. That's the number-one source of login frustration.

Much has been written about the importance of choosing a secure password, mixing uppercase and lowercase letters with punctuation marks, ensuring that you have a long password, and so on. When choosing a strong password, there's no need to overthink it. Remember two key rules: Never write your password on a sticky note near your computer, and avoid common, easily guessed passwords. Instead, try creating a simple sentence you can remember and swap out some letters for numbers, like G00dGr1efTerry. Another option is to think of a phrase and use only the first letters, such as towasautf! for "there once was a story about unicorns that flew!" These methods help you create strong, memorable passwords. However, using a PIN, facial recognition, or a fingerprint login can be even more secure and convenient than traditional passwords.

- **Change the Account Type:** You can use this option to change accounts from administrator to standard and back again.
- **Delete the Account:** If you're deleting a Windows 11 account, the account itself still lives — it just won't be permitted to log in to this computer. Windows offers to keep copies of the deleted account's Documents folder and desktop, but warns you quite sternly and correctly that if you snuff the account, you rip out all the email messages, user files, and other settings that belong to the user — definitely not a good way to make friends. Oh, and you can't delete your own account, of course, so this option won't appear if your PC has only one account.
- **Manage Another Account:** Displays the list of accounts so you can choose another user and modify the user's account with the options just described.

Switching Users

Windows 11 allows you to have more than one person logged in to a PC simultaneously. Picture this: You're knee-deep in an epic game of Minesweeper, sweating over whether that next click will reveal a flag or blow your virtual world to bits. Suddenly, your child bursts in, desperate to finish their last-minute book report on "The History of Watching Paint Dry." Meanwhile, your spouse is itching to order that life-changing pasta maker they saw in a mid-movie ad break on MAX. Just as you're about to clear that tricky corner, the cat decides your mouse hand is the perfect spot for an impromptu nap.

When using multiple user accounts, everyone can dive into their digital emergency without derailing your quest to become the neighborhood's Minesweeper champion. It's like having separate lanes on the information highway for each family member's unique brand of urgency.

Getting back on a serious note, the capability to have more than one user logged in to a PC simultaneously is called *fast user switching,* and it has advantages and disadvantages:

- **On the plus side:** Fast user switching lets you keep all your programs going while somebody else pops onto the machine for a quick computing session. When that person is done and logs off, you can pick up precisely where you left off before you got bumped.
- **On the minus side:** All idle programs left sitting around by the inactive (bumped) user can bog things down for the active user, although the effect isn't drastic. You can avoid the overhead by logging off before the new user logs in.

To switch users:

1. **Click or tap the Start icon.**
2. **Click or tap your username or picture in the bottom-left corner of the Start menu.**

   You see a menu with your username, picture, and other details such as your OneDrive cloud storage space (shown only for Microsoft accounts).
3. **Click or tap the three dots on the upper side of the newly opened menu.**

   The options shown in Figure 5-10 appear.
4. **Choose Sign Out. Then, on the sign-in screen, choose any user in the list and log in.**

TIP

If you're at work, it's a good idea to lock your computer whenever you're not at your desk. To do that, during Step 2, click or tap the power icon and choose Lock. Or press Windows+L.

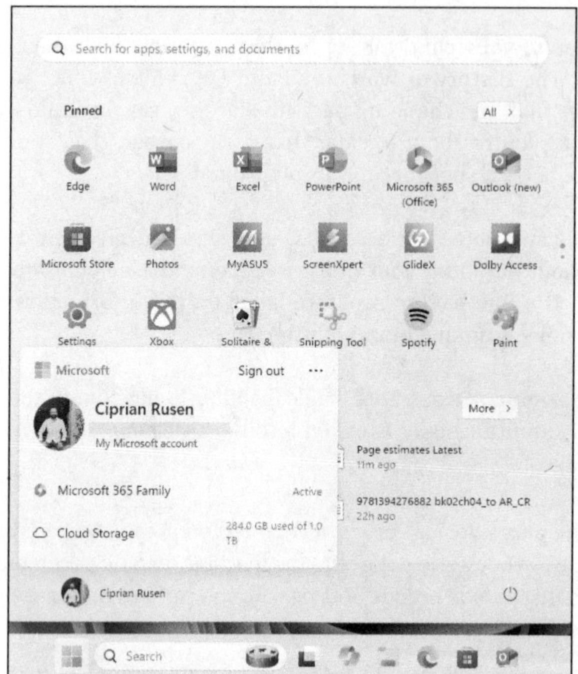

FIGURE 5-10: The options you have for switching users.

Removing User Accounts from Windows 11

If you no longer need to use an account on your Windows 11 computer or device, you can delete it. However, you can do this only from an administrator account. Before removing the account, ensure that you're signed out from it. Also, if the account has any data you want to keep, copy it to an external hard drive, a large USB flash drive, or a cloud storage solution. When all these aspects are taken care of, follow these steps:

1. **Click or tap the Start icon, followed by Settings.**

   The Settings app appears on the screen.

2. **On the left, choose Accounts. On the right, select Other Users.**

   A list of all the accounts on the computer appears (refer to Figure 5-3).

3. **Click or tap the user account you want to remove.**

   Under it, you see the options shown previously in Figure 5-8.

4. **Click or tap Remove.**

   The dialog shown in Figure 5-11 appears. You're informed that deleting the selected account will remove all its data. If this data hasn't been backed up or saved to another location, it will be lost in the removal process.

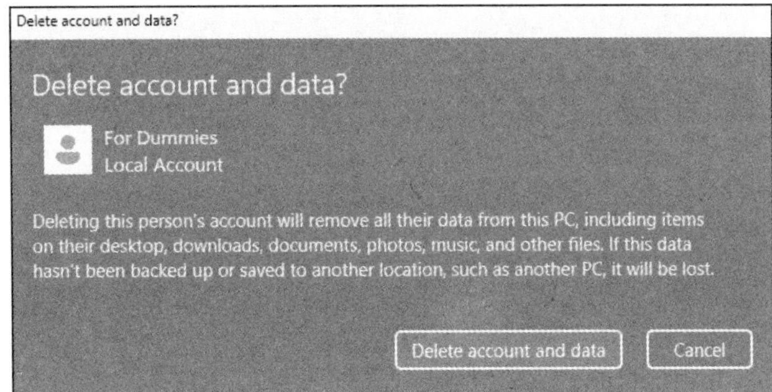

Delete account and data?
Delete account and data?
For Dummies
Local Account
Deleting this person's account will remove all their data from this PC, including items on their desktop, downloads, documents, photos, music, and other files. If this data hasn't been backed up or saved to another location, such as another PC, it will be lost.
Delete account and data
Cancel

FIGURE 5-11: Deleting a user account from Windows 11.

5. **To proceed, choose Delete Account and Data.**

   Windows takes time to remove the user account, and then you return to the screen shown previously in Figure 5-8. Note that the selected user is now gone.

6. **Close Settings.**

IN THIS CHAPTER

» Understanding Microsoft Family Safety

» Adding a child account

» Setting time limits for children

» Blocking inappropriate content

Chapter 6
Setting Up Your Family

This chapter is about the family-friendly side of Windows 11 and how to childproof the computers in your home. But instead of locking away the mouse and keyboard, I share how to set up virtual guardrails to keep your little ones safe when using Windows 11. Let's face it, handing your child an unrestricted computer is like giving them the keys to a candy store — exciting for them, but potentially disastrous for everyone involved. That's where Microsoft Family Safety comes in, a useful tool in the never-ending battle of "just 10 more minutes, please!"

In this chapter, I start by explaining a common point of confusion: the difference between Microsoft 365 Family and Microsoft Family Safety. Then, I walk you through adding child accounts to Windows 11, setting time limits for how long children can use their computer(s), and blocking inappropriate apps, games, and content.

By the end of this chapter, you'll become a superhero of screen time management, armed with the power to thwart late-night gaming sessions and protect your children from the darker corners of the web. Let's turn your Windows 11 computers and devices into safe havens for your children.

Comparing Microsoft Family Safety with Microsoft 365 Family

Microsoft has several services in its lineup of family products. The most popular is the Microsoft 365 Family subscription, which gives you and another five people access to the suite of Office programs (Word, Excel, PowerPoint, Outlook, and so on), OneDrive, Clipchamp, and Microsoft Defender. Each member in a Microsoft 365 Family subscription can use these products on five devices simultaneously and receives 1 TB of cloud storage space in OneDrive. To sweeten the deal, they also get access to Microsoft's Outlook email service, ad-free, and receive 60 minutes of calls to mobile phones and landlines per month on Skype.

A second, less-known product is Microsoft Family Safety or Microsoft Family (as named in Windows 11), which includes tools for families with children. With Microsoft Family, parents can set filters for web and search on the devices used by their children, so they don't access content inappropriate for their age. These filters work only when using the Microsoft Edge browser on Windows 10 and Windows 11, or when using Android smartphones with the Microsoft Family Safety app installed, as well as Xbox consoles. Another important feature is that you can use Microsoft Family to set screen time limits, in addition to apps and games.

TIP

Few people know that Microsoft Family Safety can also help you set up a family email and calendar that helps everyone stay organized, and a family OneNote notebook for grocery lists, family vacation plans, or shared notes (read Book 4, Chapter 5 to learn about using OneNote).

While the Microsoft 365 Family subscription costs $99.99/year, Microsoft Family Safety is a free service that can be used separately or together with a Microsoft 365 Family. The two are well integrated and, if you've bought a subscription, the same accounts are used for both services, and for managing your family and its devices.

Adding Child Accounts to Microsoft Family

If you want to manage your family, you must sign in to Windows 11 with a Microsoft account set as an administrator. Then, you can either add existing Microsoft accounts to your family or create new ones, including for your children. Unfortunately, the wizard for creating a Microsoft account for your child and adding it to Microsoft Family involves many steps and requires a bit of attention to avoid setting up things the wrong way. Therefore, arm yourself with some patience and follow these steps closely:

1. **Click or tap the Start icon, followed by Settings.**

   You see the Home tab of the Settings app.

2. **On the left, choose Accounts. On the right, scroll down and click or tap Family.**

   The screen shown in Figure 6-1 appears.

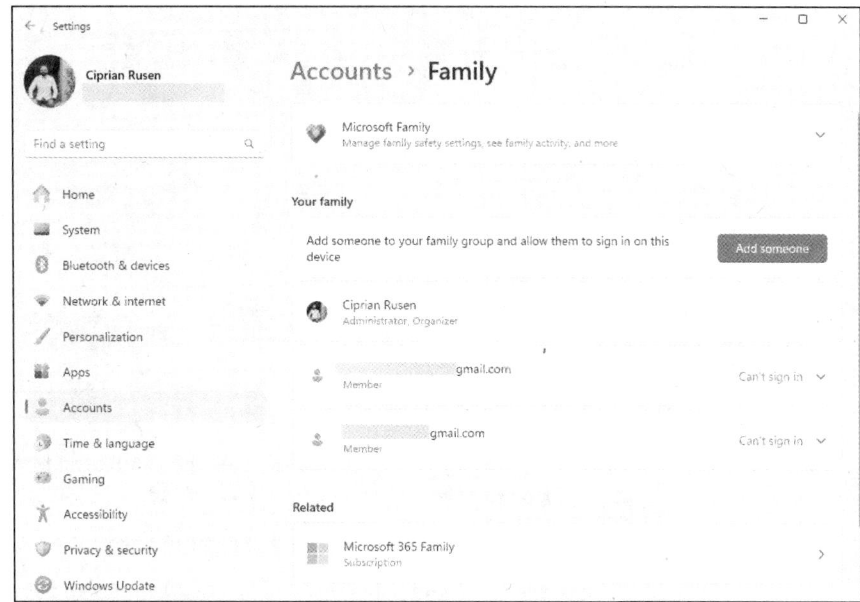

FIGURE 6-1: You add family members in Windows 11 from the Settings app.

3. **In the Your Family section, click or tap Add Someone.**

   The wizard shown in Figure 6-2 appears.

4. **Click or tap the link for Create One for a Child.**

5. **Type the email address you want to use and then click or tap Next.**

   You are asked to create a password for your child.

6. **Type the password you want for your child and deselect the box that allows Microsoft to send you information, tips, and offers. Click or tap Next.**

   You're requested to enter the name of your child.

7. **Enter your child's first name and last name, and then click or tap Next.**

   To set up the appropriate filters for your child, you're asked about their birthdate.

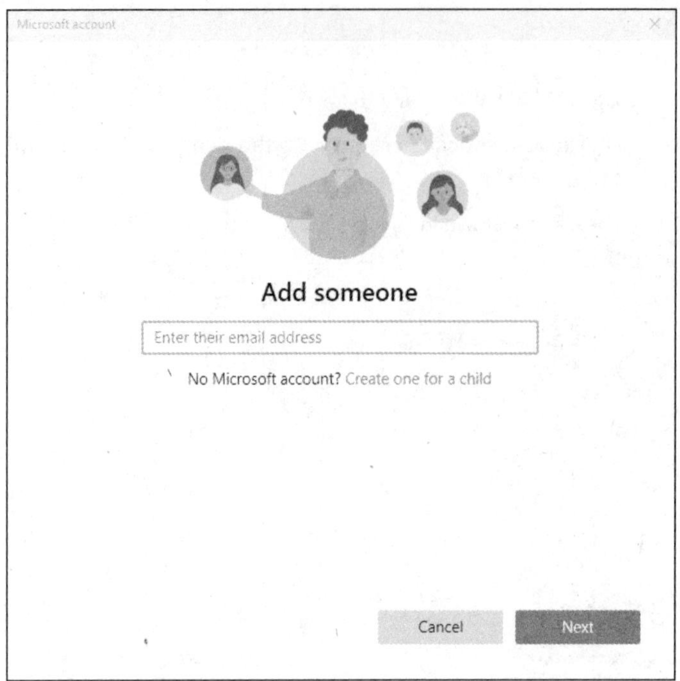

FIGURE 6-2: The wizard for adding someone to your family.

8. **Select the country where you live, enter the requested birthdate, and click or tap Next.**

   You're asked to solve some puzzles and confirm that you're not a robot.

9. **Click or tap Next and solve the puzzles. Don't forget to submit your solution for each.**

   When the verification is complete, you're asked to sign in with the account you've just created.

10. **Type your child's Microsoft account email and password, and then click or tap Sign In.**

    You're asked to specify whether you're a parent or guardian, as shown in Figure 6-3.

11. **Choose I'm a Parent or Guardian and then click or tap Continue.**

    You're asked to sign in with your Microsoft account (not your child's).

12. **Type the email for your Microsoft account, click or tap Next, provide your password, and sign in.**

    If you're using two-step verification, you're asked to confirm your sign-in.

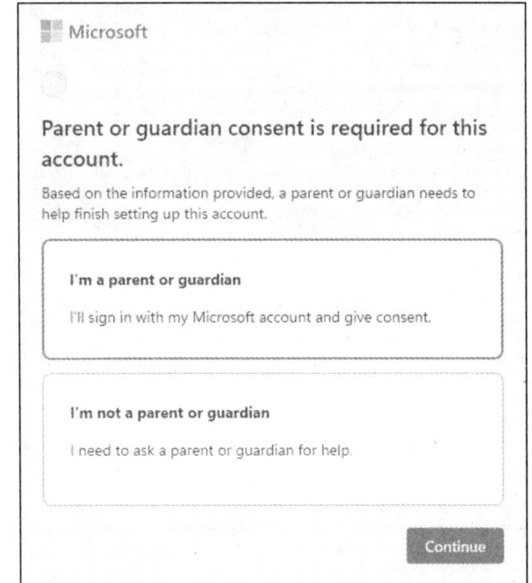

Microsoft
Parent or guardian consent is required for this account.
Based on the information provided, a parent or guardian needs to help finish setting up this account.
I'm a parent or guardian
I'll sign in with my Microsoft account and give consent.
I'm not a parent or guardian
I need to ask a parent or guardian for help.
Continue

FIGURE 6-3: Selecting whether you're a parent or guardian is a must.

13. **Approve your sign-in, confirm you want to stay signed in, and give your consent for your child's Microsoft account.**

    You're asked if you want to allow your child to sign in to non-Microsoft apps.

14. **Select the option you prefer, click or tap Continue, and then Family Safety.**

    The Microsoft Family Safety portal opens in Microsoft Edge, similar to Figure 6-4. Here, you see which protection features are turned on and how Microsoft's filters will use the child's age to decide what is appropriate content.

15. **Click or tap Done and close both Microsoft Edge and the Microsoft Account window.**

    You child is now part of your family and can sign in to Windows 11 on the same computer, using the account you've just created.

TIP

If you have more than one child, repeat the same steps for each. And if your children use different computers than the one(s) you're using, you should install Windows 11 and add your Microsoft account as administrator to those computers. After that, add your child's Microsoft account, as a standard account without administrator permissions.

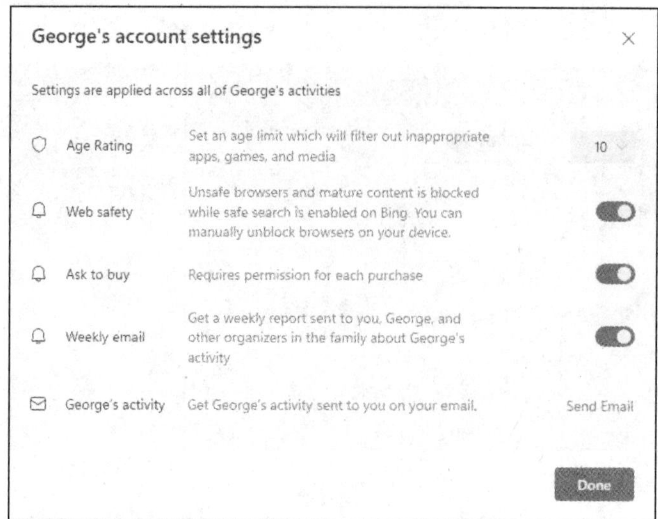

FIGURE 6-4: Your child's account is now part of Microsoft Family Safety.

Setting Time Limits for Children

In Microsoft Family Safety, only one account is the administrator, while the others can be members or organizers. The administrator is the Microsoft account which added all the others to the family.

Children accounts are members, but for them, the organizer(s) and the administrator can enforce rules regarding how long they can use their devices or what content they can access. If you're a parent and have added a child account using the steps from the preceding section, you can then turn on and configure time limits for your child. Here's how:

1. **Sign in with your organizer or administrator Microsoft account, click or tap the Start icon, and then click or tap Settings.**
2. **On the left side of the Settings app, choose Accounts. On the right, scroll down and click or tap Family.**

   You see the options shown previously in Figure 6-1.
3. **If necessary, click or tap Microsoft Family to expand it, and then click or tap Open Family Settings.**

   The Family Safety portal opens in Microsoft Edge. First, you see the list of family members.
4. **Click or tap the name of your child.**

   You see a report about your child's screen time, as shown in Figure 6-5.

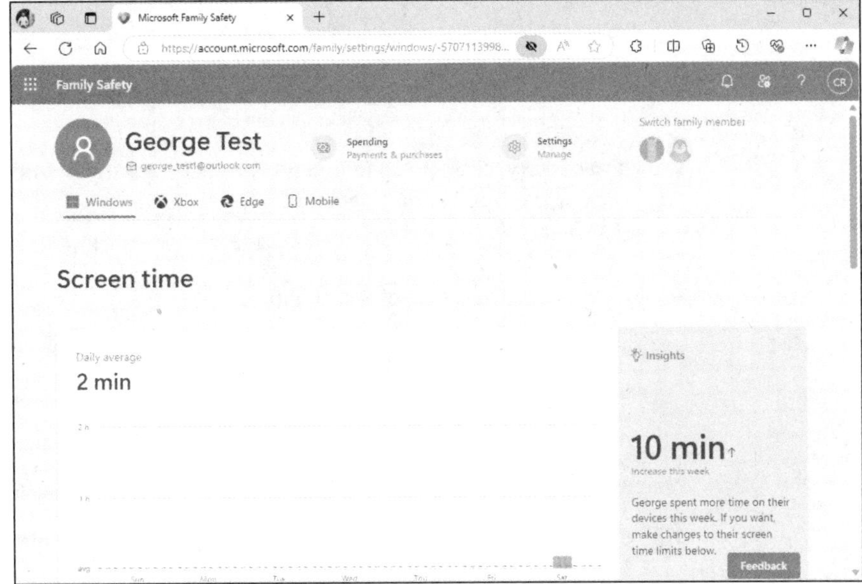

FIGURE 6-5: Setting up your child's account with Microsoft Family Safety.

5. **Ensure that Windows is selected as the platform you want to configure, scroll down, and click or tap Turn Limits On.**

   A list is shown with all the days of the week. You can set individual time limits for each of them.

6. **Click or tap Monday and choose how long your child can use their Windows computer(s), as well as the schedule of available times.**
7. **Click or tap Done, and then repeat Step 6 for all the days in the week.**
8. **When you've finished setting time limits, close Microsoft Edge and the Settings app.**

   From now on, your child can use their Windows computer only during the schedule of available times and for the maximum time allowed by their parent.

Blocking Access to Inappropriate Sites

While Microsoft Family Safety does a reasonably good job of detecting mature content on the web and blocking access to it, you can also add your own websites that shouldn't be visited by your child. Here's how it works:

1. **Sign in with your organizer or administrator Microsoft account, click or tap the Start icon, and then click or tap Settings.**

2. **In the Settings app, choose Accounts. On the right, scroll down and click or tap Family.**

   The Settings page shown previously in Figure 6-1 appears.

3. **If necessary, click or tap Microsoft Family to expand it, and then click or tap Open Family Settings.**

   The Family Safety portal opens in your Microsoft Edge browser.

4. **Click or tap the name of your child.**

   You see a report about your child's screen time (refer to Figure 6-5).

5. **In the options under your child's name, select Edge instead of Windows.**

   A report is shown about your child's internet browsing activities.

6. **Scroll down to the Filter Settings section, shown in Figure 6-6.**
7. **If necessary, click or tap the switch for Filter Inappropriate Websites and Searches to turn it on.**
8. **Click or tap in the Blocked Sites text box, type the URL of the website you want blocked, and then click or tap the plus sign (+) to add it to the list.**
9. **Repeat Step 8 for all the websites you want blocked, and then close Microsoft Edge.**

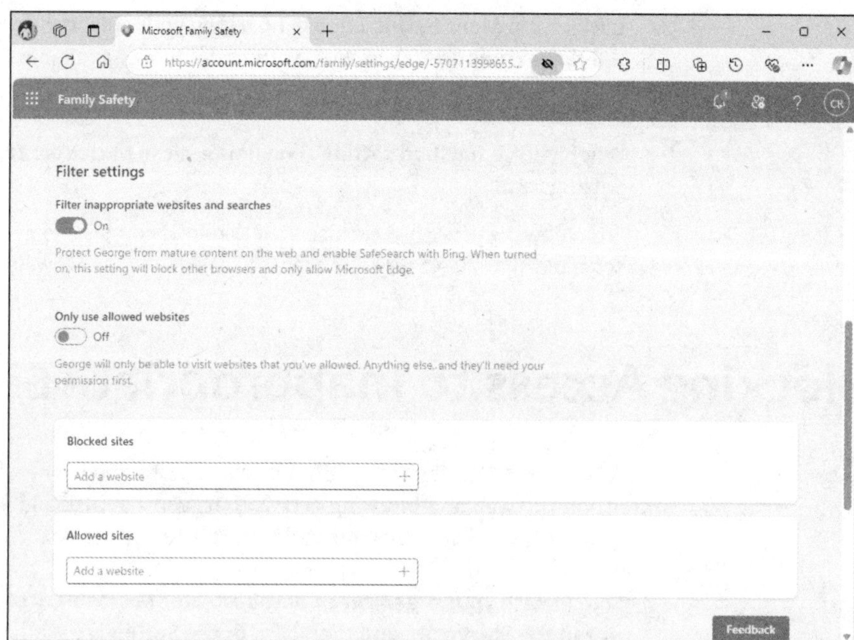

FIGURE 6-6: Filtering websites with Microsoft Family Safety.

From now on, your child will no longer be able to access the websites you've blocked. Microsoft Family Safety also adds its own protection by using its database of inappropriate content and blocking access to it automatically.

Blocking Inappropriate Apps and Games

It's easy for children to get addicted to a game if they're left unchecked in front of their computer. And if they get access to a browser other than Microsoft Edge, they can circumvent the web browsing protections enabled in Microsoft Family Safety. To ensure that your kids are not exposed to inappropriate content and don't spend too much time in one game or app, you can also set limits on an app or game basis. Here's how it works:

1. **Sign in with your organizer or administrator Microsoft account, click or tap the Start icon, and then click or tap Settings.**
2. **In the Settings app, choose Accounts. On the right, scroll down and click or tap Family.**
3. **If necessary, click or tap Microsoft Family to expand it, and then click or tap Open Family Settings.**

   The Family Safety portal opens in your Microsoft Edge browser.
4. **Click or tap the name of your child.**

   You see a report about your child's screen time (refer to Figure 6-5).
5. **Select Windows if it isn't already selected, and then scroll past the screen time report.**
6. **Click or tap Apps and Games, next to Devices.**

   A list is shown, with all the apps and games installed on your child's account, their daily average of use, and existing limits.
7. **Click or tap on the game or app that you want to block.**

   I selected Google Chrome to ensure that the child can't browse the web unchecked. A report appears about how much it was used, and you're given options to set limits or block it, as in Figure 6-7.

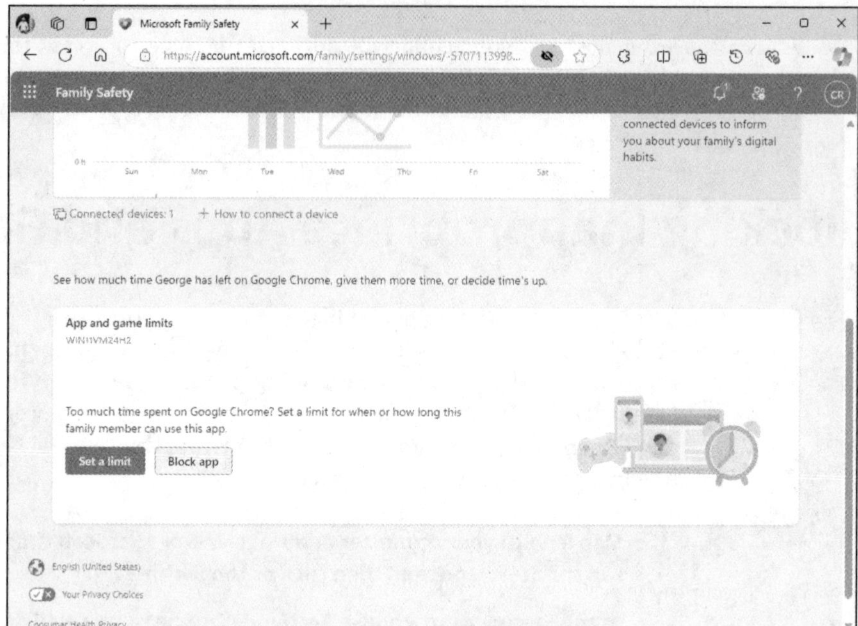

FIGURE 6-7: Setting limits for apps and games.

8. **Click or tap Block App and then To App and Games.**
9. **Repeat Steps 7 and 8 for all the apps and games you want to block, and close Microsoft Edge.**

The next time your child tries to use the apps and games you've blocked, they're closed automatically and a Microsoft Family Safety prompt appears, sharing that they must ask for permission from their parent(s).

IN THIS CHAPTER

» Finding out why privacy is important

» Viewing and limiting the data collected from Windows 11

» Reducing the ads you see

» Blocking location tracking

Chapter 7
Protecting Your Privacy

"The best minds of my generation are thinking about how to make people click ads. That sucks."

— JEFF HAMMERBACHER, EARLY FACEBOOK EMPLOYEE

When you work with so-called free services — search engines such as Google and Bing; social networks such as X, Instagram, or LinkedIn; online storage services such as OneDrive or Google Drive; email services like Gmail, `Outlook.com`, or Yahoo! Mail — these services may not charge you, but they're hardly free. You pay for them with your privacy. Every time you go to one of these sites or use one of these products, with a few noteworthy exceptions, you leave a trail that companies are eager to exploit, primarily for advertising.

If it's free, you're the product, not the client. There's a reason why you buy something on, say, Amazon, and then find ads for Amazon appearing on all sorts of websites. One of the big advertising conglomerates has your data: perhaps your IP address or the history of your web searches or data from a third-party cookie. They've connected enough dots to know that whatever site you happen to be on at the moment, you once bought something on Amazon.

Even when you log in to Windows 11 using a Microsoft account, you leave another footprint in the sand. (I talk about Microsoft accounts in Book 2, Chapter 4.) This isn't horrible. It isn't illegal either — although laws in different countries differ widely, and lawsuits are reshaping the picture even as we speak.

In this chapter, I give you an overview of privacy settings — and some privacy shenanigans — in Windows 11. You learn about the data collected by Microsoft when you use Windows 11, how to limit it, and also how to view it yourself. Then I talk about ads in Windows 11 and how to see fewer of them. Finally, I cover the location tracking we've grown accustomed to because of our smartphones.

Handling Your Privacy in Windows 11

Some people are increasingly aware of how the internet and social media erode their privacy, while others aren't concerned. A few get paranoid to the point of blocking anything with a remote chance of tracking them. Odds are that you're somewhere between the two extremes.

Windows 11 users need to understand that this operating system pulls in data from all over the web, similar to Windows 10. Every time you connect to a Microsoft service, you're helping the company's data-collection routines. If you use a Microsoft account, data collection is even more productive.

I'm not implying that Microsoft is trying to steal your data or somehow use your identity for illegal purposes. It isn't. Microsoft mostly wants to identify your interests, so it can serve you ads that you will click for products you will buy. Google, Meta, and Amazon do the same.

TIP

To keep this book at a reasonable size, I can't cover the topic of privacy extensively. However, I can recommend an authoritative discussion of privacy issues on the Electronic Frontier Foundation's Defending Your Rights in the Digital World page, at `www.eff.org/issues/privacy`.

Although Windows 11 can collect a large set of data about your activities compared to previous versions of Windows, it also offers the largest collection of controls for protecting your privacy. You can set detailed privacy permissions for more than 30 aspects of your daily computing activities, starting with general Windows 11 advertising and moving on to speech recognition, diagnostics and feedback, and which apps are allowed to take screen shots or download files automatically. Although most people will find the list of privacy controls intimidating, it's good to know where to find them:

1. **Click or tap the Start icon, followed by Settings.**

   You see the Settings app.

2. **On the left, click or tap Privacy & Security.**

   The Privacy & Security settings appear, as shown in Figure 7-1.

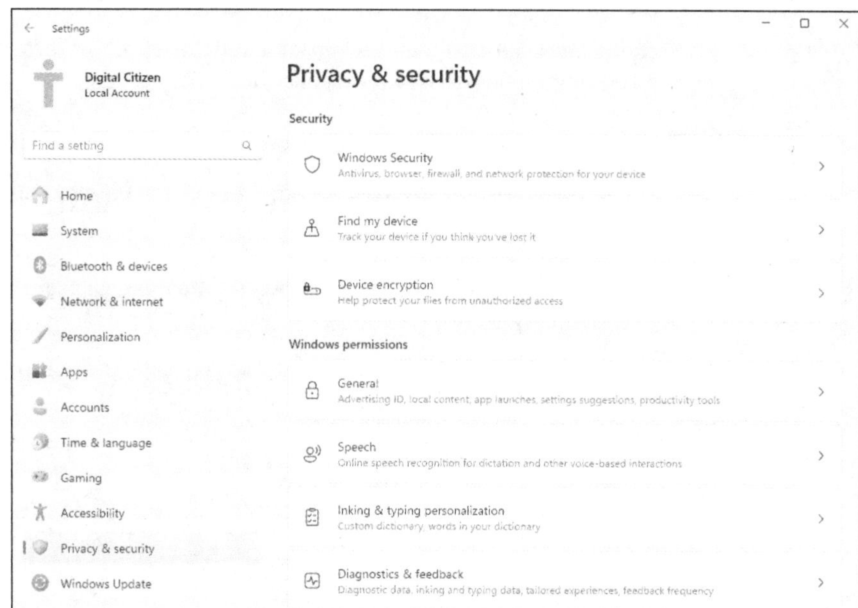

FIGURE 7-1: Windows 11's privacy and security settings.

3. **Scroll down the Windows Permissions section on the right and see the big categories of privacy settings available.**

   There aren't many, but they're all important, and you should look at how your permissions are set.

4. **Scroll further down to the App Permissions section.**

   This list is incredibly long. Simply scroll through it to understand just how many things you can set about your privacy in Windows 11.

Limiting diagnostics and feedback data collection

Most of the snooping in Windows 11 is happening for its diagnostics and feedback collection, or the usual telemetry used for monitoring how software products work and improving them. Windows 11 collects data about the events that take place when you use it, the errors that show up, when users log in, crashes, and the settings you change. Microsoft has a detailed description of its telemetry collection policy at `https://learn.microsoft.com/en-us/windows/privacy/configure-windows-diagnostic-data-in-your-organization`.

To limit the diagnostics and feedback data collection performed by Windows 11, you can set its telemetry to basic, like this:

1. **Click or tap the Start icon and then Settings.**
2. **On the left side of the Settings app, click or tap Privacy & Security.**

   The Privacy & Security settings appear (refer to Figure 7-1).
3. **In the Windows Permissions section on the right, click or tap Diagnostics & Feedback.**

   The types of data collected appear in a list similar to the one in Figure 7-2.

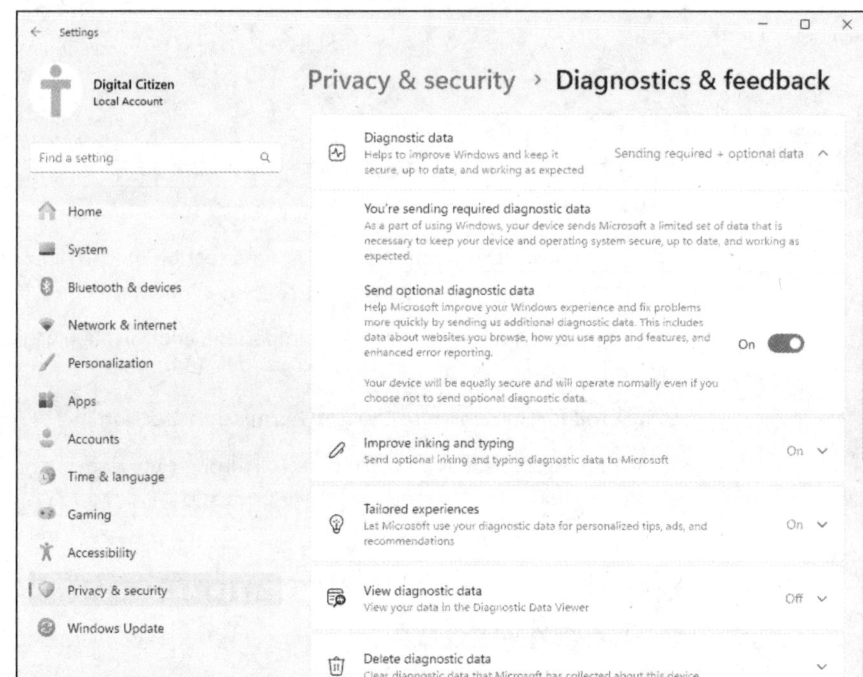

FIGURE 7-2: Configuring the Windows 11 telemetry data collected by Microsoft.

4. **Click or tap Diagnostic Data to display the section's contents and set the Send Optional Diagnostic Data switch to off.**

   Microsoft will now collect only the basic telemetry data it needs about Windows 11.
5. **Click or tap Improve Inking and Typing to expand it and set its switch off.**

   You've stopped Microsoft's data collection when you're using a pen or the touchscreen.

WHAT, EXACTLY, IS BASIC TELEMETRY?

It probably won't surprise you to find out that Microsoft collects, as part of its Basic telemetry, roughly 2,000 data points per computer, updated every day. You can see the list for basic-level telemetry in Windows 11 on this web page: `https://learn.microsoft.com/en-us/windows/privacy/required-diagnostic-events-fields-windows-11-22h2`. A similar list for the optional telemetry data that Microsoft might collect is found on `https://learn.microsoft.com/en-us/windows/privacy/optional-diagnostic-data`.

6. **Similarly, click or tap Tailored Experiences and set its switch off.**

   Microsoft will no longer collect data for personalized ads and product recommendations.

7. **When you're done, close Settings.**

   Your settings are saved automatically.

TIP

If you want to delete all diagnostic data collected by Microsoft on your Windows 11 PC, in the Diagnostics & Feedback window, click or tap Delete Diagnostic Data and then the Delete button.

Viewing the diagnostic data sent to Microsoft

Here's what I know:

- Microsoft collects telemetry, which is data about your use of Windows 11. You can minimize the data collected (the basic setting described in the nearby sidebar), but you can't stop the flow unless you're connected to a corporate domain.
- The data sent to Microsoft is encrypted. That means anyone who's snooping on your connection won't be able to pull out any useful information. Microsoft also offers the free Diagnostic Data Viewer app, which allows people to view the data sent to the company's servers.

To enable Diagnostic Data Viewer and use it to see the data sent to Microsoft, do the following:

1. **Click or tap the Start icon and then Settings.**
2. **On the left, choose Privacy & Security. Then on the right, go to Diagnostics & Feedback.**

   The options shown previously in Figure 7-2 appear.
3. **Click or tap View Diagnostic Data to expand this section, and then set the Turn on Diagnostic Data Viewer switch on.**
4. **Click or tap the Open Diagnostic Data Viewer button.**

   Most probably, the app is not installed on your Windows 11 PC, and you are taken to its Microsoft Store page.
5. **Click or tap Get or Install, depending on the button you see.**

   Wait for the Diagnostic Data Viewer app to be installed on your PC.
6. **Click or tap Open, and then browse the data displayed by the Diagnostic Data Viewer app shown in Figure 7-3.**

   As you can see, the data is technical, and most people don't understand a thing of what's being collected.

FIGURE 7-3: Diagnostic Data Viewer shows you the telemetry data collected by Microsoft.

TIP

If you need help understanding what Diagnostic Data Viewer is displaying, check out the following article on my blog: `www.digitalcitizen.life/diagnostic-data-viewer-windows-10`. Although the article was originally written for Windows 10, it has been updated for Windows 11.

WARNING

If you want to minimize identifiable data harvested from you and don't feel comfortable with the fact that Microsoft collects data about you, it's best to switch to Linux. Then, avoid Google Chrome and use Firefox, use DuckDuckGo instead of Google Search and Bing, and always run a VPN (see Book 9, Chapter 3). Of course, you'd have to avoid using a smartphone and pay with cash or Bitcoin only. You'd also need to avoid walking in public, given the current state of facial recognition.

Knowing What Connections Windows Prefers

If you use Windows 11, parts of the operating system are integrated well with services from other companies, while others are not. That's because Microsoft plays favorites with some companies and shuns others as much as it possibly can:

- **Microsoft owns part of Meta.** You see some Meta apps here and there in Windows 11. There's a reason: Microsoft owns a 1.6 percent share of Meta (at the time of writing). But Meta is ambivalent about Microsoft, at best.
- **Microsoft doesn't play well with Google.** Windows 11 has some hooks into Google, but invariably, they exist to pull your personal information out of Google (for example, your browsing history) and put it in Microsoft's databases. Google doesn't like Microsoft and actively sabotaged Microsoft products such as the former Windows Phone. Therefore, it isn't willing to share data with Microsoft.
- **Microsoft gives lip service to Apple.** There's no love lost between the companies. Microsoft makes software for Mac, iPhone, and iPad. (For example, Office for iPad is a treat, OneNote runs on any iPhone, and Office has been on the Mac for longer than it's been on Windows!) Apple makes little software for Windows. They're both fiercely guarding their turf. Don't expect to see any user information being shared between the two companies.
- **Microsoft is a key investor in OpenAI.** Microsoft has invested billions into OpenAI and its large language models. It has also integrated its Azure cloud infrastructure with OpenAI products, and the company is the exclusive cloud provider for all OpenAI workloads. Microsoft's Copilot is based on ChatGPT, the main product created by OpenAI, and it sells Azure OpenAI cloud services to their customers. Even though OpenAI doesn't necessarily love Microsoft, ChatGPT allows users to sign in to their products using Microsoft accounts.

And, of course, you know that Microsoft also owns Skype, `Outlook.com` (formerly known as Hotmail), Xbox, Clipchamp, and OneDrive, right?

Your information — aggregated, personally identifiable, or vaguely anonymous—can be drawn from any of those sources and mashed up with what Microsoft already has in its databases.

Seeing Fewer Ads in Windows 11

Ads are a major annoyance in Windows 11. Microsoft has decided to plaster them all over the place, starting with your Start menu. For example, as soon as you install Windows 11 and open the Start menu, you see shortcuts to apps that are not installed, such as Photoshop Express, Clipchamp, or LinkedIn. They're sponsored apps that Microsoft recommends to you. If you click or tap their shortcuts, these apps get installed automatically from the Microsoft Store.

Then, when you log in with a Microsoft account, the company creates an advertising ID for you that can be used to show you personalized ads. If you want to see fewer ads in Windows 11, or at least less personalized ones, here's what you have to do:

1. **Click or tap the Start icon, followed by Settings.**

   The Settings app opens.

2. **On the left, choose Privacy & Security. On the right, choose General.**

   The settings shown in Figure 7-4 appear.

3. **Set to off the switch for Let Apps Show Me Personalized Ads by Using My Advertising ID.**

4. **Set to off the switch for Let Websites Show Me Locally Relevant Content by Accessing My Language List.**

5. **Set to off the switch for Show Me Suggested Content In The Settings App.**

6. **In the column on the left, choose Personalization.**

   You see all the personalization options for Windows 11.

7. **On the right, scroll down to Device Usage and click or tap it.**

   You see several switches, as shown in Figure 7-5. They represent activities you can perform on your Windows 11 PC, for which Microsoft can show personalized ads. The list includes Development, Gaming, Family, and Creativity.

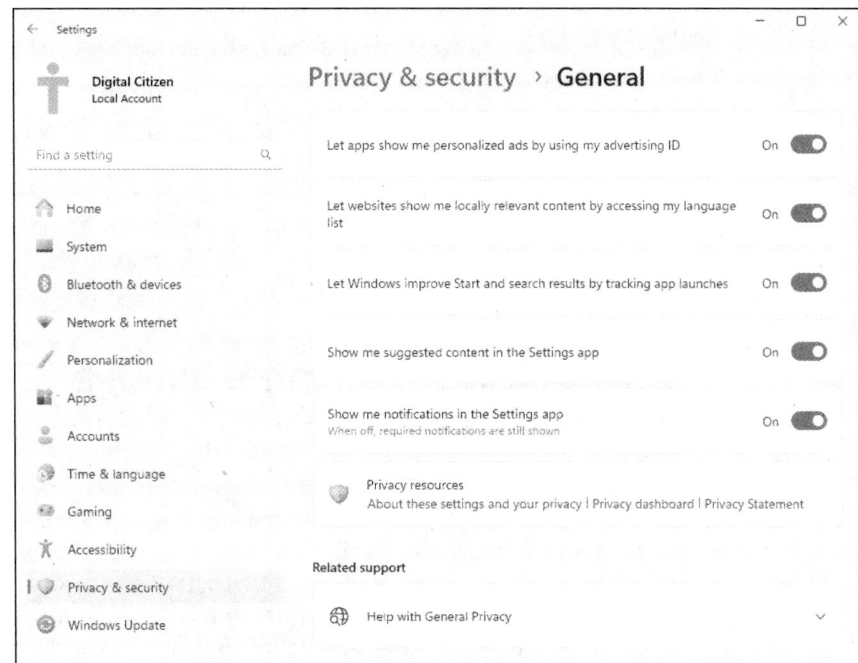

FIGURE 7-4: You can disable some personalized ads in Windows 11.

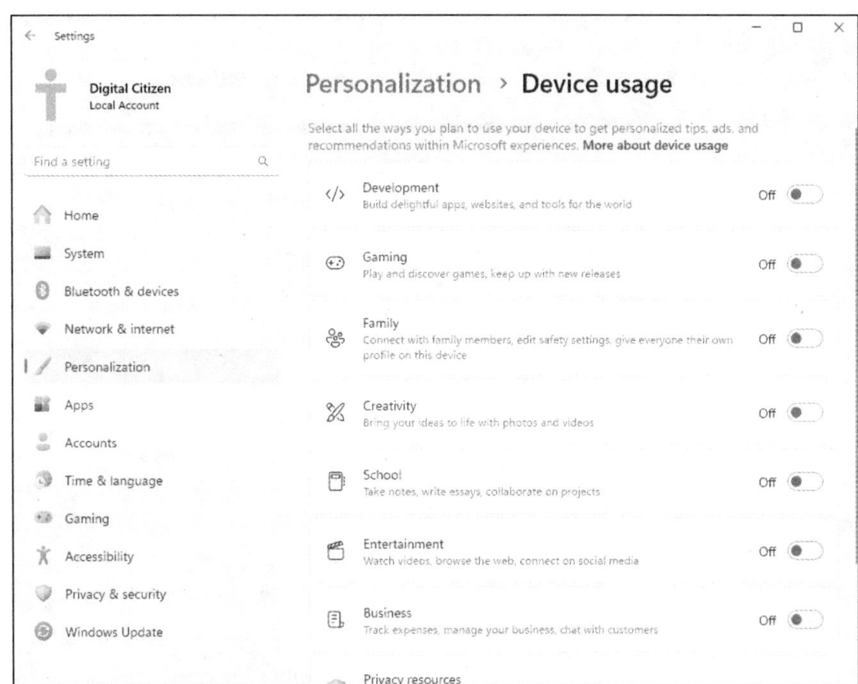

FIGURE 7-5: Stop Windows 11 from showing ads and tips about various apps and services.

8. **Set to off all the switches, starting with Development and ending with Business.**

   Your settings are applied immediately, and you can close Settings when you're done.

TIP

To get rid of a pinned shortcut from the Start menu that's an ad for an app you don't want, right-click or press and hold on the shortcut, and then choose Unpin from Start. That ad (pardon, app) is gone, and it won't come back.

Getting fewer Welcome dialogs in Windows 11

Microsoft has become more aggressive promoting its products to their Windows 11 users. One way they do this is by displaying a welcome experience dialog now and then, usually after you install an update. This welcome experience promotes Microsoft products such as OneDrive, Microsoft 365 subscriptions, the Microsoft Edge browser, and Xbox Game Pass subscriptions. What Microsoft promotes on your Windows 11 device varies depending on their goals at the time, the data they have about you, and what interests you.

If you want to limit encountering such experiences, follow these steps:

1. **Click or tap the Start icon and then Settings.**
2. **Choose System on the left and Notifications on the right.**

   You see a long list of settings about how Windows 11 handles your notifications.
3. **Scroll down the list until you see Additional Settings, and click or tap it to expand this section.**

   The settings shown in Figure 7-6 appear.
4. **Deselect the boxes next to the following settings:**
   - Show the Windows welcome experience after updates and when signed in to show what's new and suggested
   - Suggest ways to get the most out of Windows and finish setting up this device
   - Get tips and suggestions when using Windows
5. **Close Settings.**

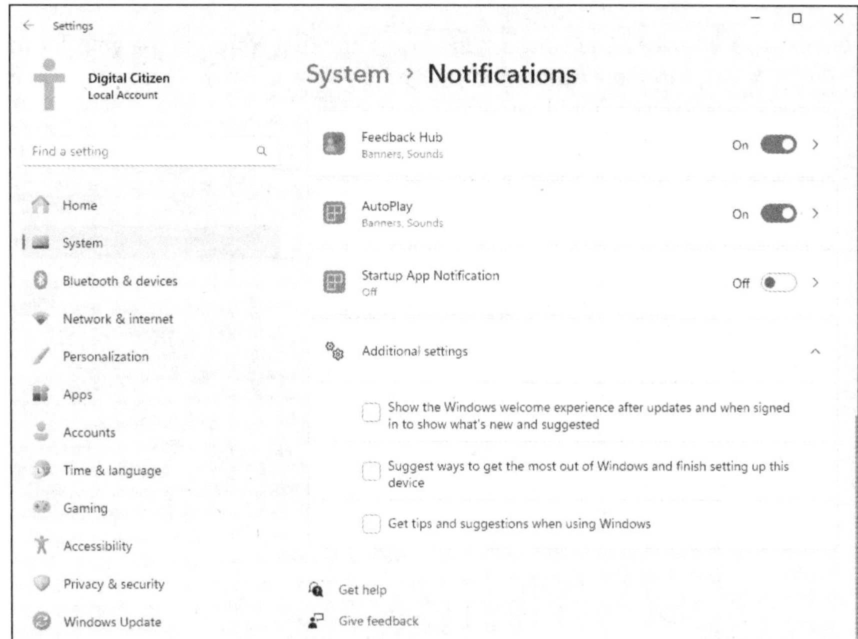

FIGURE 7-6: Stopping the welcome experience from showing up.

Controlling Location Tracking

Just like all the other major operating systems, Windows 11 has *location tracking.* You must tell Windows 11 and specific applications that it's okay to track your location, but if you do, those apps — and Windows itself — know where you are. Like any technology, location tracking can be used for good or not-so-good purposes, and your opinion about what's good may differ from others'. Also, location tracking isn't just one technology, it's several, working together.

For example, if your PC has a *GPS* (Global Positioning System) chip — they're common in tablets and some laptops but rare in desktops — the GPS is turned on, and you've authorized a Windows app to see your precise location, the app can identify your location within a few feet.

If your Windows 11 laptop doesn't have a GPS chip or it has one that isn't turned on, but you do allow apps to track your location, Windows 11 approximates where your internet connection is coming from based on your IP address (a number that uniquely identifies your laptop's connection to the internet). In many cases, that can be miles away from where you're actually sitting, but your actual region or city is identified accurately.

When you start a Windows 11 app that wants to use your location, you may see a message asking for your permission to track it, like the one in the Weather app shown in Figure 7-7.

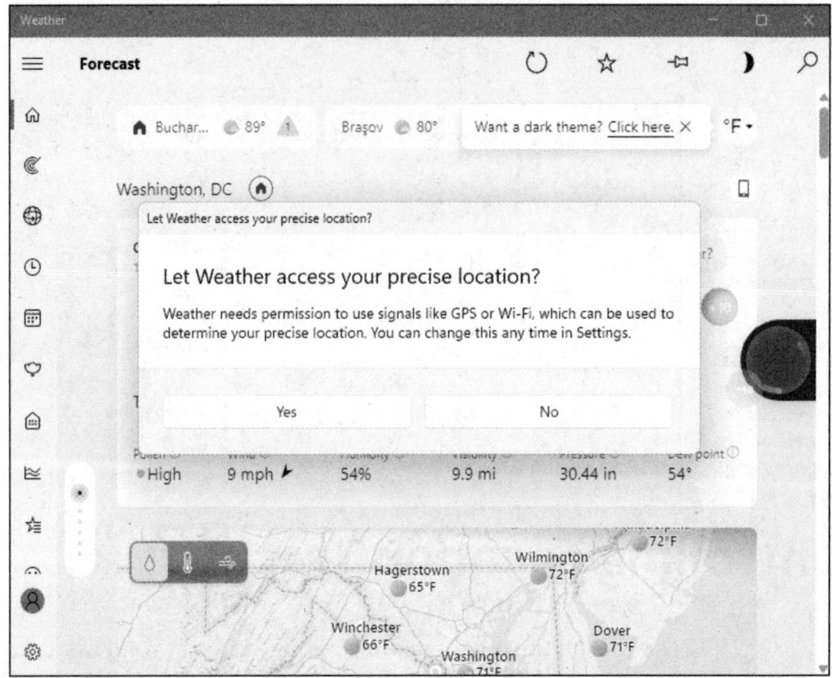

FIGURE 7-7: The Weather app wants your precise location to show you the forecast.

If you've already turned on location services, each time you add another app that wants to use your location, you see a notification that says, "Let Windows 11 app access your precise location?" You can respond either Yes or No. The following sections explain how you can control location tracking in Windows 11.

Blocking all location tracking in Windows 11

To keep Windows 11 from using your location in *any* app — even if you've already turned on location use in some apps — follow these steps:

1. **Click or tap the Start icon and then the Settings icon.**

   The Settings app opens.

2. **On the Settings app's left side, click Privacy & Security.**

3. **On the right, scroll down to App Permissions, and click or tap Location.**

   The Location settings appear, as shown in Figure 7-8.

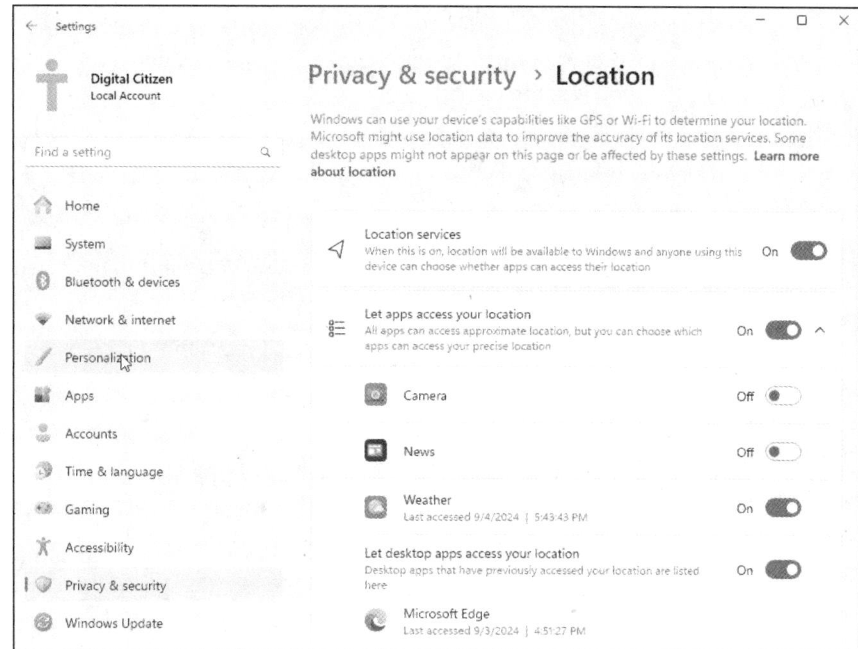

FIGURE 7-8: This is where you turn Windows 11's location tracking on and off.

4. **Set the Location Services switch off and confirm your choice by choosing Turn Off.**

   That's all it takes to turn off location tracking — even if you've already given your permission to various apps to track your location.

TIP

As a bonus, scroll down and click or tap the Clear button next to Location History, near the bottom of the screen. This deletes the recent location history stored by Windows 11.

Blocking location tracking in an app

You may not want to turn off location tracking for all apps in Windows 11, but only for some. To block location tracking for a specific app, do the following:

1. **Click or tap the start icon and then Settings. Or press Windows+I.**
2. **Choose Privacy & Security on the left and scroll down to App Permissions on the right.**

3. **Click or tap Location.**

   The Location settings appear (refer to Figure 7-8).

4. **Ensure that the switches for Location Services and Let Apps Access Your Location are turned on.**

5. **Under Let Apps Access Your Location, scroll down until you find the app you want to cut off.**

   If the list is not expanded, click or tap anywhere on Let Apps Access Your Location.

   You see the list of apps that can request access to your precise location.

6. **Find the app whose location tracking you want to block, and click or tap its switch to set it off.**

   The app loses its permission to access your location.

Minimizing Privacy Intrusion

Although it's true that using Windows 11 exposes you to some privacy concerns, you can reduce the amount of data kept about you by following a few simple rules:

- **Add a local account to Windows 11.** To increase your privacy, you may want to use a local account instead of a Microsoft account. Yes, you will be forced to install and set up Windows 11 with a Microsoft account. But after that, you can add a local account and use it moving forward. This way, Microsoft has fewer logs about what you do. Read Book 2, Chapters 4 and 5, for details.
- **Use private browsing.** In Microsoft Edge, it's called *InPrivate;* Google Chrome calls it *Incognito;* Firefox says *Private Browsing.* Turning on private browsing keeps your browser from leaving cookies around and wipes out download lists, caches, browser history, forms, and passwords. Realize, though, that your browser still leaves some crumbs: If you use Google to look up something, for example, Google still has a record of your IP address and what you typed.
- **If you use the Office apps from Microsoft 365, turn off their telemetry.** In any Office program (Word, Excel, and so on), choose File ➪ Options ➪ Trust Center. Click or tap the Trust Center Settings button. On the left, choose Privacy Options and then click or tap Privacy Settings. Deselect all the boxes you see and click or tap OK. The options displayed are ways for Microsoft to collect additional data about what you do in Microsoft Office.

IN THIS CHAPTER

» Enhancing text visibility

» Adjusting the mouse pointer and text cursor

» Zooming in with Magnifier

» Using Voice Access

» Enabling color filters

Chapter 8

Making Windows 11 Accessible

It's time to explore how to customize your Windows 11 experience to make the operating system easier to use, no matter what your needs might be. Whether you're having trouble reading small text, spotting your mouse cursor, or distinguishing between colors, Windows 11 has you covered.

In this chapter, I walk you through a few simple tweaks that can make a big difference, like bumping up the text size or changing the mouse pointer style to something much more visible. For those who need a bit more help, I present the Magnifier tool, which can zoom in on parts of your screen and even read text aloud. And if you've ever dreamed of controlling your computer with just your voice, you'll be happy to hear about Voice Access, a nifty new feature in Windows 11.

I wrap things up by looking at color filters, which can be a game-changer for folks with color blindness. By the end of this chapter, you'll have a toolbox full of tricks to make your Windows 11 PC work better for you.

Increasing Text Size

Many individuals struggle with visual clarity when using high-resolution displays, which are now ubiquitous. Even though these people may wear glasses, they still have trouble seeing clearly the text displayed on their computer's screen.

One way to make things more visible is to lower the screen resolution (read Book 3, Chapter 1). However, this method affects all elements on your screen, not just text size. For those satisfied with their current display resolution, but seeking larger text, Windows 11 offers a more targeted solution. You can adjust text size independently, as follows:

1. **Click or tap the Start icon and then Settings.**

   The Settings app opens.

2. **In the left sidebar, choose Accessibility.**

   On the right, the Settings app displays many options for improving accessibility. They are divided into the following categories: Vision, Hearing, and Interaction.

3. **Under Vision, click or tap Text Size.**

   You see the Text Size slider from Figure 8-1.

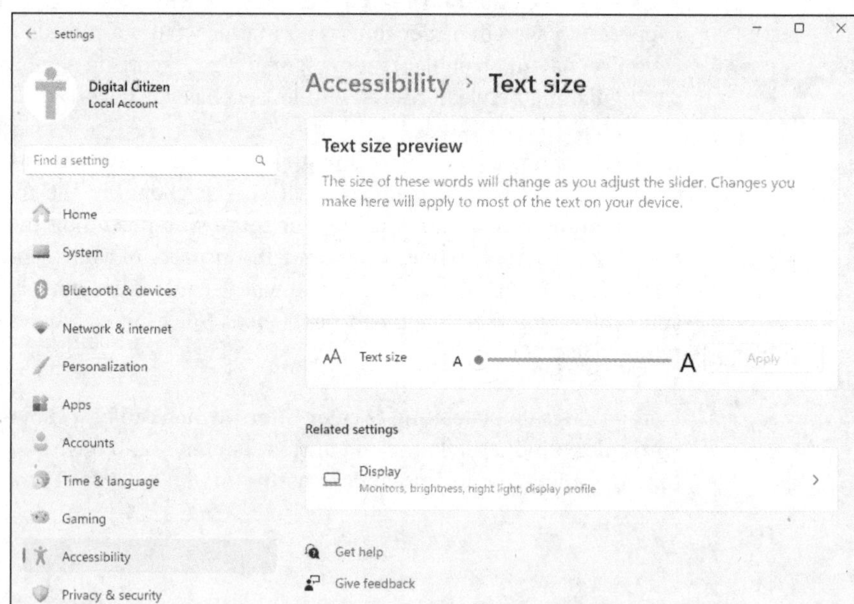

FIGURE 8-1: Setting the text size in Windows 11.

4. **Move the Text Size slider to the right. Stop when the text shown in the Text Size Preview above the slider reaches the size you prefer.**
5. **Click or tap Apply.**

   The size of the text changes throughout Windows 11, its apps, dialogs, and other user interface elements.
6. **Close Settings by clicking or tapping X in the top-right corner.**

Making the Mouse Pointer More Visible

The default Windows 11 mouse pointer is a white arrow with a thin black outline, suitable for most users. However, on certain displays or in bright environments, the pointer may be difficult to see. It also happened to me when I was testing a laptop with an OLED display while using it outdoors. Suddenly, I couldn't figure out where the mouse was because the screen reflected too much sunlight. If you experience this issue, you can easily change the mouse pointer style and size to improve visibility, like this:

1. **Click or tap the Start icon, followed by Settings. Or press Windows+I.**

   The Settings app opens.
2. **In the left sidebar, choose Accessibility.**
3. **Under Vision, click or tap Mouse Pointer and Touch.**

   The options from Figure 8-2 are shown.
4. **Under Mouse Pointer Style, select another style: Black, Inverted, or Custom.**

   The default style is White. If you choose the last style in the list (Custom), you also see a list of colors. This lets you select a color you like for your mouse pointer, which you can see without problems.
5. **Move the Size slider to the right, until the mouse pointer reaches a size that's easy to see.**
6. **Close Settings and enjoy using your new mouse pointer.**

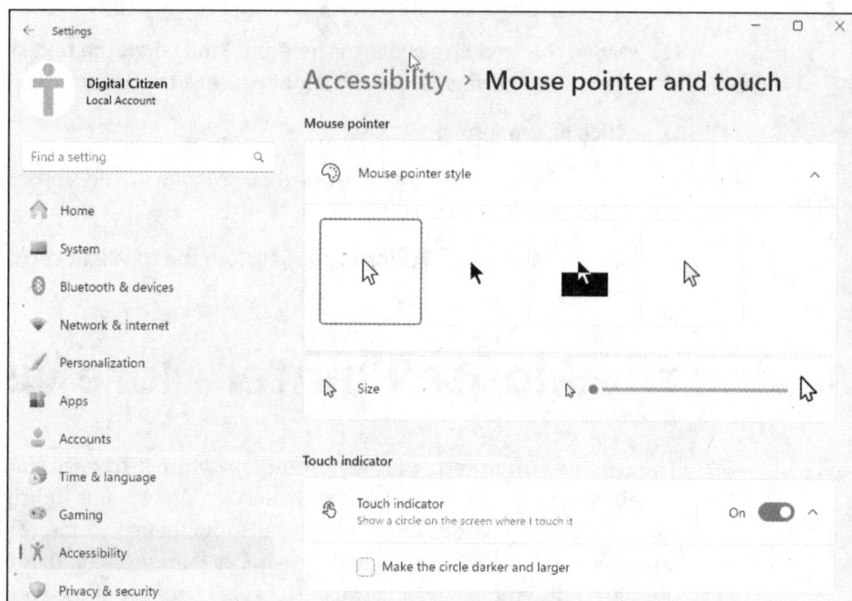

FIGURE 8-2: Setting the mouse pointer style and size.

Improving Text Cursor Visibility

If you're working with a lot of text, drafting papers, business documents, or even books like this one, you may have trouble identifying where the text cursor is, especially when it's hidden in a sea of text. Luckily, Windows 11 offers the personalization options you need to make the text cursor thicker and add a colored indicator, so it stands out and is easier to identify without staring too much at the screen. Here's how they work:

1. **Click or tap the Start icon, followed by Settings.**
2. **On the left side of the Settings app, choose Accessibility.**
3. **Under Vision, click or tap Text Cursor.**

   You see the settings from Figure 8-3.
4. **Click or tap the switch for Text Cursor Indicator to turn it on.**

   A colored indicator is shown to help your text cursor stand out.
5. **Move the Size slider to the right, to make the text cursor indicator bigger. Stop when it reaches a size you like.**
6. **Choose a color from the Recommended Colors list, so it's easier to see the text cursor indicator.**

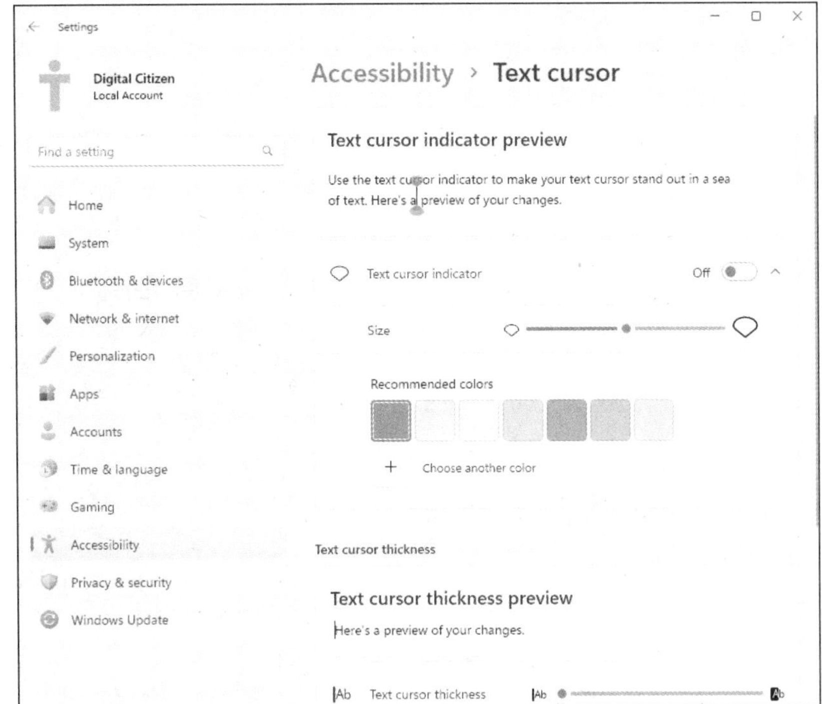

FIGURE 8-3: Improving the text cursor visibility.

7. **Scroll down to Text Cursor Thickness and move the slider to the right, to make the text cursor thicker. Stop moving the slider when the thickness reaches the size you want.**
8. **Close the Settings app and enjoy using a text cursor that is much more visible.**

Using Magnifier

Adjusting the text size may not be enough to help people with more severe visual impairments see what's on their computer screen. To help them out, Windows 11 includes an app named Magnifier. With it, you can zoom in and enlarge a part of your screen by 200 percent, 300 percent, or more.

REMEMBER

You can turn on Magnifier by pressing the Windows+plus sign (+) keys. Magnifier immediately appears on the screen, as shown in Figure 8-4. The screen is zoomed in to 200 percent, and you can use the plus (+) and minus (–) buttons to zoom in or zoom out. Magnifier also includes some buttons for asking it to read what's on the screen. When you're done using Magnifier, press Windows+Esc, and the app closes immediately.

Previous sentence Next sentence Settings

Magnifier

200%

Zoom out Zoom in Play/Pause Read from here

FIGURE 8-4: Magnifier can zoom in on your screen and read text aloud.

Here's a brief tour of how to use Magnifier in Windows 11:

1. **Open a document or web page that you want to read.**
2. **Press Windows+plus sign (+).**

   Magnifier appears (refer to Figure 8-4).
3. **Set the zoom level you want by pressing the plus (+) or minus (–) icons on Magnifier.**
4. **Click or tap where the text you want to hear begins. Then, click or tap the Play button in Magnifier, or press Ctrl+Alt+Enter.**

   Magnifier starts reading that text aloud. A blue rectangle highlights each word, and Magnifier automatically moves through the text it reads.
5. **To stop reading, click or tap the Pause button on Magnifier, or simply click or tap anywhere on the text.**
6. **When you've finished using Magnifier, press Windows+Esc.**

Controlling Windows 11 with Your Voice

Voice Access is a new app for Windows 11 that allows you to control your PC using your voice. It was created to help people with disabilities or limited mobility use their computers more easily, but anyone can benefit from it.

To use Voice Access, you need a computer with a microphone, and most laptops fit this requirement. You also need an internet connection to set it up, but once it's configured, you can use it offline.

One cool feature is that Voice Access works on the Windows 11 sign-in screen. This means you can log in to your computer by using your voice. If you find yourself using Voice Access often, you can set it to start automatically whenever you boot up your PC. This way, you'll always have voice control at your fingertips — or rather, at the tip of your tongue!

Here's how to set up Voice Access in Windows 11:

1. **Click or tap the Start icon and then Settings.**
2. **In the left sidebar, choose Accessibility.**
3. **Scroll down to the Interaction section and then click or tap Speech.**

   You see the Speech settings shown in Figure 8-5.

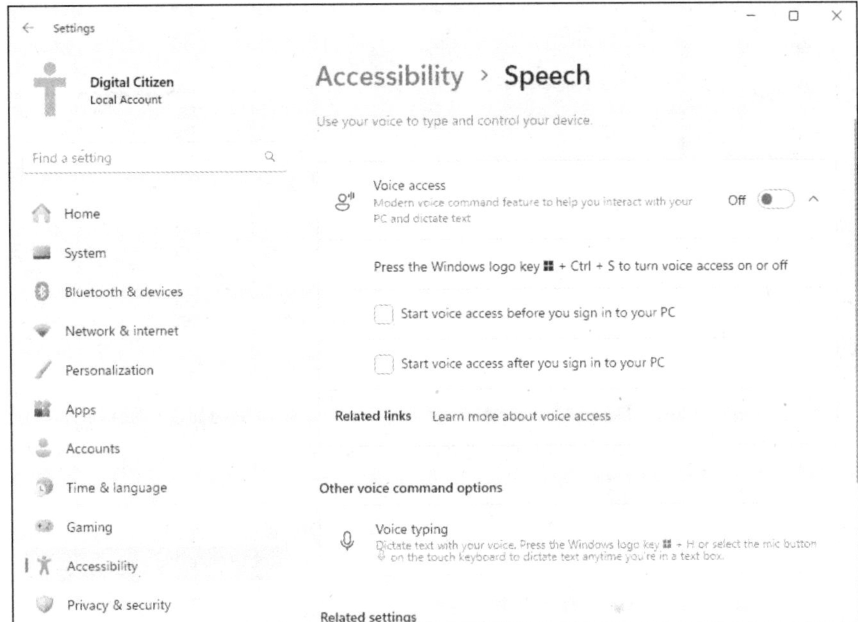

FIGURE 8-5: Enabling Voice Access is done from Settings.

4. **Click or tap the Voice Access switch to turn it on.**

   A toolbar appears, asking you to set up Voice Access to continue.

5. **In the toolbar at the top, click or tap Download.**

   Voice Access downloads the language model it will use to understand what you speak. After it finishes, it loads the Voice Access Guide shown in Figure 8-6.

6. **Select the microphone you want to use, and then click or tap Next.**

   Voice Access informs you that you're all set and shares a couple of things you can do with it.

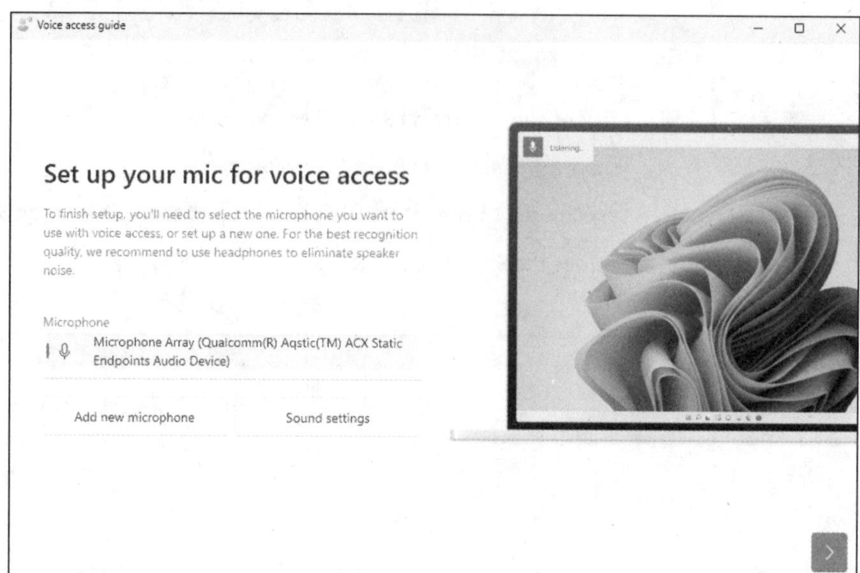

FIGURE 8-6: Setting up Voice Access isn't difficult.

7. **Click or tap Start Guide to learn how to use Voice Access.**

   Voice Access shares a few steps that you need to perform.

8. **Do as Voice Access instructs, so that you learn how it works. When you're finished following a set of instructions, click or tap Next to move to the next set.**

   In total, there are three instruction sets. When you're finished with the instructions, you see a Congratulations prompt.

9. **Click or tap Done.**

   Now you can start using Voice Access using the things you learned during its initial setup.

TIP

If you feel the need for more step-by-step guidance on how to use Voice Access, my team at Digital Citizen has a useful tutorial at `www.digitalcitizen.life/voice-access-windows-11/`.

Dealing with Color Blindness

Color perception varies from person to person, even among people without diagnosed visual impairments. However, a significant portion of the global population experiences a more pronounced difference in color vision. This condition, known as color blindness or color vision deficiency (CVD), affects approximately

300 million people worldwide, according to the National Eye Institute. CVD is not evenly distributed across genders. It disproportionately affects men, with about 1 in 12 experiencing some form of color blindness. In contrast, only about 1 in 200 women are affected.

At its core, color blindness is a result of differences in how the eyes process incoming light. People with CVD have an altered perception of colors due to variations in how their eyes receive and interpret light signals. This can lead to difficulty distinguishing between certain colors or, in rarer cases, seeing the world in shades of gray.

When someone suffering from color blindness uses a computer, they won't see it as most people do and may have trouble understanding what's shown on the screen. To help them out, Windows 11 offers color filters that deal with such vision deficiencies.

Here's how to enable color filters in Windows 11:

1. **Click or tap the Start icon, followed by Settings.**
2. **On the left side of the Settings app, choose Accessibility.**
3. **Under Vision, click or tap Color Filters.**

   The settings for color filters appear as shown in Figure 8-7.

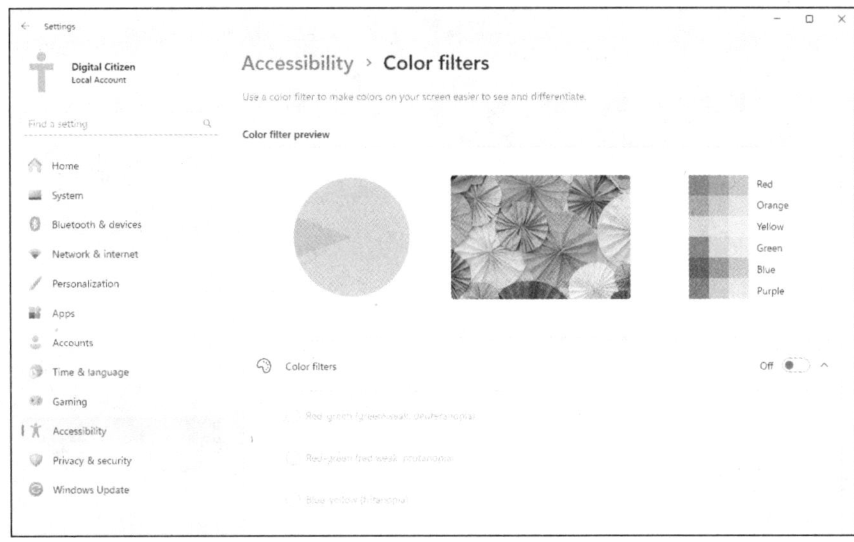

FIGURE 8-7: Enabling and adjusting color filters for people with CVDs.

4. **Click or tap the switch next to Color Filters to turn it on.**

   The settings under this switch no appear dimmed and can be changed.

5. **Choose the color filter appropriate for your CVD.**

   If you're unsure which is best, select them one by one and look at the color filter preview at the top of the window. When you find a color filter that you're happy with, move on to the remaining settings.

6. **Use the Intensity slider to adjust the intensity of the filter you selected.**
7. **Do the same with the Color Boost slider.**
8. **Click or tap to turn on the switch for Keyboard Shortcut for Color Filters.**
9. **When you've finished setting the color filters, close the Settings app.**

TIP

You can now enable or disable color filters by pressing Windows+Ctrl+C.

3 Working on the Desktop

Contents at a Glance

IN THIS CHAPTER

» Personalizing the desktop

» Enabling HDR, configuring the resolution, scaling and more

» Configuring the mouse and the touchpad

» Recovering files from the Recycle Bin

» Adjusting the sound volume and managing sound devices

Chapter 1

Running Your Desktop from Start to Finish

Each time you use Windows 11, you interact with the desktop, so why not make it your own? Personalize it by changing the wallpaper and theme to match your style. And if you love dark mode on your mobile devices, you can bring that sleek look to your Windows 11 PC too.

Next, fine-tune your display settings. Adjust for blue-light filtering to protect your eyes at night, enable HDR for vivid colors, set the screen resolution and scaling for optimal clarity, choose the display orientation that suits you, and tweak the refresh rate — especially crucial if you're a gamer.

Interacting with the desktop involves using a mouse, touchpad (on a laptop), or both. Customize their sensitivity and button settings, and then decide if you want the touchpad to disable automatically when you connect a mouse.

If you're a Windows 10 veteran, you might already know about virtual desktops and how they help you organize your tasks. If not, it's time to explore this feature, which has seen some great improvements in Windows 11.

Once you're comfortable with the desktop, adding shortcuts will make your life easier. Quickly access files, apps, or your favorite folders right from the desktop. And don't forget to master your computer's sound settings. Make sure the volume is just right and that sound is played or recorded using the appropriate devices.

This chapter is packed with tips to make Windows 11 look and behave exactly how you want it to. It's a long chapter, but it's definitely worth reading for a personalized and efficient computing experience.

Working with the Desktop

To begin, sign into Windows 11. Follow the instructions in Book 2, Chapter 2, if necessary. Are you staring at a screen like the one in Figure 1-1? Good! Windows 11 shows you this screen, called the *desktop*, every time you log in.

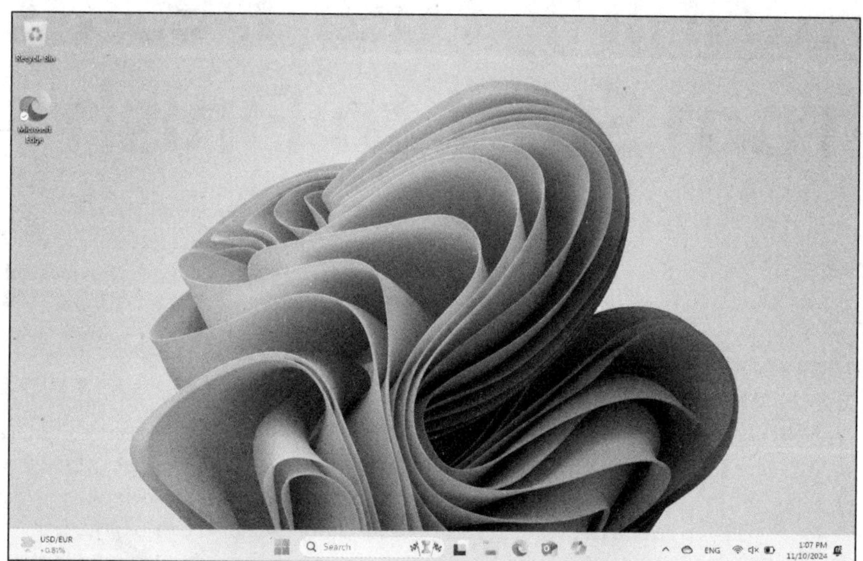

FIGURE 1-1: You start everything from the Windows 11 desktop.

The desktop has a beautiful background, with the Recycle Bin icon at the top left to hold all recently deleted files and folders, a shortcut for the Microsoft Edge browser, and the taskbar at the bottom. You can personalize many aspects of the desktop to make it feel your own, and I cover them all in this section.

Changing the background

You can start personalizing Windows 11 by changing the *wallpaper* or the desktop background. If you bought a new computer with Windows 11 installed, your background might not be as beautiful as the one in Figure 1-1. Instead, it might promote a company like HP, Dell, or Lenovo. That's pretty dull, isn't it? Change your wallpaper by following these steps:

1. **Right-click or press and hold an empty part of the desktop, and then choose Personalize.**

   You see the Personalization section in Windows 11's Settings app.

2. **Click or tap Background.**

   The settings shown in Figure 1-2 appear, starting with recent images used as a desktop wallpaper.

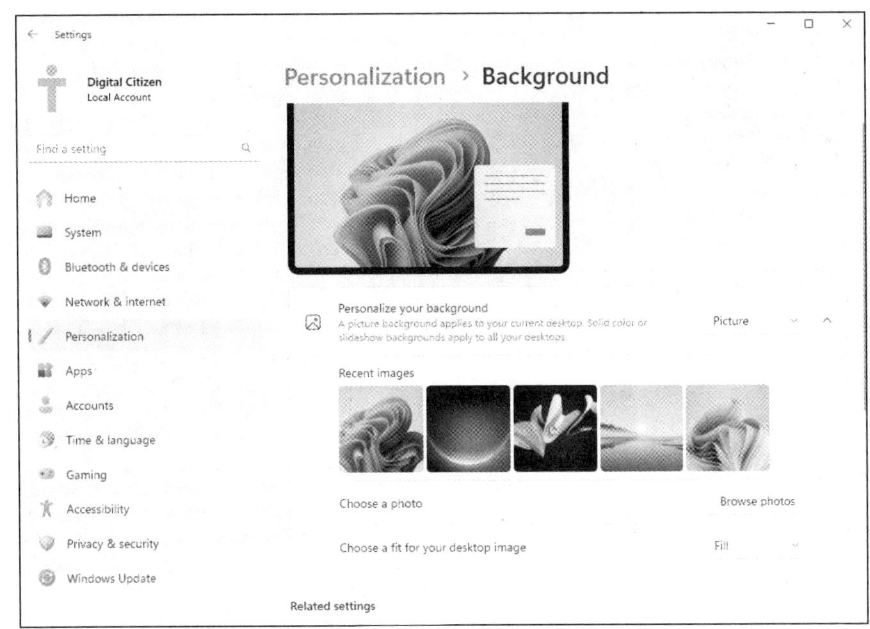

FIGURE 1-2: Choose your desktop background.

3. **Click or tap a background image you like.**

   The image is applied immediately. You can choose one of the pictures that Windows 11 offers, a solid color, or a slideshow of the photos in your Pictures folder.

4. **Next, find a different background by clicking or tapping Browse Photos next to Choose a Photo. When you find a picture you like, select it and click or tap Choose Picture.**

5. **If the picture looks like a smashed watermelon or is too small, click or tap the Choose a Fit for Your Desktop Image drop-down list and make a selection:**

   - Fill the screen. Windows 11 may stretch or crop the image to make this happen.
   - Fit the image to the available space on the screen.
   - Stretch the image to have the same dimensions as your screen.
   - Tile the image. Windows 11 puts the image on the screen multiple times to fill the space. See Figure 1-3 for an example.
   - Center the image on the desktop.
   - Span the image across multiple displays if you have two or more.

FIGURE 1-3: Tiling can be a bit excessive.

6. **To get a new background from Microsoft daily, choose Windows Spotlight in the Personalize Your Background drop-down list.**

   This is the best option in my view and is how I set the background on all my Windows computers and devices.

7. **To close the Settings app, click or tap the close icon (X).**

   Your new wallpaper settings take effect immediately.

Switching Windows 11 themes

A *theme* is what Windows names the combination of a desktop background, a dominant color for the user interface, and a set of mouse cursors and system sounds. Windows 11 has seven built-in themes, and you can switch among them easily. If you're bored by the default theme, here's how to change it:

1. **Right-click or press and hold an empty part of the desktop, and then choose Personalize.**

   You see the Personalization section of the Settings app.

2. **On the right side of the Settings app window, click or tap Themes.**

   The Windows 11 themes settings shown in Figure 1-4 appear.

FIGURE 1-4: For more personalization, consider changing the theme.

3. **In the list under Current Theme, click or tap the available themes, one by one.**

   The desktop wallpaper, taskbar, Settings app, and Start menu change immediately.

4. **After you try all the available themes, click or tap the one you like.**

   I prefer the Windows Spotlight theme because it provides me with a new, beautiful wallpaper each day.

TIP

If you're not satisfied with the built-in themes, during Step 4, click or tap the Browse Themes button and navigate to the Microsoft Store, where you can find plenty of free themes for Windows. (I like the Forest for the Trees theme from the Microsoft Store.) Click or tap the Get button for the theme you want to try, and then click or tap Open.

Battling dark mode and light mode

Dark mode is a thing for smartphone users. I have many friends who want the screens of their mobile devices black at all times. Apparently, many believe that dark mode benefits their eyes and extends the battery of mobile devices. The battery improvements are measurable and provable, but I'm not so sure about the benefits for your eyes. Using a dark screen requires your pupils to dilate, which can make it harder to focus. I prefer light mode, which is the opposite of dark mode, using brighter and crisper colors.

While the world debates whether to go dark or light in Windows 11, let me show you how to switch between the two quickly:

1. **Right-click or press and hold an empty part of the desktop and choose Personalize.**
2. **In the Settings app window, click or tap Colors.**

   You see the settings shown in Figure 1-5.
3. **Click or tap the drop-down list for Choose Your Mode and select Light or Dark.**

   If you select Custom, you see additional options for choosing between dark mode and light mode for Windows and for apps separately. The colors used by Windows 11 change as soon as you've made a choice.

TIP

Changing between Dark Mode and Light Mode in the Colors settings window doesn't affect the wallpaper, sounds, and other elements. If you want the full dark mode or light mode experience, use the steps for changing the theme shown in the preceding section, and choose between the Windows (Light) and Windows (Dark) themes.

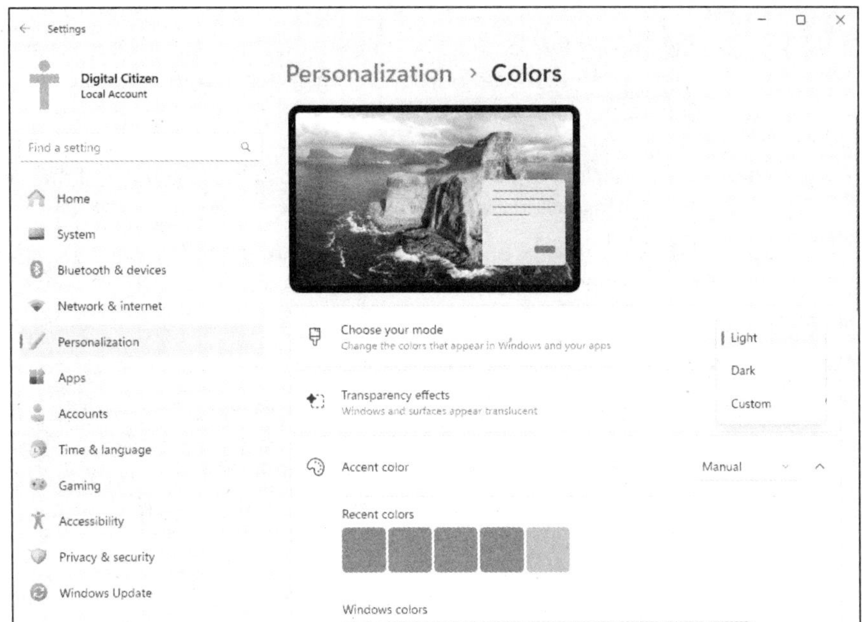

FIGURE 1-5: Choose between light mode and dark mode.

REMEMBER

Switching from dark mode to light mode via themes does more than change the look of Windows 11. It changes the sounds as well. Sounds are soft and relaxing in dark mode but energetic and crisp in light mode. This offers people with visual impairments different experiences when using the two modes.

Setting Up Your Display

Technically, the desktop is only what you see after you log into Windows 11, although people think about the desktop as their screen or computer display, too.

How text, icons, and app windows are displayed on the desktop depends on your screen settings. In this section, you become familiar with the night light, HDR, screen resolution and scaling, refresh rate, brightness, and more. These topics will help you be more productive and protect your eyesight.

Switching the night light on and off

If you use your laptop, tablet, or PC during the evening or at night, you might notice that it takes you longer to fall asleep. To help with this problem, Windows 11 includes a night light feature. When activated, it makes the screen display warmer colors, acting like a blue-light filter. The display is supposed to reduce eye fatigue at night and improve sleep cycles. Here's how to enable and configure the night light in Windows 11:

1. **Click or tap the Start icon (shown in the margin) and then Settings, or press Windows+I.**
2. **On the left of the Settings window, choose System. On the right, click or tap Display.**

   You see the Display settings shown in Figure 1-6.

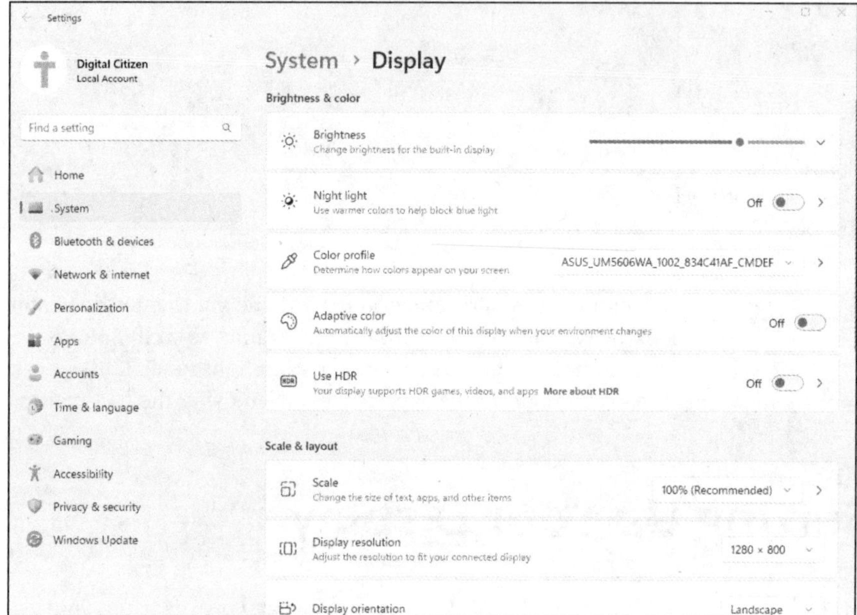

FIGURE 1-6: It's a good idea to enable the night light.

3. **To turn on the night light immediately, click or tap its switch on.**

   The colors on the screen should change immediately to filter out the blue light.
4. **If you want to configure the night light:**

   (a) *Click or tap its name, not its switch.* The strength slider and scheduling settings appear, as shown in Figure 1-7.

   (b) *Configure the strength of the night light and its schedule.*

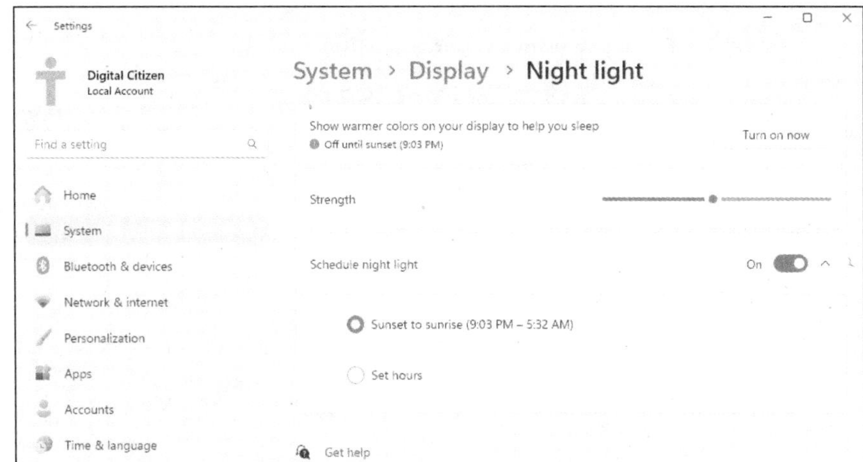

FIGURE 1-7: Change the night light strength and schedule.

Enabling HDR and auto HDR

HDR, or high dynamic range, is a display technology that offers a richer, more colorful viewing experience. With HDR turned on, you see more detail both in the shadows and highlights of a scene. You also get a brighter, more vibrant, and more detailed picture compared to a standard display. HDR is great for immersive video experiences, including movies and games. If you have a new laptop or PC with Windows 11 and its screen has support for HDR, you should turn it on.

If you're a gamer, you may also want to take advantage of the auto HDR feature built into Windows 11, which takes DirectX 11 or DirectX 12 non-HDR games and intelligently expands the color and brightness range up to HDR. This seamless feature gives you a new gaming experience that takes full advantage of your HDR monitor's capabilities. You enable this feature with a single switch.

If I've made you curious and you have a computer equipped with an HDR display, follow these steps to enable HDR and auto HDR:

1. **Click or tap the Start icon and then Settings.**
2. **On the left of the Settings window, select System. On the right, click or tap Display.**

   The Display settings appear (refer to Figure 1-6).
3. **To turn on HDR immediately, click or tap the Use HDR switch to turn it on.**

   The colors on the screen change immediately to offer a more vibrant viewing experience.

4. **If you want to configure HDR:**

   (a) *Click or tap the Use HDR text, not its switch.*

   (b) *Scroll down until you find the HDR settings shown in Figure 1-8.*

   (c) *Turn on the switches for Use HDR, and Auto HDR.*

   HDR is now enabled for all types of activities, including watching videos and playing games.

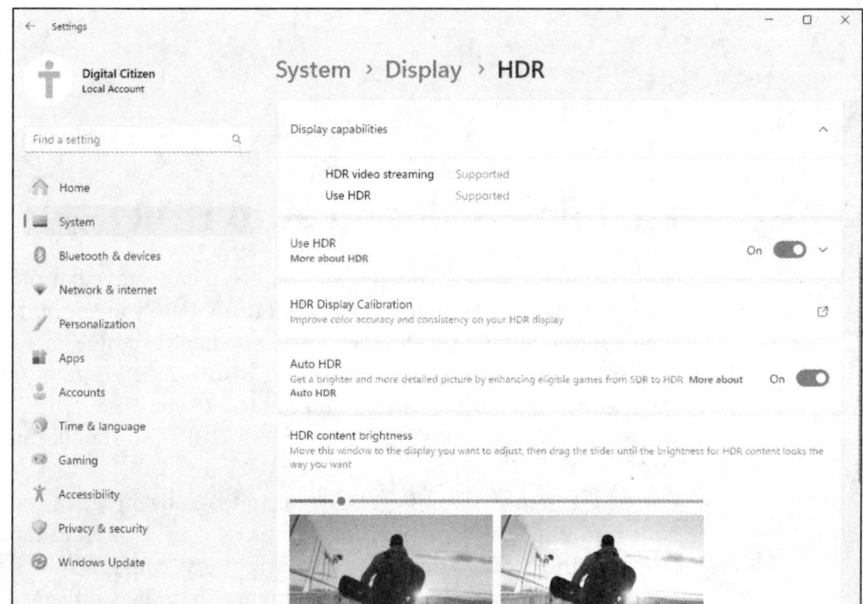

FIGURE 1-8: If you have an HDR-compatible display, be sure to enable HDR.

TIP

For more about the gaming features included in Windows 11, read Book 4, Chapter 9.

Setting the screen resolution

If you have a 4K display and want to take full advantage of the screen space it has to offer, set its screen resolution to the maximum. However, when you do, the icons and text change size and might be so small that you can't read them, especially if you view the display from a distance.

In addition, video takes more time to render at higher resolutions, so video-intensive workloads such as games might be slower, especially if your video card can't meet the demands of the game. Other hardware components can negatively affect the experience too, but the video card plays a critical role. Because of these reasons, you may want to adjust the screen resolution to something more balanced. Here's how:

1. **Right-click or press and hold an empty space on the desktop.**
2. **In the menu that opens, choose Display Settings.**

   The Display settings appear (refer to Figure 1-6).
3. **Click or tap the Display Resolution drop-down list.**

   All available screen resolutions appear, as shown in Figure 1-9. The list depends on your display, its hardware specifications, the drivers installed, and the capabilities of your computer's graphics card.
4. **Click or tap the resolution you want in the list.**

   Windows 11 changes the resolution and asks you to confirm that you want to keep this setting.
5. **Do one of the following:**
   - If you're happy with how everything looks, click or tap Keep Changes.
   - If you're not happy with how everything looks, click or tap Revert or don't do anything for 15 seconds. The screen reverts to the previous resolution, and you can repeat from Step 3.
6. **When you're done, close the Settings app by clicking or tapping X in the top-right corner.**

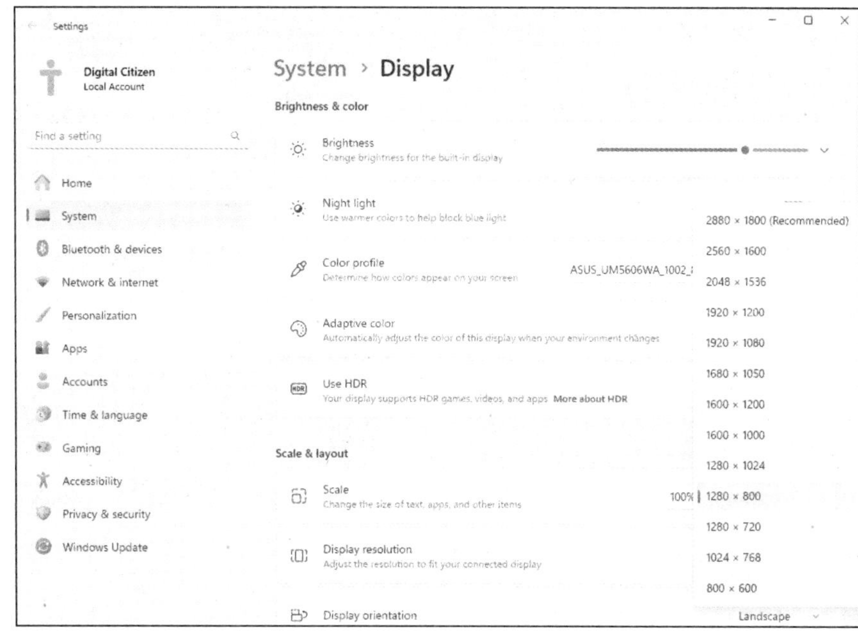

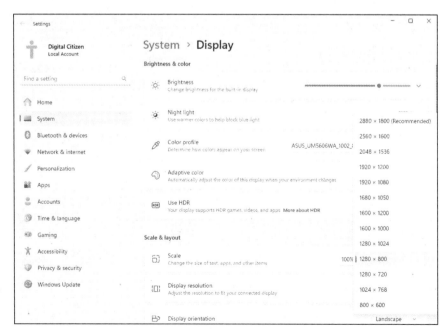

FIGURE 1-9: Changing the resolution can improve or lower the visibility of items on the screen.

Changing the size of text, apps, and other items

When you increase the resolution, you get more space on the screen and can use more apps side by side. However, if you're using a 4K display, the icons and text may get ridiculously small and put a strain on your eyes. You can fix this problem by lowering the resolution (and losing some of the screen real estate) or by changing the scaling. I prefer the latter approach. Here's how to adjust the scaling to improve the size of text, apps, and other items:

1. **Right-click or press and hold an empty space on the desktop.**
2. **In the menu that opens, choose Display Settings.**

   The Display settings appear (refer to Figure 1-6).
3. **Click or tap the Scale drop-down list and choose a scaling factor (such as 100% or 125%), as shown in Figure 1-10.**

   Your changes are applied immediately. Try different scaling factors until you find the one that's best for your eyesight. Remember that the higher the scaling, the bigger the text and icons on the screen.

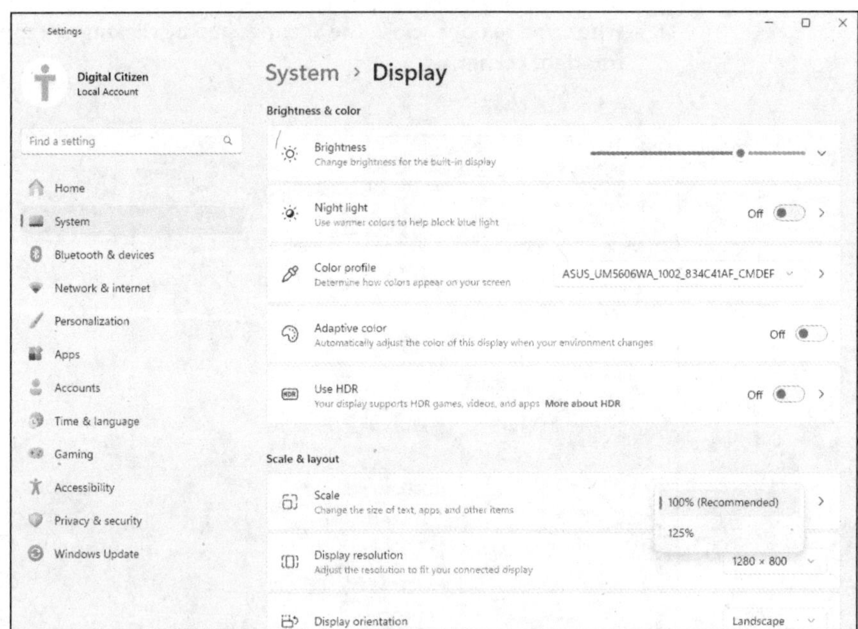

FIGURE 1-10: If you have a high-resolution display, it's a good idea to increase the scaling.

Adjusting the refresh rate

The *refresh rate* tells you how many times per second the image displayed on the screen is updated. By default, Windows 11 sets a 60 Hz screen refresh rate on all computers, meaning that the image is updated 60 times per second. However, gaming laptops or desktop PCs have screens that can reach much higher refresh rates, such as 120 Hz, 144 Hz, or 165 Hz. The refresh setting is important in gaming because it affects motion handling. The higher the refresh rate, the more information reaches your eyes in the same amount of time, leading to smoother-looking motion.

If you have a computer with a display that's capable of high refresh rates, you can change the rate like this:

1. **Right-click or press and hold an empty space on the desktop.**
2. **In the menu that appears, choose Display Settings.**

   You see the Display settings (refer to Figure 1-6).
3. **On the right, scroll down and click or tap Advanced Display.**

   You see the display information from Figure 1-11.
4. **Click or tap the drop-down list next to Choose a Refresh Rate, and then choose the value you want.**

   The screen refresh rates you see depend on your specific monitor.

   Windows 11 changes the refresh rate and asks you to confirm that you want to keep these settings.
5. **Do one of the following:**
   - If you're happy with how everything looks, click or tap Keep Changes.
   - If you're not happy with the screen, click or tap Revert or don't do anything for 10 seconds. The screen reverts automatically to the previous refresh rate, and you can repeat from Step 4.
6. **Close the Settings app by clicking or tapping X in the top-right corner.**

TIP

Some displays from newer, premium devices can use dynamic refresh rate that changes based on the content you're viewing. If this setting is available below the Choose a Refresh Rate setting, enable its switch. You will enjoy a good balance between the appropriate refresh rate based on your laptop's battery level and what you are doing on the laptop.

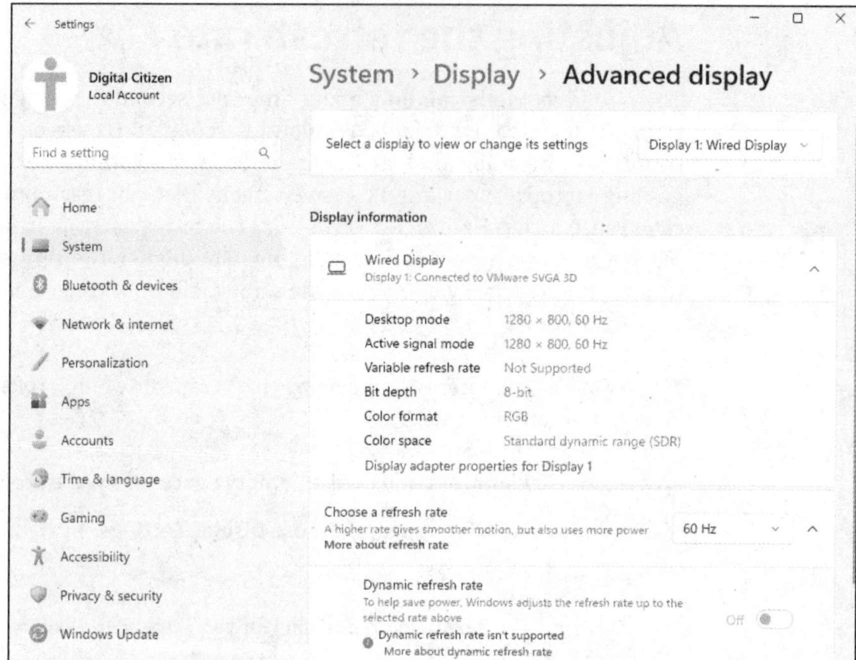

FIGURE 1-11: Increasing the refresh rate is a good idea for gaming.

Adjusting the display orientation

Many Windows 11 2-in-1 devices are on the market. For example, the ASUS Zenbook S 16 looks like an Ultrabook but also features a touchscreen that can be used not only with your fingers but also with a digital ASUS Pen. However, unlike some 2-in-1 devices, it can't change the display orientation automatically. Here's how to do so manually:

1. **Right-click or press and hold an empty space on the desktop.**
2. **In the menu that opens, choose Display Settings.**

   The Display settings appear, similar to those in Figure 1-12.
3. **Click or tap the Display Orientation drop-down list and choose the orientation you want: Landscape, Portrait, Landscape (flipped), or Portrait (flipped).**

   Your changes are applied immediately.
4. **If you're happy with how everything looks, click or tap Keep Changes. Otherwise, click or tap Revert, or don't do anything for 10 seconds.**

   The screen reverts automatically back to its previous orientation, and you can repeat from Step 3.
5. **If you want to lock the selected orientation and force Windows 11 to always use it, click or tap the Rotation Lock switch to enable it.**

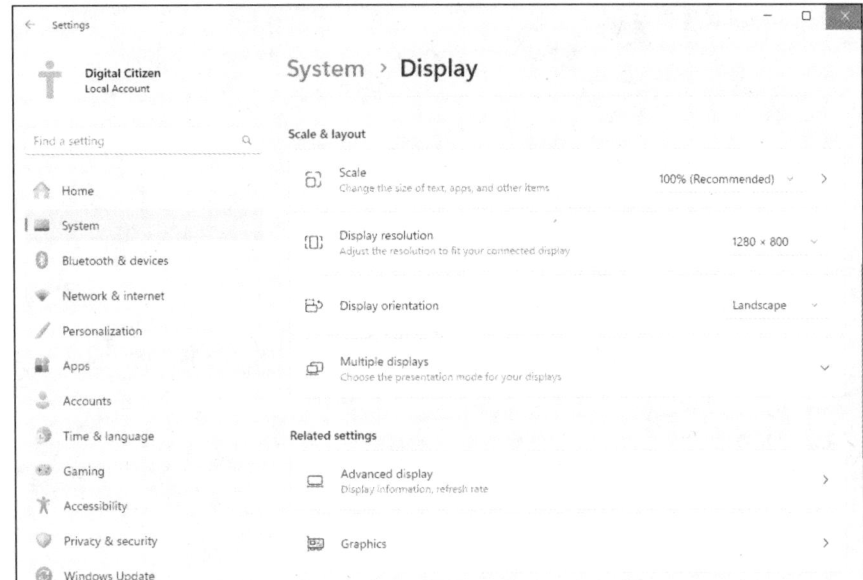

FIGURE 1-12: The display settings on my ASUS Zenbook S 16.

TIP

The display orientation can be changed on traditional laptops too, as well as desktop PCs. However, you don't get the Rotation Lock that's present on devices with a touchscreen.

Adjusting the brightness

One of the things every computer user does regularly is adjusting the brightness of the screen, especially when working on a portable device like a laptop or tablet. You may want to increase the brightness on your laptop because of glare or reduce brightness to lessen the burden on your eyes during the night. Luckily, the brightness can be adjusted in many ways. But the most reliable method is to do it straight from Windows 11, like this:

1. **Click or tap one of the icons in the bottom-right corner of the taskbar (Wi-Fi, volume, battery) or press Windows+A.**

   The Quick Settings panel appears, similar to Figure 1-13.

2. **In Quick Settings, drag the brightness slider (sun icon) to the left or right.**

   Moving the slider to the left decreases the brightness while moving it to the right increases the brightness.

3. **When you reach the brightness level you want, click or tap outside the Quick Settings panel.**

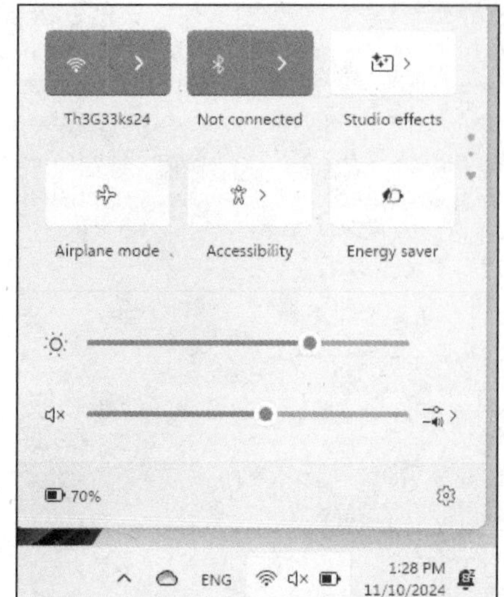

FIGURE 1-13: Adjusting the brightness is done from Quick Settings.

TIP

Another way to adjust the brightness level is to use the shortcut keys present on the keyboards of many laptops. For example, on an ASUS TUF Gaming F15 gaming laptop, you press Fn+F7 to lower the brightness and Fn+F8 to increase it. On an HP Spectre X360, you press the F2 key to reduce brightness and the F3 key to increase it. On a Microsoft Surface Pro, use Fn+Del to increase brightness, and Fn+Backspace to lower it. Laptops from different manufacturers use other brightness shortcut keys but they generally put a sun icon next to the keys you should use.

Working with a Mouse and a Touchpad

If you have the budget for a more expensive device with a touchscreen, Windows 11's Multi-Touch technology allows you to use all fingers simultaneously on your screen, making you look like Tom Cruise in *Minority Report*. But for the rest of us, the mouse and the touchpad remain the input device of choice. That's why, in this section, I show you how to set up and use the mouse and touchpad to help you be productive.

Snapping app windows

Windows 11 includes several gesture features that can save you lots of time. Foremost among them is a window docking capability called *snap*.

REMEMBER

If you click and hold the title bar of a window and drag the window all the way to the left side of the screen, as soon as the pointer hits the edge of the screen, Windows 11 resizes the window to take up the left half of the screen, docking it to the left edge. The same happens for the right side. Try it out and see how easy it is to drag and put a Word document and an Excel spreadsheet side by side or a favorite Spotify playlist alongside a favorite website in Microsoft Edge, as shown in Figure 1-14.

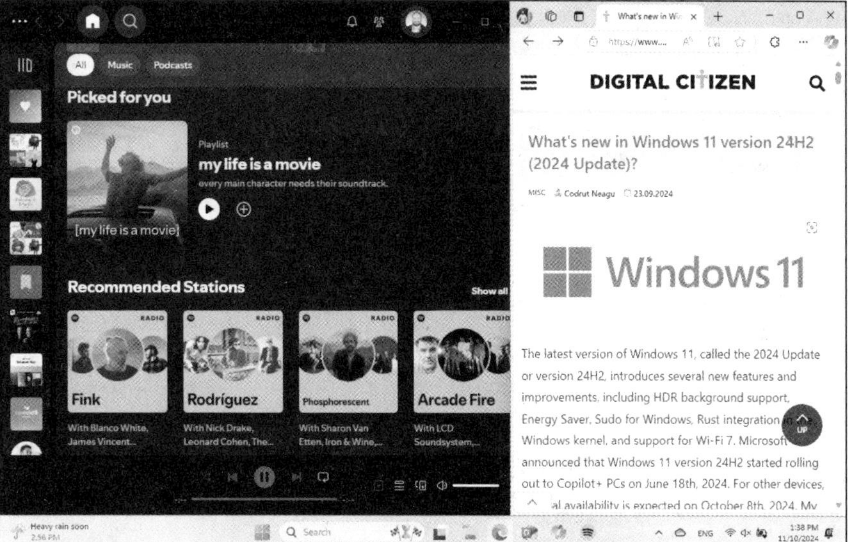

FIGURE 1-14: It's easy to arrange two apps side by side.

The Snap Assist feature makes snapping easier than ever. If you snap one app window to an edge, Windows 11 displays thumbnails of all other running programs (see Figure 1-15). Click or tap a window, and it occupies the vacant part of the screen.

You can also drag to the corners of the screen and snap four app windows into the four corners.

These aren't the only navigation tricks. If you drag a window to the top of the screen, it's *maximized,* so it occupies the entire screen. (Yeah, I know. You always did that by double-clicking the title bar.) And, if you click a window's title bar and shake it with the mouse (or your finger), all other windows on the screen move out of the way: They *minimize* themselves as icons on the taskbar.

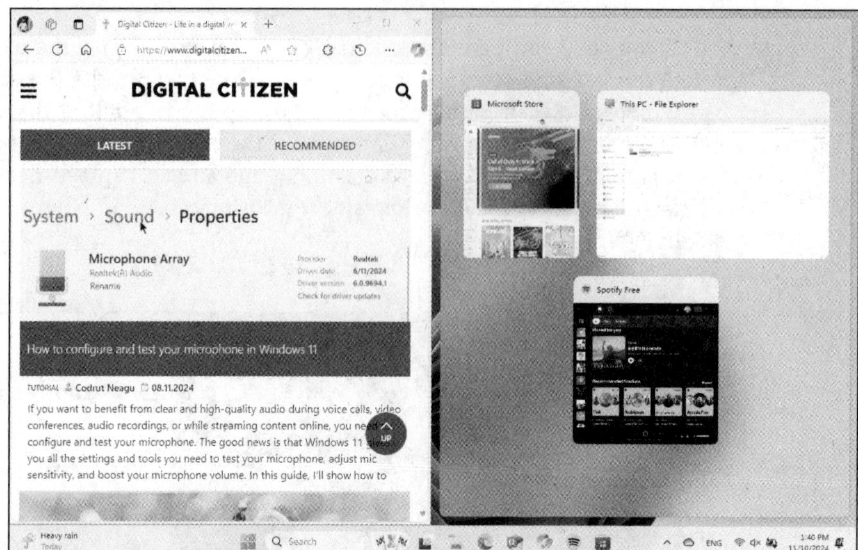

FIGURE 1-15: Snap Assist helps you put two windows side by side.

TIP

If you prefer using the keyboard, you can achieve the same results with the following key combinations:

- » **Snap left:** Windows+left arrow
- » **Snap right:** Windows+right arrow
- » **Maximize:** Windows+up arrow

TIP

All these snapping features are controlled via the Settings app. Click or tap the Start icon, Settings, System, and then Multitasking. You see all the settings for snapping app windows, and you can enable or disabling snapping with a simple switch.

Configuring the mouse

If you're left-handed, you can interchange the actions of the left and right mouse buttons — that is, you can tell Windows 11 that it should treat the left mouse button as though it were the right button and treat the right button as though it were the left. You can also reduce the mouse pointer speed (useful when you're older or not able to utilize your Windows computer normally), change how scrolling works, and so on.

To find all your mouse settings, do the following:

1. **Click or tap the Start icon and then Settings.**
2. **On the left of the Settings window, select Bluetooth & Devices.**
3. **On the right, click or tap Mouse.**

   The mouse settings appear, as shown in Figure 1-16.
4. **Change the mouse settings that interest you, and then click or tap X to close Settings.**

   One setting you'll probably want to adjust is how many lines you scroll at a time.

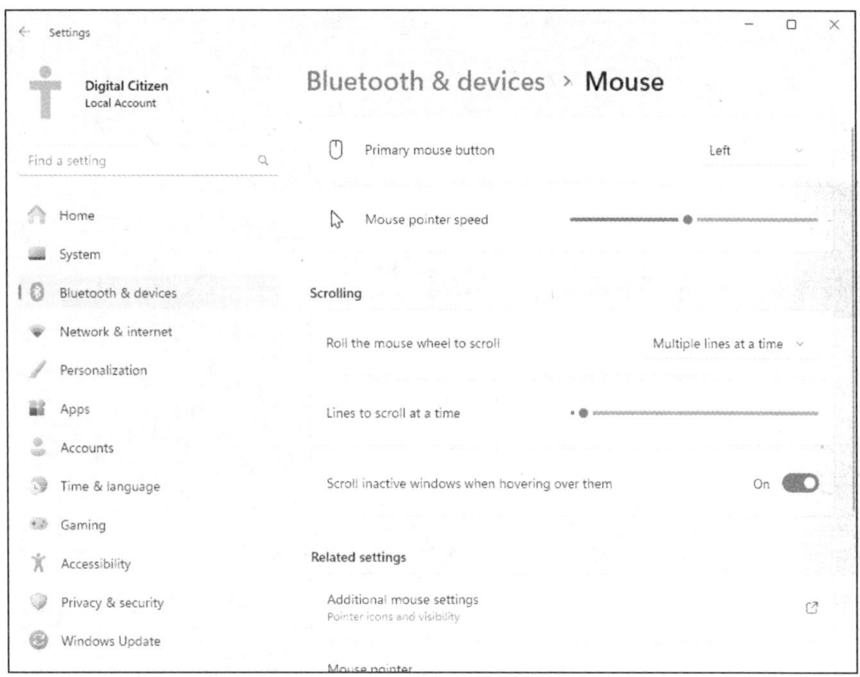

FIGURE 1-16: Configuring how your mouse works makes you more productive.

Setting up the touchpad

All Windows 11 laptops come with precision touchpads that enable you to do all kinds of gestures, even with three or four fingers, that perform actions such as switching between apps and desktops. Whether or not you like using a touchpad, it's useful to know how to turn the touchpad on and off, as well as where to find all touchpad-related settings:

1. **Click or tap the Start icon and then Settings.**
2. **On the left of the Settings window, select Bluetooth & Devices.**
3. **On the right, click or tap Touchpad.**

   You see all touchpad settings, as shown in Figure 1-17. The settings you see depend on your laptop model and its touchpad's capabilities.

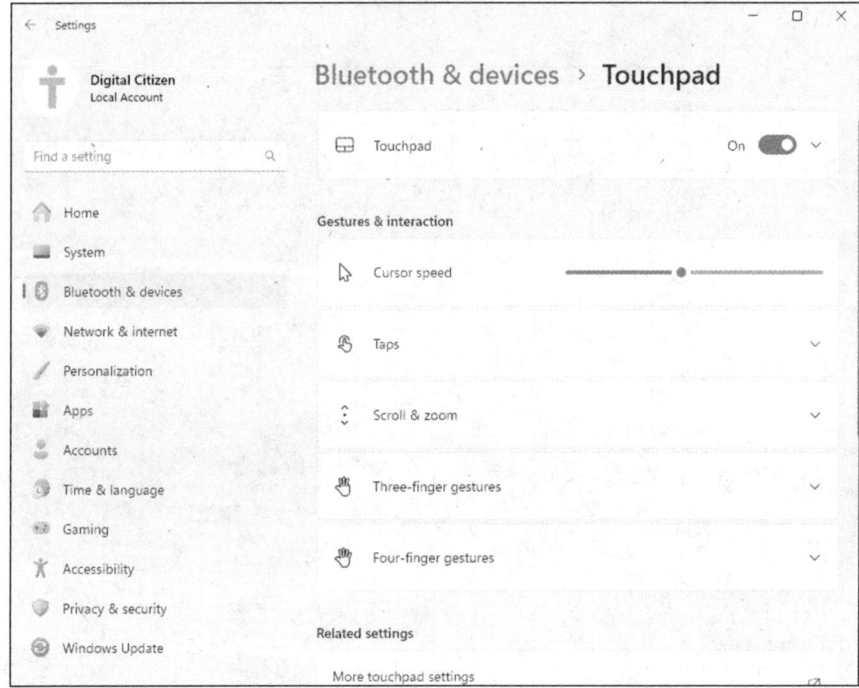

FIGURE 1-17: Enable or disable the touchpad and adjust its settings.

4. **To disable the touchpad, set its switch to off.**
5. **If you keep the touchpad on, feel free to adjust the cursor speed and all the settings available for it.**
6. **If you connect a mouse to your laptop on a regular basis and you don't want the touchpad enabled when the mouse is connected, do the following:**

   a. *Click or tap Touchpad (the text, not the switch) to expand this section.* You see two additional options, as shown in Figure 1-18.

b. Deselect Leave Touchpad On When a Mouse Is Connected.

From now on, the touchpad will be enabled only when you disconnect the mouse from your laptop.

7. **To close Settings, click or tap X.**

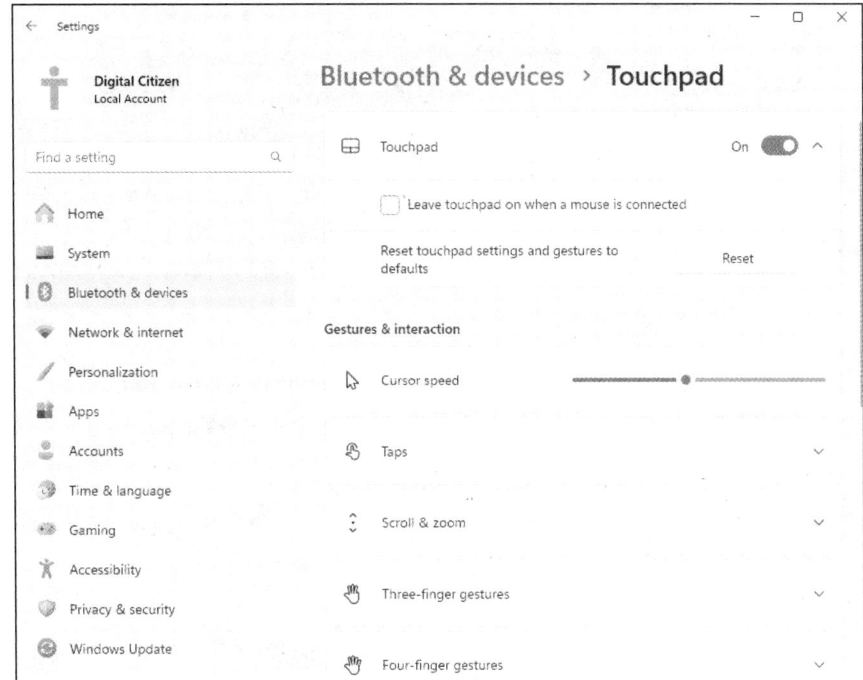

FIGURE 1-18: Disabling the touchpad when a mouse is connected.

Using Virtual Desktops

Just like Windows 10, Windows 11 can work with multiple desktops in parallel. One desktop can display your work, another your games, another your social media, and so on. Each desktop can have a specific name and background, and you can switch between them with ease. Microsoft calls this feature *virtual desktops.*

To use virtual desktops, you first need to create one, like this:

1. **Click or tap the task view icon (shown in the margin) on the taskbar.**

   Task view displays the apps you have open and any desktops you've created, as shown in Figure 1-19. The current desktop is Desktop 1, which is the desktop that Windows creates by default each time you sign in.

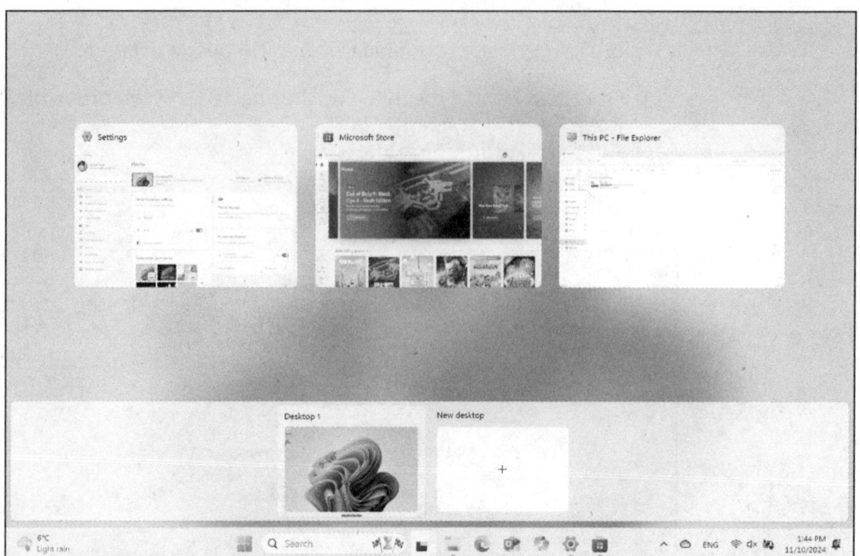

FIGURE 1-19: Virtual desktops help you organize your work.

2. **To create a virtual desktop, tap or click New Desktop +.**

   Desktop 2 is added to the list at the bottom of task view.

3. **Click or tap Desktop 2 to open it.**

   Note that the new virtual desktop is empty and has no running apps.

4. **To rename a desktop:**

   (a) *Click or tap the task view icon.*

   (b) *Right-click (or press and hold) the desktop you want and then choose Rename from the contextual menu.*

   (c) *Type a name for the virtual desktop. Press Enter or click or tap outside the list of virtual desktops.*

TIP

In task view, if you right-click the name of a virtual desktop, you see the Choose Background option. You can then change the wallpaper for only that desktop, making it easier to tell them apart.

Moving apps between virtual desktops

For virtual desktops to be useful, you need to be able to move apps between them. Here's how to do it:

1. **Create two virtual desktops, as shown in the preceding section, and select Desktop 1.**
2. **Open Microsoft Edge by clicking or tapping its icon on the taskbar.**

3. **Click or tap the task view icon on the taskbar.**

   Task view is shown with the Microsoft Edge window in the middle.

4. **Right-click or press and hold the Microsoft Edge app preview in task view.**

   The contextual menu shown in Figure 1-20 appears.

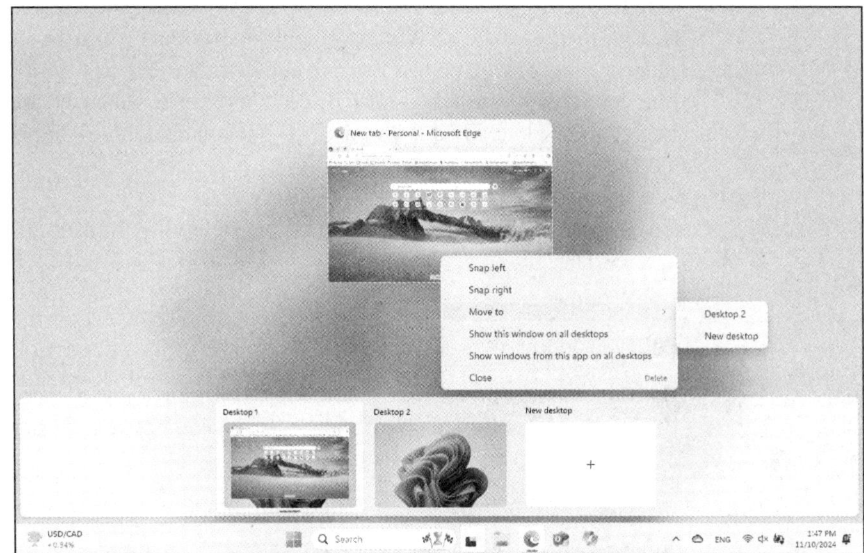

FIGURE 1-20: Moving apps from one desktop to another is easy.

5. **Choose Move To, and then click or tap the name of the desktop you want to move the window to.**

   The Microsoft Edge window is moved to the virtual desktop you chose.

6. **In task view, click or tap the name of the desktop where you moved Microsoft Edge.**

   Note how the Microsoft Edge window moved to the virtual desktop you selected.

REMEMBER

This trick works with all apps and games, not just those made by Microsoft.

Managing Icons and Shortcuts

When you first use Windows 11, you should see only one or two icons on the desktop: the Recycle Bin and perhaps Microsoft Edge. However, as you use Windows 11, you may want to add more shortcuts to your favorite apps, documents that you're working on, games, websites, and so on. In this section, I show you how to create shortcuts on the desktop and arrange them, and then tell you the basics about using the Recycle Bin.

Creating shortcuts

Sometimes, life is easier with shortcuts. (As long as the shortcuts work, anyway.) So, too, in the world of Windows, where shortcuts point to things such as files, folders, apps, or web pages. You can set up a shortcut to a Word document and put it on your desktop. Double-click or double-tap the shortcut, and Word starts with the document loaded as if you double-clicked or double-tapped the document in File Explorer.

You can set up shortcuts that point to the following items:

- Windows programs and apps of any kind
- Web addresses, such as `www.dummies.com`
- Documents, spreadsheets, databases, PowerPoint presentations, and anything else that can be started in File Explorer by double-clicking or double-tapping
- Folders from anywhere on your computer
- Drives (hard drives, Blu-ray drives, and USB drives, for example)
- Other computers on your network, and drives and folders on those computers, as long they're shared
- Printers (including printers attached to other computers on your network), scanners, cameras, and other pieces of hardware

You have many different ways to create shortcuts. One way to create shortcuts to files and folders is from File Explorer, like this:

1. **Click or tap the File Explorer icon on the taskbar to open it.**
2. **Navigate to the file to which you want to create a shortcut, and right-click or press and hold it.**

   You see a contextual menu with a few options.
3. **Choose Show More Options.**

   The old-school right-click menu from Windows 10 loads, as shown in Figure 1-21.

4. **Choose Send To and then choose Desktop (Create Shortcut).**

   A shortcut to your file is placed on the desktop.

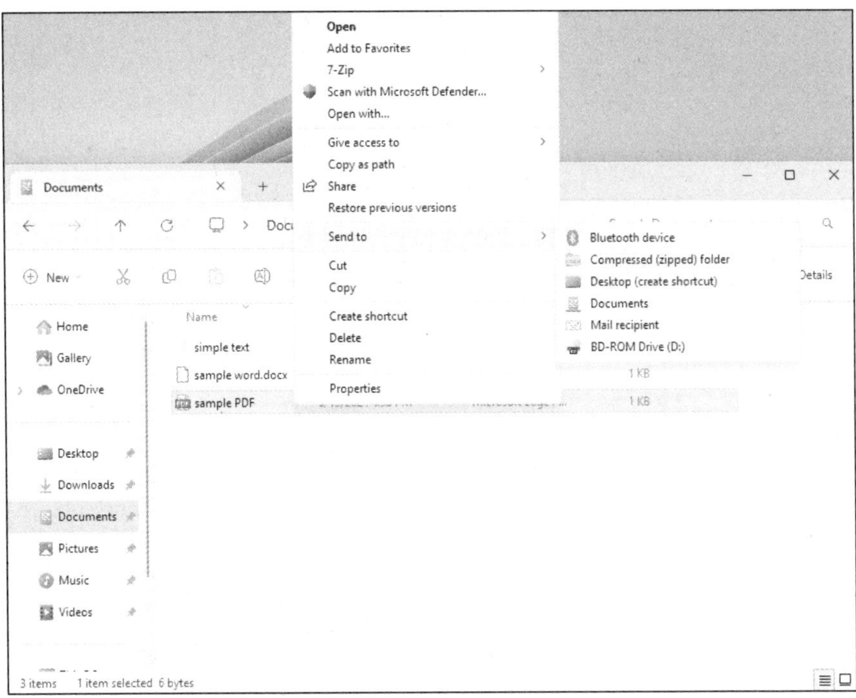

FIGURE 1-21: The old right-click menu is hidden in Windows 11.

If you want to create shortcuts for other things, such as websites, shared folders, or computers on your network, use a more general-purpose method:

1. **Right-click or press and hold a blank area on the desktop and choose New ➪ Shortcut.**

   The Create Shortcut wizard appears, as shown in Figure 1-22.

2. **In the location field, type the name or location of the program, file, folder, drive, computer, or internet address.**

   You can also click or tap Browse, and then choose the item you want the shortcut to point to.

3. **Click or tap Next.**

   Windows asks for a name for the shortcut.

4. **Give the shortcut a memorable name and click or tap Finish.**

   Windows 11 places an icon for the program, file, folder, drive, computer, website, document — whatever — on the desktop.

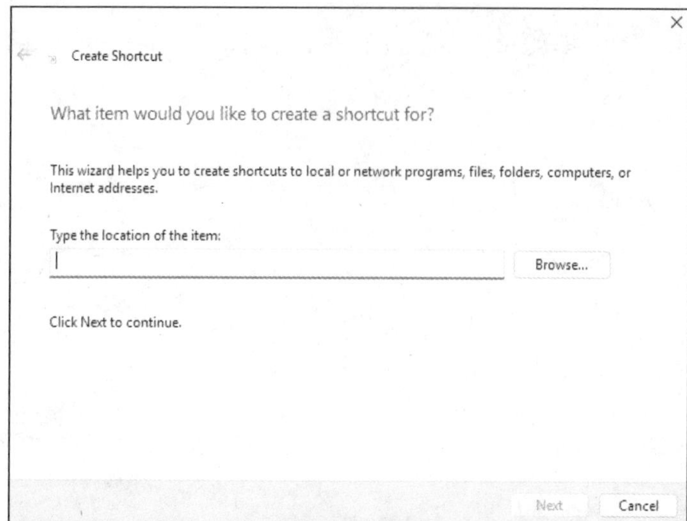

FIGURE 1-22: Create shortcuts the old-fashioned manual way.

TECHNICAL STUFF

Believe it or not, Windows thrives on shortcuts. They're everywhere, lurking just beneath the surface. For example, every entry on the Start menu is a (cleverly disguised) shortcut. The icons on the taskbar are all shortcuts. Most of File Explorer is based on shortcuts. Even the Windows 11 app icons work with shortcuts. So, don't be afraid to experiment with shortcuts. Worst-case scenario, you can always delete them. Doing so gets rid of the shortcut; it doesn't touch the original item that the shortcut pointed to.

Arranging icons on the desktop

You can change the position of the icons on your desktop by dragging them with the mouse, your laptop's touchpad, or your finger (if you use a device with a touchscreen). Simply drag and drop any icon around the desktop, and it will remain there.

However, if you're not happy with the icon's size or alignment, you can change it as follows:

1. **Right-click or press and hold a blank area on the desktop and choose View.**

   The options shown in Figure 1-23 appear.

2. **Choose an icon size (large, medium, or small).**

   The change is applied immediately.

3. **To arrange the icons on your desktop a bit, repeat Step 1 and choose Auto Arrange Icons.**

   Note how your desktop icons are arranged in a different order.

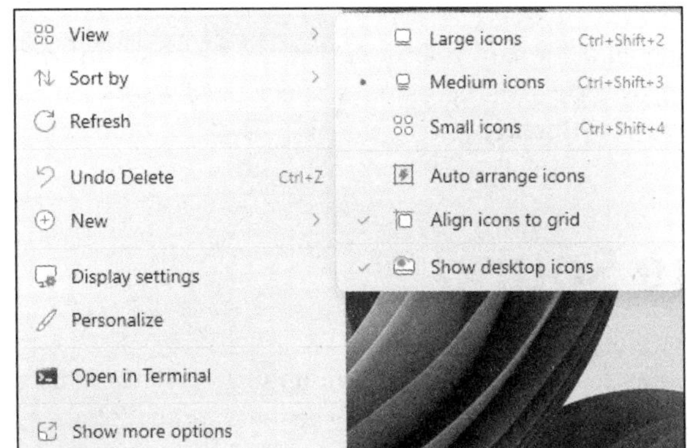

FIGURE 1-23: Choose how you want to view your desktop icons.

The Recycle Bin

The Recycle Bin is a special folder with a trash can icon that stores deleted files and folders. When you delete items from your computer or device, they're not removed permanently. Instead, they're moved to the Recycle Bin. Windows does this as a precaution in case you delete something by mistake or later discover that you need a certain discarded file or folder.

Physically, deleted files continue to occupy the same space as before on your hard drive(s). However, once an item is deleted, you can't see it in the same location on your system, and Windows displays it in the Recycle Bin. The Recycle Bin keeps the references to deleted files and folders until they're permanently removed from your PC. Each hard drive in your computer has a Recycle Bin, but all the files you delete are displayed in this one folder on your desktop, represented by the trash can icon. If nothing has been deleted, the icon looks like an empty trash can. If at least one file or folder is deleted, the trash can looks full, as shown in Figure 1-24.

FIGURE 1-24: Go to the Recycle Bin to find deleted files and folders.

REMEMBER

To completely remove all your deleted files, right-click or press and hold the Recycle Bin icon on the desktop, and then choose Empty Recycle Bin.

If you want to recover a deleted file, open the Recycle Bin, right-click (or press and hold) the file, and choose Restore. You then see the file in its initial location. This command can be used at any time, as long as you didn't empty the Recycle Bin. You can also drag a file from the Recycle Bin to another folder on your computer instead of restoring it to its original location.

TIP

If you've deleted a file and then emptied the Recycle Bin, there might still be a chance of recovering the file using a specialized app such as Recuva. To learn more, see Book 10, Chapter 4.

Setting Up the Sound

It's time to master sound control in Windows 11. Whether you're trying to silence pesky notification dings, switch from speakers to headphones, or fine-tune your audio settings, you're in the right place. In this section, I show how to master Volume Mixer — a powerful tool that's your key to customizing the sound on your PC. You'll be muting the sound, mixing volume levels, and modifying sound settings like a pro.

Muting your computer

Sometimes, you'll find yourself in a quiet environment and you won't want to bother anyone around. In that case, it's a good idea to mute your Windows 11 computer so that it doesn't play any sound, including annoying ads that auto-play a sound on a website you're visiting.

Traditionally, most laptops and desktop computers have keyboard shortcuts for muting the sound. For example, on my HP laptop, I press the F6 key, while on my desktop PC, I press Fn+PrintScreen. The keyboard shortcuts vary from computer to computer, but a more universal method is to mute your computer from Windows 11, like this:

1. **Click or tap the speaker icon in the bottom-right corner of the taskbar, or press Windows+A.**

   The Quick Settings panel shown in Figure 1-25 appears.

2. **Click or tap the speaker icon.**

   When you hover your mouse cursor over the icon, it says Mute Volume. Note how the speaker icon now has a mute symbol next to it.

When you want to unmute your computer, simply repeat the same steps.

TIP

You can use the slider next to the speaker icon to change the sound volume.

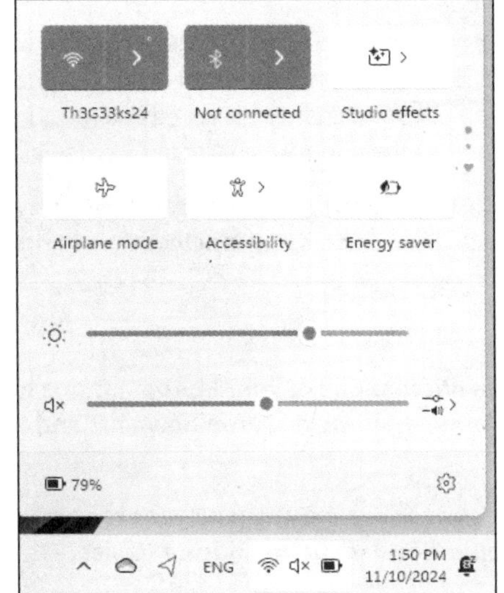

FIGURE 1-25: You can mute the sound from Quick Settings.

Setting the volume and your sound devices with Volume Mixer

In Windows 10, Volume Mixer was a popular feature because it allowed users to adjust sound output on an app level rather than just on a system level. However, Microsoft has significantly changed Volume Mixer in Windows 11. The feature is now part of the Settings app and lets you set the default sound for input and output devices, adjust the system volume, and control the volume and sound devices on an app level. This way, you can set your laptop to play sounds through its speakers while having a specific app, such as Microsoft Teams, output sound only to your headset. It's a useful feature, don't you think?

To use Volume Mixer to adjust the sound devices and sound level, follow these steps:

1. **Right-click or press and hold the speaker icon in the bottom-right corner of the taskbar, and choose Open Volume Mixer.**

   The Volume Mixer settings shown in Figure 1-26 appear. They're organized as follows:

   - The System section at the top is where you change the system volume and the sound output and input device. What you change here applies to Windows and all your apps on a system level.

- The Apps section lists all the apps you're using and which work with sound. If you click or tap the name of each app in this list, you can set the sound devices that the app uses and change its sound volume. The changes you make here apply only to the app you've selected.

2. **If your computer doesn't play the sound on the correct device, click or tap the Output Device drop-down list and select the sound device you want.**

   In most cases, you should select Speaker(s).

3. **If you've plugged in a microphone or your laptop has one built in but it's not used, click or tap the Input Device drop-down list and choose your microphone.**

4. **In the Apps section, click or tap the app you want to configure, and then change its sound volume and input and output device.**

   Your settings are applied immediately.

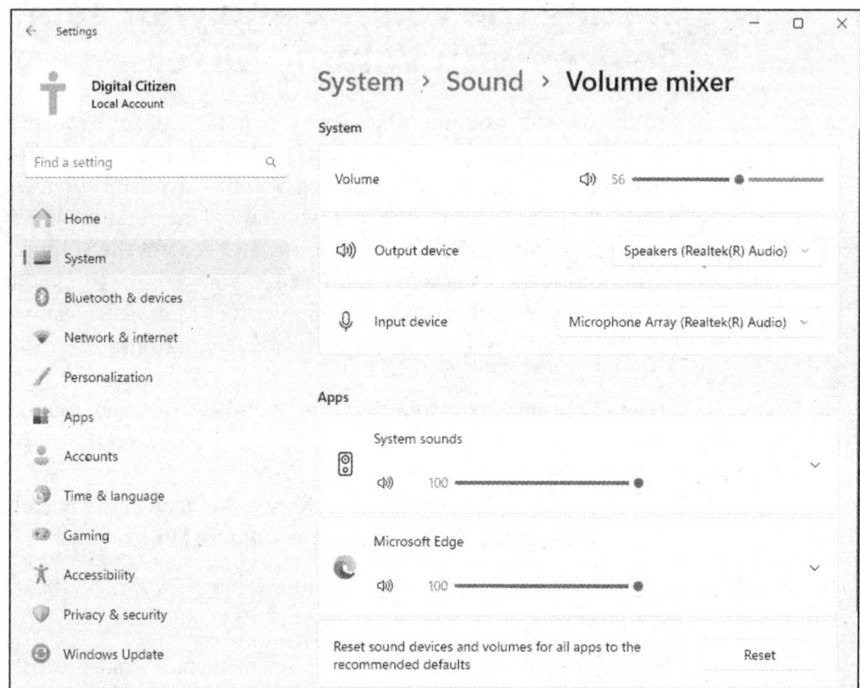

FIGURE 1-26: You can adjust sound settings in Volume Mixer.

IN THIS CHAPTER

» Navigating the Windows 11 Start menu

» Adding apps and folders to the Start menu

» Making the Start menu yours

» Changing the position of the Start menu

Chapter 2

Personalizing the Start Menu

When it comes to the desktop, Windows 11 copied the approach used by Apple on the Mac. As a result, the Start menu and the taskbar are centered and the icons on the taskbar behave in a similar way to those on macOS. I like this approach, and I especially like the new Start menu, which is organized differently than it was in Windows 10, with new sections and items. Gone are the tiles from Windows 10, and back are the classic shortcuts from Windows 7. Hooray, right?

However, there are also downsides to the new Start menu, as well as a few annoyances. In this chapter, I give you a tour of the Windows 11 Start menu, explain how it's organized, and show you how to navigate it. You also find out how to personalize the different sections, add and remove folders, disable some of the things that might annoy you, and align the Start menu to the left, like it was in older versions of Windows.

Touring the Start Menu

After you sign in to Windows 11, you see the desktop, your desktop icons, and the taskbar, with icons in its center. On the left side of the taskbar is the widgets icon, and then the first one in the center grouping is the Start icon (shown in the margin).

When you click or tap the Start icon, the first thing you see is the Start menu, as shown in Figure 2-1. This is Microsoft's first centered Start menu in a Windows operating system, and it is quite different from the one in Windows 10. But don't worry, navigating it is a breeze. I walk you through it step by step, so you can feel confident and comfortable using it.

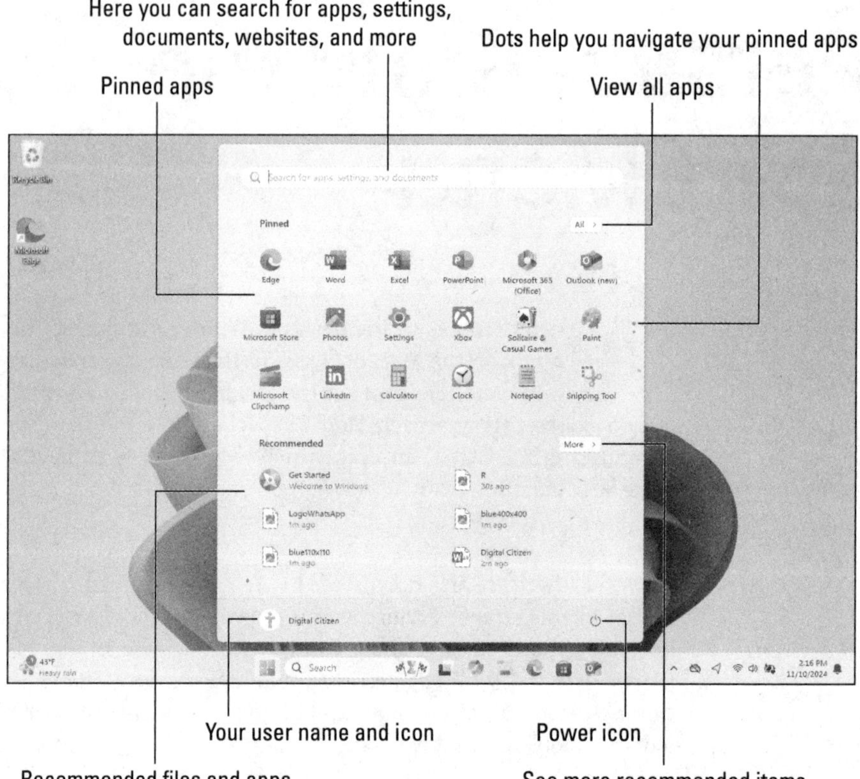

FIGURE 2-1: The Start menu in Windows 11.

Here's how the Start menu is organized:

- » At the top of the Start menu is a Search box that you can use to find anything from installed apps, settings, files on your computer, and websites on the internet.
- » Next is the Pinned section, which includes three rows of shortcuts to installed apps. These shortcuts are automatically set up by Windows 11, but you can personalize the list. Windows defaults to 18 shortcuts, but you can have more than the default. To navigate to the next screen of shortcuts, click or tap one of the dots to the right of the Pinned section. If you don't have any dots as shown in Figure 2-1, you have 18 or fewer apps pinned to your Start menu.
- » In the top right, just above the Pinned list, is the All button. A click or tap on it opens the list of all the apps in Windows 11, as shown in Figure 2-2. Note the Back button in the top right, which returns you to the Start menu.
- » Next is the Recommended section, which contains recently added apps, your most-used apps, and recently opened items. If you have more apps and items than can fit on the screen, you'll see a More button to the right of the section. Click or tap it to open a longer list filled with the same type of items.
- » The bottom of the Start menu has your username and picture on the left and the power icon on the right. Clicking or tapping your username reveals a menu where you can manage your Microsoft account, sign out, and switch the user. When clicking the power icon, you get access to a menu from where you can shut down your computer, restart it, lock it, or put it to sleep.

REMEMBER

A frustrating aspect of the Windows 11 Start menu is that it can't be resized like the one in Windows 10. You're stuck with its default size and sections.

Right-clicking Start for the WinX menu

If you right-click (or tap and hold) the Start icon, it reveals a hidden menu with many useful links, as shown in Figure 2-3. The menu doesn't have a standard name, but some people, including myself, call it the WinX menu because you can access it also by pressing Windows+X. Others call it the power user's menu, while some call it the Quick Link menu.

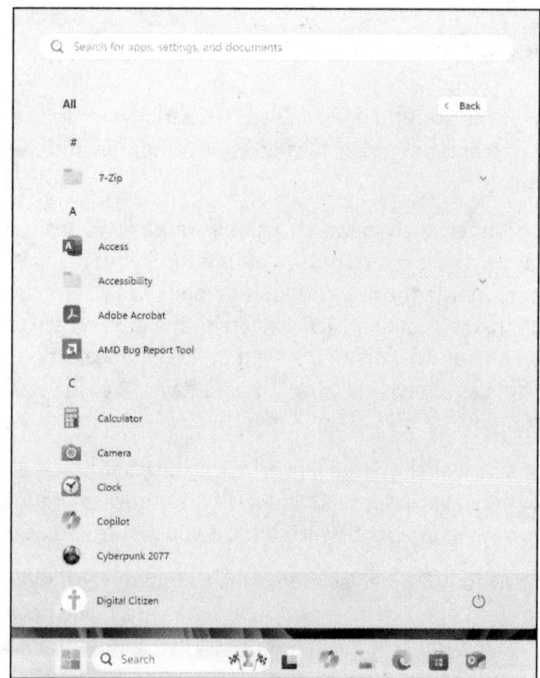

FIGURE 2-2: The All apps list displayed by the Start menu.

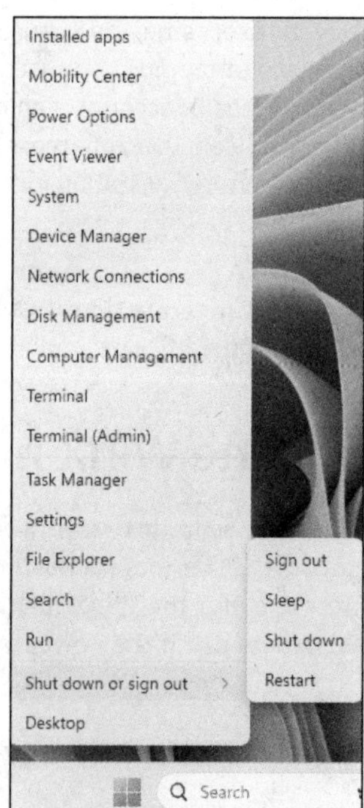

FIGURE 2-3: The WinX menu is very useful.

Even though this menu is not customizable, it's useful because it includes links to the most useful management and troubleshooting tools: Disk Management, Computer Management, Event Viewer, and Windows Terminal. At the top of the list is a useful shortcut to the Installed Apps page in Settings, from where you can quickly remove the apps you don't want. Many will appreciate the Shut Down or Sign Out menu item, which allows you to restart or sign out from Windows 11 quickly. Try it out, and I'm fairly sure you'll love using it. I know I do, and I find it a better option than the Start menu when I want to sign out, switch user accounts, or simply shut down my Windows 11 computer.

Modifying the Start Menu

You can customize many things about the Windows 11 Start menu: Add or remove apps from it, change how much space each section occupies, create folders of pinned apps, and more. Let's take each option, one by one, and see how to personalize it.

Adding, moving, and removing pinned apps

The first thing you may want to do with the Start menu is remove the pinned app shortcuts you don't want, pin shortcuts to apps you use regularly, and change the position of pinned shortcuts. The process is simple:

1. **Click or tap the Start icon.**

   The Start menu opens.

2. **To unpin an app, do the following:**

   a. *Right-click (or press and hold) the app shortcut.* The menu shown in Figure 2-4 appears.

   b. *Click or tap Unpin from Start.* The shortcut is no longer pinned, and another takes its place.

3. **To pin an app, follow these steps:**

   a. *Click or tap the All button.* You see a list of all apps installed in Windows 11.

   b. *Scroll down the list of apps and right-click (or press and hold) the app.* A menu appears with options to Pin to Start, More, and Uninstall.

   c. *Choose Pin to Start.* The app is pinned to the Start menu.

   d. *Click or tap the Back button to see the app in the Pinned list.*

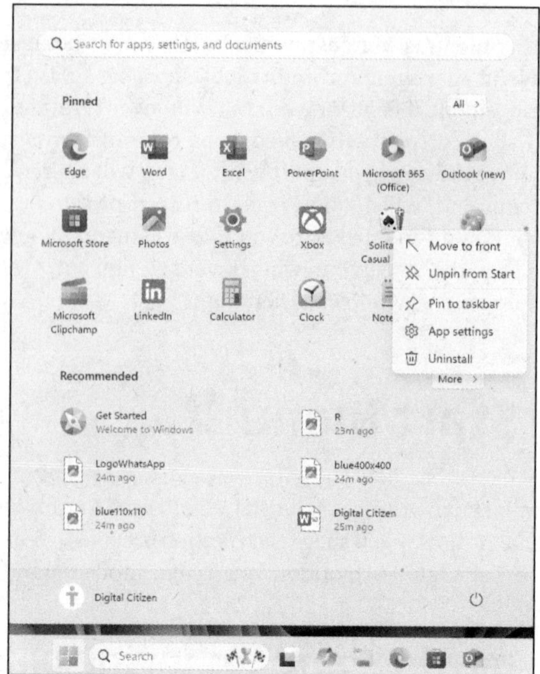

FIGURE 2-4: Removing a pinned app from the Start menu.

You can pin an app to the Start menu from other places too. For example, if you navigate your files in File Explorer (read Chapter 4 in this book to learn more), you can right-click the executable file of the app you want on your Start menu and choose Pin to Start. You can do the same when using search, simply right-clicking the search result you want and choosing Pin to Start.

TIP

If you don't see the app you just pinned in the Pinned section of the Start menu, it was added to the end of the list. Use the dots on the right side of the Pinned section to navigate to it.

TIP

To move a pinned app to the top of the list, drag it around with the mouse or your finger if you have a touchscreen. You can also right-click (or press and hold) its shortcut in the Pinned section and choose Move to Front. The shortcut will now be the first in the Pinned section.

Creating folders with pinned apps

One lesser-known capability of the Windows 11 Start menu is allowing users to group pinned apps into folders. You can name those folders and arrange them in the Pinned section like any app. Here's how to create a folder with two or more pinned apps:

1. **Click or tap the Start icon.**

   The Start menu opens.

2. **Click and hold (or press and hold) an app from the Pinned section and drag it over to another app that you want to have in the same folder. Release the app on top of the other.**

   The two apps are now placed inside a folder named Folder, as shown in Figure 2-5.

3. **Click or tap on the folder you've just created.**

   The folder opens, and you're presented with the option to edit its name.

4. **Click and or tap Edit Name.**

   A text box appears where you can type the name you want.

5. **Type the name for your folder, and then click or tap outside the folder.**

   The next time you open the Start menu, you'll see the folder alongside your pinned apps.

You can add more apps to the pinned folder simply by dragging their icons on top of the folder. You can also remove apps from the folder by opening it and dragging the app you want outside the folder.

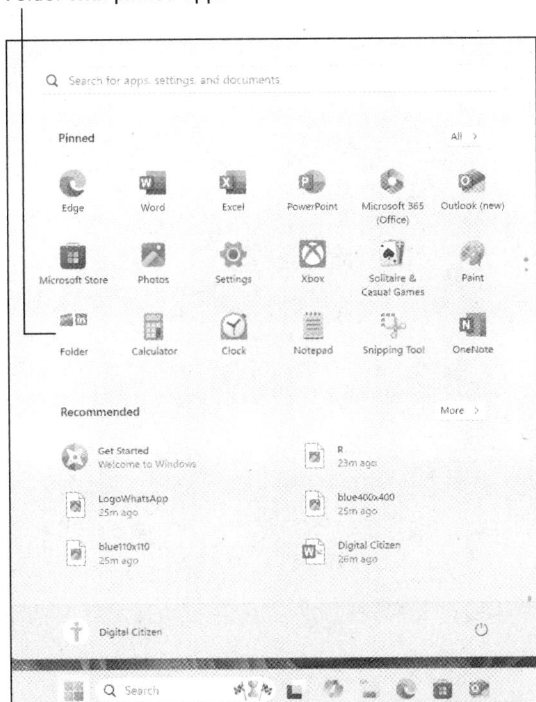

FIGURE 2-5: You've just created a folder with pinned apps.

TIP

If you want to delete a folder from your Pinned apps, either drag out all the apps inside, or right-click or tap and hold each of them and choose Unpin from Start. When all the apps from the folder are removed, the folder is deleted from the Start menu.

Adding and removing Start menu folders

By default, the bottom-right corner of the Windows 11 Start menu displays only the power icon. However, you can add several folders next to it to serve as quick shortcuts to places you visit frequently. You can add shortcuts to Settings, File Explorer, Documents, Downloads, Music, Pictures, Videos, Network, and the Personal folder (your user account folder). Here's how to add and remove folders from the Start menu:

1. **Open the Start menu and click or tap Settings.**
2. **In the Settings app, click or tap Personalization, Start, and then Folders.**

   You see all the folders that can be added to the Start menu, as shown in Figure 2-6.

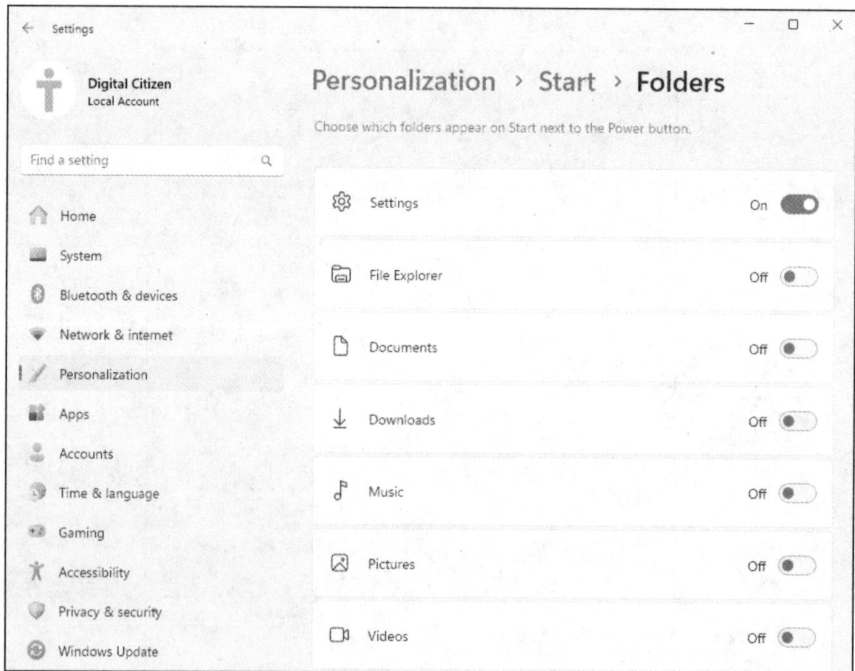

FIGURE 2-6: Adding folders to the Start menu.

3. **For each folder you want on the Start menu, click or tap the switch to set it on.**
4. **For the folders you don't want on the Start menu, set their switches to off.**
5. **When you're finished, close Settings.**

   When you open the Start menu, you see the selected folders next to the power icon.

TIP

If you add all the available folders, the Start menu gets crowded, making it difficult to tell each one apart. Therefore, it's best to enable only the folders you visit frequently, such as Documents, Downloads, Pictures, and Settings.

Choosing the Start Menu layout

When Windows 11 was introduced, you couldn't change how the Start menu was split into sections. After several updates, Microsoft introduced the ability to display more pins or more recommendations, depending on what you want. However, you can't choose to turn off a section if you don't need it. You can only make it take less space on the Start menu, like this:

1. **Open the Start menu and click or tap Settings.**
2. **In the Settings app, click or tap Personalization, and then Start.**

   You see all the settings available for personalizing the Start menu, as shown in Figure 2-7.
3. **In the Layout section, choose between More Pins or More Recommendations, depending on your preference.**
4. **When you're finished, close Settings.**

   When you open the Start menu, you see that the Pinned and Recommended sections have been resized according to your selection.

TIP

To reset the Start menu back to its initial layout, repeat the same steps and choose Default in the Layout section.

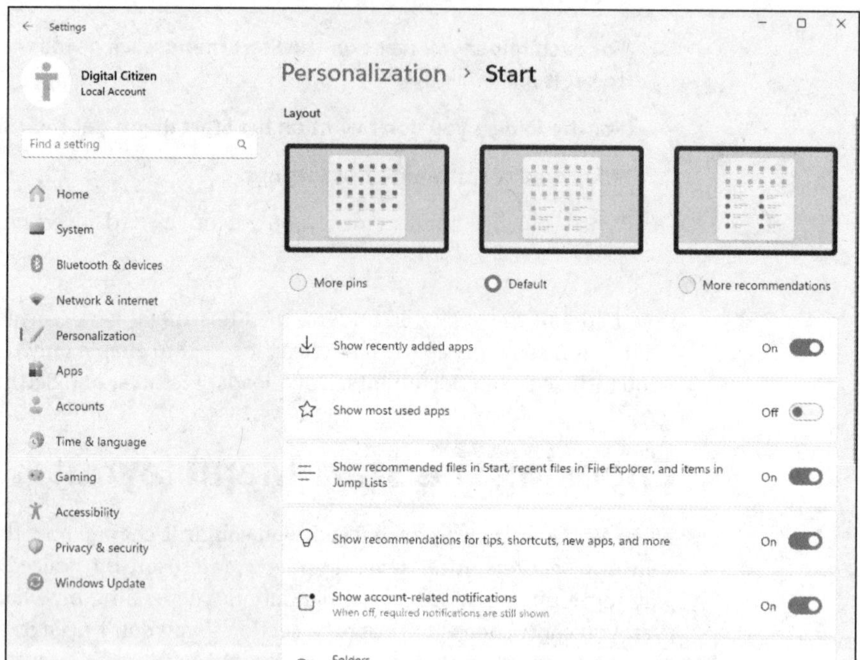

FIGURE 2-7: Choosing the layout for the Start menu.

Personalizing the Start menu

By default, Windows 11 shows your recently added apps and opened items in the Recommended section of the Start menu. It can show your most-used apps there too. Here's how to customize the Recommended section and other parts of the Start menu:

1. **Open the Start menu and click or tap Settings.**
2. **On the left side of the Settings app, choose Personalization.**

   You see an extensive list of settings on the right.
3. **Scroll down and click or tap Start.**

   The Start menu settings appear, as shown in Figure 2-7.
4. **Depending on what you want, set the following switches on or off:**
   - *Show Recently Added Apps:* It's useful to keep this setting enabled because you can quickly start recently added apps.
   - *Show Most Used Apps:* Windows analyzes the apps that you frequently use and displays them in the Start menu. I usually add them to the Pinned section, so I don't need this setting turned on.

- *Show Recommended Files in Start, Recent Files in File Explorer, and Items in Jump Lists:* This setting affects all Windows 11 apps that can display recommended or recently opened items, not only the Start menu. For example, File Explorer is also affected by this setting.
- *Show Recommendations for Tips, Shortcuts, New Apps, and More:* When enabled, Windows 11 will annoy you with additional messages and ads for new apps that Microsoft recommends installing. My advice is to set this off.
- *Show Account-Related Notifications:* When enabled, you see additional messages in the Start menu with recommendations about backing up your data to OneDrive, messages related to your Microsoft 365 subscription, and more. Again, I recommend setting this off.

5. **When you're done, close Settings.**

   There's no Save button to press. The next time you open the Start menu, the *Recommended* section will display only the items you enabled.

Moving the Start menu and taskbar to the left

In Windows 11, the taskbar and the Start menu are centered. This is different from Windows 10 and older versions of Windows, and you may want a more familiar setup, with everything aligned to the left side of the screen. Here is how to change the position of the taskbar and Start menu:

1. **Open the Start menu and click or tap Settings.**
2. **In the Settings app, click or tap Personalization and then Taskbar.**

   The taskbar personalization options shown in Figure 2-8 appear.
3. **Scroll down to Taskbar Behaviors and click or tap this section.**

   The section extends, as shown in Figure 2-9.
4. **Click or tap Taskbar Alignment and choose Left.**

   Both the taskbar and the Start menu are now aligned to the left side of the screen. To return to the new layout, choose Center.

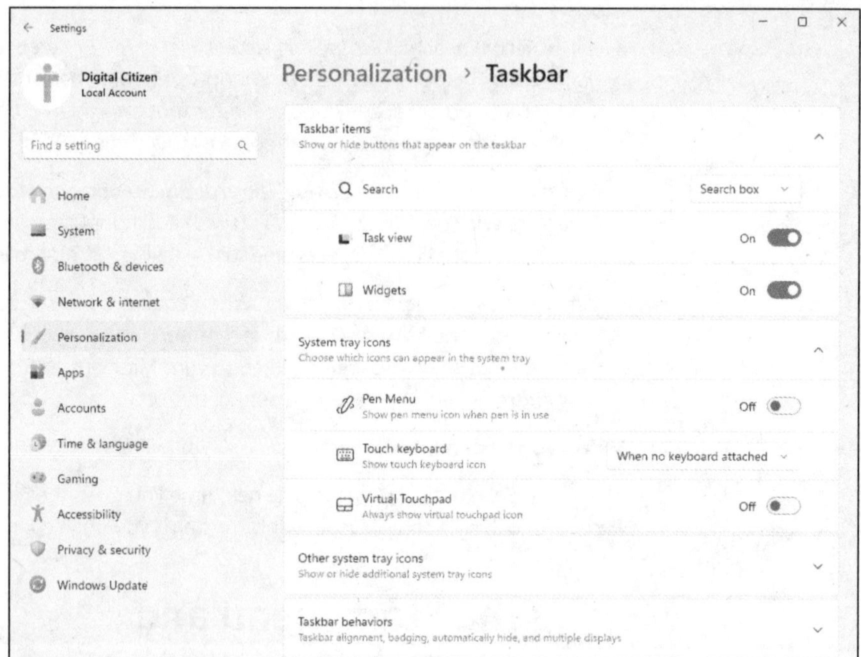

FIGURE 2-8: Here is where you personalize the taskbar.

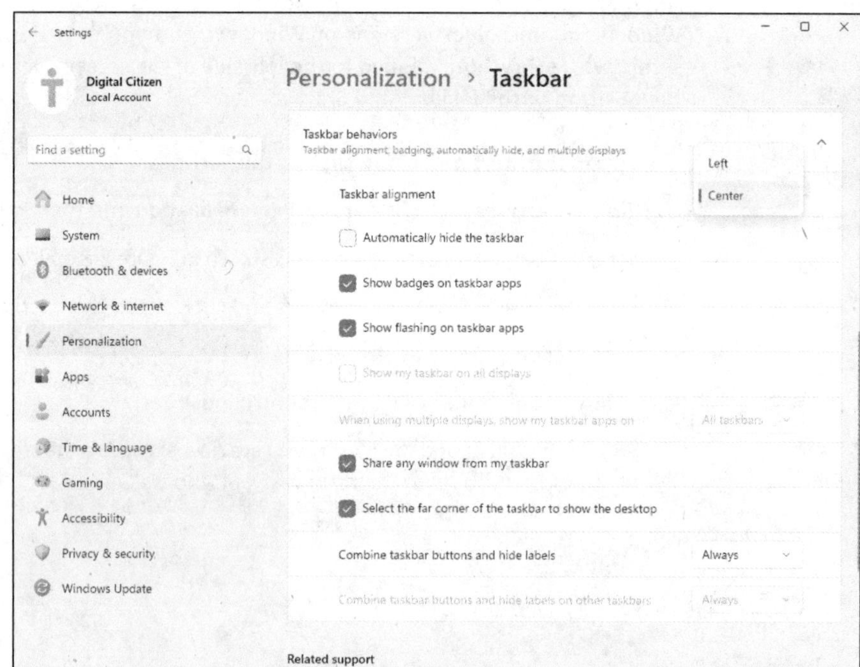

FIGURE 2-9: Choosing the alignment for the taskbar and the Start menu.

IN THIS CHAPTER

» Using Search in Windows 11

» Starting apps using Search

» Improving your search results

» Using the taskbar

» Customizing the taskbar in unexpected but useful ways

Chapter 3
Exploring Search and the Taskbar

Are you tired of playing hide-and-seek with the files and apps on your Windows computer? We've all been there. After a while, even the neatest among us can struggle to find that one document or app that isn't on the desktop or the taskbar. Enter the hero of our story: Search! This nifty feature can help you launch apps in a flash and locate files with ease. It's not perfect, but it sure is handy, and I use it all the time. Windows Search doesn't cover everything on your computer, but don't worry: I show you how to tweak that in this chapter.

Now, let's talk about the taskbar — your trusty sidekick that's always there, ready to help you access the Start menu and your favorite apps. Windows 11 has given the taskbar a makeover, and although not all the changes are for the better, I have the lowdown on how to make the most of it. In this chapter, you learn the basics of using the taskbar, discover some cool tips and tricks to boost your productivity, and find out how to pin the apps you love and ditch the icons you don't love. Plus, I show you how to personalize the taskbar to suit your style and needs. Ready to dive in?

Searching in Windows 11

The Search feature in Windows has evolved a lot over the years, and the newest version in Windows 11 is faster than its predecessors. However, it may also display content from Bing and `MSN.com`, which Microsoft is trying to promote, as well as ads for games alongside news from the web and other types of content.

In Windows 11, Search can help you find apps, settings, documents, photos, emails, files, folders, and web results from several locations: your computer, the Bing search engine, OneDrive, SharePoint, Outlook, and so on. To open Search in Windows 11, click or tap inside its box on the taskbar, next to the Windows logo, or press Windows+S. You see the Windows Search window, as shown in Figure 3-1.

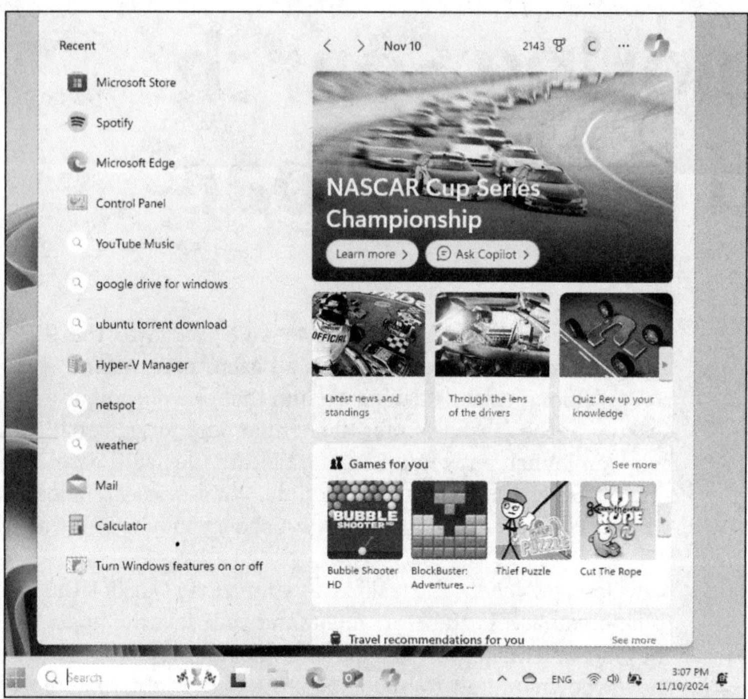

FIGURE 3-1: Windows Search helps you find what you need.

Since Windows 11 was first released, the Search window has been redesigned by Microsoft many times. It's a lot different today than it was when this operating system was first available. In its initial version, the Search window included useful filters and links to the kinds of content you may have wanted to find on your computer. Unfortunately, at the time of writing, the Search window includes only suggested content based on your previous searches and content from the web with information about the day's events, advertisements, travel recommendations, trending searches from Microsoft's web properties, trending news from the web, videos, and news from the web. This approach feels spammy and less useful than it used to be.

Now that I've complained about how this feature evolved, here are the basics of how Search works in Windows 11:

1. **Click or tap in the Search box on the taskbar.**

   Windows 11 displays the Search page (refer to Figure 3-1).

2. **Type** terminal **or another keyword for something you want to find on your computer or device.**

   The search results shown in Figure 3-2 appear. Note how the search results are split into several categories. First, you see Best Match (the result that Windows 11 assumes is what you want), then Apps, Settings, Search the Web results, and so on.

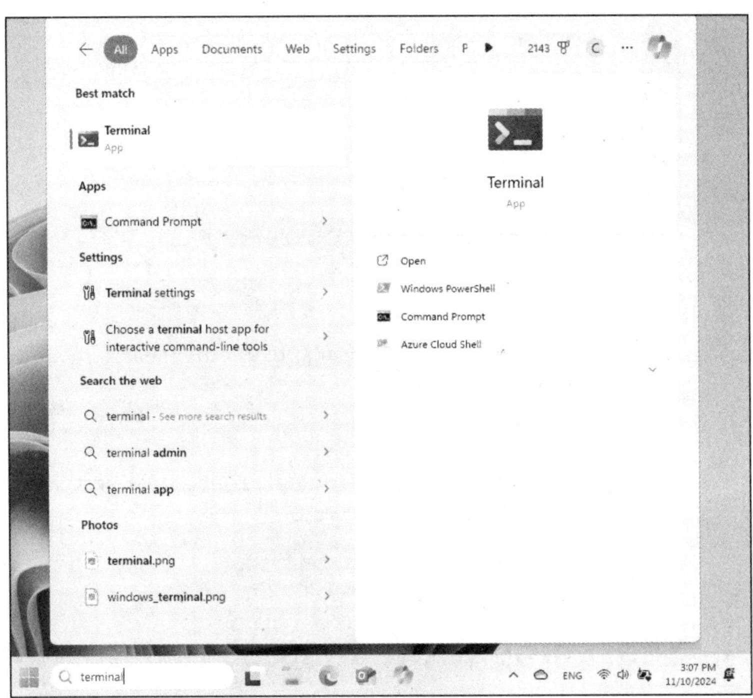

FIGURE 3-2: Search results are presented in various categories.

3. **Look at the panel to the right of the Best Match result, and note the contextual options displayed. Click or tap the downward-pointing arrow to expand the list.**

   The list includes even more options for what you can do with the Best Match result, as shown in Figure 3-3.

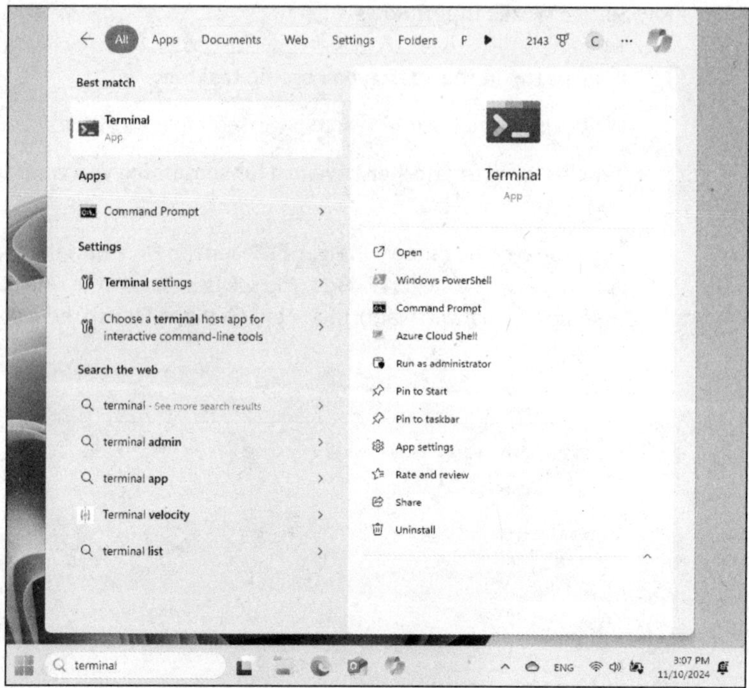

FIGURE 3-3: Note how many things you can do with a search result.

4. **Click or tap the right arrow next to another search result to see more information about it.**

   You see the contextual options for that result.

5. **Click or tap the Windows Terminal result (under Best Match) or the search result that interests you.**

   Search opens the result you've selected.

Searching is the fastest way to start apps

If you pin apps to the Windows 11 taskbar, you can start them quickly with a simple click or tap on their icon. However, pinning too many items on the taskbar makes it annoying to use. Luckily, you can use Windows Search to start any app you want in seconds. Here's how it works:

1. **Press the Windows key on your computer's keyboard.**

   The Start menu opens. This step may seem odd, but it will make sense in a moment.

2. **Type the name of the app you want to open. To follow along with the example, type** edge**.**

   Windows Search displays Microsoft Edge as the Best Match, as shown in Figure 3-4. As you see, you don't have to type the full name of an app for Search to find it.

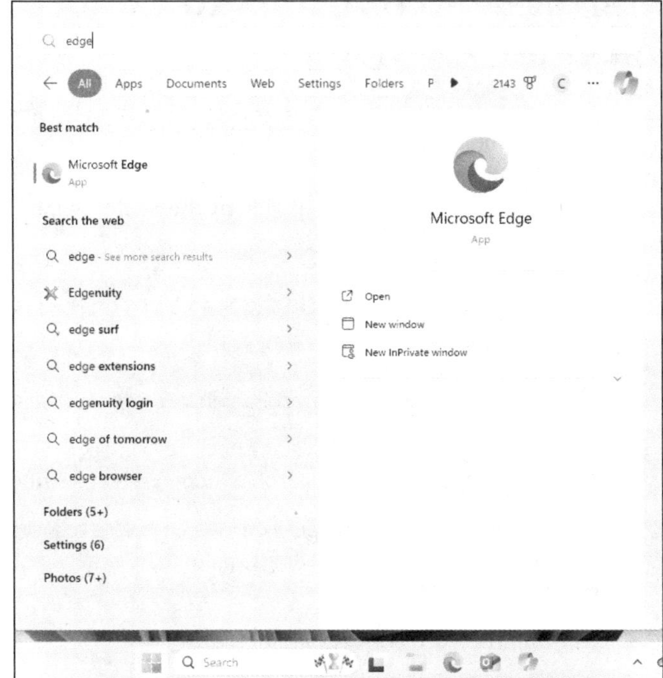

FIGURE 3-4: After you press the Windows key, you can start searching for stuff in Windows 11.

3. **Press Enter on your keyboard, and Microsoft Edge opens immediately.**

   Repeat these steps with other keywords for apps you want to start. This will train Windows Search to remember your searches and always provide the appropriate Best Match.

TIP

Note how both the Start menu and the Windows 11 Search window have a Search box. The Start menu has it at the top, while Windows Search has it at the bottom. You can use this box to start searches from both places. Also, as you've seen, after opening the Start menu or the Search window, you can also start a search by typing a keyword.

REMEMBER

When you type a search term, don't skip the first letter or letters. In my previous example, I typed *edge* and got Microsoft Edge as the best match. If I had typed *dge* instead of *edge*, Search would not have returned Microsoft Edge. Similarly, if I type *Microsoft*, I get search results with all the apps whose names start with this keyword: Microsoft Edge, Microsoft Teams, Microsoft Store, and so on. However, if I type *oso* instead, I get none of these results.

Filtering search results to find what you need

You can do many things with search results in Windows 11, some more useful than others. For example, you might be looking for a setting that's buried inside the Windows 11 Settings app. To find what you want more quickly, you can use the filters listed automatically at the top side of the Search window after you type a keyword. Here's how it works:

1. **Press the Windows key or click in the Search box on the taskbar.**
2. **Type the word** mouse.

   Windows Search displays search results split by categories: Best Match, Settings, Search the Web, and so on.

3. **In the filters at the top of the Search window, select Settings.**

   Note how Windows Search changes your search results to include all mouse-related settings, both from the Settings app and Control Panel, as shown in Figure 3-5.

4. **Click or tap the search result that interests you.**

   The mouse setting you selected is shown on the screen.

REMEMBER

Using the filters in Windows Search helps you fine-tune the results you get so that it's easier to find what you want: apps, documents, web results, settings, folders, and photos. Don't hesitate to try them out.

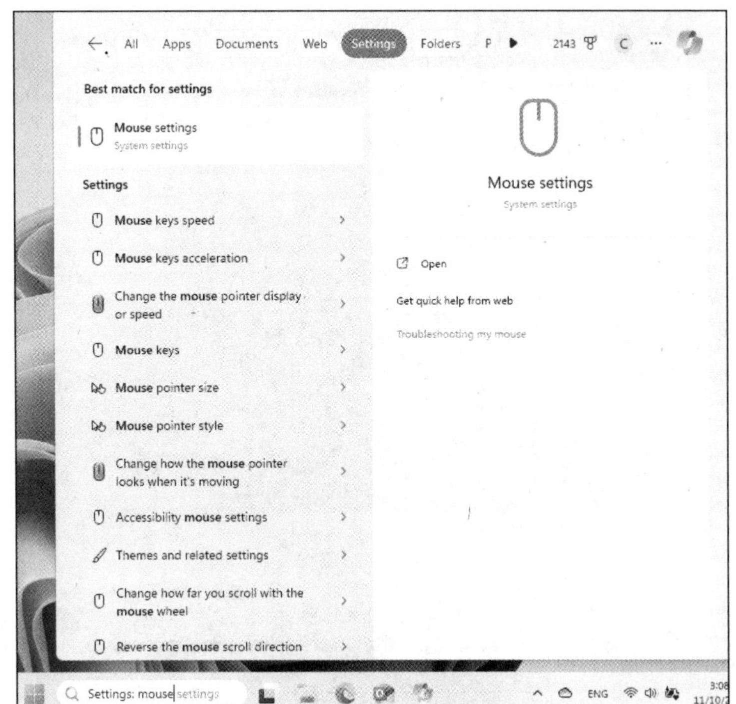

FIGURE 3-5: Don't be afraid to use filters when you search for something.

TIP

You can also search for files with a particular file extension by typing it into the Search box like this: *.*ext*, substituting *ext* with the file extension. For example, you can search for *.docx to return all documents with this file extension or *.png to return all images with this extension. The asterisk (*) is a wildcard in Windows file searches and represents any number of characters before the text that follows it.

Starting apps as admin from a Windows search

By default, apps run in Windows 11 with standard permissions, meaning that they can't change operating system files and settings. Few people know that you can start apps with administrative permissions from Windows Search, not just the Start menu. This allows apps to make all the changes they want. Let's assume that you want to start PowerShell as an administrator. Here's what you must do:

1. **Press the Windows key or click in the Search box on the taskbar.**
2. **Type the word** powershell.

   Windows Search displays search results split by categories: Best Match, Apps, Settings, and Search the Web, as shown in Figure 3-6.

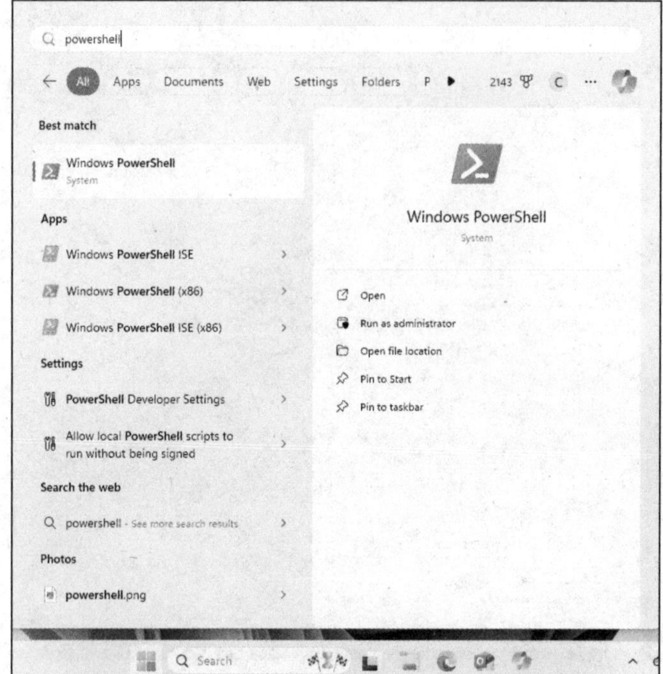

FIGURE 3-6: For each search result, you have several contextual actions to its right.

3. **To the right of the Windows PowerShell search result, click or tap Run as Administrator.**

   Windows 11 asks if you want to allow this app to make changes to your device. These changes can be anything, from modifying system files to changing Windows settings.

4. **Click or tap Yes.**

   Windows PowerShell opens with administrator permissions.

TECHNICAL STUFF

This procedure works for starting any desktop program with administrator permissions. You can't do this for Windows 11 apps designed for tablets and touchscreens, which can run only with standard permissions.

Setting Search to index your entire PC

When it comes to searching for files and folders on your Windows 11 computer or device, Search looks in only a few places, such as your user folders, the desktop, apps, and the Start menu. If you have a computer with several partitions, it doesn't look on your other drives. However, you can set it to do that:

1. **Click or tap in the Search box on the taskbar.**
2. **In the Search window, click or tap the three dots in the top-right corner.**

   The menu shown in Figure 3-7 appears.

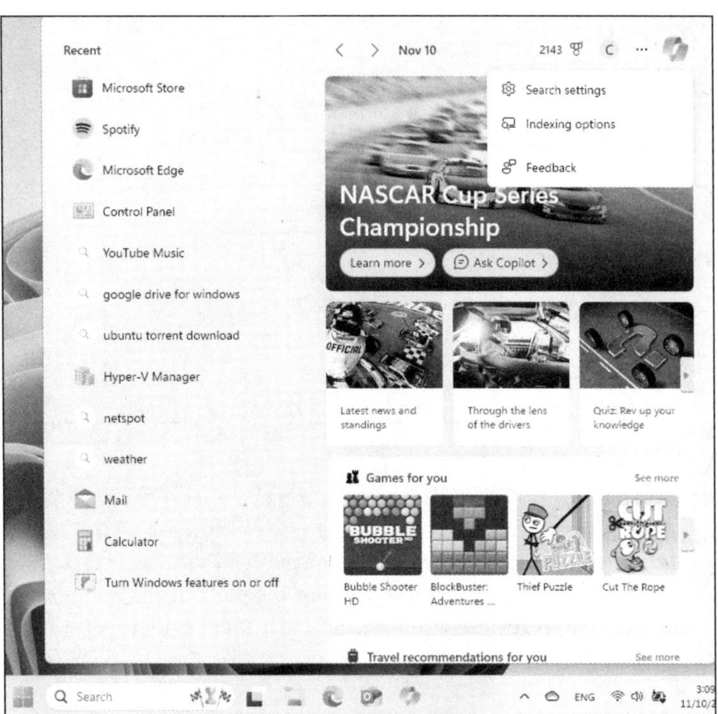

FIGURE 3-7: Accessing indexing options.

3. **Choose Indexing Options.**

   The Searching Windows page appears, as shown in Figure 3-8. At the top is Indexing Status, with how many files were indexed by Windows Search and how many are still pending.

4. **Under Find My Files, select Enhanced instead of Classic.**

   Windows Search will now index all the files on your PC from all partitions to provide you complete search results. See the progress of the indexing process in the Indexing Status section at the top of the window.

5. **Close Settings.**

   Indexing may take several hours, so don't expect to see any meaningful changes in your search results minutes after you've enabled this setting.

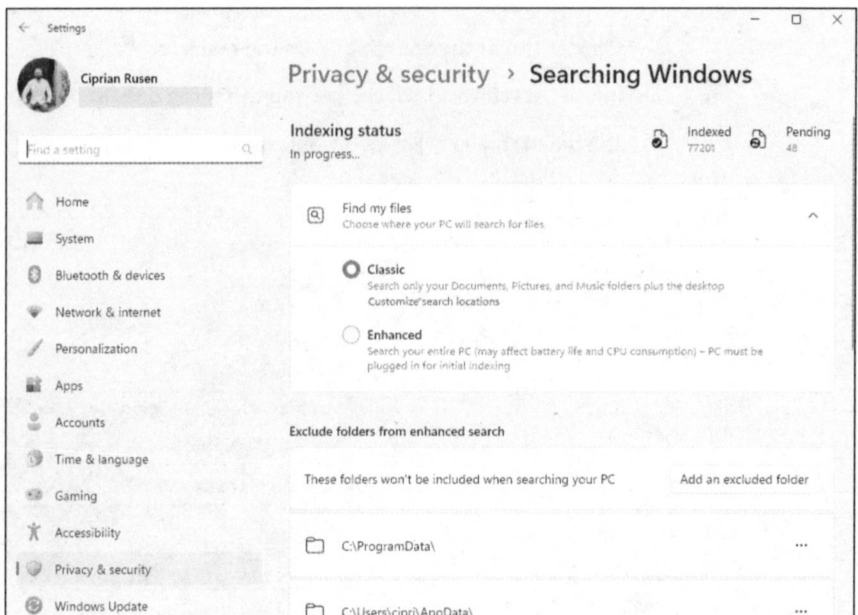

FIGURE 3-8: Changing how Windows Search works.

TECHNICAL STUFF

If you turn on this setting on a laptop or tablet, enhanced indexing is started only after you plug in your device to a power outlet. The initial indexing affects battery life and requires more CPU resources than the classic indexing. However, at the end of this lengthy process, you'll benefit from Windows being able to return useful search results from all the partitions, folders, and files on your computer or device.

TIP

If you look carefully at the options in Figure 3-8, you'll notice the section named Exclude Folders from Enhanced Search, which already contains some folders such as the Windows folder. You can remove any of those folders by clicking or tapping the three dots next to their location and choosing Remove. You can also add folders to be excluded by clicking Add an Excluded Folder and choosing the folder you don't want to be included in the Search index.

Configuring how Search works

Like it or not, Windows Search now displays many results from the web, which are powered by Microsoft's Bing search engine. And, like all search engines, depending on what you look for, it might return results that are not appropriate for children.

Another thing that Search does in Windows 11 is return results from the apps and services where you are signed in with your user account (Microsoft, work, or school account). If you don't want that, you can turn this option off.

Here's how to configure Windows Search so that it no longer returns search results you don't want:

1. **Click or tap in the Search box on the taskbar.**
2. **In the Search window, click or tap the three dots in the top-right corner.**

   The menu shown in Figure 3-7 appears.
3. **Choose Search Settings.**

   The Search Permissions page appears, as shown in Figure 3-9.

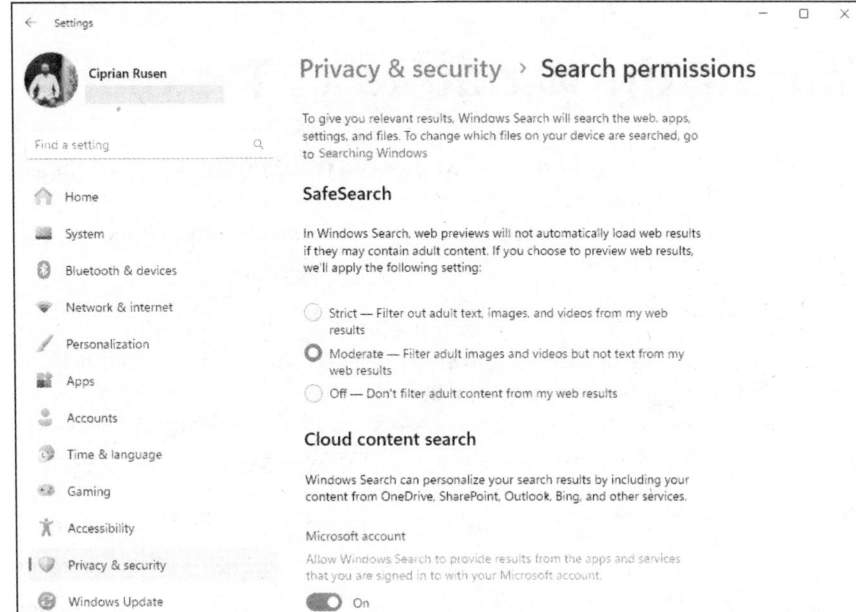

FIGURE 3-9: Setting your Search permissions is a good idea.

4. **In the SafeSearch section, choose whether you want Search to filter out adult content.**

   If your computer is going to be used by children, not just adults, it's a great idea to select Strict instead of Moderate.
5. **In the Cloud Content Search section, choose whether you want Windows Search to provide results from the apps and services where you're signed in with your Microsoft account or Work or School account by setting the switches on or off.**

   When disabling this option, you'll get fewer search results from your apps and more from your files, folders, and settings.

6. **Scroll down to the History section and choose whether you want your search history to be stored locally on your device.**

   Setting the Search History on This Device switch off stops Windows 11 from storing your search history.

TIP

If you want Windows to forget your search history and no longer suggest searches based on your previous searches, in Step 6, set the Search History on This Device switch off, and click or tap the Clear Device Search History button.

TIP

You can get to the Search Permissions page (refer to Figure 3-9) also by opening Settings and going to Privacy & Security ➪ Search Permissions.

Touring the Windows 11 Taskbar

Microsoft developers working on the old Windows 7 taskbar gave it a secret internal project name: the superbar. Although one might debate how much of the *super* in the taskbar is real, there's no doubt that the Windows 11 taskbar is a key tool for all users.

The Windows 11 taskbar is placed on the bottom of the screen, with several icons in the middle, as shown in Figure 3-10. One key difference is that it is no longer aligned to the left, like the one in Windows 10 and Windows 7. Microsoft has copied another page from Apple's workbook, and both the Windows 11 taskbar and the Start menu are centered. If you want the taskbar and the Start menu positioned to the left, read Chapter 2 in this minibook.

FIGURE 3-10: The taskbar helps you use Windows 11 productively.

If you hover your mouse cursor over an icon and the icon is associated with a program that's running, you see a thumbnail of what it's doing. For example, in Figure 3-10, Microsoft Edge is running, and the thumbnail gives you a preview of what's on offer.

WARNING

The Windows 11 taskbar is a lot less flexible than the one in Windows 10. For example, you can no longer change its size and it's stuck on the bottom of the screen, no matter what. You can drag shortcuts or executable files to the taskbar, but you can't drag documents or other types of files to it. Also, the toolbars are gone, so you can't add any. Many people dislike this a lot, but Microsoft hasn't changed its course since Windows 11 was released.

Using the taskbar

The taskbar consists of two kinds of icons:

- **Pinned icons:** Windows 11 ships with eight icons on the taskbar. These are widgets (in the left corner), Start, Search (usually a Search box, not an icon), Task View, Copilot, File Explorer, Microsoft Edge, and Microsoft Store. (Refer to the bottom of Figure 3-10.) When you install a program, you can tell the installer to put an icon for the program on the taskbar. You can also pin apps of your choice on the taskbar.
- **Icons associated with running apps and programs:** Every time a program starts, an icon for it appears on the taskbar. If you run two or more copies of the program, only one icon shows up. When the program is closed or stops running for some reason, the icon disappears.

TIP

The number of pinned icons can vary depending on the manufacturer of your PC, laptop, or tablet. While the eight icons I mentioned are always there because they're chosen by Microsoft for all Windows 11 users, the manufacturer of your device may add other icons for apps that they've preinstalled on your specific device.

To run an app from the taskbar, click or tap its icon. You can tell which icons represent running apps or programs because Windows 11 puts an almost imperceptible line under the icon for any running program. If a running app is minimized, the line below its taskbar icon gets smaller. If you have more than one copy of the program running, you see two transparent squares surrounding the taskbar icon. It's subtle. In Figure 3-10, Microsoft Edge has a line under its taskbar icon.

On the right side of the taskbar, you find other smaller icons in an area called the *system tray.* The icons you see here depend on the device you're using. On a desktop computer, you should see the icons shown in Figure 3-10: a small arrow pointing upwards that, when clicked, reveals a list with other icons for apps running in the background, a OneDrive icon, a network icon, a volume icon, the time and date, and a notifications icon (bell). The list of icons you see on a laptop or tablet will be different and will include icons for Wi-Fi or location services.

When clicked (or tapped), some of the system tray icons open apps such as OneDrive, while others open panels with quick actions or notifications. For more information on handling notifications and quick actions in Windows 11, read Book 2, Chapter 3.

Using jump lists and other taskbar tricks

If you right-click an icon on the taskbar or press and hold it, whether pinned or not, you see a bunch of links called a *jump list*, as shown in Figure 3-11.

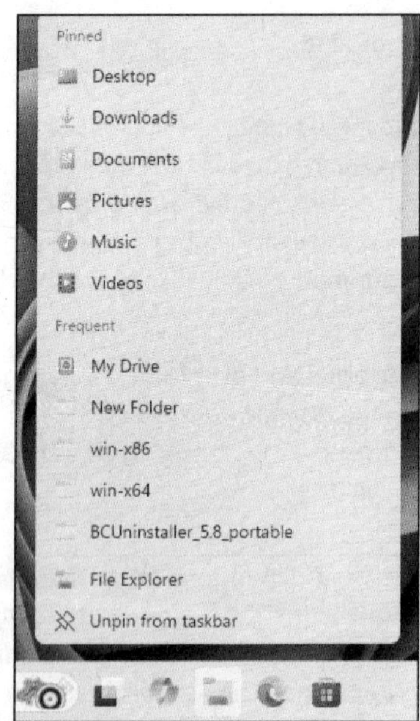

FIGURE 3-11: The jump list for File Explorer.

The contents of the jump list vary depending on the program that's running, but the bottom pane of every jump list contains the name of the program and the entry Unpin from Taskbar (or conversely, Pin to Taskbar, if the program is running but hasn't been pinned).

Jump lists can be particularly useful, especially when using apps like File Explorer or Microsoft Edge. But jump lists aren't implemented by all software developers.

Here are the jump list basics that you should remember:

- **Jump lists may show your frequent folders or files or the file history of recently opened files.** For example, the File Explorer jump list shown in Figure 3-11 displays the same Frequent list that appears inside the app. The Microsoft Edge jump list, which is shown in Figure 3-12, displays recently closed web pages as well as options for opening a new window.

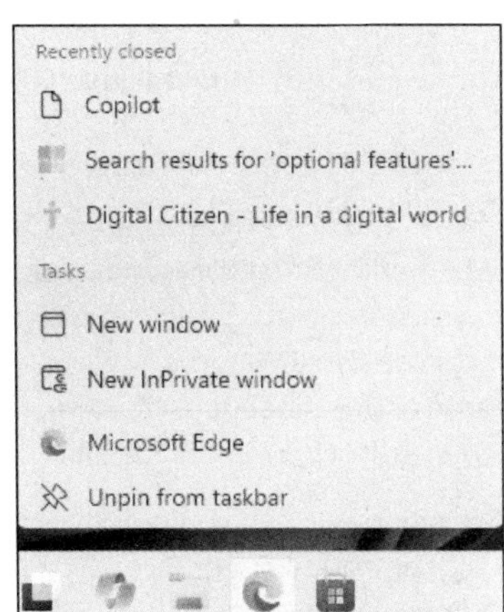

FIGURE 3-12: The jump list for Microsoft Edge lists your recently closed web pages.

- **It's easy to pin an item to the jump list.** When you open the jump list of an app and you pin an item, it sticks to the app's jump list whether or not that item is open. To pin an item, right-click (or press and hold) the app's icon on the taskbar, run your cursor to the right of the item you want to pin, and click or tap the pushpin that appears. The item is now in a separate Pinned pane at the top of the jump list for that app.
- **The jump list has one not-so-obvious use.** It lets you open a second copy of the same app. Suppose you want to copy a handful of documents from the Documents folder to a USB memory stick with the drive letter D:. Start by clicking or tapping the File Explorer icon on the taskbar, and then clicking or tapping Documents in the left pane. You can select your documents, press Ctrl+C to copy, use the list on the left of File Explorer to navigate to D:, and then press Ctrl+V to paste. But if you're going to copy many documents, it's much faster and easier to open a second copy of File Explorer and navigate to D: in that second window. Then you can select and drag your documents from the Documents folder to the D: drive.

TIP

To open a second copy of a running program without using the jump list, you can also

- Hold down the Shift key and click or tap the program's icon on the taskbar.
- Right-click the program's icon (or press and hold the icon) and choose the program's name.

In either case, Windows 11 starts a fresh copy of the program.

TIP

I've also discovered a couple of tricks with the taskbar that you may find worthwhile:

- When you want to shut down all (or most) running programs, you can tell which are running by seeing whether their taskbar icon has an underline (refer to Figure 3-10). To close all instances of a particular program, right-click or press and hold its icon and choose Close Window or Close All Windows. Sometimes, if a program is frozen and won't shut itself down, forcing the matter through the taskbar is the easiest way to dislodge it.
- Windows 11 minimizes all open windows when you move your mouse cursor to the lower-right corner and click or tap it. Click or tap the corner area again, and Windows 11 brings back all minimized windows.

Pinning apps to the taskbar

You can do several things to the taskbar:

- **Pin a program on the taskbar:** Right-click or press and hold a program on the Start menu and choose Pin to Taskbar. You can also right-click the icon of a running program on the taskbar and choose the same option.
- **Move a pinned icon:** Click or press and hold, and then drag the icon to its new position on the taskbar.
- **Drag a shortcut or .exe file to the taskbar:** Click or press and hold, and then drag the shortcut or the file to the taskbar in the position you want. That shortcut or file is pinned to the taskbar alongside all the other programs. Unfortunately, you can't do this with other types of files such as documents, pictures, and spreadsheets.
- **Unpin any pinned program:** Right-click or press and hold the icon and choose Unpin from Taskbar.

Here's how to pin an app to the Windows 11 taskbar:

1. **Click or tap the Start icon and then All.**

   You see a list of all the apps installed on your Windows 11 system.

2. **Scroll down the All apps list until you see the program you want to pin to the taskbar, and right-click or tap and hold it.**

   A contextual menu appears, as shown in Figure 3-13.

3. **In the menu, choose More➪ Pin to Taskbar.**

That's all it takes. The app's icon appears on the taskbar, and you can use it to launch the app quickly as soon as you sign into Windows.

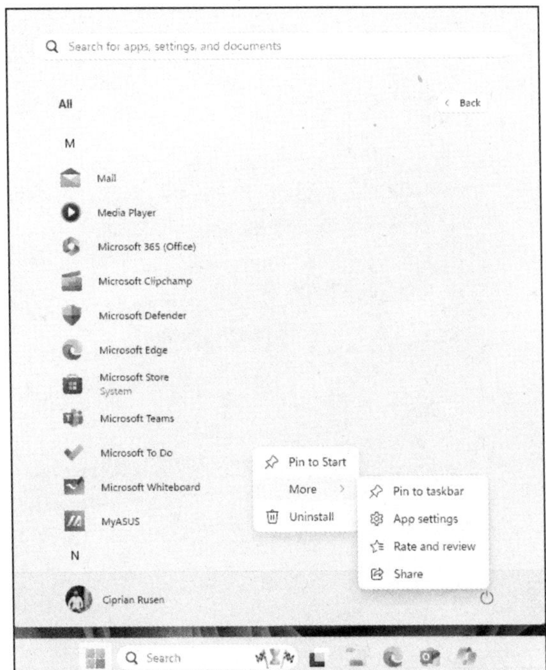

FIGURE 3-13: Pinning apps to the taskbar is a no-brainer.

TIP

While you can't turn individual documents or folders into icons on the taskbar, you can pin a folder to the File Explorer jump list, and you can pin a document to the jump list for whichever application is associated with it. For example, you can pin a Word document to the jump list.

Adding and removing taskbar items

You can show or hide some of the standard icons on the Windows 11 taskbar. And, if you have a tablet or a touchscreen, you might want to add icons for the pen menu, touch keyboard, or virtual touchpad. Here's how to add icons to and remove icons from the taskbar:

1. **Right-click or press and hold somewhere on the empty space on the taskbar and choose Taskbar Settings.**

   You see the settings for personalizing the taskbar, as shown in Figure 3-14.

2. **Under Taskbar Items, turn off the switches of the icons you want to remove from the taskbar.**

   If you don't use the widgets or task view, it's a good idea to disable their icons.

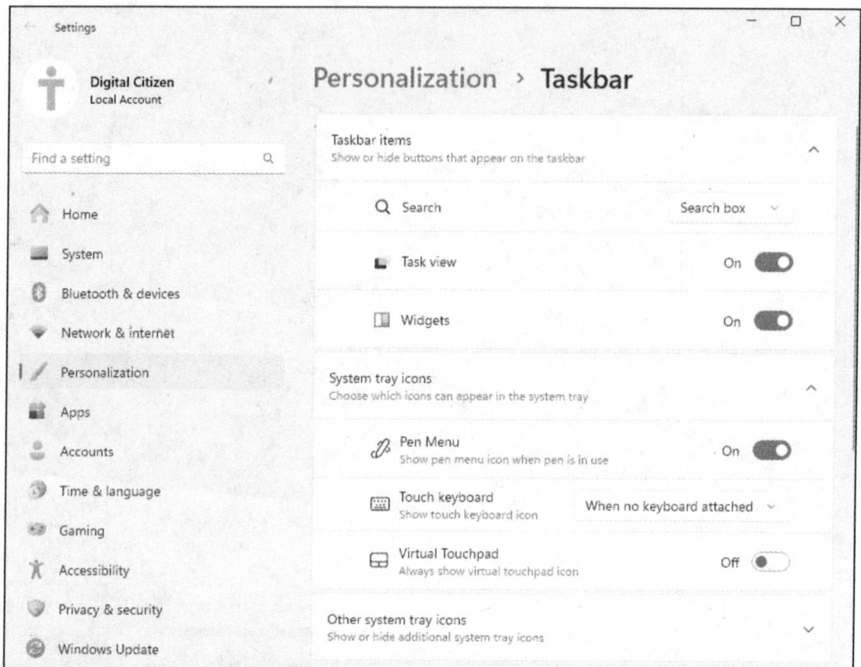

FIGURE 3-14: Displaying or hiding Windows 11 taskbar icons.

3. **If you want to hide the Search box, click or tap the drop-down list next to it, and choose Hide (which removes it) or one of the Search Icon options. If you want to see only a search icon, select Search Icon Only.**
4. **If you have a tablet or laptop with a touchscreen, turn on the icons under System Tray Icons.**

   You can choose Pen Menu (useful only if you have a pen), Touch Keyboard (works well with all touchscreens), and Virtual Touchpad. If turned on, these icons are displayed on the right side of the taskbar.
5. **When you've finished, close Settings by clicking or tapping X in the top-right corner.**

Adding or removing system tray icons

You can further personalize the taskbar by choosing which system tray icons you want to see, like this:

1. **Right-click or press and hold somewhere on the empty space on the taskbar and choose Taskbar Settings.**

   Windows displays the settings for personalizing the taskbar (refer to Figure 3-14).

2. **Scroll down and click or tap on Other System Tray Icons to expand this section.**

   You see the settings for personalizing the system tray, as in Figure 3-15.

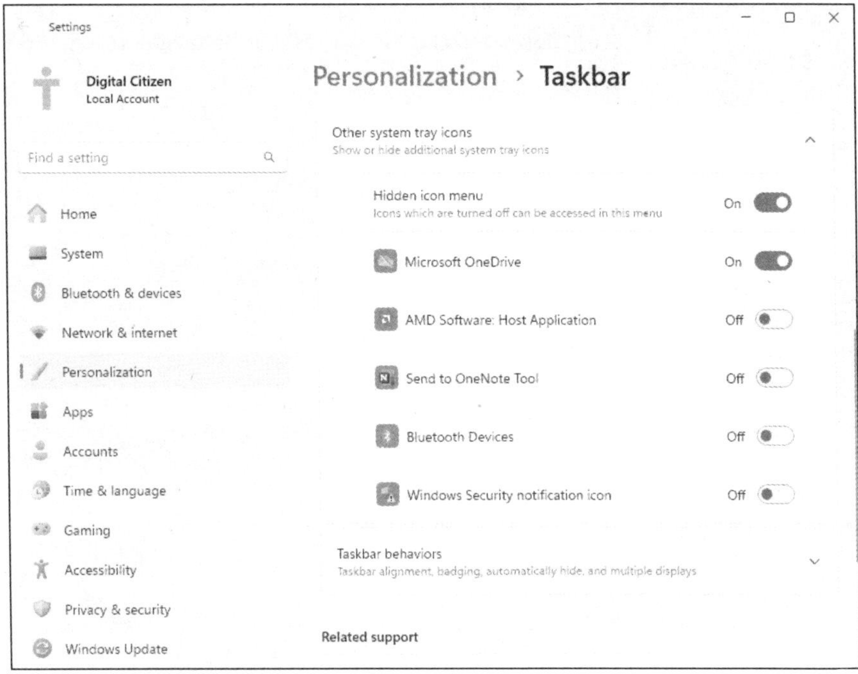

FIGURE 3-15: Displaying or hiding system tray icons.

3. **If you want to remove from the system tray the arrow pointing upwards, which reveals background apps, set the Hidden Icon Menu switch off.**

4. **For all the apps shown in the list, set their switch to on or off, depending on whether you want to see them in the system tray.**

   Your settings are applied instantly.

Personalizing how the taskbar behaves

You can tweak the taskbar in Windows 11 to match your style and needs:

Want the taskbar to disappear when you're not using it? No problem! Do you have multiple displays and want the taskbar on all of them? You got it! Or maybe you're a time fanatic who needs to see the seconds ticking away on the clock? The Windows 11 taskbar has you covered.

No matter how you want to customize your taskbar, here's where you'll find the settings for personalizing its behavior:

1. **Right-click or press and hold somewhere on the empty space on the taskbar and choose Taskbar Settings.**

   You see the settings for personalizing the taskbar (refer to Figure 3-14).

2. **Scroll down and click or tap Taskbar Behaviors to expand this section.**

   You see the settings for personalizing the taskbar's behavior, similar to Figure 3-16.

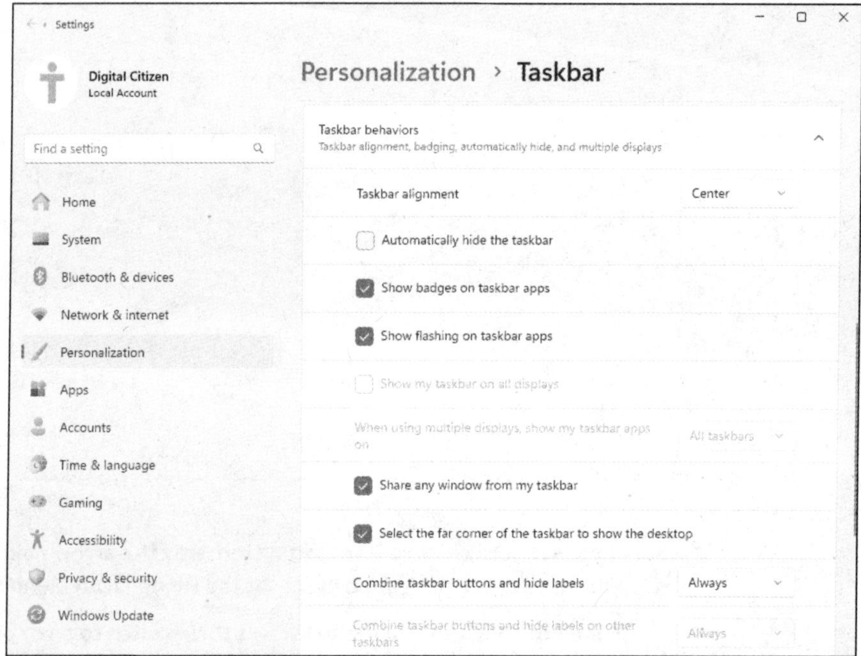

FIGURE 3-16: Personalizing how the taskbar behaves in Windows 11.

3. **If you want to hide the taskbar, select Automatically Hide Taskbar.**

   The taskbar disappears from the bottom of the screen, and you can view it only if you move your mouse cursor over its former position or press the Windows key.

4. **If you want to add the seconds to the taskbar clock, select Show Seconds in System Tray Clock (Uses More Power).**

   Note how the clock in the right corner of the taskbar starts displaying the seconds.

5. **If you have two or more displays and want to see the taskbar on them all, select Show My Taskbar on All Displays.**

   Note how the taskbar is now fully visible and functional on all your displays.

6. **Browse through all the other settings and select or deselect those that interest you.**

   Your changes are applied immediately.

7. **When you've finished, close Settings by clicking or tapping X in the top-right corner.**

IN THIS CHAPTER

» Using File Explorer

» Navigating and searching files and folders

» Personalizing aspects of File Explorer

» Creating and extracting ZIP archives

» Using the new right-click menu

Chapter 4

Working with Files and Folders

File Explorer and the right-click menu have received a major redesign in Windows 11. Compared to Windows 10, they look simpler and are easier to use, at least when it comes to accessing the most common things people do on their computers. File Explorer is also a lot more useful thanks to the inclusion of some new features, including the ability to work with multiple tabs in the same window, just like web browsers do. However, not everything is simpler, and you may feel lost for a time until you get the hang of it.

To help you out, I give you a tour of all the basics you need to know about File Explorer: how to navigate it, view, open, and create files and folders, view your pictures, search for the stuff you need, sort and group files and folders as you like, and personalize the Home section.

I also share some useful tricks on how to make File Explorer always display the extensions of your files, how to add check boxes that are useful for selecting stuff, and how to make File Explorer show hidden files.

Then, I cover the new ways of sharing items in Windows 11, and how to handle file archives in File Explorer. Lastly, I cover the changes introduced by Microsoft to the right-click menu, and how to access the old one when you need to.

Using File Explorer

The File Explorer app from Windows 11 includes many changes. The ribbon is gone, in favor of a minimalist user interface, with icons for the most common actions shown on the top. There's also a new Home section, shown by default each time you start File Explorer, which includes Quick Access shortcuts, your favorite files, and your recent ones, as shown in Figure 4-1. You can also work with multiple tabs and multiple File Explorer windows open and move tabs around, both in the same window and from one window to another.

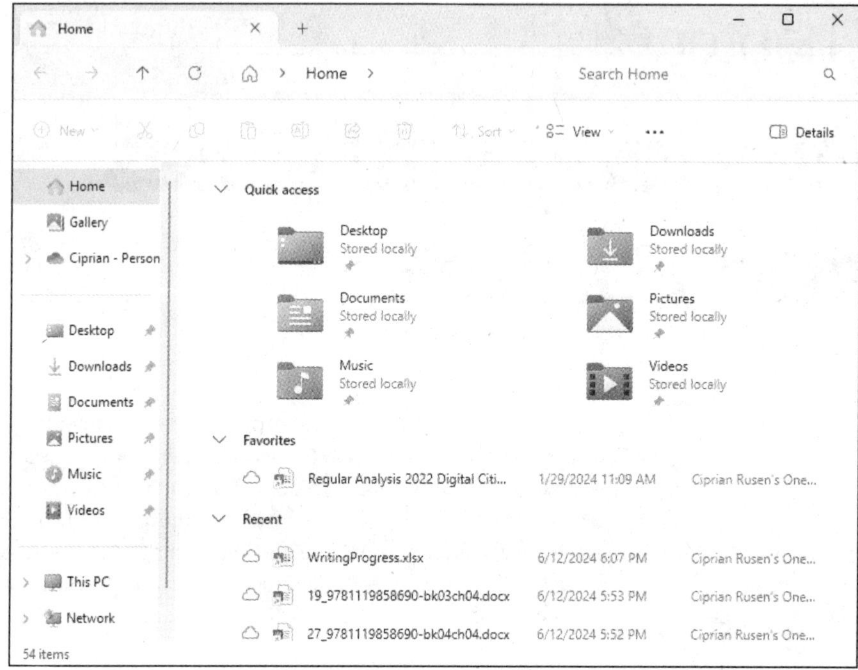

FIGURE 4-1: The File Explorer user interface changed in Windows 11.

I prefer the new File Explorer to the old, and I think most people will like it too. However, there's a learning curve to get used to the latest version, so this section takes you through most of the significant changes to help you make sense of things.

Navigating File Explorer

First, you should know how to start and navigate the File Explorer app in Windows 11. Here's a quick tour:

1. **Click or tap the File Explorer icon on the taskbar or open the Start menu and choose File Explorer.**

   The File Explorer app window appears (refer to Figure 4-1). The app starts by displaying its Quick Access section, which includes shortcuts to useful places like the desktop, the Downloads folder, and your recent files.

2. **On the left, in the sidebar with shortcuts to places you can navigate on your computer, click or tap This PC.**

   You see your user folders (Desktop, Documents, Downloads, Music, Pictures, and Videos), your devices, and drives.

3. **In the Devices and Drives section, double-click or double-tap the C: drive.**

   The files and folders on your C: drive are displayed.

4. **To go back to the previous location, click or tap the back arrow in the top-left corner of File Explorer.**

5. **To see the contents of the C: drive again, as in Step 3, click or tap the forward arrow (next to the back arrow).**

   Note how the address bar next to the back and forward arrows changes to display the current path, as shown in Figure 4-2. You can use the address bar in File Explorer to jump to a specific location.

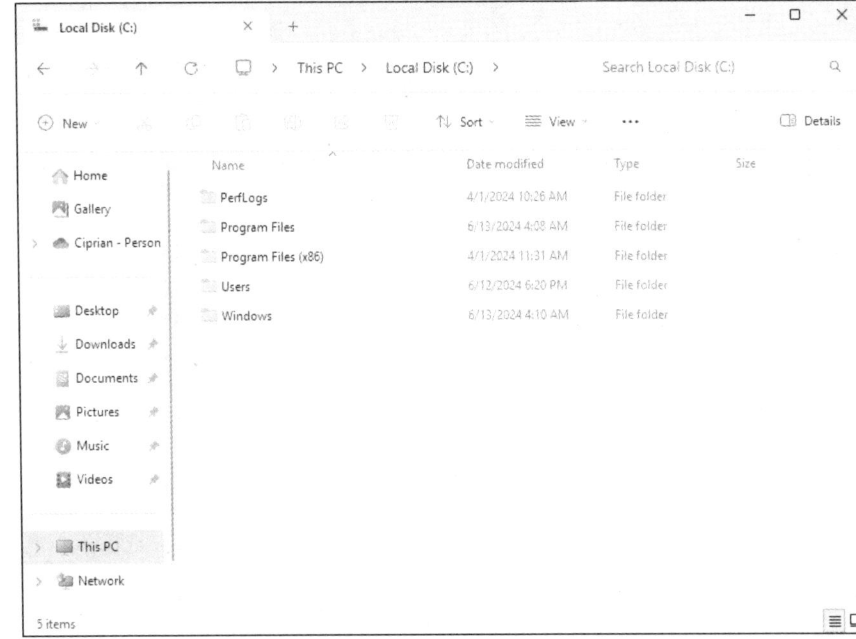

FIGURE 4-2: Use the address bar and the arrows at the top to quickly jump between folders and locations.

6. **To see how the address bar works, click or tap This PC in the address bar, not in the column on the left.**

   You can do this with any folder or location displayed in File Explorer's address bar. This is a quick way to navigate your computer.

7. **To create a new tab, click or tap + on the top, next to the current tab, which is displaying the current location.**

   A new tab opens in the Home section.

8. **To close File Explorer, click or tap the X in the top-right corner.**

   You return to the desktop.

TIP

You can use the address bar in File Explorer to run commands quickly. For example, navigate to a folder you want, click or tap inside the address bar, type **cmd**, and press Enter on your keyboard. This action opens a Command Prompt tab inside Windows Terminal, using the current folder from File Explorer. This way, you save some time changing the current folder in Command Prompt using the **cd** (change directory) command.

TIP

You can create multiple tabs by clicking or tapping + at the top. You can change their order by dragging and dropping them to the desired position. You can also drag a tab outside the current File Explorer window and create a new window, just like you do in a web browser such as Microsoft Edge or Google Chrome.

Viewing and opening your files and folders

As you noticed in the preceding section, if you want to open one of the places shown on the left side of the File Explorer app window, you just click or tap its name. However, if you want to open a folder or a file shown on the right, you must double-click or double-tap. The double-click or double-tap applies to everything from folders to drive, and partitions to files.

When you double-click (or double-tap) a file, it opens the file in the app set by Windows to open that file's type. For example, if you double-click a picture, it will open in the Photos app. If you double-click a PDF file, it will open in Microsoft Edge or Adobe Reader, depending on which app is set to open PDF files. Similarly, if you double-click a document, it will open in Microsoft Word, and so on.

By default, when you open a folder such as Downloads on your Windows 11 PC, File Explorer displays the files and subfolders inside, as shown in Figure 4-3. For each file, you see its icon, name, date modified, type, and size. For each subfolder, you see its icon, name, and date modified.

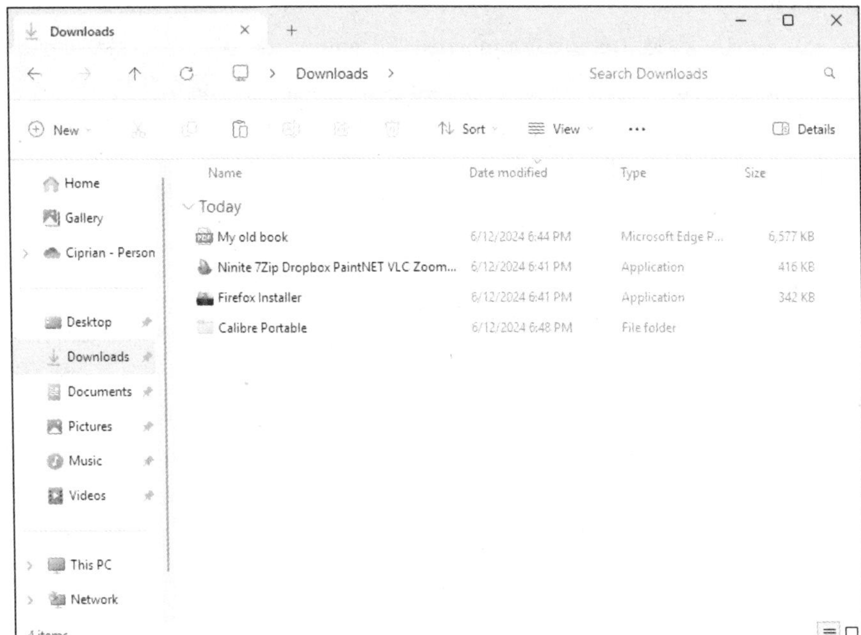

FIGURE 4-3: When you double-click a folder, you see its files and subfolders.

Depending on how the folders are set, they can show you more or less information about the files found inside. File Explorer applies different views to your folders, based on their content. For example, File Explorer applies the details view to your Downloads folder, but the large icons view to your Pictures folder. The menu in Figure 4-4 lists the views available in File Explorer:

- **Extra Large Icons:** Offers the best previews of graphic and video files, and I recommend this view for pictures, media files, and PowerPoint presentations.
- **Large Icons:** Useful when you want to see your photos without opening them. While its thumbnails are not as big as the ones you get with the extra-large icons view, they're larger compared to the other views. They're helpful because you can see more of them at once.
- **Medium Icons:** Displays thumbnails large enough to give you an idea about the content of media items but not big enough to distinguish among several similar graphics files. You're better off using the two previous views.
- **Small Icons:** Displays items in columns with a tiny thumbnail. The icons next to your files differ based on their type, and the only other information you get is the filename.
- **List:** Displays just the filenames and the icon associated with each file. Your files and folders are displayed as small icons, which makes this view nearly indistinguishable from the small icons view.

» **Details:** Provides detailed information about your files and folders, split by columns: Name, Date, Type, Size, Tags, and so on.

» **Tiles:** Displays medium-sized icons for your files and folders, as well as basic details. Use it to display thumbnails and information about the type and size of your files. While not as detailed as the content and details views, the tiles layout is a useful mix between the medium icons and content views.

» **Content:** Lists files and folders in separate rows. For each item, you see details such as the filename, size, date modified or date taken (shown for pictures). This layout is a mix between the tiles and details views, although its thumbnails are slightly smaller than those used by the tiles view.

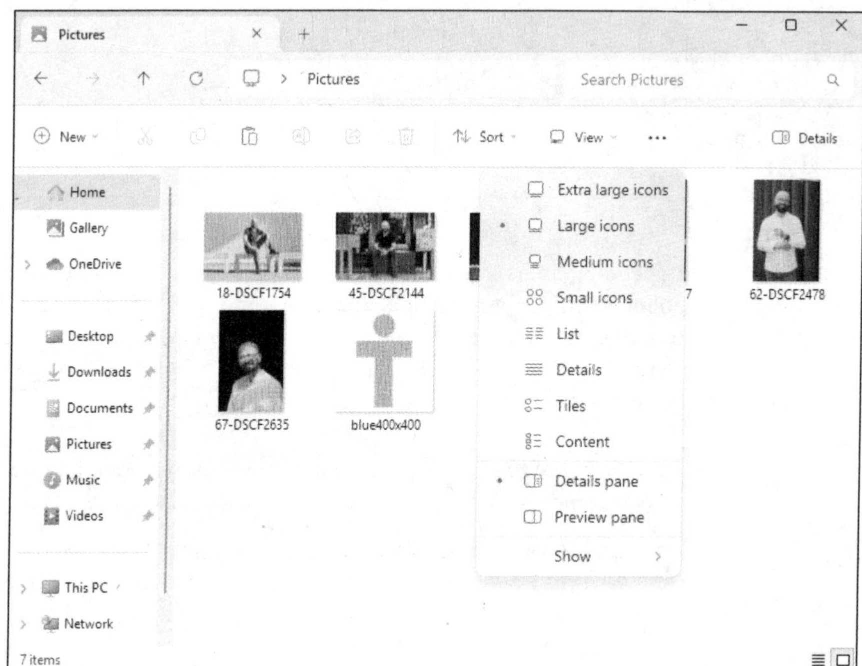

FIGURE 4-4: The different ways in which you can view your files in File Explorer.

Here's how to switch between the views available in File Explorer:

1. **Click or tap the File Explorer icon on the taskbar, or press Windows+E.**
2. **Click or tap your Pictures folder on the left.**

   You see all the subfolders and pictures in your Pictures folder.

3. **At the top of the screen, click or tap View.**

A menu appears with all available File Explorer views (refer to Figure 4-4). For your Pictures folder, the default view is large icons.

4. **On the View menu, select Extra Large Icons.**

   Note the change in the way your pictures are displayed. This view is useful for previewing the contents of multimedia files such as pictures and videos.

5. **Click or tap View and select List.**

   See how the list view differs from the extra-large icons view, displaying only the icon and name of each file and folder.

6. **Click or tap View and select Content.**

   Note how this view is different from the previous ones.

7. **Click or tap View and select Large Icons.**

   You return to the initial view of the contents of your Pictures folder.

TIP

You can switch between the different views using keyboard shortcuts too. See the following table for details:

Ctrl+Shift+1	Extra-large icons
Ctrl+Shift+2	Large icons
Ctrl+Shift+3	Medium icons
Ctrl+Shift+4	Small icons
Ctrl+Shift+5	List
Ctrl+Shift+6	Details
Ctrl+Shift+7	Tiles
Ctrl+Shift+8	Content

Creating and managing files and folders

The toolbar at the top of File Explorer makes it easy to work with files and folders in Windows 11. The New button opens a menu for creating new folders, shortcuts, and files, as shown in Figure 4-5. Keep in mind that the options you see depend on your location in File Explorer and the apps you've installed. Some apps may add entries to this menu.

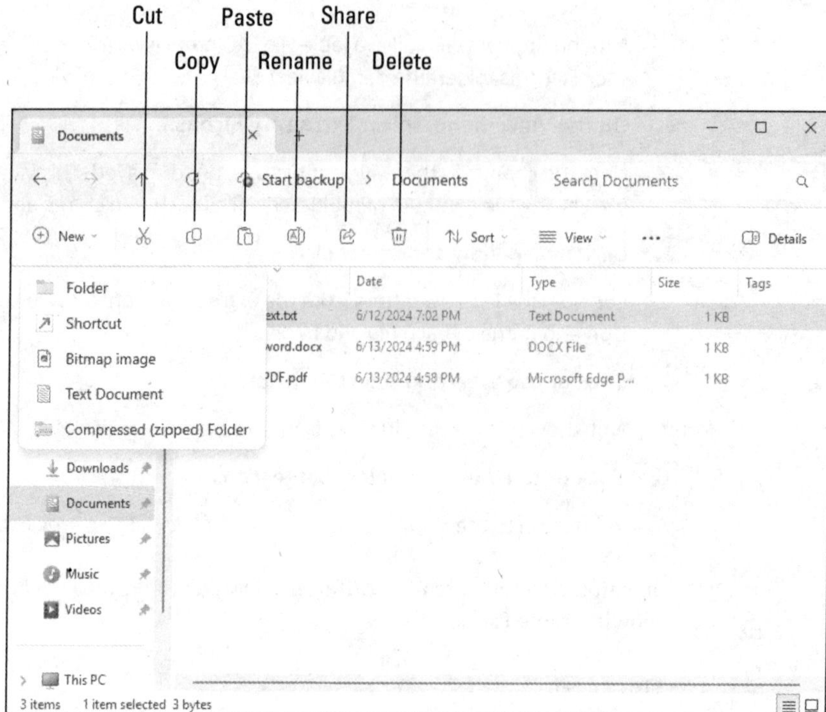

FIGURE 4-5: Use the New menu to create folders, shortcuts, and files.

To the right of the New button, you have icons for cut, copy, paste, rename, share, and delete (labeled in Figure 4-5). If you don't select anything, these icons aren't active and appear dimmed. If you select a file or folder with a click or tap on its name, these icons become usable. Here's how to use them:

1. **Start File Explorer and then click or tap your Pictures folder.**
2. **In the top-left corner of File Explorer, click or tap New.**

   You see the New menu (refer to Figure 4-5).
3. **In the menu, choose Folder.**

   A new folder is created, waiting for you to edit its name, as shown in Figure 4-6.
4. **Type the name you want for the new folder and press Enter.**
5. **With that folder still selected, click or tap the rename icon.**

   The rename icon is the fourth icon after the New button. The folder's name becomes editable again, and you can type a new name.
6. **Type a new name and press Enter.**

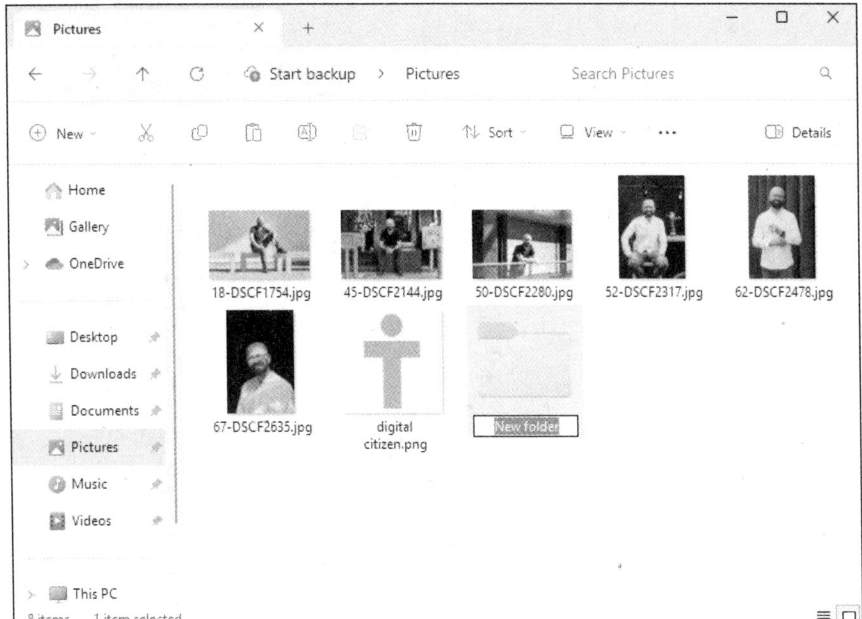

FIGURE 4-6: Renaming folders and files is easy.

7. **With that folder still selected, click or tap the delete icon.**

   The folder is deleted immediately, without any confirmation. You can find it in the Recycle Bin, on your desktop.

REMEMBER

You can always undo your previous action (delete, cut, paste, rename, and so on) by pressing Ctrl+Z.

TIP

You create files the same way you create folders. The only difference is that in Step 3, choose Bitmap Image or Text Document, depending on the type of file you want to create. If you installed Microsoft Office, some Office apps have been added to this menu, which you can use to create new files. No matter what type of file you select, when it's created, the file is empty, and you can add content to it by opening it, editing it, and then saving it.

Using Gallery

On September 26, 2023, Microsoft introduced a feature in File Explorer named Gallery. Its purpose is to make it easier to view all the pictures in your Pictures folder and its subfolders, sorted by date, in descending order, with the most recent pictures listed first. To view Gallery, simply click it on the top left side of the File Explorer window. Your pictures will be shown in a way that is similar to Figure 4-7.

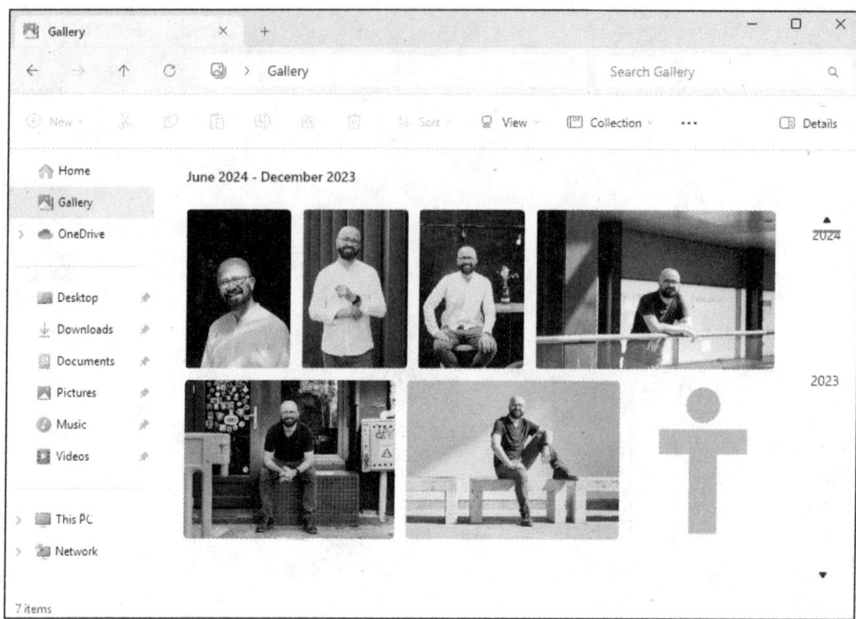

FIGURE 4-7: Check out your Gallery of pictures.

When accessing Gallery, you can't sort your pictures in a different way, nor can you rename them. However, you can copy pictures from Gallery and paste them elsewhere, you can delete them (and they'll get deleted from their original location, too), and you can share them with others.

The only customization you can do in Gallery is adding or removing the folders included in its *collection*, as Microsoft calls it. Here's how to add a folder to your Gallery:

1. **Start File Explorer and then click or tap Gallery on the left.**
2. **On the toolbar, click or tap Collection and choose Manage Collection.**

   You see the Gallery Locations window in Figure 4-8.
3. **To add a folder to Gallery, click or tap Add, navigate to and select the folder you want, and click or tap Include Folder.**

   The folder is added to your Gallery Locations and your Pictures library.
4. **Click or tap OK.**

   Gallery now displays the pictures from the selected folder alongside those in the Pictures folder.
5. **To see only the pictures from the folder you just added, click or tap Collection and select the folder from the list.**
6. **To see all pictures, click or tap Collection and choose Show All.**

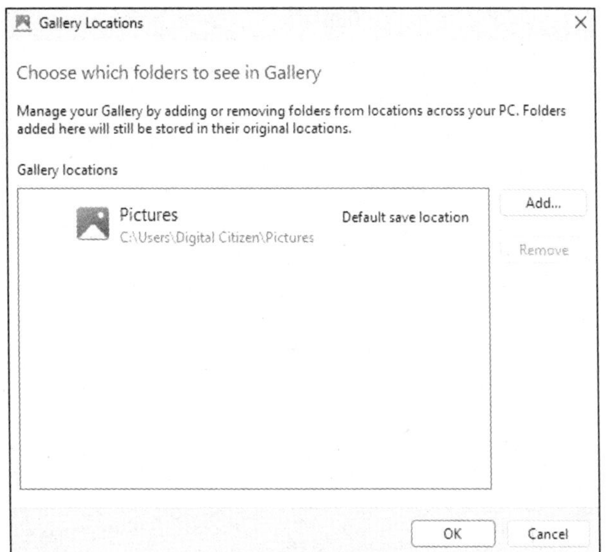

Gallery Locations
Choose which folders to see in Gallery
Manage your Gallery by adding or removing folders from locations across your PC. Folders added here will still be stored in their original locations.
Gallery locations
Pictures
C:\Users\Digital Citizen\Pictures
Default save location
Add...
Remove
OK
Cancel

FIGURE 4-8: Adding folders to Gallery is easy.

TIP

If you want to remove a folder from Gallery, follow Steps 1 and 2. In Step 3, select the folder you want removed, and choose Remove, followed by clicking or tapping OK.

Deleting files and folders

When you delete a file, folder, or shortcut from Windows, it goes into the Recycle Bin. This is a special folder that provides protection against the accidental erasure of files. Read Book 3, Chapter 1, to learn more about how it works.

For now, follow these steps to delete files and folders from File Explorer so that they get to the Recycle Bin:

1. **Start File Explorer and then click or tap Downloads on the left.**
2. **On the toolbar, click or tap New and choose Text Document.**

   A new New Text Document file is created on your computer.
3. **Press Enter to create the file using the name proposed by File Explorer.**
4. **With the file still selected, click or tap the Delete icon, which is highlighted in Figure 4-9.**

   The file is deleted and moved to the Recycle Bin without confirmation.
5. **Repeat Steps 2 and 3 to create another file.**
6. **With the file still selected, press the Delete key on your keyboard.**

   Notice how the file is deleted and disappears from File Explorer.

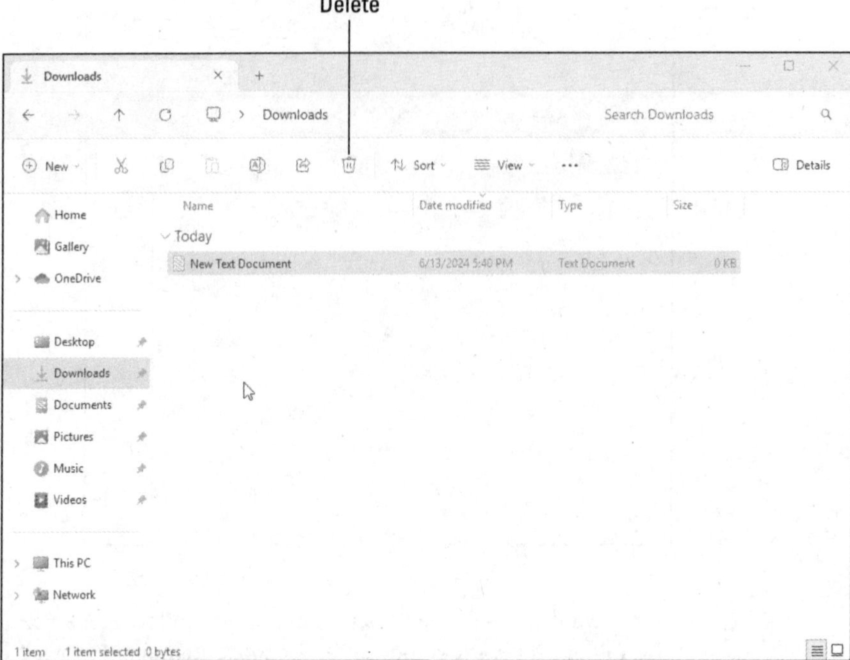

FIGURE 4-9: Deleting files and folders is easy.

TIP

If you are at the desktop and want to delete a file or folder, you don't have a Delete icon available. However, you can right-click (or press and hold) the item and choose Delete in the menu.

TIP

If you want to delete an item and not have it moved to the Recycle Bin, select it and press Shift+Delete. You see a dialog asking you to confirm that it's okay to delete this file permanently. Choose Yes, and you're done.

Searching for files and folders

One of the most useful features of File Explorer is search. If you want to find anything, use the Search box on the top right, like this:

1. **Start File Explorer and then open the partition (drive) or the folder where you want to find stuff.**
2. **In the top-right corner of File Explorer, click or tap in the Search box.**
3. **Type the name or partial name of the file or folder you want to find.**

   After a few seconds, your search results are displayed, as shown in Figure 4-10.

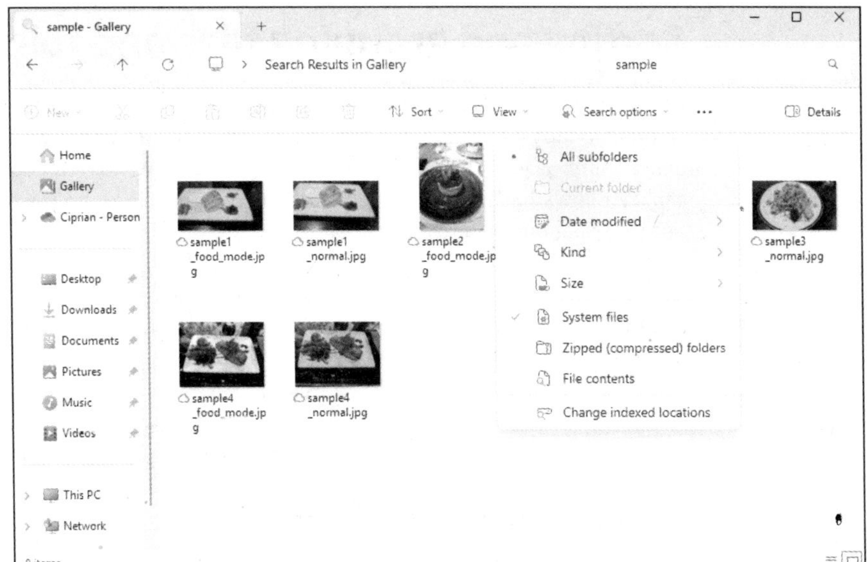

FIGURE 4-10: If you want to find something, don't hesitate to use the Search box.

4. **If you're not satisfied with the results, click or tap Search options on the toolbar and filter the results by characteristics — Date Modified, Kind, Size and so on — using the menu options.**
5. **After you've found what you're looking for, double-click or double-tap the item you want to open.**

WARNING

The text you type as a search term must appear at the beginning of a word. For example, entering *str* returns items containing words such as *strong*, *straw*, and *strip* but does not return items containing words such as *ostrich*, *abstract*, and *backstrokes*.

REMEMBER

The Search box in File Explorer searches only for items in the folder or location you're currently in. This approach narrows the search and returns your results faster. However, it's not helpful when you have no idea about the location of the item you're looking for. For example, if you search for a file in your Documents folder but the file is in your Downloads folder, you won't find it because you searched in the wrong place. If you don't have an idea about the location of a file, simply open the C: drive and make a search starting from there. Be warned that searching your entire C: drive will take much longer than using a specific folder. A better idea is to run your search in the Search box on the taskbar. Read Chapter 3 in this minibook to see how it works.

Sorting and grouping files and folders

By default, File Explorer sorts your files and folders in ascending order by name (alphabetically), except for the items in the Downloads folder, which is sorted in descending order by date modified, with the newest downloads displayed at the top. Windows has approximately 300 sorting criteria to help you organize things, but most people only need the basics.

In addition to sorting files and folders, you can also group them. When using grouping, File Explorer organizes all the items in a folder, breaking them into separate sections based on the criteria you choose (name, size, date, and so on). By default, items are not grouped in any way.

To familiarize yourself with how sorting and grouping work, do the following:

1. **Start File Explorer and then open a folder with lots of files.**

   The Downloads folder might be an excellent choice.

2. **At the top of the screen, click or tap the Sort icon.**

   The menu shown in Figure 4-11 appears. It includes the sorting and grouping options available in File Explorer.

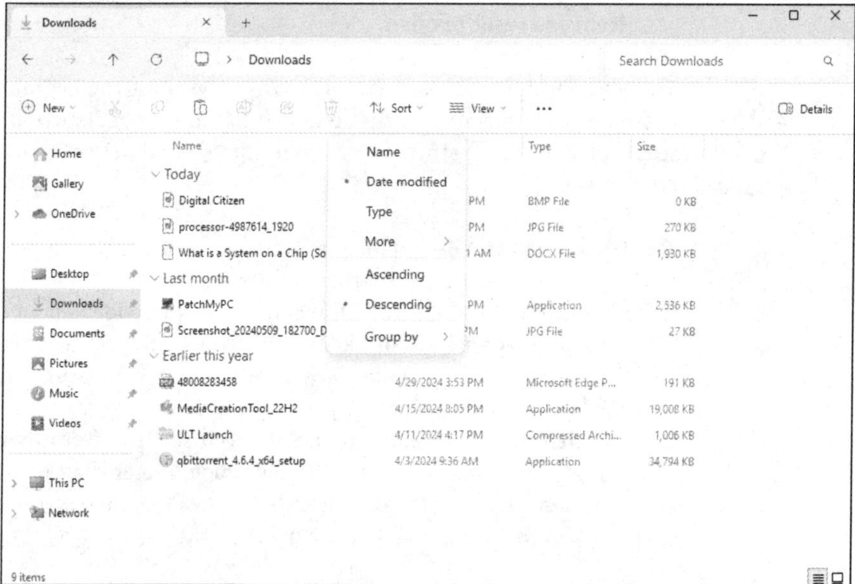

FIGURE 4-11: The sorting options present in File Explorer.

3. **In the Sort menu, choose Type.**

   Note how your files and folders are reorganized by type: file folder, JPG file, ZIP archive, and so on.

4. **To change the order, click or tap Sort again, and choose Ascending or Descending.**

   Everything in the current folder is sorted again, based on the order you selected.

5. **To group items, click or tap Sort and then Group By.**

   The grouping options shown in Figure 4-12 appear.

6. **In the Group By menu, choose the grouping criteria you want.**

   For example, if you want to identify the largest files quickly, choose Size, and you'll see the largest files in the current folder first, grouped based on their size: gigantic files (bigger than 4 GB), huge files (between 1 and 4 GB), large files, and so on.

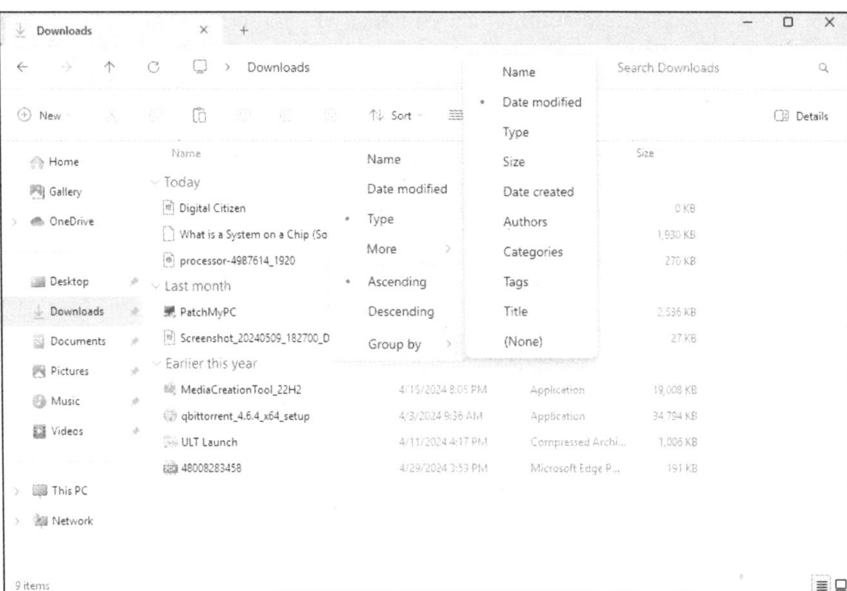

FIGURE 4-12: Grouping items can be useful too.

Displaying file extensions

A file, or filename extension, is a suffix at the end of a file on your computer. It comes after the period and is usually two to four characters long (for example, archive.7z, textfile.txt, picture.jpeg, or document.docx). Most files have extensions, and if you've opened a document or viewed a picture, you've probably noticed similar suffixes at the end of its name.

Windows uses the file extension to identify the app associated with the file. It then uses that app to open the file. When you double-click or double-tap a file in Windows, the operating system looks for the app associated with its file extension, opens that app, and then loads the file in the app. For example, PNG or JPEG files are opened by the Photos app, .xlsx files are opened by Excel, PDF files are opened by Microsoft Edge or Adobe Reader, and so on. However, these associations can be changed by the user or installed apps at any time.

By default, File Explorer doesn't display the extension of your files. For example, you don't see that Word documents have the file extension .doc or docx. Therefore, when you view a file named document.docx in File Explorer, you don't see the .docx part at the end. This is not necessarily a problem unless you're dealing with malware. Malicious files use this behavior of Windows to hide their real file extension. Therefore, you might end up with a file named document.docx.exe, but File Explorer displays only document.docx without the .exe part at the end, which is the real file extension. When you double-click or double-tap the file, it's executed automatically instead of opening in Word. If the virus is smart enough, the moment you run the file, your computer is infected.

To avoid such problems, you can set File Explorer to always display the file extension for all files:

1. **Start File Explorer.**
2. **Click or tap the View button in the toolbar at the top.**

   The View menu shown in Figure 4-13 appears.
3. **In the View menu, choose Show ⇨ File Name Extensions.**

   File Explorer displays the file extension for all your files.

TIP

To learn more about securing Windows 11 against viruses, read Book 9, Chapter 1.

Viewing hidden files

By default, File Explorer displays only files and folders that are not marked as hidden. The files you create as a user are never marked as hidden and are always visible. The same happens with the files created by most apps. However, Windows itself, device drivers, and some apps may create files that are marked as hidden and cannot be seen when you browse your computer with File Explorer.

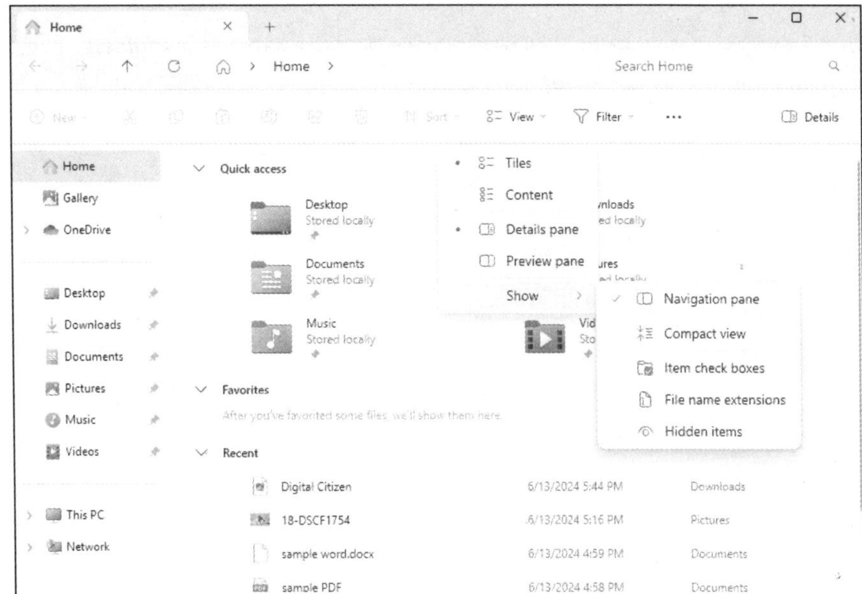

FIGURE 4-13: The View menu enables you to display file extensions for all your files.

Luckily, you can set File Explorer to display all files and folders, including hidden ones, like this:

1. **Start File Explorer.**
2. **Click or tap the View button, and then choose Show ➪ Hidden Items.**

   File Explorer now displays hidden files too.

Managing the Home section

Home in File Explorer is split into three sections: Quick Access, Favorites, and Recent. By default, Quick Access lists the following folders: Desktop, Downloads, Documents, Pictures, Music, and Videos. You can use them to organize your files according to their type. The Favorites section has only files you've marked as your favorites, while the Recent list is dynamic and is populated automatically with whatever file you open. You can add (pin) or remove (unpin) folders from Quick Access, and you can manually set what you want to see in Favorites.

Here's how to pin a folder to Quick Access and add a file to Favorites:

1. **Start File Explorer and navigate to a folder you want pinned to Quick Access.**

2. **Right-click or press and hold the name of the folder.**

   The right-click menu appears, as shown in Figure 4-14.

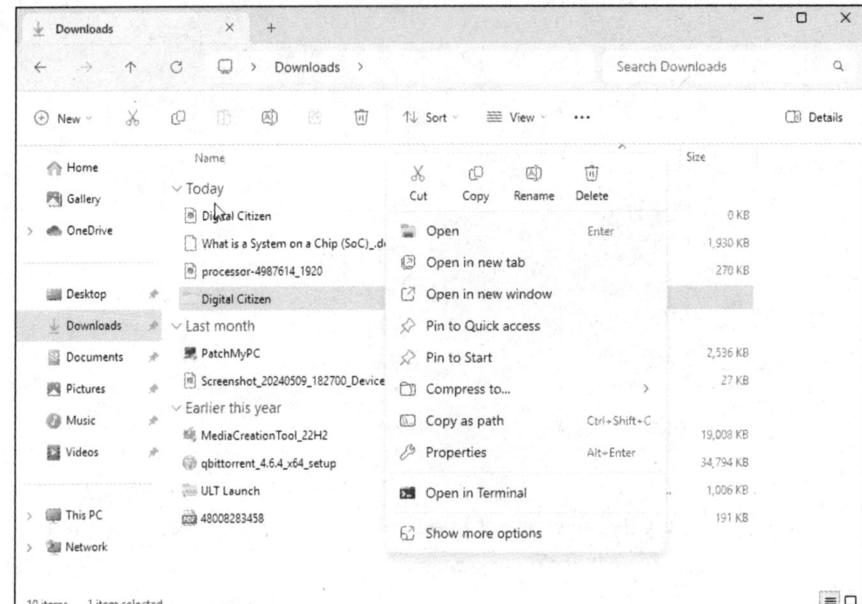

FIGURE 4-14: Right-clicking a folder gives you access to many useful options.

3. **Choose Pin to Quick Access.**

   The folder is added to Quick Access.

4. **Navigate to a file you want to see in Favorites.**
5. **Right-click or press and hold the name of the file.**

   The right-click menu appears.

6. **Choose Add to Favorites.**

   The selected file appears under Favorites.

7. **Click or tap Home.**

   You see the effects of your changes.

TIP

To remove a folder from Quick Access, navigate to the Quick Access section, right-click (or press and hold) the folder's name, and choose Unpin from Quick Access. Similarly, to remove a file from Favorites or Recent, navigate to Favorites or Recent, right-click (or press and hold), and choose Remove from Favorites or Remove from Recent.

Enabling and disabling check boxes for files and folders

If you have a Windows 11 laptop or tablet with a touchscreen, you'll notice that all files and folder icons in File Explorer have a check box that becomes visible when you hover over them with the mouse cursor or when you click or tap them, as shown in Figure 4-15. This check box is useful when you want to select multiple items and then perform actions such as deleting them or copying them to another location.

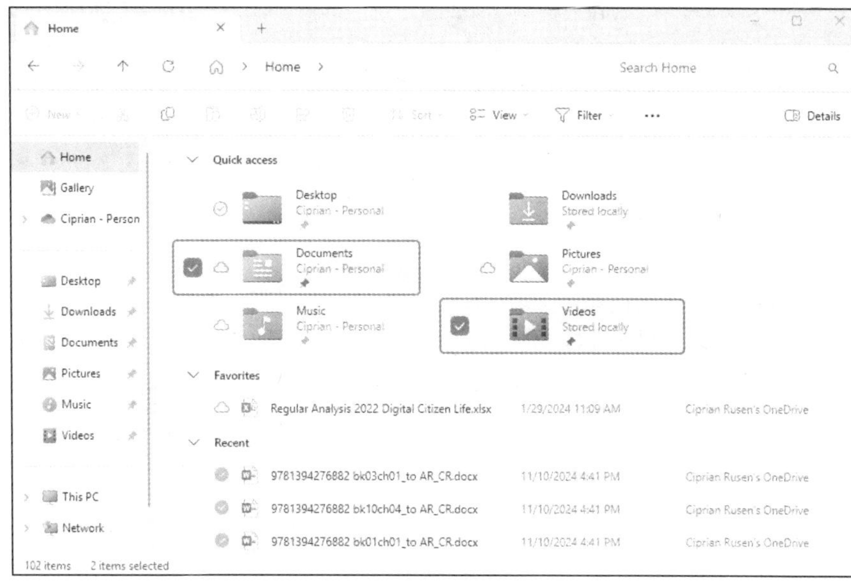

FIGURE 4-15: On devices with touchscreens, items in File Explorer have a check box next to them.

You may want to enable check boxes on a PC without a touchscreen because you consider them useful. Or you may not like this feature and prefer to disable it. Both are done using the same procedure:

1. **Start File Explorer.**
2. **Click or tap the View icon and then choose Show ➪ Item Check Boxes.**

   If this feature was initially enabled, it will be disabled and vice versa.

Sharing files

Windows 11 no longer promotes the concept of home networks and the old way of network sharing between your computers. Instead, it focuses on the cloud and promotes sharing through other means: Nearby Share, OneDrive, Outlook, Phone Link, and the other apps installed in Windows.

If you're navigating your OneDrive folders and files, sharing works is detailed in Book 4, Chapter 6. If you're browsing other parts of your computer that are not linked to OneDrive, the sharing options you get are limited to those in Figure 4-16:

- **Email a Contact:** Email your contacts from the Outlook app. Read Book 4, Chapter 3 for details.
- **Nearby Share:** Share with nearby computers that have Windows 10 or Windows 11 installed. This option is similar to Quick Share on Android devices and AirDrop on Apple devices.
- **Share Using:** Share using some of your Windows apps, such as WhatsApp, Feedback Hub, Instagram, and Microsoft Teams.

Here's how to share a file that's not in your OneDrive folder using Nearby Share:

1. **Start File Explorer.**
2. **Navigate to the file you want to share, which is not stored in your OneDrive folder. Select the file by clicking or tapping its name.**
3. **Click or tap the share icon at the top of the File Explorer window.**

   The share icon is to the left of the trash can icon. You see the Share dialog box (refer to Figure 4-16).
4. **If you see a Turn On button, click or tap it.**
5. **In the Nearby Share section, choose the computer you want to send the file to.**
6. **On the computer where you're receiving the file, click or tap Save.**

   The file is automatically transferred to the Downloads folder of the computer you selected.

TECHNICAL STUFF

When transferring content with Nearby Share, Windows uses Wi-Fi only if the receiving Windows 10 or Windows 11 PC is connected to the same private Wi-Fi network. Otherwise, the sharing happens over Bluetooth and will be much slower. You can send any number of files, documents, photos, and so on. If the computer you want to send files to is not in the list, make sure that it's using Windows 10 or Windows 11, that it's updated to the latest version, and that Nearby Share is turned on.

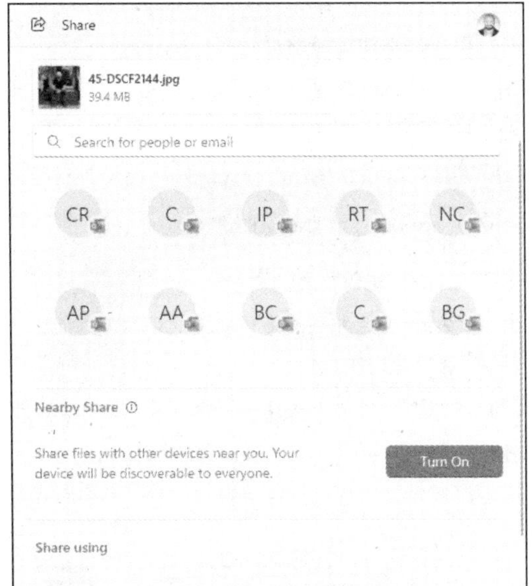

FIGURE 4-16: Sharing in Windows 11 is quite different.

Working with ZIP Files

A ZIP file is an archive that contains one or more files and folders. The concept of archiving files by combining them into one file and compressing the space used in the process was born in the early years of the internet, when reducing the space used by a file was a big deal, resulting in many minutes saved in transferring files over slow dial-up internet connections. The ZIP file and the high-performance compression that it enabled received widespread support because its specifications were made public, so that anyone could create apps to work with ZIP files.

Windows 11 can natively work with ZIP files, so you don't have to install a third-party app such as 7-Zip or WinRAR. To make things even better, the 24H2 update also added support for 7z and TAR file archives. However, support for the RAR file archives is still missing, so you'll need a specialized third-party app for those files. Luckily, for most people, this isn't a problem because they use only ZIP files to archive stuff.

Creating a ZIP file

If you want to archive several files and send them to someone else in a ZIP file archive, follow these steps:

1. **Start File Explorer and then navigate to the file or files you're interested in archiving.**

2. **Click or tap the file you want to archive.**

   If you need to archive more than one file, click or tap the first file, hold down the Ctrl key, and click or tap the additional files you want to include in your selection.

3. **At the top of the File Explorer window, click or tap the three dots icon.**

   The See More menu appears, as shown in Figure 4-17.

4. **In the menu, choose Compress to ZIP File.**

   A ZIP file is created. Windows gives the file a default name and selects it, so that you can type a new name.

5. **Type a name for the ZIP file, and then click or tap outside its name.**

   You can then cut and paste the ZIP file where you want or use the sharing options described in the previous "Sharing files" section to send the ZIP file to someone.

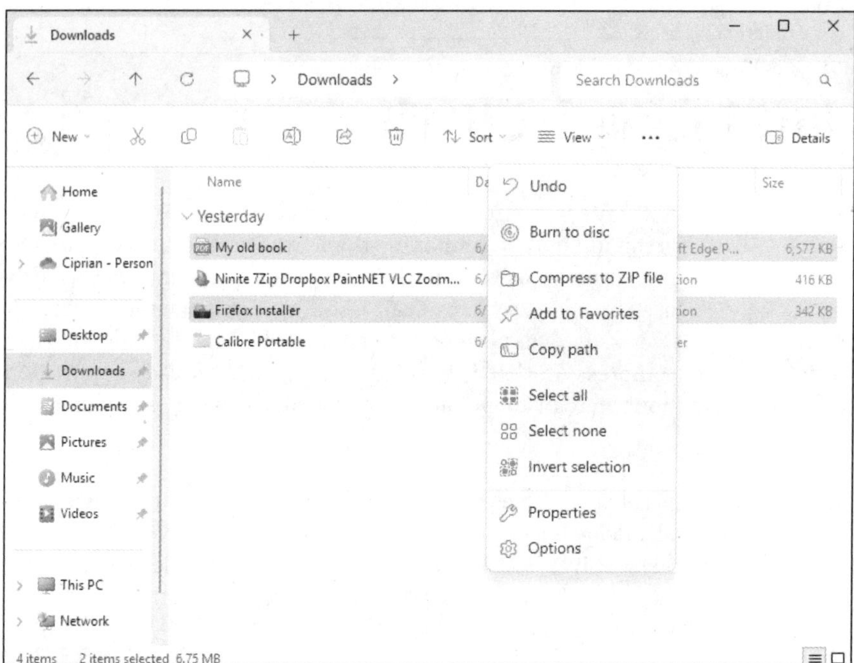

FIGURE 4-17: Clicking the three dots icon reveals an additional menu.

Creating more advanced file archives

If you want to create a file archive using another format and choose the compression method (the algorithm used for compressing the files) and the compression level (which controls the size of the resulting archive), Windows 11 offers several useful options. Here's how to create a file archive using a specific format, compression method, and compression level:

1. **Start File Explorer and navigate to the file or files you're interested in archiving.**
2. **Click or tap the file(s) you want to archive.**

   If you need to archive more than one file, click or tap the first file, hold down the Ctrl key, and click or tap the additional files you want to include in your selection.
3. **Right-click or press and hold your selection.**

   The right-click menu appears, as shown in Figure 4-18.

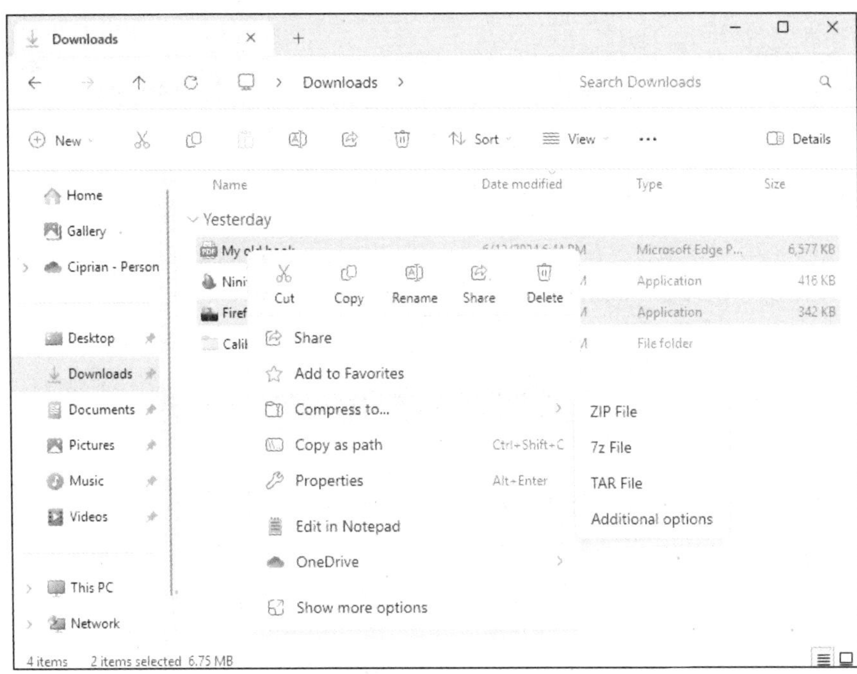

FIGURE 4-18: You can use multiple formats for archiving files in Windows 11.

4. **Choose Compress To ➪ Additional Options.**

   The Create Archive wizard appears, as shown in Figure 4-19.
5. **Click or tap Browse, select where you want to save the archive, type its name, and click or tap Save.**

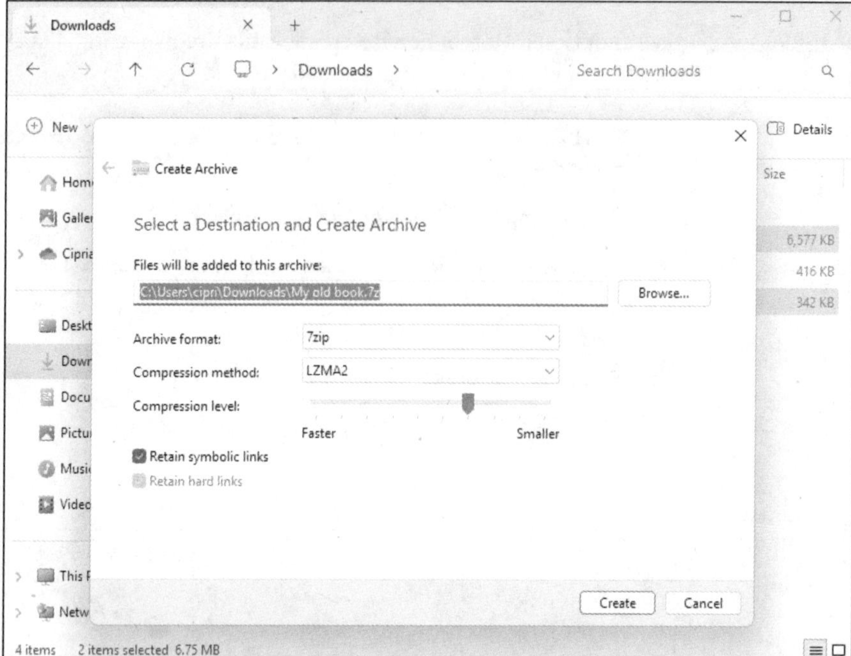

FIGURE 4-19: Setting up how you want to archive your file(s).

6. **In the Archive Format drop-down list, choose the format: 7zip, tar, or ZIP.**
7. **In the Compression method drop-down list, choose the method you prefer.**

   If you don't know what to choose, the default selection should work fine.
8. **Move the Compression Level slider to the desired level.**
9. **Click or tap Create.**

   The file archive is created where you selected. If you're archiving many files or larger ones, the process may take a while.

Extracting a ZIP file

If you have received a ZIP file and want to see its contents, you can double-click or double tap it, and it opens in File Explorer like a folder. If you want to extract its contents, do the following:

1. **Start File Explorer and navigate to the ZIP file you're interested in.**
2. **Double-click or double-tap the ZIP file to open it.**

   You see the files inside the ZIP file, as shown in Figure 4-20.

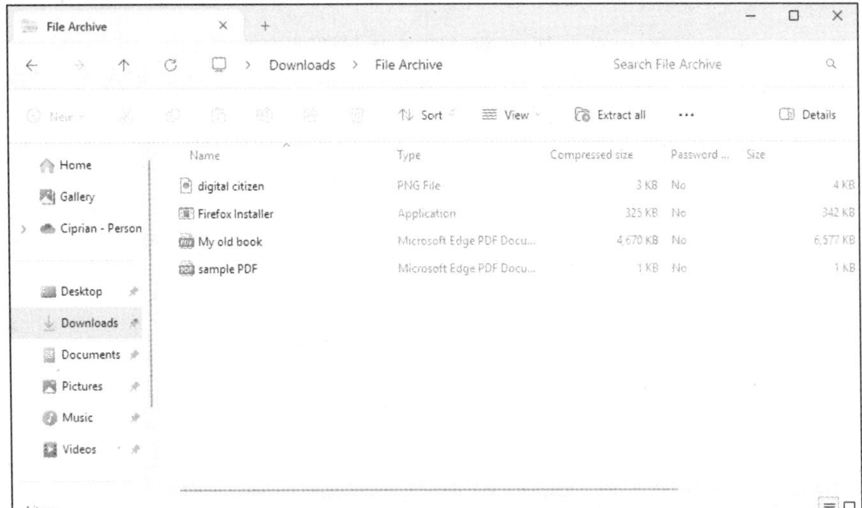

FIGURE 4-20: File Explorer can open ZIP files and show you what's inside.

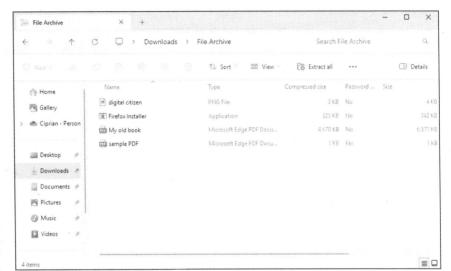

3. **At the top of the window, click or tap the Extract All icon.**

   The Extract Compressed (Zipped) Folders wizard appears.

4. **Choose the location where you want to extract the contents of the ZIP file and then click or tap Extract.**

   The contents of the ZIP file are extracted and displayed in a separate File Explorer window.

Right-Clicking in Windows 11

The right-click menu provides shortcuts for actions you might want to take. You access it by pressing the right button on your mouse once or, if you're using a touchscreen, by pressing and holding the item whose menu you want to open. Because the action list changes depending on the item that you right-click (or press and hold), it's also called a contextual menu.

The problem with the right-click menu is that, over time, it has become increasingly difficult to navigate, especially on systems with lots of apps. This is because many apps add their respective action shortcuts to this menu. As a result, the most-used commands (cut, copy, paste, and so on) are far from the mouse pointer when you right-click, and the menu is difficult to use. Because of these issues, Microsoft decided to redesign the right-click menu in Windows 11. Look at Figure 4-21 to see how it looks when you right-click (or press and hold) a file in File Explorer.

The new right-click menu is less cluttered than the one in Windows 10. It has a new toolbar with icons close to the position of your mouse cursor (or finger), which contains the simplest and most common actions, such as cut, copy, rename, share, and delete.

Below the toolbar is a list of contextual actions, which vary based on the right-clicked item. This section is consistent and contiguous, as opposed to Windows 10, where the actions would sometimes be separated or split up.

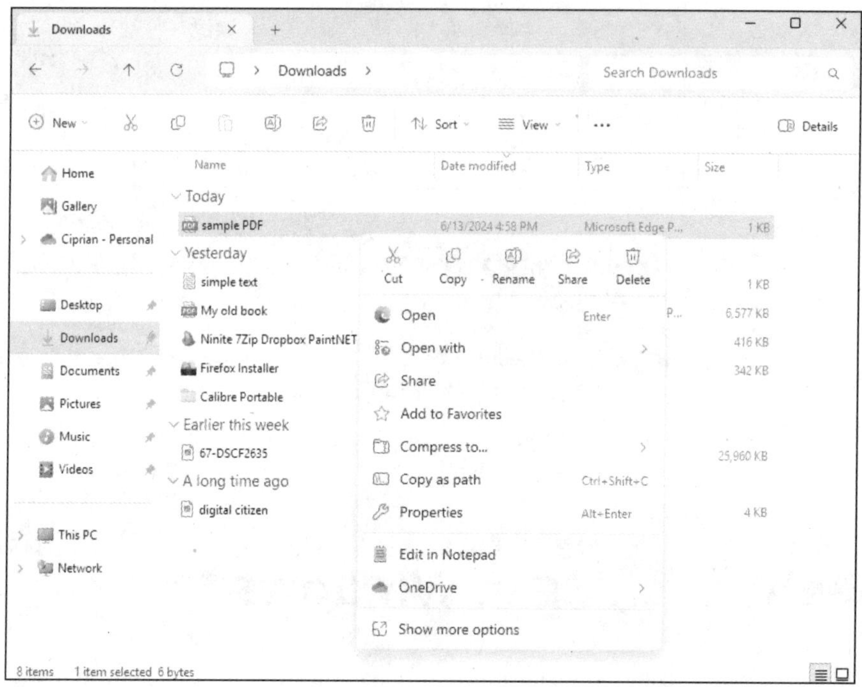

FIGURE 4-21: The right-click menu in Windows 11 has been redesigned.

To keep the right-click menu simpler and more productive in Windows 11, Microsoft enforces stricter rules for the apps that want to add their own actions. This should, in theory, make right-clicking (or pressing and holding) more useful than it was in older versions of Windows.

The old right-click menu is not completely gone from Windows 11, just hidden. You need to perform an additional action to access it, like this:

1. **Start File Explorer and right-click or press and hold on a file.**

   The right-click menu appears (refer to Figure 4-21).

2. **In the menu, choose Show More Options.**

   The old right-click menu appears, as shown in Figure 4-22.

3. **Click or tap the option that you want to use from the old right-click menu.**

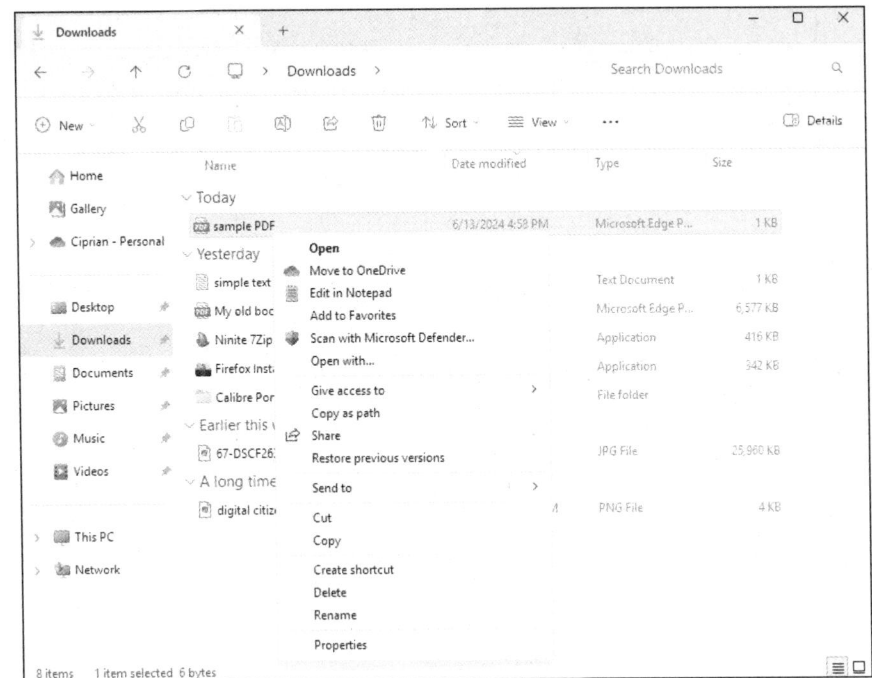

FIGURE 4-22: The old right-click menu is one additional click away.

TIP

This trick works on the desktop too, not just in File Explorer. If you don't see the option you want in the new right-click menu, choose Show More Options.

IN THIS CHAPTER

» Connecting your Windows 11 PC to an Ethernet network

» Dealing with Wi-Fi and hidden Wi-Fi

» Setting the network location

» Troubleshooting networking problems

Chapter 5

Connecting to Wi-Fi and the Internet

No PC or device is truly useful without an internet connection. How else could you check out your friend's latest Facebook post or scroll through Rihanna's X feed? More importantly, how could you hunt for a new job on LinkedIn or work from home?

Don't worry, connecting to the internet isn't rocket science. Just plug a network cable into your PC and your home router, or connect to Wi-Fi on your Windows 11 laptop and — *bam!* — you're online.

But wait, not all Wi-Fi networks are visible. Some are hidden, making them tricky to connect to. And what about those times when you forget the Wi-Fi password? No problem! You can use the WPS standard to connect by simply pushing a button on your router to send the connection details to your Windows 11 laptop.

Once you're connected, there's still more to do. For example, you need to set the network location so that you can share with others. Plus, you'll need to know how to deal with Wi-Fi connection issues.

In this chapter, I walk you through all these topics step-by-step. Let's get started!

Connecting to the Internet

To use the internet, you first must be connected to a network that is, in turn, connected to the internet. At home, a wireless router handles this task for you. At work, the network setup is a lot more complex, involving several routers, network switches, servers, and so on. However, to keep things simple, remember this: If you want internet access, you must connect to a network. If you use a desktop PC, you probably need to use a cable to connect it to a network. If you're using a laptop or a tablet, Wi-Fi is the way to go.

Connecting a desktop PC to the network

If you have a desktop PC and want to browse the internet, you need to connect the PC to your home router or your company's network. Many desktop PCs don't have a wireless network card, but they do have an Ethernet port on the back. Plug one end of the network cable into the Ethernet port on the back of your PC and plug the other end into one of the empty ports on the back of your home router (see Figure 5-1) or the Ethernet port on a wall plate at work.

FIGURE 5-1: Connect the Ethernet port on your PC to a LAN port on your router.

After you connect your desktop PC to the network, note how the network icon appears next to the time and date, in the bottom-right corner of the desktop. Before connecting, the icon was a small globe with a disconnected sign on it. Now it's shaped like a PC with a network cable next to it. If you hover your mouse cursor over it, you see the text *Network Internet Access*, as shown in Figure 5-2.

Your PC is connected to the network and the internet. You can then fire up Microsoft Edge (read Book 4, Chapter 1) and browse the web.

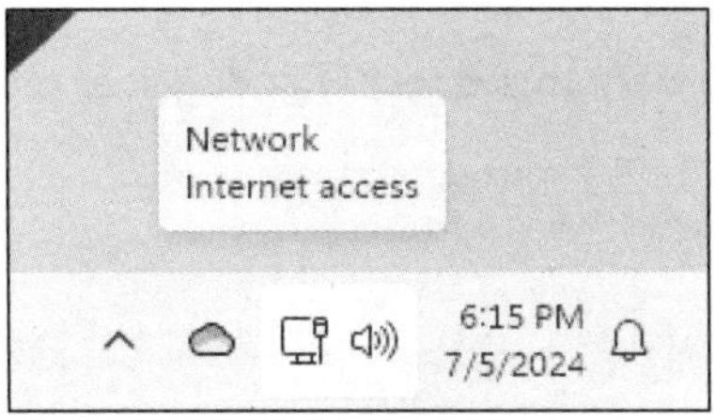

FIGURE 5-2: Your desktop PC is connected to the network and the internet.

Connecting to Wi-Fi

If you have a laptop or a tablet with Windows 11, you must connect it to Wi-Fi before you can go online. The process for doing this isn't rocket science, but it does take slightly longer than it did in Windows 10. Here's how it works:

1. **Click or tap the globe icon (internet or network) in the bottom-right corner of the desktop or press Windows+A on the keyboard.**

   The Quick Settings panel appears, as shown in Figure 5-3.

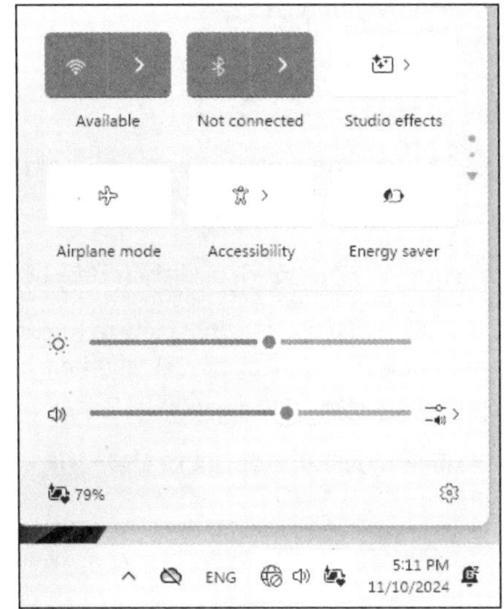

FIGURE 5-3: First check whether the Wi-Fi icon appears dimmed.

2. **If the Wi-Fi icon in the Quick Settings panel is dimmed, click or tap it to activate the Wi-Fi chip on your laptop or tablet.**
3. **Click or tap the right arrow (>) next to the Wi-Fi icon.**

   Windows 11 displays the list of Wi-Fi networks available in your area.

4. **Locate the network you want to connect to and click or tap its name.**

   The options shown in Figure 5-4 appear.

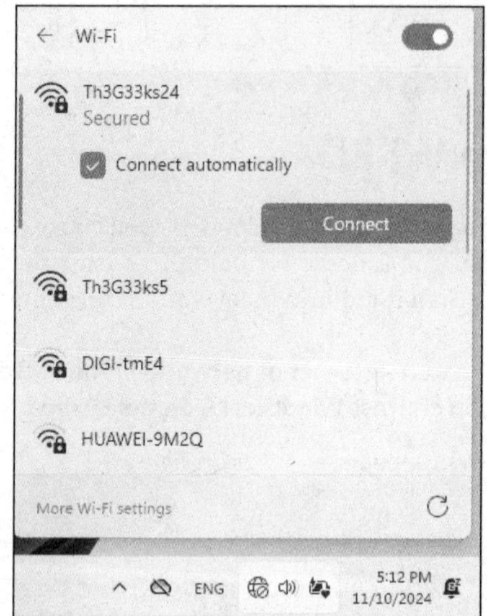

FIGURE 5-4: Choose your Wi-Fi network and connect to it.

5. **Select the box next to Connect Automatically and click or tap Connect.**

   You're asked to enter the network security key.

6. **Type the password of your Wi-Fi network and then click or tap Next.**

   Windows 11 tells you that it's verifying and connecting to the Wi-Fi network you chose. If everything works well, the connection is established, and *Connected* appears under the Wi-Fi network you chose.

7. **Click or tap an empty space on your desktop to close the Quick Settings panel, and you're done.**

   You're connected to Wi-Fi and can navigate the web.

Connecting to hidden Wi-Fi

Some people choose to hide their wireless networks. Hidden Wi-Fi networks are not truly hidden because they can still be detected using the right tools, and hackers know how to find them with ease. However, a hidden Wi-Fi doesn't broadcast its name, and most people and devices don't see it and therefore won't try to connect to it.

REMEMBER

If you do have a hidden Wi-Fi you want to connect to, you must know the following details before trying to connect:

- » The exact name of the network, which is case sensitive (uppercase and lowercase letters are different)
- » The Wi-Fi connection password, which is also case sensitive

After you have these details, do the following to connect to a hidden Wi-Fi from Windows 11:

1. **Click or tap the globe icon in the bottom-right corner of the desktop or press Windows+A.**

   The Quick Settings panel appears (refer to Figure 5-3).

2. **If the Wi-Fi icon in the Quick Settings panel appears dimmed, click or tap it to activate the Wi-Fi chip on your laptop or tablet.**
3. **Click or tap the right arrow (>) next to the Wi-Fi icon.**

   Windows 11 displays a list of the Wi-Fi networks available in your area.

4. **Scroll to the end of the list, and choose Hidden Network, as shown in Figure 5-5.**

   WARNING

   If you don't see Hidden Network in the list of available networks, your Windows 11 laptop, tablet, or 2-in-1 device can't detect hidden Wi-Fi in your area. Click or tap the refresh icon and check whether a Hidden Network entry appears. If not, then you're out of luck.

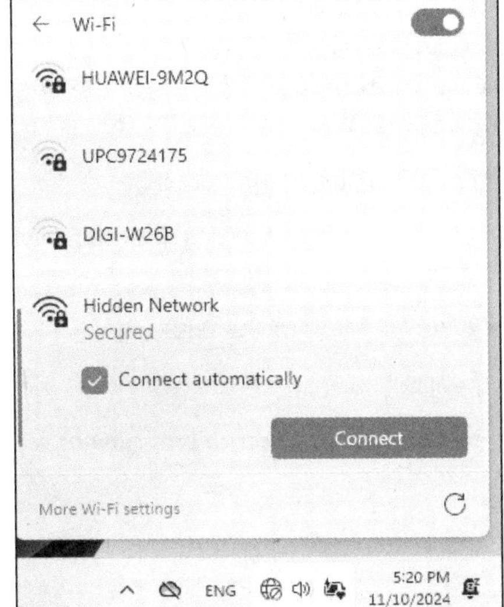

FIGURE 5-5: Connecting to a hidden Wi-Fi network takes a bit more work.

Connecting to Wi-Fi and the Internet

5. **Select Connect Automatically, and then click or tap Connect.**

   You are asked to enter the network name.

6. **Type the name of the hidden network, and then click or tap Next.**

   You are asked to enter the password for the selected Wi-Fi.

7. **Type the password for connecting to the hidden Wi-Fi, and then click or tap Next.**

   If everything worked okay, the connection will be established, and you see the word *Connected* under the network's name.

8. **Click or tap anywhere on an empty space on your desktop to close the Quick Settings panel.**

   You're now connected to the hidden Wi-Fi.

Connecting to Wi-Fi through WPS

If you don't know the Wi-Fi password but you have access to the router emitting the wireless signal for your network, you can still connect by using the WPS (Wi-Fi Protected Setup) standard, which is turned on and available on most routers.

REMEMBER

Before you use WPS to connect a Windows 11 laptop or tablet to Wi-Fi, you should know where to find the WPS button on your router. It is usually on the back of the router and is labeled WPS. On older wireless routers, the WPS button is marked by an icon that looks like two arrows forming a circular shape.

After you locate the WPS button on your router, do the following to connect your Windows 11 device to Wi-Fi:

1. **Click or tap the globe icon (internet or network) in the bottom-right corner of the desktop or press Windows+A.**

   The Quick Settings panel appears (refer to Figure 5-3).

2. **If the Wi-Fi icon in the Quick Settings panel is dimmed, click or tap it to activate the Wi-Fi chip on your laptop or tablet.**

3. **Click or tap the right arrow (>) next to the Wi-Fi icon.**

   Windows 11 displays the list of Wi-Fi networks available in your area.

4. **Locate the network you want to connect to and click or tap its name.**

5. **Select the box next to Connect Automatically (refer to Figure 5-4), and click or tap Connect.**

   You're asked to enter the network security key. Under the password field, there's a notice informing you that you can connect also by pushing the button on the router. That's the WPS button you identified earlier.

6. **Walk to the wireless router and push and hold its WPS button for a few seconds.**

7. **Get back to your Windows 11 laptop or tablet and note how it's getting settings from the router.**

   After the WPS connection is established, you see the word *Connected* under the network's name.

8. **Click or tap anywhere on an empty space on your desktop to close the Quick Settings panel.**

   You're now connected to Wi-Fi.

Setting the Network Location

When you connect to a new or unfamiliar network (through Wi-Fi or Ethernet) in Windows 11, your computer automatically labels it as public. This means Windows doesn't trust the network, and your computer stays hidden from others. In public mode, you can't share files or printers with others on the network. But what if you're on a network you trust and want to share things with family members, friends, or co-workers? No problem — you just have to change the network to private. Here's how:

1. **Click or tap the Start icon, and then Settings. Or press Windows+I.**

   The Settings window appears.

2. **On the left, select Network & Internet, and then select Wi-Fi on the right.**

   The wireless networking settings shown in Figure 5-6 are shown.

3. **Under Wi-Fi, find your network's name followed by the word *properties*, and then click or tap this entry.**

   The properties of your current Wi-Fi connection appear, as shown in Figure 5-7.

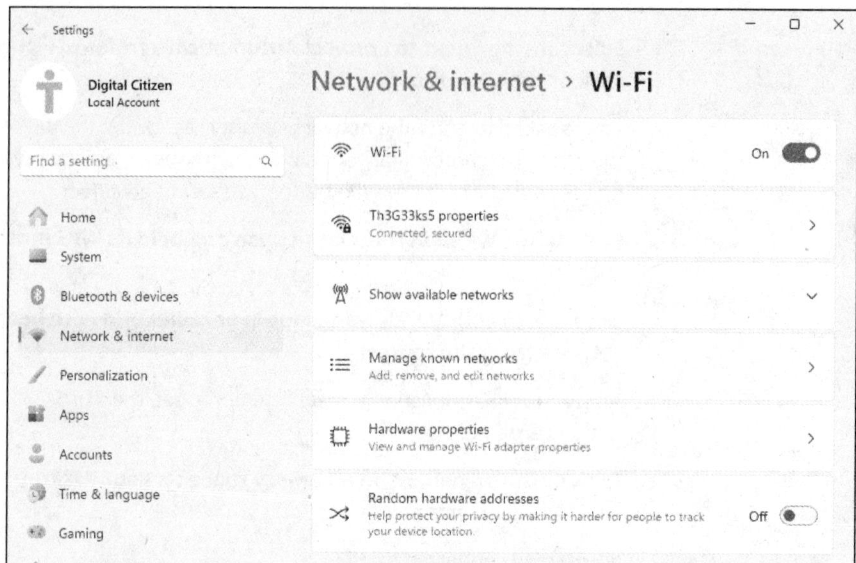

FIGURE 5-6: Here is where you see all Wi-Fi settings.

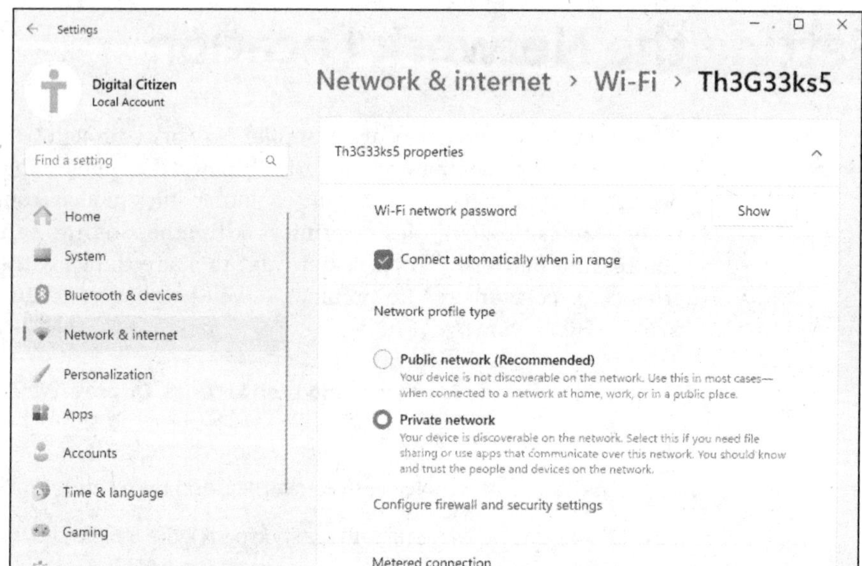

FIGURE 5-7: Setting the network to private instead of public.

4. **Under Network Profile Type, select Private Network instead of Public Network.**

   The network is now set as private, and Windows 11 allows you to share content with other computers and devices on the same network using the instructions presented in Chapter 4 of this minibook.

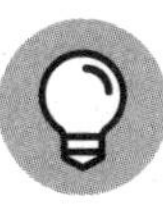

TIP

If you need to set a wired network connection as private, follow the same steps but choose Ethernet instead of Wi-Fi in Step 2. You then see the network's properties and can change its profile.

Troubleshooting Network Connections

From time to time, you may encounter problems connecting to Wi-Fi. This can happen for many reasons. Perhaps the network administrator changed the connection password, or you entered the wrong password when you tried to connect the first time. Or maybe the router managing the network was replaced, or some of its settings were altered and connections no longer work using the old settings stored by Windows 11.

To solve such problems, you can do a number of things, starting with asking Windows to forget the Wi-Fi network you have problems connecting to and trying again.

Forgetting a Wi-Fi network

If you can't connect to a Wi-Fi network but you could in the past, it's a good idea to ask Windows 11 to forget it. Here's how to do this:

1. **Click or tap the Start icon, and then Settings. Or press Windows+I.**

   The Settings window appears.

2. **On the left, select Network & Internet, and then select Wi-Fi on the right.**

   The wireless networking settings appear (refer to Figure 5-6).

3. **Click or tap Manage Known Networks.**

   A list of all the wireless networks known to your Windows 11 device appears, as shown in Figure 5-8.

4. **In the list, find the network you're having trouble connecting to and click or tap Forget next to its name.**

   The Wi-Fi you selected is immediately forgotten by Windows 11.

You can now reconnect to the same Wi-Fi network using any of the methods shared earlier in this chapter.

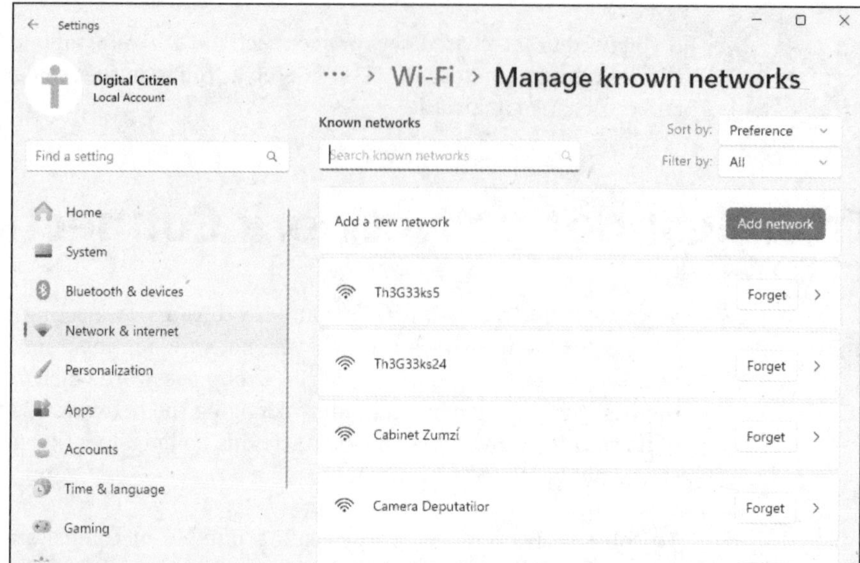

FIGURE 5-8: All the Wi-Fi networks known to your Windows 11 device.

Resetting network adapters

If you still have problems connecting to a wireless or Ethernet network, you can opt for a hardline approach and reset all the network adapters in your Windows 11 laptop or computer. This forces Windows to reset all your network adapters and network components to their original settings, which could solve your problems. Here's how it works:

1. **Click or tap the Start icon, followed by Settings.**
2. **On the left, select Network & Internet, and then select Advanced Network Settings on the right.**

   You see a list with all the network adapters on your computer, as shown in Figure 5-9.
3. **Scroll down and choose Network Reset.**

   You are given the option to reset all network adapters and are informed about what this process entails, as shown in Figure 5-10.
4. **Click or tap Reset Now and confirm your choice by pressing Yes.**

   You are informed that you are about to be signed out and that Windows will shut down in 5 minutes. Close all your apps and documents before those 5 minutes run out. When they do, Windows 11 reboots.
5. **Wait for Windows 11 to start and sign in with your account.**

   After you see the desktop, you can try to connect to the network.

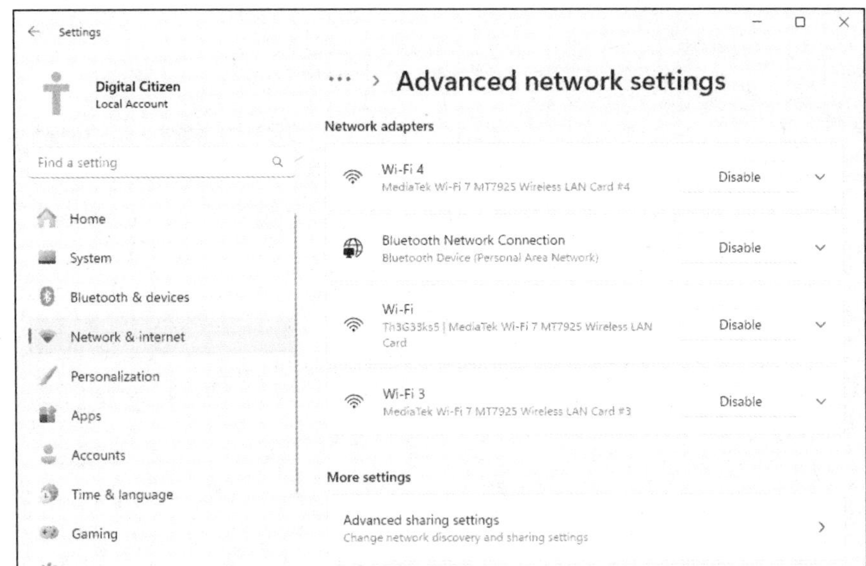

FIGURE 5-9: Your laptop may also have many more network adapters than you would expect.

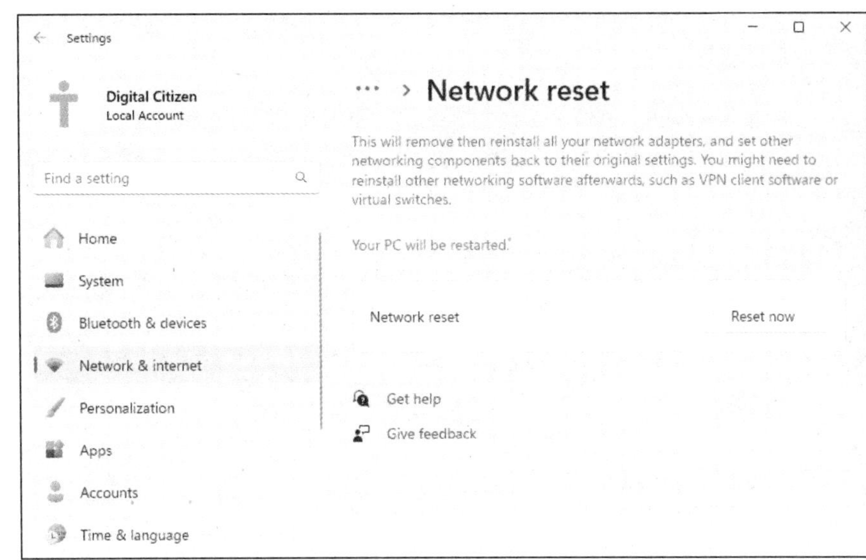

FIGURE 5-10: Here is where you reset your network adapters.

WARNING

The downside to using this troubleshooting method is that Windows 11 forgets all the network connections and settings you've used before. Therefore, each time you go to a new location, you must reconnect to its Wi-Fi or network all over again. This requirement might a problem if you forgot the connection password for one or more locations.

4 Using Windows Apps

Contents at a Glance

IN THIS CHAPTER

» Using Microsoft Edge to browse the web

» Enabling vertical tabs in Microsoft Edge

» Browsing the web privately with Edge

» Using other web browsers in Windows 11

» Switching to Google Chrome or another browser

Chapter 1
Browsing the Web

Microsoft Edge has come a long way since its release back in 2015. After this browser's initial failures in Windows 10, Microsoft decided to switch course in 2019. Edge no longer used its own rendering engine and switched to Chromium — the open-source engine used by Google Chrome, Opera, and other web browsers. This ushered in a new era for Microsoft Edge, in which it enjoyed steady progress and an increasing number of useful features. Today, Edge stands tall as one of the best web browsers out there, and it uses less memory than Chrome. It also includes useful features such as vertical tabs, and it's friendlier with your laptop's battery, allowing you to use it for longer on a single charge.

In this chapter, I share the basics of browsing the web in Windows 11 using Microsoft Edge. Whether you're looking to group your tabs like a pro, browse incognito, or just figure out what the buttons in Microsoft Edge do, I've got you covered.

But wait, there's more! I know that not everyone wants to stick with the factory settings, so I also share how to switch things up if Microsoft Edge isn't your cup of tea. From Google Chrome to Firefox and other browsers, I also walk you through the process of changing your default browser faster than you can say "cookies and cache."

So, buckle up, grab your favorite beverage, and get ready to dive into the nitty-gritty of web browsing in Windows 11.

Getting to Know Microsoft Edge

Microsoft Edge works just like any other web browser, and its user interface should be familiar, especially if you've used Google Chrome. However, to make sure you feel right at home, let's go together through a tour of its user interface:

1. **Click or tap the Microsoft Edge icon on the taskbar or from the Start menu.**

   The browser loads its user interface. Look at the icons and other elements highlighted in Figure 1-1 to understand what they do.

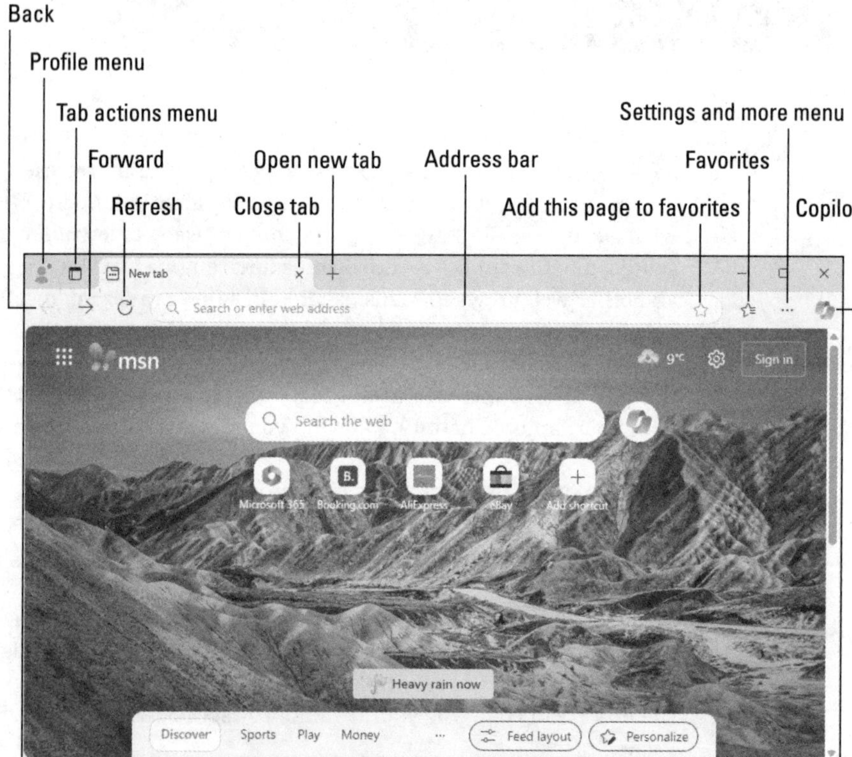

FIGURE 1-1: The most important icons and user interface elements in Microsoft Edge.

2. **In the address bar at the top, type** digitalcitizen.life **and click or tap Enter.**

   The Digital Citizen website loads in Microsoft Edge.

3. **Click or tap + to the right of the current tab.**

   Microsoft Edge opens a new, empty tab.

4. **Click or tap the browser essentials icon at the top right.**

   A menu appears that presents details about your browser's performance, how it protects your safety, and options for enabling the VPN service built into the browser, which is named Microsoft Edge Secure Network.

5. **Click or tap the same browser essentials icon to close the menu.**

6. **In the address bar, type** `dummies.com` **and press Enter.**

   The *Dummies* website loads in the tab.

7. **Click or tap the settings and more menu icon (three horizontal dots) in the top-right corner of Microsoft Edge.**

   The menu shown in Figure 1-2 appears. From this menu, you can access Edge's settings, favorites, extensions, and other tools and options.

8. **To close Microsoft Edge, click or tap X in the top-right corner.**

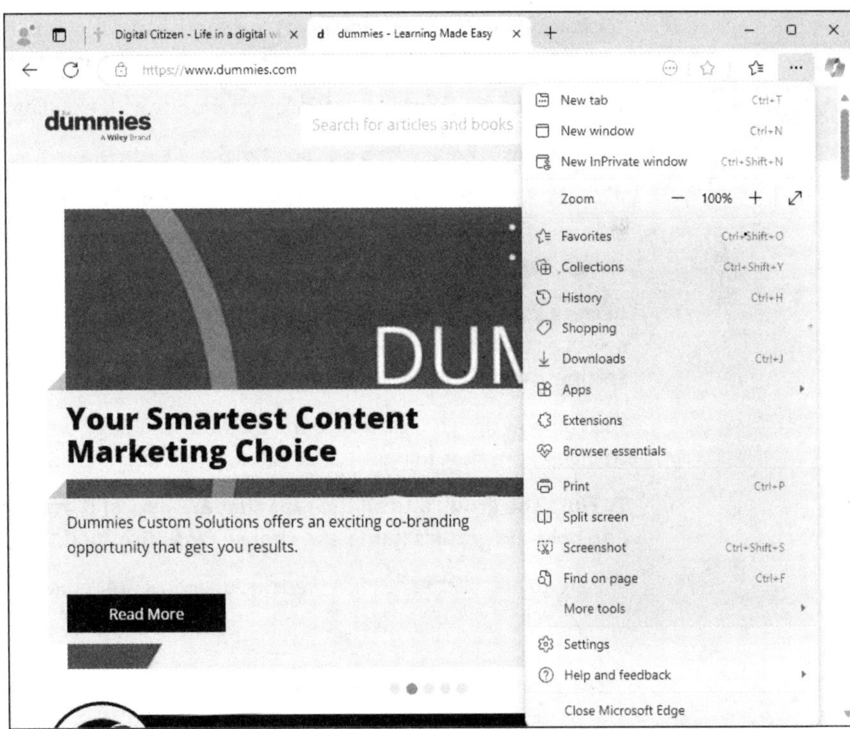

FIGURE 1-2: The Settings and More menu is quite long and filled with options.

Grouping tabs in Microsoft Edge

A feature I like about Microsoft Edge is that it allows me to group two or more tabs, name the groups I create, and choose different colors to tell them apart. Then I can drag around a group as if it were just a tab, minimize it, close it, or move it to a new Microsoft Edge window. I use groups to organize my tabs more efficiently and separate them based on what I want to do: perform my work for Digital Citizen, do the research required for writing this book, or kill time online on social media and news sites. Here's how to create a group in Microsoft Edge and manage it:

1. **Click or tap the Microsoft Edge icon on the taskbar or from the Start menu.**

   The browser loads its user interface. Refer to the icons highlighted in Figure 1-1 to understand what they do.

2. **In the address bar at the top, type** digitalcitizen.life **and press Enter. Then, open two more tabs and load** `dummies.com` **and** `bing.com`**.**

3. **Click and hold (or press and hold) the last tab you created and drag it to the left side of the tab where you loaded `dummies.com`.**

   Notice how the tab changed its position.

4. **Click and hold (or press and hold) the same `bing.com` tab and drag it on top of the first tab you created, where you loaded digitalcitizen.life.**

   The two tabs are now highlighted together using a blue outline.

5. **Release the `bing.com` tab on top of digitalcitizen.life.**

   A group named Group 1 is created, and you see the properties of the group, as shown in Figure 1-3. Read all the options to familiarize yourself with what you can do with this group.

6. **In the group properties menu, type the name you want for the group and select a color. Then click or tap outside the group's menu to apply your settings.**

   You can now drag the group around the Microsoft Edge browser window and change its position, minimize it, or extend it by clicking or tapping its name.

7. **To close the group and all the tabs that are part of it, right-click or press and hold the group's name and choose Close Grouped Tabs.**

   The group and all the tabs that were included in it are removed.

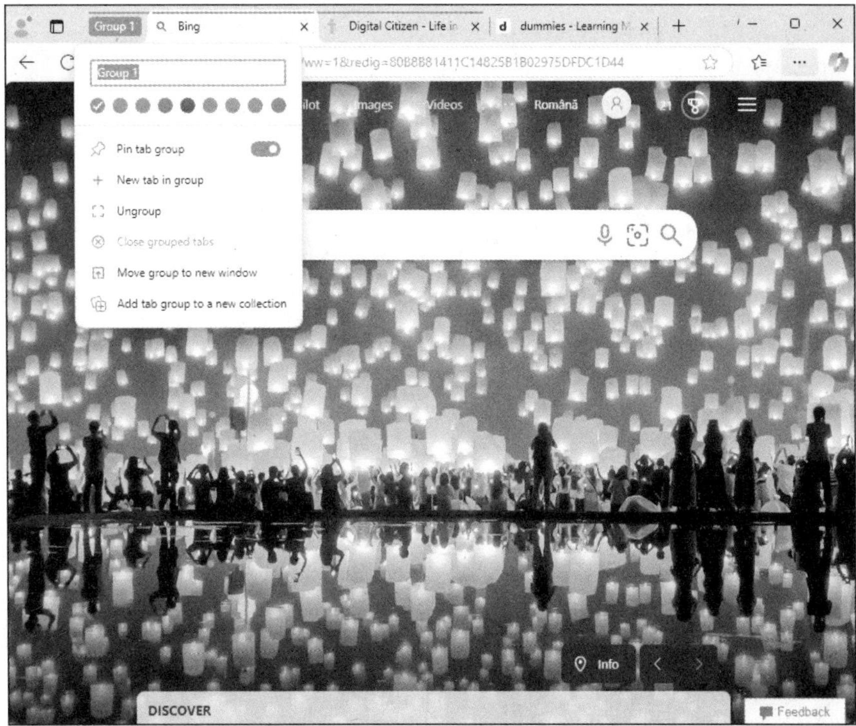

FIGURE 1-3: Creating and working with groups is easy.

Enabling vertical tabs in Microsoft Edge

By default, Microsoft Edge displays its tabs horizontally, on the top side of its window. However, you can also use vertical tabs on the left side of the browser. Many users say that using vertical tabs allows them to browse the web more efficiently. If this sounds appealing to you, do the following to enable vertical tabs:

1. **Click or tap the Microsoft Edge icon on the taskbar or from the Start menu.**
2. **Click or tap the tab actions menu icon (refer to Figure 1-3) on the top-left side of the browser window.**

   The menu shown in Figure 1-4 appears.
3. **In the menu, choose Turn on Vertical Tabs.**

   Your tabs move to the left side of Microsoft Edge.

TIP

If you want the horizontal tabs back, repeat the same steps, but in Step 3, choose Turn off Vertical Tabs. Alternatively, you can press Ctrl+Shift+, (comma) to toggle vertical tabs on or off.

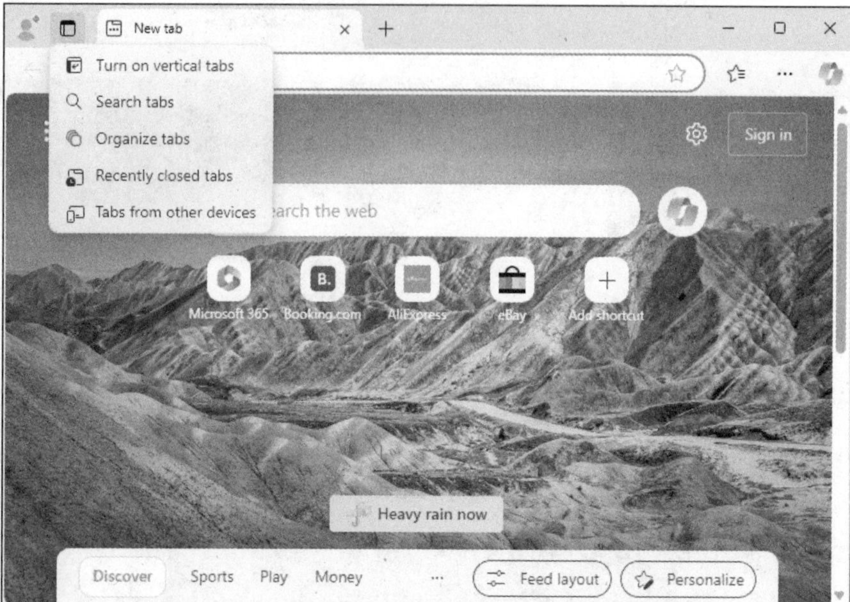

FIGURE 1-4: Enabling vertical tabs in Microsoft Edge.

Changing the default search engine

The default search engine used by Microsoft Edge is Bing. In recent years, it has become a solid choice, especially in English-speaking countries such as the US, UK, and Australia. Starting in February 2023, Bing was integrated with Copilot (initially named Bing Chat), its personal AI assistant, and is now more useful than ever. If you haven't used it, I recommend you try it. To learn more about Copilot, read the next chapter in this minibook.

From my experience, Bing has become better than Google at promoting content from smaller independent publishers, and many people are happy with their search results.

However, if you don't like Bing, you can change the default search engine used by Microsoft Edge like this:

1. **Open Microsoft Edge using its icon on the taskbar or from the Start menu.**
2. **Click or tap the settings and more icon (three horizontal dots) in the top-right corner.**

   The Settings and More menu appears.

3. **In the menu, choose Settings.**

   A new tab opens showing the Settings page.

4. **On the left, choose Privacy, Search, and Services.**

   You see a long list of settings, as shown in Figure 1-5.

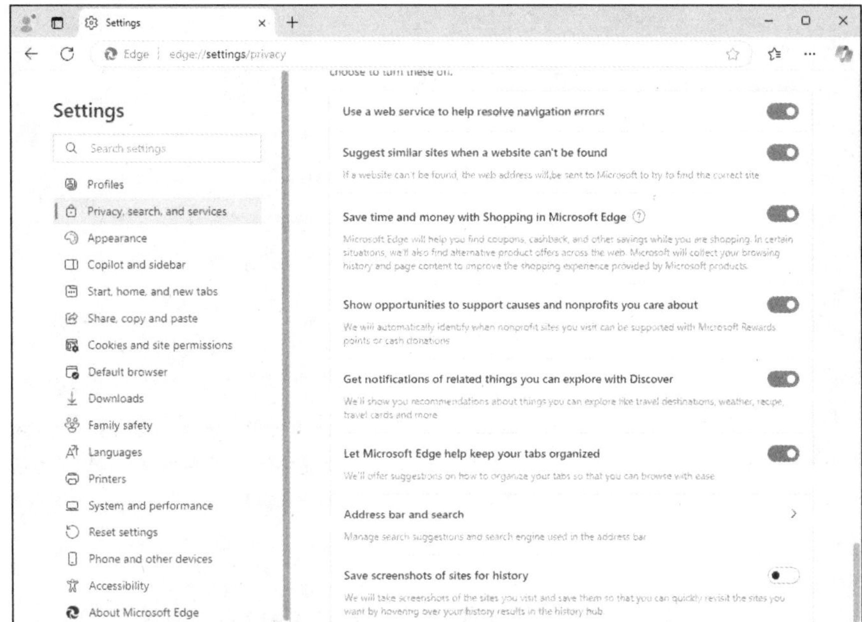

FIGURE 1-5: Accessing the Settings page in Microsoft Edge.

5. **On the right, scroll down until you find Address Bar and Search, and click or tap it.**

   You see the options for managing the search engines used by Edge, as shown in Figure 1-6.

6. **Click or tap the dropdown list next to Search Engine Used in the Address Bar, and then select the one you want: Bing, Yahoo!, Google, DuckDuckGo, or Yandex.**

   Microsoft Edge will use the search engine you've selected the next time you search for something in its address bar.

7. **Close the Settings tab in Microsoft Edge and resume browsing the web.**

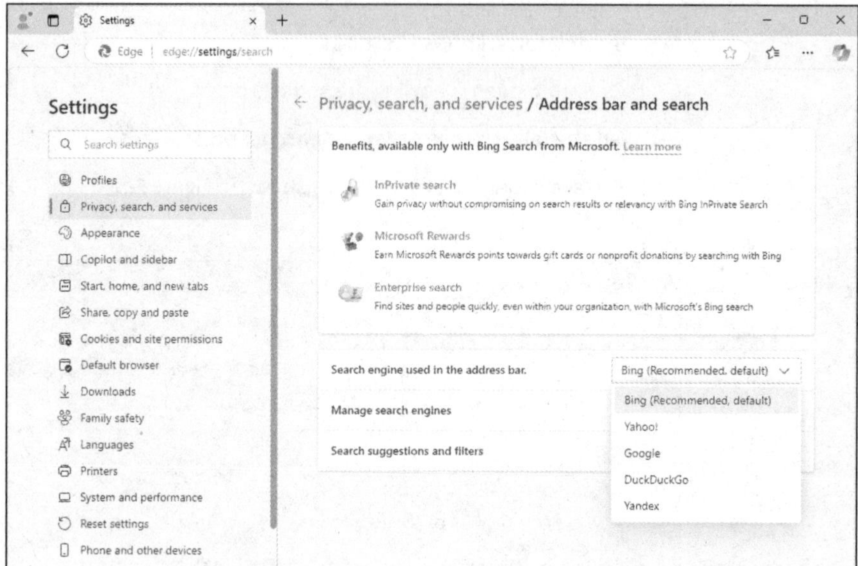

FIGURE 1-6: Changing the default search engine isn't overly complicated.

REMEMBER

The default search engine you've selected is used only for searches made in the address bar of Microsoft Edge. Each time you open a new tab in this browser, you see a Search box in the middle of the tab and a Copilot logo next to it. All the searches made using this box go through Bing; you can't change the search engine for this Search box.

InPrivate browsing with Microsoft Edge

InPrivate is the name given by Microsoft to Edge's private browsing mode. It provides a slightly more private way of browsing the web compared to normal web browsing. After you use InPrivate in Microsoft Edge to browse the web and close all private browsing tabs and windows, the browser does the following:

- Deletes the cookies stored when using InPrivate browsing. If you log into Facebook, Gmail, YouTube, or some other website and later close all private browsing tabs and windows, all the cookies generated by the sites you visited are deleted, and you're automatically signed out. If someone else tries to visit the same websites in a new browsing window, they're not automatically logged in with your account(s).
- Deletes its records of all the data you typed in forms, such as sign-up pages, login pages, and contact pages.
- Deletes temporary files and the cache from your browsing session. When you visit a website, files such as images and styling files are downloaded to your

computer or device. These files are stored on your computer for the duration of your private browsing session to make browsing faster. When you close all private browsing tabs and windows, these files are deleted, so they can't be accessed and used by anyone else.

- Deletes the browsing history from your browsing session. This way, other people with access to the same computer or device (and the same Windows user account) can't know what you have visited on the web just by looking at your web browser.
- Does not store the search history from your browsing session. In all web browsers, you can search the web straight from the browser's address bar. You type some keywords and press Enter, and the keywords are sent automatically to the default search engine to return results. In regular browsing sessions, this data is stored for later reuse to help you browse the web faster. In private browsing, this data isn't stored, so others can't reuse it when accessing the same computer or device.

All these features enhance your privacy and confidentiality because other people who have access to the same computer don't know what you're doing online. However, private browsing doesn't mean that no one can track you. Your internet service provider still knows what you did online, as well as your network administrator, if you're at work. If you want to be private, you need to use a VPN with a strict no-logs policy. For more on that, read Book 9, Chapter 3.

REMEMBER

Few people know that you can use both normal and InPrivate browsing windows at the same time. They're separate, and the cookies stored in one window don't affect the other. To make it stand out and easier to separate from normal browsing, the InPrivate browsing windows use a special dark theme.

If you want to browse privately with Microsoft Edge, do the following:

1. **Click or tap the Microsoft Edge icon on the taskbar or from the Start menu.**
2. **Click or tap the settings and more icon (three horizontal dots) in the top-right corner.**

   The Settings and More menu appears.
3. **In the menu, choose New InPrivate window.**

   You see a new InPrivate Browsing window, as shown in Figure 1-7.
4. **To further enhance your tracking protection, click or tap to enable the switch for Always Use "Strict" Tracking Prevention when Browsing InPrivate.**

   You can now start browsing the web using the InPrivate tab that you've just opened.

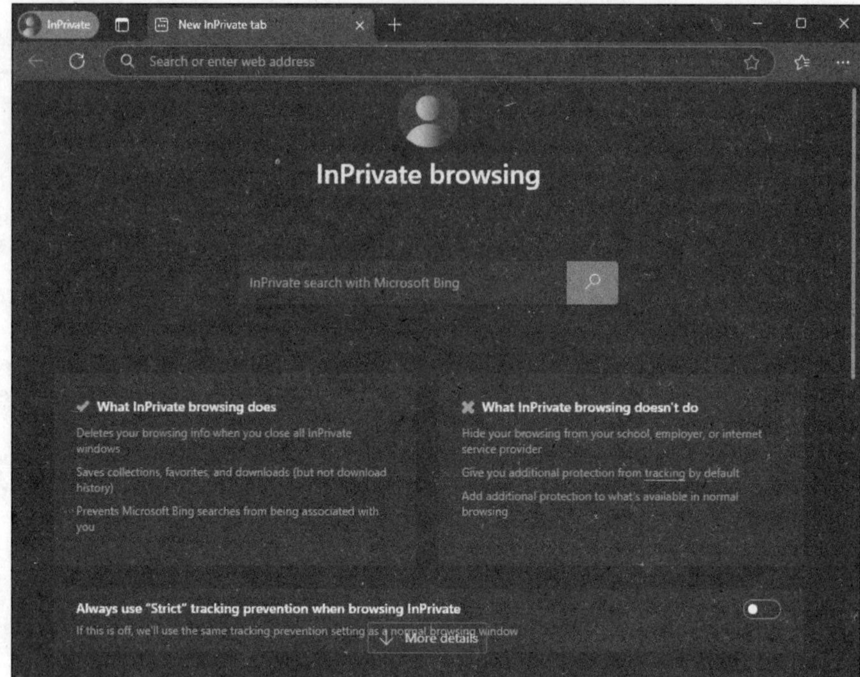

FIGURE 1-7: Microsoft Edge's InPrivate Browsing window uses a special dark theme.

REMEMBER

When browsing in a Microsoft Edge InPrivate window, any tab you open uses the same private browsing mode. The private browsing session ends only when you close the entire InPrivate browsing window and all its tabs.

TIP

You can open a new InPrivate browsing window by using the keyboard shortcut Ctrl+Shift+N.

Adding extensions to Microsoft Edge

You can customize Microsoft Edge by adding extensions or add-ons that interest you. They are a great way to enhance your browsing experience and boost your productivity. For example, you can use Microsoft Edge extensions to add a password manager, such as Bitwarden (read more in Book 9, Chapter 3), a TikTok video downloader, or a spelling and grammar checker.

Here's how to add extensions to Microsoft Edge:

1. **Start Microsoft Edge.**
2. **Click or tap the three dots icon in the top-right corner. Alternatively, you can press Alt+F.**

   The Settings and More menu opens.

3. **In the menu, choose Extensions, and then click or tap Manage Extensions.**

   A new tab opens displaying the Extensions page, and you see all installed extensions, as shown in Figure 1-8.

TIP

   If you want to install Google Chrome extensions in Microsoft Edge, click or tap the Allow Extensions from Other Stores switch, which is on the left side of the Extensions page.

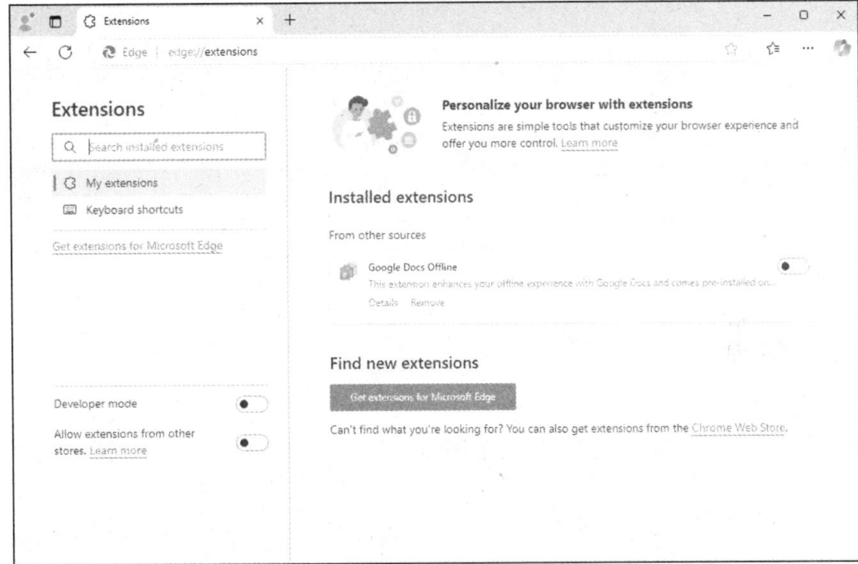

FIGURE 1-8: This is where you manage extensions in Microsoft Edge.

4. **Click or tap the Get Extensions for Microsoft Edge button.**

   The Microsoft Edge Add-Ons web portal loads in a new tab. You can browse through the extensions on the home page or search for a specific extension.

5. **Click or tap in the Search box at the top left, and type** Bitwarden.
6. **In the list of search results, choose Bitwarden Password Manager.**

   A page appears with screenshots and details about that extension, including reviews from other users.

7. **Click or tap the Get button, and then Add Extension.**

   The extension is installed in Microsoft Edge, and you can start using it.

TIP

If you are using Windows 11 at work and need to browse dated internal websites that require Internet Explorer, you can enable and use the Internet Explorer mode built into Microsoft Edge. To learn how it works, read the tutorial published on Digital Citizen at `www.digitalcitizen.life/internet-explorer-mode-microsoft-edge/`.

Using Other Web Browsers

Some people ask themselves, "Which browser is best?" Others simply don't care — and for good reason: All web browsers do the same things, with fewer differences than ever. You could stick with the Microsoft Edge browser and never miss a thing — especially because it now shares the same rendering engine as Google Chrome and Opera and can also use the same Chrome extensions.

However, here's how I view things:

- **Microsoft Edge** is a good browser, with cool features such as vertical tabs, strict private browsing, and Copilot built-in (read Book 4, Chapter 2). It evolves at a fast pace, and I strongly recommend you try it before moving to another browser.
- **Google Chrome** is the king of web browsers mostly due to its integration with Google's services: Gmail, Google Docs, Google Drive, YouTube, and so on. If you're an Android user, it makes sense to use Chrome on all your PCs and devices and have it synchronized through your Gmail account. However, you can also install Microsoft Edge on your mobile devices and have it synchronized.
- **Opera** is another great browser I used before migrating to Microsoft Edge. It uses the same rendering engine as Edge and Chrome, and it has some cool integrations with WhatsApp, Facebook, X, and other services. If you want to chat or interact on social media while doing your usual web browsing in a productive manner, Opera is a smart choice. It, too, can use Chrome extensions.
- **Mozilla Firefox** has faded from the headlines and users' attention. It is not backed by any big corporation and not pushed by any major platform except Linux. It also uses its own rendering engine, which may be problematic in some situations, as fewer websites will support it. While Firefox is still a great browser, I expect it to become a niche product like Opera and continue to lose market share to Microsoft Edge and Google Chrome.
- **Arc** is a new niche browser that's making headlines. While it uses the same rendering engine as Microsoft Edge and Google Chrome, it comes with a unique user interface and a new approach to handling web browsing. If you're tired of using traditional web browsers, then you should try Arc.

Changing the Default Browser in Windows 11

One annoying thing in Windows 11 is that Microsoft aggressively pushes its Edge browser so that users don't switch to another browser. I like Edge and use it daily, but this approach is not cool. If you want to switch your default browser from Microsoft Edge to Google Chrome (or some other browser), here's what you must do:

1. **Click or tap the Start icon and then Settings, or press Windows+I.**

   Windows 11 displays the Settings app.

2. **On the left, choose Apps. On the right, click or tap Default Apps.**

   This is where you set the defaults for applications in Windows 11.

3. **Scroll down the list of apps on the right until you find Google Chrome or the browser that interests you. Click or tap its name.**

   You see a list of all the file types and link types that can be opened by Google Chrome. At this point, the default for most of them should be set to Microsoft Edge, as shown in Figure 1-9.

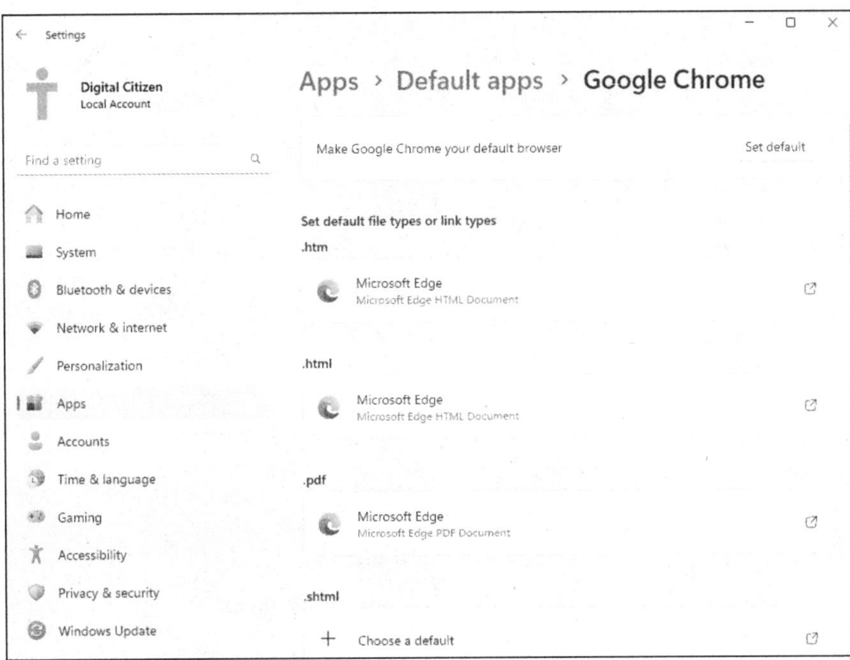

FIGURE 1-9: Changing the default browser in Windows 11.

4. **At the top, click or tap Set Default next to Make Google Chrome Your Default Browser.**

   Google Chrome is then set as the default app for opening files such as .htm or .html. However, Microsoft Edge remains the default for other types of files such as .pdf or .svg.

5. **If you want to change the default app for other file types, scroll the list, and for each of them, click or tap Microsoft Edge. Then, select Google Chrome followed by Set Default.**

6. **Repeat Step 5 for all entries where you see Microsoft Edge as the default instead of Google Chrome.**

   After you set Google Chrome as the default for all these entries, this browser will be your new default. Your changes are applied immediately.

   Follow the same procedure to set the default browser to Arc, Firefox, or Opera. The only difference is that you select your browser instead of Google Chrome.

IN THIS CHAPTER

» Getting started with Copilot

» Accessing older Copilot conversations

» Ending a conversation with Copilot and starting a new one

» Using Copilot on the web and mobile devices

» Understanding Copilot's paid options

Chapter 2
Enhancing Your Productivity with Copilot

Artificial intelligence (AI) has been the buzzword of 2024, and it's likely to stay in the spotlight for years to come. While AI products may not be as smart as their creators claim, they are becoming increasingly integrated into our lives and the way we work.

Microsoft has made significant investments in AI, resulting in the development of Copilot, a product based on the renowned ChatGPT language model. Copilot is now an integral part of Windows, Microsoft Edge, Paint, Photos, Snipping Tool, Windows Search, and even Microsoft 365 subscriptions, which also include the well-known Office apps and Teams.

One standout feature of Copilot is its continuous connection to Bing, Microsoft's search engine. This integration allows Copilot to provide up-to-date information from the web, making it a robust research tool that can offer links to valuable online sources.

To broaden Copilot's appeal, Microsoft has made it available not only on Windows, but also on mobile and web platforms. This ensures seamless integration across devices, so you can use Copilot as your helpful assistant on Android, iPhone, and the web.

If the free version of Copilot doesn't meet your needs for speed, precision, or accuracy, you can use one of Microsoft's paid versions. These provide access to newer language models, improved performance, and enhanced integrations with Microsoft 365.

In this chapter, I explore the basics of using Copilot in Windows 11. You learn how to start and end conversations with Copilot, as well as access previous chats you had with it. You then see how to access Copilot from your web browser and mobile devices. Finally, I present the paid options Microsoft offers for those who need more from Copilot.

Chatting with Copilot

When you click or tap the Copilot icon on the taskbar or the Start menu, or you press the Copilot key that was enforced by Microsoft on all Copilot+ PC devices, you start the Copilot app. Initially, Copilot was a sidebar that always showed up on the right side of the screen. But with Windows 11 version 24H2, it became a standalone Windows 11 app, which can be resized, snapped to the left of the screen (instead of the right), closed, minimized, and so on. The Copilot app now looks a lot different than the initial sidebar. You can see Copilot in action in Figure 2-1.

Inside the chat prompt in the middle of the Copilot window, you can type text and ask it questions, upload images, or click or tap the microphone icon and start talking to it. The good news is that the free version of Copilot does not limit how much you can chat with it. However, if you want it to generate images, it will create only 15 images per day.

One of the things I appreciate about Copilot is its constant connection to Bing, Microsoft's search engine. Thanks to this connection, every time it provides answers, it also displays its sources from the web. At the time of writing, other large language models such as ChatGPT and Google's Gemini don't do this, which I find unethical. After all, these AI models are trained using data from the web, and content creators should not only be recognized as the true source of knowledge but also compensated for their work. Microsoft does a good job of acknowledging their sources, though they (and their competition) don't share revenue with content creators. I hope this will change in the future. Until then, let's dive into how you interact with Copilot in Windows 11:

1. **Click or tap the Copilot icon on the taskbar or press the Copilot key on your keyboard (if you have one).**

   The Copilot app window appears (refer to Figure 2-1).

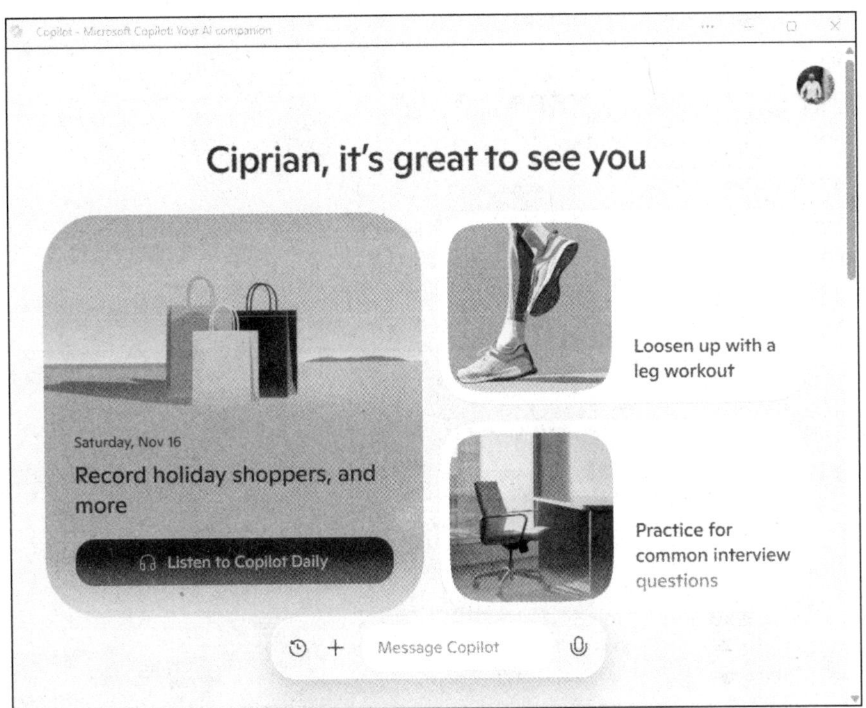

FIGURE 2-1: Initially, Copilot looks like a glorified chat window.

2. **Click or tap inside the Message Copilot field and type the following:** Hey Copilot, give me a summary of what you can do. **Press Enter to submit your input.**

   Copilot starts displaying its answer. Read what it can do for you.

3. **Type the following and press Enter:** Please explain Newton's law of inertia in a kid-friendly way.

   Read the answer presented by Copilot and notice its many references to its sources.

4. **Click or tap the plus (+) icon next to the Copilot logo.**

   You see a menu with the options shown in Figure 2-2.

5. **Select Upload Image, choose a picture from your Pictures folder, and then click or tap Open.**

   Keep in mind that the picture you select is uploaded to Microsoft's servers. You may not want to use a picture of yourself or your family.

6. **In the Add a Message field, type** Analyze this image for me. **Click or tap Submit Message or press the Enter key on your keyboard.**

   Copilot displays its analysis of your picture.

7. **Click or tap X in the top-right corner of the Copilot window to close it.**

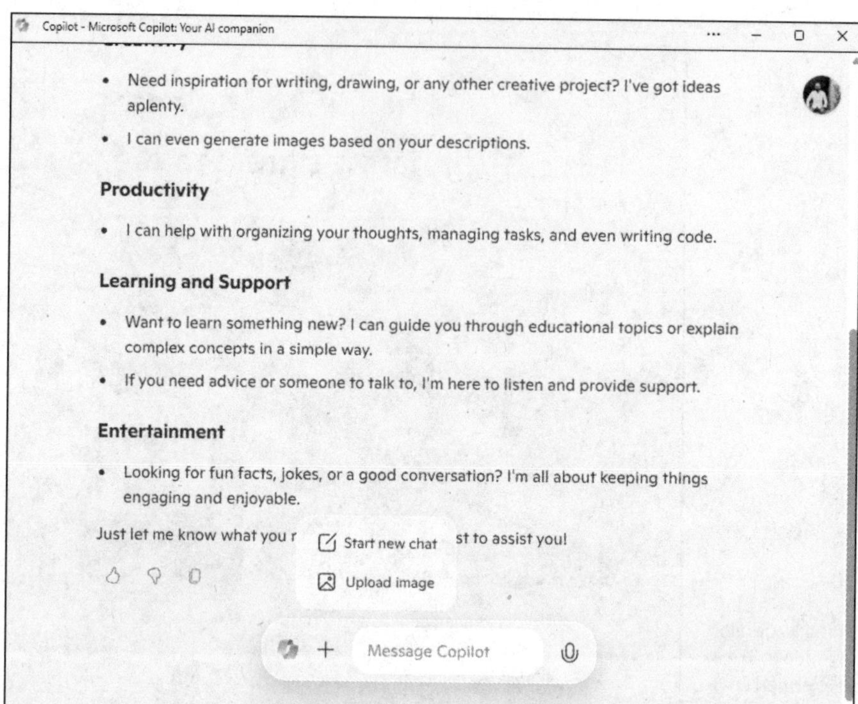

Copilot - Microsoft Copilot: Your AI companion
Need inspiration for writing, drawing, or any other creative project? I've got ideas aplenty.
I can even generate images based on your descriptions.
Productivity
I can help with organizing your thoughts, managing tasks, and even writing code.
Learning and Support
Want to learn something new? I can guide you through educational topics or explain complex concepts in a simple way.
If you need advice or someone to talk to, I'm here to listen and provide support.
Entertainment
Looking for fun facts, jokes, or a good conversation? I'm all about keeping things engaging and enjoyable.
Just let me know what you r
st to assist you!
Start new chat
Upload image
Message Copilot

FIGURE 2-2: You can upload pictures to Copilot.

TIP

Analyzing uploaded images is not the only thing Copilot can do. It can also identify text from an image and translate it into another language, and even generate new images based on the ones you provide and the text input you provide.

Accessing previous chats

Your Copilot conversations are automatically stored, so that you can access them later and continue from where you left off. However, when you start Copilot, you don't see them immediately. Instead, you see the Copilot home page (refer to Figure 2-1), which gives you suggestions about topics of conversation you could have with it. These topics change regularly, and some are interesting. But if you want to access previous chats, here's how it's done:

1. **Click or tap the Copilot icon on the taskbar or press the Copilot key on your keyboard (if you have one).**

   The Copilot app window appears (refer to Figure 2-1).

2. **Click or tap in the Message Copilot field, but don't type anything.**

   Copilot displays the previous conversation, as shown in Figure 2-3.

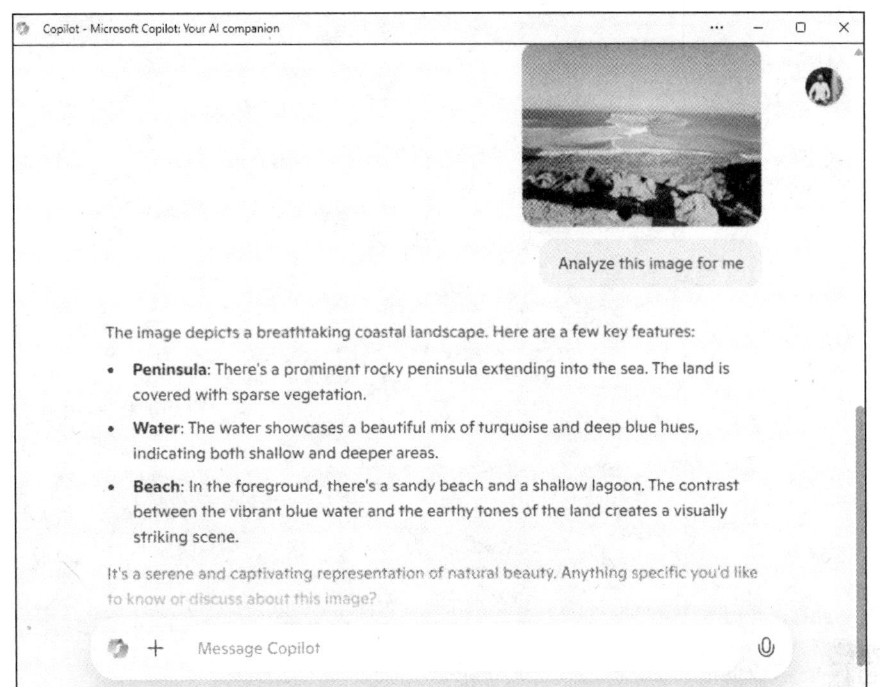

FIGURE 2-3: Copilot displays your previous conversations, in descending order.

3. **If you want to access other past conversations, click or tap the Copilot logo, followed by the View History icon.**

   A menu with past conversations appears, as shown in Figure 2-4.

4. **Click or tap on the conversation you want to access.**

   The conversation is loaded, with all the questions you 've asked and the answers you've received.

5. **Repeat Steps 3 and 4 to view all past conversations that interest you. When you're done, close Copilot.**

TIP

When accessing the menu shown in Figure 2-4, you can delete conversations by clicking or tapping the delete icon (trash can) next to them.

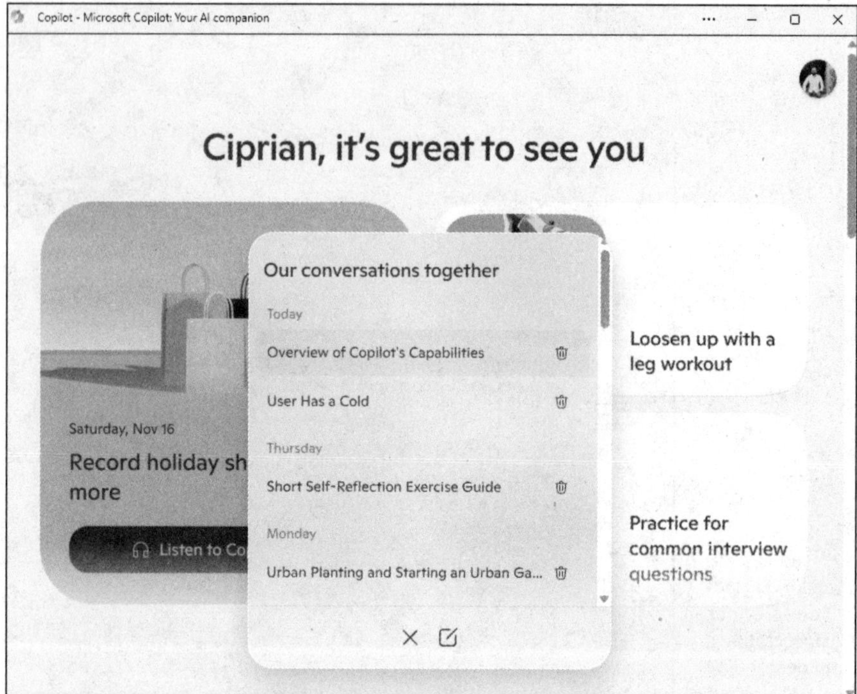

FIGURE 2-4: Copilot shows the history of your chats together.

Ending a chat and starting a new one

Each time you open Copilot, you start a conversation, either by asking it something or selecting a topic from those that it proposes. If you keep typing questions, even ones on a different subject, they are included in the same chat started earlier. If you want to start a new conversation, which will be shown as a separate entry in your chat history, here's what to do:

1. **Click or tap the Copilot icon on the taskbar or press the Copilot key on your keyboard (if you have one).**

   The Copilot app window appears (refer to Figure 2-1).

2. **Click or tap any of the subjects of conversation it proposes to start a new chat.**

   Copilot shares information on the subject you selected, and this is considered a conversation. You can continue the conversation by asking it questions on this topic, if you find it interesting.

3. **When you are done with this conversation and want to start a new one, click or tap the plus (+) icon next to the Copilot logo.**

   The menu shown previously in Figure 2-2 appears.

4. **Click or tap Start New Chat.**

   A new chat starts.

5. **Type the message you want to share with Copilot, and then and press Enter on your keyboard or click or tap the submit message icon (arrow).**

   Copilot answers your query.

6. **Continue the conversation for as long as you want. When you're finished, close Copilot.**

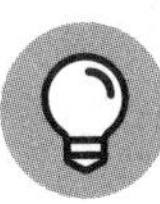

TIP

All the companies investing heavily in AI are experimenting and frequently changing their products and models. This is true of Copilot too. For example, while writing this book, Copilot was redesigned three times. If the instructions don't match what you are experiencing, I recommend that you visit `www.digitalcitizen.life` and look for Copilot tutorials there. My team will do their best to update our Copilot tutorials on a regular basis.

Using Copilot while Browsing the Web

Copilot is embedded in many places into Windows 11, from Photos to Paint, Snipping Tool, and Microsoft Edge. One of the places where it can be most useful is Microsoft Edge, because Copilot can function as an assistant while browsing the web. (Read Chapter 1 in this minibook to learn more about Microsoft Edge.) You can use Copilot to generate a summary of a long web page you're visiting or translate it into another language. Here's how these features work:

1. **Click or tap Start and then Edge.**

   Microsoft Edge opens.

2. **In Microsoft Edge, navigate to** `www.digitalcitizen.life/screenshot-windows/`.

3. **When the article loads in Microsoft Edge, click or tap the Copilot icon in the top right.**

   Copilot appears in a sidebar on the right, as shown in Figure 2-5.

4. **In the Message Copilot text box in the lower right, ask Copilot to generate a summary, and then click or tap the submit message icon (arrow).**

   See how Copilot reads the entire article and shares the key points.

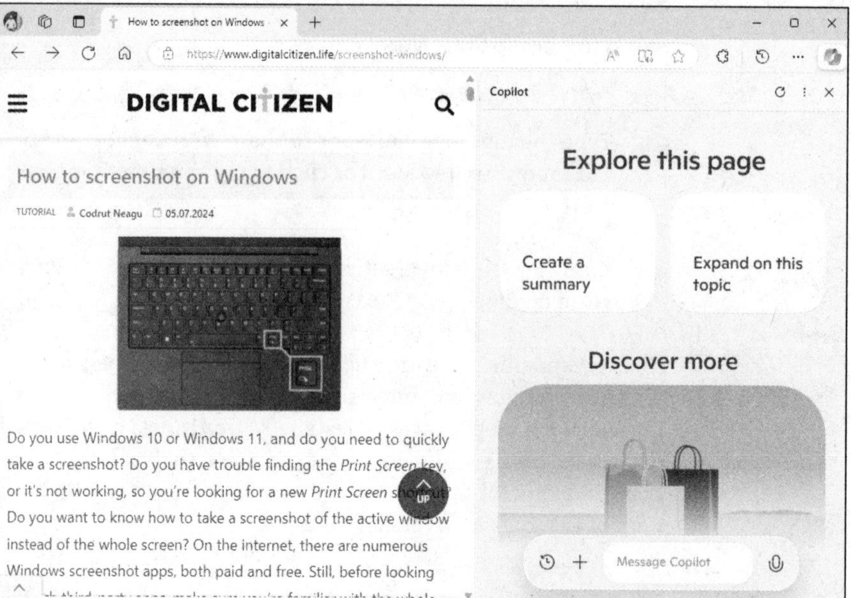

FIGURE 2-5: Copilot has its own icon and sidebar in Microsoft Edge.

5. **In the Message Copilot text box in the lower right, ask Copilot to create a social media post promoting this article, and then click or tap the submit message icon.**

   Copilot generates a social media post, with key points from the article, and relevant hashtags, as shown in Figure 2-6.

6. **In the Message Copilot text box, ask it to write an invitation to your birthday party, which you want to post on a WhatsApp group.**

   Don't forget to give it instructions on the tone of voice you want to use and the length of the invitation.

7. **Click or tap the submit message icon.**

   Copilot generates and displays the invitation.

8. **If you like the generated text, copy and paste it where you want to use it. If not, give it additional instructions.**

9. **When you're done, click or tap the Copilot icon at the top right.**

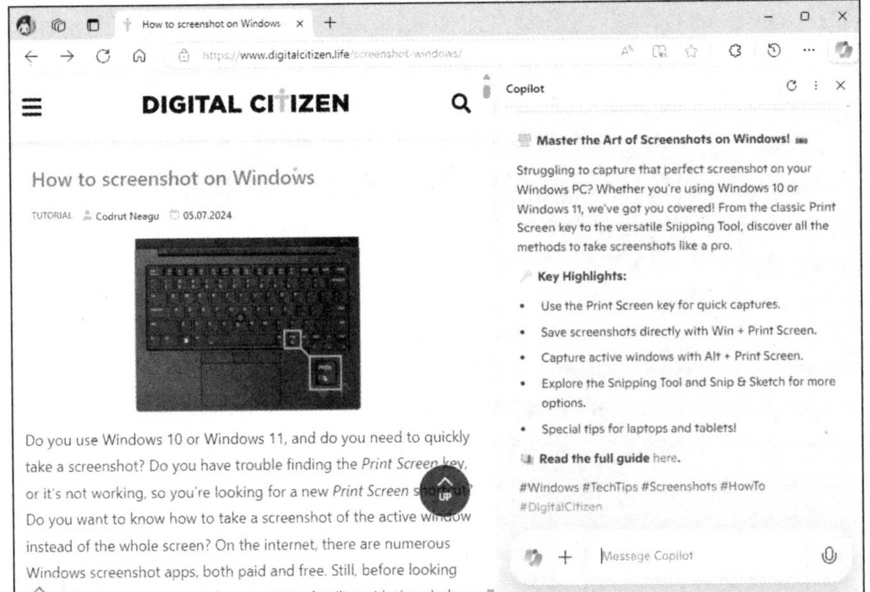

FIGURE 2-6: Copilot can compose social media posts straight from Microsoft Edge.

TIP

A useful way to use Copilot in Microsoft Edge is when you read something for which you want more information. Select the text that interests you, right-click (or press and hold) it and choose Ask Copilot. Copilot shows up on the right side of Microsoft Edge, starts looking for information on your text selection, and provides a detailed answer, complete with links to its sources.

TIP

If you don't like using Microsoft Edge and you prefer Google Chrome, Mozilla Firefox, or some other web browser, you can still use Copilot. Simply visit `copilot.microsoft.com` and sign in with your Microsoft account (read Book 2, Chapter 4). You then have access to the same options as in the Copilot app from Windows 11, even though you may be using a computer with another operating system, such as Linux or macOS.

Adding Copilot to Your Phone

Microsoft wants as many people as possible to use Copilot, so it expanded its availability not only to Windows and the web but also to mobile devices such as Android smartphones, iPhones, and iPads. If you want to give it a try, look it up on your device's app store or visit `www.microsoft.com/en-us/copilot-app` on your device and use the download options shared by Microsoft.

The mobile Copilot app has the same user interface (shown in Figure 2-7), and it does pretty much the same things as the Windows app. After you sign in with your Microsoft account, you can access previous conversations you had on other devices and ask it to do anything you want, from helping you create a plan for a vegetable garden and giving you travel recommendations to creating "realistic images" of flamingos standing in the Arctic Ocean and telling you jokes.

FIGURE 2-7: Copilot is available on mobile devices too.

Copilot is embedded in the mobile version of Microsoft Edge, and works similarly to its desktop counterpart. To access it, tap the Copilot icon at the bottom of the Microsoft Edge app, as shown in Figure 2-8.

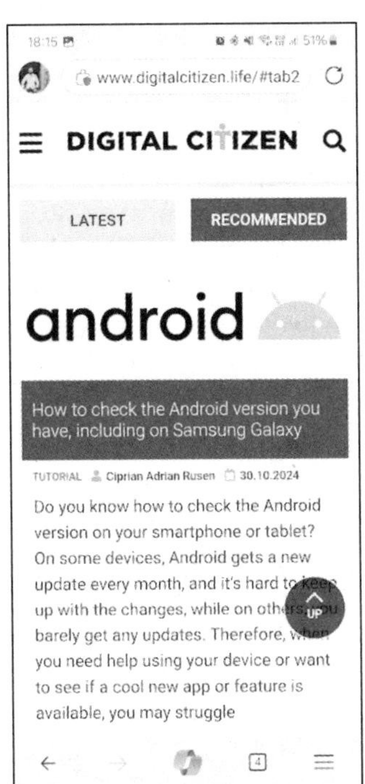

FIGURE 2-8: Check out the large Copilot icon in Microsoft Edge for Android.

Copilot Pro and Copilot for Microsoft 365

Microsoft developed Copilot to be a profitable product, so it's no surprise that they offer a Copilot Pro version for $20 per user per month. Copilot Pro includes all the features of the free version, plus some exciting extras:

- Faster responses during peak usage times
- Enhanced image creation, which generates images more rapidly and using better image generation models
- Access to better AI models that provide more accurate results, including during peak usage times
- Microsoft 365 integration, which allows Copilot to read and summarize your emails in Outlook, generate formulas and analyze data in Excel, or assist in creating presentations in PowerPoint

If you need to generate a lot of images, Copilot Pro is your go-to because it allows up to 100 images per day, compared to the 15-image limit in the free version. Another handy feature is the ability to create and configure a Copilot chatbot tailored to a specific skill or resource. To learn more about Copilot Pro and purchase the subscription, go to `www.microsoft.com/en-us/store/b/copilotpro`.

For business organizations, there's a paid Copilot version integrated into Microsoft 365 subscriptions. This version works with Microsoft Teams to track discussions in real-time and generate conversation summaries. It can also resolve scheduling conflicts based on calendar appointments from Outlook. For details, including pricing, visit `www.microsoft.com/en-us/microsoft-365/business/copilot-for-microsoft-365`.

IN THIS CHAPTER

» Adding email accounts to Outlook

» Creating and searching email messages

» Using the Calendar in Outlook

Chapter 3
Using the Outlook App

In 2024, Microsoft started pushing to their Windows 11 users a new email app that replaces the Mail & Calendar app. This new app is Outlook, and it's a web app, not a desktop app like the old Outlook from Microsoft 365. The new Outlook looks and works quite differently from the old one.

The Outlook app for Windows 11 has been controversial since its preview version, with many users criticizing its user interface, the lack of a unified inbox experience, and the app's inefficient use of hardware resources. Another downside is that Outlook collects more data about your emails than Mail & Calendar and sends it to Microsoft. If privacy and performance are significant concerns for you, you may want to skip using the new Outlook app from Windows 11 and opt for an open-source app like Thunderbird.

However, if you want to try the new Outlook, this chapter has you covered. I dive into the basics of setting up Outlook, starting with adding one or more email accounts. I also explain how to check your emails, search your inbox for older messages, and ask Outlook to check for new ones. Additionally, I give you a tour of Outlook's Calendar capabilities and show you how to navigate it and add new appointments. Are you ready to become an Outlook wizard? Grab your digital wand (that's your mouse or touchpad), and jump right in. Who knows? You might even find that mythical "Inbox Zero" people like to dream about.

Understanding Email

Email is no longer what it used to be in the early days of the internet. Today, email has many different incarnations:

- **Email programs,** commonly called *email clients, email apps,* or *email readers,* run on your computer or device. They reach out to your email, which is stored somewhere on a server (in the cloud, which is to say, on your email company's computers), bring it down to your device, and help you work on it there. Messages get stored on your PC and, optionally, removed from the server when you retrieve them. When you write a message, it too gets stored on your machine, but it also gets sent out via your email provider. Your email client interacts with your email company's server through strictly defined processes called *protocols.* The most common protocols are POP3, SMTP, and IMAP. As is the case with most computer acronyms, their names don't mean anything useful to most people.
- **Online email** (most commonly Gmail, `Outlook.com`, or Yahoo! Mail, but there are many others) works directly through a web browser or a program that operates much like a web browser but runs on your computer. You see mail on your computer, but it's stored on your email company's servers. You can log in to your mail service from any web browser, anywhere in the world, and pick up right where you left off.
- **Hybrid systems** combine local mail storage on your computer or device with online email. Just as email clients are getting more online email characteristics, so too are online email systems adopting limited local storage. For example, Gmail can be set up to store mail on your machine, so you can work on email while away from an internet connection.

All the popular email services have mobile options, too. For example, Microsoft has Outlook apps for Windows 11, iPhone, iPad, and Android, and their email service also works directly through an internet browser on any kind of device.

Google, similarly, has Gmail apps for Android, iPhone, and iPad, although Windows access to Gmail goes through a browser. Unlike Outlook, Gmail consistently offers the same interface and the same behavior on all its different platforms. The free version of Gmail is identical to the organizational version, but organizations are required to sign up for (and pay for) Google Workspace.

Surprisingly, thanks to POP3 and IMAP, both Outlook and Gmail work well with about any email account. You can use @gmail.com email addresses with Outlook and @outlook.com (and @hotmail.com, @msn.com, @live.com, and so on) addresses with Gmail. The people reading your messages will never know that you're consorting with the enemy. Now that you have a basic understanding of the different ways in which email can be used, let's get practical and use the Outlook app from Windows 11.

Setting Up Outlook

The first time you click or tap the Outlook shortcut from the Start menu, you're given the chance to add an account. If you're signed into Windows using a Microsoft account, the app automatically suggests it for you. If you're using a local account, you have to type it yourself. Here's how to set up Outlook in Windows 11 and add your first account:

1. **Click or tap the Start icon and then Outlook.**

   The Outlook app appears, as shown in Figure 3-1. Your Microsoft account is automatically suggested for use.

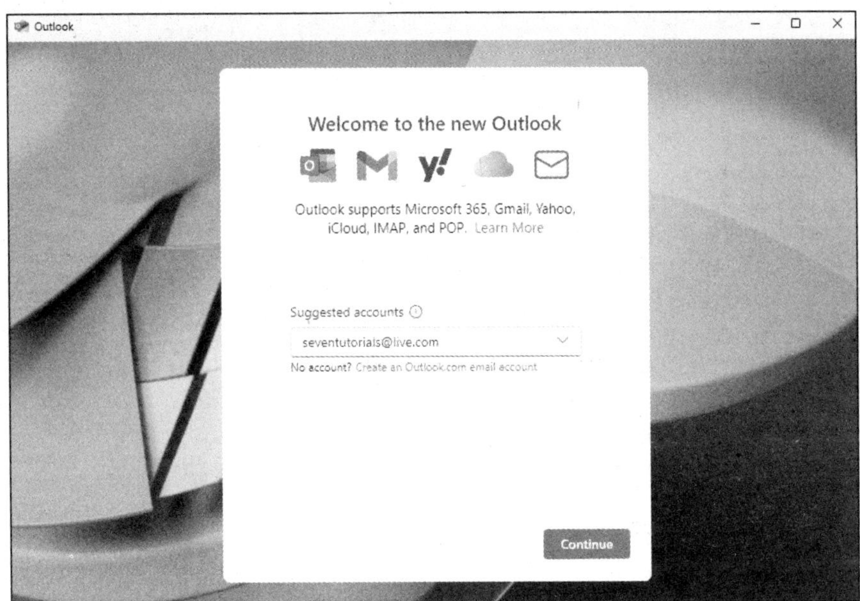

FIGURE 3-1: The Outlook app works with about any kind of email account.

2. **Leave the suggested account as is or type a new one, and then click or tap Continue.**

   Outlook takes some time to set things up. If you're using the suggested Microsoft account to sign in to Windows 11, no password is required. The sign-in is performed automatically.

3. **If you're using another account, you are also asked to type the password and other authentication details. Click or tap Sign In after entering the requested information.**

   When Outlook is done setting up your email account, you see your inbox, as shown in Figure 3-2.

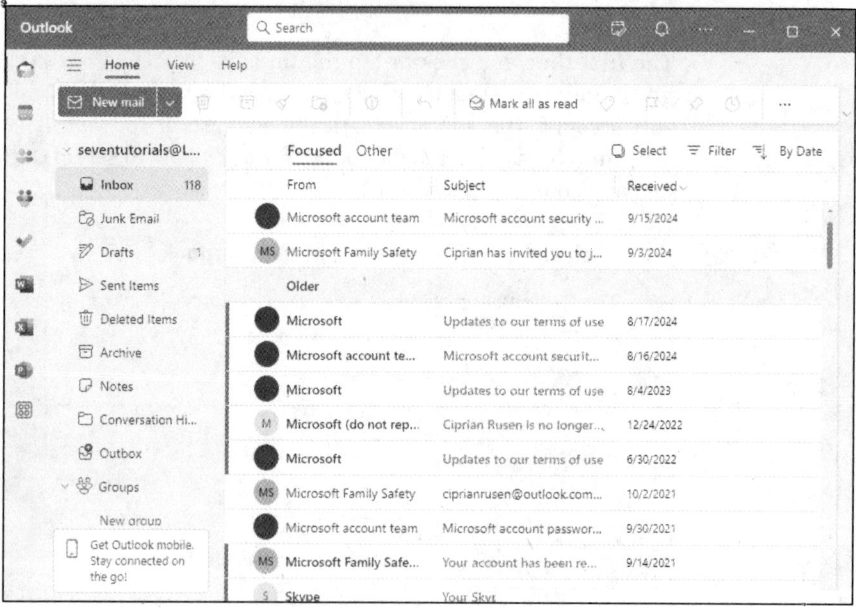

FIGURE 3-2: Outlook presents your inbox.

4. **Click the latest email received from the Outlook Team, which has a subject that starts with the word *Welcome*.**

   The email presents you with the latest features available with your email account.

You can start using the Outlook app to send and receive emails using the account that you just set up.

Adding Other Email Accounts

The Outlook app can connect to any `Outlook.com`, Gmail, Microsoft 365, Yahoo!, iCloud, or IMAP or POP account. You can also add any number of different types of accounts. For example, you can add two different Gmail accounts or multiple `Outlook.com` accounts.

To add a new account alongside the default one, do the following:

1. **Open the Outlook app, and then click or tap View followed by View Settings.**

   The Settings window shown in Figure 3-3 appears.

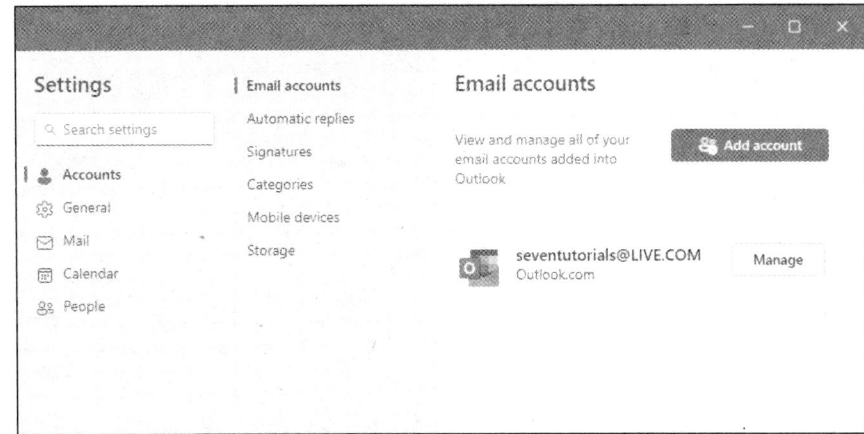

FIGURE 3-3: This is where you set up your email accounts in Outlook.

2. **Select Accounts and then Email Accounts.**

   You see a list of the accounts that were already added to Outlook.

3. **Click or tap Add Account.**

   Outlook displays the Add All Your Email Accounts dialog box, where it may suggest another account. However, you can remove the suggestion and add any account you want, including one that's not from Microsoft.

4. **Type the email address of the account you want to add, and then click or tap Continue.**

   I added my personal Gmail account. Depending on the type of account you add, you may be informed that your emails, calendar, events, and contacts will be synced to the Microsoft Cloud.

5. **Click or tap Continue.**

   Depending on the email account you're adding, a web browser window may be loaded. You're asked to sign in with your account.

6. **Type the necessary authentication details (email, password, and so on), and then click or tap Sign In.**

   Some email services, such as Gmail, may show a prompt informing you that, by continuing, they will share your name, email address, language preference, and profile picture with Microsoft apps and services, as shown in Figure 3-4.

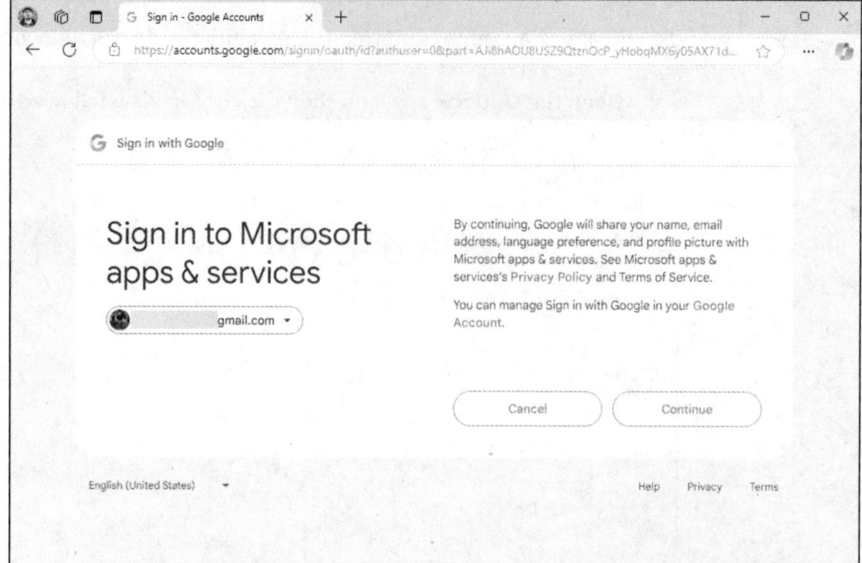

FIGURE 3-4: Gmail requires many confirmations before setting up your account in `Outlook.com`.

7. **Click or tap Continue as many times as necessary to finalize the setup process and give it any permission it requires.**

   The Outlook app informs you that your emails are now synchronized.

8. **Click or tap Done.**

   The new account is shown in the Email Accounts list. To add other accounts, repeat Steps 3 to 8.

9. **Close the Settings window.**

Checking Your Emails

After you've added all the email accounts you want to use in the Outlook app, it's time to start exploring how to use it. This app is similar to web-based email services like `Outlook.com` or Gmail. Here's how it works:

1. **Click or tap the Start icon, followed by Outlook.**

   You see your inbox, as in Figure 3-2.

2. **Select the email account you want to navigate, and expand it to see its folders.**

   Under the name of each email account, you'll see email folders such as Inbox, Junk email, Drafts, and Sent Items.

3. **Click or tap the Inbox folder of the email account that interests you.**

   On the right, Outlook lists your emails in descending order. Unread emails have a bold, blue subject line.

4. **Click or tap on an email message to view its content.**

   Outlook displays the content of your email, as shown in Figure 3-5. For each email, you see its title (or subject line), who sent it, to whom it was sent, and the content.

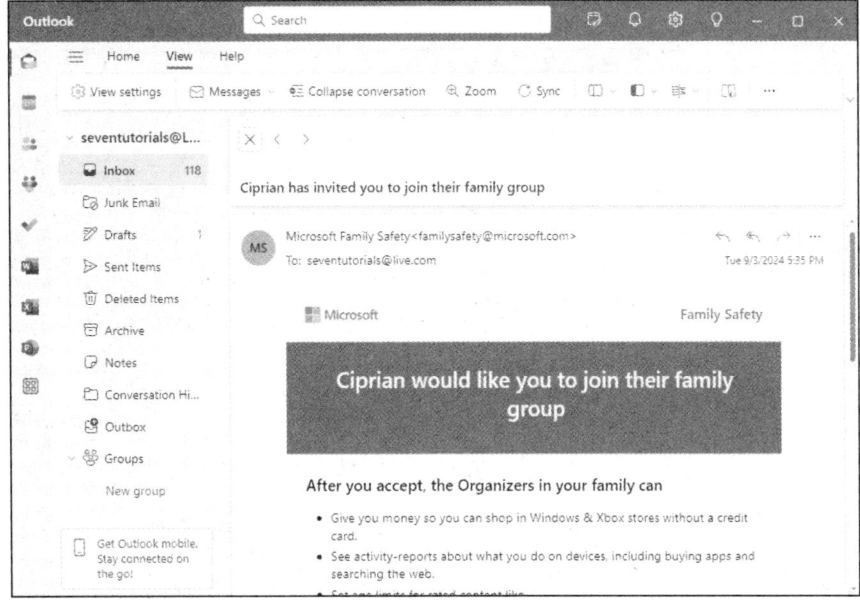

FIGURE 3-5: Viewing an email in your inbox.

5. **Click or tap the X icon above the email's title to get back to the previous folder.**

   You return to the list of emails.

6. **Select the View tab at the top, and then click or tap Sync.**

   Outlook checks for new emails that were sent and received and updates your account. You can check your email folders to see if there's anything new.

Creating an email message

To write an email in Outlook, simply click or tap the New Mail button at the left end of the Home tab. You can also select Reply or Reply to All when viewing a message you've received in your inbox. Whether you reply or start a new message, simply start typing. By default, everything you type is saved automatically as a draft message that can be continued at any time, as shown in Figure 3-6.

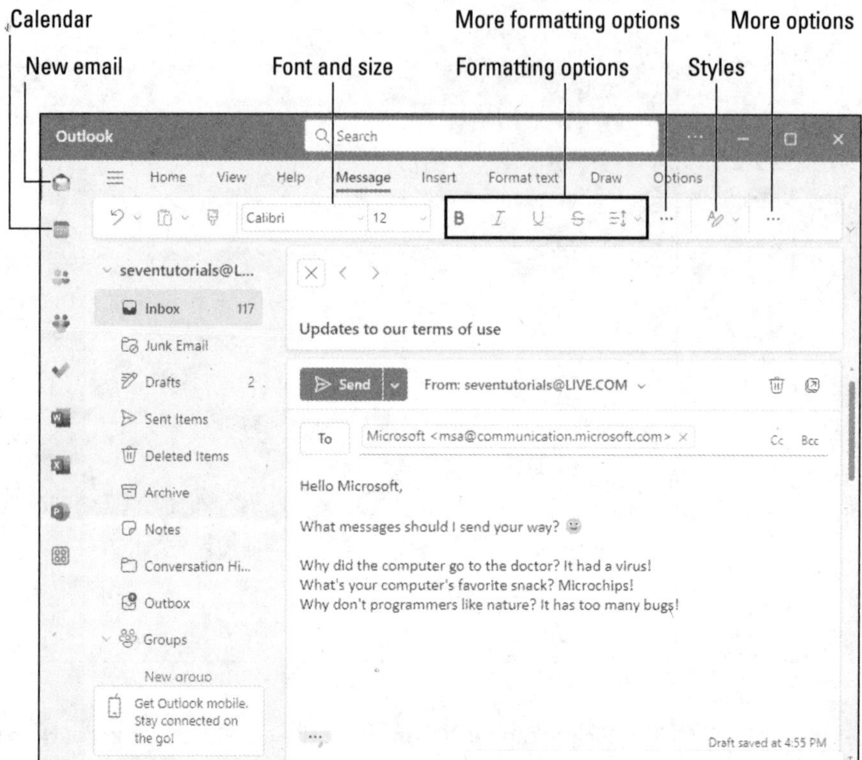

FIGURE 3-6: When you reply to a message or compose a new email, Outlook gives you these options.

Here's a quick tour of the features available to you as you create your email message:

» **Format the text:** The text you type appears in Calibri 12-point type, which is a good all-around, middle-of-the-road choice. If you want to format the text, select it, and then use the formatting options at the top of the Outlook app, shown in Figure 3-6. You can change the font and size.

Those who have a keyboard and know how to use it will be pleased to know that many of the standard formatting keyboard shortcuts still work. Here are the most-used shortcuts for formatting:

- *Ctrl+B* toggles bold on and off.
- *Ctrl+I* toggles italic on and off.
- *Ctrl+U* toggles underline on and off.
- *Ctrl+Z* undoes the last action.
- *Ctrl+Y* redoes the last undone action.

(In addition to the old stalwarts Ctrl+C for copy, Ctrl+X for cut, and Ctrl+V for paste, of course.)

You'll be happy to know that your old favorite emoticons work, too. Type :-) and you get a smiley face.

» **Create bulleted or numbered lists or apply other paragraph formatting:** Select the paragraph(s) you want to change, click or tap the more formatting options icon (three vertical dots), and choose from the many formatting options available, as shown in Figure 3-7.

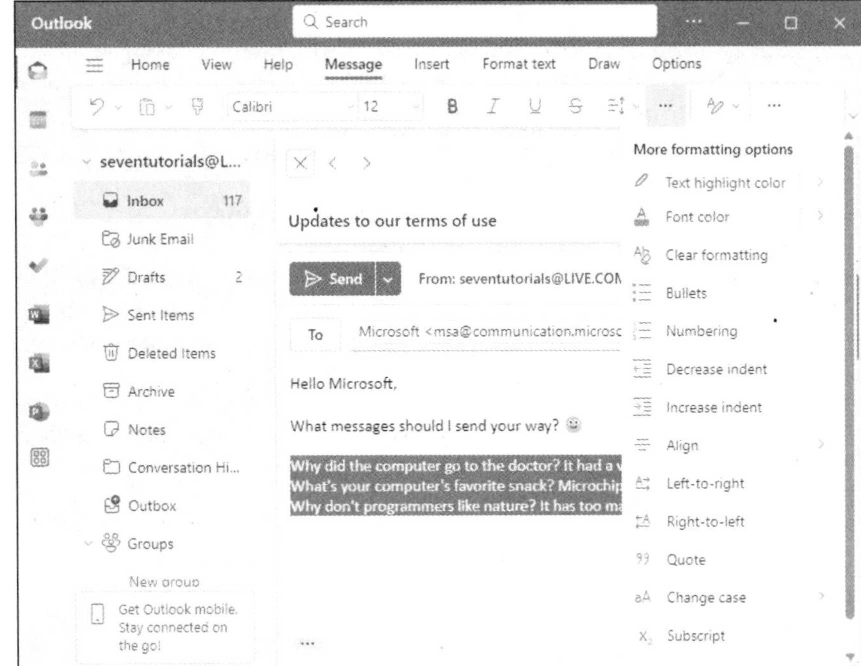

FIGURE 3-7: To create a bulleted list, type the paragraphs, select them, and then the bullets style from More Options.

- **Add an attachment:** At the top, click or tap the attach icon (paperclip). You see a menu where you can choose the location of the file you want to attach. Click or tap the file to select it, and then click or tap Open.
- **Add a message priority indicator:** At the top, choose the Options tab and set the message to either high (exclamation point) or low (down arrow) priority.
- **Send the message:** Click or tap the Send icon next to the From field, and the message is queued in the outbox and ready to send. You can also click or tap the arrow next to Send, choose Schedule Send, and then set the day and time when your message will be sent by Outlook.
- **Delete the message:** If at any time you decide that you don't want to send a message, click or tap the delete icon (trash can) to the right of the From field.

The Outlook app's editing capabilities are impressive, with many of the features you would expect in Microsoft Word. Styles, tables, fancy formatting, and easy manipulation of inline pictures top the most-used list.

Searching for an email

REMEMBER

Searching for mail is easy if you remember one important detail: When you're using multiple accounts, navigate to the account you want to search before you perform the search. If you search while you're looking at the `Gmail.com` inbox, for example, you won't find anything in your `Outlook.com` account.

To search for email messages:

1. **Click or tap the Start icon and then Outlook.**

   Your inbox appears.

2. **If you have more than one email account, select a folder in the account you want to search.**
3. **At the top, click or tap in the search field.**
4. **Type your search term, and press Enter or click or tap the magnifying glass icon.**

   Your results appears where you usually see your emails.

5. **To load a message, click or tap it in the list of results.**

BEYOND EMAIL

Email is changing a lot. Most of us have used Facebook, Instagram, X, Teams, Slack, and WhatsApp for interactions that are more or less similar to email. The distinction between texting and email is disappearing — in fact, the line between video calls and email is crumbling too.

Don't lock yourself out of new ways to communicate using WhatsApp, Discord, Threads, Slack, Instagram, Teams, Zoom, and many others. Each has a slightly different approach, and in some situations, they're better than good old emails.

Working with Outlook's Calendar

The Outlook app automatically connects to your calendar when you add an email account. Therefore, if you add your Gmail account, your `Outlook.com` account, and your work email account to it, you can see the calendar for each of them. Here's how it works:

1. **Click or tap the Start icon and then Outlook.**

   Your inbox appears.

2. **In the left column, click or tap the calendar icon (labeled in Figure 3-6).**

   You see the calendar for all your accounts, displayed by default in monthly view, as shown in Figure 3-8. If you have added multiple accounts, the appointments and events from each account have a different color.

3. **To switch between calendar views, use the options at the top and click or tap them in the following order: Week, Work Week, and Day.**
4. **To see the details of a calendar appointment, simply click or tap it.**

   Calendar displays all information added to the appointment, such as name, date, time, and location.

To add an appointment or another calendar item, click or tap New Event button in the upper-left corner of the Outlook Calendar app. The New Event window shown in Figure 3-9 appears.

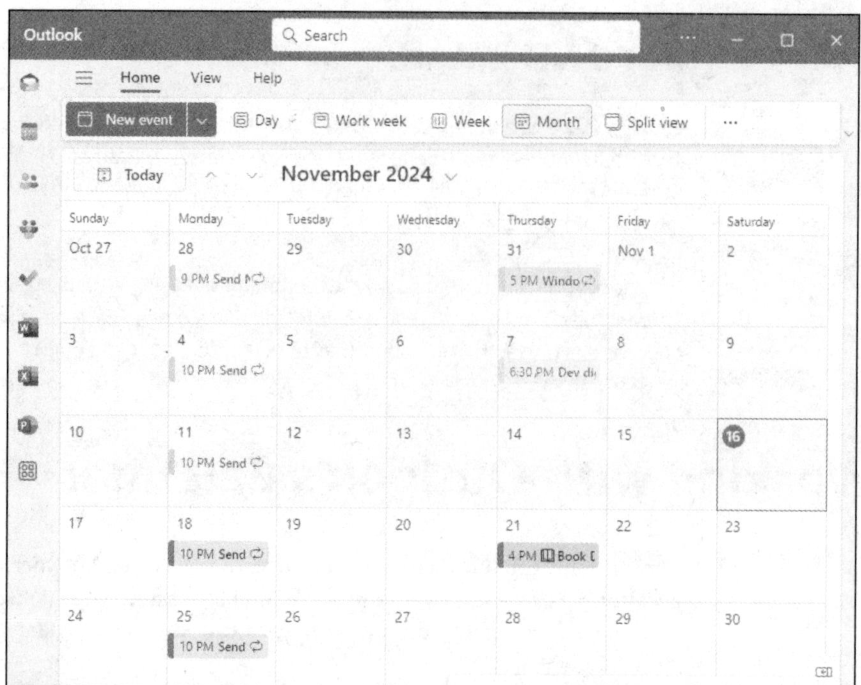

FIGURE 3-8: Viewing your calendar in Outlook.

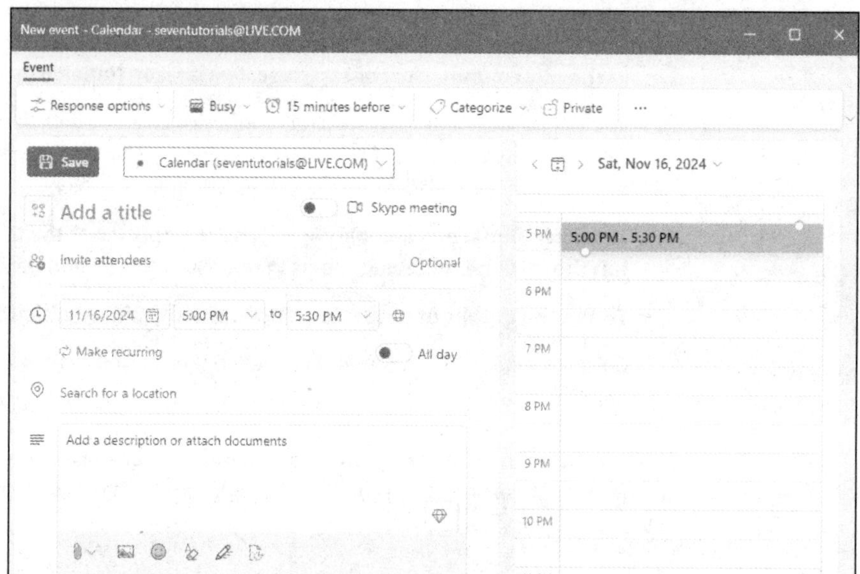

FIGURE 3-9: Create an appointment or a calendar entry.

Most of the entries are self-explanatory, except these:

REMEMBER

- **You must choose a calendar — actually, an email account — that will be synchronized with this appointment.** As soon as you enter the appointment, Outlook logs in to the indicated account and adds the appointment to the account's calendar.
- **You may optionally specify email addresses in the People box.** If you put valid email addresses in the Invite Attendees field, Outlook generates an email message and sends it to the recipients, asking them to confirm the appointment.

TIP

If you click or tap the Make Recurring option, Outlook lets you choose how often to repeat and when to end the repetition.

When you're finished, click or tap Save or Send (in the upper-left corner), depending on whether you're setting the appointment or setting it and sending invitations.

IN THIS CHAPTER

» Viewing pictures with the Photos app

» Adding photos in several ways

» Editing pictures with the Photos app

» Creating pictures using AI

» Navigating your Pictures folder

Chapter 4

Working with Photos

The Photos app in Windows 11 has been redesigned with rounded corners, updated typography styling, new theme-specific color palettes, and more. It's not just about looks, though — there are quite a few new features compared to the Windows 10 version, including some AI tricks that only work on the latest Copilot+ PCs.

This app is meant to give you a pleasing, straightforward way to look at your picture collection, coupled with some easy-to-use photo-editing capabilities. I find that it does a good job at these tasks and that few alternatives offer a better experience. However, if your expectations go beyond that, you'll be disappointed.

In this chapter, I walk you through what Photos can do, starting with how to view pictures in the app and navigate its user interface. Then, I explain how to add images from different sources, how to use the editing tools, and how to tweak some of its settings. If you have a fancy new Copilot+ PC device infused with AI capabilities, you can also learn how to use Photos to create images with the help of AI.

Lastly, I show you how to navigate your folders with pictures straight from the Photos app so that you can find what you're looking for faster than when using the built-in search.

Viewing Pictures with the Photos App

The Windows 11 Photos app is a central hub for the images and videos stored on your computer, OneDrive, and even iCloud, and it offers a straightforward way to manage and view those pictures and videos. You can organize your collection by date or browse through the folder structure on your computer. For users with newer laptops or PCs equipped with a Neural Processing Unit (NPU), Photos includes AI-powered tools for creating images based on text prompts. This mix of basic organizing features and modern AI capabilities can turn Photos into a handy tool for photo management.

To get you familiarized with the Photos app, let's start with a mini-tour and see how you can view pictures from your computer:

1. **In the Start menu, click or tap the Photos shortcut. If you can't find it, go to All and then Photos.**

   The main screen of the Photos app appears, displaying the Gallery section, similar to Figure 4-1.

TIP

   The collection is a simple reverse chronological view of all the pictures and videos in your computer's Pictures folder and its subfolders, combined with all your pictures and videos in the OneDrive Pictures folder and its subfolders. Note that pictures outside your Pictures folder aren't included.

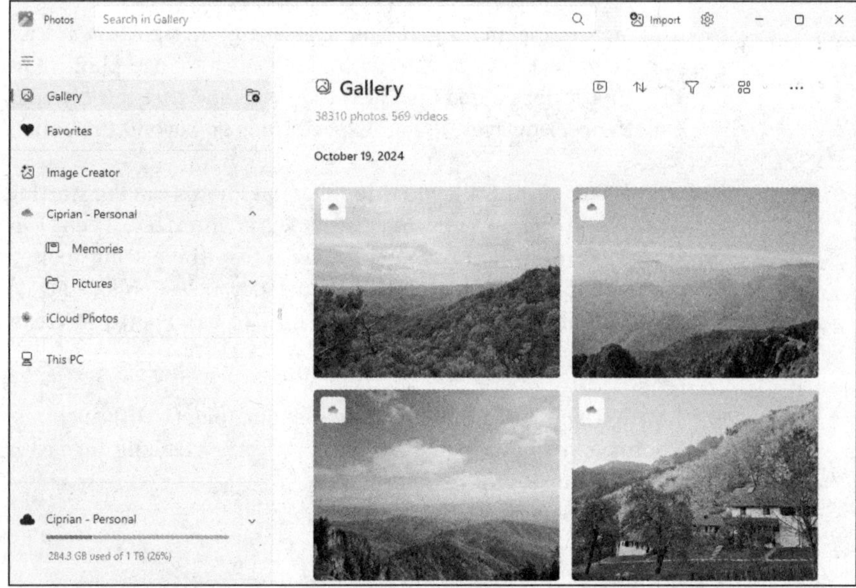

FIGURE 4-1: Your pictures are displayed in reverse chronological order.

2. **If you want to search for a specific photo, use the slider on the right to scroll and find the date the photo was taken.**

   You can also search for people, places, or things by using the Search box at the top.

3. **To view a picture from the Photos app, double-click or double-tap it.**

   The picture opens in a different window, similar to Figure 4-2. At the top, you see icons for editing, rotating, deleting, printing, sharing, and starting a slideshow with the image. Towards the top right, you also have icons for browsing all photos and videos by returning to the Photos app and using other Microsoft tools such as Designer, Clipchamp, or OneDrive.

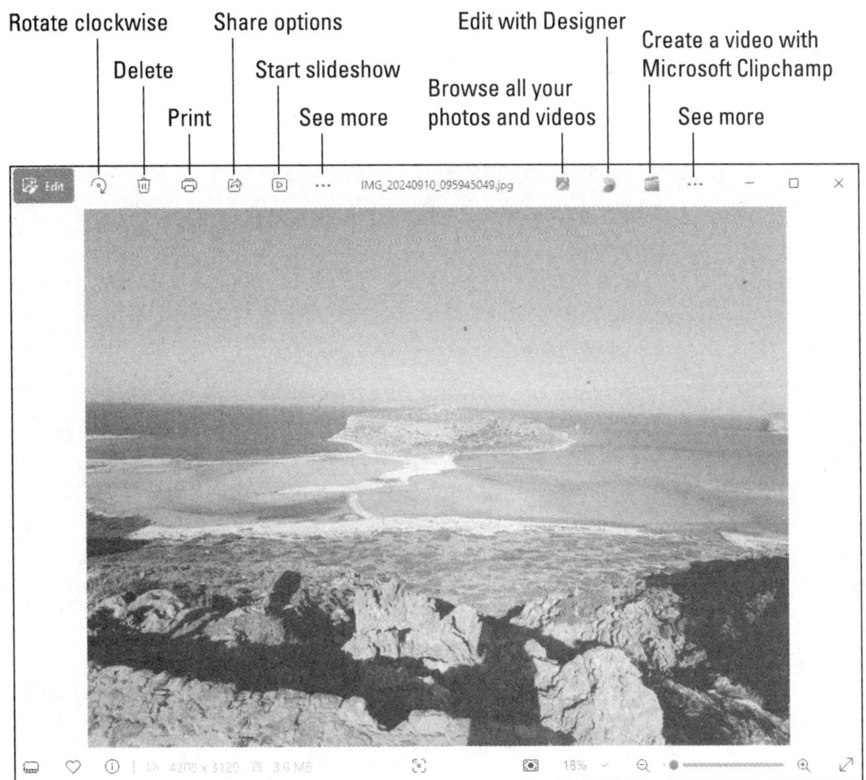

FIGURE 4-2: The icons available when viewing a picture in the Photos app.

4. **Navigate your pictures by clicking or tapping the right margin to move to the next picture or the left margin to move to the previous picture. Or press your keyboard's left or right arrow key.**

5. **To return to your Pictures collection, click or tap the Photos icon in the top right.**

Working with Photos

TECHNICAL STUFF

The Photos app can display an enormous variety of picture and video formats, including AVI, BMP, GIF (including animated GIFs), JPG, MOV, MP4, MPEG, MPG, PCX, PNG, many kinds of RAW (full-quality photos), TIF, WMF, and WMV files. That covers most picture and movie formats you're likely to encounter.

REMEMBER

By default, the Photos app in Windows 11 uses dark mode for its user interface. In this chapter I use light mode so that the printed figures in the book will be clearer.

Adding Photos

You can add pictures to your collection in the Photos app in three ways:

- **Add photos to OneDrive.** Putting photos into the OneDrive Photos folder is a simple drag and drop. File Explorer is great for this task. However, you can set OneDrive to back up the pictures from your smartphone automatically, like I do. Once they're synchronized with Microsoft's cloud storage, they will automatically pop up in the Photos app of your Windows 11 device.
- **Import photos from a connected device.** You can import pictures from a camera or any removable device, including a USB drive, an SD card, or even an external hard drive. See the next section, "Importing pictures from a camera or an external drive," for details.
- **Add pictures to your Pictures folder.** I call this the old-fashioned way, and it's how I add pictures to the Photos app (in addition to OneDrive). Simply use File Explorer to move photos and videos in your Pictures folder. Remember that videos in your Videos folder don't show up in the Photos app at first. You need to add the Videos folder to the Photos app folder watchlist using the instructions in the "Adding folders to the Photos app" section, later in this chapter.

Importing pictures from a camera or an external drive

It's easy to import pictures from a camera or any external data source, including a USB-attached hard drive, an SD card, or a smartphone connected to your computer through USB. Attach the camera, plug in the micro SD card or the external drive, and wait for Windows 11 to recognize it. Then, do the following:

1. **Click or tap the Start icon and then Photos.**
2. **At the top right of the Photos app, click or tap the Import button.**

   The action opens the menu shown in Figure 4-3. It displays a list of devices connected to your Windows 11 PC.

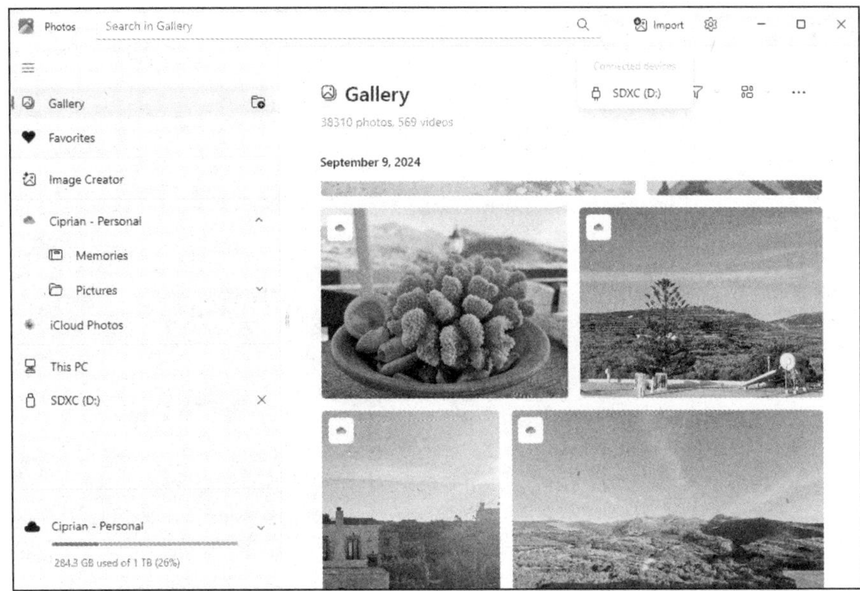

FIGURE 4-3: It's easy to import pictures from anywhere by using the Photos app.

3. **Click or tap on the name of the device you want to import from.**

   The Photos app takes some time to scan for pictures on your selected device.
4. **Select the pictures you want to import, and then click or tap the Add button, which shows the number of photos you've selected.**

   The Photos app asks you to choose a folder where you want to import the selected picture(s).
5. **Choose the folder, click or tap Import, and you're done.**

   When you go back to All Photos, you'll see the new pictures in your Photos collection.

Adding folders to the Photos app

By default, the Photos app from Windows 11 scans only your local Pictures folder and the OneDrive Pictures folder (if you're using a Microsoft account). When you open the app, you can't see pictures and videos from other folders. Even the video files from your Videos folder are ignored. To fix that and add other locations for the Photos app to scan and manage, do the following:

1. **Start the Photos app and select Gallery on the left.**

   You see the Gallery with your pictures, similar to Figure 4-4.

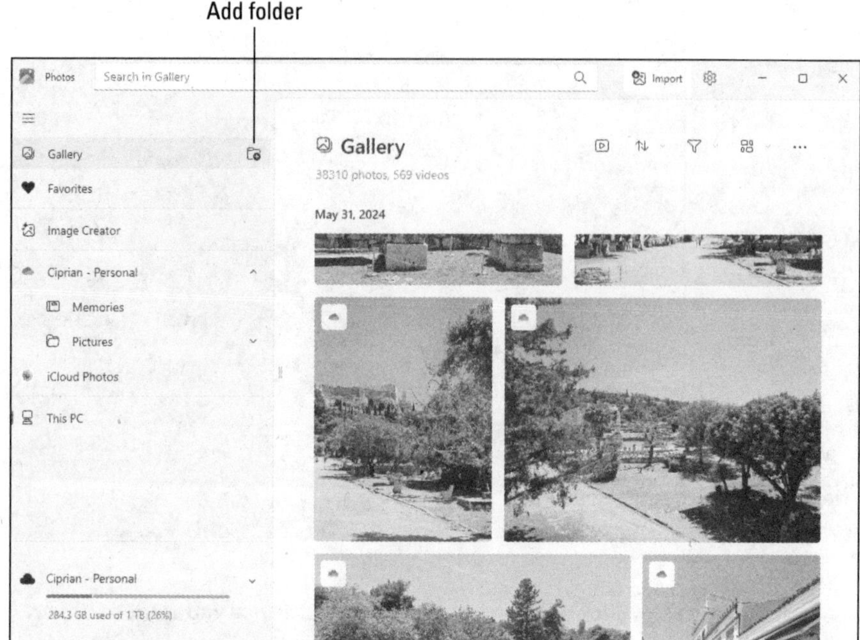

FIGURE 4-4: From the Gallery you can add more folders to the Photos app.

2. **Click or tap Add a Folder icon next to Gallery.**

   You see the Select Folder dialog.

3. **Browse your computer and select the folder you want to add. Then, click or tap Select Folder.**

   The selected folder is now listed in the Folders list that the Photos app is using.

4. **Repeat Steps 2 and 3 until you've added all the folders you want.**

   Your collection now includes the pictures and videos from the folders you've added to the Photos app.

Dealing with pictures from OneDrive or iCloud

If you use a Microsoft account to sign into Windows 11 (read Book 2, Chapter 4) the Photos app automatically looks for any pictures and videos you've stored on your OneDrive and displays them automatically, as long as they're stored in the Pictures folder. Pictures and videos stored in other folders in your OneDrive, such as Documents or Personal Vault, aren't displayed in your All Photos collection.

TIP

If you are using an iPhone or iPad and want to add your pictures and videos from iCloud, you can. Click iCloud Photos in the Photos app, install iCloud for Windows from the Microsoft Store, sign in with your Apple ID, and choose Photos to view them in the Photos app.

If you don't use iCloud or OneDrive, you may want to remove their content from the Photos app. You can make these changes as follows:

1. **Start the Photos app and click or tap the settings icon (gear) in the top right.**

   The settings shown in Figure 4-5 appear.

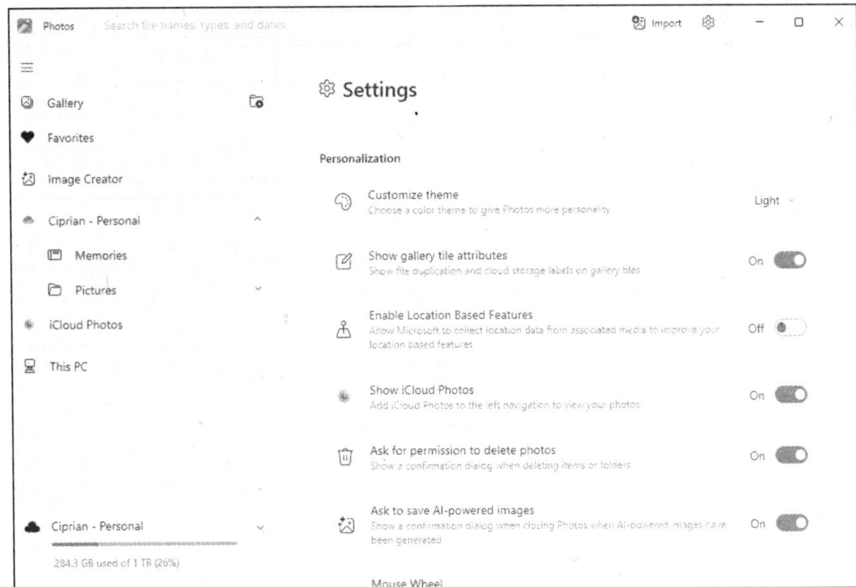

FIGURE 4-5: Here you can change the settings for the Photos app.

Working with Photos

2. **Click or tap the switch for Show iCloud Photos to set it off.**

   Note how the iCloud Photos section is instantly removed from the Photos app.

3. **Scroll down to OneDrive Accounts, and click or tap yours to expand it.**

   You see additional settings for managing and removing OneDrive albums.

4. **Click or tap Remove next to Remove OneDrive Albums, Search by Content, and Memories.**

   The OneDrive section can't be removed from the Photos app. However, all the content from OneDrive has been removed and is no longer available.

5. **Click or tap Gallery to see your pictures and videos without the cloud content included.**

TIP

Do you want to switch the color theme that the Photos app uses? After getting to the settings page shown in Figure 4-5, click or tap the drop-down list next to Customize Theme and select Light.

Editing Photos

Although searching for pictures in the Photos app isn't the best experience, editing can be surprisingly good. And if you have a Copilot+ PC device with a Neural Processing Unit (NPU), you can even use AI-based tools to restyle images and remove or replace backgrounds.

Here's how to use the Photos app to edit a picture:

1. **Navigate to the photo in the Photos app and click or tap it.**

   The picture opens in a separate window, and a bar is shown at the top of its window, with the options presented previously in Figure 4-2.

2. **Click or tap the edit icon in the top left.**

   Each of the many icons at the top represents a tab that reveals additional editing options: Crop, Adjust, Filter, Markup, Erase, Background, and Restyle, as shown in Figure 4-6.

3. **To see the filter options, click or tap the filter icon (labeled in Figure 4-6).**

   You have various options for applying enhancement techniques to the picture in a manner that resembles an Instagram experience. You can use filters that can increase the contrast of your photo, make it black and white, or add more punch to its colors.

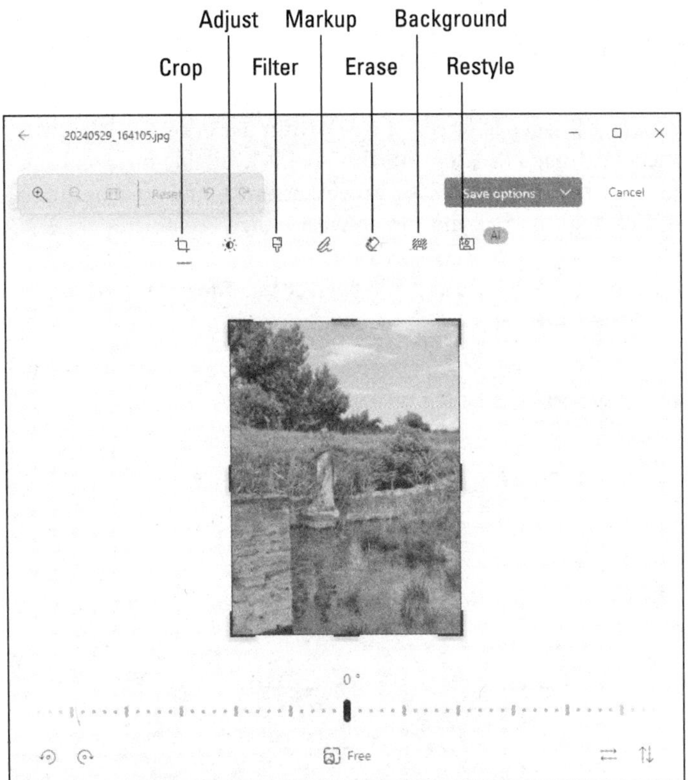

FIGURE 4-6: The editing options offered by the Photos app.

4. **To remove an area from your picture, click or tap the erase icon (labeled in Figure 4-6).**

   You see options for adjusting the brush size.

5. **Move the slider for the brush size until you find the size you want, and then click or tap the area you want to remove from your picture.**

   Note how the Photos app uses AI to remove that area from the picture and fill it with something it thinks makes sense.

6. **To save your changes, click or tap Save Options followed by Save as Copy.**

   The Save As dialog appears.

7. **Name your new picture, choose its location, and click or tap Save.**

   You drop out of editing mode and see the resulting picture.

When you're ready to return to your pictures collection, click or tap the Photos icon in the top right of the picture you're viewing.

Using Image Creator

Creating images is one of the most fun uses of AI in Windows 11. The Photos app includes Image Creator, but this tool is available only on Copilot+ PC devices, not laptops and PCs with older processors without AI capabilities. If you have such a device, here's what you can do with Image Creator:

1. **Start the Photos app and click or tap Image Creator on the left side of the app.**

   You see a text prompt that you can use to generate images, followed by a list of visual ideas, as shown in Figure 4-7.

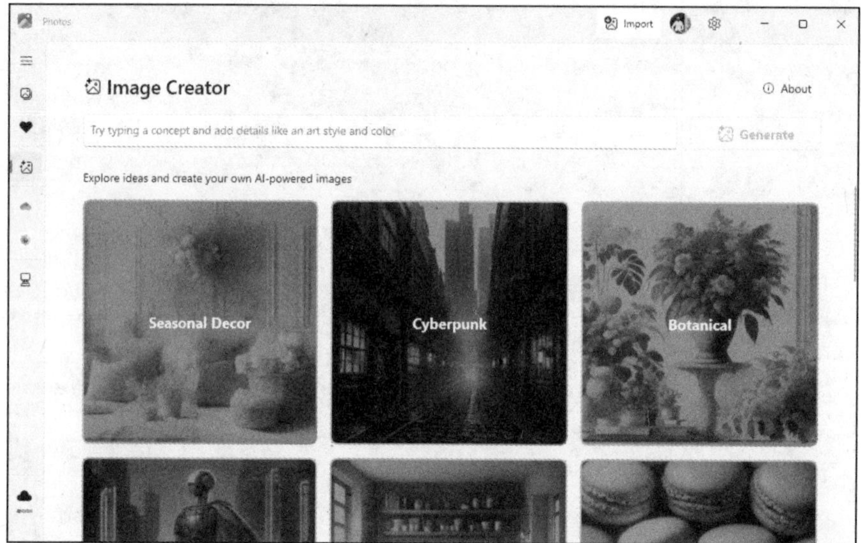

FIGURE 4-7: Using Image Creator in the Photos app.

2. **To get you started, choose one of the ideas in the list.**

   For example, I selected Sci-fi Book Covers.

   The Photos app displays the prompt it uses for Image Creator and starts generating images that fit that description. You have some controls at the top for adjusting the creativity of the image generation process and its style.

3. **Scroll down the list of AI-generated pictures and select the picture or pictures you like.**

4. **When you're done, click or tap the Save button in the top right.**

   The Select Folder dialog appears.

5. **Select the folder where you want to save the picture.**

   The folder is saved with an automatically generated name.

6. **To return to your pictures, click or tap Gallery in the top left.**

   If you saved the AI-generated picture in your Pictures folder (or any of its subfolders), the picture appears in your collection.

Browsing Folders with Photos

Some people don't find the search capabilities built into Photos precise enough to find what they're looking for. Others don't like the default All Photos view and its way of organizing pictures and videos. If you're in a similar situation, you can navigate to specific folders on your computer or OneDrive, straight from the Photos app like this:

1. **Start the Photos app. To ensure that you have enough room to navigate, maximize Photos by clicking or tapping the square icon in the top-right corner.**

2. **To navigate the pictures found on your OneDrive, click or tap on the OneDrive icon on the left, and then Pictures.**

   Note how the folders on the left side of the app window expand into a tree-like structure.

3. **Navigate to the subfolder you want to view.**

   On the right side of the Photos app, you see the pictures from the folder you've just selected, as shown in Figure 4-8.

4. **Scroll down the list of pictures on the right until you find the one you're interested in, and then double-click or double-tap to open it.**

5. **When you've finished viewing the picture, click or tap X in the top right.**

6. **To navigate the pictures found on your computer, select This PC on the left, and then repeat Steps 3 to 5.**

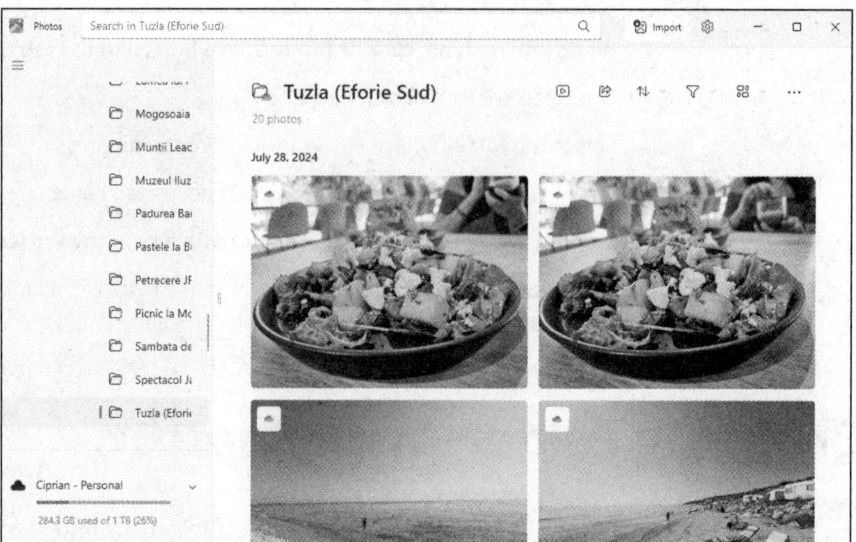

FIGURE 4-8: Using the Photos app to browse folders of pictures.

IN THIS CHAPTER

» Getting started with OneNote

» Adding a notebook, sections, and pages

» Adding content to your notes

» Sending web pages to OneNote

» Tweaking OneNote's settings

Chapter 5
Note-Taking with OneNote

If you haven't used OneNote, you've missed out on Microsoft's premier example of a cloud-first, mobile-first application. OneNote started as a small app in the Office suite. It's grown a lot over the years, and when Windows 11 was launched, it came preinstalled with the operating system. The problem is that we had two OneNote apps for Windows: OneNote (part of the Office suite) and OneNote for Windows 10, which was bundled with the operating system. This confused many people, and for good reason.

In August 2021, Microsoft announced that it would combine its multiple OneNote apps into a single Windows application. In October 2022, the company removed the OneNote for Windows 10 app from the Microsoft Store and introduced a new OneNote app. This app is also part of Office and Microsoft 365 subscriptions. However, the new OneNote app is no longer part of Windows 11 as default. To make things even more confusing, the previous OneNote for Windows 10 app will reach the end of support in October 2025.

Therefore, if you have an old PC with Windows 11, you may have an app named OneNote for Windows 10 on it. If you installed Microsoft 365 on the same computer, you would also have a second OneNote app. And if you just bought a new Windows 11 laptop or 2-in-1, you may not have any OneNote apps.

REMEMBER

OneNote isn't Windows-only, far from it. OneNote is available on the Mac, iPhones, iPads, Android smartphones and tablets, and other mobile devices. You can use OneNote to talk to yourself and synchronize all sorts of things between your computers and devices. You can access it even on an Apple Watch or smartwatches with Android Wear. The OneNote interface makes working with those things surprisingly easy, and your OneNote gets synchronized with the help of OneDrive and a Microsoft account.

In this chapter, I don't cover everything there is to know about using OneNote. I show you only the basics of using OneNote. First, you learn how to start it and add an account to it so that it can sync your notes. Then, you see how to add content to OneNote and send stuff over from Microsoft Edge. Finally, you can browse OneNote's settings to change how it works.

Getting Started with OneNote

TECHNICAL STUFF

If you don't have a OneNote app, I recommend that you head to `www.onenote.com` in Microsoft Edge or any other web browser you prefer, download it, and install it from there. Or get OneNote from the Microsoft Store by following the instructions in Book 5, Chapter 1. The second approach is best for reasons I outline in that chapter. If you have two OneNote apps, I recommend uninstalling OneNote for Windows 10 using the instructions I provide in the same chapter. Keep the app named OneNote instead because it's the one that Microsoft will keep updating and improving.

If you have OneNote already installed with Windows 11, you can start using it. Otherwise, download it from the Microsoft Store or from `www.onenote.com` and install it.

You need to set up OneNote before you can start taking notes with it. OneNote works great if you use a Microsoft, work, or school account. It syncs all your notes through the cloud between all your devices, and it needs one of these three types of accounts to tie them together. If you have a local account, you can use OneNote but your notes won't be synchronized across devices. The notes remain stored locally, on the computer you're using. You must switch to another type of account or create a new Microsoft account for OneNote to sync your notes, as shown in Figure 5-1. For details about working with user accounts, read Book 2, Chapter 4.

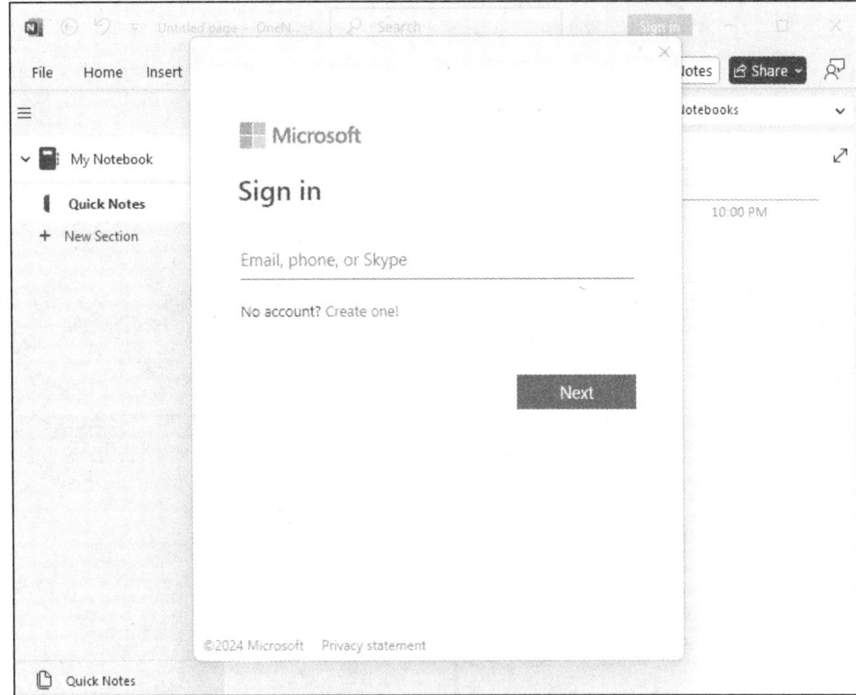

FIGURE 5-1: On a home computer, OneNote asks you to use a Microsoft account.

Here's how to start OneNote and configure your account:

1. **Click or tap the Start icon and then All.**

   You see all the apps from your Start menu.

2. **Scroll down the apps list to those that start with letter *O* and click or tap OneNote.**

   The OneNote app appears, asking you to sign in, as shown in Figure 5-2.

3. **Click or tap Sign In.**

   A pop-up window appears where you must enter your Microsoft, work, or school account (refer to Figure 5-1).

4. **Type your account's email or phone number and click or tap Next.**

   OneNote verifies whether your account exists. If it detects that your Microsoft 365 subscription has expired, you're informed about this issue. However, you can ignore this warning if you only want to view and print files from OneNote. Remember that you'll need such a subscription to create and edit files. If everything is okay with your subscription, you see the license agreement shown in Figure 5-3.

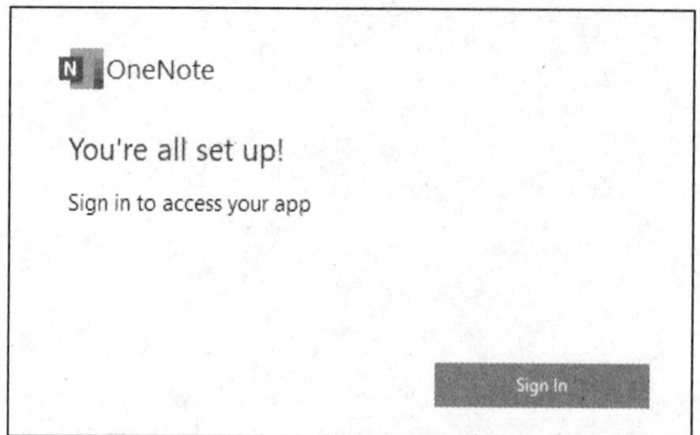

FIGURE 5-2: Sign in before using OneNote.

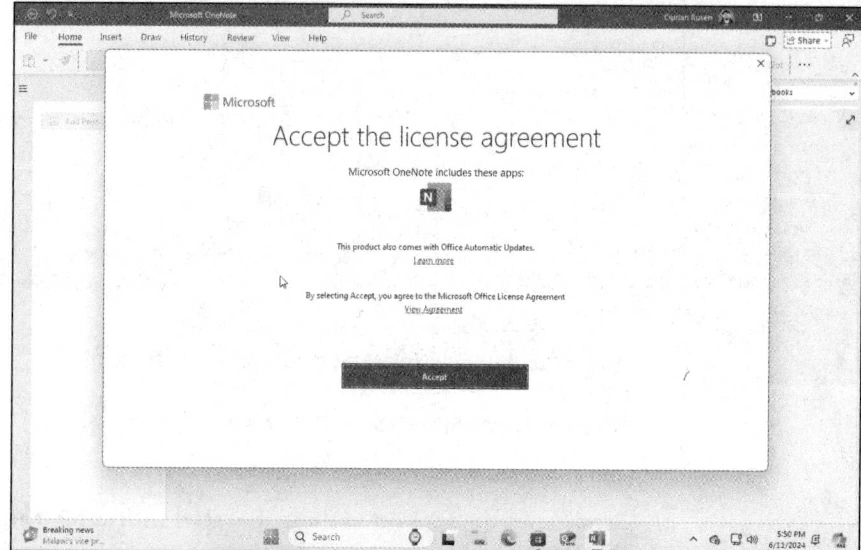

FIGURE 5-3: OneNote asks you to accept the license terms.

5. **Click or tap Accept.**

   A pop-up informs you about the data collected by Microsoft and your privacy settings. If you want more detailed information, click any of the links in this window.

6. **Click or tap Next to continue.**

   You're asked whether you want to send optional diagnostic and usage data to Microsoft.

7. **Select Don't Send Optional Data.**

   Microsoft tells you that Office includes experiences that connect to online services to help you work more effectively, and it also lets you know what this means, with links to pages where you can learn more.

8. **Click or tap Done to start using OneNote.**

   The OneNote app loads and displays the Untitled Page with an empty note and a welcome message, as shown in Figure 5-4.

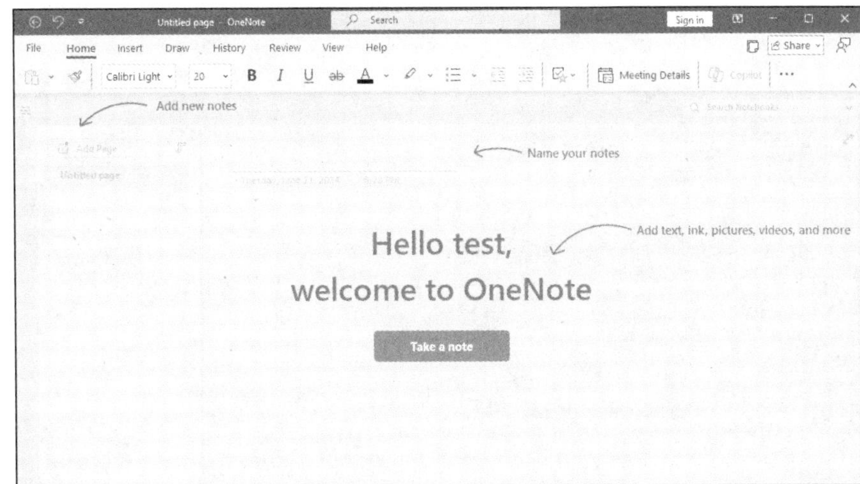

FIGURE 5-4: Welcome to OneNote.

TIP

Here's a tip for owners of Microsoft Surface devices who have a digital pen and have set up Windows 11 to start by using Hello face recognition (see Book 2, Chapter 2). After your machine is turned on, you may be able to run OneNote by simply clicking the top of the pen. That's a convenient shortcut because it's easy to start Windows 11 on a OneNote page, ready to take notes.

Adding Notebooks, Sections, and Pages

OneNote works with notebooks like Word works with documents, Excel with workbooks, and PowerPoint with presentations. A OneNote notebook contains sections, and each section contains pages. Each page can contain many things: typed notes, screenshots, photos, voice recordings, marked-up web pages, tables, attached files, and web links. Lots and lots of digital things. Only your imagination limits what you can add to a OneNote page.

Here's how to get going with your very own notebook:

1. **Get OneNote fired up by clicking or tapping the Start icon, All, and then OneNote. Or if you have a fancy pen, click it.**

   If you've used OneNote before, you see the main screen shown in Figure 5-5.

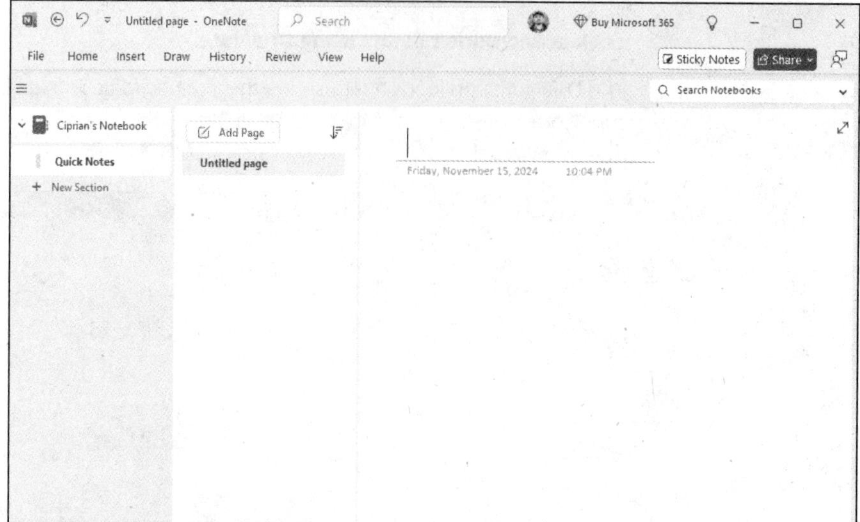

FIGURE 5-5: OneNote opens a new untitled page when you use it for the first time.

2. **Click or tap File.**

   A menu with several options appears, as shown in Figure 5-6.

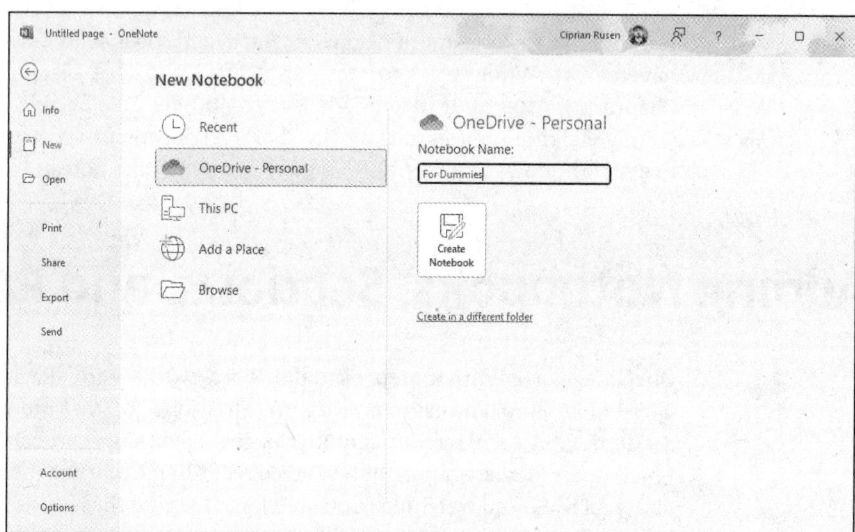

FIGURE 5-6: Creating a notebook.

3. **Choose New, and then type a name in the Notebook Name field to the right.**
4. **Click or tap Create Notebook.**

5. **If Microsoft OneNote invites you to share the notebook with others, choose what you want.**

   OneNote creates a notebook and puts a link to it in your OneDrive's Documents folder. In Figure 5-7, the new notebook appears as For Dummies (the filename extension is .one, although you can't see it).

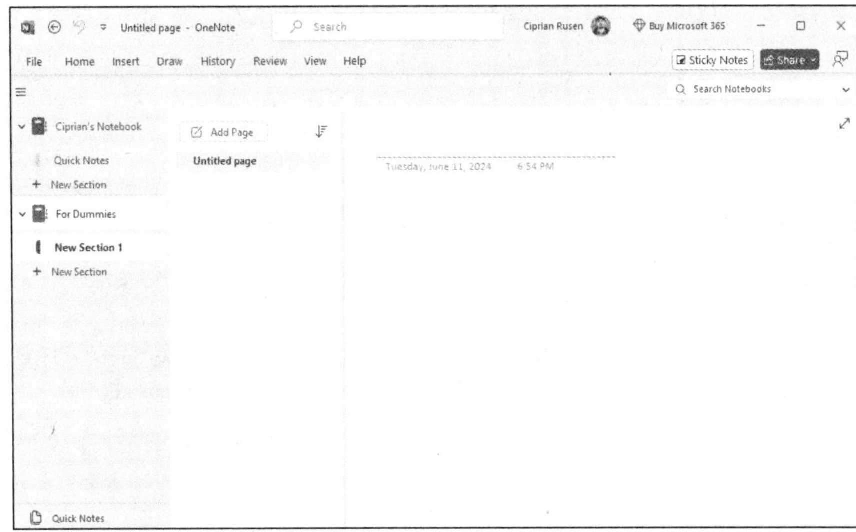

FIGURE 5-7: The new notebook is created and saved to your OneDrive.

REMEMBER

One weird aspect of OneNote is that your notebooks are saved not locally on your Windows 11 computer but in your OneDrive's Documents folder. Unless you set OneDrive to synchronize your local Documents folder with its Documents (see Book 4, Chapter 6), you won't see your OneNote notebooks in your File Explorer's Documents folder. But if you log in to OneDrive (`www.onedrive.com`), you'll see them.

Now that you have a new notebook, let's add a couple of sections. Like adding tabs in a web browser, adding new sections is flat-out simple:

1. **Make sure the new notebook is selected. If it isn't, click or tap its name.**
2. **Right-click or tap and hold New Section 1, and choose Rename.**

   You can also delete the section, move it to another notebook, merge it into another section, change the section color, and do much more, as shown in Figure 5-8.

3. **Type a new name and press Enter.**

   The new name appears on the tab.

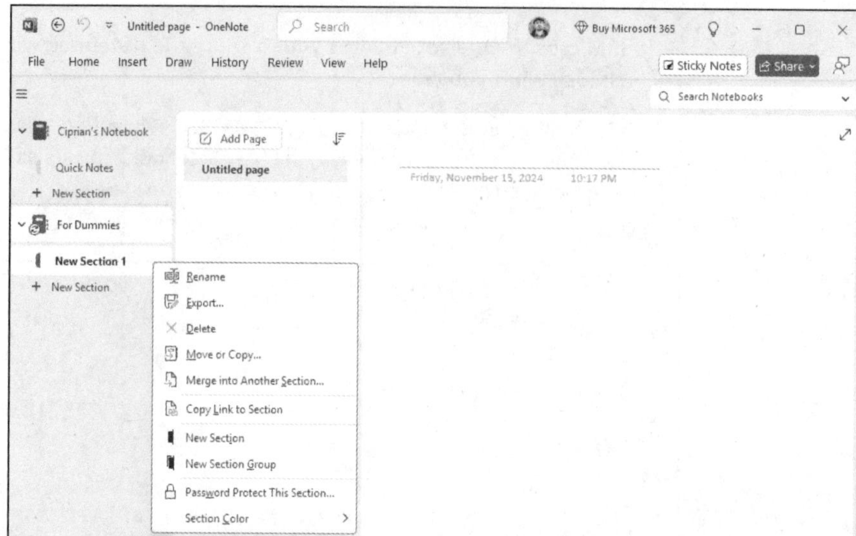

FIGURE 5-8: Rename a section by right-clicking.

4. **To add another section, click or tap the + New Section link at the bottom of the list of sections. Then rename it, and press Enter.**

   If you've ever worked with tabs in a browser, you already know all you need.

5. **To add pages to a section, select the section you want to use and click or tap Add Page at the top of the list of pages.**

   A new, empty, and untitled page appears, ready for you to fill in.

REMEMBER

OneNote saves everything automatically as you type or paste stuff into it. There's no Save button as in Word or Excel.

Adding Content to a OneNote Page

Writing in a OneNote page is done the same way as in Word, Notepad, or any other text editor. The typing, formatting, and editing controls at the top work just as expected. On the Home tab, you can change the font and font size used for your notes, and then use basic formatting tools such as bold, italic, and underline. In Figure 5-9, I typed text in a resizable box by simply typing on the keyboard, and then formatted the text by using the controls in OneNote.

You might think that you need a pen to draw in OneNote — and, believe me, a good pen helps! — but you can doodle with your finger on a touch-sensitive computer or with a mouse or trackpad if necessary. The lines and doodles you create with a pen look much more refined than they do with a mouse because the pen is easier to control and most pens are sensitive to pressure.

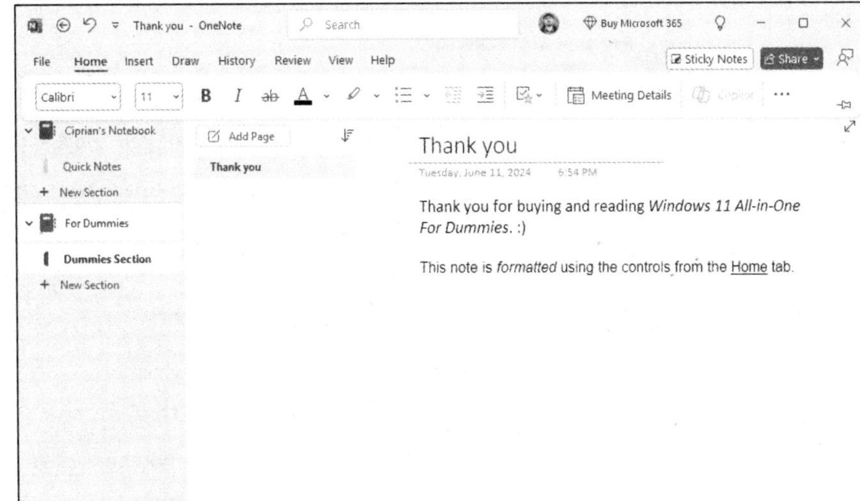

FIGURE 5-9: Typing and formatting a OneNote page is easy.

Here's how to draw on a OneNote page:

1. **Start with whatever OneNote page you want. Then click or tap the Draw tab at the top.**

   OneNote responds with the tools and palette shown in Figure 5-10.

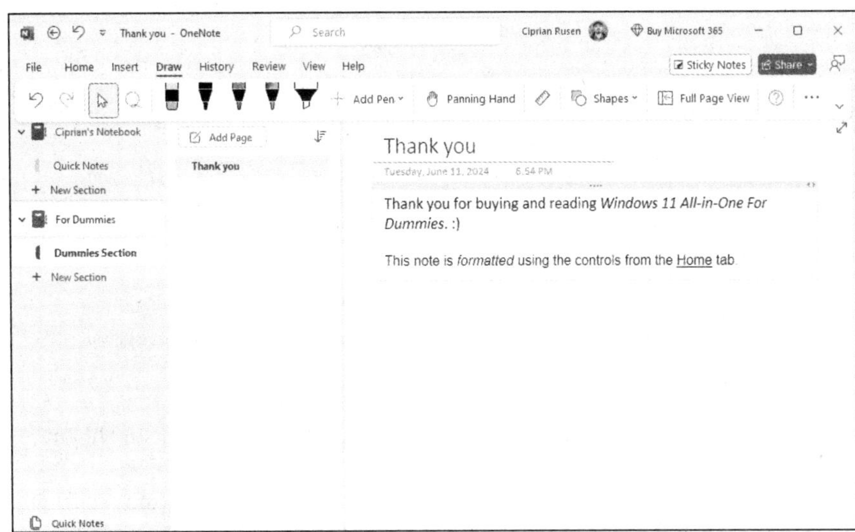

FIGURE 5-10: Extensive drawing tools work better with a pen, but they'll do okay with a mouse.

2. **Prepare for drawing:**

   (a) *Select a pen — narrow, highlighter, multicolor.*

   (b) *Click or tap the down arrow at the bottom of the pen icon and choose a color.*

   (c) *Adjust the thickness of the pen by clicking or tapping the plus and minus signs or by choosing a bigger or smaller dot.*

   The cursor turns into a circle.

3. **Draw away on the OneNote page on the right.**

   See the quick drawing I made in Figure 5-11.

4. **If you don't like what you just drew, press Ctrl+Z.**

   That deletes the drawing you just made on the notebook page and lets you start all over.

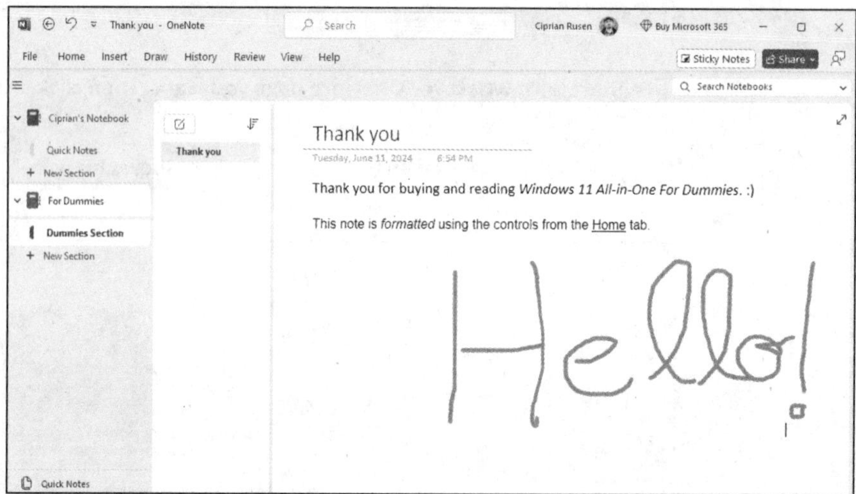

FIGURE 5-11: Drawing — even with a mouse — is easy.

Remember that everything is saved for you automatically; you don't need to do a thing.

On the Draw tab (refer to Figure 5-10), find the icon shown in the margin. If you hover your mouse cursor over it, it says Select Objects or Type Text. Use this icon to select text (say, to apply formatting from the Home tab) or to create a box into which you can type or insert a picture.

The icon next to it, which looks like a lasso, is lasso select. Use it to select items to move, copy, or delete as a group.

The icon that looks like a ruler adds a ruler to your page, which you can rotate how you want and then use to draw lines and align objects against its straight edge. Pretty neat!

The icon that looks like an eraser is an eraser. After selecting it, you can use it to erase anything you have drawn on the page.

Sending Sites from Microsoft Edge to OneNote

Very few people know that it's easy to take a snapshot of a web page from Microsoft Edge (and other web browsers) and send it to OneNote. Here's how it works:

1. **Open Microsoft Edge and browse to a website you like.**

   I chose my blog: `www.digitalcitizen.life`.

2. **Click or tap the three dots icon in the upper-right corner of Microsoft Edge and choose Print.**

   OneNote displays the Print dialog shown in Figure 5-12.

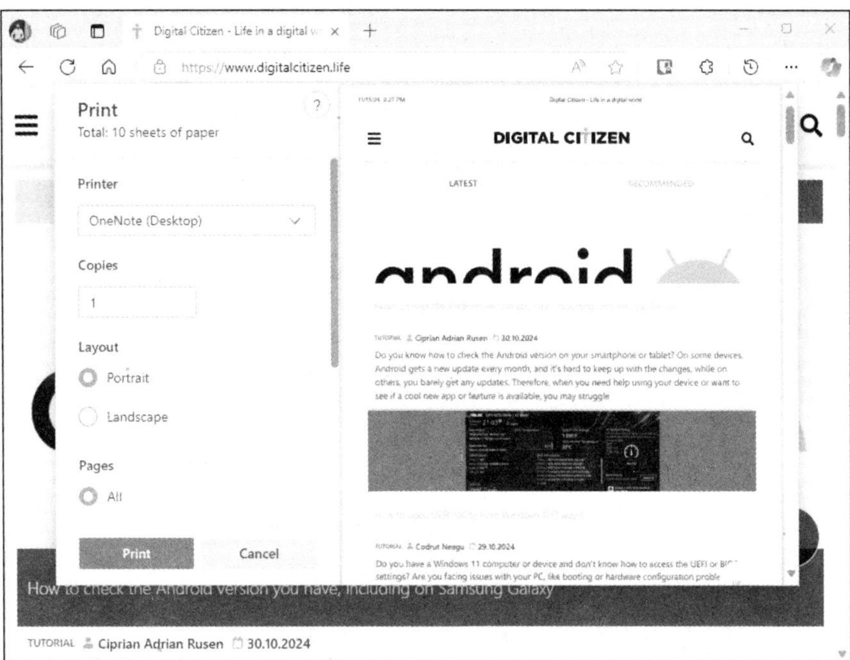

FIGURE 5-12: Saving a web page in OneNote.

3. **Click or tap the Printer drop-down list and choose OneNote (Desktop).**

   A preview of the page that will be created inside OneNote appears.

4. **Click or tap Print, and then go to OneNote.**

   Inside OneNote, you're asked to select the location to save this web page.

5. **From the list, choose the notebook, the section, and then a page, if you want. Click or tap OK.**

   The web page is now stored in the notebook you chose.

Configuring OneNote's Settings

OneNote has a handful of settings you might want to try someday. Or maybe not. To see them, follow these steps:

1. **Inside OneNote, click or tap File.**

   A menu appears (refer to Figure 5-6).

2. **Choose Options.**

   The OneNote Options window shown in Figure 5-13 appears.

3. **Scroll down the list of settings and change what you want.**

   You can change anything from the default font and size used for your notes to the pasting options. You can also change where OneNote stores and backs up your notebooks.

WARNING

   I don't recommend disabling the Sync Notebooks Automatically setting in the Sync section because doing so will stop sending your notes to OneDrive, and they won't be accessible on your other devices.

4. **To close the OneNote Options window, click or tap OK.**

This chapter just scratched the surface of OneNote's capabilities. You'll find that the app itself has many different guises in many different locations — OneNote online is different from OneNote for the iPad, which is different from OneNote for Android, and from OneNote on Windows, and so on. Install the app on all your devices, sign up with the same account on all of them, and try it out. I'm sure you'll find it useful. And who knows, maybe you'll even love using it.

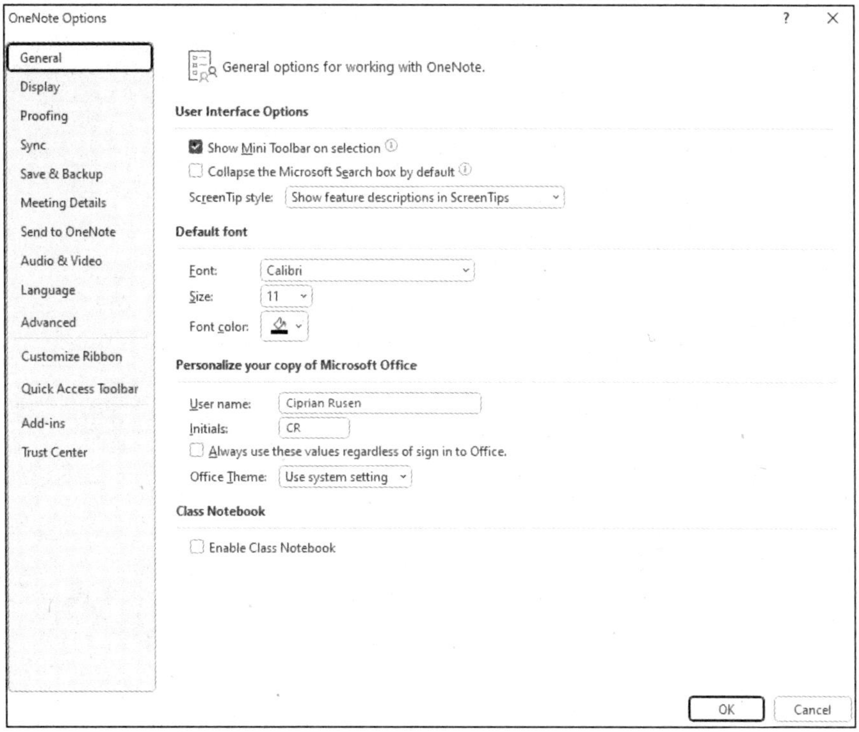

FIGURE 5-13: Configure how OneNote works in the OneNote Options window.

IN THIS CHAPTER

» Working with OneDrive through File Explorer

» Understanding the states of OneDrive data

» Configuring OneDrive and synchronizing your data

» Sharing files and folders with OneDrive

» Protecting files in Personal Vault

Chapter 6

Storing and Syncing Your Data with OneDrive

Let's start with the basics: OneDrive is an online storage service, sold by Microsoft, which has some features woven into Windows to make it easier to work with your files stored on Microsoft's servers in the cloud. (*Cloud* is another word for the web or the internet.) "In the cloud" is just a euphemism for "stored on somebody else's computer."

If you have a Microsoft account (such as an `Outlook.com` ID, a Hotmail ID, or any other kind of Microsoft account — see Book 2, Chapter 4), you already have free OneDrive storage space ready for you to use.

OneDrive has many competitors — Dropbox (which I used for this book), Google Drive, iCloud, Box, and many others. These competitors all have advantages and disadvantages — and their feature lists change constantly. However, OneDrive is here to stay, and it's embedded into Windows 11.

If you also use Office or have a Microsoft 365 (formerly known as Office 365) subscription, you may want to use OneDrive, and use it productively. That's why, in this chapter, I show you just about everything you need to know to make OneDrive work for you: how to set it up, add files and folders, and share files and folders. You also learn about the states of OneDrive data and how to protect sensitive files with OneDrive's Personal Vault.

What Is OneDrive?

OneDrive is an internet-based storage platform created and managed by Microsoft. It can be used with a Microsoft account, as well as with a school or work account. Think of it as a hard drive in the cloud, which you can share, with a few extra benefits thrown in. Two of the primary benefits: OneDrive hooks into Windows 11 and Windows 10, and it offers 5GB of free storage space. Microsoft, of course, wants you to buy more storage, but you're under no obligation to do so.

REMEMBER

At the time of writing, OneDrive gives everyone with a Microsoft account 5GB of free storage (down from 15GB free in 2015), with the option to expand it to 200GB for $1.99/month or to 400 GB for $3.99/month. Many Microsoft 365 subscription levels have 1TB (1024GB) OneDrive storage per person.

The free storage is there even if you never use OneDrive. In fact, if you have a Microsoft account, you're all signed up for OneDrive, and you can access it straight from File Explorer by clicking or tapping the OneDrive icon (blue cloud). (The OneDrive icon is under Gallery.) You can see my OneDrive folder in Figure 6-1.

REMEMBER

Here are the keys to using OneDrive effectively:

- OneDrive does what all the other cloud storage services do — it gives you a place to put your files on the internet. You need to log in to OneDrive with your Microsoft account (or work, or school account) to access your data.
- OneDrive keeps a history of all changes you made to files over the past 30 days. This feature can be useful — and a lifesaver if you get hit by ransomware.
- If you log in to a different device or computer (Windows, Mac, iPad, Android) using the same account, you have access to all your OneDrive data.
- You can share files or folders stored in OneDrive by sending or posting a link to the file or folder to whomever you want. So, for example, if you want Aunt Emma to be able to see the folder with pictures of little William, OneDrive creates a link for you that you can email to her. You can also set a file or folder as Public, so anyone with the link can see it.

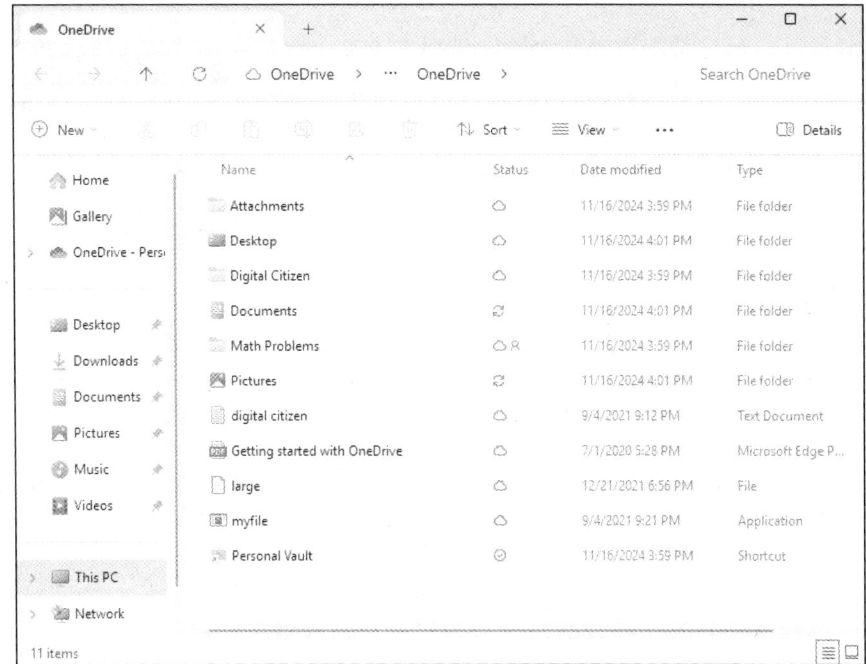

FIGURE 6-1: OneDrive files look and act a lot like everyday files.

- To work with the OneDrive platform on a mobile device, you can download and install one of the OneDrive apps — OneDrive for Mac, iPhone, iPad, or Android. The mobile apps have many of the same features that you find in Windows 11.
- In Windows 11, you don't need to download or install a OneDrive app — it's already baked into the operating system.
- If you have OneDrive installed, as soon as you connect to a network, the app syncs data among computers, smartphones, and tablets that are set up using the same account. For example, if you change a OneDrive file on your iPad and save it, the modified file is put in your OneDrive storage area on the internet. From there, the new version of the file is available to all other computers with access to the file. The same is true for Android devices.

Setting Up a OneDrive Account

If you sign in to Windows 11 with a Microsoft account, File Explorer automatically uses the same Microsoft account ID and password you use to sign in and connects you to OneDrive.

But if you're using a local account (see Book 2, Chapter 5), life isn't so simple. You must either create a Microsoft account or sign into an existing Microsoft account (and thus an existing OneDrive account). Follow the advice in Book 2, Chapter 4 to get a Microsoft account set up. After you have a Microsoft account, here's how to set up OneDrive. Don't worry, you need to do this only once:

1. **On the taskbar, click or tap the File Explorer icon.**

   You see File Explorer.

2. **On the left, click or tap OneDrive.**

   You get a Set Up OneDrive splash screen, as shown in Figure 6-2.

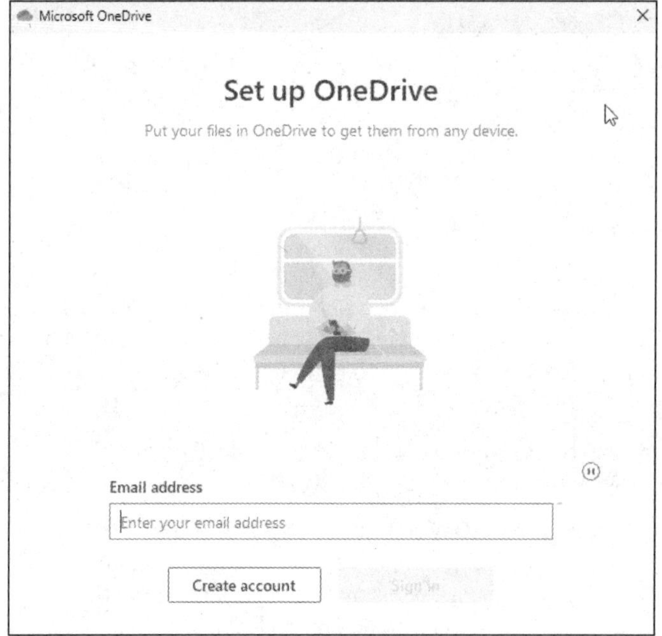

FIGURE 6-2: If you're using a local account, hook it into OneDrive with a Microsoft account.

3. **Type the email address of your Microsoft account, and then click or tap Sign In.**
4. **Enter the password and click or tap Sign In one more time.**
5. **If you're asked to choose whether you want to use this account everywhere on your device, choose Microsoft Apps Only.**

   OneDrive shares the location of the OneDrive folder. As you can see in Figure 6-3, it creates a OneDrive subfolder in your user folder.

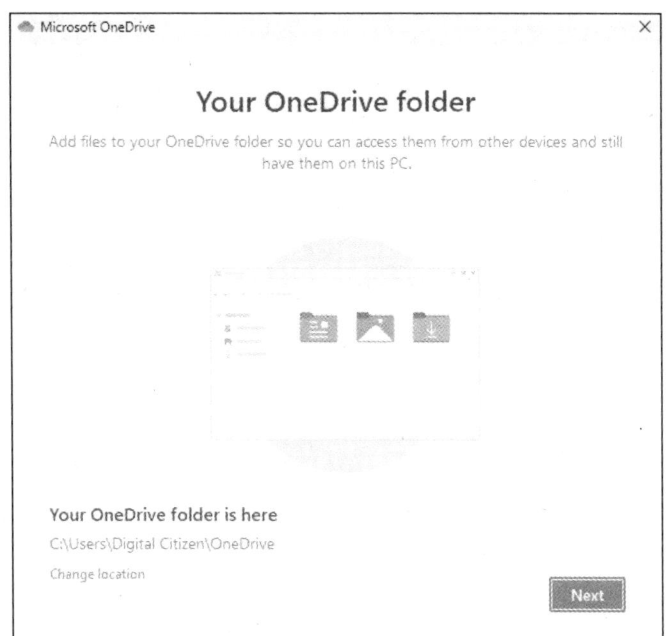
Microsoft OneDrive
Your OneDrive folder
Add files to your OneDrive folder so you can access them from other devices and still have them on this PC.
Your OneDrive folder is here
C:\Users\Digital Citizen\OneDrive
Change location
Next

FIGURE 6-3: Choose where you want your OneDrive folder.

6. **If you're happy with the default location, click or tap Next. Otherwise, click or tap Change Location and select another folder on your Windows 11 machine.**

   OneDrive informs you that it's going to back up user folders such as Desktop, Documents, and Pictures.

7. **If you're happy with OneDrive backing up your user folders, leave their switches enabled (I recommend that you do) and click or tap Start Backup. Otherwise, disable their switches by clicking or tapping them, before choosing I'll Do It Later.**

   If you're using the free storage for OneDrive, you may see an ad for upgrading to Microsoft 365 Personal.

8. **If you see the ad, click or tap Not Now followed by Next.**

   OneDrive teaches you how to share files and folders through a brief animated movie, how to add items to OneDrive, and more. Pay attention when you see the screen about All Your Files, Ready and On-Demand, as shown in Figure 6-4. See the next section for details.

9. **Click or tap Next to navigate through all the screens, while paying attention to the information displayed.**

10. **When encouraged to Get the Mobile App, click or tap Later.**

    You're presented with an opportunity to open your OneDrive folder.

11. **Click or tap Open My OneDrive Folder.**

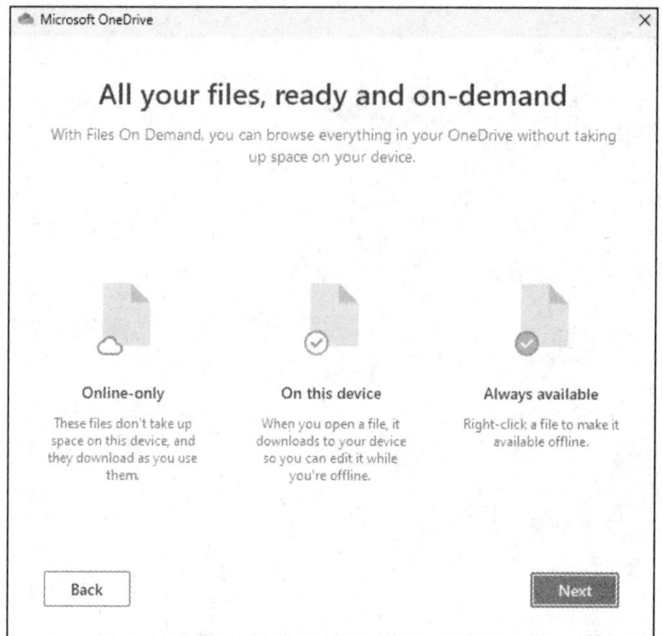

FIGURE 6-4: A brief explainer for Files On-Demand.

Now you're ready to set up synchronization between your PC and your mobile devices, if you install the OneDrive app on them and sign in with the same account you just used in Windows 11.

The Four States of OneDrive Data

On any given computer or device, all data in OneDrive exists in one of four states:

- **Online-only:** Files you've stored in your OneDrive cloud storage but not downloaded locally. You can see a list of these files, even if you don't have an internet connection, but you can open them only if you have internet access. These files use only cloud storage, not local storage.
- **On this device:** Files from your OneDrive space that you have opened, and File Explorer has downloaded and stored them locally. These files can be reopened and used even when you don't have an internet connection. They are taking up space both in your local storage and OneDrive. They get synchronized each time you're connected to the internet.

» **Always available:** Files from your OneDrive that you've explicitly set to always be available offline. They are permanently taking up space on your local storage but are also always available for use, regardless of whether you have an internet connection. They get synchronized each time you're connected to the internet.

» **In sync:** Files found in the middle of the synchronization process between your machine and OneDrive cloud storage.

That's the story behind the options shown previously in Figure 6-4, and it's an important story to remember.

TIP

Why wouldn't you choose to sync all your files and folders? Because the amount of data in your OneDrive storage could be enormous (5GB, just for starters). Syncing that data on your machine takes up not only disk space but also time and internet bandwidth because missing files will be downloaded and altered files will be uploaded every time you're connected to the internet.

However, if you have lots of available disk space, and your internet connection is reasonably fast (and not hampered by ridiculous data caps), there's little reason to keep OneDrive files sitting stranded in the cloud and not copied to your machine.

WARNING

An important caveat: If you have OneDrive files or folders that you use all the time, you probably want to make them always available. That way, if your internet connection is unavailable — say, you hop on a flight or a cruise with exorbitant Wi-Fi fees — you can continue to work on the files while the internet goes on without you. When you connect to the internet again, your files get synced with OneDrive in the cloud.

File Explorer tells you the status of every file and folder in your OneDrive by using tiny icons in the Status column, as shown in Figure 6-5:

» **Blue cloud icon:** The file or folder is available when online and is stored in the cloud, not on your machine.

» **Green circle with white in the middle and a green check mark:** The item is available locally on your machine, not just on Microsoft's servers.

» **Green icon with a white check mark:** The item is set to always be available on your device.

» **Person icon:** The shared file or folder can be accessed by others. This icon is displayed alongside other status icons.

» **Blue refresh icon:** The file is in the process of synchronizing with OneDrive.

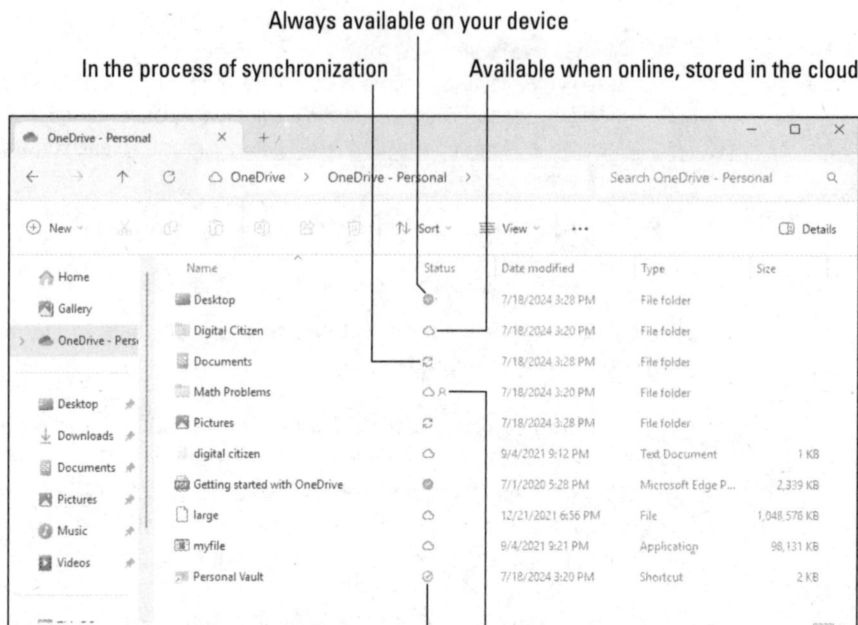

FIGURE 6-5: The status icons for folders and files stored in OneDrive.

Configuring OneDrive

To get OneDrive working as you want and synchronizing what you want, follow these instructions to step through its settings:

1. **Click or tap the OneDrive cloud icon on the right side of the taskbar, next to the time.**

   If you don't see the OneDrive cloud icon, click or tap the up arrow first. You see the OneDrive pane shown in Figure 6-6.

2. **Click or tap the help & settings icon (gear) in the top-right corner and choose Settings.**

   The OneDrive Settings window appears.

3. **If it isn't already selected, on the left, choose Sync and Backup.**

   You see the options shown in Figure 6-7.

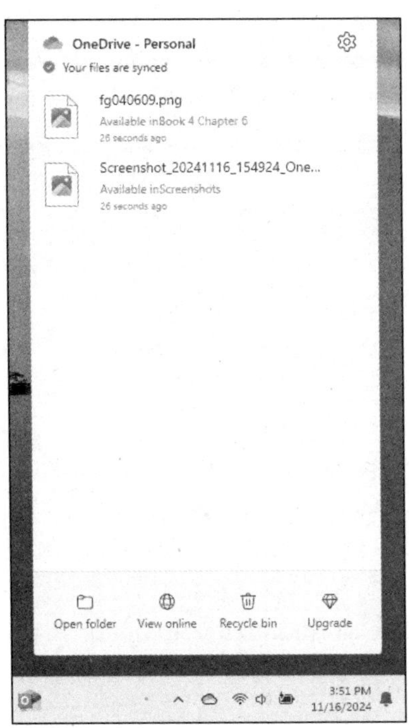

FIGURE 6-6: The OneDrive app.

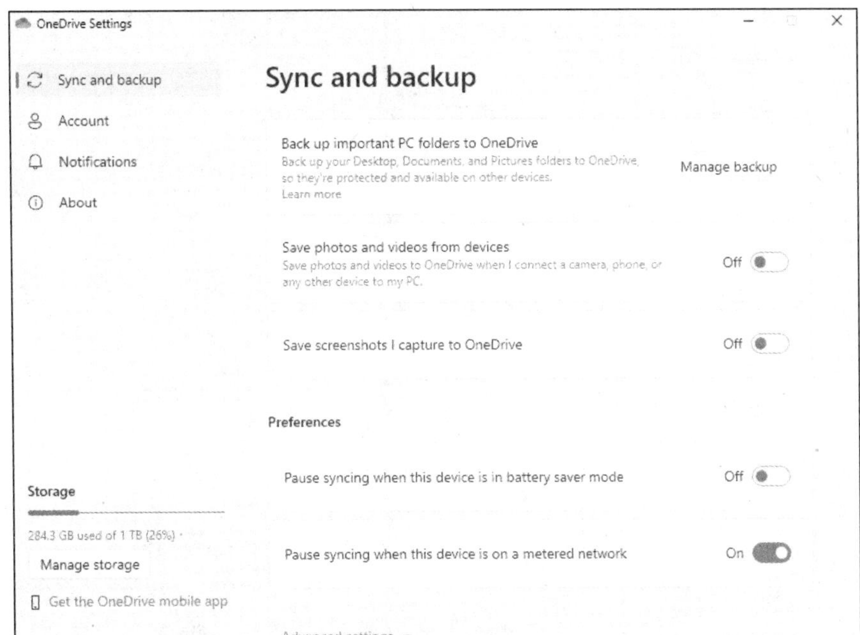

FIGURE 6-7: Configuring how OneDrive syncs and backs up your data.

4. **Choose whether you want to enable or disable the following features by clicking or tapping their switches:**

   - *Save Photos and Videos from Devices:* Useful only if you have a paid Microsoft 365 subscription and you often need to import pictures and videos from your smartphones, digital camera, and so on.
   - *Save screenshots I Capture to OneDrive:* Useful if you want your screenshots synchronized across devices.
   - *Pause Syncing When This Devices Is in Battery Saver Mode:* If you want to increase battery life, I recommend that you set this on.
   - *Pause Syncing When This Device Is on a Metered Network:* A great idea when you're connected to a capped Wi-Fi or internet connection.

5. **If you want to change which local user folders are backed up to OneDrive, click or tap Manage Backup, make your choices, and then click or tap Save Changes.**

6. **To select which folders get synchronized from OneDrive to your PC, select Account on the left, and then click or tap Choose Folders.**

   The Choose Folders dialog box appears, as shown in Figure 6-8.

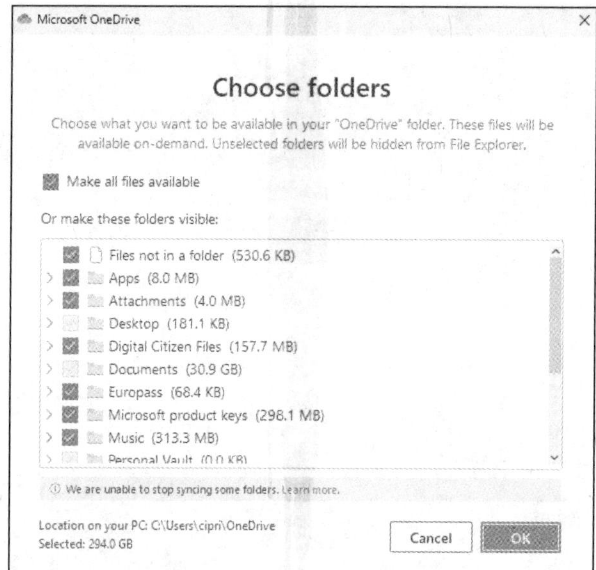

FIGURE 6-8: Sync all OneDrive data or choose which folders get the Files On-Demand treatment.

7. **Do one of the following:**

   - If you have a lot of room on your PC and have a reasonably good internet connection, select the Make All Files Available box. Click or tap OK. To help you make this decision, look at the Selected field in the bottom-right corner, which tells you how many gigabytes of files you're going to sync to your PC.
   - If you don't want to sync all OneDrive files on this particular PC, deselect the Make All Files Available box, and select the boxes next to the folders you want to sync. Click or tap OK.

8. **When you've finished setting OneDrive the way you want, click or tap OK.**

   It may take a while for OneDrive to sync, but when it's finished, all folders you've chosen to sync appear in File Explorer with the appropriate status icons (refer to Figure 6-5).

TIP

If you want to change the kind of notifications you get from OneDrive, do the following: After Step 6, click or tap Notifications, choose the notifications you want, and disable those you don't.

Adding Files and Folders to OneDrive

When you access OneDrive in File Explorer, from the screen shown previously in Figure 6-5, you can add files to any of the folders on OneDrive. Then, anything you can do to files elsewhere, you can do in the OneDrive folder. For example, you can:

- Edit, rename, and copy files, as well as move vast numbers of them. The OneDrive folder in File Explorer is by far the easiest way to put data into and take data out of OneDrive.
- Add subfolders in the OneDrive folder, rename them, and delete them; move files around; and drag and drop files and folders in to and out of the OneDrive folder to your heart's desire.
- Change file properties (by right-clicking or by pressing and holding if you have a touchscreen).
- Print files from OneDrive just as you would any other file in File Explorer.

TIP

What makes the OneDrive folder in File Explorer unique is that when you drag files into it, the files are copied into the cloud. If you have other computers or devices connected to OneDrive with the same Microsoft account, those may or may not get copies of the files (depending on whether the Make All Files Available option in their OneDrive app is selected), but they can all access them and set them to become always available.

It may take a minute or two to upload the files, and then they appear everywhere, magically. Larger files may take hours to get uploaded, depending on the speed of your internet connection.

If you have other computers (or tablets or smartphones) that you want to sync with your computer, now would be a good time to go to those other computers and install whichever version of the OneDrive app is compatible with the device. Remember that a OneDrive app is available for Windows, Mac, iPad and iPhone, and Android smartphones and tablets.

WARNING

When you remove an online-only folder or file, it's permanently deleted — no backup copy remains. However, OneDrive provides a safety net by keeping deleted files in a recycle bin for 30 days. You can access this recycle bin online at `https://onedrive.com/`, or by clicking or tapping the OneDrive icon on the taskbar and then the Recycle Bin icon. Keep in mind, if the contents of your recycle bin exceed 10 percent of your total OneDrive storage, the retention period may be shortened. Conversely, if the recycle bin stays under this 10 percent threshold, all deleted files and folders remain available for the full 30 days. For those using a work or school account, OneDrive keeps deleted items in the recycle bin for 93 days, unless an administrator has changed the setting.

Changing the States of OneDrive Data

It's remarkably easy to switch between the four states of OneDrive data:

- In the cloud only
- On your machine, synced
- On your machine, synced, and you've told OneDrive that you *always* want a copy of it on your machine
- On your machine but not yet synced (a synchronization may be in progress)

In general, all you must do is right-click (or press and hold) a file or folder — even the entire OneDrive folder — and choose the correct option. For example, in Figure 6-9, I right-clicked the Math Problems folder, which is already synced.

From this point, I have two state-changing choices:

- » If I select Always Keep on This Device, OneDrive will change the state to Always Available and keep a copy on the PC.
- » If I select Free Up Space, OneDrive will remove the copy of data currently on the PC and set the state to Online-Only.

In general, after OneDrive has stopped syncing, you can change from one state to another by right-clicking (or pressing and holding).

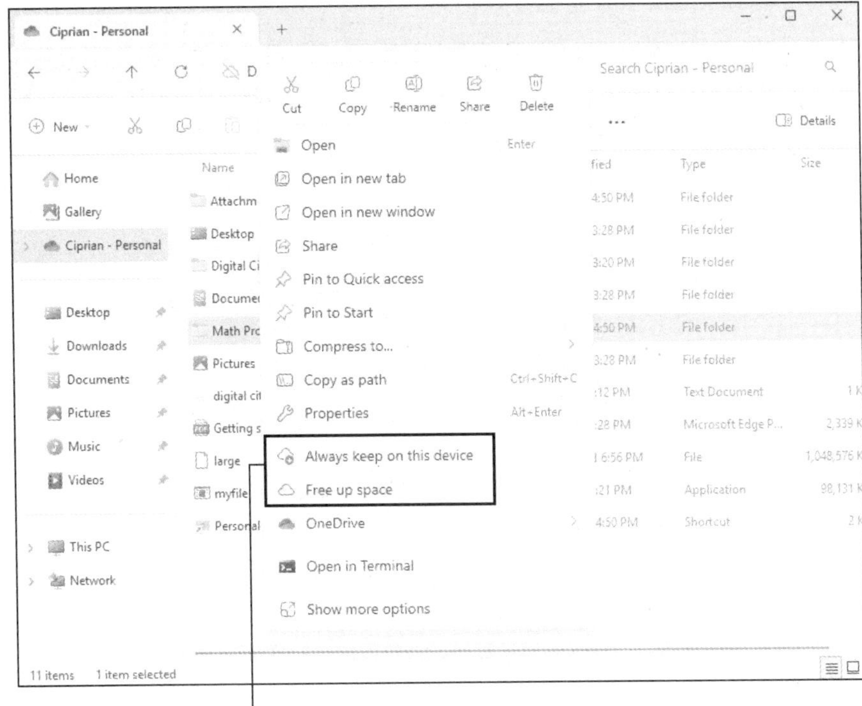

FIGURE 6-9: Changing the OneDrive state of a folder.

Synchronizing and Pausing OneDrive

Normally, the OneDrive app detects when you change something in your OneDrive folder, and automatically synchronizes the change to Microsoft's cloud storage servers and then to your other devices. However, sometimes you may want to stop OneDrive from syncing your files, such as when you're working on a video-editing project with large 4K videos and high-resolution images. Having OneDrive sync everything while your work is not finished may generate problems. In this situation, it's a good idea to temporarily pause OneDrive, like this:

1. **Click or tap the OneDrive cloud icon on the right side of the taskbar, next to the time.**

   You see the OneDrive pane (refer to Figure 6-6).

2. **Click or tap the help & settings icon (gear) in the top-right corner,**

   A menu with options appears, as shown in Figure 6-10.

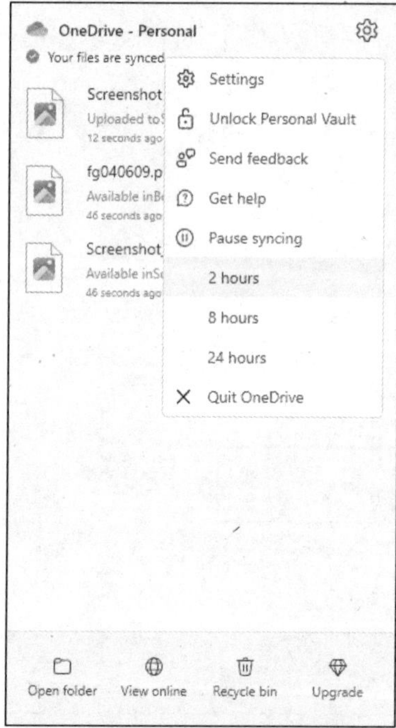

FIGURE 6-10: Pausing OneDrive from syncing your files.

3. **Click or tap Pause Syncing to expand it, and choose the 2, 8 or 24 hours option.**

   OneDrive stops syncing your files for the selected period and informs you that your files are not currently syncing. After the selected period ends, OneDrive resumes syncing your files automatically.

TIP

If you finished your work earlier, you could set OneDrive to resume syncing by repeating Steps 1 and 2 and then clicking or tapping Resume Syncing.

REMEMBER

Every time OneDrive doesn't sync a file or folder as fast as you want, you can force it to do so by pausing syncing and then resuming it manually, using the instructions shared earlier.

Sharing OneDrive Files and Folders

Sharing files and folders with OneDrive couldn't be simpler. All it takes are just a few clicks (or taps). Here's how it is done:

1. **Open the OneDrive folder in File Explorer.**
2. **Navigate to the file or folder that you want to share, and right-click (or press and hold) it.**

   The right-click menu opens, with several contextual options, as shown in Figure 6-11.

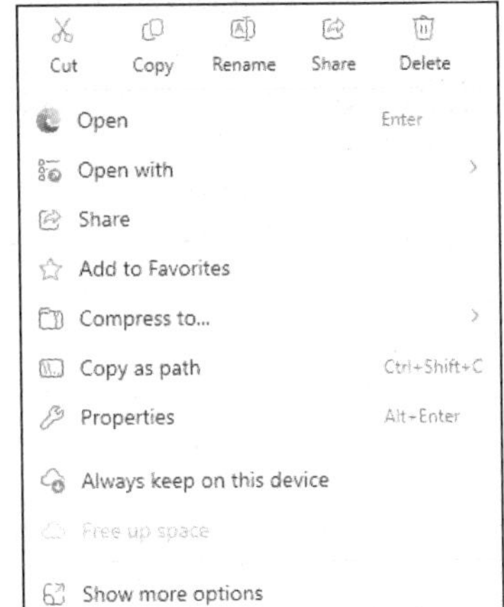

FIGURE 6-11: The right-click menu holds the Share option.

3. **Choose Share.**

   You can share the file or folder via email, copy a link to it that you can paste into a chat app or some other place, set the sharing permissions, and more, as shown in Figure 6-12.

WARNING

If you don't see the options shown in Figure 6-12, you're either trying to share an item that is not stored on your OneDrive account or OneDrive syncing is paused and you must resume it before trying again.

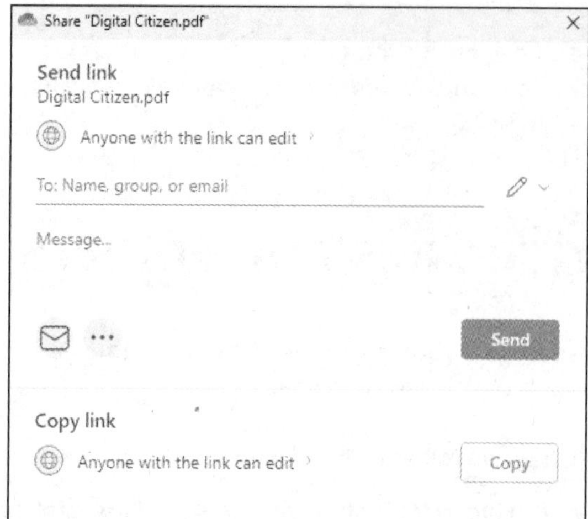

FIGURE 6-12: The OneDrive Share dialog.

4. **Click or tap Copy.**

   You see the sharing link generated by OneDrive.

5. **Paste the sharing link from OneDrive anywhere you want (email, chat window, web browser, and so on).**
6. **When you're done, close the OneDrive Share window by pressing X in the upper right.**

TIP

After Step 3, if you click or tap Anyone with the Link Can Edit, you can also set an expiration date for the share and an access password. However, this option works only for premium (paid) versions of OneDrive. You can also set the sharing link to allow people to only view the item you're sharing, instead of editing it.

Protecting Files with Personal Vault

Personal Vault is a secure folder in OneDrive that requires strong authentication or a second factor of identity verification, such as your fingerprint, face, PIN, or a code sent via SMS or generated by the Microsoft Authenticator app. Without this verification, Personal Vault stays locked, ensuring that even if someone gains access to your device or OneDrive account, they can't open Personal Vault without your authorization.

The data inside Personal Vault is automatically encrypted, making it a safe place to store not only sensitive files but also passwords. This feature is one of the best ways to password-protect folders on Windows or any other platform where OneDrive is available.

Whether you're using OneDrive for free or with a Microsoft 365 subscription, you can store files in Personal Vault and access them from any device with OneDrive, including Windows 10 and Windows 11 PCs, Macs, Android devices, iPhones, and iPads. However, free accounts are limited to storing up to three files in Personal Vault, while Microsoft 365 subscribers can store an unlimited number of files.

If this feature sounds useful to you, follow these steps to enable and use OneDrive's Personal Vault in Windows 11:

1. **Click or tap the OneDrive cloud icon on the right side of the taskbar, next to the time.**

   You see the OneDrive pane.

2. **Click or tap the help & settings icon (gear) in the top-right corner.**

   A menu with options appears (refer to Figure 6-10).

3. **Click or tap Unlock Personal Vault.**

   The first time you access Personal Vault, you are greeted by a wizard that briefly shows you what it's all about and walks you through the initial configuration steps, as shown in Figure 6-13.

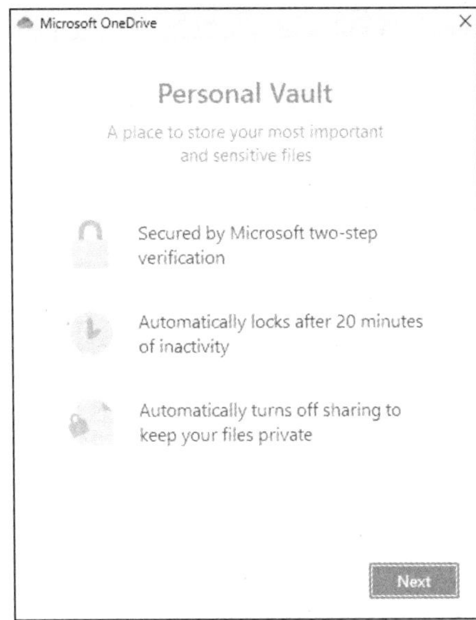

FIGURE 6-13: Setting up your Personal Vault isn't complicated.

4. **Click or tap Next.**
5. **Click or tap Allow.**

   You may see a User Account Control prompt, asking whether you want to allow OneDrive to make changes to your device.

6. **Choose Yes.**

   OneDrive makes the preparations for your Personal Vault.

7. **Enter the information requested from you and follow the necessary authentication steps.**

   You're asked to set up a verification method. Depending on how you've configured your Microsoft account, you may need to enter your PIN, authenticate with a fingerprint, use face recognition, type your password, or enter a code sent by email or generated by the Microsoft Authenticator app on your phone.

   When you finish the verification steps, OneDrive opens Personal Vault in File Explorer.

You can add, edit, and remove files and folders in your Personal Vault just like you would with any other files or folders. You can create files, drag and drop items from your Windows computer or other OneDrive folders, and more. Personal Vault automatically locks after 20 minutes of inactivity or when you sign out of Windows. Once it's locked, you'll need to verify your identity again to access your files and folders.

IN THIS CHAPTER

» Working with widgets in Windows 11

» Adding and removing widgets

» Customizing your widgets

» Removing the news feed

Chapter 7
Using Widgets

Let's talk about a less-known feature of Windows 11: widgets. Microsoft borrowed this concept from the smartphone world, but it's doing things differently, as always. First, widgets are tied to a Microsoft account. While they work with a local account, any personalization you make doesn't get saved. Second, although their purpose is to provide you with news that interests you or data that's useful to you, they also promote Microsoft's services, websites, and Edge browser. You may not like this, but it's how things are.

The widgets load only when you click or tap their icon on the taskbar, and they're just as fast (or slow) no matter how many you add. The only things that might slow them down are your internet connection and how long it takes to refresh their data.

To help you get the most out of widgets, I explain what widgets are and how they work. You also learn how to change their size and customize the data they display. You also find out how to remove and add widgets and get rid of the spammy news feed shown on the right side of the widgets board. And, for those who don't like the widgets, I also share how to remove their icons from the taskbar.

Working with Widgets

In Windows 11, a *widget* is a small app designed to display information that you might find useful, such as the weather forecast, stock market data, or news. This feature is inspired by the News and Interests widget introduced in Windows 10, which is similar to a personalized news feed. This concept was expanded in Windows 11 to allow other apps to install and display widgets, not just the ones built by Microsoft.

To open the widgets in Windows 11, click or tap the widgets icon in the left corner of the taskbar or press Windows+W. The widgets board appears on the left side of the screen, occupying a large portion of it, as shown in Figure 7-1. Note how all the widgets are displayed as cards with different sizes and how the widgets icon on the taskbar changes regularly to display new information, such as today's weather forecast and stock market updates.

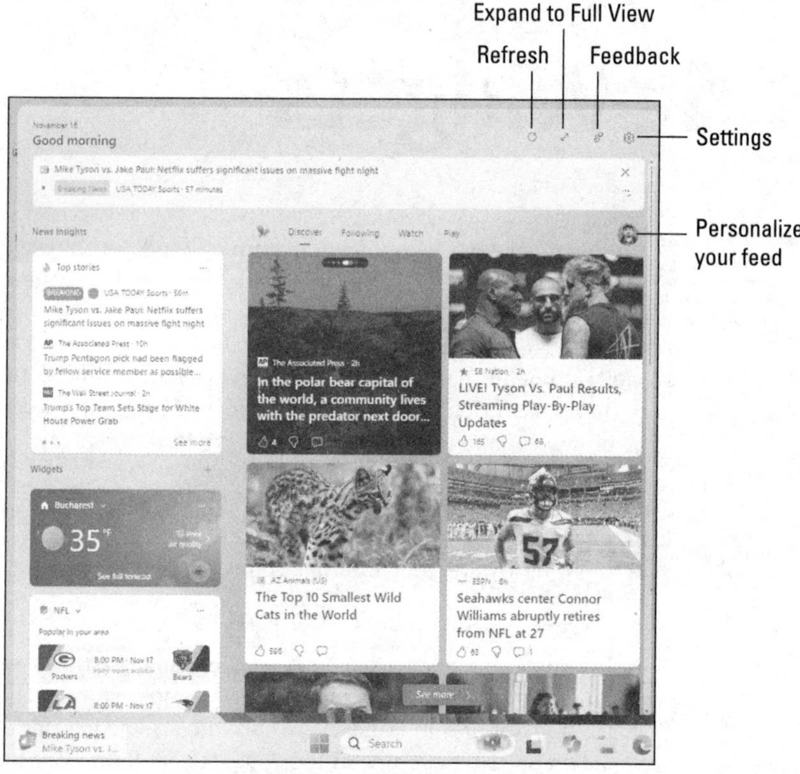

FIGURE 7-1: The Windows 11 widgets in all their glory.

On the top of the widgets board, you see the current date and a few icons. The first is a refresh icon, followed by expand to full view, feedback, and settings. Each of them does what their name implies. Below the settings icon is your Microsoft account picture. This is the button for personalizing the feed associated with your account.

The widgets take up only the smaller left-side column of the widgets board. The larger section to the right is reserved for your feed and is split into several sections that Microsoft may change over time: Discover, Following, Watch, and Play. Unfortunately, this large section to the right not only occupies a lot of space but also presents a lot of spammy content. This is the reason most Windows 11 users dislike widgets. Luckily, you can turn off this feed; I show you how later in this chapter.

Scroll down the list of widgets to see more of them, including news articles. Remember that Windows adds some widgets by default. When you manually pin widgets to this board, they are positioned at the top of the list, above the ones chosen by Microsoft. For each news article, you see a picture, the title, the name of its publisher, and reaction icons (thumbs up, thumbs down, comment). Microsoft learns what information to display based on how you use the reaction icons. Widgets contain clickable information. Unfortunately, most of them take you to a Microsoft site such as `msn.com`.

WARNING

Because Microsoft is fighting Google for market share in the online space, it has decided that Windows 11 widgets ignore your default browser setting and load into Microsoft Edge everything you click. I find this annoying. Don't you?

Adding Widgets

Microsoft is slowly expanding the list of widgets you can add and is also trying to convince other companies to create widgets. So far it hasn't succeeded much and, at the time of writing, only Spotify has created a cool widget that people could use in Windows 11. Even so, this doesn't mean that there are no useful widgets for you to consider.

If you want to try other widgets than the ones displayed by default, you first need to add them. The process for adding a widget isn't difficult, even though you may not know where to start. But that's why I'm here, to show you how:

1. **Click or tap the widgets icon on the taskbar or press Windows+W.**

   Windows 11 displays the widgets board.

2. **In the top-right corner of the widgets board, click or tap the Settings icon.**

   The Settings pane from Figure 7-2 pops up.

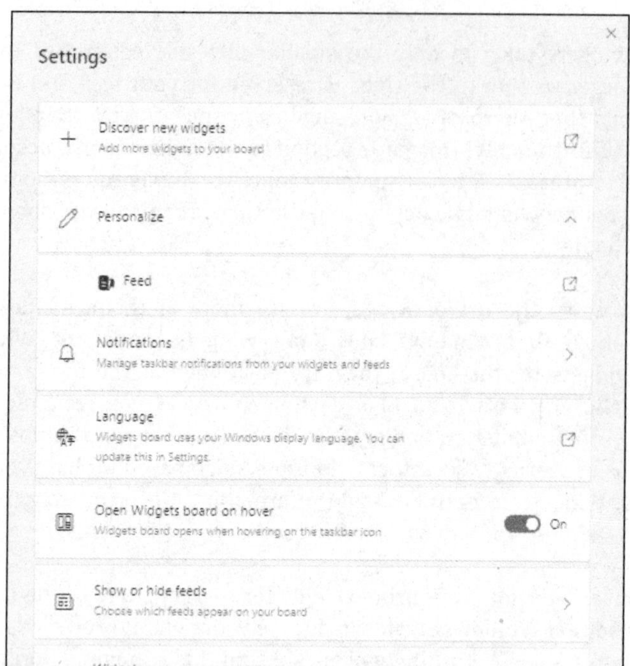

FIGURE 7-2. The settings available for the widgets in Windows 11.

3. **Click or tap + Discover New Widgets.**

   You see a list of widgets as in Figure 7-3. For each widget, you see its name and how it looks.

4. **Select a widget and check out its preview on the right.**
5. **After you find a widget you like, click or tap the Pin button below its preview.**

   When you open the widgets board again, you see the newly added widget. Don't hesitate to drag and drop it to the position you want in the list.

REMEMBER

If you try to drag and drop a widget to a new position and it simply won't move, you haven't pinned it to the board first, using the steps shared earlier. Therefore, first pin a widget, and then drag and drop the widget to change its position. All the widgets that you haven't manually pinned are placed below your pinned widgets and can't be moved around with drag-and-drop.

TIP

Widgets can be added by the apps you install. For example, you won't see a Spotify widget available in the list shown in Figure 7-3 until you install the Spotify app from the Microsoft Store.

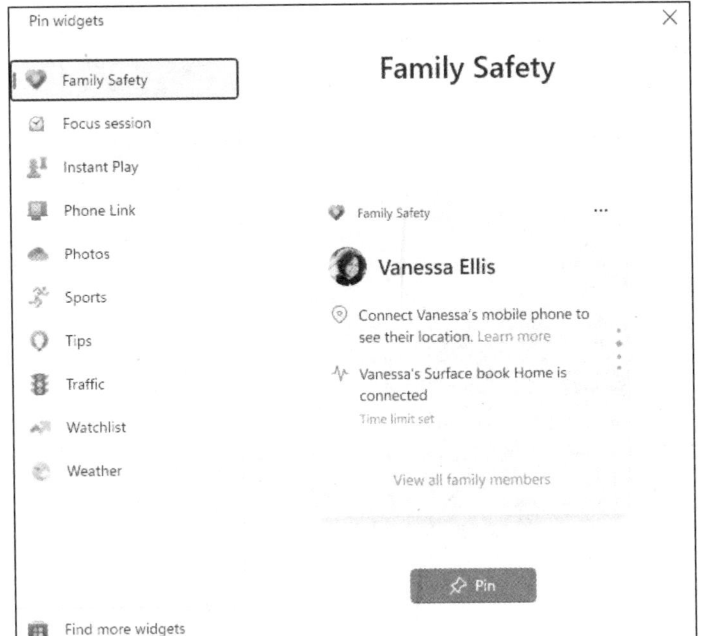

FIGURE 7-3: From here you can add widgets to Windows 11.

Removing Widgets

If you don't like a widget on your widgets board, you can remove it easily like this:

1. **Click or tap the widgets icon on the taskbar or press Windows+W.**

   Windows 11 displays the widgets board.

2. **Scroll down the list of widgets until you find the one you want removed.**

   Windows 11 displays the widgets board.

3. **Click or tap the three dots in the top-right corner of the widget you want gone.**

   A menu appears with several options, as shown in Figure 7-4

4. **Choose Hide This Widget or Unpin Widget, depending on what option you see.**

   The widget is removed.

REMEMBER

The option to Unpin Widget is shown only for widgets that are manually pinned by the user to the board. The Hide This Widget option is shown for widgets that are populated on your board by Windows automatically, without your manual intervention.

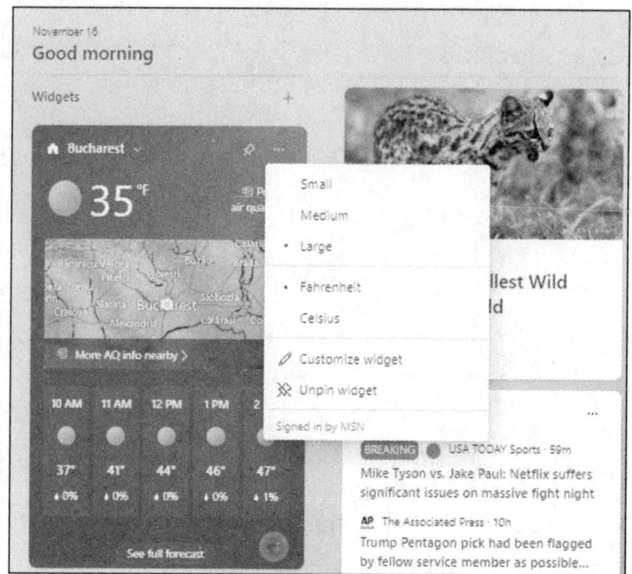

FIGURE 7-4: Configuring or removing a widget is easy.

TIP

To remove the widgets icon from the taskbar, open the Settings app, go to Personalization, and then go to Taskbar. Click or tap to turn off the switch next to Widgets. To learn about using the Settings app, see Book 7, Chapter 1.

Customizing Widgets

After you pin widgets to the board, they can be dragged-and dropped to any position you want, using both the mouse and touch. However, you can also change their size, customize the data they display, or remove them from the board. Here's how to do all that, using the Weather widget as an example:

1. **Click or tap the widgets icon on the taskbar.**

   Windows 11 displays the widgets board on the left side of the screen.

2. **In the top-right corner of the Weather widget, click or tap the three dots icon.**

   The menu shown previously in Figure 7-4 appears.

3. **Choose Small, Medium, or Large as the size of the Weather widget.**

   Note how the Weather widget gets smaller or larger, depending on what you choose.

4. **Click or tap the same three dots icon to the right of the Weather widget and choose Customize Widget.**
5. **Type the location for which you want to see the weather forecast and click or tap the plus (+) sign next to its name. If you want this location to become the default, also click or tap the home icon next to its name.**
6. **Click or tap the X in the top-right corner of the Weather widget.**

   The Weather widget updates its forecast to add the location you entered alongside the default one.
7. **Click or tap the same three dots icon to the right of the Weather widget and choose between Fahrenheit and Celsius.**

   The weather forecast is updated to use the units of measure you selected.

TIP

Customizing other widgets works in a similar way, but the customization options differ. Some widgets, such as Photos or Games, don't offer a Customize Widget option. You can change only their size and position in the feed.

Removing the Feed from Widgets

Many people, including myself, don't like the feed shown on the right side of the widgets board. When this feature was introduced, you couldn't remove it. However, after negative feedback from users, Microsoft has built a way to disable this feed. Here's how it works:

1. **Click or tap the widgets icon on the taskbar or press Windows+W.**

   Windows 11 displays the widgets board.
2. **In the top-right corner of the widgets board, click or tap the Settings icon.**

   The Settings pane shown previously in Figure 7-2 pops up.
3. **Click or tap on Show or Hide Feeds.**

   You see only an entry named Feed, with a switch next to it set on.
4. **Click or tap the switch next to Feed to turn it off.**

   You are informed that this will change how your widgets board looks.
5. **To go ahead with this change, choose Turn Off.**

   The next time you access the widgets board, the feed will be gone, and you'll have room only for the widgets you want to use.

IN THIS CHAPTER

» Playing media files with Windows Media Player Legacy

» Ripping audio CDs

» Setting up a Spotify account

» Playing audio and video files with Media Player

» Creating homemade videos

Chapter 8

Handling Music, Movies, and Videos

I listen to music daily, especially when writing tutorials for Digital Citizen. I've listened to songs even while drafting some of the chapters in this book. You may consider music a distraction, but it's how I get myself into a creative zone and become a productive writer. Music also enhances my mood and allows me to enjoy my day even more.

Whether you're a music junkie like me or just someone who wants to kick back listening to their favorite songs or watching videos from their holidays, Windows 11 has you covered. In this chapter, I walk you through the Windows apps that can play audio and video content.

I start with the old and reliable Windows Media Player Legacy. Yes, it's still alive and kicking, and it can still play the songs and videos stored on your computer or in your OneDrive. Not only that, but it can also play your old-school CD music collection and even back it up on your computer by transforming it into MP3 files.

Is streaming more your style? I show you how to set up Spotify and listen to music with a free account. Then I check out the new kid on the Windows block, the modern Media Player app, and share how you can use it to play music and videos. And for all you budding YouTubers out there, I introduce you to Microsoft Clipchamp, a nifty video editor built right into Windows 11.

Whether you're a casual listener, a media maven, or a wannabe content creator, let's explore how Windows 11 can amp up your digital entertainment.

Using Windows Media Player Legacy

While few people know about Windows Media Player Legacy and even fewer use it, the program has survived in Windows 11. It hasn't changed in many years, doing the same things it did in Windows 8 and Windows 10: It plays music and videos and can even be used as a picture viewer. When you start Windows Media Player Legacy, it looks for content automatically in your local Pictures, Music, and Videos folders as well as those found on your OneDrive. If it finds anything in the many formats it can play or view, you can interact with that content.

Here's how to use Windows Media Player to play music and videos:

1. **Click or tap in the Search box on the taskbar and type** media player.
2. **Choose the Windows Media Player Legacy search result.**

   If this is the first time you start the program, you see a welcome message asking you to choose the initial settings.
3. **If you see the welcome page, choose Recommended Settings, and click or tap Finish.**

   You finally see the Windows Media Player program, as shown in Figure 8-1. The app spends some time scanning your Music, Videos, and Pictures folders, both locally and on your OneDrive.
4. **Click or tap Music on the left, and then double-click or double-tap a song you want to play.**

   The song starts to play immediately, and you can use the controls at the bottom to pause, play, skip to the next song, and so on.
5. **Click or tap Videos, and then double-click or double-tap a video you want to watch.**

   The video opens in a special window, with useful controls at the bottom, as shown in Figure 8-2.
6. **To close Windows Media Player Legacy, click or tap X.**

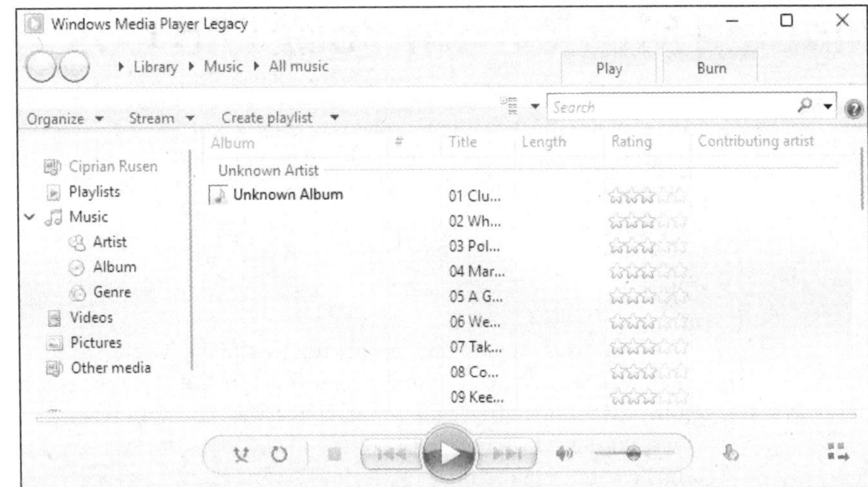

FIGURE 8-1: Windows Media Player Legacy can play both music and videos.

FIGURE 8-2: Watching a video with Windows Media Player Legacy.

TIP

Windows Media Player hasn't been updated in years, and it shows. If you want the best media player for movies that works with all formats, check out VLC Media Player. For more on why I recommend it, see Book 10, Chapter 4.

Ripping Music from Your Old CDs

Do you have a large music collection stored on CDs? I do, and I love my Pink Floyd, Beatles, Leonard Cohen, and Bob Dylan albums. The problem is that CDs wear over time and become unusable after several years. If you don't want to lose the songs stored on CDs, one solution is to rip them and store them on your PC. You might even want a cloud backup for your music on OneDrive or another cloud storage platform.

The process of *ripping* means copying the music from a CD to a computer in a format such as MP3. Once you've ripped a CD, you can take the resulting MP3 files, move them anywhere you want, and listen to them without using the CD. This way, you can prolong the life of the CD by using it less frequently and playing the music you ripped from it instead.

However, if your computer, like most these days, doesn't have a drive for reading optical discs, you have to buy an external DVD drive such as the ASUS ZenDrive. It costs around $35 and is easy to find on Amazon and other online shops.

To rip the music from a CD you own, plug it into the DVD/Blu-ray drive of your computer, and follow these steps:

1. **Click or tap in the Search box on the taskbar and type** media player**.**
2. **Select the Windows Media Player Legacy search result.**
3. **Wait a few seconds for Windows Media Player Legacy to read the disc, and then click or tap its name on the left, below Other Media.**

   Windows Media Player Legacy displays your CD's tracks and album cover.
4. **To configure the ripping process, click or tap Rip Settings in the toolbar on the top side of the app window.**

   The menu shown in Figure 8-3 appears.
5. **To set the format for your music files, choose Format, and then choose the format you want.**

   I prefer MP3. Most probably you do, too.
6. **In the same Rip Settings menu, choose Audio Quality, and then go for a high value, such as 320 Kbps (Best Quality).**

   You want your music to sound great, don't you?
7. **Click or tap Rip CD.**

   Windows Media Player displays the ripping status for each track on your CD. All your songs should be ripped and stored on your PC in just a few minutes.

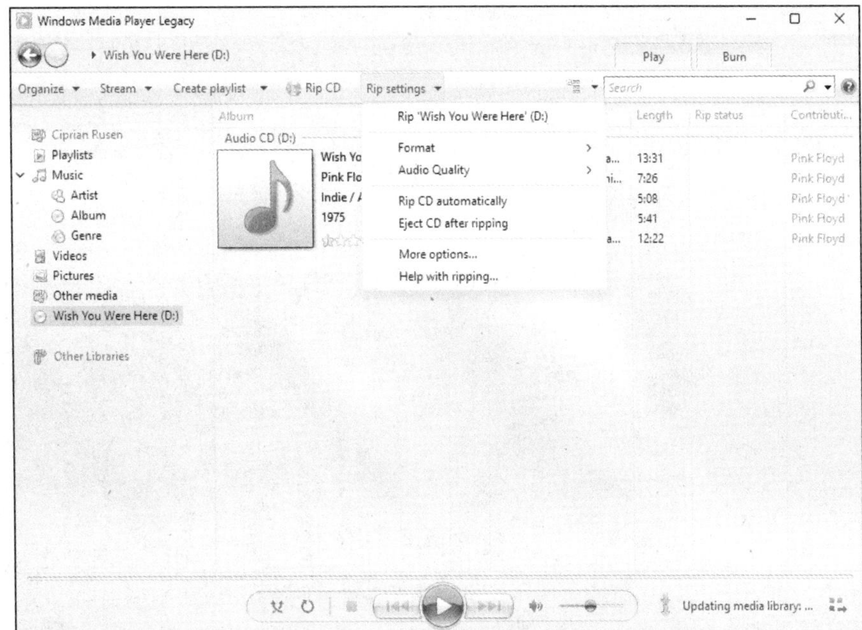

FIGURE 8-3: Configuring the CD ripping settings in Windows Media Player Legacy.

8. **When the ripping process is over, click or tap X to close Windows Media Player Legacy, and then eject your CD.**

   You'll find all your songs in the Music folder, in a folder named after the artist whose songs you've ripped. You can play them in Windows Media Player Legacy or any other media player app.

Setting Up Spotify

Back when Windows 10 was launched, Microsoft launched Groove Music as a music-streaming service that competed with the likes of Spotify, Tidal, and Apple Music. Groove Music lost the battle, and Microsoft discontinued it. You won't find it if you look for it in Windows 11. Instead, Microsoft has partnered with Spotify and actively promotes this music service, including on the Windows 11 Start menu.

If you want to stream music online for free, you can sign up to Spotify directly from Windows 11, like this:

1. **Click or tap the Start icon and then the Spotify shortcut.**

   If you see a progress bar below the Spotify shortcut, Windows 11 is downloading the app from the Microsoft Store.

2. **When the Spotify app opens, click or tap Sign Up Free.**

   The Spotify website opens in your web browser, displaying the options shown in Figure 8-4.

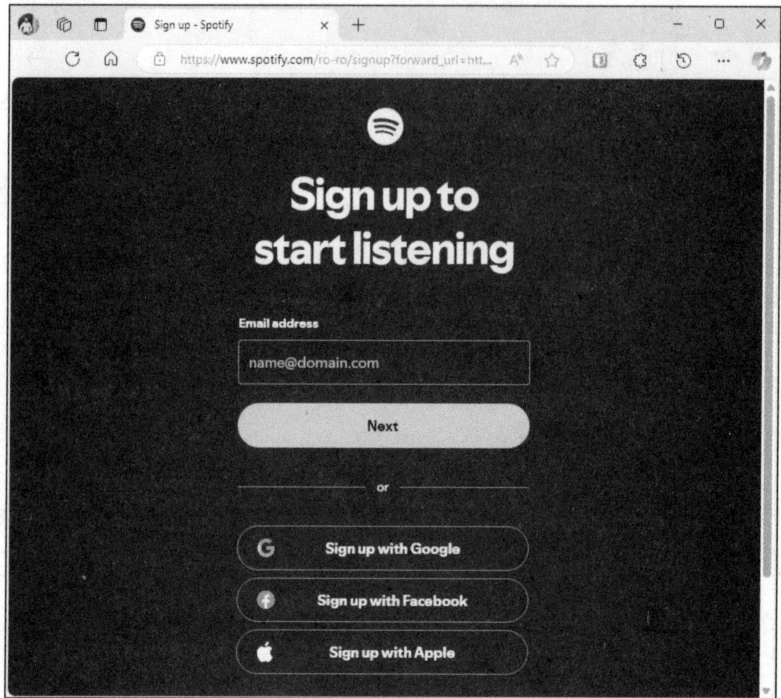

FIGURE 8-4: To join Spotify, you must provide some personal details.

3. **Type your email (a real address, please) and password, clicking or tapping Next after each one.**

   You're asked to provide your name, date of birth, and gender.

4. **Type your name, choose your date of birth and your gender, and then click or tap Next.**

   You're asked to accept the terms and conditions for using Spotify.

5. **Don't select any boxes for accepting news, offers, or marketing content; click or tap Sign Up instead.**
6. **Click or tap Continue to the App.**

   Spotify loads its library of hits and featured charts, as shown in Figure 8-5.

7. **Select one of the featured charts and click or tap the play icon.**

   Music starts playing, and you see the track controls at the bottom. They're like those from any other media player, so you should feel right at home.

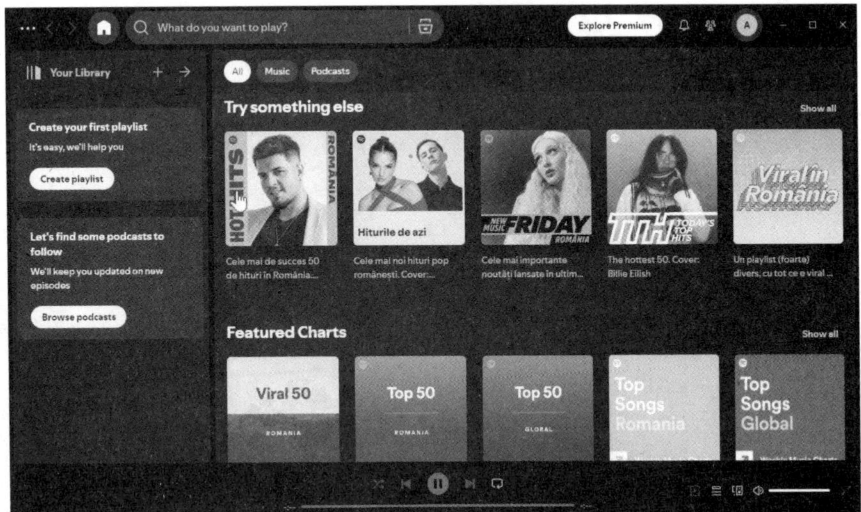

FIGURE 8-5: Welcome to Spotify. Start playing music.

TIP

Spotify doesn't cost a thing to get started. You can listen to music for free for as long as you want. The two important downsides to the free plan are that you have to listen to ads every few songs, and the music streaming quality is set to low. However, an individual plan ($11.99 per month) gets rid of ads and sets the audio quality to the maximum available. There are also plans for two people, families (of up to six people), and students (only $5.99/month).

Using the Media Player App

Because Windows Media Player Legacy is on its way out of Windows, Microsoft decided to give us a modern replacement that can do most of the things the old app can do. And this is why we now have the Media Player app in Windows 11. It's a modern counterpart that can be used to play songs and videos in different formats that you can store locally on your computer or in your OneDrive account. When you open the app, it scans your Music and Videos folders, and if it finds anything, it automatically displays them and allows you to play them. While most people use music and video streaming services nowadays, a minority still rely on local files and multimedia collections. If you're one of them, follow these steps to use the Media Player app in Windows 11:

1. **Click or tap in the Search box on the taskbar and type** media player.
2. **Choose the Media Player search result, not Windows Media Player Legacy.**

   You see the Media Player Home page shown in Figure 8-6. The app encourages you to open audio and video files that it can play for you or explore your personal libraries.

3. **Click or tap Music Library on the left.**

   You see the audio files stored in your Music folder.

4. **Double-click or double-tap any audio file you want to listen to.**

   The file starts playing, and the Media Player app displays a few controls on the bottom of its window, as shown in Figure 8-7. You can use them to go to the previous audio file, pause the audio file, or skip to the next one.

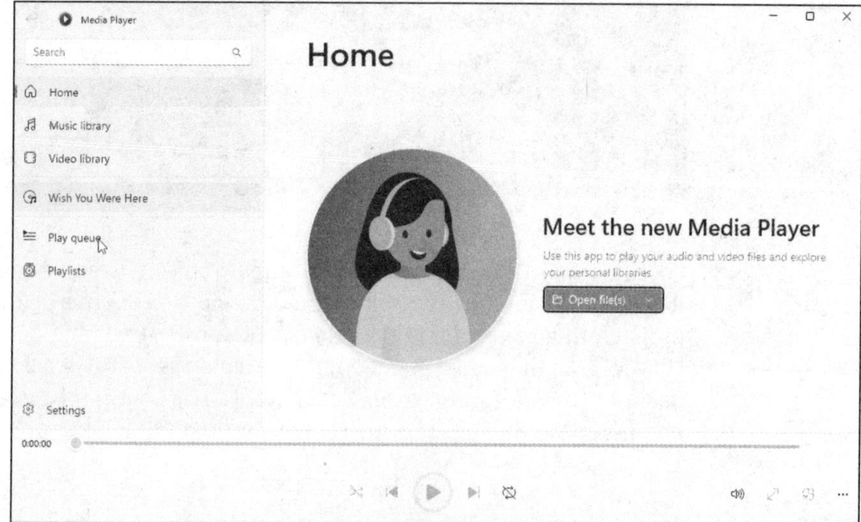

FIGURE 8-6: The Media Player app can play both audio and video files.

5. **Select Video Library on the left**

   You see the video files in your Videos folder if there are any.

6. **Double-click or double-tap the video file you want to watch.**

   The file starts playing, and the Media Player app shows controls at the bottom of its window for pausing and resuming the video, skipping the next 30 seconds, changing the volume, adding subtitles, and so on. For details about what each button does, refer to Figure 8-8.

7. **When you're finished watching, click or tap X to close the app.**

TIP

If you want Media Player to scan for music and video files in other folders, click or tap the Settings icon on the left, and then click or tap Add Folder next to Music Library Locations or Video Library Locations, depending on what you want. Then select the folder you want to add to your collection.

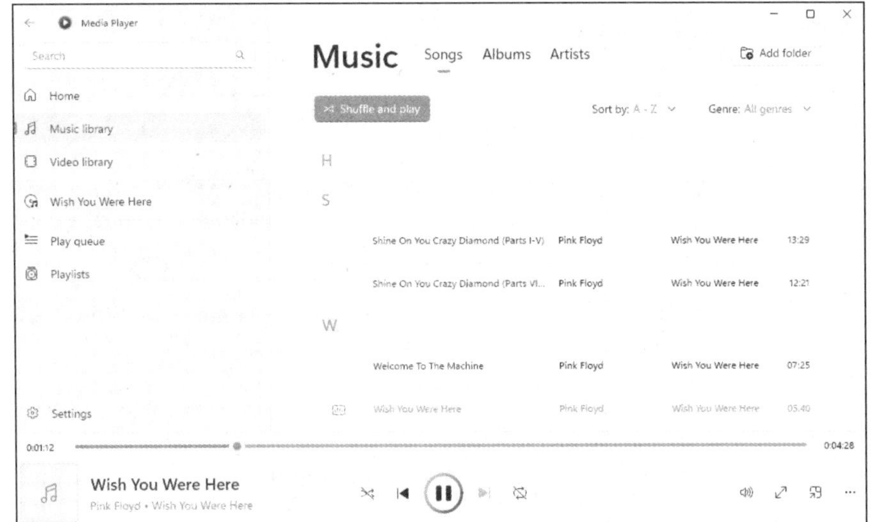

FIGURE 8-7: Listening to some of the songs I've ripped from my old CDs.

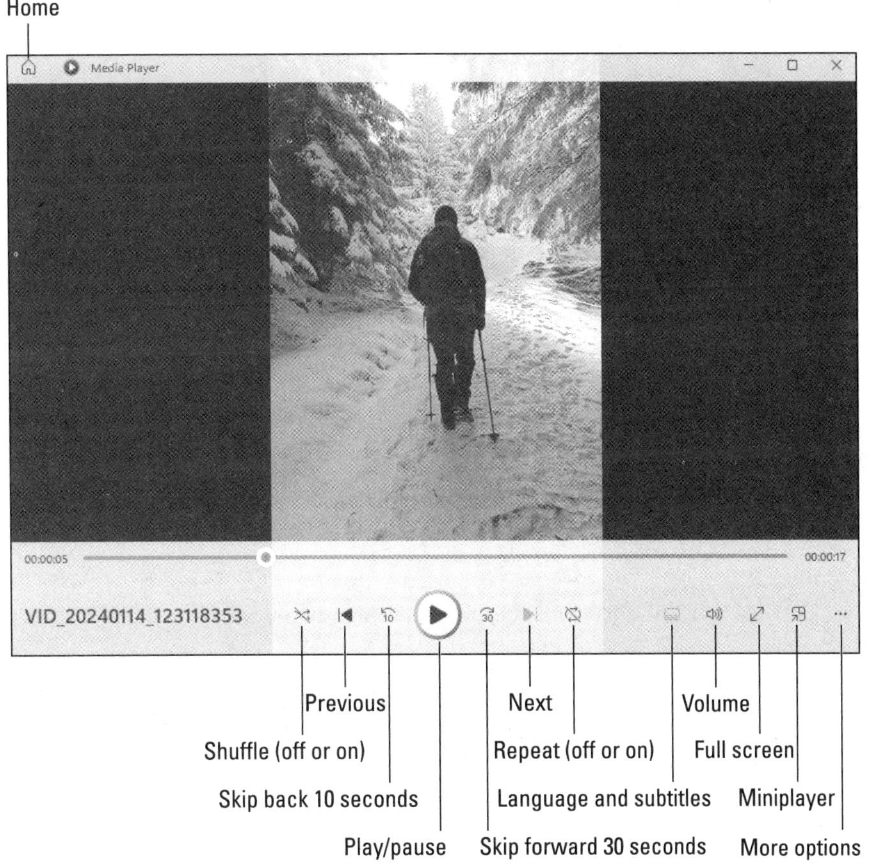

FIGURE 8-8: The controls for watching videos with Media Player.

Creating Videos

Clipchamp, originally a web-based video editor, was acquired by Microsoft in 2021. Since then, it has become a free app in Windows 11 that helps people create videos without needing a degree in video editing. You can use this app to blend videos you've recorded with your smartphone, images, and audio files into professional-looking clips you can upload on YouTube, video stories you can upload to Instagram, or video content you can post on TikTok. The app has easy-to-use templates, stock multimedia content, filters, and effects that can turn you into a creative video editor.

Microsoft Clipchamp is freemium, meaning it's free to install and use as long as you create only 1080p HD content and are okay with using its free filters and stock media. If you want to delve into 4K video editing, premium stock media content, and premium filters and effects, you need to pay for a subscription ($11.99 per month).

Even though it is not complicated to use, Microsoft Clipchamp includes many tools and options for creating videos. Here's a basic tour of how to use it to create a video:

1. **Click or tap the Start icon, followed by Microsoft Clipchamp.**

   If you see a progress bar under the Microsoft Clipchamp shortcut, Windows 11 is downloading the app from the Microsoft Store.

2. **Decline any offers that the app may display and accept the cookie prompt, if you see one.**

   You finally see the Home tab of the Microsoft Clipchamp app, as shown in Figure 8-9.

3. **Choose Create a New Video and enter a name for your project in the top-left corner of the app window.**

4. **Click or tap Import Media, browse your computer, select the file(s) you want to add to your video, and click or tap Open.**

   Your media is imported to the Microsoft Clipchamp app. Feel free to repeat this step until you add all the files you want in your video. They can be pictures, videos, and audio files.

5. **Drag and drop the files you imported onto the storyboard on the bottom left. Arrange them in any order you prefer.**

   Remember that the items on the storyboard can be dragged and dropped to change their order. The result should be something similar to what you see in Figure 8-10.

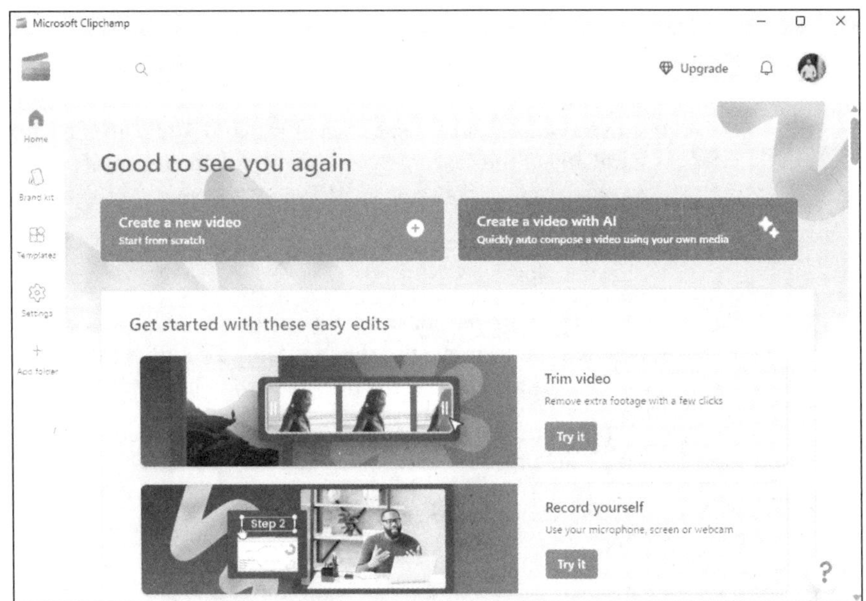

FIGURE 8-9: Microsoft Clipchamp is a freemium app for editing videos.

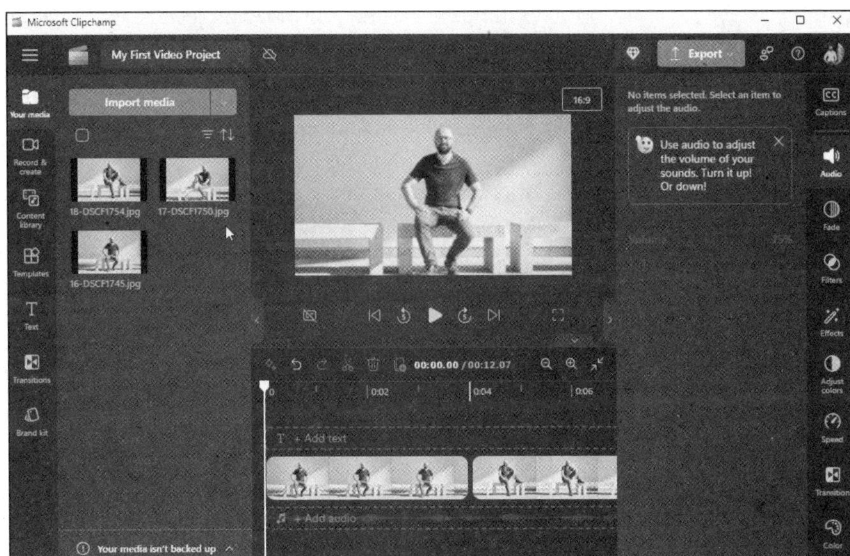

FIGURE 8-10: Adding media content to the Clipchamp storyboard.

6. **If you want to add text, click or tap Add Text on the storyboard and use the options on the left side of the app window.**
7. **If you want, you can also click or tap Add Audio on the storyboard and add any of the featured content displayed on the left side of Microsoft Clipchamp.**

   Clipchamp has a reasonably good selection of audio content that can be added to your clips.
8. **If you want to play back what you've added so far to see how the video is coming along, move the slider on the storyboard to the left, and then click or tap the play icon in the middle of the Microsoft Clipchamp window.**
9. **When you're finished adding content to the video, click or tap Export in the top right.**

   You see a menu with several video quality options, such as 480p, 720p, 1080p, 4K, and GIF.
10. **Choose the resolution you want for your video.**

    I recommend 720p for a smaller file size or 1080p for better quality. Microsoft Clipchamp starts generating your video project using the name you chose. When it' done, it saves the video in your Downloads folder.
11. **Click or tap X to close Microsoft Clipchamp, and then open your video file found in the Downloads folder.**

TIP

You can use Microsoft Clipchamp to make decrease a video file's size. Simply import the file into the video editor using the steps shared earlier, add it to the storyboard, and click or tap Export. Choose a lower resolution than the original. Usually, 720p offers a good balance between video quality and file size.

IN THIS CHAPTER

» Searching for games in the Microsoft Store

» Playing with game mode

» Using the game bar

» Setting the default graphics card for your game(s)

» Finding old games, reborn

Chapter 9 Playing Games

Microsoft promoted Windows 11 as a game-changer for PC gaming. However, although Windows 11 introduces some new features, the overall gaming experience is similar to that of its predecessor, Windows 10. The most interesting innovations for gamers are DirectStorage and Auto HDR.

DirectStorage is a technical advancement that allows your PC to bypass the processor when loading data from an NVMe solid-state drive (a fast type of SSD) to the graphics card. This reduces the CPU processing required during the loading of textures, resulting in faster game load times. However, adoption has been slow because developers must implement DirectStorage in their games. Despite Windows 11 launching on October 5, 2021, games supporting DirectStorage only began to appear in 2023, with Forspoken being the first. Since then, more popular titles such as Diablo IV, Forza Motorsport, and Horizon Forbidden West have started to utilize this technology.

Auto HDR is particularly intriguing because it employs an algorithm to convert standard game images into HDR (high dynamic range). It does this by analyzing SDR (standard dynamic range) luminance (intensity of light) data and enhancing the image quality — not by increasing the resolution but by improving luminance. If you have an HDR-capable monitor, enabling Auto HDR can enhance your visual experience.

Aside from these features, Windows 11 retains most of the gaming tools from Windows 10, such as the Microsoft Store for game distribution, game mode, and the game bar. In this chapter, I focus on the aspects that matter most to you, the user. You learn how to navigate the Microsoft Store to find and play games, enable game mode, access the game bar, and make the most of its widgets. If you're using a gaming laptop, you learn how to set the default graphics card for your favorite games.

Finally, for casual gamers who miss classics like Solitaire and Minesweeper, I wrap up the chapter by showing you how to bring these games back to Windows 11.

Searching the Microsoft Store for Games

You can get games for Windows on many platforms, the most popular being Steam. However, you can also try `www.gog.com`, the Epic Games Store, or the Humble Bundle, to name a few. Microsoft is also trying to carve out some market share in the distribution and selling of games for Windows through its Microsoft Store. While its portfolio isn't as large as that of its competitors, you can find some good games on it.

Here's how to use the Microsoft Store to find games and install them on your Windows 11 computer:

1. **Click or tap the Microsoft Store shortcut on the taskbar or from the Start menu.**

   The Microsoft Store appears.

2. **On the left, click or tap Gaming.**

   An array of games and offers appears, as shown in Figure 9-1. At the top are the latest offers from Microsoft. Below them, you find many games organized by categories such as Best Selling Games, Best of Game Pass, and Top Free Games.

3. **Scroll down to Top Free Games and click or tap this category to expand it.**

   You see the free games that are popular.

4. **Browse the list and click or tap any game that interests you.**

   I chose Angry Birds 2, as shown in Figure 9-2. The Microsoft Store displays a description of the game and allows you to install it. The description may include a notice that you can buy stuff inside the game (offers In-Game Purchases). Scroll down further, and the game description includes the Additional Information section, which indicates what's available and how much it costs.

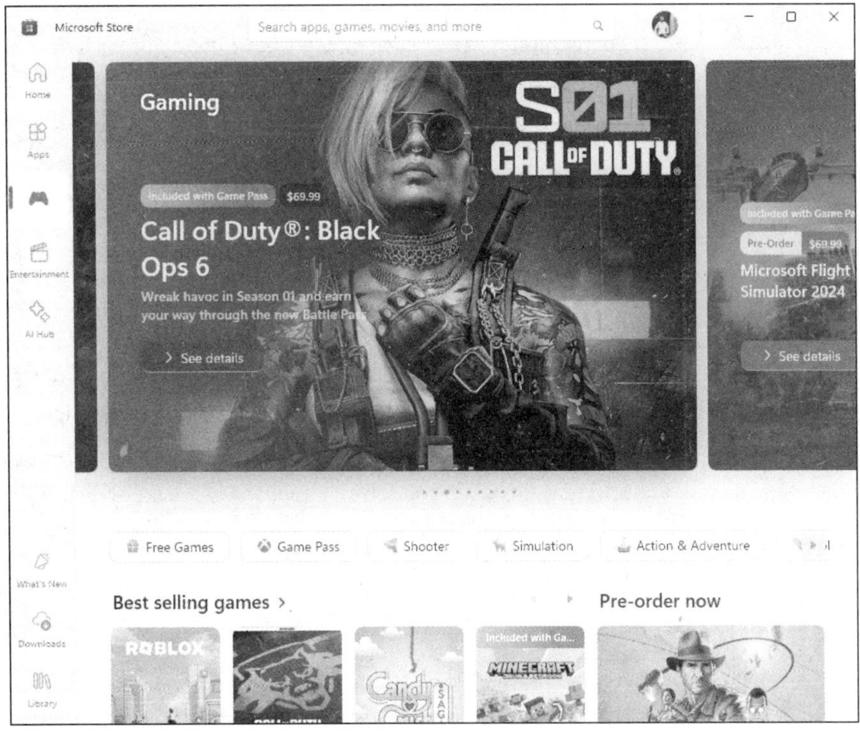

FIGURE 9-1: The Games section in the Microsoft Store.

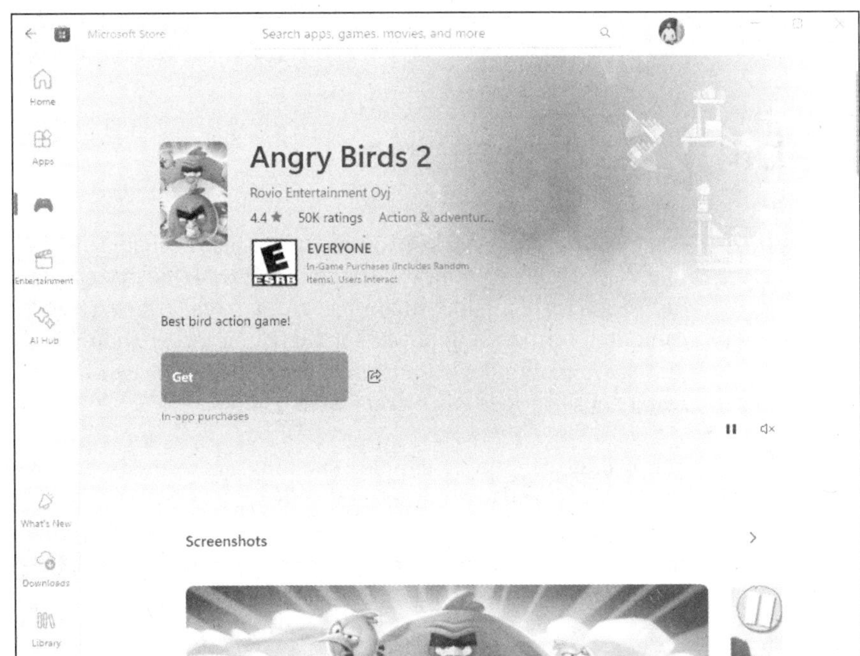

FIGURE 9-2: If a game tickles your fancy, install it.

5. **To install the game, click or tap Get or Install (if it's free) or Buy (if it's not free).**

   If you browse other game categories, you see the Buy button with the price.

6. **Free games start downloading and installing right away. When choosing a paid game, first verify your billing details and then click or tap Buy again.**

   While the game is downloading, you see a progress bar in the Microsoft Store.

   REMEMBER

   Games marked Included with Game Pass are free as long as you have an Xbox Game Pass Ultimate or PC Game Pass associated with your Microsoft account.

7. **To run the game after it's downloaded and installed, click or tap the Play button that appears on the game's Microsoft Store page.**

   The game appears also in the Recommended list on the Start menu, just like any newly installed Windows 11 app. The game is also in the All list.

As you can see, downloading and installing a game is easy. Finding them and winning are anything but.

TIP

Serious gamers should consider subscribing to Steam, the internet's largest digital game distribution center. While the Microsoft Store is a decent distribution platform, it doesn't get close to Steam when it comes to the number of available titles. Steam works for PC, Mac, and Linux. It has built-in social networking, automated saved game backups, in-game achievement tracking, micro-payments, and more. Visit `https://store.steampowered.com`.

Enabling Game Mode

Game mode, introduced in Windows 10 and also available in Windows 11, is designed to enhance your gaming experience by optimizing system performance. According to Microsoft, game mode boosts in-game frame rates by prioritizing your computer's processing power for the game rather than for background tasks. It also prevents Windows Update from performing driver installations and sending restart notifications while you play.

The overall concept is simple: Enabling game mode helps prevent issues like significant slowdowns, frame rate drops, and interruptions from notifications, making your gaming sessions smoother. While Windows 11 is supposed to automatically activate game mode when it detects a game, this doesn't always happen, particularly with older titles.

To check to see if game mode is enabled — and to enable it if necessary — follow these steps:

1. **Click or tap the start icon and then Settings.**

   The Windows 11 Settings app opens.

2. **On the left, click or tap Gaming. On the right, choose Game Mode.**
3. **Set the Game Mode switch on, as shown in Figure 9-3.**
4. **Close Settings and start the game.**

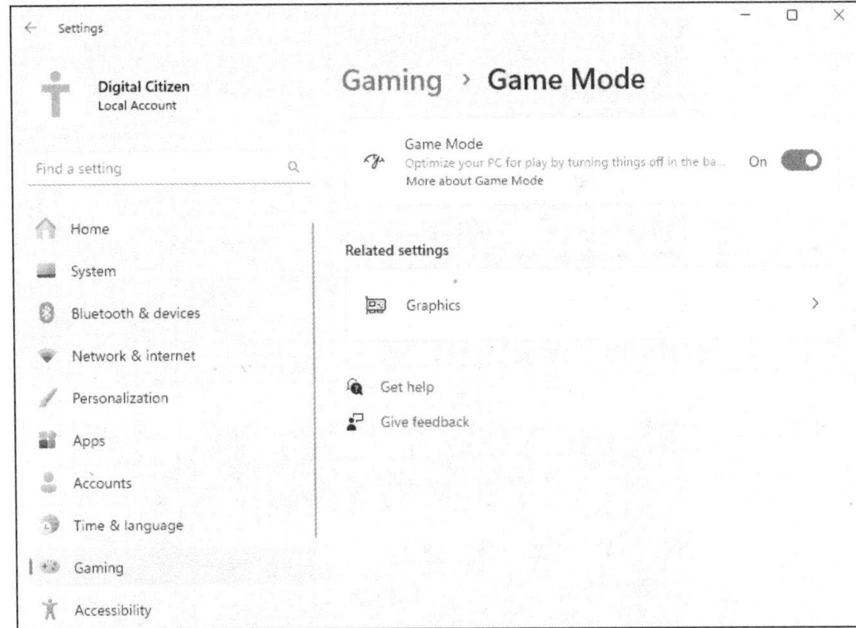

FIGURE 9-3: Turning game mode on or off.

If you're playing an older game, and it doesn't look like Windows 11 is enabling game mode for it, do this:

1. **While the game is running, press Windows+G.**

   The game bar appears on the top of the screen, as shown in Figure 9-4. Alongside the game bar, you also see some widgets for various features included in the game bar.

2. **Click or tap the settings icon (gear) on the game bar.**

   The Settings window appears, as shown in Figure 9-5.

3. **On the General tab, select the Remember This Is a Game option.**

   This tells Windows 11 that you're playing a game, and it should enable game mode. If you don't see this option, the game is already on the list of officially supported titles, and everything is okay.

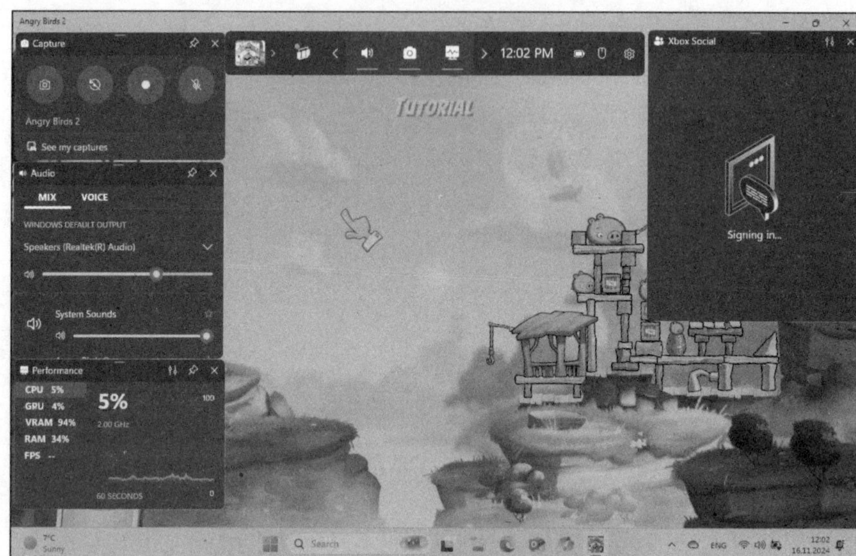

FIGURE 9-4: The game bar appears at the top of the screen alongside other widgets.

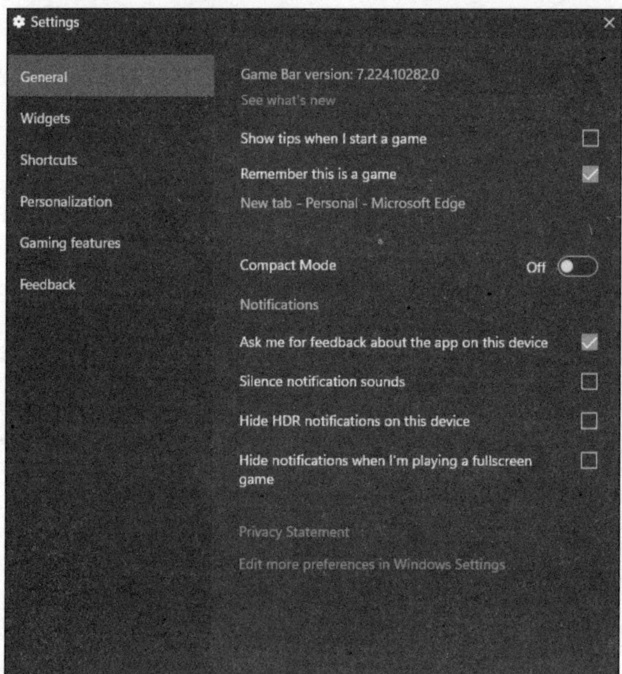

FIGURE 9-5: Telling Windows 11 that you are playing a game and want game mode.

Using the Game Bar

Game mode in Windows 11 comes with a useful tool called the game bar. When you start a game, press Windows+G. The game bar appears over your game, with several widgets that offer useful settings and data, as shown in Figure 9-4.

To become familiar with the game bar, follow these steps:

1. **Start a game that you want to play, and then press Windows+G.**

   The game bar appears (refer to Figure 9-4).

2. **On the game bar, click or tap the widgets menu icon (labeled in Figure 9-6).**

   A menu with widgets that can be enabled and disabled is shown. A star to the right of a widget's name indicates that it's enabled. Click or tap their name to enable or disable them.

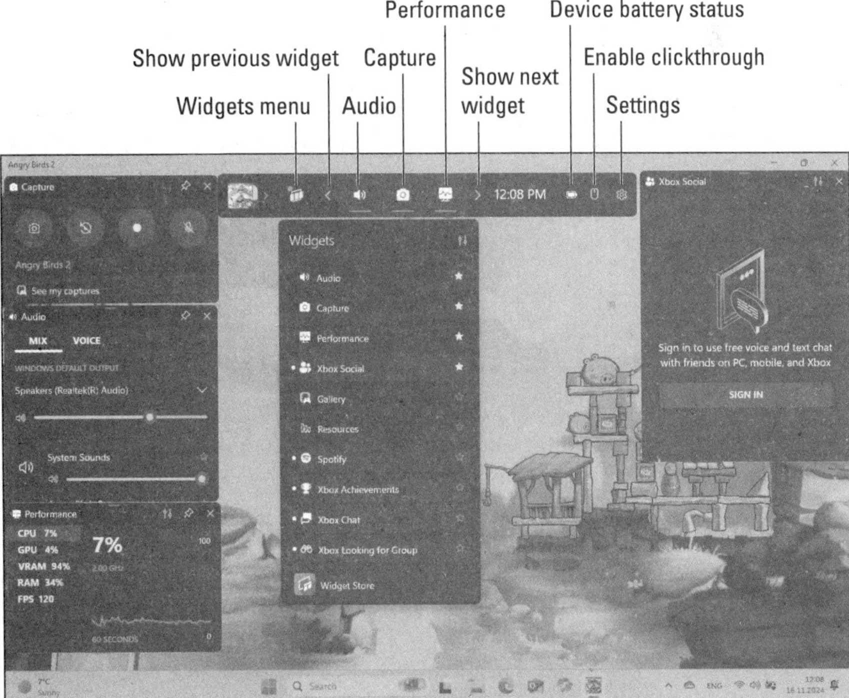

FIGURE 9-6: Adding or removing widgets.

3. **Click or tap the audio icon to see how audio devices are set for your game. Change the settings if necessary.**

4. **Click or tap the capture icon.**

   The capture widget is displayed, with buttons for taking screenshots of your game, recording the last 30 seconds of gameplay, recording a video of your gameplay, and turning the microphone on and off.

5. **Click or tap the performance icon.**

   The performance widget is displayed with real-time data about processor (CPU) usage, graphics card usage (GPU), RAM consumption, and the number of frames per second rendered on the screen (FPS). This data is useful to gamers who play demanding video games.

6. **Click or tap the Xbox Social icon. If you don't see this icon, click or tap > (show next widget icon) until you do.**

   The Xbox Social widget gives you tools to chat with friends, see who is online, invite them to a party, and so on.

7. **Click or tap the settings icon (gear).**

   You get access to settings that you can use to personalize the game bar and Windows 11's gaming features.

8. **To hide the game bar, click or tap anywhere outside it or press Windows+G.**

TIP

If you have a powerful gaming PC or laptop and a display with HDR support, you'll want to enable HDR for your games. To learn how to do that, go to Book 3, Chapter 1, and read the section about HDR in Windows 11.

Setting the Default Graphics Card

Many gaming laptops have two video cards: an integrated graphics chip that helps them provide basic video features at low power consumption and a dedicated video card for more demanding apps and games. By default, Windows 11 does a respectable job of using the correct video card based on the apps you run and the games you play. However, sometimes Windows might use the wrong card, or you might want to force Windows 11 to use a specific graphics card for a specific game.

Here's how to set the default graphics card for a specific game that's installed on your PC:

1. **Click or tap the start icon, followed by Settings.**

   The Settings window opens.

2. **Select System on the left, and then choose Display on the right.**
3. **Under Related Settings, click or tap Graphics.**

   You see a list of apps and games, as shown in Figure 9-7.

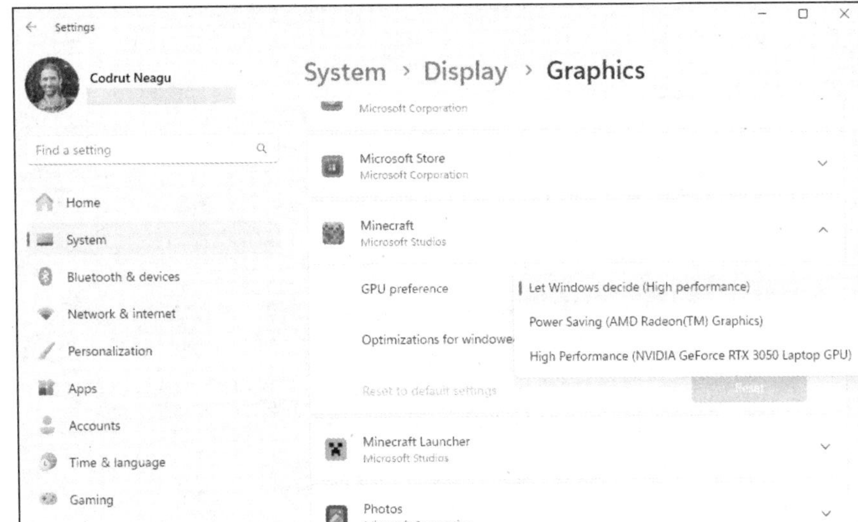

FIGURE 9-7: The list of apps and games for which you can set the default graphics card.

4. **Click or tap the name of the game for which you want to set the default graphics card to expand it.**

TIP

   If you don't see the game you want in the list, click or tap Add Desktop App and choose its default .exe file.

5. **Click or tap the GPU Preference drop-down list and choose between Power Saving (which uses the integrated graphics chip) and High Performance (which uses the dedicated video card).**

   From now on, each time you play that game, Windows 11 uses the graphics card you chose, even if it may not be the optimal choice.

Bringing Back the Classics

Admit it. You want to play Solitaire on your new Windows 11 machine. And Minesweeper. Just like people did in Windows 7. Well, you're in luck — and they're easy to find if you know where to look.

Just crank up the Microsoft Store, and in the Search box at the top, type **Xbox Game Studios**. Press Enter. In the Games section, you get a list of all the games published by Microsoft and its gaming studios, as shown in Figure 9-8.

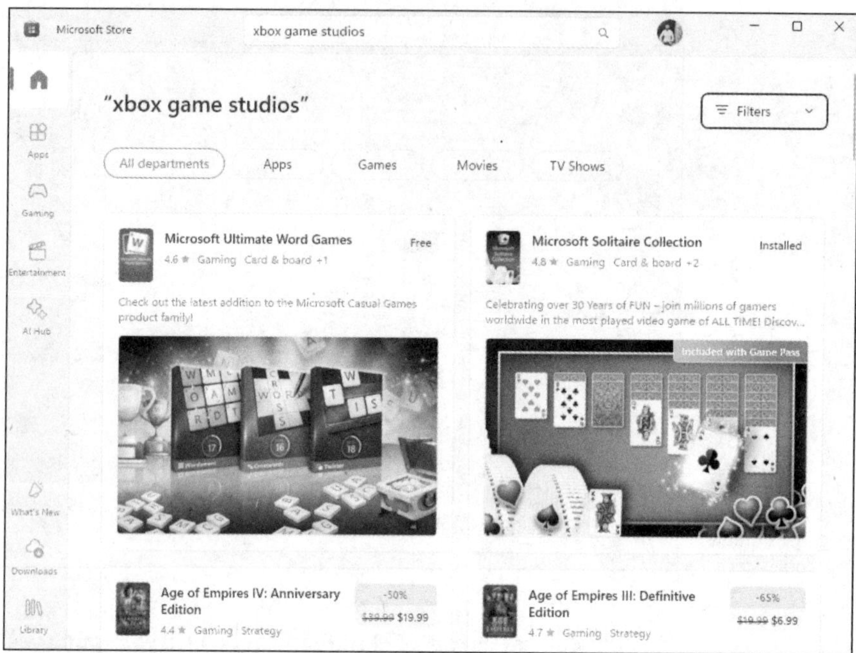

FIGURE 9-8: These games are published by Microsoft's Xbox Game Studios.

If you're an experienced Windows user, you might want to pick up some or all these free games:

- **Microsoft Solitaire Collection** includes Klondike (the game you no doubt remember as Solitaire, shown in Figure 9-9), Spider Solitaire, FreeCell, Pyramid, and TriPeaks. As mentioned in the "What is freemium?" sidebar, if you want your Solitaire Collection without ads, you must pay for the privilege.

  None of the old cheats work in Solitaire — you can't switch how many cards you flip in the middle of a hand or peek — but you can still play with hints or choose between one-card and three-card draws.
- **Microsoft Minesweeper,** the game that Bill Gates loved to hate, works very much like it has for many years.
- **Microsoft Mahjong** brings the classic click-clack to the screen.
- **Microsoft Sudoku** is another classic game that's easy to play, even on low-end PCs.

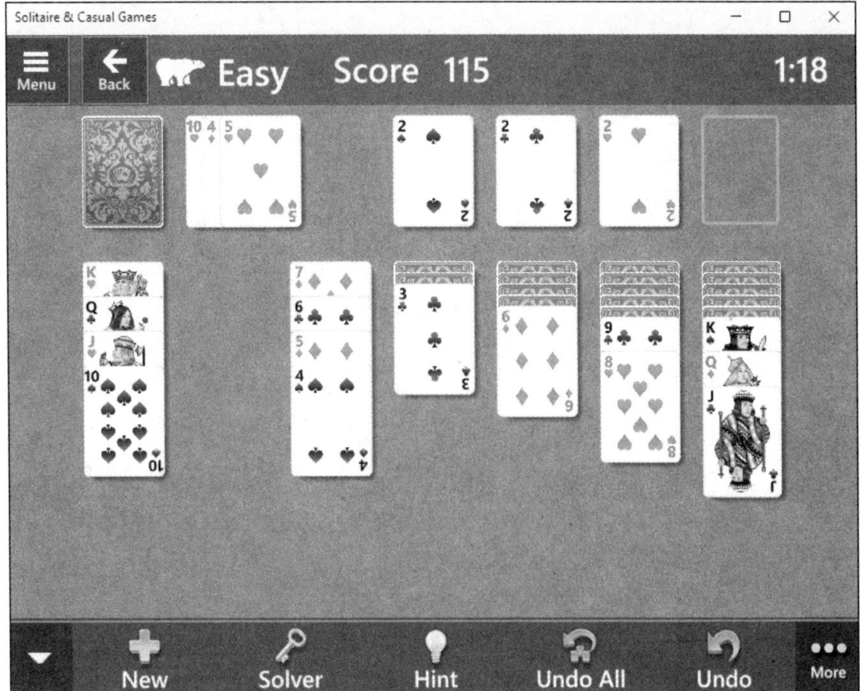

FIGURE 9-9: Klondike, the game you remember from when you were a kid.

There are many more, but those Xbox Game Studios games should keep you going for hours.

WHAT IS FREEMIUM?

Microsoft has shifted to freemium games to drive new income from its classic (and traditionally free) games. *Freemium* means that you can get the basic game for free, but you must pay to get more features or — as is the case with Microsoft Solitaire Collection — to get rid of ads.

You can download and play Microsoft Solitaire forever without having to pay for it. But if you want to get rid of the ads, you pay $14.99 a year for the Premium Edition. Is it worth the money? Good question.

IN THIS CHAPTER

» Taking screenshots and recording your screen

» Editing text files

» Editing or creating images

» Understanding Sticky Notes

» Setting new default apps

Chapter 10

Working with Apps

Welcome to the unpredictable world of Windows 11 apps, where old favorites get facelifts, niche Microsoft apps get removed without much explanation, and new features sneak in when you least expect it. In this world, taking screenshots is snappier than ever, editing text files has regained its cool factor, sticky notes stick around (in the cloud, no less), the weather forecast has become even more complex, and Paint has a fresh coat of . . . well, paint.

In this chapter, I explore some of the most popular apps built into Windows 11: Snipping Tool and its new screenshot and screen-recording capabilities; the new Notepad, with tabs support and auto-saving features; and the Paint app, which has been infused with tools based on artificial intelligence. I continue this chapter by exploring what's going on with Sticky Notes and how it's likely to be radically changed in the future, as well as the Weather app, which has received a new presentation and much more data than it used to have.

Last but not least, I also share how to tell Windows which apps should open which files. After all, sometimes Microsoft Edge isn't the best tool for working with complex PDF documents, no matter how much it insists otherwise. So grab your Windows 11 computer, and let's explore some of its apps.

Taking Screenshots with Snipping Tool

In Windows 11, if you want to take a snapshot of your desktop, you simply press the Print Screen key on your keyboard. Your screen dims, and you see a toolbar with screen-capturing options at the top of the screen, as shown in Figure 10-1. They're added there by Snipping Tool, the default screenshot app in Windows 11.

FIGURE 10-1: Snipping tool can take screenshots or record a video of your screen.

REMEMBER

Depending on your keyboard, the Print Screen key may be labeled PrtScn, Print Scrn, Prnt Scrn, Prnt Scr, Prt Scrn, Prt Scr, Prt Sc, Pr Sc, or simply PS. On some keyboards, the Print Screen key has a Snipping Tool logo to tell it apart, while on many laptops it needs to be pressed alongside the Fn key. Therefore, expect to press two keys instead of one: Fn+Print Screen, or Fn PrtScn, and so on.

By default, the photo camera icon is selected, signaling that you are about to capture an image of what's on your screen. This *snip*, or screenshot, can be rectangular, a screenshot of a window, a fullscreen snip, or a freeform one. Here's how to take a screenshot in Windows 11:

1. **Open an app that you want to capture in a screenshot, say Microsoft Edge.**
2. **Press the PrtScr or Print Screen key on your keyboard. If you're using a laptop, you may need to press Fn+PrtScr instead.**

   The screen dims, and you see the toolbar shown previously in Figure 10-1.
3. **Ensure that the photo camera icon is selected, and then click or tap the rectangle icon.**

   The menu shown in Figure 10-2 opens.

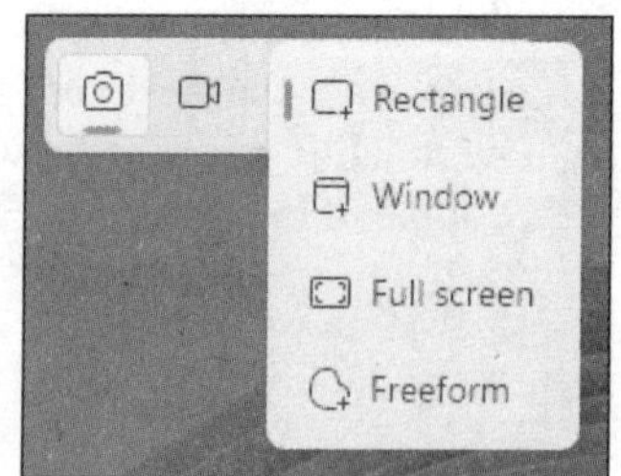

FIGURE 10-2: Choosing how you want to take the screenshot.

4. **Choose Window, and then click or tap the app window you want to capture.**

   To follow along with the example choose the Microsoft Edge window. You see a notification that the screenshot was copied to the clipboard.

5. **Click or tap the notification.**

   The screenshot is displayed in the Snipping Tool app. You can edit the screenshot, select Edit in Paint and work with it there, or save it anywhere you want. By default, the screenshot is automatically saved in your Pictures\Screenshots folder, even if all you do is capture the screenshot.

6. **Click or tap X in the top-right corner to close Snipping Tool.**

TIP

While this is the default way to take screenshots in Windows 11, you can try other methods as well:

» **Press Alt+Print Screen:** Windows 11 puts a screenshot of the currently active window on the clipboard. From there, you can open Paint (or another picture-savvy program), paste, and do what you want with the screenshot.

» **Press Windows+Print Screen:** Windows takes a screenshot of the entire screen, converts it to a PNG file, and stores it in your Pictures\Screenshots folder.

Recording the Screen with Snipping Tool

If a picture or screenshot is worth a thousand words, a video of the screen in action must be worth a thousand and one at least, right?

You'll probably be happy to know that Microsoft has updated Snipping Tool to include screen recording. The resulting recordings can include not only what happens on the screen but also your voice when speaking into your microphone and the sounds the system makes. Such recordings are useful if you encounter problems with your computer and need to show what's happening to someone more technical than you, or when you want to create useful how-to content, such as these steps on how to use screen recording in Windows 11:

1. **Press the Print Screen key.**

   The screen dims and the toolbar shown previously in Figure 10-1 appears.

2. **Click or tap the video camera icon, and then draw the area you want to capture with your mouse (or your finger on a touchscreen).**

   The selected area brightens, and you see new options on the toolbar at the top, as shown in Figure 10-3. The toolbar gives you the option to start the recording, mute or unmute your microphone (if you have one), and mute or unmute the system audio. Furthermore, the recording area can be dragged around and also made larger or smaller by using the controls on its margins.

3. **Make your selections and click or tap Start.**

   You may be asked to let Snipping Tool access your microphone.

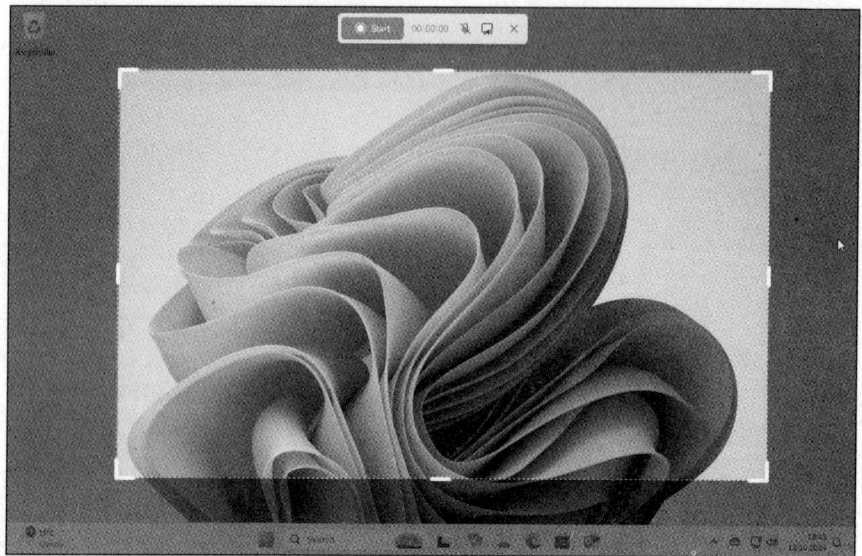

FIGURE 10-3: Selecting the area for the screen recording.

4. **Give Snipping Tool the necessary permissions.**

   After a countdown, the recording starts. The toolbar at the top changes to display the options shown in Figure 10-4.

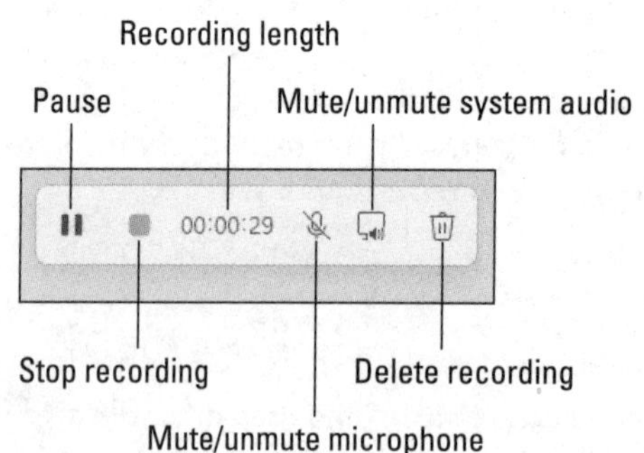

FIGURE 10-4: Your options for controlling the recording.

5. **When you're done, click or tap the stop recording icon.**

   The recording is opened in Snipping Tool, and you're informed that it was automatically saved in your Videos\Screen Recordings folder. You can't edit the recording in Snipping Tool, but you have the option to edit it in Clipchamp.

6. **To close Snipping Tool, click or tap X in the top-right corner.**

TIP

When you click or tap the stop recording icon, Snipping Tool saves the video as an MP4 file and stores it in the Videos\Screen Recordings folder. There's no need to use the Save option in Snipping Tool.

Editing Text Files with Notepad

Notepad made its debut in 1983, during the MS-DOS era, which predated the Windows operating system. For over four decades, this computer program has maintained its core functionality, becoming an integral part of every Windows version. Despite its longevity, Notepad remained largely unchanged until the arrival of Windows 11, when Microsoft finally invested time in transforming it into a modern app, with a few new features that its users are likely to appreciate:

- **Tabs support:** You no longer need to open multiple text files in separate Notepad windows, even though you can. You can now work with them using tabs, just like you do with web pages in your favorite web browser.
- **Automatic word wrapping:** The text no longer extends way off to the right side of the screen. Notepad skips to a new line only when it encounters a line break or when you press Enter, which typically occurs at the end of every paragraph.
- **Search with Bing:** You can select text, open the Edit menu, and then select Search with Bing. This action opens a Microsoft Edge browsing window and performs a search using the selected text.
- **Spell checking:** Notepad automatically checks your spelling as you type text into it.
- **Autocorrect:** Just like the keyboard on every smartphone or tablet, Notepad automatically corrects your typos when you enable spell checking.
- **Continue previous session:** When you start Notepad, it automatically opens the files used previously and allows you to resume where you left off. If you don't like this behavior, you can turn it off from the app's settings.

Although Notepad's appearance and feature-set in Windows 11 differ from its predecessors, it remains a basic yet efficient tool for writing and editing plain text. Its minimalist approach provides a distraction-free environment ideal for quick note-taking, coding, or any task requiring pure text manipulation.

However, it's important to note that Notepad handles only plain, unformatted text — essentially, the characters you see on your keyboard. It doesn't support text formatting, such as bold or italics, nor can it embed pictures or other media.

If you're interested in exploring Notepad, here's a brief tour on how to use it:

1. **Click or tap the Start icon, All, and then Notepad.**

   The Notepad app opens, displaying an empty Untitled tab, where you can input text, as shown in Figure 10-5.

FIGURE 10-5: As you can see, Notepad is a very simple text editor with a modern look.

2. **Open Microsoft Edge or another web browser, visit a website you like (say, Wikipedia), and then copy and paste the content of a web page into Notepad.**

   Note how the text is copied to Notepad without formatting or images.

3. **To change how the text is displayed in Notepad, click or tap the gear icon (Settings) in the top right.**

   The Settings page appears.

4. **Under Text Formatting, click or tap Font.**

   You see the text formatting options presented in Figure 10-6.

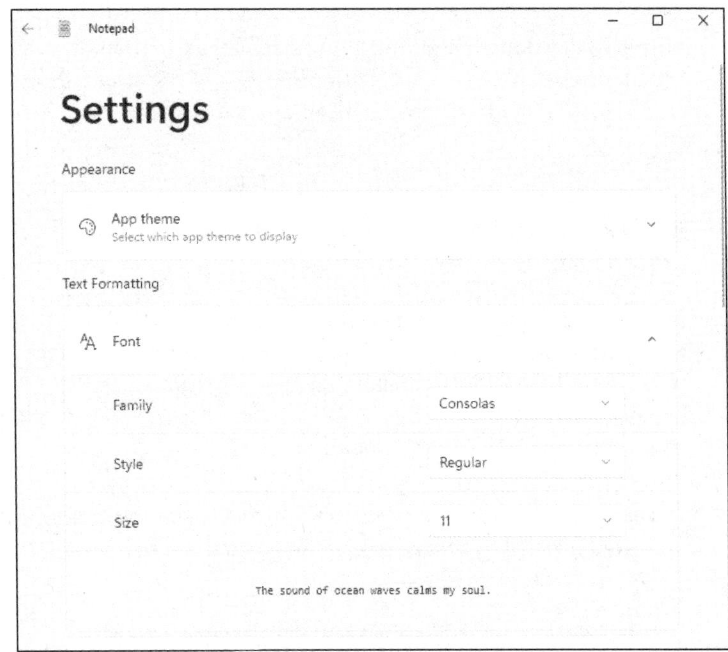

FIGURE 10-6: Notepad's Settings page is where you change how it works.

5. **Click or tap Family and select the font you want. Then choose the style and its size.**
6. **To return to your text, click or tap the back arrow in the top left.**

   Notice how the text is displayed using your new formatting settings.

7. **To create a new tab, click or tap the plus sign (+) next to the current tab.**

   Notepad opens a new Untitled tab where you can enter text.

8. **Click or tap X on the right of the new Untitled tab to close it.**

   You're back to your initial text.

9. **To save the text in a file, click or tap File, choose Save, enter the file name you want to use, select its location, and click or tap Save.**

   Notepad creates a TXT file with the name you've typed and in the location you selected.

10. **To close Notepad, click or tap X in the top-right corner.**

REMEMBER

Although the text you see in Notepad is in a specific font that you chose in its settings, the characters in the file itself aren't formatted. The font you see on the screen is the one Notepad uses to display the text in a file. The stuff in the file itself is plain, unformatted text.

TIP

Software developers may need more advanced text editors, and one of the most popular alternatives is Notepad++. You can check it out at `notepad-plus-plus.org/downloads/`. It's free, open source, and works well.

Using Paint

Microsoft has also redesigned the Paint app for Windows 11. The new version is a modern spin on the classic app, with a new user interface with rounder corners. Initially, it didn't get any major new features, but starting with Microsoft's exploration of artificial intelligence (AI) and the introduction of Copilot, Paint has received significant improvements:

- **Background removal:** With the help of AI, Paint can analyze a picture of an area selected by the user, separate objects, and remove only the background, turning it transparent.
- **Layers:** You can add, remove, or hide layers to create images and drawings in a more productive and professional manner.
- **Image Creator:** Use Microsoft's AI services to generate digital images based on your instructions. It's like having a digital artist doing the work for you. Alongside your text input, you can also choose a drawing style. Create photorealistic images or drawings in pixel art, paintings, sketches, and more. This feature works with all Windows 11 computers and devices, unlike the next feature.
- **Cocreator:** Use this AI-based service to generate digital images. While you start by providing a text description of what you want to create, Cocreator also acts like a real-time drawing assistant. You can draw on top of the image drafts it creates, adjust the creativity level and style, and update your image in real time. Cocreator may be useful to people who want to learn how to become digital artists, as well as professionals who want to sketch ideas for clients and have little time available for this task. Unfortunately, this requires a Copilot+ PC device.

TIP

If you want to experiment with using Image Creator to create images based on your input, you can find a detailed step-by-step tutorial at Digital Citizen: `https://bit.ly/4841Jfk`.

If you want to fire up Paint and see how it looks, click or tap the Start icon, All, and then Paint. You see the new app in all its glory, as shown in Figure 10-7.

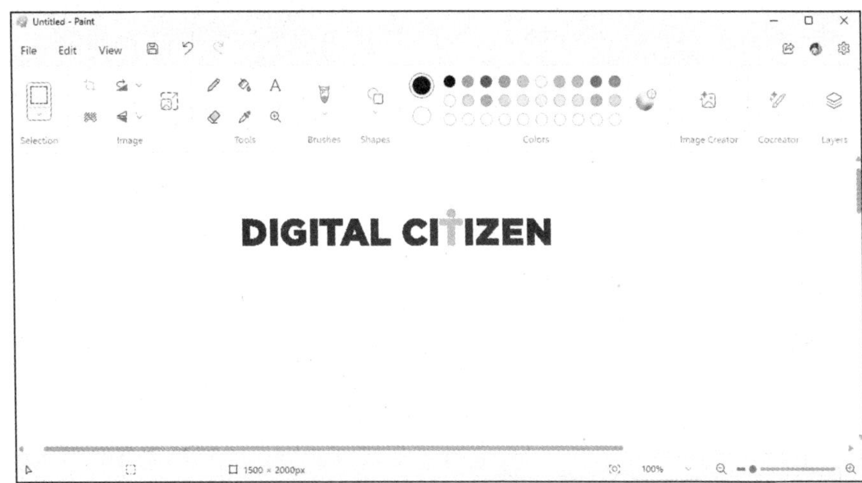

FIGURE 10-7: Paint has received a fresh coat of paint and new features.

We no longer have a ribbon with several tabs, as in the Windows 10 version of Paint. All the tools are at the top, logically organized, and easy to use on touchscreens as well as with the mouse. The File, Edit, and View menus are easily accessible in the top-left corner. The toolbar is simplified, with new icons, a rounded color palette, and a new set of drop-down menus for tools such as brushes, stroke size, and flip and rotate controls.

Try it out and see the kinds of drawings and images you can create with the new Paint.

Creating Sticky Notes

The Sticky Notes app in Windows is the digital equivalent of real-life Post-it notes that stick anywhere, starting with your fridge and ending with your computer monitor. When you try to use the app, Windows asks for a Microsoft account, even though local accounts can still create sticky notes. Microsoft does this because it takes your notes to the cloud, backs them up regularly, and synchronizes them across your PCs and devices via OneDrive.

However, if you also have a Microsoft 365 subscription, it's likely that you have two Sticky Notes apps on your Windows 11 computers and devices. Don't believe me? Click or tap in the Search box on the taskbar, type **sticky notes**, and see how many apps are shown in the list of results. Most probably, you'll see Sticky Notes and Sticky Notes (New), as shown in Figure 10-8.

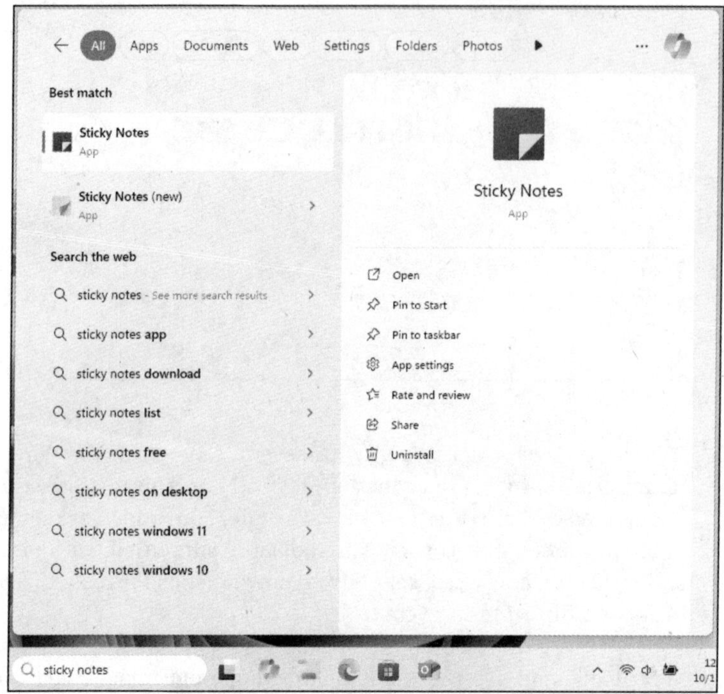

FIGURE 10-8: Microsoft has created confusion about the Sticky Notes app.

If you open them both, you'll notice that they're different, as shown in Figure 10-9. The one on the left is the classic Sticky Notes app you've grown accustomed to from Windows 10. To create a note, click or tap + (plus) and start typing the note. You have some formatting options at the bottom of the note, and you can also add images. When you close a note, it's saved in the list shown in the middle of the Sticky Notes app.

The Sticky Notes (New) app is shown on the right side of Figure 10-9. While it looks like a new app, it's actually a new feature of OneNote. As its name implies, Sticky Notes (New) brings new capabilities to your note-taking, such as adding a screenshot to a note with one click, automatic source capture, and a dedicated keyboard shortcut: Windows+Alt+S.

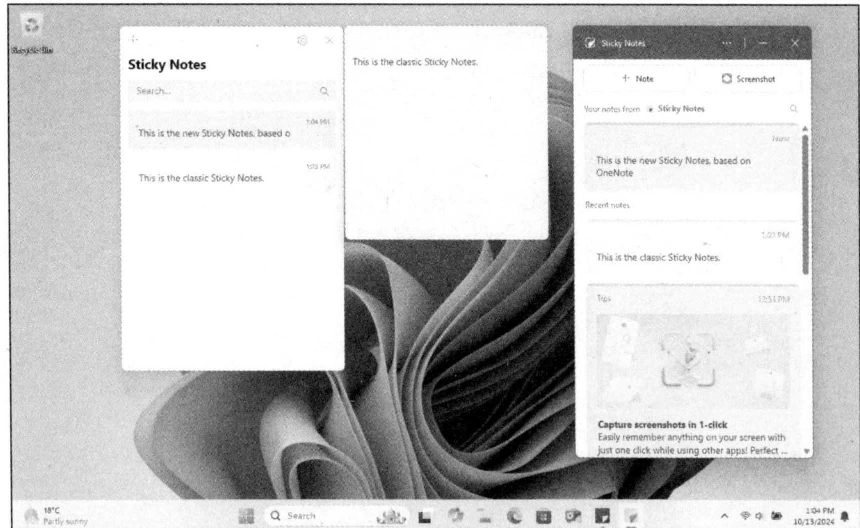

FIGURE 10-9: The classic Sticky Notes versus Sticky Notes (New).

Both Sticky Notes apps are synchronized using your Microsoft account, and the content you add in one shows up automatically in the other. To differentiate between the Sticky Notes app you've used to take the original note, the notes have different colors: yellow for the classic Sticky Notes versus purple for Sticky Notes (new).

Microsoft hasn't clarified if and when it intends to replace the old Sticky Notes app with the new. For now, it keeps both in Windows 11, making the user experience more confusing. I suspect Sticky Notes (New) will replace the old one in the future. And if you like OneNote (read Chapter 5 in this minibook to learn more about it), I think it's best to uninstall the classic Sticky Notes and use the new one instead.

Getting Weather Forecasts

The Weather app in Windows 11 has also received changes and improvements. It has a redesigned home page, which presents weather data in a better way and provides you with more weather information than ever before. You can see the Weather app in action in Figure 10-10.

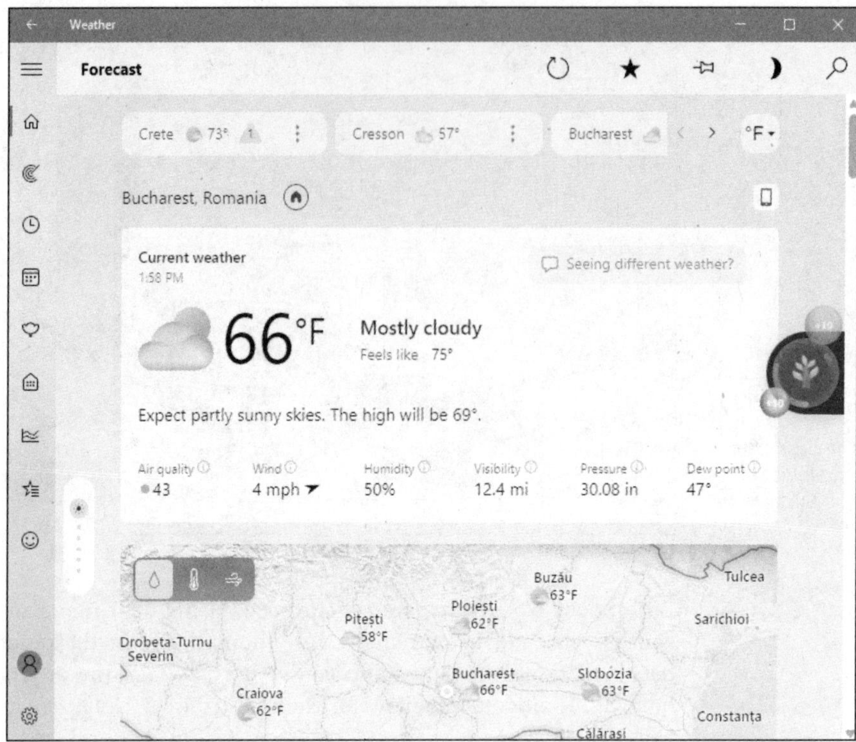

FIGURE 10-10: The Weather app delivers the basics you need for a weather forecast.

You can have the app access your precise location and display its 10-day forecast, or you can check the forecast for locations all over the world. On the left side of the app are several icons that give you access to the distinctive features of the app:

- **Home:** Takes you to the app's home screen, displaying the default location you set for the weather forecast.

- **Maps:** Displays different weather maps for any location you want. You can see how temperatures evolve over different regions, how the clouds move (viewed from satellites), precipitation maps, and more. It's like the weather maps you see on TV. Unfortunately, this section also includes ads and news recommendations.

- **Hourly forecast:** Shares the detailed hourly forecast for any location you want, with data about precipitation, ultraviolet levels, humidity, and wind.

- **Monthly forecast:** Shares the weather forecast for the current month, as well as the following 11 months.

- **Pollen:** You see the pollen forecast for your area, coupled with recommendations on whether you should wear a mask when outdoors, how to dress, and so on.

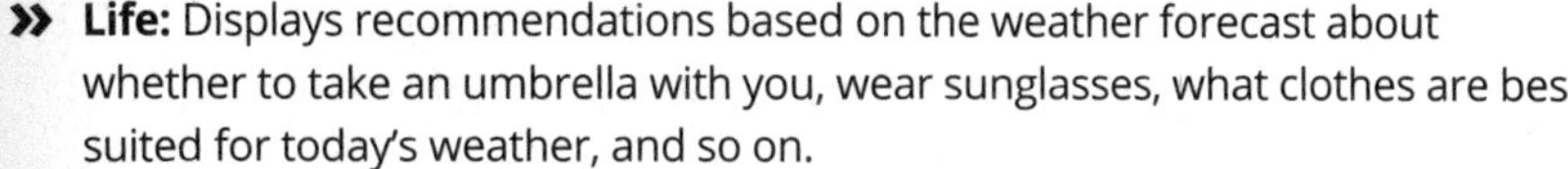

- **Life:** Displays recommendations based on the weather forecast about whether to take an umbrella with you, wear sunglasses, what clothes are best suited for today's weather, and so on.

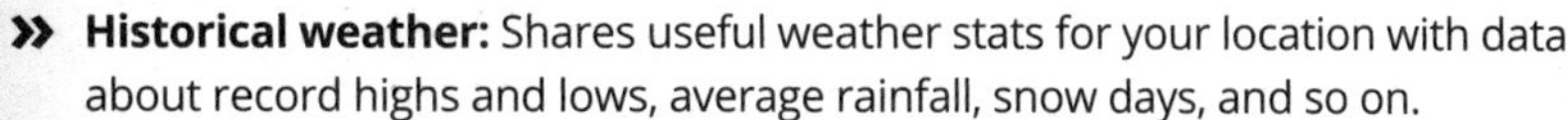

- **Historical weather:** Shares useful weather stats for your location with data about record highs and lows, average rainfall, snow days, and so on.

- **Favorites:** Enables you to set several locations from all over the world as favorites and have them available for easy access.

- **Send feedback:** Opens the Feedback Hub app, which you can use to give feedback to Microsoft about the Weather app and other Windows features.

While I like the Weather app, I dislike how Microsoft is experimenting with displaying ads and adding news content from its online properties. On the upside, the Weather app has a solid database that works well for most countries, not only the United States. If you're based in Europe, Asia, or another continent, you won't be disappointed with how many locations are available and how much weather information you get from this app.

Setting Default Apps

Your Windows 11 computer or device contains many file types, from images and videos to music, text files, documents, spreadsheets, and executable applications. Each file format stores information uniquely and requires a specific app to open it. To simplify this complexity, Windows automatically assigns default apps to various file types. While these preset associations generally suffice, you may want to modify some as you explore alternative applications and discover new preferences.

One likely example is that you may want to use a different app than Microsoft Edge to open PDF documents. If you work with digitally signed PDF files, you'll surely want to use Adobe Acrobat instead.

Here's how to set a new default app for a file type in Windows 11:

1. **Click or tap the Start icon, followed by Settings.**

   The Settings app opens and displays its Home tab.

2. **On the left, select Apps. On the right, click or tap Default Apps.**

   You see a list of the applications installed on your Windows 11 computer or device.

3. **Scroll down or use the Search Apps field at the top of the list to find the app whose default settings you want to change.**

   I selected Adobe Acrobat because I want to ensure that it's used as the default PDF reading app. You see the default file types and link types that the selected app can open, as shown in Figure 10-11.

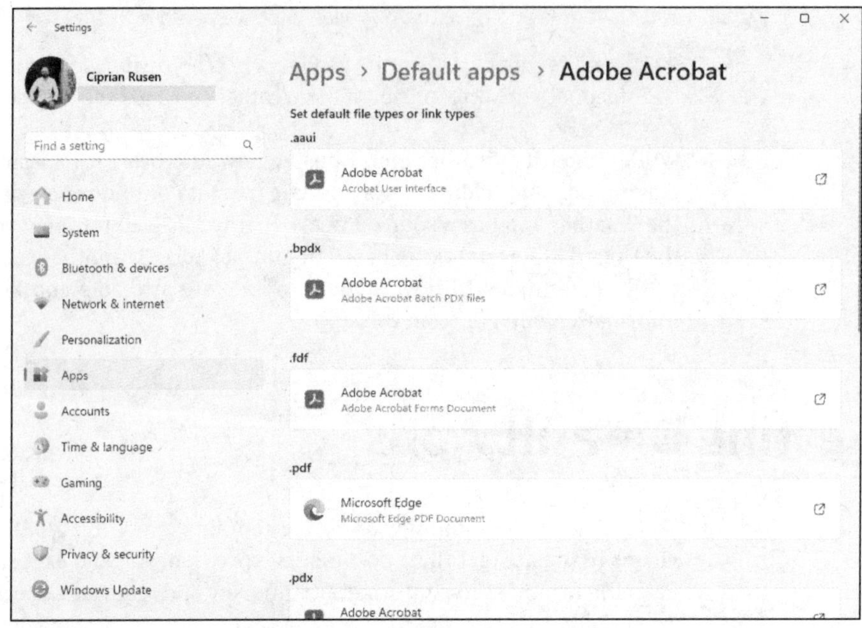

FIGURE 10-11: The file types and link types that Adobe Acrobat can open.

4. **Click or tap the file type for which you want to set the default.**

   I chose .PDF. You see a list of apps that can open the file type you've selected.

5. **Choose the app you want from the list, and then click or tap Set Default.**

   I selected Adobe Acrobat. Note how the default app for the selected file type has changed.

6. **To close Settings, click or tap X in the top-right corner.**

REMEMBER

This procedure works for all file types and link types. For example, you can follow the same steps to change the app used to open videos in Windows 11 from Media Player to VLC Media Player or something else.

IN THIS CHAPTER

» Accessing Windows Terminal

» Setting the default profile

» Executing commands in Command Prompt

» Running Windows PowerShell cmdlets

Chapter 11

Rocking the Command Line

While the graphical world of Windows 11 is mostly intuitive and user-friendly, there's a powerful world beneath all those clickable icons and menus: the command line. The user interface Microsoft promotes for working with the command line is Windows Terminal — a modern app that consolidates various command-line tools into a single, customizable interface.

In this chapter, I share how to access and configure Windows Terminal, set your preferred default profile (and choose between Command Prompt and Windows PowerShell), and navigate between different command-line environments. To keep things simple, I explore only the two primary command-line interfaces: the traditional Command Prompt and the newer and more advanced Windows PowerShell. I walk you through a few essential commands and cmdlets, demonstrating how to perform tasks such as navigating the file system, managing processes, and querying system information.

So, put on your geek hat (don't worry, it's invisible), and let's explore the text-based world of Windows 11.

Opening Windows Terminal

One of the best features of Windows Terminal is its capability to work with multiple tabs. Not only can you open as many tabs as you need, but each tab may also host a different command-line shell. (A *shell* is the command-line interface that allows users to interact with an operating system through textual commands rather than a graphical user interface.) Since PowerShell is the command-line interface favored by Microsoft, when you open Windows Terminal, its default tab hosts Windows PowerShell. However, you can open new tabs hosting Command Prompt or Azure Cloud Shell. Here's how to access Windows Terminal and open tabs using the command-line shell you want:

1. **Right-click or press and hold the Start icon on the taskbar. Or press Windows+X.**

   You see the menu shown in Figure 11-1.

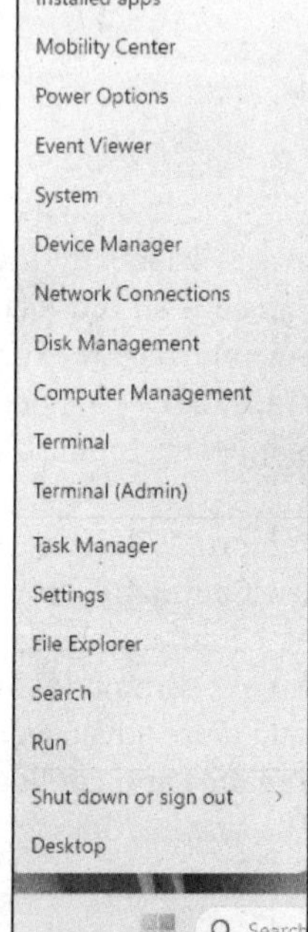

FIGURE 11-1: This menu includes many useful shortcuts, including two for Windows Terminal.

2. **If you need to open Windows Terminal with administrator permissions, choose Terminal (Admin) and click or tap Yes when you see the UAC prompt. Otherwise, simply select Terminal.**

The Windows Terminal app opens, as shown in Figure 11-2. Initially, it hosts a Windows PowerShell tab. If you've opened it with administrator permissions, the default tab will have the word Administrator in its name.

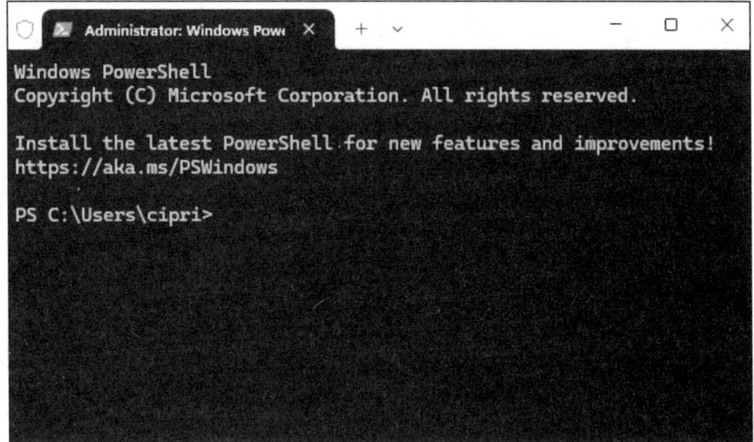

FIGURE 11-2: Windows Terminal hosts a Windows PowerShell tab.

3. **To open a new tab, click or tap the plus sign (+) next to the current tab.**

Windows Terminal opens a new tab hosting Windows PowerShell, which is the default shell.

4. **To open a Command Prompt tab, click or tap the down arrow to the right of the plus sign, and choose Command Prompt.**

A third tab is loaded, this time using the Command Prompt command-line shell. These tabs can be reordered, opened, and closed, just as you would when working with tabs in your favorite web browser.

5. **When you're done working with Windows Terminal, click or tap X in its top-right corner.**

TIP

You can also use the keyboard to open new tabs in Windows Terminal. When the app is open, press Windows+Shift+1 to open a new Windows PowerShell tab, and Windows+Shift+2 to open a new Command Prompt tab. To move forward and backward through your open tabs, press Ctrl+Tab or Ctrl+Shift+Tab.

Setting the Default Profile in Windows Terminal

Some people might not appreciate that each time they open Windows Terminal, it loads a Windows PowerShell tab by default. If you find it frustrating, you can set the default profile to Command Prompt, Azure Cloud Shell, or something else, in just a few clicks:

1. **Right-click or press and hold the Start icon on the taskbar.**

   You see the menu shown previously in Figure 11-1.

2. **In the menu, select Terminal.**

   The Windows Terminal app opens (refer to Figure 11-2).

3. **Click or tap the down arrow to the right of the plus sign and choose Settings. Or press Ctrl+comma (,).**

   The Settings tab opens, as shown in Figure 11-3. On its left, you see a list of icons, one for each category of settings: startup, interaction, appearance, and so on. The startup icon is selected by default.

TIP

   To see what each icon stands for, click or tap the icon with three horizontal lines in the top left. A menu opens with labels for each icon.

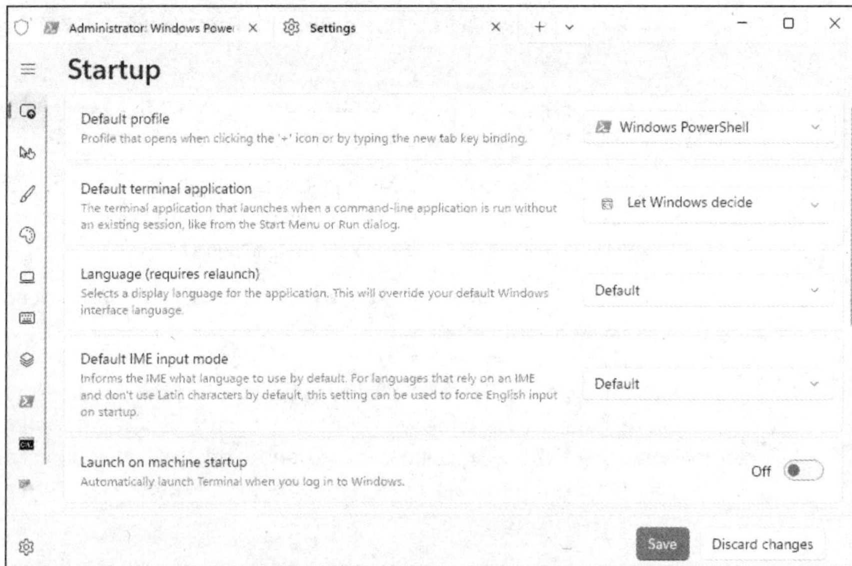

FIGURE 11-3: Windows Terminal has many settings that can be personalized.

4. **In the Startup settings for Windows Terminal, click or tap the drop-down list next to Default Profile and select the shell you want: Windows PowerShell, Command Prompt, or Azure Cloud Shell.**
5. **Click or tap Save so that your settings get applied.**
6. **When you're done, click or tap X in the top-right corner.**

TIP

I encourage you to explore the settings of Windows Terminal. You'll find many things that can be personalized, including how to interact with it and options to change its appearance. If you want to learn the keyboard shortcuts you can use while working in Terminal, during Step 4, click or tap the actions icon (keyboard) on the left to see a list with all keyboard shortcuts and what they do.

Running Commands in Windows Terminal

You can start Windows Terminal and run commands in any shell you want: the classic Command Prompt, the newer Windows PowerShell, or Azure Cloud Shell. If you install Windows Subsystem for Linux, you could use that too inside Terminal, as well as newer versions of PowerShell, if you download them from the internet. But let's not get ahead of ourselves. In this section, we stick to the basics: running commands using Command Prompt or Windows PowerShell.

Working with Command Prompt

First, let's dip our toes into using the Command Prompt shell inside Windows Terminal to execute a few commands. When you open a Command Prompt tab, it uses your user folder as the default path. However, you can change the working folder to anything you want and execute the commands that interest you. Here's a brief tour of navigating Command Prompt:

1. **Right-click or press and hold the Start icon on the taskbar and select Terminal (Admin). Click or tap Yes to allow it to run.**
2. **To open a Command Prompt tab, click or tap the down arrow to the right of the plus sign, and choose Command Prompt.**

   A second tab is loaded using the Command Prompt command-line shell. Note how the current folder is your user folder.
3. **Type** cd\ **and press Enter.**

   This command takes you to the top of the directory tree. In this case, it takes you to the C: drive and sets it as the working folder, as shown in Figure 11-4.

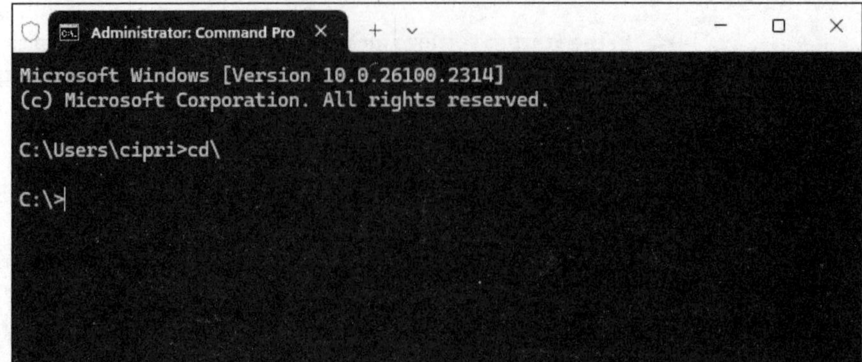

FIGURE 11-4: Navigating to the top of the directory tree in Command Prompt.

4. **Type** cd windows\system32\ **and press Enter.**

   The working folder changes to windows\system32\. This is how you change the directory used by Command Prompt to the one you want.

5. **Type** dir **and press Enter.**

   This command displays a list of the files and folders in the working folder, their size, and the date and time when they were last modified.

6. **Type** cd\ **and press Enter to get back to the top of the directory tree.**
7. **Type** mkdir DigitalCitizen **and press Enter.**

   This command creates a folder named DigitalCitizen on your C: drive. The folder is empty.

8. **Type** rd DigitalCitizen **and press Enter.**

   This command deletes the folder named DigitalCitizen from your C: drive.

9. **Type** help **and press Enter.**

   TIP

   If a particular command interests you, type **help** followed by the name of that command. Or type the command's name followed by the **/?** parameter.

10. **When you're done, click or tap X in the top-right corner.**

Working with Windows PowerShell

Microsoft designed Windows PowerShell as a tool for automating and solving time-consuming administration tasks. For example, you can use PowerShell to display all the USB devices installed on one or multiple computers in a network and configure them in a specific way, or you can set a time-consuming script to run in the background while you work on something else.

PowerShell commands are called *cmdlets.* Their names are typically easy to understand and even memorize, as their syntax is similar to a regular sentence. This makes cmdlets user friendly, when compared to the commands used in classic shells such as Command Prompt. For instance, I bet you can easily remember and understand what a PowerShell cmdlet, such as Get-Process or Copy-Item, is all about.

Here's a brief tour of how to use PowerShell from Windows Terminal:

1. **Right-click or press and hold the Start icon on the taskbar and select Terminal.**

   The Windows Terminal app opens (refer to Figure 11-2) to a Windows PowerShell tab.

2. **Type** get-process **and press Enter.**

   You see a list of all the processes running on your PC, as shown in Figure 11-5.

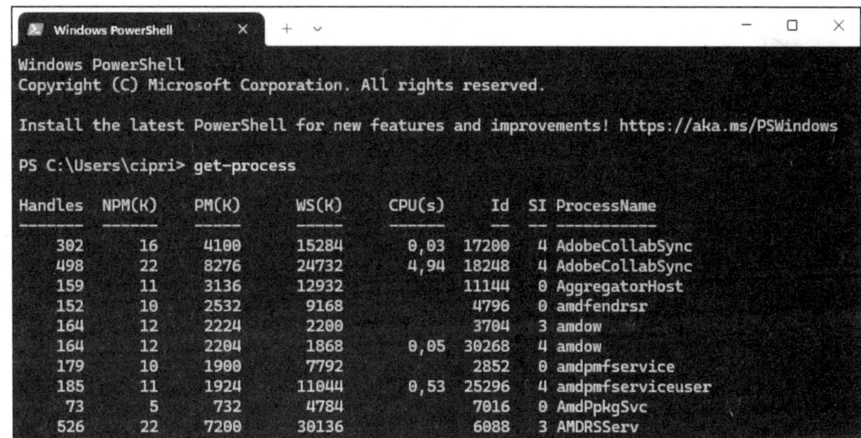

FIGURE 11-5: Checking the running processes using Windows PowerShell.

3. **Type** get-process -name explorer **and press Enter.**

   You see the running processes named explorer.

4. **Type** get-service **and press Enter.**

   This command lists all the services on your Windows 11 computer, their status, name, and display name.

5. **Type** get-service | Format-List **and press Enter.**

   Note how the list of services is now formatted differently and displays a lot more information for each service on your computer.

6. **Type** get-command **and press Enter.**

   PowerShell lists all the cmdlets that you can use.

7. **To get more information about a specific cmdlet, type** get-help **followed by the name of the cmdlet, and then press Enter.**

   For example, I typed **get-help Stop-Service**. Help information is shown about the cmdlet I selected. In this situation, PowerShell is helping me learn how to use the Stop-Service cmdlet to stop any of the running services I've identified at Steps 4 and 5.

8. **When you're done, click or tap X in the top-right corner of Windows Terminal.**

TIP

If you want to learn more about PowerShell, I recommend Microsoft's documentation at `https://learn.microsoft.com/en-us/powershell/scripting/learn/ps101/00-introduction`.

5 Managing Apps

Contents at a Glance

IN THIS CHAPTER

» Exploring the Microsoft Store and its content

» Installing apps from the Microsoft Store

» Finding AI apps in the Microsoft Store

Chapter 1

Navigating the Microsoft Store

If you've ever purchased apps from Apple's App Store or Google's Play Store, you're probably familiar with most of the features you'll find in the Microsoft Store. However, the selection, variety, and quality of apps are better in the App Store and the Play Store thanks to their larger user bases and potential for greater profits for developers.

Although the Microsoft Store originally featured only Windows apps designed for touchscreens and traditional computers, it now offers a wide range of apps, including desktop programs and progressive web apps. The store also includes games, movies, and AI-powered apps.

In this chapter, you learn how to navigate the Microsoft Store and install the apps and games you want. Additionally, I show you how to play games from the Microsoft Store without installing them on your Windows 11 computer or device.

Understanding What a Windows 11 App Can Do

Microsoft Store was slow to evolve and grow. However, over the years, it managed to gather a respectable number of apps. As is the case with all app stores, each app must meet a set of requirements before Microsoft allows it to be published in the Microsoft Store. Here's a condensed version of what you can expect from any app you buy (or download) from the Microsoft Store:

- **You can get both Windows 11 apps (which are supposed to run on any type of PC or device) and desktop apps (or computer programs) from the Microsoft Store.** If you want a new program for the desktop, you may be able to find it in the Microsoft Store, or you may be able to get it through all the old sources, such as its official website or specialized download sites. But if you want a Windows 11 app, you must get it through the Microsoft Store — unless you're an employee with a computer that's part of a corporate network, in which case apps are sideloaded (installed from the company's network) by the administrators of that network, using specialized tools and services.
- **Windows 11 apps can be updated only through the Microsoft Store.** When an update is available, the Microsoft Store automatically manages the upgrade process without any intervention from you. Read Chapter 3 in this minibook for details.
- **Apps that use any internet-based services must request permission from the user before retrieving or sending personal data.**
- **Each app must be licensed to run on up to ten devices at a time.** For example, if you buy the latest version of Minecraft, you can run that same version on up to ten Windows 11 devices — computers, tablets, laptops, Xbox One consoles, and so on, at no additional cost.
- **Microsoft won't accept apps with a rating over ESRB *Mature,* which is to say adult content.** ESRB, or Entertainment Software Rating Board, is a content rating system that helps users understand the age-appropriateness of apps and games, similar to movie ratings.
- **Apps must start in 5 seconds or less and resume in 2 seconds or less.** Microsoft wants apps to be speedy, not sluggish.

In addition to the basic requirements for any app, you're also likely to find that the following is true of most apps:

TIP

- **Microsoft's tools help developers create trial versions of their apps so you can try them before you buy.** The trial version can be limited in many ways — for example, it works only on a certain number of pictures, messages, or files, or only for a week or a month — before requiring payment. The developer must explain precisely what has been limited and what happens if you decide to purchase the app.
- **If an app breaks, you can complain to Microsoft, but the support responsibility lies 100 percent with the developer.** Although Microsoft acts as an agent in the distribution and sale of apps, Microsoft doesn't buy or sell or warrant anything at all.
- **Many apps (and especially games) attempt to get you to buy more — more levels, more features, more content.** Microsoft has that covered, just like Apple and Google: Orders generated by the app must go through the Microsoft Store. Only Microsoft can fulfill the orders.

Browsing the Microsoft Store

When you're ready to venture into the Microsoft Store for Windows 11 apps and games, open the Start menu and click or tap the Microsoft Store shortcut. The app shown in Figure 1-1 appears.

Moving around in the Microsoft Store isn't difficult. The navigation sidebar on the left contains shortcuts to types of content like apps, games, arcade games, movies, and AI-powered apps. On the right, you see the content itself organized by categories and offers.

The following tips can help you move around and find what you're looking for:

- **You no longer need a Microsoft account to get anywhere beyond basic searching and browsing, as you did in Windows 10.** Fortunately, Microsoft has lifted this restriction in Windows 11. Now, both local and Microsoft accounts can have a similar experience, as long as they only use free apps, games, and content. Attempting to make a purchase, however, still requires a Microsoft account, as shown in Figure 1-2.

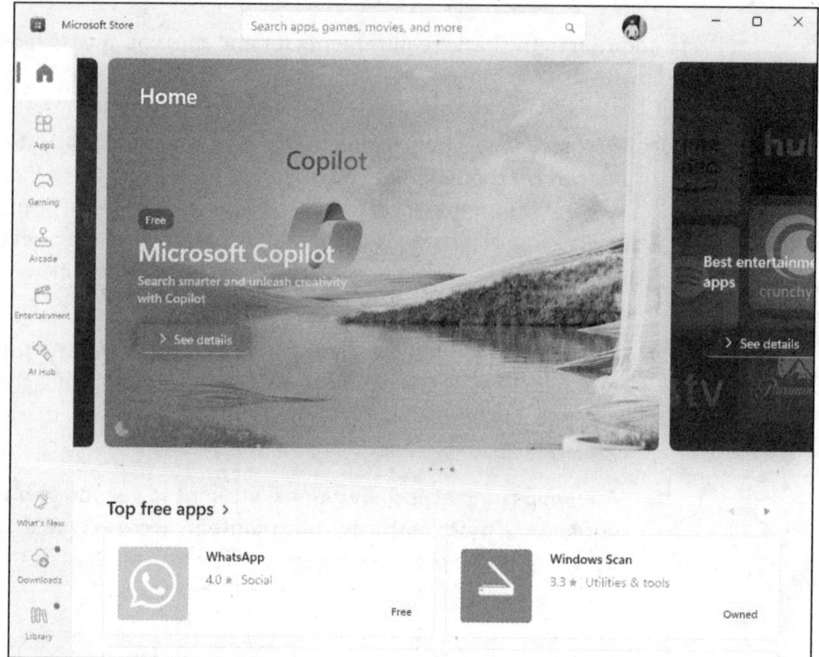

FIGURE 1-1: Here's a peek at the Microsoft Store.

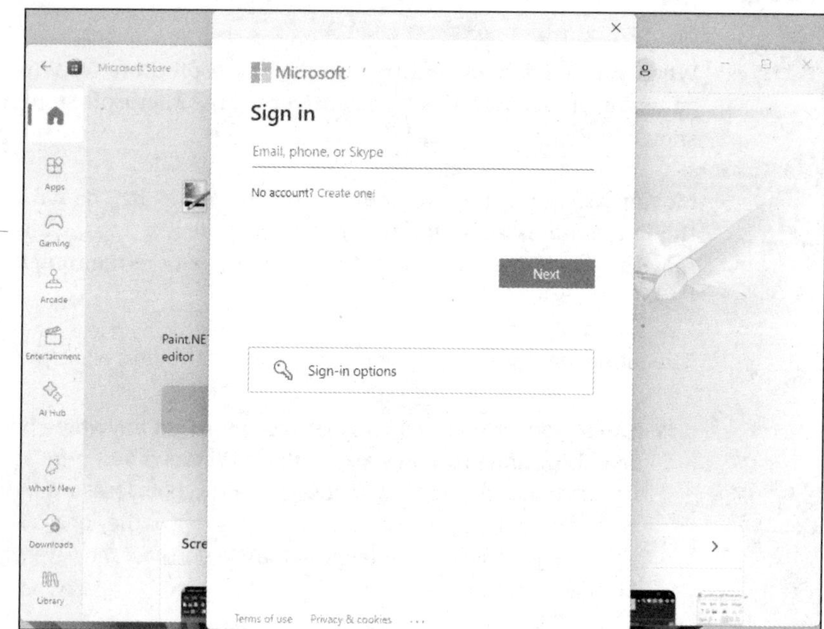

FIGURE 1-2: You can't buy stuff from the Microsoft Store with a local account.

» **To order an app or a game, click or tap its name**. The Microsoft Store takes you directly to the ordering screen for the app. For example, if you click or tap the Paint.NET app, you see the ordering page displayed in Figure 1-3. At the top is an overview of the app and its price. Scroll down, and you see screenshots, a description, ratings from other users, system requirements for using it, and additional information about its developer, release date, size, and so on.

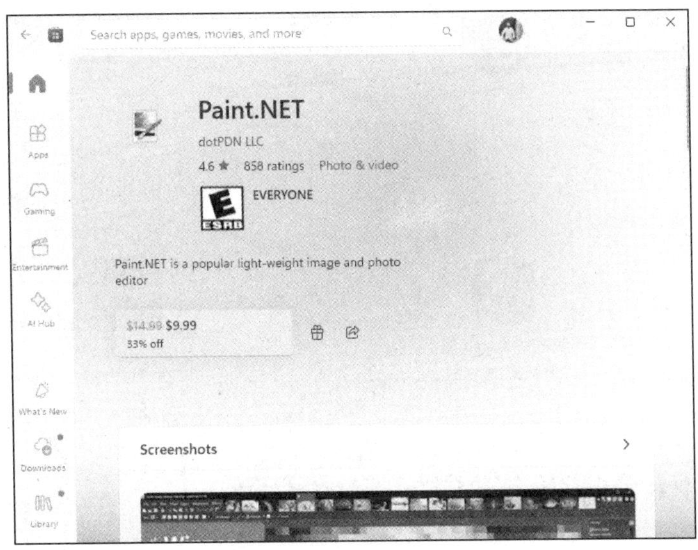

FIGURE 1-3: The app-ordering page for the Paint.NET app.

TIP

» **Use categories to find apps quickly.** If you scroll down the Apps section, you see all kinds of categories created by Microsoft: Best Selling Apps, Essential Apps, Creativity Apps, Top Free Apps, and so on. For each category, click or tap its name to see everything inside that group. Check out Figure 1-4 to see what Microsoft considers Essential Apps. I don't know about you, but TikTok and Threads surely aren't essential to me.

TIP

If you read the system requirements of the apps you want to install from the Microsoft Store, you'll notice that some say "Architecture: neutral," others say "Architecture: x64," while others mention "Architecture: X86 X64 ARM." Those listed as "neutral" are Progressive web apps (see the "Progressive web apps" sidebar), those with x64 are classic desktop programs, and the others are Windows 11 apps.

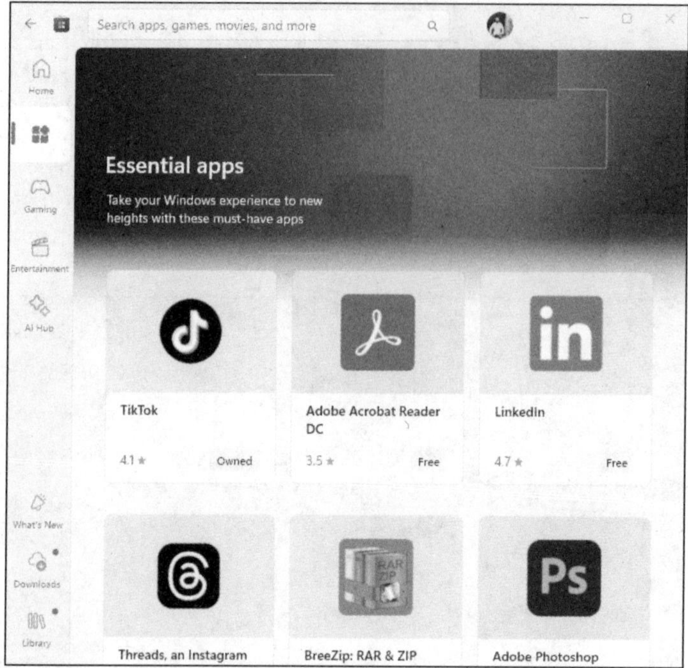

FIGURE 1-4: Apps in the Store are organized by groups chosen by Microsoft.

PROGRESSIVE WEB APPS

A revolution is going on – from web apps running in a browser to web apps running outside the browser, to hosted web apps, which are downloaded dynamically on execution, to progressive web apps, which blur the distinction between web-based apps and native apps.

Progressive web apps (PWAs) are a genuine attempt to make browser-based applications look and feel more like regular old apps. Chances are good that you've never seen a PWA in action, but they're here, including in the Microsoft Store. For example, TikTok and Threads don't offer native Windows 11 apps but PWAs. Any company that doesn't want to develop a specific app for Windows can easily make a PWA.

The theoretical benefits of PWAs are interesting. Just for starters, Windows 11 apps can run only in the stripped-down Windows 11 environment. PWAs, on the other hand, should be able to run on anything that supports a browser — Microsoft Edge, Google Chrome and Chrome OS. Yes, that includes Chromebooks.

Installing Apps and Games from the Microsoft Store

If you want to find a specific app in the Microsoft Store, you can search for it using the Search box as the top, or you can browse the built-in categories. Here's how to install a free app, like the incredibly useful VLC Media Player:

1. **Click or tap the Start icon and then Microsoft Store.**
2. **In the Search box at the top, type the name of the app you want to find.**

   In my case, I typed *vlc*. Microsoft Store displays a list of app suggestions, as shown in Figure 1-5.

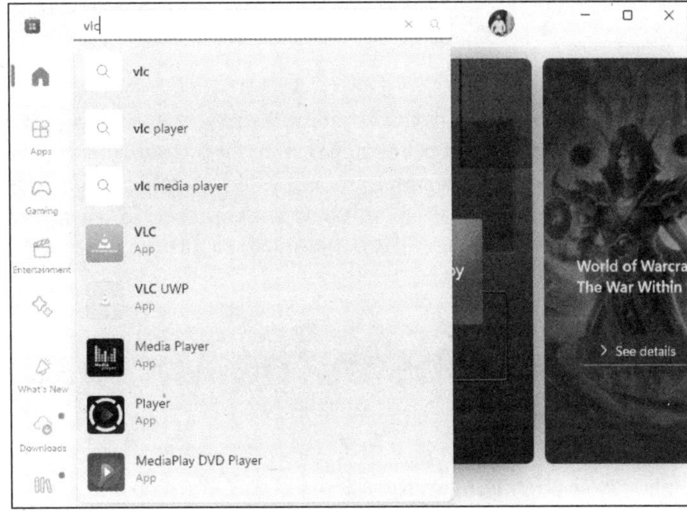

FIGURE 1-5: Searching for *vlc* in the Microsoft Store.

3. **Click or tap the name of the app you want.**

   In my case, I chose VLC, not VLC UWP (which is a different app). The Microsoft Store loads the app's page with plenty of details, screenshots, user reviews, and system requirements, as shown in Figure 1-6.

4. **Click or tap the Get or Install button.**

   Inside the button, you see the progress of the app's download and installation. You can minimize the Store and do something else while it handles everything for you. When the installation is complete, the app's shortcut appears in the Start menu's All apps list.

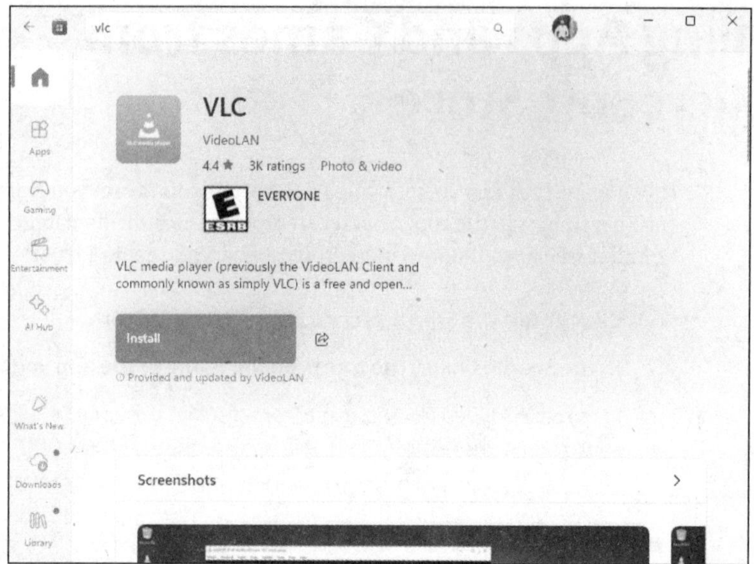

FIGURE 1-6: The app's page includes plenty of details you should look at.

TIP

If you're installing a desktop program from the Microsoft Store, at some point during the installation process, you may see a User Account Control (UAC) prompt asking you to allow the app to make system changes. If you don't click or tap Yes, the installation will fail. Read Book 9, Chapter 2, to learn more about UAC. This prompt is never shown for Windows 11 apps or PWAs.

Discovering AI Apps in the Microsoft Store

Microsoft has invested heavily in artificial intelligence (AI), and this is evident in many ways, including in the Microsoft Store, which added an AI Hub in the summer of 2023. This section of the store offers a curated selection of apps powered by AI. These apps are by Microsoft and third-party developers, and include chatbots, apps for musicians, apps for digital artists creating animations, videos or doing image editing, and accessibility apps for people who are blind or have low vision.

Here's how to get apps powered by AI from the Microsoft Store:

1. **Click or tap the Start icon and then Microsoft Store.**
2. **On the left, click or tap AI Hub.**

   You see a list of apps with AI capabilities for you to use.

3. **Browse the apps from the AI Hub until you find one that interests you, and then click or tap its name.**

   You see the app's page from the store, sharing details such as its rating, description, and screenshots.

4. **Click or tap the Get or Install button.**

   The app is downloaded and installed on your Windows 11 computer. The progress of the download is shown inside the button.

5. **After the app is installed, click or tap Open.**

   Enjoy using the AI-powered app that you've chosen.

TIP

One AI-powered app I recommend is Reading Coach from Microsoft, which helps people learn how to read and improve their literacy using AI. Another useful choice is Canva, which helps people design beautiful presentations, social media graphics, posters, flyers, and more.

IN THIS CHAPTER

» Adding or removing Windows features

» Downloading programs and desktop apps safely

» Checking downloaded apps for viruses

» Uninstalling apps and desktop programs

Chapter 2

Adding and Removing Apps and Windows Features

When you install Windows 11 on your computer or device, it comes equipped with a standard set of tools, apps, and features. However, for some users, the magic lies in the optional features you can add on demand. For instance, if you're a Linux enthusiast, you might want to install the Windows Subsystem for Linux, which enables you to use Linux in Windows. Or, if you need to test various environments, you can add Hyper-V to your Windows 11 Pro or Enterprise machine to run virtual machines.

Using Windows in its default state is just the beginning. Although the built-in apps and the Microsoft Edge browser offer a lot of functionality, they might not cover all your needs for productivity or entertainment. You may find yourself needing specialized tools such as a PDF editor, a cloud-storage app beyond One-Drive, a media viewer, an image editor, a 3D modeling app, or a video editor.

In this chapter, I guide you through adding and removing features in Windows 11. I recommend how to handle downloading apps from the internet, and show you how to verify their safety. Finally, I walk you through the process of uninstalling apps you no longer need.

Adding or Removing Windows 11 Features

Windows 11 has optional features that can be added to the operating system (such as additional fonts, language packs, server tools, group policy management tools, and TPM diagnostics tools) and Windows features that contain tools and services that can be added to the operating system (Hyper-V, the Windows Subsystem for Linux, and Print and Documents Services). While their purpose is the same, optional features can be added and removed from the Settings app, and Windows Features can be added or removed through the Control Panel. Both, however, can be added or removed by using PowerShell commands. (Read Book 4, Chapter 11 to learn about PowerShell.) First, I show you how to deal with optional features.

Adding or removing optional features

Some features were developed by Microsoft independently from Windows and then transformed into optional features. Although some of these features are pre-installed with Windows 11, such as Notepad or Windows Hello Facial Recognition, others are available for installation on demand. Here's how to add an optional feature to your Windows 11 computer or device:

1. **Click or tap the Start icon and then Settings. Or press Windows+I.**

   The Settings app opens.

2. **On the left, choose System. On the right, scroll down to Optional Features and click or tap this section.**

   You see the list of optional features installed on your computer or device, as shown in Figure 2-1.

3. **In the top right, click or tap the View Features button.**

   Windows lists the available optional features, as shown in Figure 2-2.

4. **Scroll down the list to see all the features, one by one. Select the one(s) you want to install.**

   I chose Wireless Display because it allows my Windows 11 laptop to be used as a wireless display for other devices through Miracast (a wireless display standard that lets you mirror your device's screen to another display). You can select more than one feature.

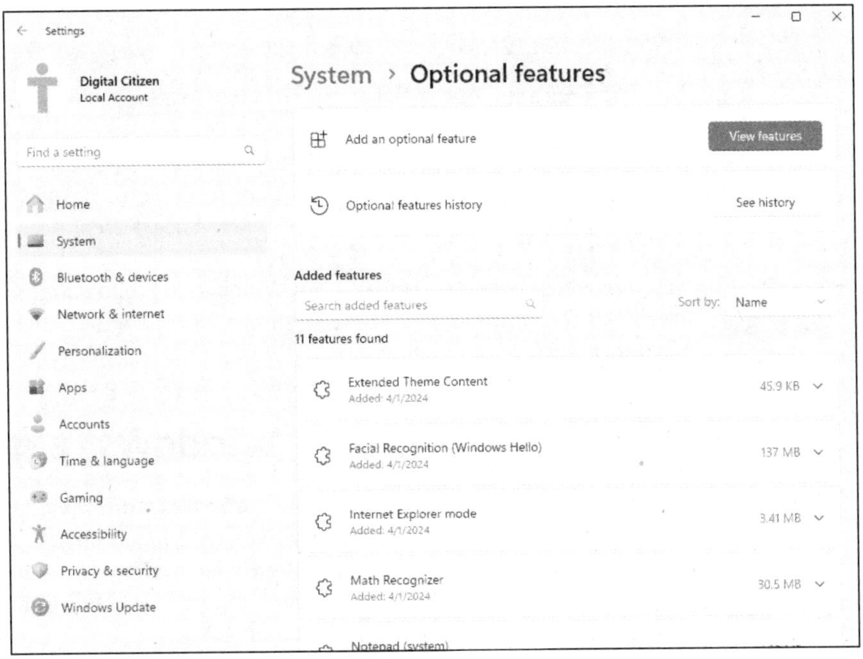

FIGURE 2-1: A list of optional features installed on your computer or device.

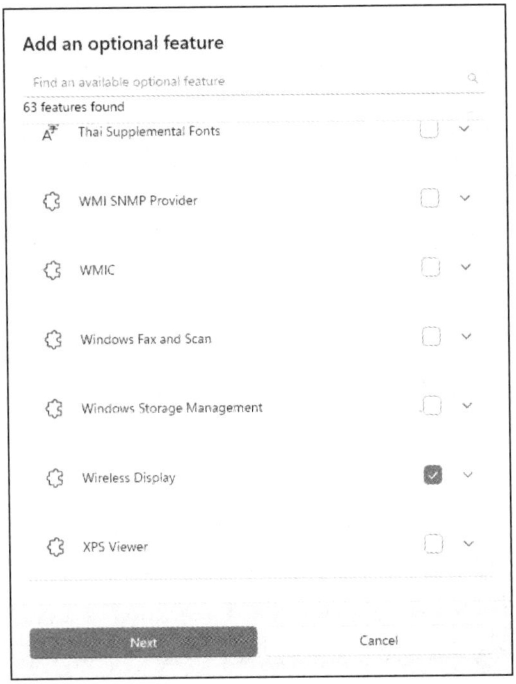

FIGURE 2-2: Select which Optional Feature to add.

5. **Click or tap Next.**

   You see a summary of what you are about to add to Windows 11.

6. **Click or tap Add.**

   The selected feature starts downloading from Microsoft's servers. When the status of the progress bar is Added, you can use the feature.

TIP

To remove an optional feature from Windows 11, follow Steps 1 and 2. When you arrive at the Optional Features list shown in Figure 2-1, click or tap the feature and then click or tap Remove.

Adding or removing Windows features

Windows 11 has another list of features inherited from previous versions, including Windows Sandbox (a temporary, isolated virtual environment in which you can safely run untrusted software), the Hyper-V virtualization platform, and legacy services such as SMB File Sharing Support. To add or remove those features, you must run the Windows Features tool:

1. **Click or tap in the Search box on the taskbar and type** windows features.

   A list of search results is shown.

2. **Click or tap Turn Windows Features On or Off.**

   The Windows Features dialog box shown in Figure 2-3 pops up.

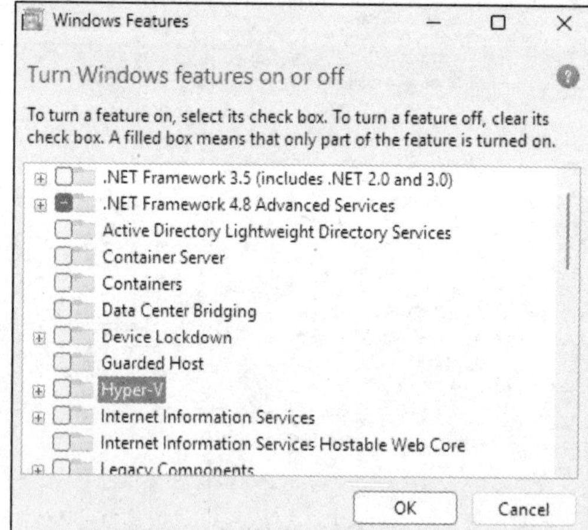

FIGURE 2-3: Adding or removing Windows Features.

3. **Scroll down the list of features, select those you want to install, and deselect those you want to remove.**

   I am adding Hyper-V. Read Book 10, Chapter 3, to see how to use it to run virtual machines in Windows 11.

4. **Click or tap OK.**

   Windows spends some time applying your settings and informs you when it is done making the changes you requested.

5. **Close any open files and apps, and then click or tap Restart Now.**

   Windows 11 restarts and spends some time adding or removing the feature(s) you selected. When it is done, you can sign in again and resume using your computer or device.

TIP

The Windows Features tool can be accessed also by running the OptionalFeatures.exe file in the C:\Windows\System32 folder.

Finding Safe Places to Download Desktop Apps

The first place to look for Windows 11 apps, including classic desktop programs, is the Microsoft Store, covered in Chapter 1 of this minibook. It's a safe place because all apps are reviewed by Microsoft, and you can install only the app you want without other bundled apps you don't need. Not only that, but the Microsoft Store also keeps your desktop apps automatically updated without any effort on your part. Unfortunately, you may not find all the desktop apps you want in the Microsoft Store. In this situation, performing an internet search for the name of the app you want to download is the way to go.

WARNING

Be wary when you download an app from someplace other than the Microsoft Store. The safest option is to download the app from its official site. Using third-party download sites such as `softonic.com` or `filehippo.com` can be a frustrating experience, filled with ads that promote something other than what you want. Look at Figure 2-4, where I tried to download Google Chrome and got a large ad instead, recommending me to download Opera. Yes, Opera is a good web browser, but I wanted Google Chrome. Note how you barely see the link to refuse this offer and continue to download Google Chrome. If you don't pay attention, you'll fill your new computer with bloatware in no time.

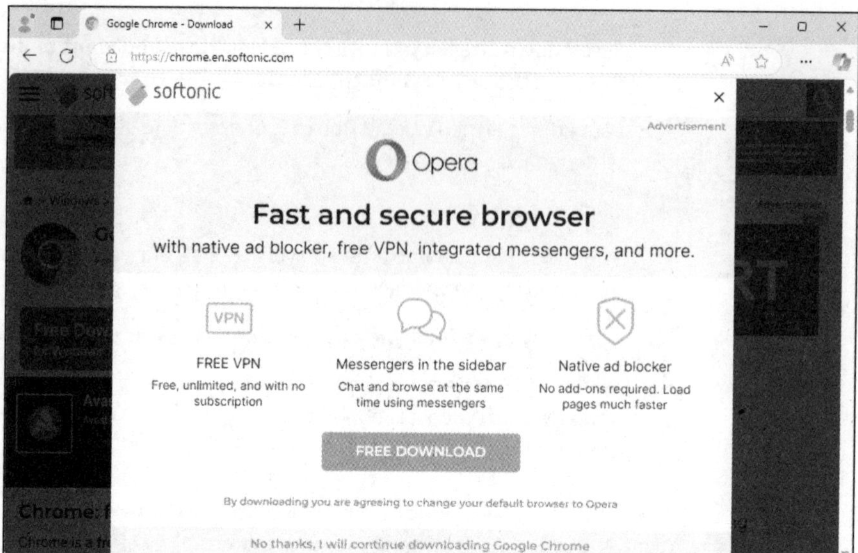

FIGURE 2-4: While trying to download Google Chrome, you get offers for other apps.

TIP

To make things simpler and easier, following are the locations I recommend for downloading desktop apps:

- The Microsoft Store app from Windows 11
- The official website of the app
- Safe(r) download sites such as `microsoft.com` (for everything made by Microsoft), `softpedia.com`, `download.com`, and `github.com`

To navigate the process, let's download Paint.NET, a free app that you can use to edit pictures and images, with support for layers, special effects, and more. You can find it in the Microsoft Store too, but it's available as a paid app there, not a free one:

1. **Open Microsoft Edge and navigate to** `www.bing.com`**.**
2. **Type** paint net **and press Enter.**

   Bing shows you a list of links, as shown in Figure 2-5.
3. **Scroll down the list of search results.**

   Note how the first result is from `www.getpaint.net/download.html`, while others farther down are from `techspot.com`, `softonic.com`, and other locations.

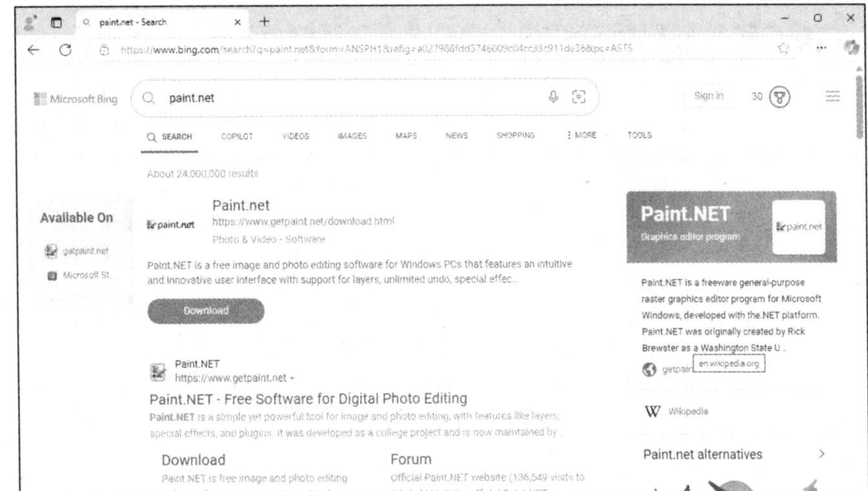

FIGURE 2-5: Searching for Paint.NET on Bing (or Google) reveals many download locations.

4. **Get back to the first result,** `www.getpaint.net/download.html`**, and click or tap it.**

   Your browser should display a page where you see information about the system requirements of `Paint.NET` and a list of download options.

5. **Click or tap the Download Now button for the version that is listed as Free.**

   An ad may be shown before you can download the app.

6. **Click or tap the X button in the top-right corner of the advertisement to close it.**

   You see a page with information about the app.

7. **Click or tap the download link under Free Download Now.**

   The link includes the app name followed by a version number such as 5.0.13 or higher. The Paint.NET app is now downloaded on your computer.

When Paint.NET finishes downloading, you can install it on your Windows 11 PC by extracting it from its ZIP archive. (Read Book 3, Chapter 4 if you need help handling file archives.) The setup file for this app should have a name such as paint.net.5.0.13.install.anycpu.web.exe. Double-click or double-tap this file to start installing it.

WARNING

When downloading desktop apps on Windows 11, pay attention to the ads that are loaded. Some of them include a Download button, but it's for not the app you want but the app promoted by the ad. Close the ad first before looking for the correct Download button.

Checking Apps for Malware

If you want to make sure that an app you just downloaded is safe to use, run an antivirus scan on it. To do so, navigate to `www.virustotal.com` and upload the file you want to scan. This site is particularly useful because it analyzes your file using all the major antivirus software on the market, from the likes of Bitdefender, Avast, TrendMicro, and many others.

If you think that using VirusTotal is too cumbersome or time-consuming, Windows Security (which includes Microsoft Defender alongside other security tools) from Windows 11 is a good choice. Here's how to use it to check whether a file you just downloaded is secure:

1. **Open File Explorer and double-click or double-tap Downloads.**
2. **Right-click or press and hold on the file you want to check, and then choose Show More Options.**

   If you downloaded `Paint.NET` in the preceding section, you can right-click or press and hold on the paint.net.5.0.13.install.anycpu.web file.

   The right-click menu extends to include more options, as shown in Figure 2-6.
3. **Choose Scan with Microsoft Defender.**

   The Windows Security app opens, displaying the results of the scan and whether it found any threats inside the file you scanned.

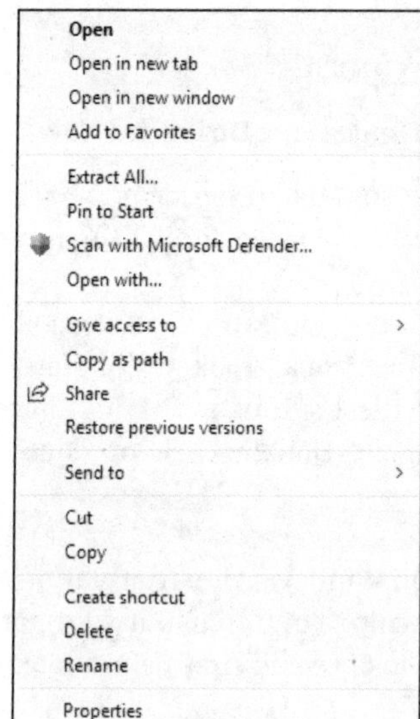

FIGURE 2-6: The extended right-click menu includes the option to Scan with Microsoft Defender.

WARNING

If Windows Security tells you that threats were found inside the file you scanned, delete that file immediately. Never run it. It's highly likely that the file contains malware (such as a virus, trojan, or ransomware) that will harm your computer.

Uninstalling Apps

If you no longer want to use an app, you can remove it from Windows 11 to save space and optimize your system performance. Unfortunately, the process for removing desktop apps is different from the one required for uninstalling apps, and it requires a few more steps.

TIP

If you feel confused about the terms *apps* and *desktop apps,* read Chapter 1 in this minibook to learn more about the differences between apps and desktop apps or programs.

First, here's how to remove an app from Windows 11:

1. **Click or tap the Start icon and then All, at the top right of the Start menu.**

   You see the list of apps that are available on your computer or device.

2. **In the list of apps, find the one you want to remove and right-click (or press and hold) on its name.**

   You see the contextual menu shown in Figure 2-7.

3. **In the menu, choose Uninstall and confirm by pressing Uninstall again.**

   The app is removed from Windows 11 and from the All apps list.

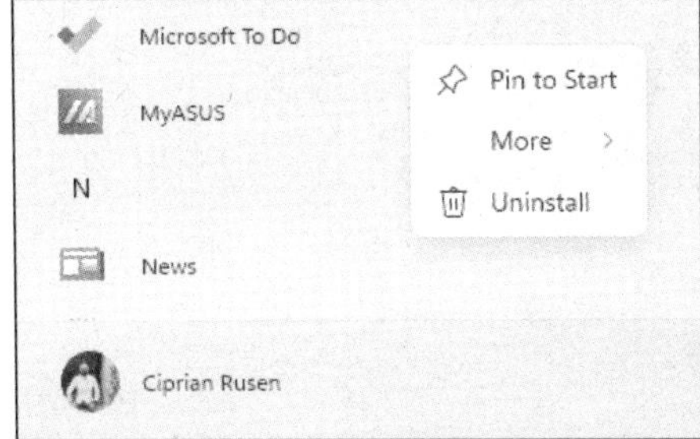

FIGURE 2-7: Uninstalling apps is easy.

Next, let's see one of the many ways to remove a desktop app in Windows 11:

1. **Click or tap in the Search box on the taskbar and type** add remove.

   Windows 11 displays a list of search results.

2. **Click or tap Add or Remove Programs.**

   The Settings app opens to the Apps > Installed Apps section. You see the list of apps installed on your device, as shown in Figure 2-8.

3. **Find the app you want to remove, and click or tap the three dots to the right of its name.**

4. **Click or tap Uninstall, and then click or tap it again.**

   A User Account Control prompt is shown, asking you to confirm that you want to allow the app to make changes to your device.

5. **Click or tap Yes, and follow the program's Uninstall wizard.**

   This process usually means clicking or tapping buttons such as Next, Uninstall, Confirm, and Finish. The options you see differ from program to program.

As you can see, the process is not that difficult, and your Windows 11 computer or device now has more free space for you to use for other things.

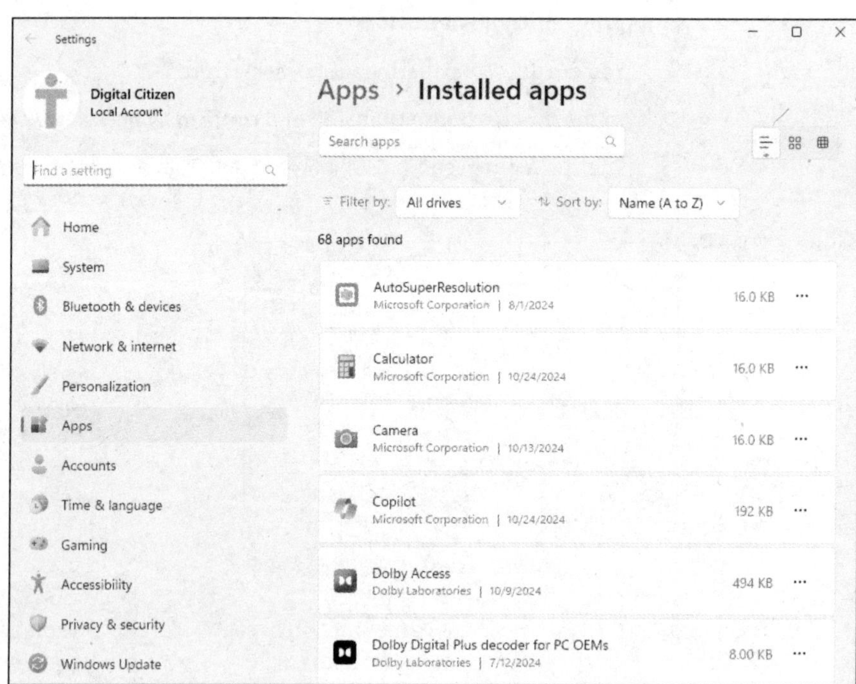

FIGURE 2-8: The Installed Apps section is where you go to uninstall programs and apps alike.

IN THIS CHAPTER

» Updating apps from the Microsoft Store

» Keeping desktop programs and games up to date

» Updating drivers in Windows 11

Chapter 3
Keeping Apps and Drivers Up to Date

One of the most important advantages of mobile platforms such as Android and iOS is that they have an app store where you can find apps to install on their devices. Google and Apple review these apps to meet their software development standards, and they also get a commission from all paid apps and services available in their app stores. Users don't have to do anything special to ensure they have the latest version of their apps because they're updated automatically through Google Play and the App Store.

Unfortunately for Microsoft, and also for us users, things are not as straightforward on Windows. If you want to keep your PC as secure as possible and working in tip-top shape, it's not enough to keep only Windows 11 up to date with the latest patches and feature updates. You must also update your apps, desktop programs, and device drivers.

Apps and desktop programs get regularly updated by their developers to offer new features, fix bugs and security glitches, and more. Drivers for hardware components like graphic cards or network cards receive similar updates. Driver updates are especially important if you are a gamer and want to play the latest titles with maximum performance and without lag. Often, new graphics drivers implement support for the newest games and offer specific optimizations that increase frame rates and overall performance. In addition, new driver versions for your Wi-Fi network card can increase the speed or lower the latency (the delay between the player's action and when that action takes effect) you get when playing games online.

Microsoft tries to simplify the software updating experience by using the Microsoft Store. If the app and game developers distribute their creations through it, and users install them from there, Microsoft will handle the update process automatically. Unfortunately, some important software developers, such as Google, intentionally keep their apps (such as Google Chrome) outside the Microsoft Store.

Microsoft handles driver updates through Windows Update. It does a decent job updating drivers, especially for laptops, but it doesn't update drivers for all the hardware inside your computer. For example, getting new driver versions from Windows Update is not good enough for gamers who require the latest drivers for their NVIDIA, Intel, or AMD video cards.

To help you manage this complexity, this chapter covers the essentials of keeping Windows 11 apps, desktop programs, games, and device drivers updated regularly.

Updating Your Microsoft Store Apps

Microsoft updates the apps and games you purchased or downloaded from the Microsoft Store as well as built-in Windows 11 apps. For instance, Notepad has received multiple updates since the release of Windows 11, not through Windows Update as you might anticipate but via the Microsoft Store. The same applies to Paint, Clock, and others.

Another aspect to keep in mind is that Microsoft Store updates apps (as well as itself) automatically, but the process doesn't always work or updates may be provided slower than you'd like. If you read in the news that Microsoft has released a new feature for an app that interests you but you don't have it available on your Windows 11 computer, you should check that you have the latest updates for absolutely everything, including the Microsoft Store. Here's how:

1. **Click or tap the Start icon and then Microsoft Store.**

   Or click the Microsoft Store icon on your taskbar, if one is available.

2. **In the lower part of the left sidebar, click or tap Downloads.**

   You see all your Windows 11 apps and those with updates available for installation. The latter are placed at the top of the list. In some cases, the Microsoft Store automatically updates some of your apps when you access the library.

3. **Click or tap Get Updates.**

   Any waiting updates start installing, as shown in Figure 3-1.

4. **If the Microsoft Store is updating your apps too slowly and seems to ignore your request to Get Updates, click or tap Update All in the top-right corner.**

   This action forces the Microsoft Store to focus on updating all your apps right now.

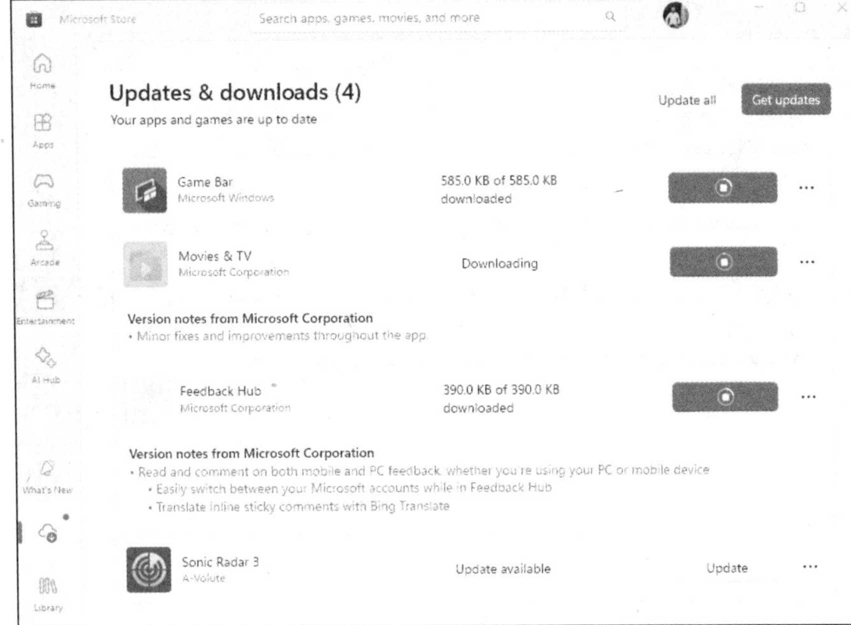

FIGURE 3-1: Downloads is where you see available updates and the progress of app updates.

In the normal course of events, you'll want to update all your apps, but if you know of a bad update (and they happen occasionally), you can choose which apps you want to bring up to date.

From time to time, you'll hit a problem with an update, and an error will appear, as shown in Figure 3-2. To see more information, click or tap the app's name and then See Details. Check that your internet connection is working, and then try again by clicking or tapping the Retry button next to the app whose update has failed. If that doesn't work, do a web search for the error details (the error code will be especially useful) or try contacting the app manufacturer. Good luck!

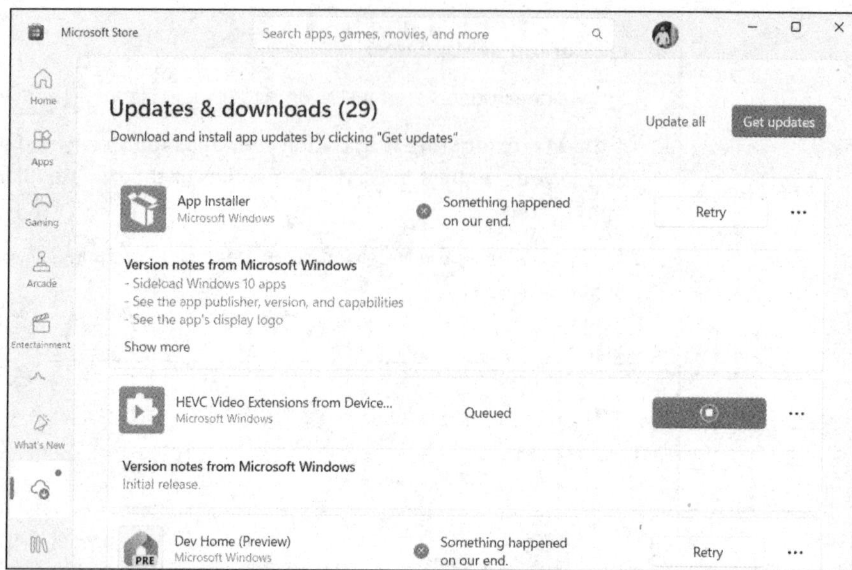

FIGURE 3-2: Occasionally, even app updates fail.

Updating Programs and Desktop Apps

Keeping your computer programs up to date used to be a hassle, especially in the good old days of Windows 7. In recent years, the process has been easier for several reasons. One is that many desktop apps, especially web browsers, have their own update checker running in the background. When your web browser upgrades to a new version, it loads a new tab to inform you that the browser is up to date and gives you a summary of what's new, similar to what Google Chrome did in Figure 3-3.

I like this approach because it ensures that I always use the latest version of my web browser and that my device as secure as possible with the latest bug fixes and security improvements.

Some Microsoft apps, such as the Office apps from Microsoft 365, can be updated through Windows Update. However, they don't do that by default; you must enable the Receive Updates for Other Microsoft Products setting in Windows Update. For details, read Book 7, Chapter 2. Keeping Office updated is important because its security bugs are often used for complex attacks, especially in business environments.

When you start other desktop programs like Paint.NET, Discord, or Slack, they check for updates automatically. If they find any, they inform you and give you the option to update them now or later. It is generally a good idea to update them as soon as possible.

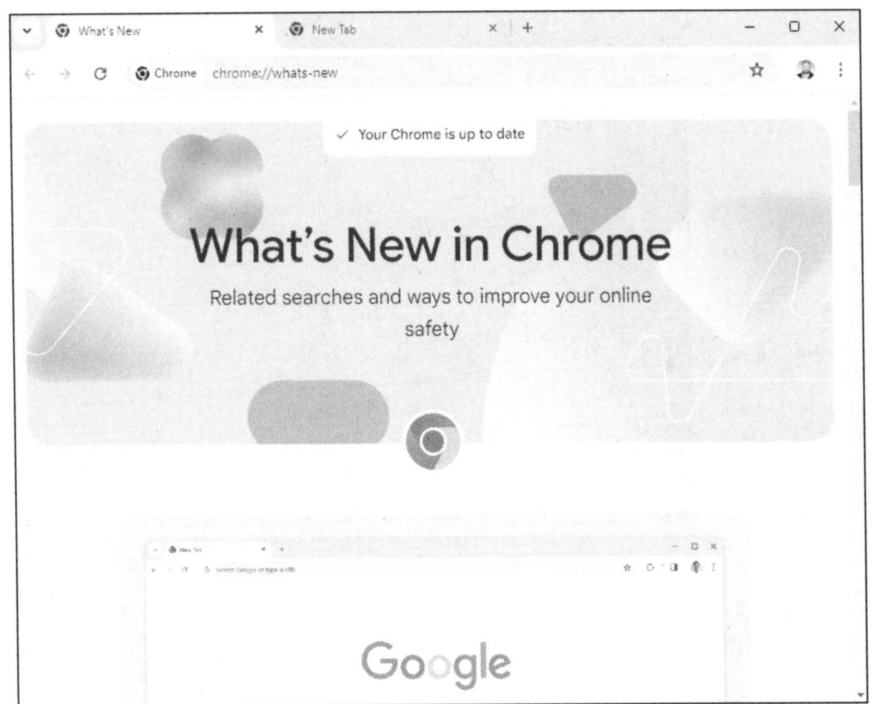

FIGURE 3-3: All web browsers for Windows update themselves automatically.

Fortunately, an increasing number of apps and desktop programs are now distributed through the Microsoft Store, so Windows 11 updates them automatically in the background. And, if the Microsoft Store hasn't updated them for some reason, you can do it yourself using the steps in the preceding section. The automatic app-updating service is the main reason why I hope the Microsoft Store in Windows 11 will finally catch on with developers and users alike.

Lastly, you can use software updating programs. Some are decent, but most are junk, filled with adware, trialware, and other stuff you don't want. One of the best is Patch My PC Home Updater at `https://patchmypc.com/home-updater`. The program is free, has a database of over 300 desktop apps that it checks regularly for updates, and lets you know which programs are outdated, as shown in Figure 3-4. A bonus is that it can update all your programs with just one click.

Another bonus is that Patch My PC Home Updater can be set to create a scheduled task in Windows 11, allowing it to run at a frequency of your choosing. Simply go to its Scheduler section and set things up as you want. If you want to know more about working with scheduled tasks in Windows, read Book 8, Chapter 5.

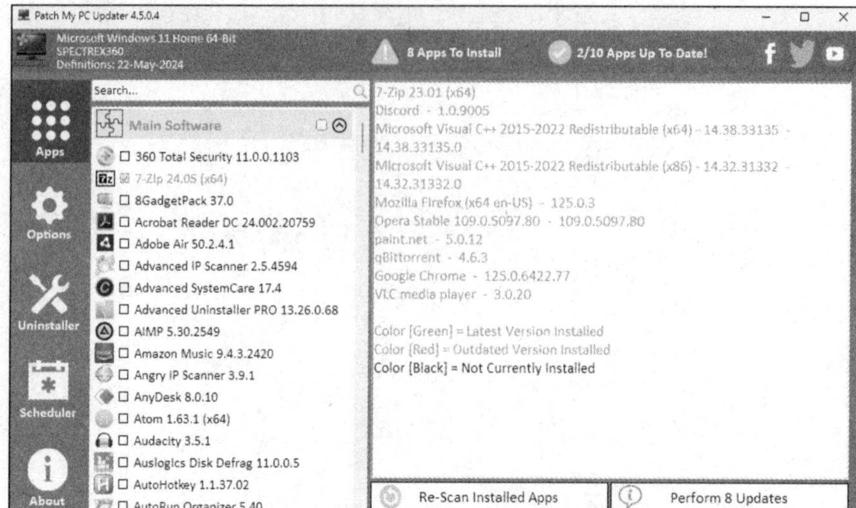

FIGURE 3-4: Patch My PC Home Updater can help you keep your programs up to date.

TIP

If you are a gamer and buy your games from Steam, `GOG.com`, or Epic Games, keeping your games up to date is easy. Start the platform you're using, and it automatically downloads the latest updates for the games you've installed on your gaming rig.

Updating Drivers

A *driver* is software that allows your operating system to start, use, and control a specific hardware device. For example, while your laptop may look like a single device, it contains many hardware components, each with its responsibilities. The graphics card handles displaying the image on the screen, the processor takes care of all kinds of complex calculations, the network card handles Wi-Fi connectivity, and so forth. Drivers are vital because they act as translators: When Windows (or any other operating system) wants a hardware device to do something, it uses its driver to make the request so that the hardware understands what it has to do.

Updating drivers is somewhat simpler than updating apps or programs because Windows 11 handles the process automatically through Windows Update. Windows does this for all kinds of devices, such as network cards, printers, video cards, and monitors. However, what you get from Windows are the latest drivers approved by Microsoft, not necessarily the latest drivers available from the manufacturer of each component. If you want the latest driver, you have to check the official site of the company that manufactured the component.

Getting the latest driver for graphics cards is especially important for gaming. If you're a gamer, don't stick with what Windows 11 offers. Instead, manually download the latest driver for your graphics card. Here are the support sites for the most important manufacturers of video cards:

- **AMD:** www.amd.com/en/support/download/drivers.html
- **NVIDIA:** www.nvidia.com/Download/index.aspx
- **Intel:** www.intel.com/content/www/us/en/download-center/home.html

If you're a laptop user, you can simplify the process of updating your drivers by using a specialized app made by the laptop's manufacturer. Here are the apps used by each major laptop manufacturer:

- **Lenovo:** Lenovo System Update, at www.lenovo.com/us/en/software/lenovo-system-update/
- **HP:** HP Support Assistant, at https://support.hp.com/us-en/help/hp-support-assistant
- **Dell:** SupportAssist, at www.dell.com/support/contents/en-us/category/product-support/self-support-knowledgebase/software-and-downloads/support-assist
- **Acer:** Control Center, at https://apps.microsoft.com/detail/9mzpx5wcbmwt?hl=en-us&gl=US
- **ASUS:** MyASUS, at www.asus.com/support/myasus-deeplink/

WARNING

When downloading a driver, it's vital to choose one made for your operating system (in this case, Windows 11, not Windows 8 or older) and the exact model of the hardware component you're using. If you install a driver for the wrong component or the wrong operating system version, Windows 11 could crash. If that happens, boot Windows 11 in safe mode (read Book 8, Chapter 3) and uninstall the driver you just installed.

Let's assume that a hardware component in your computer isn't working well, and you suspect the driver is outdated. Use Windows 11 to search for updates, like this:

1. **Right-click or tap and hold the Start icon. Or press Windows+X.**

   The WinX menu opens.

2. **Choose Device Manager.**

   The Device Manager program opens, as shown in Figure 3-5. You see all the hardware inside your computer and the devices connected to it organized by type. You can expand each hardware category with a double-click or double-tap.

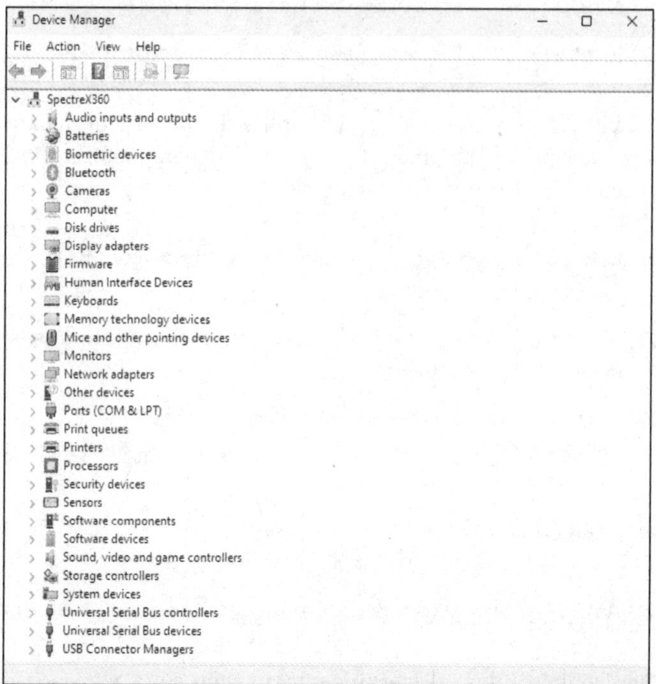

FIGURE 3-5: Device Manager shows you all the hardware in your computer.

3. **Expand the type of hardware whose driver you want to update.**

   For example, to update the driver for a network card, expand Network Adapters.

4. **Right-click or tap and hold the name of the hardware component you want to update, and then choose Update Driver.**

   The options shown in Figure 3-6 appear.

5. **Choose Search Automatically for Drivers.**

   Windows 11 checks for newer drivers. If it finds any, it informs you and installs them automatically.

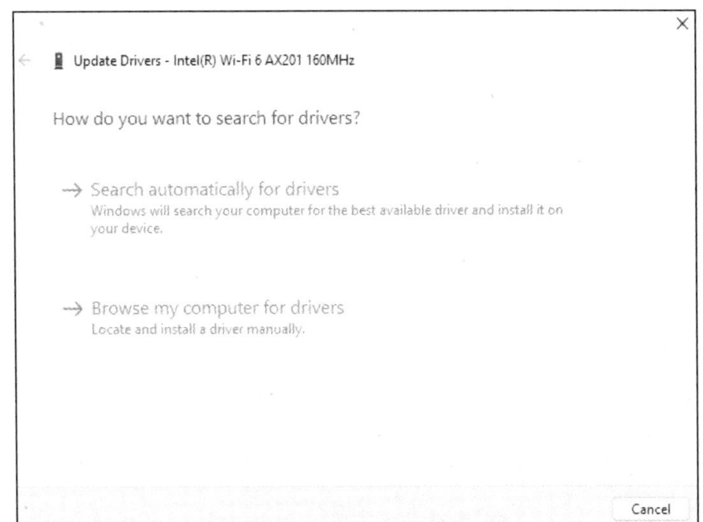

FIGURE 3-6: Tell Windows 11 you want to search for drivers.

6. **If Windows 11 tells you that you have the best drivers installed, but you want it to keep looking, click or tap Search for Updated Drivers on Windows Update.**

   Windows 11 takes you to Windows Update, where you can click or tap Check for Updates and see what updates are available.

6 Working Remotely

Contents at a Glance

IN THIS CHAPTER

- » Connecting to other displays, casting and projecting your desktop
- » Transferring files with Nearby Sharing
- » Setting up your webcam
- » Enabling a mobile hotspot on your laptop
- » Using airplane mode

Chapter 1
Working on Your Laptop

Laptops have become an indispensable part of modern life, transforming how we work, learn, and entertain ourselves. From students attending virtual classes to professionals embracing remote or hybrid work, laptops offer unparalleled flexibility and productivity. The pandemic accelerated their adoption, with many households investing in multiple laptops to meet the demands of work-from-home and distance learning. Whether you're a digital nomad working from a cozy cafe or a retiree staying connected with your family, chances are there's a laptop within arm's reach, ready to connect you to the internet.

This chapter is your guide to unlocking the potential of your Windows 11 laptop, regardless of whether you're using an older model with an AMD or Intel processor or a cutting-edge Copilot+ PC infused with AI capabilities. I explore a treasure trove of tips and tricks designed to boost your productivity and enhance your user experience.

The chapter kicks things off by showing you how to connect your laptop to external displays, perfect for supersizing your workspace or streaming your favorite shows on the big screen. Then, I dive into the world of wireless casting and projection, saying goodbye to tangled cables once and for all.

Next up is Nearby Sharing, a useful Windows 11 feature that simplifies file transfers between Windows devices. After learning how to use it, you'll wonder how you ever managed without it. Then, I tackle your webcam setup, including those fancy Studio Effects that have you looking like a Hollywood star during video calls.

To round things off, I explore how to transform your Windows 11 laptop into a mobile hotspot, sharing your internet connection with other devices. And for the frequent flyers among us, I demystify airplane mode, ensuring your laptop plays nice with aircraft systems while keeping you productive (or entertained) at 30,000 feet.

So, grab your laptop, get comfortable, and let's embark on this journey to master your Windows 11 laptop.

Connecting and Projecting to Another Screen

Working on two screens at the same time can increase productivity, regardless of whether you're at home or at the office. To connect a second display to your Windows 11 laptop or PC, first check out the ports on the display and then check the ones on your Windows device. Figure 1-1 shows you the video ports look.

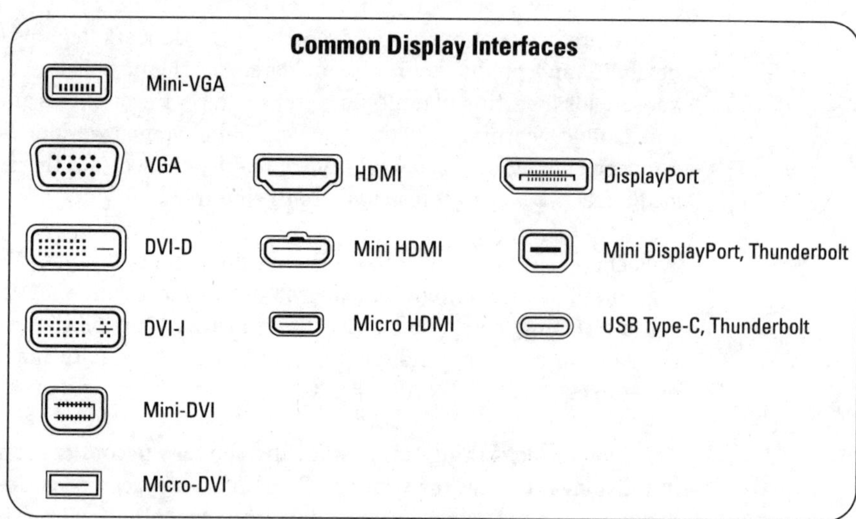

FIGURE 1-1: All the ports used by monitors, new and old.

There are two possible situations:

- **Your monitor and your laptop or PC share the same video port.** Buy a cable that has the same video port on both ends (DisplayPort, USB Type-C, and so on).
- **Your monitor and your laptop or PC do not share a common video port.** Buy an adapter to convert the video signal from your laptop or PC to the external monitor and the appropriate cable for it. Depending on what video ports you have on your laptop or PC and monitor, you might need a HDMI-to-DisplayPort, USB-C-to-HDMI, or Mini DisplayPort-to-DisplayPort adapter. You can find inexpensive adapters in electronics shops for almost any type of video connection.

After you have the necessary cable, do the following to connect the second monitor:

1. **Using the appropriate cable, connect the monitor to your Windows 11 laptop or PC.**
2. **Turn on the second monitor by plugging it into a power outlet and pressing its power button.**

   Windows 11 takes a few seconds to detect the external monitor. Note that the external monitor may not display anything after it's detected.
3. **Press Windows+P to display the Project options (see Figure 1-2).**

   You can view the desktop only on your PC screen (the main display) or only on your second screen, view the same desktop on both screens, or extend the desktop and have two different desktops side by side.

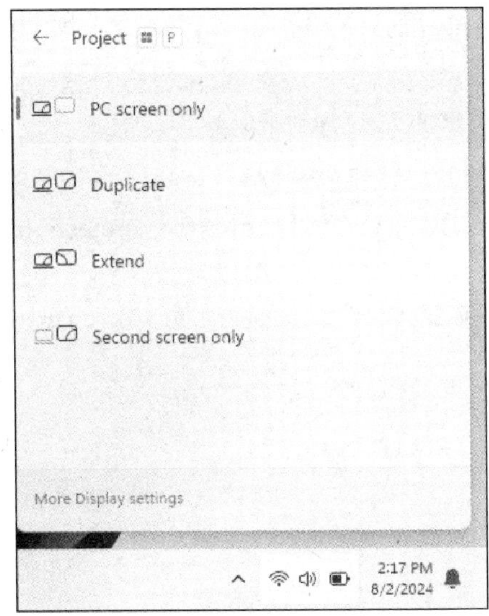

FIGURE 1-2: Your options for projecting the image on a second display.

4. **Press Windows+P to cycle through the Project options and view the results.**

   You can also click or tap to select an option. The image changes with each selection.

TIP

When delivering a presentation, you may need to connect to a projector instead of a computer monitor. Luckily, the procedure for connecting your Windows 11 laptop to a projector and displaying the image on it works the same as the one for connecting to a monitor. However, modern projectors also include wireless projection capabilities using the Miracast standard. Connecting to them works differently and is detailed in the next section.

TIP

You can access the Project dialog shown in Figure 1-2 also by using Quick Settings. Read Book 2, Chapter 3, to learn more.

Casting wirelessly

Windows 11 includes support for a useful wireless display technology called Miracast. Developed by the Wi-Fi Alliance back in 2012, Miracast allows users to project their screen to compatible devices without the need for cables. Many Smart TVs and projectors, particularly those used in corporate settings, support Miracast, which allows users to mirror the display of one device onto another, such as streaming a laptop's screen to a TV, projector, or monitor. If you're using a Windows 11 laptop, it's already Miracast-compatible, giving you the ability to project your screen wirelessly. Here's how it all works:

1. **Turn on the Smart TV or projector with wireless display capabilities.**
2. **Press Windows+K to display the Cast options (see Figure 1-3).**

   Windows 11 takes a few seconds to detect displays to which you can connect through Miracast and displays those that it finds.

3. **Click or tap on the name of the display you want to connect to.**
4. **If you see a message asking you to approve the connection, do so on the wireless display.**

   Windows 11 takes a few seconds to display the desktop on the wireless display you just connected to.

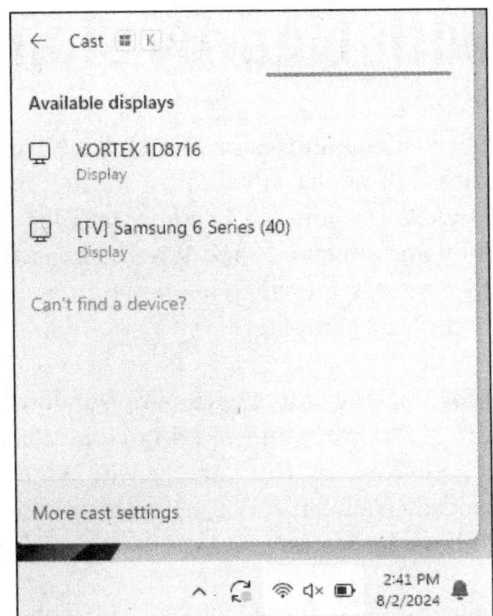

FIGURE 1-3: Connecting to a wireless display using the Cast dialog.

After you connect to a wireless display, you can set how you want to project your image on it by pressing Windows+P and using the instructions shared in the preceding section. Or press Windows+K and choose one of the options shown in Figure 1-4.

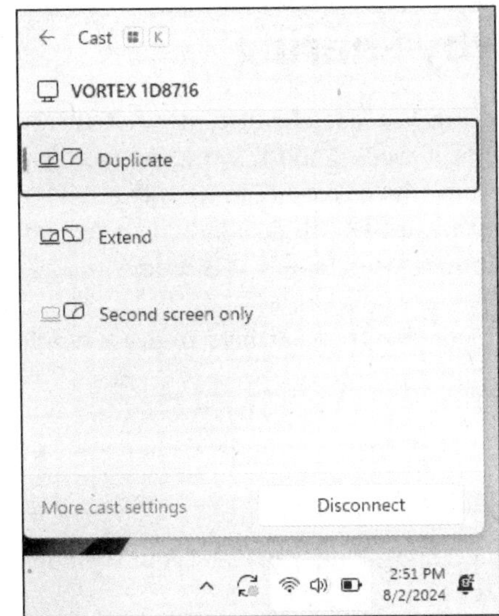

FIGURE 1-4: After connecting to a wireless display, set how to project the image onto it.

TIP

You can access the Cast dialog (refer to Figure 1-3) also from Quick Settings. Read Book 2, Chapter 3, to learn more.

Transferring Files with Nearby Sharing

Do you want to say goodbye to email attachments and the transferring of large files over USB memory sticks? Windows 11's Nearby Sharing is your magic wand for sending files wirelessly. It lets you zap documents, files, photos, and even links to nearby devices by using Bluetooth and Wi-Fi. I even used it to transfer many of the screenshots I've made for this book between an ASUS Vivbook S 15 Copilot+ PC and my trusty desktop computer.

Here's the cool part: Nearby Sharing works with both Windows 10 and Windows 11 devices. They're all part of the same file-sharing club. When you're sending something, if the receiving device is on the same private Wi-Fi network, Nearby Sharing uses Wi-Fi for a speedy transfer. If not, no problem! Bluetooth steps in to save the day, even though it's a lot slower.

Windows 11 users are in luck because Nearby Sharing is ready to go right out of the box. Windows 10 folks need to make sure that they're running version 1803 or newer (April 2018 Update for Windows 10) to use Nearby Sharing.

So the next time you need to share a file, forget the old-school methods, let Nearby Sharing do its thing and watch your files hop from one device to another in a few seconds.

Enabling Nearby Sharing

Even though Nearby Sharing is a cool feature, it's not turned on by default in Windows 11. To ensure that it works, and it works as fast as possible, you must set your current Wi-Fi connection as private instead of public (read Book 3, Chapter 5), enable Nearby Sharing, and configure how it makes your Windows computer or device visible to others. Here's how it is done:

1. **Click or tap the Start icon and then Settings, or press Windows+I.**

   The Settings app appears.

2. **On the left, choose System. Then on the right, choose Nearby Sharing.**

   You see the Nearby Sharing configuration options shown in Figure 1-5.

3. **Under Nearby Sharing, choose how you want your Windows 11 computer to be visible to others:**

   - *Off:* Stops Nearby Sharing, and your computer is not visible to others when using this feature.
   - *My devices only:* Your computer is visible only to other Windows devices on which you use the same Microsoft, work, or school account.

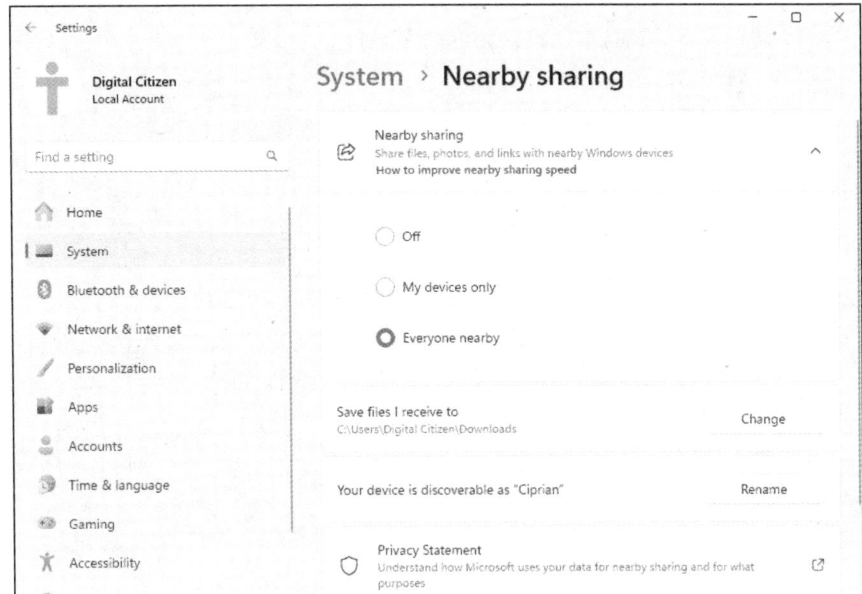

FIGURE 1-5: Turning on Nearby Sharing.

- *Everyone nearby:* All other Windows 10 and Windows 11 computers that are near you can see your computer and share files and other items through Nearby Sharing.

4. **If you want to change where files are downloaded through Nearby Sharing, do the following:**

   a. *Click or tap the Change button next to Save Files I Receive To.* The Select Folder dialog opens, as shown in Figure 1-6.

   b. *Browse your computer, select the new folder that you want to use for receiving files, and choose Select Folder.*

5. **Close the Settings window.**

Sharing files nearby

Ready to become a Nearby Sharing wizard? Great! Just remember, it takes two to tango. Make sure this feature is switched on for both the sending and receiving computers. It's like making sure both dance partners know the steps before you hit the floor.

Now that you have Nearby Sharing all set up, let's walk through the simple steps of sending a file from one Windows laptop to another:

1. **Click or tap the File Explorer icon on the taskbar or press Windows+E.**

   The File Explorer app opens.

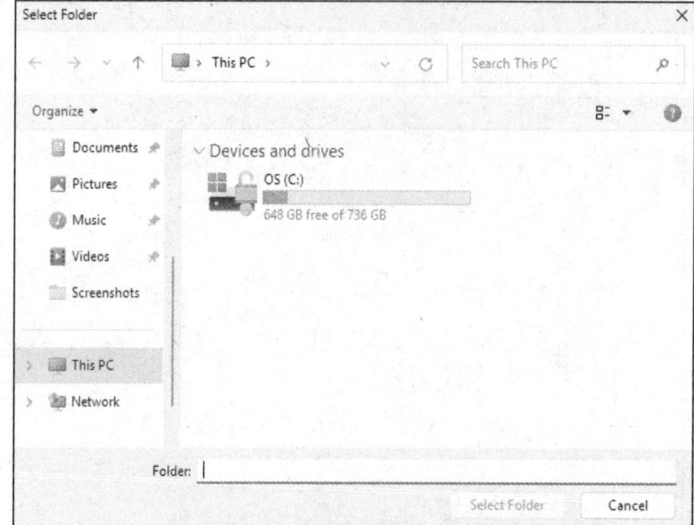

FIGURE 1-6: Selecting where Nearby Sharing downloads files.

2. **Browse your computer to find the file you want to send to another computer. Select it with a click or tap on its name.**

   On the toolbar in the top side of File Explorer, you see the options shown in Figure 1-7.

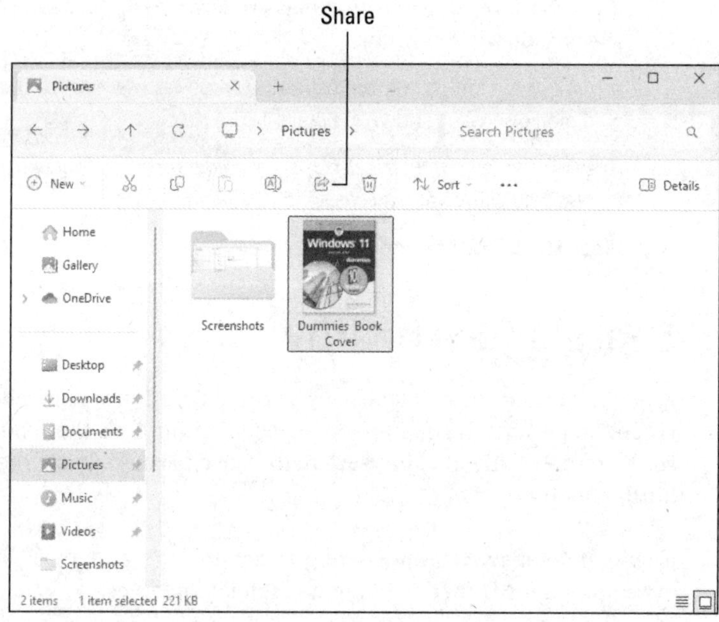

FIGURE 1-7: Selecting the file(s) you want to transfer in File Explorer.

3. **Click or tap the share icon on the toolbar, to the left of the trash icon.**

   Windows 11 displays the Share dialog shown in Figure 1-8.

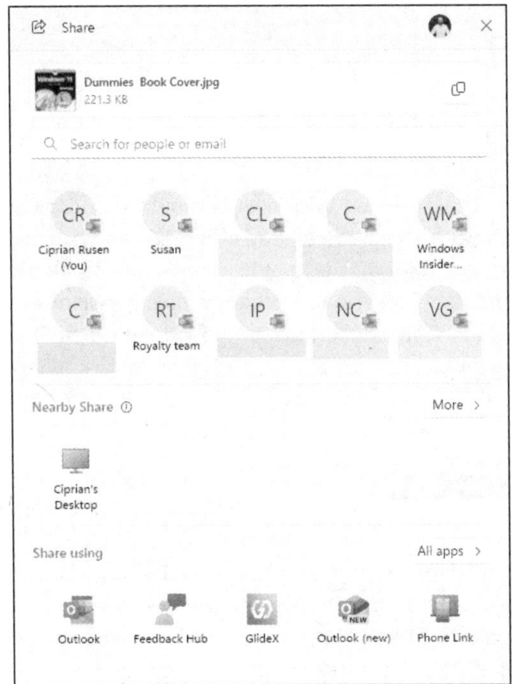

FIGURE 1-8: Choosing the PC to send the file to in the Nearby Sharing section.

4. **In the Nearby Share section, click or tap the name of the computer where you want to send the file.**

   On the receiving computer, you see a notification similar to Figure 1-9, asking whether you want to save the file or decline the transfer.

5. **Click or tap Save or Save & Open, depending on what you want to do.**

   The file is transferred from one computer to another, and you're notified when the transfer ends.

WARNING

You can repeat the same steps to transfer another file or more than one file. However, Nearby Share doesn't work when you want to send files stored in your OneDrive folder. If you follow the same steps for sharing a file stored on your OneDrive, you get OneDrive's Share dialog instead. Read Book 4, Chapter 6, to learn how OneDrive sharing works.

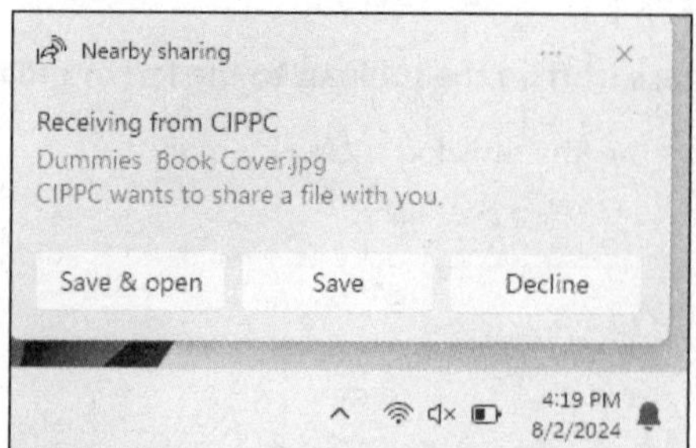

FIGURE 1-9: Accepting the Nearby Sharing transfer.

TIP

Nearby Share was designed for Windows computers and devices, and it doesn't share files with smartphones, tablets, and other devices with mobile operating systems such as iOS or Android. On the upside, Google has developed a Quick Share app for Windows, which you can use to exchange files between Android smartphones and tablets as well as Windows laptops. To download Quick Share for Windows get the app, visit `www.android.com/better-together/quick-share-app/`.

Setting Up a Webcam

Webcams surged in popularity during the COVID-19 lockdowns as remote work became widespread and as people used them to communicate with friends and family. While the work-from-home trend has decreased, hybrid and remote work options persist, maintaining the relevance of webcams. Fortunately, modern laptops with Windows 11 come equipped with built-in webcams, reducing the need for separate devices.

However, for those seeking a stand-alone webcam, a full HD model typically suffices for most users, as a 4K resolution for video recording is often unnecessary. Installation is straightforward: Simply connect the webcam to a USB port and allow Windows 11 to detect and install drivers automatically.

One of my favorite webcams is the Microsoft Modern Webcam (shown in Figure 1-10), offering all the features most people need (full HD video recording, HDR support, automatic light adjustment, and Microsoft Teams compatibility) at an affordable price, with plug-and-play functionality.

Some webcams include software to activate features that you might find useful. That's why it's a good idea to do a Bing search for the support page of the webcam's manufacturer and download from there the latest software and drivers for your webcam model. Install the webcam's software, and you should have no problems using it for Microsoft Teams or Zoom video calls.

FIGURE 1-10: Microsoft Modern Webcam.

Image source: Microsoft.com

TIP

I prefer webcams from proven manufacturers, such as Microsoft, Logitech, Dell, or Razer. Their webcams have many options at diverse price points.

Using a webcam shield

Webcams are vulnerable to hacking through specialized malware known as Remote Access Trojans (RATs). These trojans can allow attackers to silently access, monitor, and record your activities through your webcam. For more information on trojans and other types of cybersecurity threats, refer to Book 9, Chapter 1.

The frequency of webcam hacking incidents is higher than many users realize. This issue gained significant media attention following high-profile cases involving public figures. For example, in 2013, Miss Teen USA, Cassidy Wolf, fell victim to such an attack, followed by actress Jennifer Lawrence in 2014. Each year, at least one new high-profile case makes the headlines.

These incidents sparked notable trends in user behavior and industry response. For example, many individuals, including high-profile tech executives like Facebook CEO Mark Zuckerberg, began covering their webcams with tape (reported by the *New York Times* in 2016). In response, laptop manufacturers started incorporating built-in webcam covers into their designs. Even stand-alone webcams for desktop computers now often feature physical covers that can block the camera lens, preventing unauthorized recording even if the device is remotely activated.

To protect yourself from webcam hacking, use security software such as the Windows Security app in Windows 11, be cautious when downloading software or clicking links, consider using a physical webcam cover when the webcam is not in use (see Figure 1-11), and keep your operating system and applications up to date.

If you're using a Windows 11 laptop, read its user manual and look for a webcam switch, which you can press to turn off the camera and its recording capabilities.

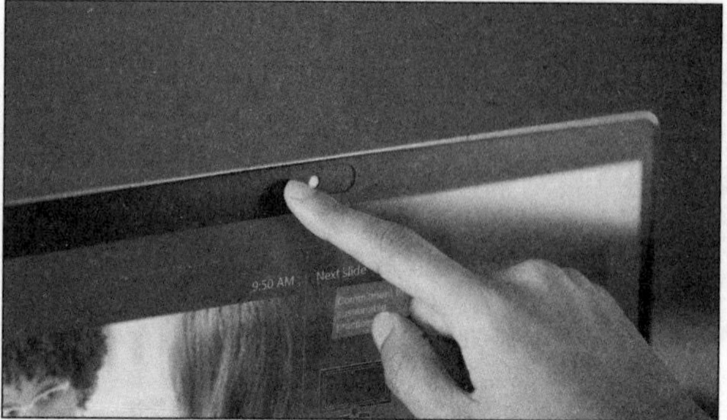

FIGURE 1-11: The webcam cover for HP EliteBook laptops.

Image source: HP

REMEMBER

If your webcam has support for Windows Hello face recognition, using the webcam cover or switch also disables face recognition capabilities. Therefore, if you can't sign in with your face on your Windows 11 laptop, check whether the webcam is turned off. After the webcam cover is removed, you should be able to sign in again just by looking at your laptop.

Configuring the webcam

Depending on their hardware capabilities and features, webcams can be customized to work as you want them to, and you can change aspects of their functioning such as the zoom level they use to record video, the brightness, contrast, saturation, and so on. What can be customized varies from webcam to webcam, depending on its drivers and specific hardware characteristics. Luckily, Windows 11 allows you to access your webcam using the Settings app and customize the way it works:

1. **Click or tap the Start icon and then Settings, or press Windows+I.**

   The Settings app appears.

2. **On the left, choose Bluetooth & Devices. Then on the right, choose Cameras.**

   Under Connected Cameras, you see the name of your webcam.

3. **Click or tap your webcam's name in the list of connected cameras.**

   You see preview footage from your webcam, followed by a list of settings, similar to Figure 1-12. Depending on your specific webcam, you can change aspects such as the zoom, brightness, and contrast.

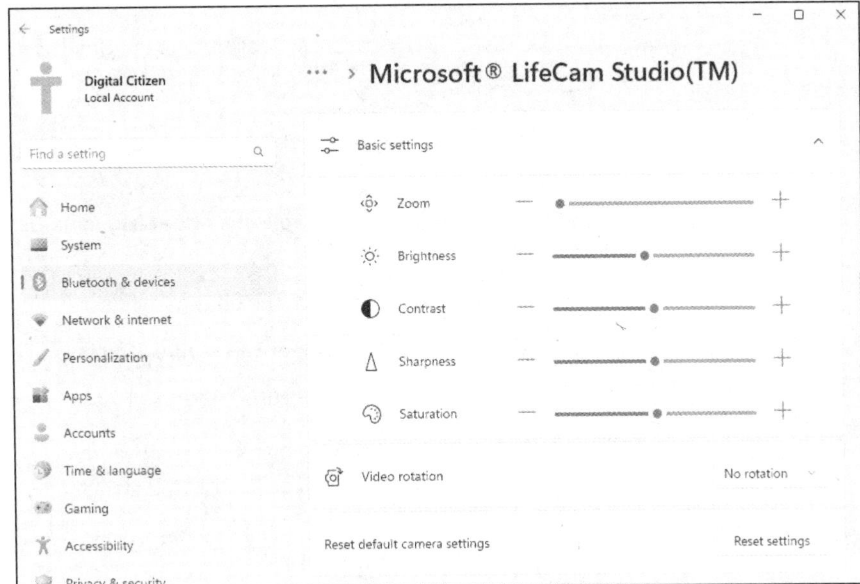

FIGURE 1-12: Changing your webcam settings.

4. **Change the aspects you're interested in and see how they affect the video recording in the preview footage above the webcam's settings.**
5. **When you've finished setting things up, close the Settings window.**

Working on Your Laptop

Using Studio Effects

As of 2024, the market has welcomed a new generation of computers known as Copilot+ PC devices. These machines are distinguished by their built-in neural processing unit (NPU), designed to handle artificial intelligence–related tasks while minimizing battery use.

One of the most notable AI-powered features in Windows 11 is Windows Studio Effects, which acts as a virtual personal stylist for your webcam and microphone. It offers several enhancements to improve your video conferencing experience. For example, background blur allows you to obscure your surroundings, maintaining privacy and professionalism during video calls with colleagues or managers, regardless of your actual environment. The Eye Contact effects use AI to adjust your gaze to appear focused on the camera, giving the impression of direct eye contact and engagement with other participants.

If you're using a Copilot+ PC laptop, such as the ASUS Vivobook S 15 (which I'm using to write this chapter), you can easily access and enable Windows Studio Effects in two primary ways. The first is through the Settings app by navigating to the Cameras page, as described in the preceding section. The second method, which provides faster access to these features, is via Quick Settings, and it works like this:

1. **Make sure that your laptop's webcam is turned on and that its cover isn't blocking it.**
2. **On the taskbar, click the Wi-Fi, volume, or battery icon. Or press Windows+A.**

   You see the Quick Settings pane on the bottom-right side of the screen.
3. **In the Quick Settings pane, click or tap Studio Effects.**

   You see a list of effects similar to Figure 1-13.

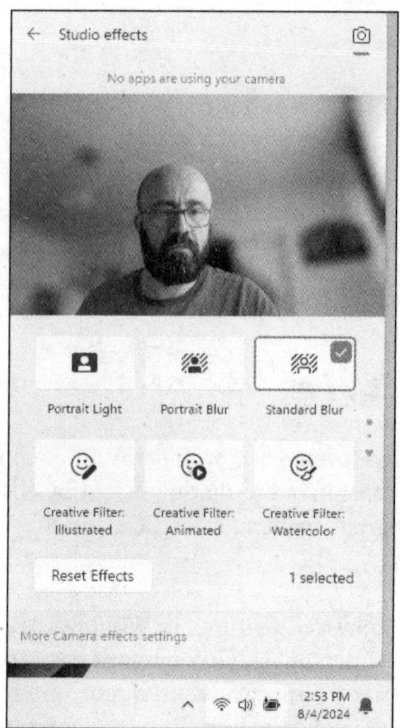

FIGURE 1-13: Enabling Windows Studio Effects for your webcam.

4. **Select Standard Blur.**

   See how the video looks in the preview footage above the list of Studio Effects.
5. **To get the video footage back to normal, click or tap Reset Effects.**
6. **Navigate the list of available effects and test them one by one.**
7. **When you've finished choosing the video effect you want, click or tap outside the Studio Effects pane.**

The selected effect will apply to all your video recordings, including all video-conferencing meetings you join using Microsoft Teams, Zoom, or another similar platform.

Creating a Mobile Hotspot

Have you ever found yourself in a situation where you needed to share your internet connection with other wireless devices? Perhaps you wanted to connect your smartphone or your colleague's laptop to the internet using your Windows 11 laptop, tablet, or 2-in-1 device as a mobile hotspot. The good news is that Windows 11 makes this process straightforward and accessible.

To set up a Wi-Fi hotspot using Windows 11, your computer or device needs to meet a few basic requirements. First, it must have at least one Wi-Fi network card or Bluetooth chip. Second, it needs to be connected to the internet, which can be done through various means such as Wi-Fi, Ethernet, a USB modem, or even a SIM card.

The versatility of Windows 11 allows you to create a mobile hotspot regardless of how your device is connected to the internet. This feature can be particularly useful when you have limited internet access, such as in a hotel, at a conference, or at a remote work location. By sharing your connection, you can ensure that all your devices — or those of your colleagues — remain connected and productive.

Here's how to set up a mobile hotspot in Windows 11:

1. **Click or tap the Start icon and then Settings, or press Windows+I.**

   The Settings app is shown.

2. **Choose Network & Internet on the left, and then click or tap Mobile Hotspot on the right.**

   Click or tap the Mobile Hotspot text, not the switch. This action opens the Mobile Hotspot settings page, as shown in Figure 1-14.

3. **In the Properties section, click or tap the Edit button.**

   You see the Edit Network Info dialog shown in Figure 1-15.

4. **Set the network name you want to use for the Wi-Fi hotspot.**

5. **Enter the network password that other devices must use to connect to your Wi-Fi hotspot.**

   You can also configure the network band and the security type used by your hotspot. However, for most people, the default values offered by Windows 11 work just fine.

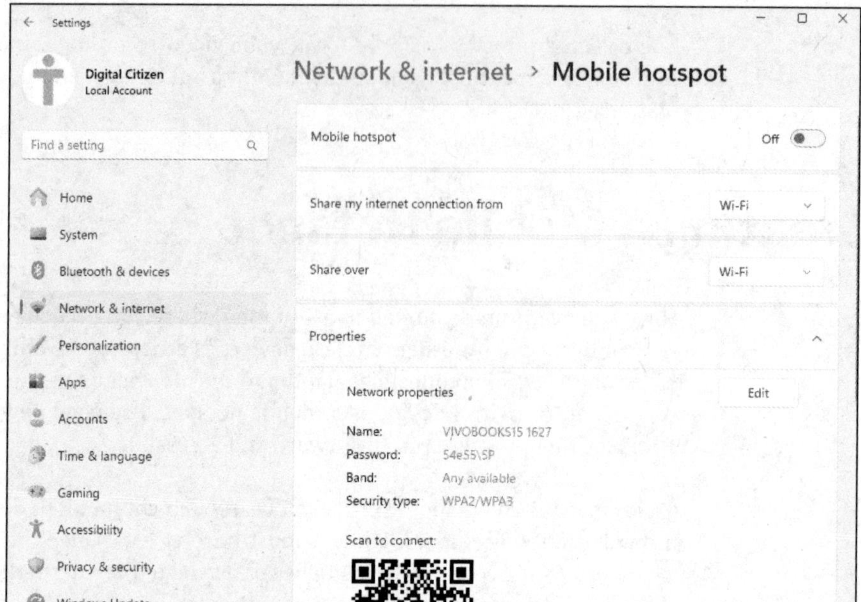

FIGURE 1-14: The Mobile Hotspot settings page.

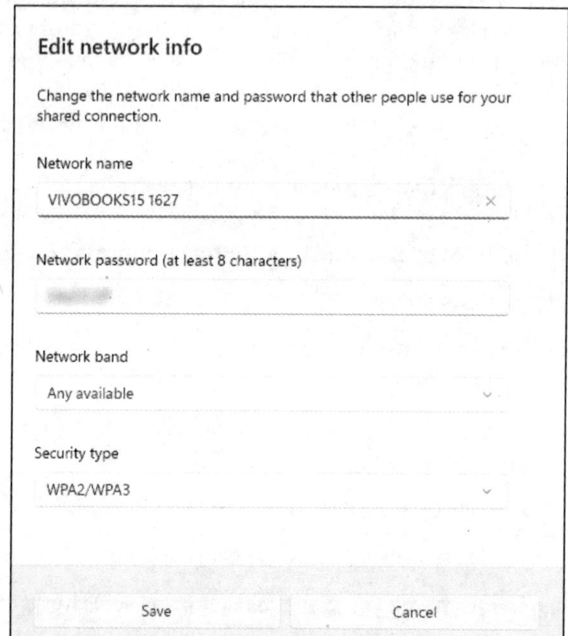

FIGURE 1-15: Choosing a custom name and password for the mobile hotspot.

6. **Click or tap Save.**

   You return to the Mobile Hotspot settings page.

7. **Click or tap the Mobile Hotspot switch on the top to turn it on.**

   Your Wi-Fi hotspot is now turned on, and other devices can connect to it using your connection settings.

When you're finished using the mobile hotspot, you can stop it by following Steps 1 and 2 and then setting the Mobile Hotspot switch off.

TIP

After setting up the mobile hotspot using the instructions shared earlier, you can quickly enable it from the Quick Settings pane. On the taskbar, click the Wi-Fi, volume, or battery icon or press Windows+A. Navigate the list of Quick Settings until you find Mobile Hotspot, and click or tap it. The hotspot is turned on immediately using the settings you've made. Disable it by following the same steps.

Using Airplane Mode

If you're a frequent flyer, you know the struggle of staying productive (or entertained) while soaring through the clouds. Fear not, sky warrior! Windows 11 has your back with a feature called airplane mode. Just like your smartphone, your Windows 11 device can go into flight-friendly mode faster than you can say: "fasten your seatbelts." No worries about interfering with important airplane equipment — you can work, play, or binge-watch your favorite shows to your heart's content.

Luckily, airplane mode isn't just for high-altitude adventures. It's also a good tool for squeezing extra life out of your battery. By putting your laptop's radio components to sleep, it sips power instead of guzzling it. So even when you're firmly on terra firma, you might want to consider toggling on airplane mode if you're in a battery crunch.

When airplane mode takes off, Windows 11 grounds quite a few systems. Your Wi-Fi waves goodbye to the internet, Bluetooth bids farewell to your accessories, and if your device has mobile data capabilities (4G/5G), those get temporarily grounded, too. Even wireless projection technologies such as Miracast and file-sharing capabilities such as Nearby Sharing take a siesta.

But don't worry; you're not completely cut off. After takeoff, you can selectively wake up Wi-Fi or Bluetooth if you need them. Just remember to keep an eye out for that little airplane icon in your system tray — it's your signal that airplane mode is on duty.

To engage airplane mode, follow these steps:

1. **Click or tap the Start icon, followed by Settings.**

   The Settings app is shown.

2. **Choose Network & Internet on the left, and then click or tap Airplane Mode on the right.**

   Click or tap the Airplane Mode text, not the switch. This action opens the settings page shown in Figure 1-16, where you see which chips will be turned off.

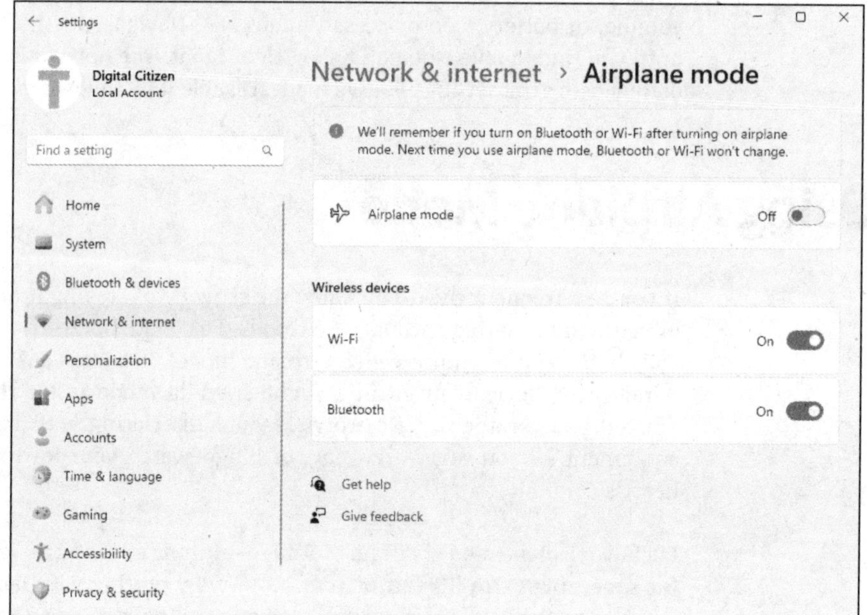

FIGURE 1-16: Enabling and configuring airplane mode.

3. **Click or tap the Airplane Mode switch to turn it on.**

   Note how the Wi-Fi and Bluetooth switches get turned off, and an airplane icon shows up on the taskbar, next to the time. You can enable Wi-Fi or Bluetooth later, after take-off, if necessary.

4. **When you've finished using airplane mode, set its switch off.**

TIP

You can also enable and disable airplane mode from the Quick Settings pane. On the taskbar, click the Wi-Fi, volume, or battery icon or press Windows+A. Navigate your Quick Settings until you find airplane mode, and then click or tap its icon.

IN THIS CHAPTER

» Understanding the basics of using Microsoft Teams

» Starting a meeting on Teams

» Connecting with Remote Desktop Connection

» Adding clocks for different time zones to the taskbar

» Improving battery life and lowering your carbon footprint

Chapter 2
Mastering Tools for Remote Work

The last time I wrote a *Dummies* book, working from home was the main trend in the workforce. Nowadays, things have changed, with companies all over the world asking their employees to return to the office and use a hybrid work model, which alternates work from home with work in the office. Even though this change is important, working remotely is still necessary for millions of people.

In this chapter, I explore a range of features and tools that help you stay connected, work efficiently, and manage your device's power consumption, whether you're in the office or working from home.

I start by diving into Microsoft Teams, the go-to communication platform recommended by Microsoft. I show you how to set it up, chat on Teams, and initiate meetings with ease. Next, I present the Remote Desktop feature, showing you how to enable it on your Windows 11 PC and connect to other computers remotely. For those working across time zones, I demonstrate how to add multiple clocks to your taskbar, ensuring you're always aware of your colleagues' local times.

Lastly, I shift gears to discuss power management, introduce you to the new energy saver that was recently added to Windows 11, and explain how to configure your device's power settings. To wrap things up, I look at how you can reduce your carbon footprint by following Windows 11's energy recommendations.

By the end of this chapter, you'll be equipped with the knowledge to work remotely and communicate effectively on Microsoft Teams, establish remote connections when needed, and manage your device's power consumption.

Contacting Others Using Microsoft Teams

When Windows 11 was introduced, Microsoft Teams was integrated into the operating system through a Chat app with a prominent icon on the taskbar, next to the widgets and File Explorer. Despite its improvements over time and the fact that it was built on the foundation of Microsoft Teams, the Chat app did not gain much traction with consumers. Consequently, in June 2023, Microsoft announced that it would be removing Chat from Windows 11 and users could install Microsoft Teams (free) instead.

However, this resulted in users dealing with two separate Teams apps: one for personal use (which works only with a Microsoft account) and another for work or school. To address users' complaints about this situation, Microsoft is slowly moving towards a unified Microsoft Teams application in Windows 11 version 24H2. During its preview phase, this unified app is called *Microsoft Teams (work or school)* but will be renamed to *Microsoft Teams* upon its final release. When that happens, the stand-alone consumer app Microsoft Teams (free) is going to be removed from Windows 11, Microsoft's download sites, and the Microsoft Store.

At the time of writing, there is no clear release date for the final unified Microsoft Teams app. To ensure that you have the latest version, you can visit Microsoft's Teams website and download it yourself: `www.microsoft.com/en-us/microsoft-teams/download-app`.

Getting started with Microsoft Teams

Before you start using Microsoft Teams, you need either a Microsoft account (if you're a home user) or a work or school account. Use that account to sign into Windows 11. Then, to get started and use Microsoft Teams, do the following:

1. **Click or tap inside the Search box on the taskbar and type the word** teams.

   You see a list of search results.

2. **Choose the Microsoft Teams search result.**

   The Teams app opens, similar to Figure 2-1. If this is the first time you're using it, it may request your permission to access your location and location history, your camera, and other items.

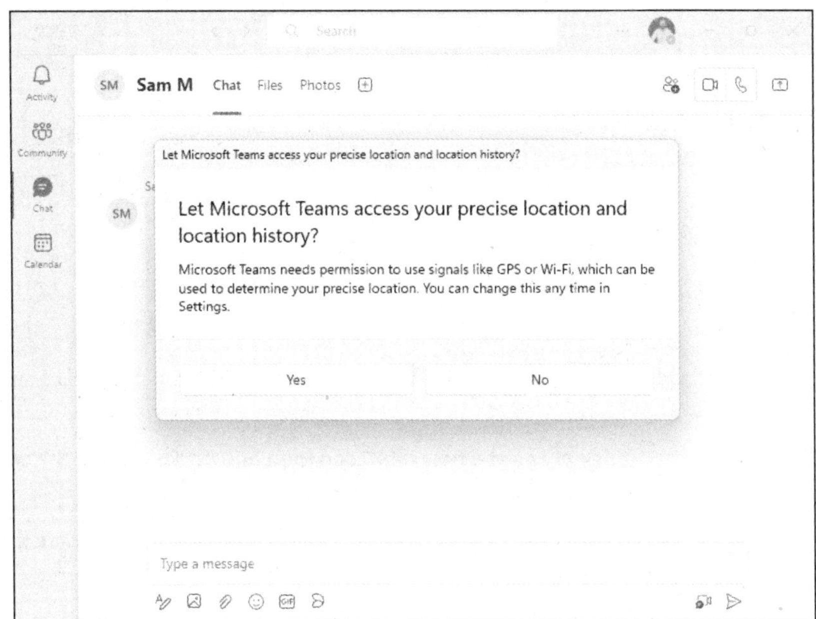

Search
Activity
Community
Chat
Calendar
SM
Sam M
Chat
Files
Photos
Let Microsoft Teams access your precise location and location history?
Let Microsoft Teams access your precise location and location history?
Microsoft Teams needs permission to use signals like GPS or Wi-Fi, which can be used to determine your precise location. You can change this any time in Settings.
Yes
No
Type a message

FIGURE 2-1: Giving Microsoft Teams the permissions required to work.

3. **Choose Yes or No for each request, depending on whether you want to give it the required permissions.**

   If you want to join video calls, you must allow it to access your camera. The Microsoft Teams app is now ready for use.

Chatting from Windows 11

After you set up Teams using the instructions in the preceding section, starting a chat conversation with someone takes a few clicks or taps:

1. **Click or tap inside the Search box on the taskbar and type** teams.
2. **In the list of results, choose Microsoft Teams.**
3. **Click or tap the Chat icon on the left.**

   You see your list of contacts, with the recent conversations on the top, as shown in Figure 2-2.

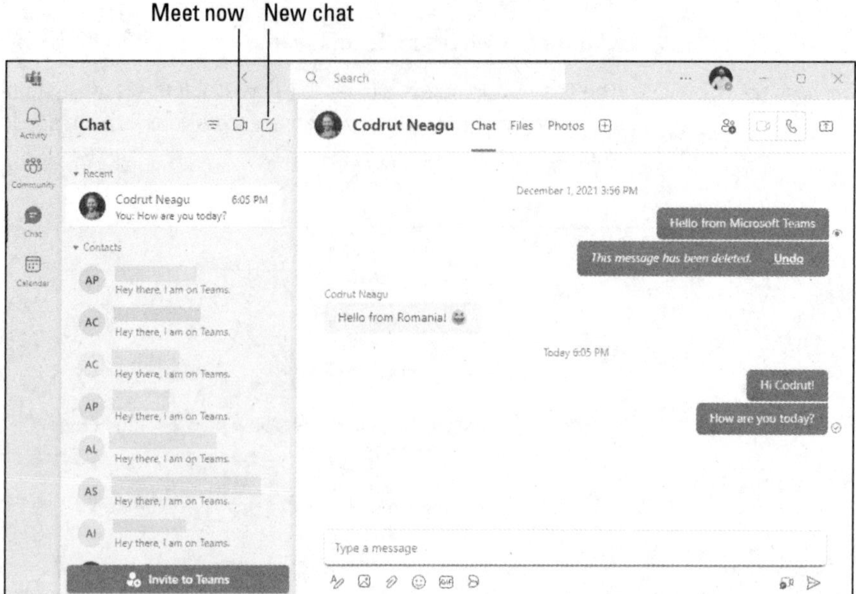

FIGURE 2-2: Chatting on Microsoft Teams.

4. **Click or tap the new chat icon (pen and paper) above the contacts list. Alternatively, you can press Ctrl+N.**
5. **In the To field at the top, type the name, email, or phone number of the person you want to find on Teams.**

   As you type, Microsoft Teams searches for people, and it may provide you with suggestions.
6. **Choose the person you want to chat with from the list.**

   You can repeat Steps 5 and 6 to add more people to the chat, creating a group chat.
7. **In the Type a Message field at the bottom of the chat window, type your message and then click or tap the send arrow in the lower-right corner or press Enter.**

   The message is sent to the people you contacted, and they receive a notification on their Microsoft Teams app, even if they are using it on a smartphone, tablet, or Mac instead of Windows.

TIP

You can start a chat also by selecting the person you want from the Contacts list on the left and simply typing your message on the right, in the Type a Message field. Once you start a conversation, don't hesitate to format your messages, attach files, or add emojis and animated GIFs. All these options are displayed as icons just below the Type a Message field.

Starting a meeting from Windows 11

Besides chat conversations on Microsoft Teams, you can quickly start a meeting. Before you do that, make sure you have a webcam installed and working. Then, start Microsoft Teams as shown in the preceding section, and follow these steps:

1. **In the Microsoft Teams app window, click or tap the Chat icon on the left.**

   You see your list of contacts, with recent conversations at the top.

2. **Click or tap the meet now icon (labeled in Figure 2-2).**

   The Start a Meeting Now dialog appears, similar to the one in Figure 2-3.

3. **Enter a new meeting name or leave the default one, and then click or tap Get a Link to Share, followed by Start Meeting.**

   The meeting link is copied to the clipboard, and you can share it with others after you start the meeting. You're also given the option to share it via email.

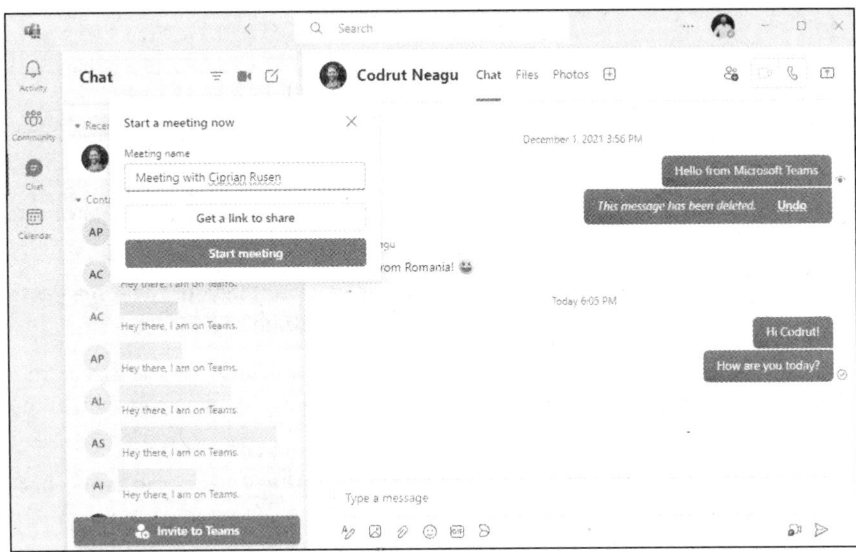

FIGURE 2-3: Starting a meeting in Microsoft Teams.

4. **Click or tap Start Meeting one more time.**

   If this is the first time you're starting a meeting, Microsoft Teams asks for your permission to access the microphone.

5. **Give Microsoft Teams the necessary permissions to start the meeting.**

   The meeting has started, but there's only one participant: you! Microsoft Teams shows you several options to invite people to join you, as shown in Figure 2-4.

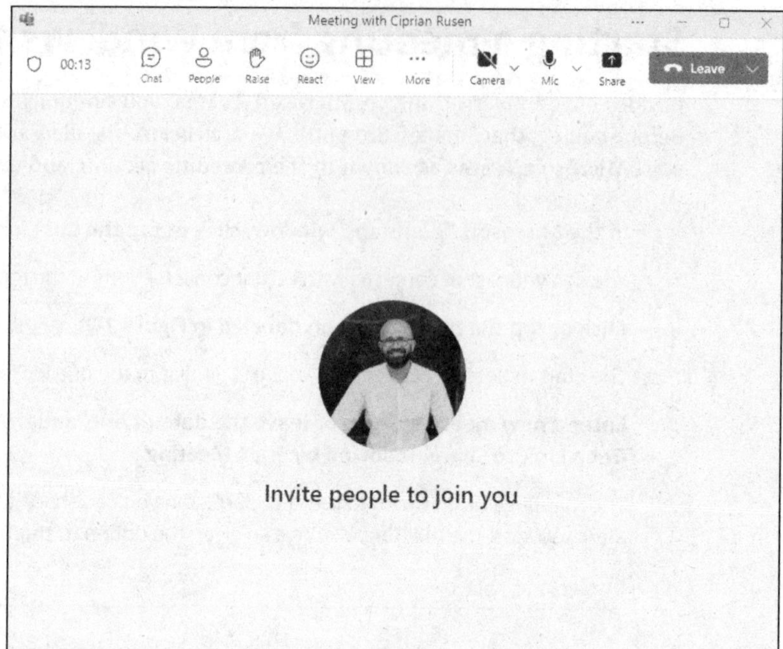

FIGURE 2-4: Teams presents easy-to-use options for handling your meeting.

6. **Make sure the Mic icon is enabled, so that others can hear you. If you want to be seen, do the same with the Camera icon.**
7. **Click or tap the Microsoft Teams icon on the taskbar and select its Chat window.**
8. **Find and select the people you want in your meeting, paste the link in the appropriate chat, and wait for them to join.**

   You can also paste the meeting link in an email message or the chat window of a different app. You can start talking with people as soon as they enter the meeting.
9. **When you want to exit the meeting, click or tap Leave, in the top right.**

Working Remotely with Windows 11

In this section, I start with how to enable Remote Desktop and use it to connect remotely to another computer. This discussion ties in with Book 9, Chapter 3, where I discuss VPN. You may have to use VPN to connect to your company's network, and then use Remote Desktop to connect to a computer in your company's office. If that's the case, this section has you covered.

Enabling remote desktop connections

Remote Desktop connections allow Windows devices to connect to one another through the internet or your local network. When you connect remotely to another Windows PC, you see that computer's desktop. You can also access its apps, files, and folders as if you were sitting in front of its screen. This feature is useful for IT professionals and business users who must work remotely.

WARNING

This procedure works only on Windows 11 Pro or Enterprise editions. If you run another edition, such as Windows 11 Home, you can't enable this feature. In Windows 11 Home, if you open the Remote Desktop section in the Settings app, you see a message stating that *Your Home edition of Windows 11 doesn't support Remote Desktop.*

If you want to use another PC to connect remotely to your own Windows 11 PC or want to let others connect to it, you must enable Remote Desktop. Here's how:

1. **Click or tap the Start icon and then Settings.**

   The Settings app opens.

2. **Choose the System category on the left, and then click or tap Remote Desktop on the right.**

   You see the Remote Desktop settings, as shown in Figure 2-5.

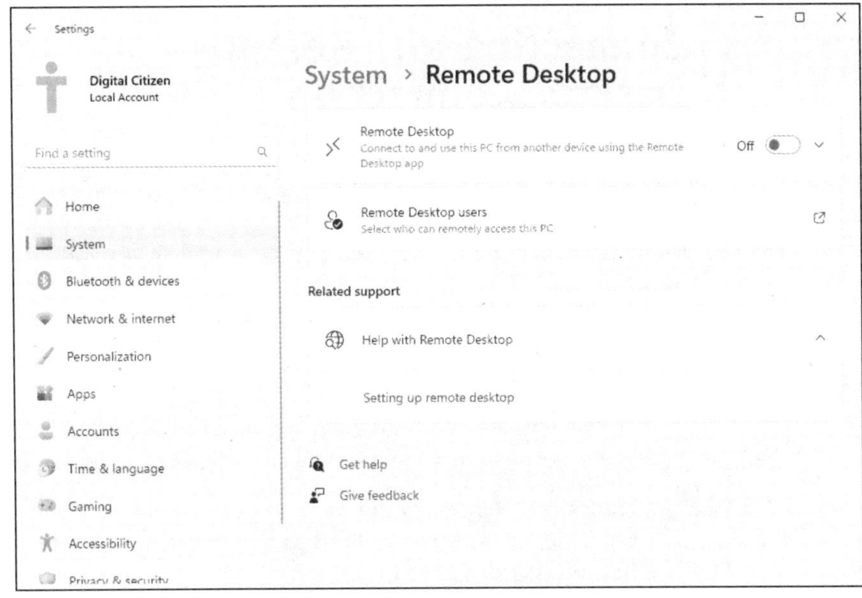

FIGURE 2-5: Enabling Remote Desktop in Windows 11.

3. **Click or tap the switch to enable Remote Desktop and then confirm your choice.**

   You or others can now connect remotely to your PC. Under the Remote Desktop switch, you see the PC name that you can use to connect remotely from another device. Keep in mind, however, that you've enabled Remote Desktop only for the user account you're using.

4. **If you have other user accounts for which you want to allow Remote Desktop connections:**

   a. **Click or tap Remote Desktop Users.** The Remote Desktop Users window is shown.

   b. **Click or tap Add, type the name of the user account you want added, and click or tap Check Names.** If the correct username is found, you see it underlined.

   c. **Click or tap OK twice.** The user account you've selected is added to the list of accounts that can remotely access your PC.

5. **Close Settings.**

REMEMBER

Don't forget that you turn on Remote Desktop to let other computers connect remotely to yours. You don't need to enable Remote Desktop if you want to connect from your computer to another. However, the PC you're connecting to must have Remote Desktop enabled for the remote connection to work.

Connecting with Remote Desktop Connection

If Remote Desktop is enabled on the PC that you want to connect to and you know the IP address and the credentials for a user account that exists on that computer, you can connect to it from your Windows 11 PC by using the built-in Remote Desktop Connection app. Here's how to establish a remote desktop connection from Windows 11:

1. **Click or tap inside the Search box on the taskbar, type** remote**, and select the Remote Desktop Connection result.**

   The Remote Desktop Connection app opens, asking you to enter the address of the computer that you want to connect to, as shown in Figure 2-6.

2. **Enter the IP address of the computer you want to connect to and click or tap Connect. If the computer is part of the same network, you can type its name instead of its IP address.**

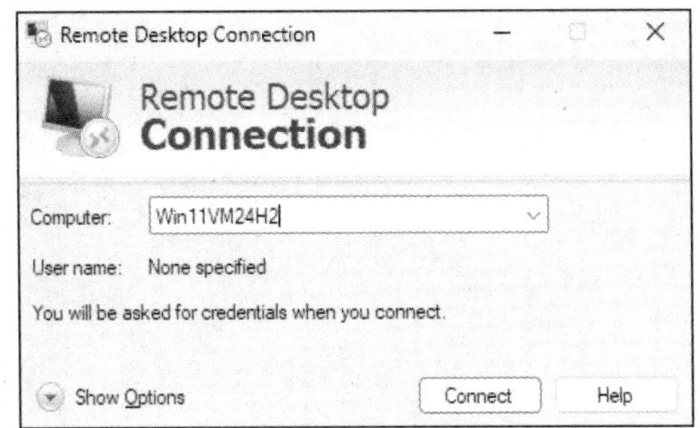

FIGURE 2-6: The Remote Desktop Connection app allows you to connect to other computers.

Remote Desktop Connection may take some time to establish the connection, after which it asks for the username and password to use to connect to that PC.

3. **Enter the details of the user account to use to connect to the remote PC, and then click or tap OK.**

   If you plan to connect frequently to the remote PC, you may want to select the Remember Me box so that your connection details are saved and automatically used each time you log in.

4. **If you see a warning message that problems exist with the security certificate of the PC you want to connect to, click or tap Yes to continue.**

   When the connection is established, you'll see the desktop of the remote PC as if it were your own. A toolbar at the top allows you to manage your connection, as shown in Figure 2-7.

5. **When you've finished working on the remote PC, click or tap X in the toolbar at the top of the screen.**

TIP

Feel free to adjust how the Remote Desktop connection functions by clicking or tapping on Show Options (refer to Figure 2-6) and adjusting the available settings. For example, you can save your username to avoid having to input it every time, choose whether you want to access the printers connected to the local computer, select if you want to share clipboard contents between the local and remote session, and decide how you want remote audio to be handled.

TECHNICAL STUFF

I've learned that it's impossible to establish Remote Desktop connections when two PCs are logged into the same Microsoft account at the same time. To create these connections, you must log in with different Microsoft accounts. A great solution is to log in with a Microsoft account on one PC and log in with a local account on another PC.

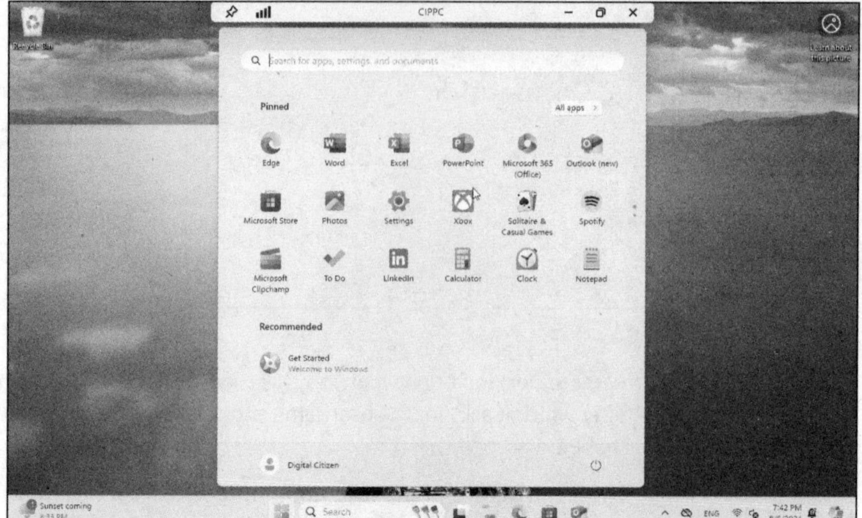

FIGURE 2-7: You see the desktop of the remote computer and can use it as your own.

Adding Clocks to the Taskbar

If you work with a team from a multinational corporation, it's a good idea to set Windows 11 to display not only the clock from your time zone but also the clock from the time zone of your colleagues. That way, you can quickly check the time in the country of your team members to ensure that you don't send them links to join your Microsoft Teams meetings outside their working hours.

Here's how it works:

1. **Right-click or press and hold the clock in the bottom-right corner of the screen.**

   A contextual menu appears with a few options.

2. **Choose Adjust Date and Time.**

   The Settings app opens, displaying options about adjusting the date and time, as shown in Figure 2-8.

3. **On the right, scroll down to Related Links and click or tap Additional Clocks.**

   The Date and Time dialog box appears, as shown in Figure 2-9.

4. **Select the Show Clock 1 box, choose a time zone from the list, and enter the name of the city, region, or country that interests you.**
5. **Select the Show Clock 2 box, choose another time zone from the list, and enter the name of the city, region, or country that interests you.**
6. **Click or tap OK.**

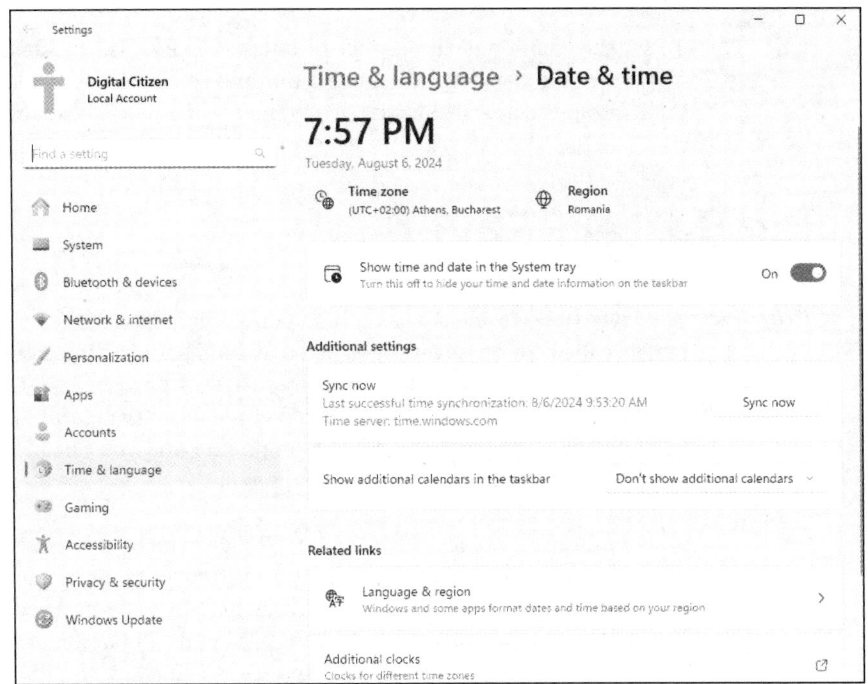

FIGURE 2-8: The Date and Time settings page.

Date and Time

Date and Time | Additional Clocks | Internet Time

Additional clocks can display the time in other time zones. You can view them by clicking on or hovering over the taskbar clock.

Show clock 1

Select time zone for clock 1:

(UTC-07:00) Arizona

Enter display name for clock 1:

Arizona

Show clock 2

Select time zone for clock 2:

(UTC+09:00) Osaka, Sapporo, Tokyo

Enter display name for clock 2:

Japan

OK | Cancel | Apply

FIGURE 2-9: The Date and Time dialog box where you add clocks to the taskbar.

TIP

To see the additional clocks, click or tap the clock on the taskbar. They appear just above the calendar. If the calendar is minimized, you see only the additional clocks. Click or tap the upward-facing arrow next to the date to expand the calendar.

Using Battery Saver

Windows 11 24H2 introduces a new power management feature for laptops and tablets called energy saver. Designed to extend battery life and reduce energy consumption, energy saver automatically manages power usage to achieve an optimal balance between performance and efficiency. This feature is especially useful when you're working remotely for long hours and you need to squeeze as much battery as possible from your work laptop.

When energy saver is active, some Windows features operate differently. For example, users can't change the power mode in Settings, and the display brightness is reduced by 30 percent. Transparency effects are disabled, and some Microsoft apps, such as OneNote, OneDrive, and Phone Link, may not synchronize. Background apps are blocked, but users can allow specific apps to run. Noncritical Windows updates are prevented from downloading, and most telemetry is blocked except for critical data. Task Scheduler tasks trigger only if they meet certain conditions: They must not be set to start only if the computer is idle, must not be set to run during automatic maintenance, and must be set to run only when the user is logged on. All other tasks are delayed until energy saver mode is turned off.

You can enable energy saver in several ways, but the fastest is from Quick Settings (read Book 2, Chapter 3). Simply click or tap the battery icon on the bottom-left side of the screen, followed by the Energy Saver button, as shown in Figure 2-10. Note how the battery icon changes to include a leaf, signaling that energy saver is turned on.

If your laptop or tablet runs out of battery and you plug it in, energy saver doesn't get disabled. You must do that manually, going through the same steps used for enabling it.

TIP

If you're browsing the web a lot and want to maximize battery life, the web browser you use matters a lot. To understand how much, my team at Digital Citizen has run several interesting benchmarks that revealed Microsoft Edge as the most energy-efficient browser. On our test laptops, it delivered an additional 60 to 70 minutes of battery life compared to Google Chrome. You can find more details about our tests at `https://bit.ly/3AZjxtD`.

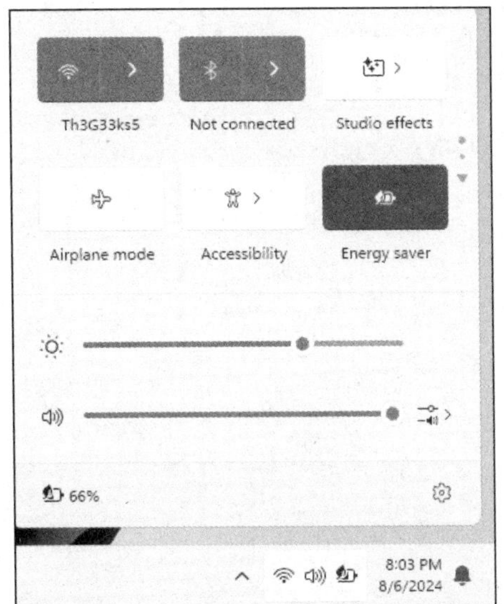

FIGURE 2-10: Enabling Energy Saver from Quick Settings.

Changing the power mode

By default, Windows 11 uses a balanced power mode, which tries to provide good performance without sacrificing too much battery life. However, you can change the power mode to deliver more performance or more power efficiency, depending on your needs, like this:

1. **Click or tap the Start icon and then Settings.**

   The Settings app opens.

2. **Choose the System category on the left, and then click or tap Power & Battery on the right.**

   You see the configuration options shown in Figure 2-11.

3. **Click or tap the drop-down list next to Power Mode and choose the mode you want: Best Power Efficiency, Balanced, or Best Performance.**

   Windows 11 applies the selected power mode.

4. **Close the Settings window.**

TIP

If you can't change the power mode and you see a message saying, "Power mode cannot be set when energy saver is on," first disable energy saver and then try again.

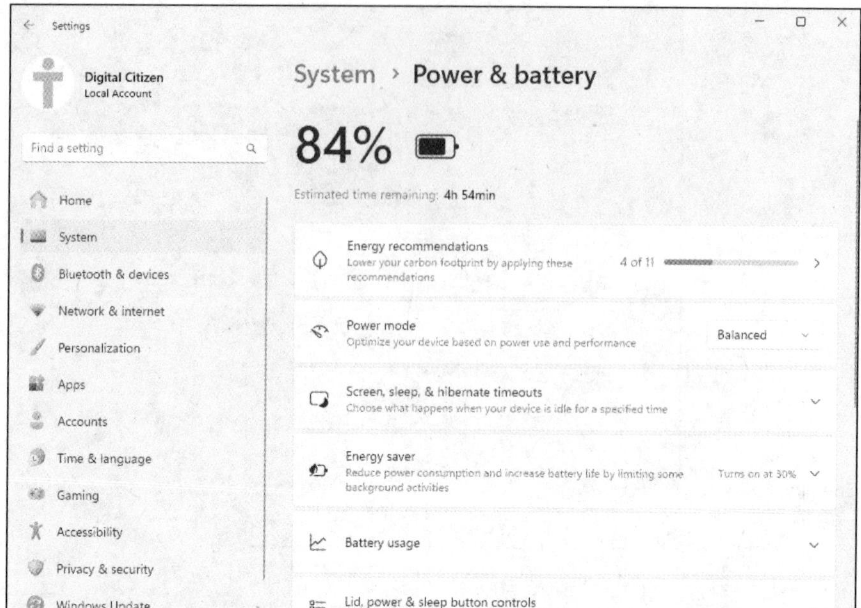

FIGURE 2-11: Setting the Power & Battery options.

Lowering the carbon footprint

How you set up your Windows 11 device can significantly affect its power consumption, its battery life, and the carbon emissions associated with electricity generation. That's why Microsoft has decided to include energy recommendations in Windows 11. Think of this feature as the dashboard for all the settings that matter regarding power use. The recommendations you get depend on your device type and whether the device is plugged in. It's like having a power-saving guru built into your computer, making it easy to lower your energy use without hunting through endless menus and settings. Give it a try and see how it works:

1. **Click or tap the Start icon, followed by Settings.**

   The Settings app opens.

2. **Choose System and then Power & Battery.**

   You see the configuration options (refer to Figure 2-11).

3. **Click or tap Energy Recommendations at the top.**

   You see a list of energy recommendations relevant to your device, similar to the ones in Figure 2-12. Remember that the recommendations you get may be different from those shown on my Windows 11 device.

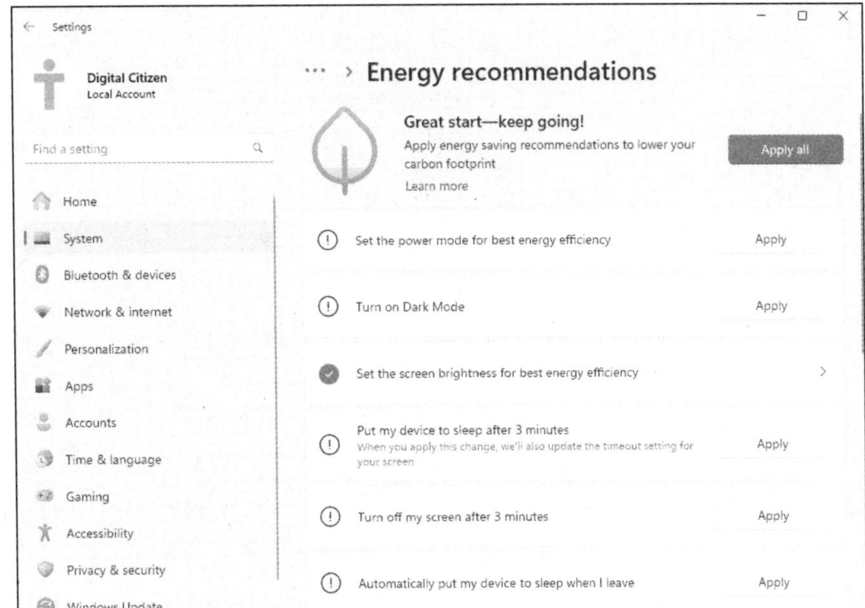

FIGURE 2-12: Following the energy recommendations increases battery life.

4. **Scroll through all the recommendations and click or tap Apply next to those you want to enable.**

   For each recommendation you follow, its Apply button is replaced by a green check mark.

5. **When you're done, close the Settings window.**

Enjoy the increased battery life of your Windows 11 laptop or tablet and lowering your carbon footprint.

7
Controlling Your System

Contents at a Glance

IN THIS CHAPTER

» Checking out the Settings app

» Finding what's left in the Control Panel

» Putting shortcuts to settings on your desktop

» Trying out God mode

» Adding and switching between languages in Windows 11

Chapter 1

Navigating Windows Settings and Languages

Windows 11 has more settings than previous versions, and that's to be expected since it has even more features than Windows 10 or Windows 8. Most settings are found in the new Settings app, which is well-organized and surprisingly easy to navigate, including on devices with touchscreens.

However, the old Control Panel still controls some aspects of how a Windows 11 PC works, although more settings are migrated from the Control Panel to the Settings app with each new major update to Windows 11. While the Settings app controls several hundred settings, the Control Panel has a smaller yet still large enough number of Windows settings. There's an overlap between the two, but some settings can be changed only in the Settings app, and other settings can be changed only in the old-fashioned Control Panel.

This chapter covers both the Settings app and the classic Control Panel. The Settings app is generally sufficient, but mastering both tools is essential for those who want to take full control of their Windows 11 machine.

For convenience, you may want to create shortcuts on your desktop to frequently used settings. In this chapter, I have some tips on how to do just that, quickly. There's also the world-famous God mode, which still works in Windows 11, and I haven't forgotten about it. You may want to try that too.

Lastly, many users need to use Windows in two or more languages. To help them out, I share how to install new languages in Windows 11 and how to switch between them, including when typing in multiple languages.

Understanding the Settings App

The Windows 11 Settings app, shown in Figure 1-1, has a remarkable collection of settings arranged in a way that's infinitely more accessible than the old-fashioned desktop Control Panel. To make it even more appealing, it's designed to work great not just on a computer with a mouse and keyboard but also on devices with a touchscreen.

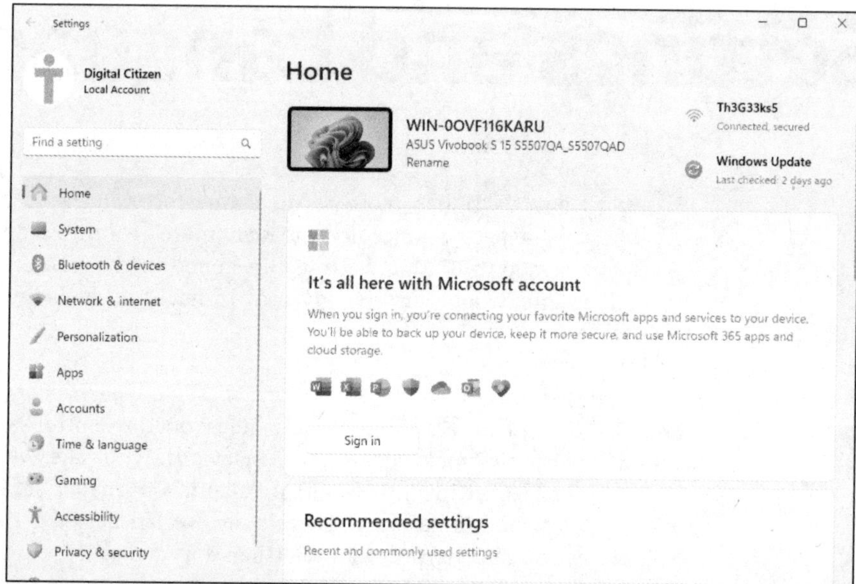

FIGURE 1-1: The Settings app is where you configure most things about Windows 11.

In 2023, Microsoft added a Home page to the Settings app, which, in theory, should be a place for you to find recommended settings based on your previous usage, as well as shortcuts to commonly used features such as Windows Update.

Unfortunately, Microsoft also decided to make the Home page a place for promoting its services. Therefore, if you sign in to Windows 11 using a local account, you are strongly encouraged to switch to a Microsoft account instead and to buy a Microsoft 365 subscription. If you do get such a subscription, the Home page of the Settings app becomes a place where you can manage both this subscription and your OneDrive cloud storage space. Because of this design choice, the Home page offers little value to users who aren't using Microsoft's services. Annoying, isn't it?

But enough complaining; click or tap the Start icon and then Settings; alternatively, press Windows+I. Either way, you'll see all Windows 11 settings organized by categories, as follows:

- **System:** This category includes settings for changing the display and sound settings, controlling notifications, focus sessions, managing the battery and storage, configuring nearby sharing, and many other things.
- **Bluetooth & Devices:** From here, you can control printers, scanners, cameras, and other connected devices, as well as turn Bluetooth on and off, change mouse settings, manipulate the pen, and specify what AutoPlay program should kick in when you insert a USB drive or memory card. You can also link your Android smartphone or iPhone with Phone Link (read Book 10, Chapters 1 and 2 to learn more).
- **Network & Internet:** This category lets you turn Wi-Fi off and on, adjust your Wi-Fi settings, and manage Ethernet (wired) network connections. You can also go into airplane mode, set up a VPN, work with a dial-up connection, and manually set a *proxy* (an intermediary server that acts as a gateway between your computer and the internet), as well as transform your Windows 11 laptop or tablet into a mobile hotspot.
- **Personalization:** This category includes settings for your desktop wallpaper, adding a new Windows 11 theme, choosing accent colors, choosing a picture for your lock screen, and controlling the Start menu, the taskbar, the touch keyboard, and installed fonts. Gamers will also appreciate the Dynamic Lighting feature found here, which allows them to control the RGB lighting on their accessories.
- **Apps:** Want to remove an app? Here's where you do it. You can also set default apps (for opening pictures and videos, for example), download offline maps, and set the websites that can open in an app instead of a browser (like on Android). Finally, you also get access to settings involving video playback and which apps run at Windows startup.
- **Accounts:** Disconnect a Microsoft account, set your account picture, and change information about your Microsoft account. Options enable you to add a new standard user, change your password and the way you sign in, and

switch between a Microsoft account and a local account. You can also set your Windows backup and sync settings through OneDrive and your Microsoft account. There are also options for adding other accounts (like children, work, or school accounts).

- **Time & Language:** Set your time zone, manually change the date and time, set date and time formats, add keyboards in different languages, add new display languages, control how Windows 11 uses speech and spoken languages, set up your microphone for speech recognition, or change the way the touch keyboard works (if your machine has a touchscreen).
- **Gaming:** Work with game mode and the game bar, as well as other gaming-related features. The Gaming category is your link to the Xbox-friendly part of your Windows 11 PC.
- **Accessibility:** Microsoft has long had commendable aids for people who need help seeing, hearing, or working with Windows. All the settings are here, and there are surprisingly many. Read Book 2, Chapter 8 for more details.
- **Privacy & Security:** This section includes an overwhelming list of options. First, this is where you access Windows Security. You can also set the Find My Device feature (useful for laptops and tablets that may be stolen or lost) and access settings for web developers creating Windows 11 apps. Then there's the Windows permissions part, where you can turn off broadcasting of your advertising ID, maintained by Microsoft to identify you. Search settings are buried in here too. You can control how Search works, whether web results are filtered, and how indexing works, so that you get the search results you want. Next, you can turn on and off location tracking, and keep your webcam and microphone locked up. You can also control what apps get access to different features and personal data, including giving Windows 11 permission to send your full computer diagnostics data to Microsoft. Privacy is a huge deal, and I discuss it in more detail in Book 2, Chapter 7.
- **Windows Update:** Control how Windows 11 updates itself, when it installs updates, when it reboots to install updates, and more.

Overall, Settings is a well-thought-out app for managing Windows 11. Navigating it is as easy as a click or tap on the sections on the left, followed by clicks or taps on the right side of the app, depending on where you want to go.

Using Search to quickly find settings

Even though the Settings app is well organized, no one can know where every setting is located, unless they were on the development team that created Windows 11. To help you find the settings you're interested in, the Settings app has a search feature of its own. Here's how it works:

1. **Click or tap the Start icon and then Settings. Or press Windows+I.**

   The Settings app opens to the Home page.

2. **In the Find a Setting Search box, in the top left of Settings, type** clipboard.

   Note how the Settings app displays several search results with links to clipboard-related settings, as shown in Figure 1-2.

3. **Click or tap the Clipboard Settings search result.**

   The Settings app takes you directly to its clipboard settings.

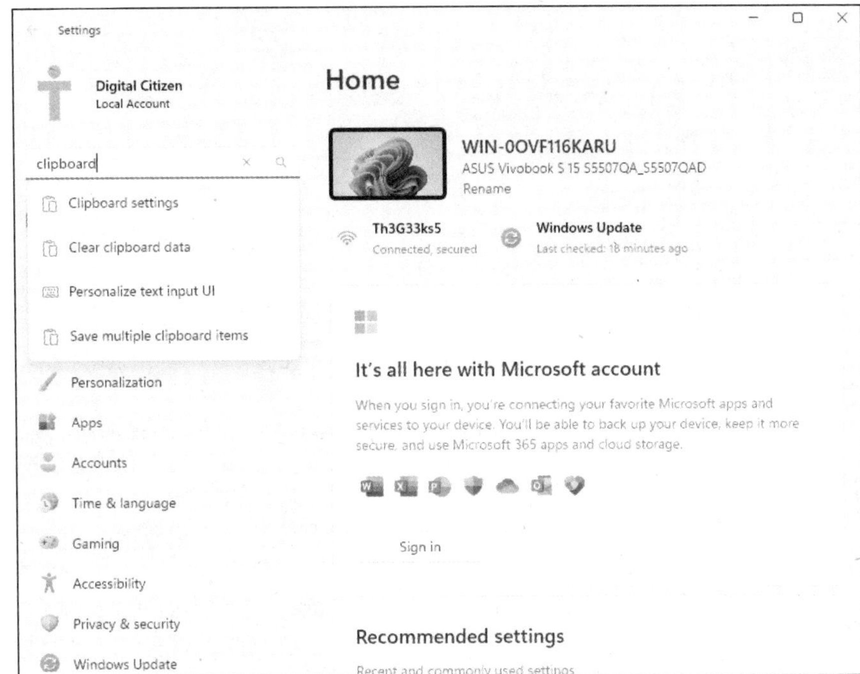

FIGURE 1-2: Don't hesitate to use search in Settings.

REMEMBER

Use the same process to find any setting that interests you, from Bluetooth and battery settings to fonts or any other setting.

Exploring the Control Panel

The inner workings of Windows 11 also reveal themselves in the Control Panel but less than they used to in previous versions of Windows. That's because the Control Panel is in the process of being phased out and replaced by Settings, and with each new version of Windows, the Control Panel gets shrunk a bit more.

You can find the Control Panel also by clicking or tapping the Search box on the taskbar and typing **Control**. Then choose Control Panel in the list of results to open the Control Panel window, as shown in Figure 1-3.

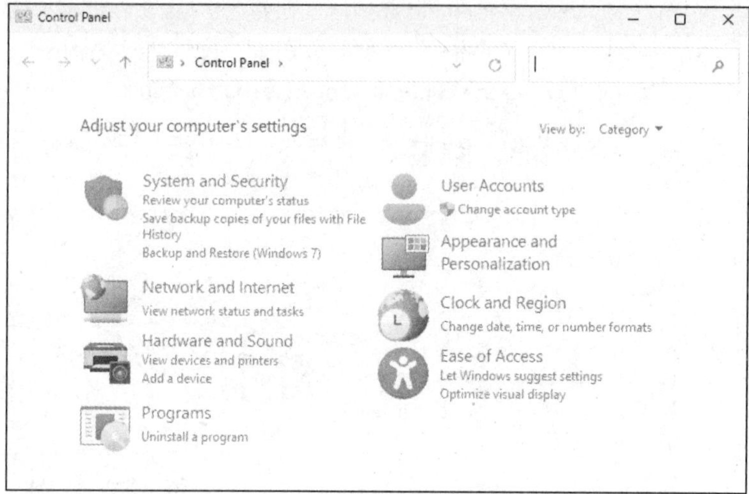

FIGURE 1-3: You may still need to use the Control Panel.

Here's an overview of the main categories of the Control Panel:

- **System and Security:** This category includes an array of tools for trouble-shooting and adjusting your PC. Check out Windows Defender Firewall and its settings, change power options, retrieve files with File History, manage BitLocker Drive Encryption, and rifle through miscellaneous administrative tools. This part of the Control Panel is the most consistent and useful of all.
- **Network and Internet:** Configure network sharing settings. Set up internet connections, particularly if you have a cable modem or digital subscriber line (DSL) service.
- **Hardware and Sound:** Add or remove printers and connect to other printers on your network. Troubleshoot printers, configure sound devices, and adjust the power settings for your laptop or tablet.
- **Programs:** Add and remove specific Windows features and uninstall programs (desktop apps only). Change the association between filename extensions and the programs that run them. Most of the functionality here is available in the Settings app, but a few laggards are still in the old Control Panel.
- **User Accounts:** This group is a limited selection of actions that Microsoft hasn't yet moved to the Settings app. Here, you can change your account type or remove user accounts. I expect this section to disappear from the Control Panel soon after this book is published.

- **Appearance and Personalization:** Font management is in this section even though it exists in the Settings app too. You also get access to the Ease of Access Center and to File Explorer options.
- **Clock and Region (and Language):** Set the time and date, your region, or tell Windows to synchronize the clock automatically. You can also change how dates, times, currency, and numbers appear.
- **Ease of Access:** Change accessibility settings to help you see the screen and better use the keyboard or mouse. You also set up speech recognition here. Most of the settings from this section have been moved to the Settings app, and many of them have received improvements compared to their Control Panel–based counterparts. That's why I recommend using the Settings app to change accessibility settings.

If you want to change a Windows 11 setting, try the Control Panel, but don't be discouraged if you can't find what you're looking for. The Settings app is growing into a better alternative each year.

TIP

The Control Panel also has a Search box in the top-right corner of its window, and it works in a similar fashion to the one found in the Settings app.

Putting Shortcuts to Settings on Your Desktop

Want to see the Windows Update settings by simply clicking or tapping a shortcut on the desktop? Change the Windows theme with two clicks? Set which apps can access your webcam? Manage your Wi-Fi settings? It's easy! Here's how:

1. **Right-click (or press and hold) any blank space on the desktop and then choose New ⇨ Shortcut.**

   You see the New Shortcut wizard.

2. **Choose one of the ms-settings apps listed in Table 1-1 and type it in the input box.**

   For example, as shown in Figure 1-4, to go to Windows Update, type **ms-settings:windowsupdate** in the box marked Type the Location of the Item.

3. **Click or tap Next, give the shortcut a name, and then click or tap Finish.**

   A new shortcut appears on your desktop. Double-click or double-tap it, and the Settings app appears, taking you to Windows Update.

TABLE 1-1 **Shortcuts to Settings App Panels**

Settings App Page	Command
Access Work or School	ms-settings:workplace
Account Info	ms-settings:privacy-accountinfo
Activation (System)	ms-settings:activation
Airplane Mode	ms-settings:network-airplanemode
Background (Personalization)	ms-settings:personalization-background
Calendar (Privacy & Security)	ms-settings:privacy-calendar
Camera (Privacy & Security)	ms-settings:privacy-webcam
Captions (Accessibility)	ms-settings:easeofaccess-closedcaptioning
Clipboard	ms-settings:clipboard
Colors (Personalization)	ms-settings:colors
Contacts (Privacy & Security)	ms-settings:privacy-contacts
Contrast Themes	ms-settings:easeofaccess-highcontrast
Date & Time	ms-settings:dateandtime
Delivery Optimization (Windows Update)	ms-settings:delivery-optimization
Devices (Bluetooth & Devices)	ms-settings:connecteddevices
Diagnostics & Feedback	ms-settings:privacy-feedback
Dial-up	ms-settings:network-dialup
Display	ms-settings:display
Ethernet	ms-settings:network-ethernet
Other Users (Accounts)	ms-settings:otherusers
For Developers	ms-settings:developers
Game Mode	ms-settings:gaming-gamemode
Inking & Typing Personalization	ms-settings:privacy-speechtyping
Keyboard (Accessibility)	ms-settings:easeofaccess-keyboard
Language & Region	ms-settings:regionlanguage
Location (Privacy & Security)	ms-settings:privacy-location

Settings App Page	Command
Lock screen (Personalization)	ms-settings:lockscreen
Magnifier	ms-settings:easeofaccess-magnifier
Manage Known Networks (Wi-Fi)	ms-settings:network-wifisettings
Microphone (Privacy & Security)	ms-settings:privacy-microphone
Mobile Hotspot	ms-settings:network-mobilehotspot
Mouse	ms-settings:mousetouchpad
Mouse (Accessibility)	ms-settings:easeofaccess-mouse
Narrator	ms-settings:easeofaccess-narrator
Night Light	ms-settings:nightlight
Notifications	ms-settings:notifications
Offline Maps	ms-settings:maps
Optional Features	ms-settings:optionalfeatures
Personalization	ms-settings:personalization
Power & Battery	ms-settings:batterysaver
Privacy & Security	ms-settings:privacy
Proxy	ms-settings:network-proxy
Sign-in Options	ms-settings:signinoptions
Speech	ms-settings:speech
Start (Personalization)	ms-settings:personalization-start
Storage	ms-settings:storagesense
Themes (Personalization)	ms-settings:themes
Typing	ms-settings:typing
VPN	ms-settings:network-vpn
Wi-Fi	ms-settings:network-wifi
Windows Update	ms-settings:windowsupdate

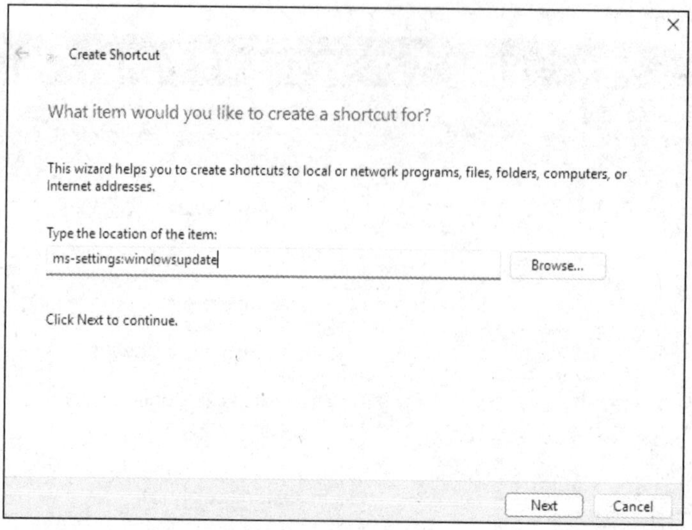

FIGURE 1-4: Create a shortcut to the Windows Update page in the Settings app.

God Mode (Still) Works in Windows 11

The Windows Vista–era power user trick named *God mode* is alive and well in Windows 11. I, for one, was quite surprised to see that God mode made the transition to Windows 11 because it's based on hooks into the Control Panel — and the Control Panel is being slowly retired. However, a significant difference exists between the God mode from the days of Windows 7, which included 278 settings, and the God Mode on my Copilot+ PC with Windows 11, which includes "just" 198. I expect the trend to continue as Microsoft moves over more settings from the Control Panel to the Settings app.

The parts of God mode that appear in Windows 11 are slightly different from the elements in Windows 10 (which, in turn, is slightly different from Windows 8.1 and Windows 7). But the overall effect is the same.

Follow these steps to access God mode on your Windows 11 desktop:

1. **Right-click (or press and hold) any empty spot on the desktop, and then choose New ➪ Folder.**

   A new folder appears on your desktop, ready for you to type a name.

2. **Give the folder the following name, and then press Enter:**

   GodMode.{ED7BA470-8E54-465E-825C-99712043E01C}

   The name you just entered is going to disappear.

TIP

The God Mode folder can be renamed to anything you want after you first create it.

3. **Double-click or double-tap the folder to display the list you see in Figure 1-5.**

   It's a massive list of direct links to all sorts of settings. Most of them work.

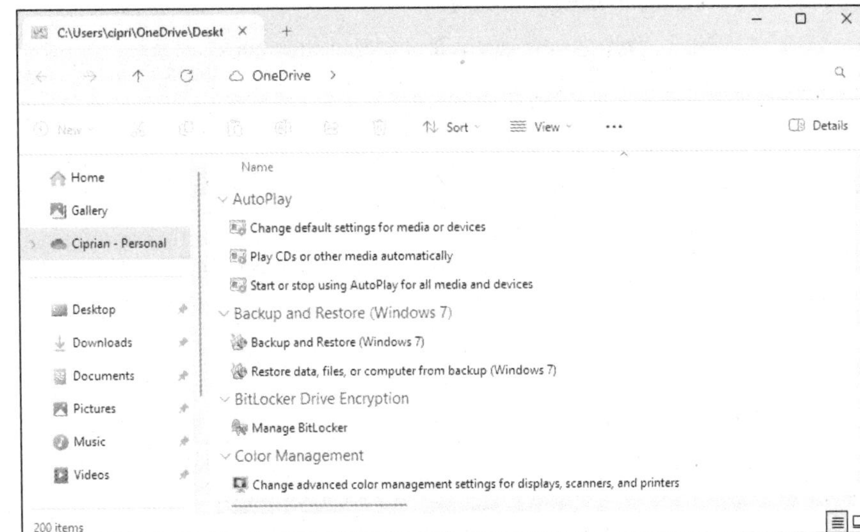

FIGURE 1-5: God mode is a massive collection of shortcuts to all sorts of Windows settings, many of which are obscure.

Some of these links may be useful. For example, the AutoPlay option, when accessed through God mode, brings up the old Windows 7–style AutoPlay dialog box, which is more advanced than the Windows 11 Settings version of AutoPlay (click or tap the Start icon, followed by Settings, Bluetooth & Devices, and then AutoPlay).

Adding Languages to Windows 11

According to the Journal of Neurolinguistics, 43 percent of the world's population is bilingual, meaning that almost half of all people utilize two languages on a regular basis, while 17 percent is multilingual, using three or more languages regularly. Therefore, it's not surprising that many people need to type in more than one language. Windows 11 excels in this area by offering 47 language interface packs (LIPs). This generous list includes popular languages such as Spanish, Arabic, and French, as well as less commonly used languages such as Georgian, Lithuanian, and Icelandic.

If you want to install a new language, Windows 11 makes the process easy. Here is how it works:

1. **Click or tap the Start icon and then Settings.**

   You see the Settings app.

2. **On the left, click or tap Time & Language. On the right, click or tap Language & Region.**

   You see the languages installed on Windows 11, as shown in Figure 1-6.

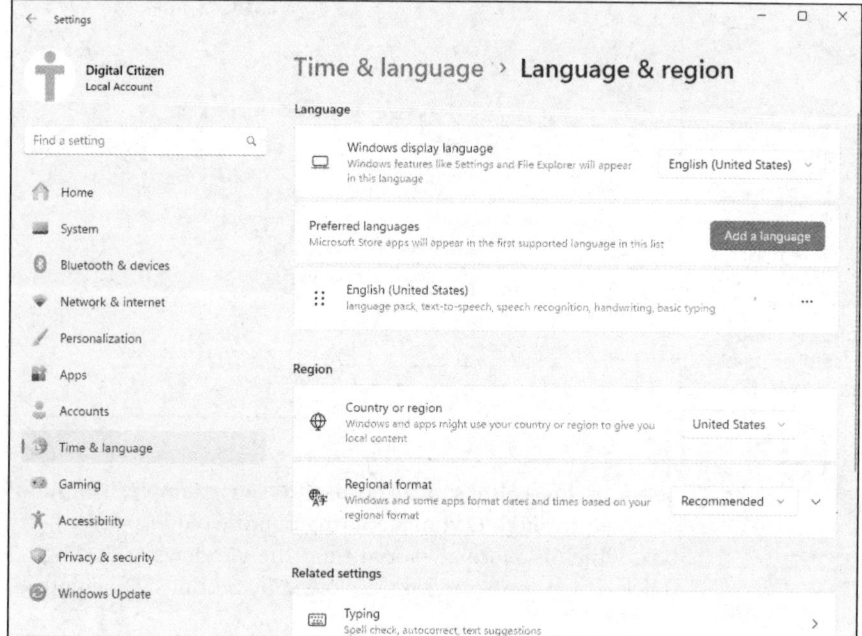

FIGURE 1-6: Here you set your language and region.

3. **Click or tap the Add a Language button next to Preferred Languages.**

   A surprisingly long list of all the available languages is displayed. Scrolling the list takes a long time, so you may want to use the Search box at the top of the language list, like I did in Figure 1-7.

4. **Find and select the language you want to install, and then click or tap Next.**

   You are shown several settings for the language, as shown in Figure 1-8. The language will be installed as both a display language and a keyboard language.

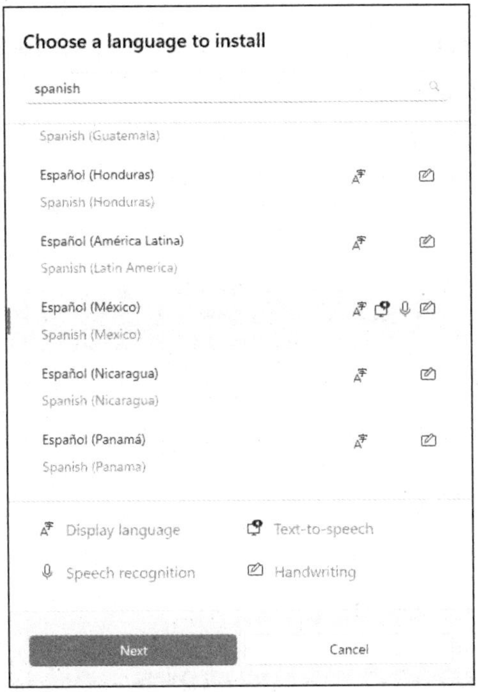

FIGURE 1-7: Choose a new language to install.

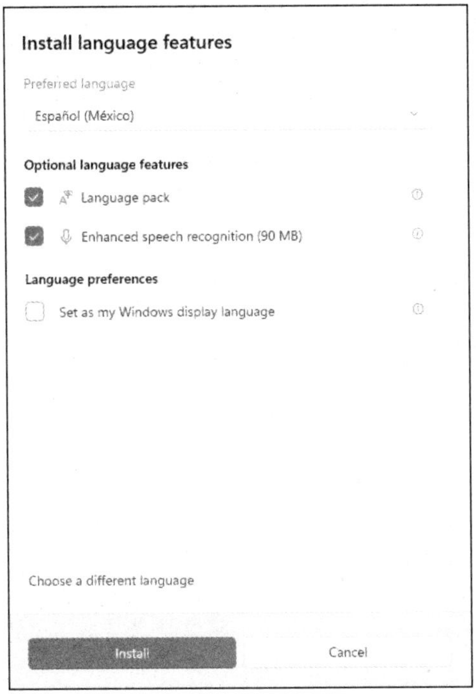

FIGURE 1-8: The settings available when installing a new language.

5. **(Optional) Select the Set as My Windows Display Language option.**
6. **Click or tap Install.**

   Windows 11 displays a progress bar, so you see how much time remains before it finishes downloading the new language and its features. When the process is over, the progress bar disappears, and you see the new language in the list of available languages.
7. **Click or tap the Windows Display Language drop-down list, choose the new language, and then click or tap Sign Out.**

   Windows 11 signs you out, applies the new display language to your account, and the next time you sign in, you'll see the operating system in the language you just installed.

REMEMBER

Languages are applied per user account. Therefore, two user accounts can use different languages. If you install a new language for one user account, it won't show up on the other account. The other user will have to install it, using the same process.

Adding keyboard languages and layouts

Before you can type in a new language, you must install that language by using the instructions provided in the preceding section. Once the language is installed, you can add a different keyboard layout for it and switch to this layout whenever you need to type using the selected language. Here's how it works:

1. **Click or tap the Start icon and then Settings, or press Windows+I.**

   The Settings app opens.
2. **Click or tap Time & Language, followed by Language & Region.**

   You see the languages installed on Windows 11 (refer to Figure 1-6).
3. **Click or tap the more options icon (three dots) next to the language you're interested in configuring.**
4. **In the menu that opens, select Language Options.**

   You see the Options page shown in Figure 1-9.
5. **Scroll down to the Keyboards section and click or tap Add a Keyboard.**

   Windows displays a list of keyboard layouts, starting with those relevant to the selected language and continuing with all the other languages available for this operating system.

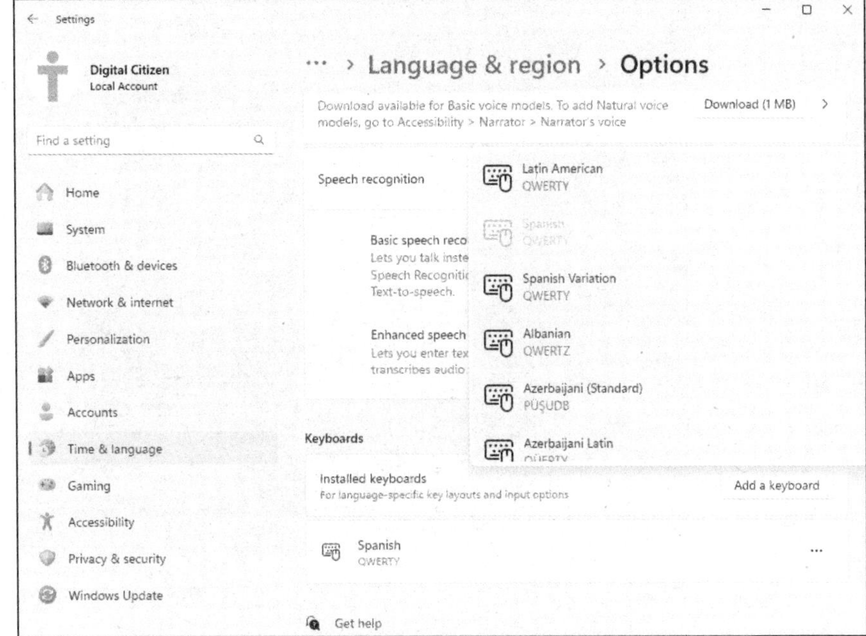

FIGURE 1-9: Adding a keyboard layout isn't complicated.

6. **Choose the keyboard layout you want from the list.**

   The selected keyboard layout is added to the Keyboards list.

7. **If you want to delete a keyboard layout, click or tap the three dots next to it and choose Remove.**

   The selected keyboard layout is immediately deleted; no confirmation is required.

8. **When you've finished adding and removing keyboard layouts, close Settings.**

Switching between languages

After you add keyboard languages and layouts, a new icon appears on the system tray area of the taskbar, next to the network and speaker icons. You see three letters representing the language you're using to type, as shown in Figure 1-10. If you click or tap these letters, you see a menu listing the languages you've installed for typing in Windows 11. Choose the language you want from the list, and start typing in the desired language, with the selected keyboard layout.

TIP

You can switch between keyboard languages and layouts by pressing and holding the Windows key, pressing the spacebar key, and then selecting the keyboard language or layout you want from the list.

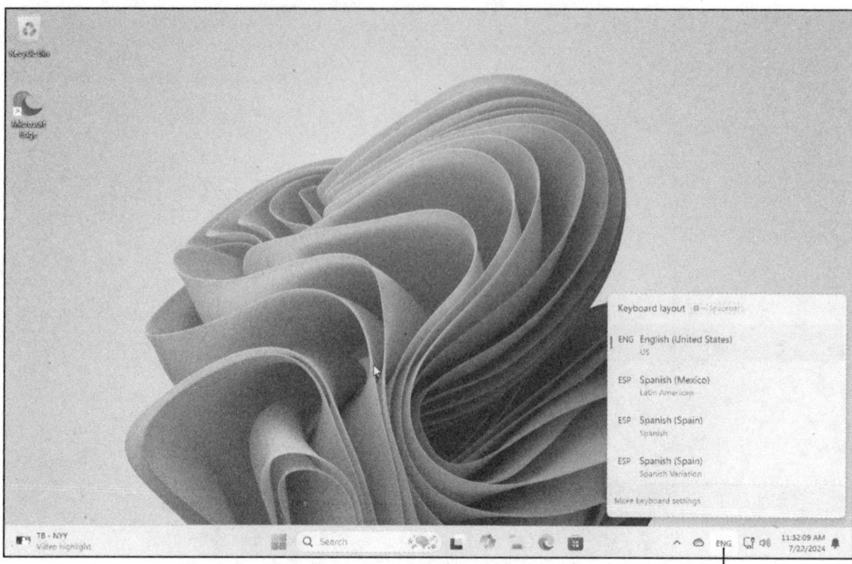

FIGURE 1-10: Switching the keyboard language and layout.

Another keyboard shortcut is left Alt+Shift. When you use it, it skips any additional keyboard layouts for the same language and switches directly to the first layout available for the next language.

Ctrl+Shift is another handy keyboard shortcut that toggles between the keyboard layouts available for the current language. This shortcut is effective only if you've added multiple keyboard layouts for the selected input language.

One problem is that these keyboard shortcuts for changing the active keyboard language and layout are not the same as the ones in older versions of Windows. For example, some experienced users have complained that they want the Ctrl+Shift shortcut to switch between all keyboard layouts and languages, not just the keyboard layouts for the current language. Luckily, you can change some of the shortcut keys (also called *hot keys*) used to switch between languages, like this:

1. **Click or tap the Start icon, followed by Settings. Or press Windows+I.**
2. **Click or tap Time & Language, followed by Typing.**
3. **On the Typing page, scroll down and click or tap Advanced Keyboard Settings.**

   You see the settings page shown in Figure 1-11.

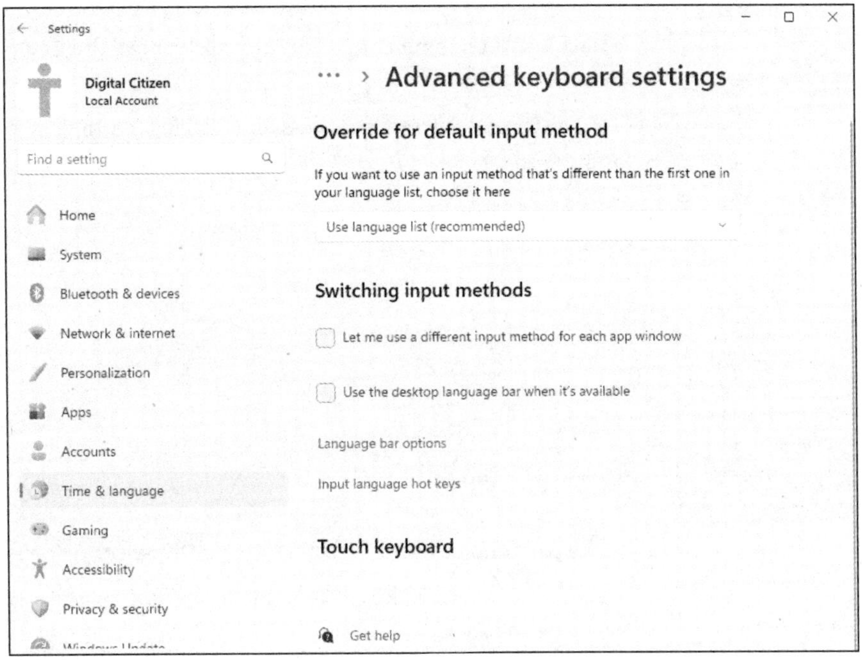

FIGURE 1-11: The Advanced Keyboard Settings page.

4. **Under Switching Input Methods, click or tap Input Language Hot Keys.**

   The Text Services and Input Languages window opens, as in Figure 1-12. This is where you can change the keyboard language shortcuts used by Windows 11.

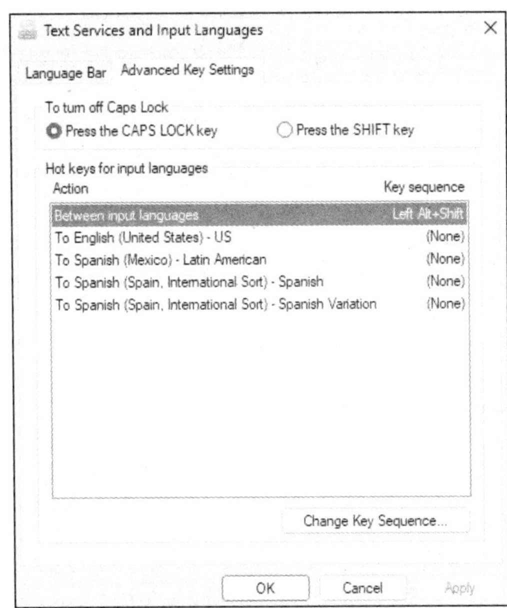

FIGURE 1-12: Setting the hot keys for changing input languages.

5. **Select Between Input Languages and click or tap the Change Key Sequence button.**

   You can choose different shortcuts for switching the input language or switching the keyboard layout, as shown in Figure 1-13.

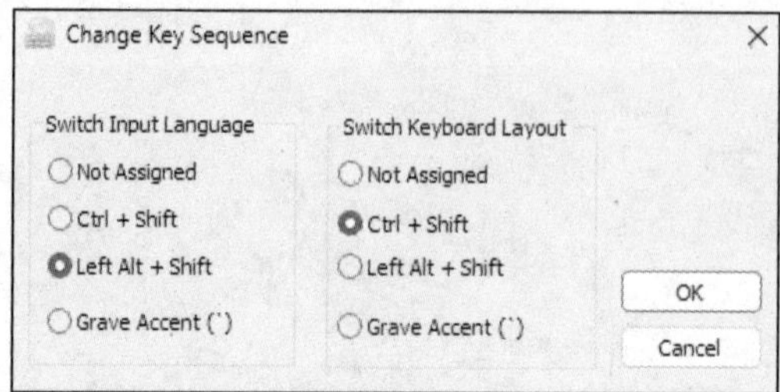

FIGURE 1-13: Choosing your own keyboard shortcuts for changing languages and layouts.

6. **Make your choices, and then click or tap OK twice.**

   Your new settings are applied and can be used to change the keyboard language and layout.

IN THIS CHAPTER

» Understanding the terminology for Windows updates

» Installing updates for Windows and Office

» Improving the download speed for Windows updates

» Stopping updates from rebooting the PC

» Pausing and blocking updates

Chapter 2

Managing Windows Updates

Windows 11 updates itself automatically in the background using criteria known only to Microsoft. Unless you change the Windows Update settings, Windows 11 assumes you want to install updates as soon as they become available.

Many users rightfully complain about Windows 11's forced patches and upgrades. Since the days of Windows 10, Microsoft has repeatedly shown that it can't always be trusted to deliver reliable software fixes. If you want a better computing experience, it's a good idea to take control by using the Pause Updates feature, especially before a new feature update is released.

While some updates can be troublesome, updating Windows 11 is necessary, and so is updating Office. Few people know that Windows Update can also be set to download and install Office updates, as well as updates for other Microsoft apps.

In this chapter, I cover all the basics of updating Windows 11 and Office. I show you how to install updates, improve their download speeds, find information about specific updates and what they do, remove problematic updates, and pause or block updates when needed.

Understanding the Terminology

When you check for updates in Windows 11, you'll encounter a variety of them, especially if you've just installed the operating system. These updates come with different names and fall into these categories:

- **Cumulative updates:** Microsoft calls these *quality updates.* These updates include a combination of security patches, bug fixes, and small changes to the operating system. Each cumulative update supersedes previous updates for that version of Windows. This means that when you install the latest cumulative update for Windows 11, it applies the most recent version of all quality updates that apply to your operating system.

  In theory, cumulative updates arrive on the second Tuesday of every month — the so-called Patch Tuesday. Reality can be messier, with some cumulative updates pulled because of the issues they generate, then re-released a couple of days later, and so on.

- **Security updates:** These fix security issues for different components of Windows, and Microsoft launches them whenever it identifies and fixes a new security problem. In most situations, you want to install security updates that are rolled out to your Windows 11 machine because they will help protect you from security problems.
- **Versions:** Microsoft calls these *feature updates,* but they're really upgrades. These move you from one version of Windows 11 to the next. New versions of Windows 11 are supposed to appear once a year, usually in the fall.
- **Changes to the updating software itself:** *Servicing stack updates* can appear unexpectedly just about any time. They're intended to improve the reliability of the update process to mitigate potential issues while installing the latest monthly security updates and feature updates. If you don't install the latest servicing stack update, there's a risk that your Windows 11 device won't be able to be updated with the latest Microsoft security fixes.
- **Security Intelligence Updates for Microsoft Defender Antivirus and the Windows Malicious Software Removal Tool (MSRT):** These updates happen all the time, and they're delivered only to increase the effectiveness of the security products built into Windows. Go ahead and install them and, read Book 9, Chapter 2, for more about the security tools built into Windows 11.
- **Driver updates:** Some Microsoft drivers are famous for creating mayhem, even though most driver updates are harmless. Windows 11 regularly distributes drivers for certain hardware manufacturers through Windows Update. It's your decision whether or not to install them.

WARNING

If you're having problems with a driver pushed by Microsoft, uninstall it (I provide instructions later in the chapter), go to your hardware manufacturer's website, and get the latest driver from them.

- **Firmware changes:** One of the joys of owning a Surface device is that Microsoft pushes system software updates — both firmware changes and driver changes — via Windows Update. However, firmware updates get delivered for other types of devices too, such as laptops made by manufacturers like ASUS, Dell, HP or Lenovo.
- **Other updates:** Microsoft occasionally pushes out patches specifically for Microsoft Edge, the .NET Framework used by software developers to create computer programs for Windows, and all sorts of other pieces of Windows 11. In general, these patches are supposed to be rolled into cumulative updates. In practice, they're sometimes delivered independently.

Microsoft delivers its updates to Windows users through what it calls *servicing channels*. Each channel has a set of devices that Microsoft deems suitable to receive a certain feature update. While I was writing this book, Microsoft used these servicing channels:

- **General Availability Channel** means that the latest "stable" version of Windows 11 found in this channel is good enough to be sent out the door, usually to consumers. In this channel, feature updates are available annually, but unlike home users, businesses can delay them for as long as they want to make sure that they won't cause havoc on their work computers.
- **Long-Term Servicing Channel** (LTSC) applies to only Enterprise versions of Windows 11. In theory, it's a more stable version of Windows, suitable for environments that need to avoid update bugs. In practice, it's difficult to get real work done on an LTSC machine. Microsoft states that LTSC is not intended for machines that run, say, Microsoft Office, and it should be used for special-purpose devices only, like ATMs, medical equipment, and point-of-sale systems.
- **The Windows Insider Program** includes people and organizations that want to test early builds for Windows 11 feature updates and provide feedback on what features will be shipped next. This channel delivers frequent updates, many of which are barely tested, and it is not intended for the faint of heart.

That's the general framework for how the Windows Update platform works. Your job, should you choose to accept it, is to make the rules work for you — not blindside you.

Installing Updates for Windows 11

Windows 11 automatically checks for updates when you use it, and you don't have to do anything to get them installed on your computer. The only thing that's necessary is a working internet connection.

However, you can manually check for updates, see what's available, and install them yourself, like this:

1. **Click or tap the Start icon and then Settings.**

   The Windows 11 Settings are shown.

2. **On the left, choose Windows Update.**

   You see the Windows Update options and a message about whether your device is up to date and when a check for updates was last made, as shown in Figure 2-1. If updates are available, you see a name and release date for each one, without any meaningful details about what it does.

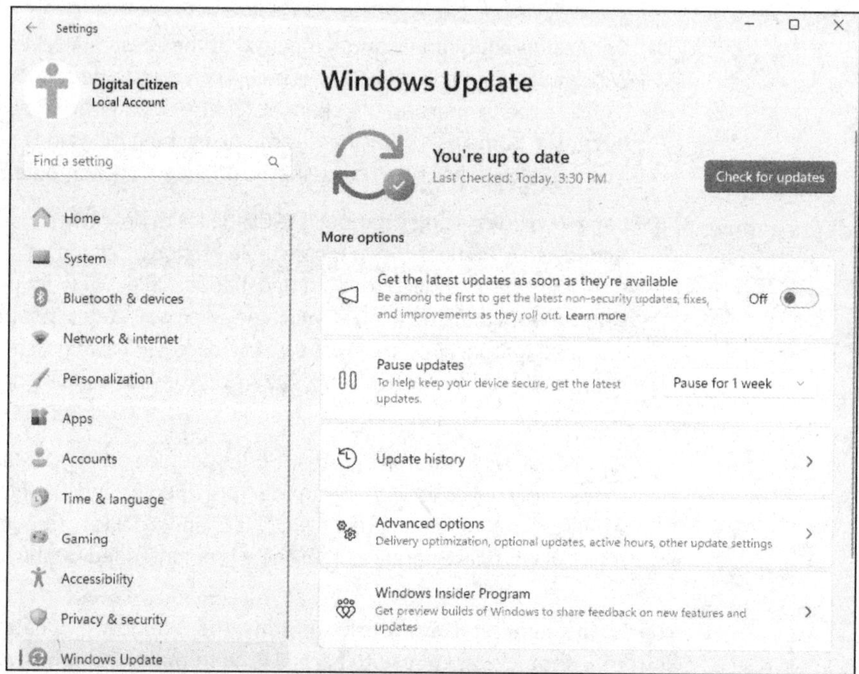

FIGURE 2-1: This is where you update Windows 11.

3. **If you want to make a manual check, click or tap Check for Updates and wait for Windows Update to display the results of its findings.**

4. **To install the latest updates, click or tap Download & Install All.**

   The progress is shown for each update, which is first downloaded from Microsoft's servers and then installed on your computer or device.

5. **If necessary to complete the installation of the updates, first close all apps and files (so you don't lose any work), and then click or tap the Restart Now button when it appears.**

   This last step is not required by all updates. Only those that change important system files require you to reboot before their installation is finished.

Making Sure You Don't Get Updates as Soon as They're Available

I think it's a good idea *not* to install updates for Windows 11 as soon as they're available. In recent years, Microsoft has dropped the ball on the quality of their updates and the company regularly makes headlines with botched updates that break things for their users.

One small thing you can do is set Windows Update to stop delivering updates the second they're made available by Microsoft, like this:

1. **Click or tap the Start icon, followed by Settings. Or press Windows+I.**

2. **On the left, choose Windows Update.**

   You see the Windows Update options (refer to Figure 2-1).

3. **If it isn't already set to off, click or tap the switch to Get the Latest Updates as Soon as They're Available.**

4. **Close Windows Update.**

TIP

Microsoft wants users to set the switch on. If you choose this, Windows Update won't wait and will prioritize your device for getting the latest non-security updates at the time they're available.

REMEMBER

Security updates are not affected by this switch. They're always delivered immediately after their release, whether you toggle on or off the capability to get the latest updates as soon as they're available.

Postponing Windows 11 Updates

Some Windows 11 feature updates can be exciting, introducing features and important improvements to the operating system. However, they often haven't been thoroughly tested before release, so it's wise to wait a bit before installing them. If you're using Windows 11 Pro, you can postpone these updates for up to five weeks (which I recommend); Windows 11 Home users can delay them for only a week. By delaying, if any issues arise with a feature update, other users will likely encounter them first, giving Microsoft time to fix them before the update reaches your machine.

To pause Windows 11 updates, do the following:

1. **Click or tap the Start icon and then Settings. On the left, choose Windows Update.**
2. **Click or tap the drop-down list next to Pause Updates.**

   You see the options shown in Figure 2-2. If you're on Windows 11 Home, you see only a Pause For 1 Week button instead.
3. **If you're using Windows 11 Pro, choose Pause for 5 Weeks. If you're on Windows 11 Home, click or tap Pause for 1 Week instead.**

   On the top side of the Windows Update window, you see the date until updates are paused.
4. **If you want to resume updating Windows 11 prior to the pause date, click or tap Resume Updates.**

WARNING

The Pause Updates option takes precedence over all other settings. If you have Pause turned on, Windows 11 stops all updates but Microsoft Defender Antivirus updates. Microsoft is careful to mention that you can't reset the Pause Updates setting. If you try to turn it off and turn it back on again, you see "This device will need to get new updates before you can pause again." However, you can resume updates anytime you want before the pause period ends.

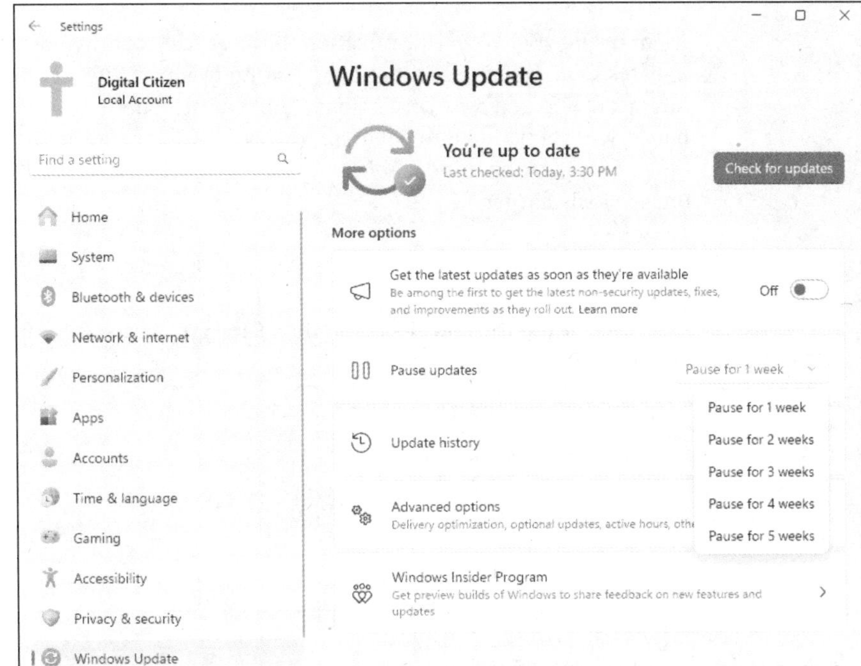

FIGURE 2-2: You can pause updates for up to five weeks on Windows 11 Pro.

Improving the Download Speed for Updates

Traditionally, Windows updates were downloaded directly from Microsoft's servers to your PC. This approach required massive infrastructure often resulting in slow download speeds. To improve this, Microsoft developed Delivery Optimization, a feature that allows computers to obtain updates from other users on the local network or the internet and upload updates to other users.

When enabled, Delivery Optimization can download Windows updates, Microsoft Store apps, Microsoft Defender updates, Microsoft Edge updates, Xbox Game Pass, and other items from computers on the same network or nearby on the internet, as well as from Microsoft. Instead of downloading the entire file from one source, it breaks the update into smaller parts, fetching some parts from other PCs and some from Microsoft to complete the process as quickly as possible. It then creates a local cache for updates, temporarily storing downloaded files for quick access and sharing with other computers on the network or the internet, depending on your settings.

As a result, Delivery Optimization reduces the bandwidth needed to deliver updates to all Windows computers, leading to lower internet bandwidth costs for Microsoft and reduced server load. Users also benefit from faster updates and network-level bandwidth savings. However, if your internet connection is billed based on usage, be mindful of how you configure Delivery Optimization to avoid unexpected charges.

Here's how to enable and configure Delivery Optimization on Windows 11:

1. **Click or tap the Start icon and then Settings. On the left, choose Windows Update.**

   The options shown previously in Figure 2-1 appear.

2. **Choose Advanced Options.**

   You see a long list of advanced options for Windows Update, like the ones shown in Figure 2-3.

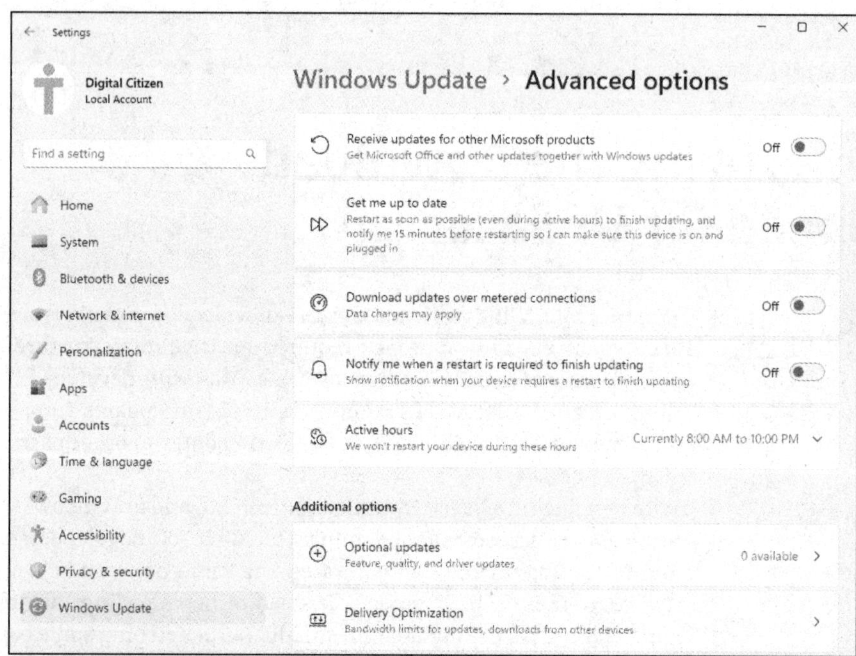

FIGURE 2-3: Windows Update has many advanced options for you to configure.

3. **Click or tap Delivery Optimization.**

   Now you can configure this feature using the options shown in Figure 2-4.

4. **Turn on the switch to Allow Downloads from Other Devices.**

   Delivery Optimization is now enabled.

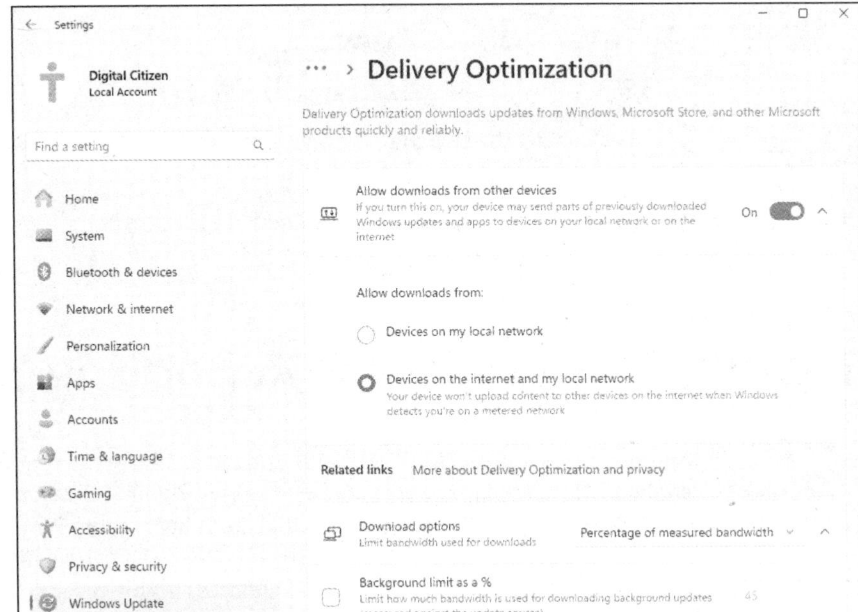

FIGURE 2-4: Enabling Delivery Optimization is easy.

5. **Under Allow Downloads From, choose the option you prefer:**
   - *Devices on my local network:* Useful for workplaces and homes with more than one Windows 11 computer.
   - *Devices on the internet and my local network:* Useful for home users who don't have other computers on their network but do have unlimited internet bandwidth.

WARNING

If your internet connection is billed based on your usage, you should never enable the second option because it allows other computers on the internet to download updates from you, which will increase your costs.

Getting Updates for Office (Microsoft 365)

If you use multiple Microsoft services and products, enabling Windows Update to manage updates for them can be beneficial. This feature is especially useful for Office but applies to other Microsoft products as well. Here's how to set Windows 11 to install updates for Office and other Microsoft apps automatically:

1. **Click or tap the Start icon, followed by Settings. On the left, choose Windows Update.**

2. **Click or tap Advanced Options.**

   You see the options shown previously in Figure 2-3.

3. **Click or tap the switch to Receive Updates for Other Microsoft Products and set it on.**

   The next time you click or tap the Check for Updates button, Windows Update will check for updates for Office and other Microsoft products.

Stopping Updates from Rebooting Your PC

Another annoying part of Windows 11 updates is that some require a reboot to get applied. Because of that, you may end up with your PC restarting while you're doing something important. To stop that from happening, Windows Update has a feature called Active Hours. You can set the interval during which you tend to use your PC, named Active Hours, and Windows 11 won't restart for updates during that time. Here's how to set it up:

1. **Click or tap the Start icon and then Settings.**
2. **In the Settings app, choose Windows Update.**
3. **Go to Advanced Options. Click or tap Active Hours to see more options.**
4. **Click or tap the drop-down list next to Adjust Active Hours and select Manually.**

   You can then change the interval for Active Hours, using the options from Figure 2-5.

5. **Set the Start Time and End Time.**

   Windows needs an interval when it is allowed to install updates, but you are allowed to have a maximum of 18 hours between the start and end times. Your settings are applied at once.

TIP

You can also let Windows 11 automatically adjust your Active Hours. It does that by monitoring how you use your PC.

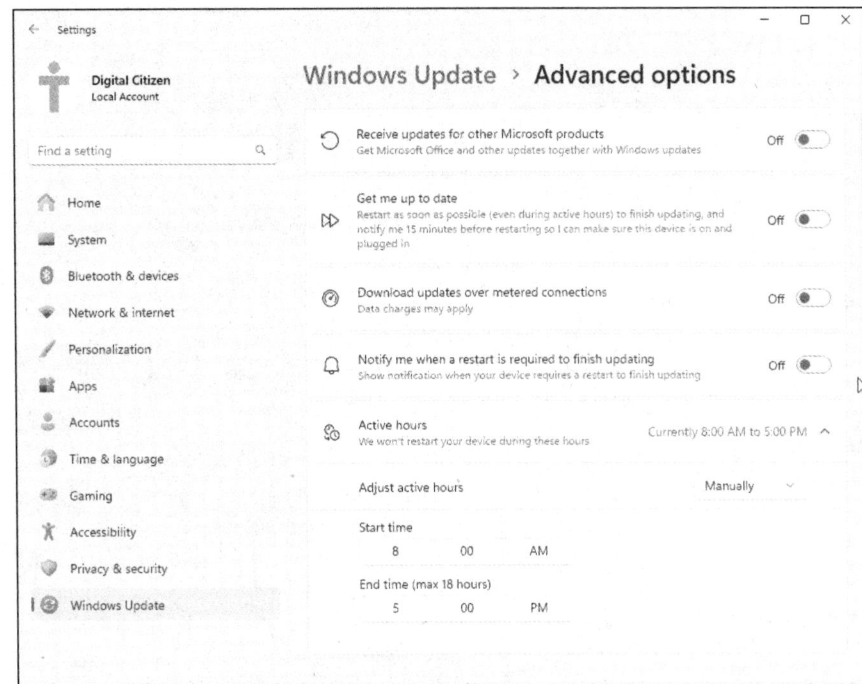

FIGURE 2-5: Setting the hours when Windows 11 doesn't restart for updates.

Getting Information about and Removing Updates

Unfortunately, Microsoft doesn't make it easy for you to learn what an update does before it gets installed. However, it does provide plenty of information after the fact. If you recently installed an update and Windows 11 is misbehaving, you can learn more about that update and then remove it like this:

1. **Click or tap the Start icon, followed by Settings. Then select Windows Update.**
2. **Click or tap Update History.**

   Windows displays all the updates installed on your machine, split by type, as shown in Figure 2-6.
3. **Expand each category of updates with a click or tap on the arrow to the right of its name.**

   For each update, you see its name, when it was installed, and a Learn More link.

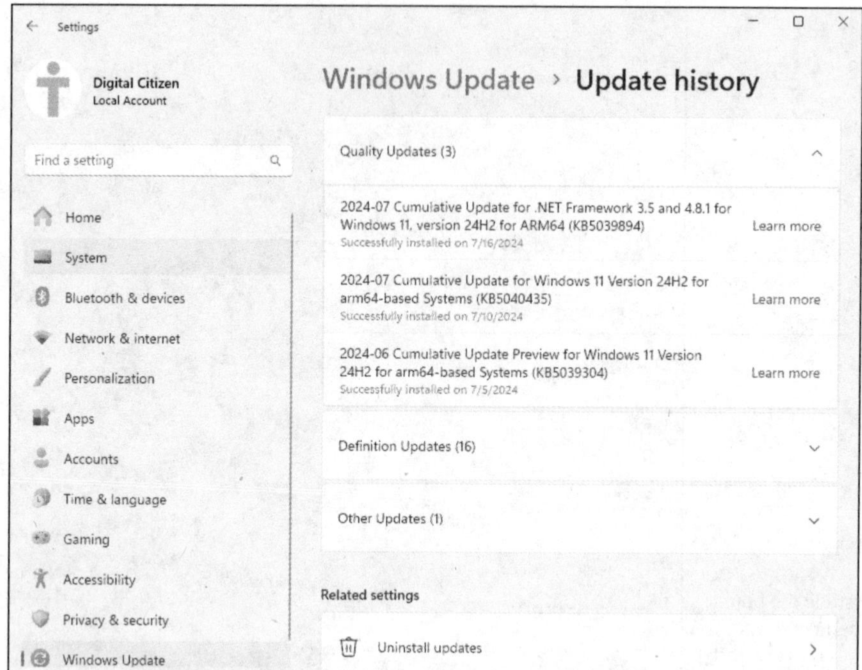

FIGURE 2-6: Your Update History reveals plenty of useful information.

4. **To find out more about a specific update, click or tap the Learn More link to its right.**

   A web page is loaded in Microsoft Edge, sharing detailed information about the update.

5. **To remove an update, get back to the Update History screen by clicking or tapping the Settings icon on the taskbar. Then, under Related Settings, click or tap Uninstall Updates.**

   A list with updates that can be removed is shown, like the one in Figure 2-7.

6. **Click or tap the Uninstall link next to the update you want to remove and confirm by clicking or tapping the Uninstall button.**

   During the uninstallation process, a progress bar appears under the selected update. When done, its status changes to Uninstalled, and a restart is required to finalize everything.

7. **Close all open apps and files and restart Windows 11.**

   When you get back to the sign-in screen, the update will have been removed from Windows.

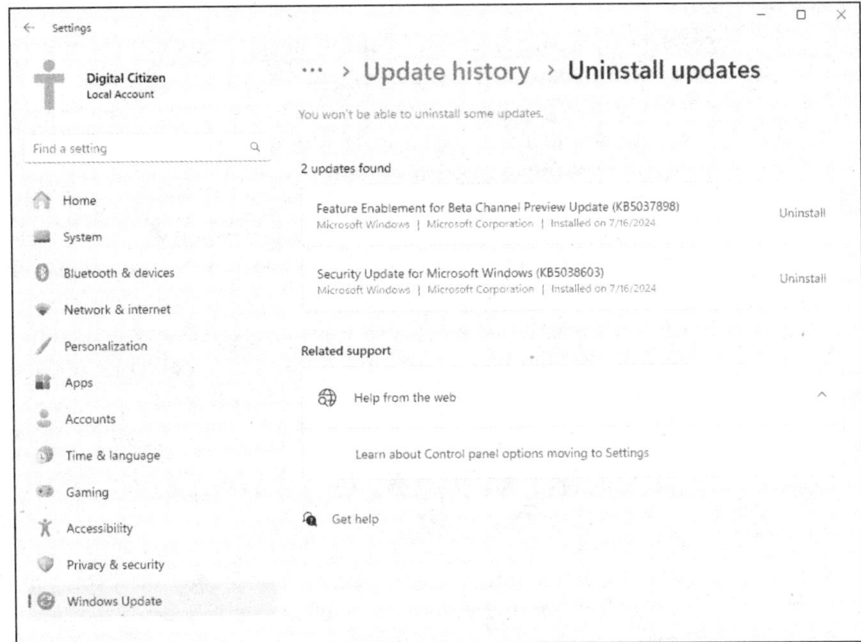

FIGURE 2-7: From here you can remove troublesome updates.

TIP

The problem with removing updates from Windows 11 is that Windows Update will install them back at some point. If you have problems with a specific update, you can block it from installing on your machine again by using Windows Update Manager — a free tool developed by a passionate developer — at `https://github.com/DavidXanatos/wumgr/releases`.

Problems with Windows Update

Unfortunately, Microsoft hasn't mastered delivering reliable Windows 11 updates. Patch Tuesdays often turn into beta-testing events where bugs appear in unexpected ways. While it's a tough job to patch an operating system as complex as Windows and Microsoft is not always to blame for the chaos, skipping automatic updates altogether would lead to a bigger mess.

Some unreliable patches can be particularly troublesome for a group of users and a minor nuisance for others. Generally, issues can be avoided if you wait a few weeks for any problem reports to settle down and for Microsoft to fix their bugs. This is why pausing updates is a good practice, especially before the next feature update for Windows 11 is released.

Even when Microsoft isn't entirely at fault, it's little consolation to those whose days are disrupted by a problematic update. However, the wait-and-watch approach does have its downsides. For example, if Microsoft patches a vulnerability and malware quickly exploits a previously unknown security hole, users deferring Windows updates might be caught off guard.

However, this scenario has become less common. Patches for zero-day exploits — security holes with known exploits — are different. Microsoft has done a good job of obfuscating its descriptions and preventing quick reverse engineering of its patched code. While a massive wave of reverse-engineered malware could theoretically roll out on some future Wednesday, automatic updates would then save the day.

Blocking Windows 11 updates

The trick to blocking updates on Windows 11 Home or Pro machines lies in a little-known setting called metered connection. Microsoft put the metered connection setting in Windows 11 to let you tell Windows that you're paying for your internet access by the bit, which means you don't want it to download anything unless it absolutely must. From that fortunate beginning arises the best option for Windows 11 users to block updates.

REMEMBER

What goes through a metered connection? Hard to say, specifically, and Microsoft has made no commitments. From my experience, the metered connection setting guards against any patches, except Microsoft Defender Antivirus updates. No guarantees, of course, but metered connection looks like a decent approach to blocking updates, even if it's not the most elegant.

If you want to (temporarily!) block updates and Windows 11 version upgrades, follow these steps:

1. **Click or tap the Start icon, followed by Settings. On the left, choose Network & Internet.**
2. **Do one of the following:**
   - *If you have a wired (Ethernet) connection, click or tap Ethernet.* You see the Ethernet configuration options shown in Figure 2-8.
   - *If you have a wireless connection, click or tap Wi-Fi and then the name of your network connection, followed by the word* properties. You see the properties of your Wi-Fi connection, similar to the ones in Figure 2-9.
3. **Set the Metered Connection switch on by clicking or tapping it.**

   Your internet connection is now set as metered and — unless Microsoft changes the rules — you're protected from both cumulative updates and version upgrades.

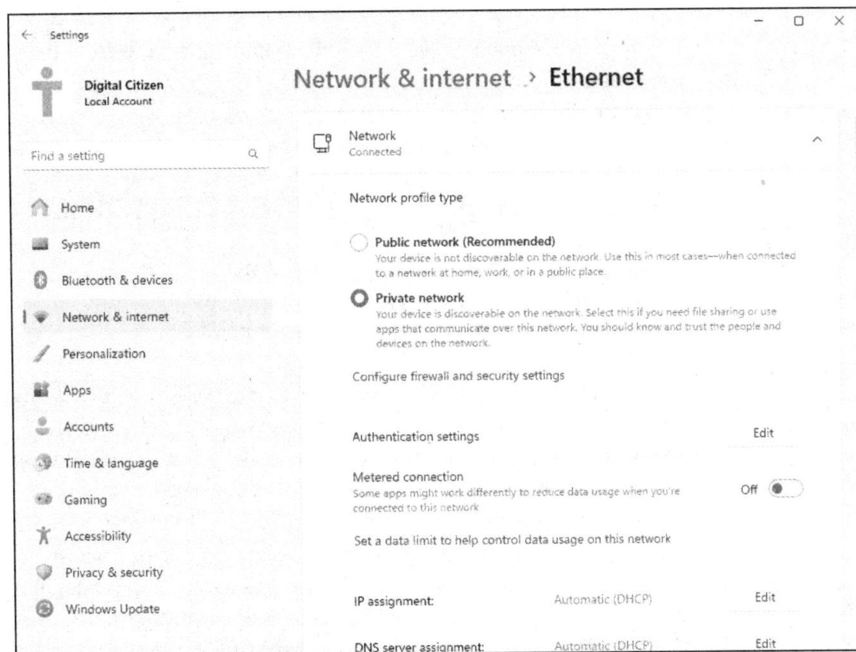

FIGURE 2-8: The properties of a wired (Ethernet) connection look like this.

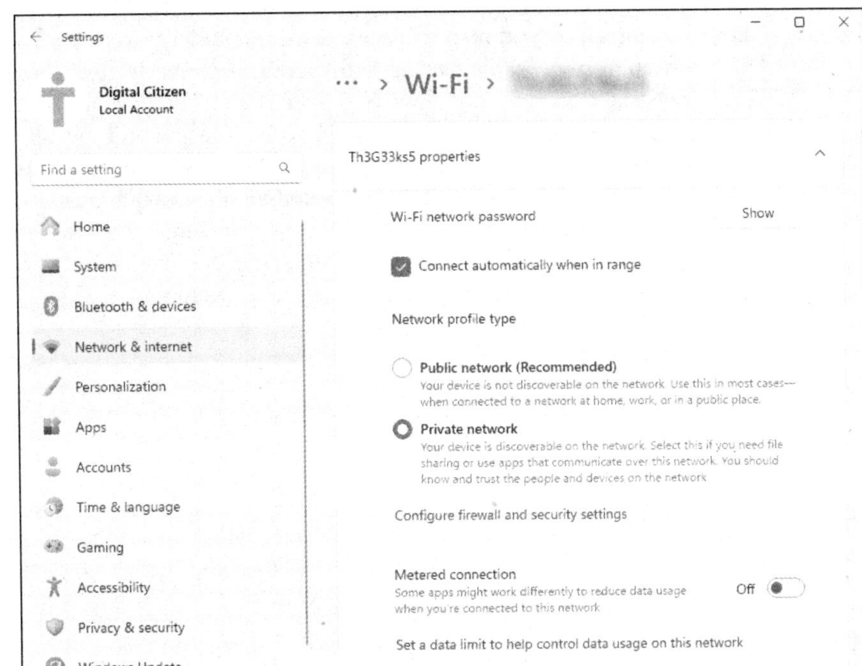

FIGURE 2-9: If you have a Wi-Fi connection, it'll look like this.

WARNING

You must install updates eventually. To resume them, follow the same steps and set the Metered Connection switch to off. Then, read the next section for advice on choosing the right time to update Windows 11 fully.

When is it a good time to unblock updates?

If you block updates, you'll eventually need to unblock them. It typically takes several days for the worst bugs in a cumulative update to surface and a few weeks for more subtle problems to be diagnosed and fixed.

Version upgrades, on the other hand, can generate problems that may not be identified immediately. It usually takes two or three months of broader testing to ensure that a new Windows 11 version is stable enough to install on your machine.

The real deadline we're up against is the one set by cyber threats. Delaying patches too long can leave your system vulnerable to serious security threats. We had a good example in February 2017, when Microsoft's patches, about six weeks after they were released, became crucial to block the WannaCry and NotPetya vulnerabilities. If you waited too long to patch in early 2017, your machine was wide open to some truly awful malware.

WARNING

Conversely, if you install all patches immediately after they're released, you risk encountering problems like those seen in January 2018. Back then, Microsoft released a slew of Meltdown and Spectre patches that many made PCs unusable. It took five days for Microsoft to find the issue and pull the patch. For weeks, they had to patch, pull patches, re-patch, and re-re-patch, all while dealing with bugs in Intel's patches as well. This created an abominable mess, leaving many Windows users bewildered and staring at blue screens. The takeaway? Every month is different. If you block updates and upgrades, you need to stay informed about the latest developments and decide when it's safe to patch.

IN THIS CHAPTER

» Using the Windows troubleshooting tools

» Fixing Windows installation and updating problems

» Getting help from Microsoft or the web

» Screen sharing with Quick Assist

» Running experiments safely with Windows Sandbox

Chapter 3
Troubleshooting and Getting Help

Welcome to the wild world of Windows 11 troubleshooting! If you've ever felt like your computer was speaking in riddles, you're not alone. This chapter is your guide to decoding the mysteries of Windows 11 troubleshooting and taming at least some of its tantrums.

First up, you bid farewell to the old Windows troubleshooters and get acquainted with the new kid on the block: the Get Help app. It's not perfect, but Microsoft has decided that this is the future of Windows troubleshooting, so I show you how to make the most of it.

Then it's time to roll up your sleeves and tackle a few hardcore troubleshooting techniques for handling problems with Windows 11 installations and forced Windows updates that break systems instead of fixing them. Have you ever heard of tools with gibberish names like CHKDSK, SFC, and DISM? You will soon, and they might just save your day.

Next, you explore the overlooked treasures of Microsoft's Support website and discover how to navigate the company's tech support maze. Then you see how to use the Quick Assist app built into Windows 11 as a remote tech support hero and to get help from someone else when you're in a pinch.

If you feel playful and are likely to endanger your computer and data, you need to be introduced to the Windows Sandbox — your personal testing ground for suspicious links, software, files, and you name it. You can use it to run everything you want, no matter how perilous, in a safe environment that doesn't negatively affect your actual computer. Finally, you learn where to find help beyond Microsoft's walled garden.

Whether you're wrestling with a stubborn update or trying to get help from a real technical expert, this chapter has your back. So grab your metaphorical hat and master the art of Windows 11 troubleshooting.

Saying Goodbye to Windows Troubleshooters

One of the best features of Windows was that it included troubleshooters to help you fix problems with almost everything that could go wrong with your computer: network and internet connectivity, audio, printing, Bluetooth, the keyboard and mouse, and more.

Unfortunately, in 2023, Microsoft announced that it was going to retire these troubleshooters because it labeled them as legacy products. And by 2025, the entire Microsoft Support Diagnostic Tool platform that runs the troubleshooters will be removed from Windows 11.

At the time of writing, Windows 11 gives you the impression that it still has some built-in troubleshooters, but when you try to start them, you end up in the Get Help app, which tries to help fix your problems by providing solutions using AI-generated content based on Microsoft's support documentation, links to community discussions on Microsoft's support forums, and articles written by Microsoft's staff. In Figure 3-1, I stumbled upon the Get Help app while trying to access the former Program Compatibility Troubleshooter.

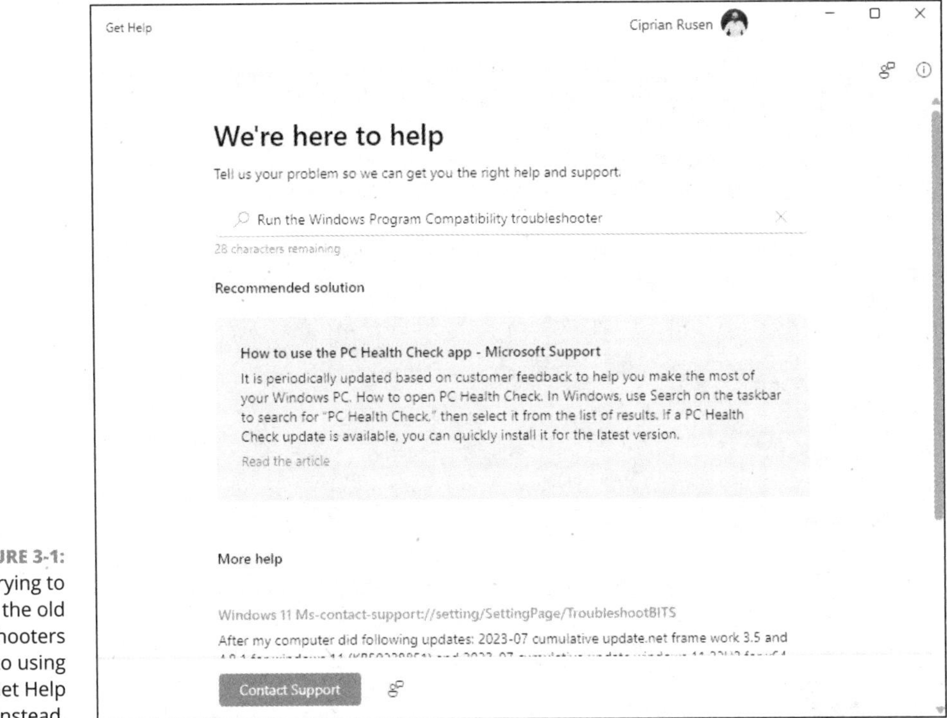
Get Help
Ciprian Rusen
We're here to help
Tell us your problem so we can get you the right help and support.
Run the Windows Program Compatibility troubleshooter
28 characters remaining
Recommended solution
How to use the PC Health Check app - Microsoft Support
It is periodically updated based on customer feedback to help you make the most of your Windows PC. How to open PC Health Check. In Windows, use Search on the taskbar to search for "PC Health Check," then select it from the list of results. If a PC Health Check update is available, you can quickly install it for the latest version.
Read the article
More help
Windows 11 Ms-contact-support://setting/SettingPage/TroubleshootBITS
After my computer did following updates: 2023-07 cumulative update.net frame work 3.5 and
Contact Support

FIGURE 3-1: Trying to run the old troubleshooters leads to using the Get Help app instead.

Here's how the new Windows troubleshooter experience works:

1. **Click or tap in the Search box on the taskbar and type** troubleshoot**.**

   A list of search results is shown.

2. **Select Troubleshoot Settings.**

   The System > Troubleshoot section of the Settings app is loaded.

3. **To see all the troubleshooters available, click or tap Other Troubleshooters.**

   The list shown in Figure 3-2 appears. Scroll down, and you'll see that it's a long list of troubleshooters that should help you fix a long range of technical problems.

4. **Click or tap Run next to the troubleshooter that you think may help with your problem.**

   The Get Help app opens and loads some content that may or may not help you fix your issue. Check this content and see whether it is helpful to you.

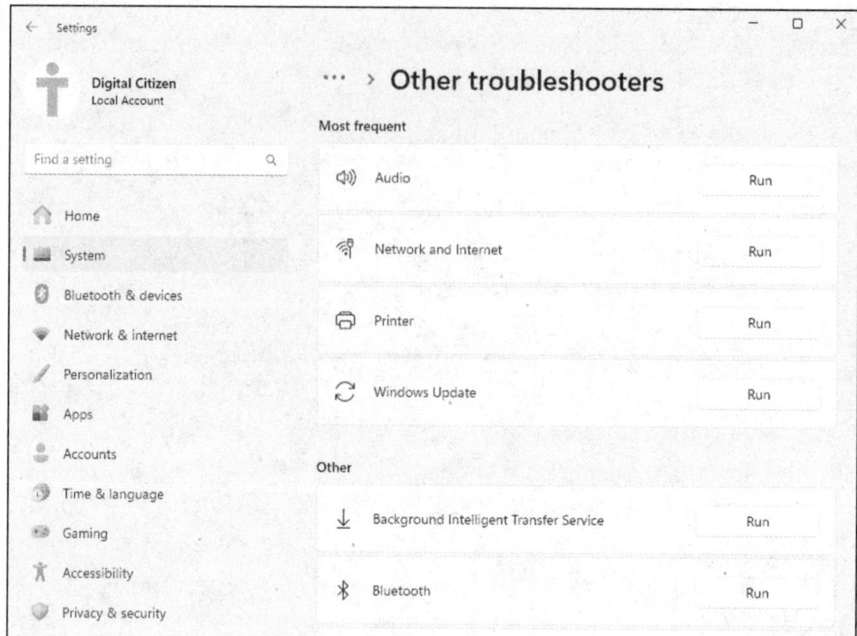

FIGURE 3-2: Windows 11 makes you think that it has many troubleshooters.

TECHNICAL STUFF

If you can't fix your issues using the content provided by the Get Help app, you may be able to unearth worthwhile information from your system's log using Event Viewer, a topic I tackle in Book 8, Chapter 4.

Using Get Help

The old Windows troubleshooters were pretty decent at fixing stuff, and I liked them a lot, but they're history now. We're stuck with the Get Help app, so we might as well figure out how to use it. The process is not rocket science: You tell the app what's busted, it provides some suggestions, maybe asks some questions, and then tries to tell you how to fix the problem. Is it perfect? Far from it, and at times it won't provide the solutions you're looking for.

Give the Get Help app a shot the next time your computer acts up. Maybe you'll get lucky and it will help you solve a problem you're having on your Windows 11 computer or device. To try it out, do the following:

1. **Click or tap the Start icon, followed by All.**

   You see the list of apps installed on your Windows 11 computer device.

2. **Scroll down to the apps that start with the letter *G* and choose Get Help.**

   The Get Help app appears, as shown in Figure 3-3. The app has a Search box in the middle that you can use to find help on the specific problem you're encountering, and it also suggests common searches people make.

3. **In the Search box, type a summary of your issue.**

   If you encounter error messages, don't hesitate to enter their exact text, as well as any error codes you see. This will help the app provide you with more specific information. To exemplify how the process works, I entered *set up microphone* as the issue I needed help with.

   The Get Help app spends some time looking for content that may be helpful and then loads.

4. **If you see a list of instructions on what to do, follow them and see if your problem gets fixed. (See Figure 3-4.) If you're asked whether the content provided helped to solve your problem, answer Yes or No, depending on your situation.**

   If you answer No, the Get Help app records your answer and then loads more content that could be useful. Check it out and see if it is helpful. In rare situations, Get Help might not return a list of instructions but it should load a list of articles. Browse through those articles or change your search query and try again.

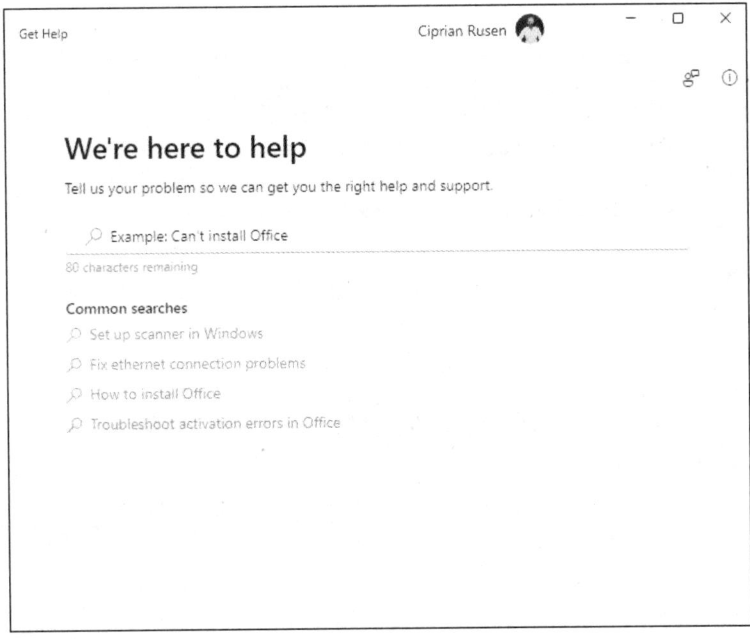

FIGURE 3-3: The Get Help app has a functional start page.

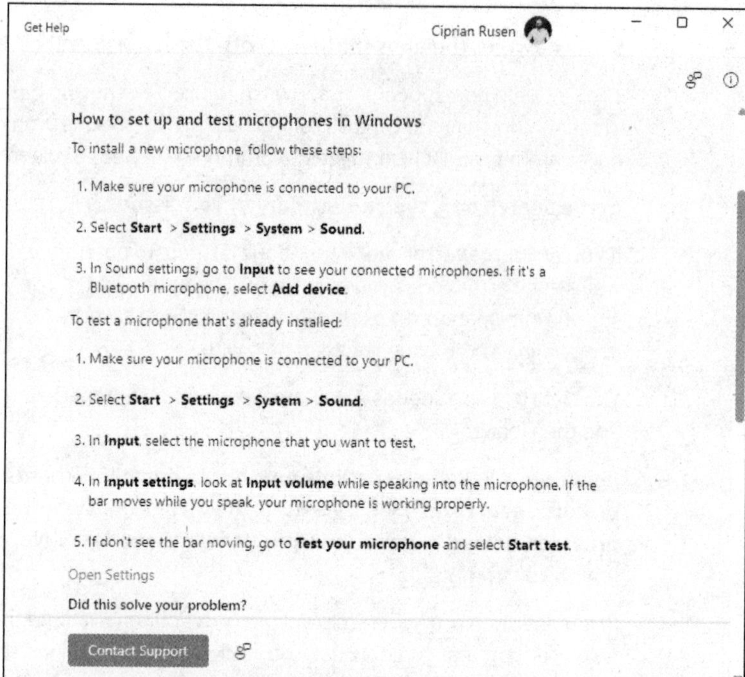

FIGURE 3-4: Get Help can provide you with many troubleshooting instructions.

Contacting Microsoft Support from Get Help

Did you use Get Help and follow the instructions but can't find a solution? Note the Contact Support button at the bottom of the app. You can use it to contact Microsoft, report your issue, and (I hope) get help from a tech support engineer. This sounds great, doesn't it? Here's how it all works:

1. **Open Get Help and try to find solutions to your problem using the instructions shared earlier.**

   At some point, after you navigate the instructions provided by Get Help, a Contact Support button appears at the bottom of the app (refer to Figure 3-4).

2. **Click or tap Contact Support.**

   A wizard appears, asking you several questions about your problem. The questions depend on the topic you searched for earlier. I looked for solutions to Windows activation problems.

3. **Choose the Product and Services that are affected by your issue, and then choose the Category and other criteria that may be shown. Then click or tap Confirm.**

   The wizard asks you to choose a support action, as shown in Figure 3-5. I was given the option to chat with a support agent in my web browser. In other regions, you may also have the option to call Microsoft's Support service. You can also see the schedule for when you can reach them.

4. **Choose the option that works for you and see if Microsoft can help fix your problem.**

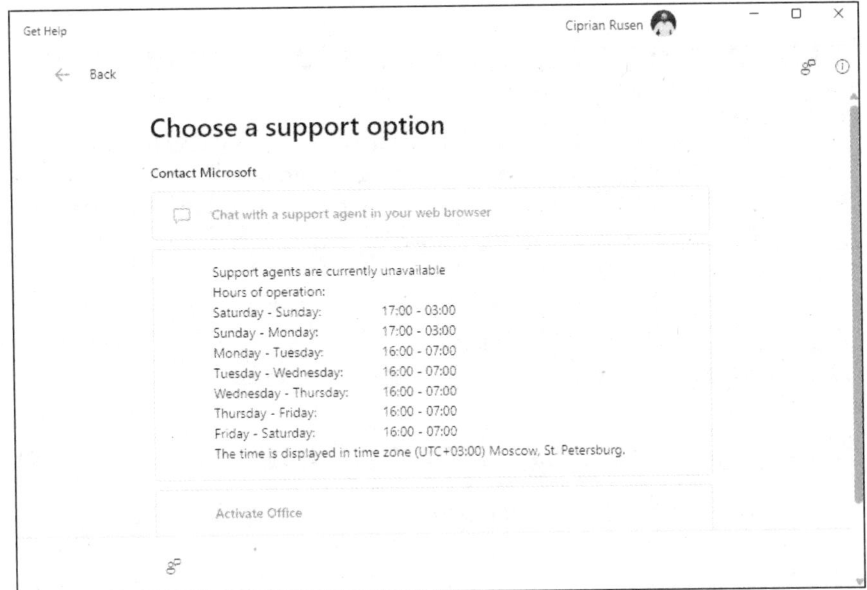

FIGURE 3-5: The Get Help app can help you contact Microsoft Support.

REMEMBER

In my experience, the best part about the Get Help app is not the instructions that it provides when you describe your problem but the option to contact Microsoft Support that appears after you start looking for solutions. Talking to a support engineer may save you a lot more time than navigating endless pages of content that is difficult to understand or may not apply to your issue.

TIP

Microsoft offers support by phone — you know, an old-fashioned voice call. You can find their service phone numbers for your country by visiting `https://bit.ly/4cpDSY8`. This is a shortened link that takes you to Microsoft's Global Customer Service page, listing all the phone numbers where you can call them.

REMEMBER

Realize that tech support people aren't frontline programmers or testers. Usually, they are quite familiar with the most common problems and have access to lots of support systems that can answer myriad questions that aren't so common. Some of them may even have copies of this book or similar ones on their desks.

Support has three levels of escalation, and in rare cases, some problems are escalated to the fourth level — which is where the product developers live. Kind of like Dante's *Inferno*. If your problem is replicable — meaning it isn't caused by bad hardware or cosmic rays — and the tech support engineer can't solve it, you should politely ask for escalation.

Troubleshooting the Hard Way

Windows 11 can be a pain sometimes, especially when installing or updating it. I'm not a Microsoft tech support engineer, but I've gathered years of technical experience. In my quest to be helpful, I've compiled two lists of fixes: one for Windows 11 installation hiccups and another for update headaches. These aren't magic bullets, but they might save you a headache or two when Windows 11 throws a tantrum. So, give these tips a shot the next time your computer acts up during a Windows 11 installation or update. They might be just what you need to get things running smoothly again.

Tackling Windows installation problems

This section is for people who are using Windows 10 and trying to upgrade to Windows 11 but can't and for those trying to move from one version of Windows 11 to the next. I have categorized some installation problems, including initial setup problems, and I offer some advice and pointers should you find yourself stuck.

You're asked for a product key but don't have one

If you're prompted for a product key and are upgrading from a genuine Windows 10 version or switching versions of Windows 11, click or tap Skip, Do This Later, or Next (depending on the dialog box). Don't bother trying to find a Windows 11 key. Chances are that Windows will recognize the error of its ways and not bother you again, although it may take a few hours for the activation routine to figure it out. Another thing that may help is to use in Windows 11 the same Microsoft account that you used in Windows 10. Usually, the product keys are linked to Microsoft accounts.

The Windows 11 installer hangs for hours or reboots continuously

If the Windows 11 installer hangs for a long time or keeps rebooting, make sure that you've disconnected any nonessential hardware. Unplug that external hard drive, disconnect peripherals that aren't absolutely necessary, including extra monitors, smart-card readers, weird keyboards, whatever. If possible, consider turning off Wi-Fi and plugging into a router with a LAN cable.

Second, make sure you have the right upgrade: Don't upgrade from 32-bit Windows 10 to 64-bit Windows 11. That won't work. This situation requires a clean installation of Windows 11, not an upgrade.

Also, if you started with Windows 10 Home, you should install Windows 11 Home. If you started with Windows 10 Pro, you should install Windows 11 Pro. If you're working with any Enterprise version of Windows 10, the upgrade isn't free; it's dependent on your company's license terms.

Then, try running the upgrade again.

If you continue to have the same problem, Microsoft's best advice is to use the Windows 11 Installation Media tool to create a USB installation drive (or an installation DVD). See the Download Windows 11 page at `www.microsoft.com/en-us/software-download/windows11` for details, but be aware that keeping your genuine license requires running the upgrade sequence correctly. Specifically, you must first upgrade the PC instead of performing a clean install to make sure your old Windows 10 license is recognized as a valid license for the free Windows 11 upgrade. If you start with a valid Windows 10 machine and use the Windows 11 Installation Media tool to move to the next version, you shouldn't have licensing problems.

For full instructions on installing Windows 11, read Book 8, Chapter 2.

Problems with installing updates

If you're frustrated with Windows 11 updates, you're not alone. I've been there too. Every update's different, but I have a few tricks that often work when things go wrong. These aren't fancy tech solutions — just practical tips that usually do the job. I'm not going to bore you with a long list of every possible problem. Instead, here's the lowdown on the most common issues and how to fix them. It's straightforward stuff that might just save your computer (and your sanity).

Turn off third-party antivirus software

The very first thing to do is to make sure your antivirus software is turned off while you're troubleshooting. If you're using Microsoft Defender Antivirus (built into Windows Security), you're fine. But if you've decided to install something different, turn it off. Then see if the errors go away or if the latest update installs correctly.

Check for mundane hardware problems

Just because your PC has problems right after you installed the latest cumulative update, it doesn't mean the update caused the problem. Consider the possibility that your problem has nothing to do with the cumulative update. At the very least, someone with a cumulative update problem should right-click or press and hold the Start icon, choose Terminal (Admin), and type the following command:

```
chkdsk /f
```

Don't forget to press Enter. If you're asked whether to schedule this volume to be checked the next time the system restarts, type **Y** for yes and reboot your computer. The command will then scan your main drive and fix any errors.

If you're having problems with a mouse, keyboard, monitor, or speaker, try plugging them into another computer to see if they're dead. This low-tech approach can save you from wasting time on a dead device.

Recover from a bricked PC

For most people, a bricked PC (a computer that has become unresponsive and unusable) is the scariest situation. The cumulative update installs itself (possibly overnight, while you aren't looking), you come back to your machine, and nothing happens. It's dead, Jim!

REMEMBER

At least half the time, you can get back to a working machine by booting into safe mode, uninstalling the cumulative update, blocking it, and then rebooting normally. For the rundown on booting into safe mode, check out Book 8, Chapter 3.

Make sure your problem isn't the latest Windows update

Try to uninstall the latest Windows 11 update and see if the problem goes away. To learn how to remove updates, read Book 7, Chapter 2. After the update is removed and you restart, you should be on the previous (presumably functional) version of Windows 11. Immediately test to see if your problem went away. If it did, see my tips in the chapter about Windows updates on how to block them from installing again. However, if your problem persists, chances are good your problem isn't with this particular update.

Run SFC and DISM

Running SFC (System File Checker) and DISM (Deployment Image Servicing and Management) seems to be everyone's go-to suggestion for cumulative update installation problems. In my experience, it works only a small fraction of the time, but when it does, you come back from the brink of disaster with few scars to show for it.

System File Checker, better known as SFC, is a Windows 11 program that scans system files, looking to see if any of them are corrupt. There are ways to run SFC with switches to tell it to replace bad versions of system files.

If SFC can't fix the problem, a second utility called Deployment Image Servicing and Management (DISM) digs even deeper. Microsoft recommends that you run both, in order, regardless of the problems dug up (or missed) by SFC.

Be aware that SFC has flagged files as broken when they weren't. You're looking for the automatic repair from SFC, not its diagnosis.

Here's how to run SFC:

1. **Right-click or press and hold the Start icon and choose Terminal (Admin).**
2. **When the UAC prompt appears, choose Yes.**
3. **In Windows Terminal, type** sfc /scannow **and press Enter.**

   Yes, there's a space between *sfc* and */scannow*. It can take a couple of minutes or half an hour, depending on the speed of your storage drive. See Figure 3-6.

   If SFC reports "Windows Resource Protection did not find any integrity violations," you're out of luck. Whatever problems you have weren't caused by scrambled Windows system files. If SFC reports that "Windows Resource Protection found corrupt files and repaired them," you may be in luck because the problem may have been fixed. If SFC reports that "Windows Resource Protection found corrupt files but was unable to fix some of them," you're having a very unlucky day.
4. **Keep the same Windows Terminal (Admin) app open, type** DISM /Online / Cleanup-Image /RestoreHealth, **and press Enter.**

   Again, remember the spaces before all the slashes, and note that there's a hyphen between *Cleanup* and *Image.* Let it run: half an hour, an hour, however long it takes. If DISM finds any corrupt system files, it fixes them. Don't close the Windows Terminal until you see a message that the operation has been completed.
5. **Reboot and see if your system has been fixed.**

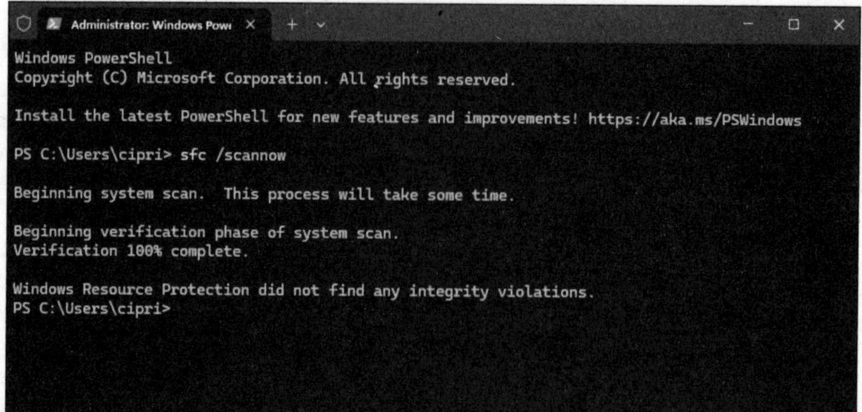

FIGURE 3-6: The sfc /scannow command scans all your system files.

The result of the scans is placed in the C:\Windows\Logs\CBS\CBS.log file. (*CBS* stands for *Component Based Servicing.*) You may want to make a ZIP of that file, in case one of Microsoft's tech support engineers needs to take a look.

Check the system event log from Event Viewer

Almost everything that happens in Windows gets posted to the system event log from Event Viewer. The biggest problem with the log? People get freaked out when they see all the errors. That's why you rarely see a recommendation to check the log. It's hard to believe that an error in a system event log is a natural occurrence.

Fair warning: Scammers frequently have customers look at their system event logs to convince them that their computer needs repair and that they have to pay for the scammer's services.

To bring up the system event log and interpret its results, look at Book 8, Chapter 4.

Refresh built-in Windows 11 apps

After the sfc /scannow run, refreshing the built-in apps is another common general recommendation for fixing a bad Windows 11 update. The command I recommend looks at each app installed in your user profile, and reinstalls a fresh, supposedly glitch-free copy:

1. **Right-click or press and hold the Start icon and choose Terminal (Admin). Or press Windows+X.**
2. **Click or tap Yes when UAC asks for your confirmation.**

3. **In the Windows Terminal window, type the following (all on one line) and press Enter:**

```
Get-AppXPackage -AllUsers | Foreach {Add-AppxPackage
   -DisableDevelopmentMode -Register "$($_.InstallLocation)\
   AppXManifest.xml"}
```

You see a bunch of red error messages (see Figure 3-7). Don't panic! Ignore them. Yes, even the ones that say "Deployment failed with HRESULT," "The package could not be installed because resources it modifies are currently in use," and "Unable to install because the following apps need to be closed."

When the Get-AppXPackage loop finishes — even with all those red warnings — you'll be returned to the Windows Terminal prompt.

4. **Close Windows Terminal, reboot, and see if the demons have been driven away.**

Although it sounds like this process will fix only misbehaving built-in Windows 11 apps, people have reported that it fixes all manner of problems with Windows 11, including icons that have stopped responding or Start menu problems.

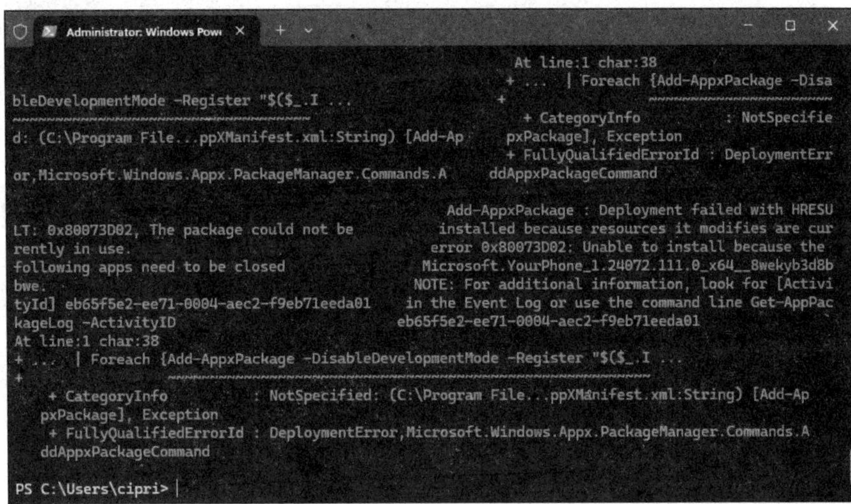

FIGURE 3-7: Don't be scared of all the red error messages you see.

Even if an app refresh doesn't fix your machine, you've now undertaken the second standard approach (after sfc /scannow) that you'll find offered just about everywhere.

Check Device Manager

Many problems can be traced back to non-Microsoft peripherals with drivers that don't work correctly. The first stop for bad devices is Device Manager:

1. **Right-click or press and hold the Start icon and choose Device Manager.**
2. **Look for yellow icons in the list of devices.**
3. **If you find any:**

   (a) *Double-click or double-tap the device that's causing problems to open its properties.*

   (b) *Click or tap the Driver tab.*

   (c) *See if you can find a newer driver by clicking or tapping Update Driver and asking Windows 11 to search automatically for drivers and find them through Windows Update, or by browsing for a driver you've downloaded locally.*

TIP

Download and install only Windows 11 drivers for your PC. If you can't find any, try Windows 10 64-bit drivers too. Don't go for Windows 8 or Windows 7 drivers because they will cause more problems than you already have.

WARNING

My previous recommendation doesn't work for laptops and computers with ARM processors. Be extra careful when using such a device and install only Windows 11 drivers for your specific architecture. Old drivers won't work on it because they weren't made for the hardware architecture you're using. They'll just crash your computer or worse.

Just walk away and forget it

It's good to keep a bit of perspective. If the latest Windows 11 cumulative update won't install (or if it breaks something) and you can get your machine back to a normal state, seriously consider doing nothing else.

I know it's heresy, but the most recent cumulative update doesn't necessarily fix anything you need (or want!) to have fixed immediately.

Yes, security patches are tossed into the giant cumulative update, but Microsoft doesn't bother to split those out so you can install them separately. So, you're stuck with an undifferentiated massive mess of fixes and security patches that may or may not be important to you.

There's no penalty for sitting out this particular cumulative update. The next one will come along, usually within a month, likely on Patch Tuesday (the anointed second Tuesday of the month), and it may well treat you and your machine better.

Tricks to Using Microsoft Support

To go straight to the source of Windows help, fire up your favorite web browser and go to the `https://support.microsoft.com` website, as shown in Figure 3-8. This is Microsoft's official support site for all its products, including Windows and Microsoft 365.

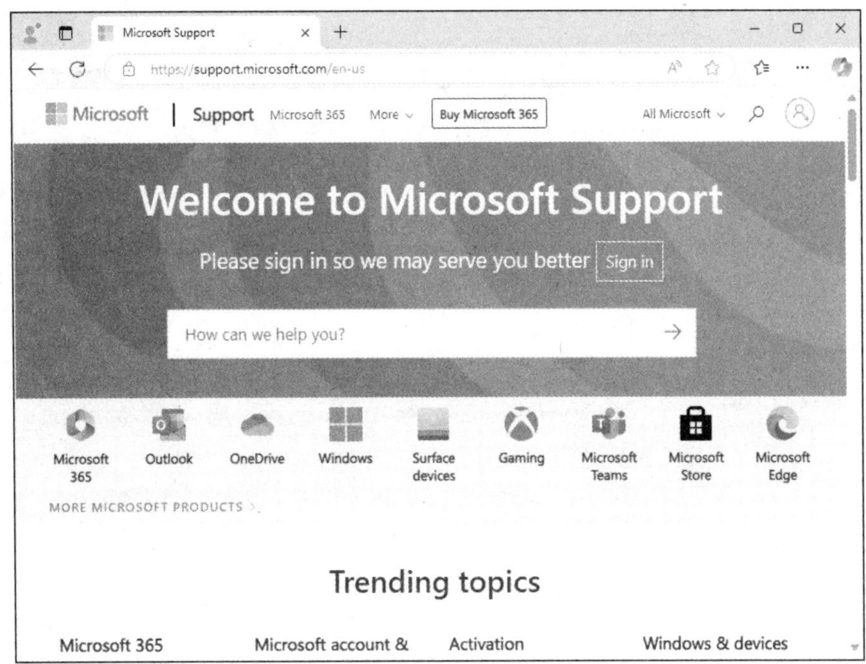

FIGURE 3-8: Microsoft's official support site.

If you click or tap the Windows category, you get to the Windows Help & Learning center, which includes how-to articles, links to Microsoft's support community, and support service.

The problems with Windows Help & Learning

Windows Help & Learning offers only Microsoft's official messaging. If a big problem crops up with Windows 11, you find only a brief report. If a product from a different manufacturer offers a better way to solve a problem, you won't find that information in Windows Help & Learning. If you're looking for in-depth technical advice and unbiased evaluations, you may not find it there. But that's why you have this book or tech blogs such as `www.digitalcitizen.life`.

Now, don't get me wrong. Microsoft isn't totally off base here. Windows Help & Learning is their way of saying, "Figure it out yourself. If you can't, maybe our articles can help or someone else can help you for free." It's all about keeping their support costs down. Smart move for them, I guess. But for you? Well, sometimes you need more than that and have to talk with an actual tech support engineer.

Managing your expectations of Windows Help & Learning

Windows Help & Learning has been set up for you to jump in, find an answer to your problem, resolve the problem, and get back to work. Unfortunately, life is not always so simple. You probably won't dive into Windows Help & Learning until you're feeling lost. Most of the content you find there falls into the following categories:

- **Overviews, articles, and tutorials:** These explanatory pieces are aimed at giving you an idea of what's going on, as opposed to solving a specific problem.
- **Tasks:** The step-by-step procedures are intended to solve a single problem or change a single setting.
- **Walkthroughs and guided tours:** These multimedia demonstrations of capabilities tend to be light on details and heavy on splash.

In my experience, Windows Help & Learning works best in the following situations:

- You want to understand what functions the big pieces of Windows 11 perform (for example, Windows 11 widgets) and aren't overly concerned about solving a specific problem.
- You have a problem that's easy to define (for example, *how to install a printer or a Bluetooth mouse*).
- You have a good idea of what you want to do (for example, use touch gestures), but you need a little prodding on the mechanics to get the job done.

This portal doesn't do much if you only have a vague idea of what's ailing your machine or if you want to understand enough details to think your way through a problem.

Using Quick Assist

Microsoft developed a new tool that allows you to remotely assist another person or receive help from someone else in a safe environment. The tool is Quick Assist, and it's now part of Windows 11. To use it, the person providing assistance must sign in with a Microsoft account. They can't use a local offline account or a work or school account.

This tool is particularly useful for troubleshooting issues, providing technical support, or guiding someone through something they want to do on their computer. Working with it involves two sides: the person providing the assistance, and the person receiving it. This section describes what each of them has to do.

Initiating the assistance process with Quick Assist

The person providing assistance must initiate a tech support session using Quick Assist, not the person receiving assistance. For that to happen, you must communicate before to the screen-sharing session so that both parties are online at the same time and each knows what they need to do.

If you want to help someone with their technical difficulties, here's how to ask them to share their screen with Quick Assist and give you permission to control their Windows 11 computer or device:

1. **Click or tap inside the Search box on the taskbar and type** assist.

   A list of search results appears.

2. **Select Quick Assist.**

   The Quick Assist app appears, as shown in Figure 3-9.

3. **Click or tap Help Someone.**

   You are asked to sign in with a Microsoft account. If you're using one, it's listed at the bottom of the sign-in page.

4. **Select your Microsoft account from the list or enter your credentials if necessary (such as email and password).**

   A code is generated for your upcoming remote tech support session, which expires in 10 minutes. Copy the code and send it to the person you want to help via chat, email, SMS, and so on.

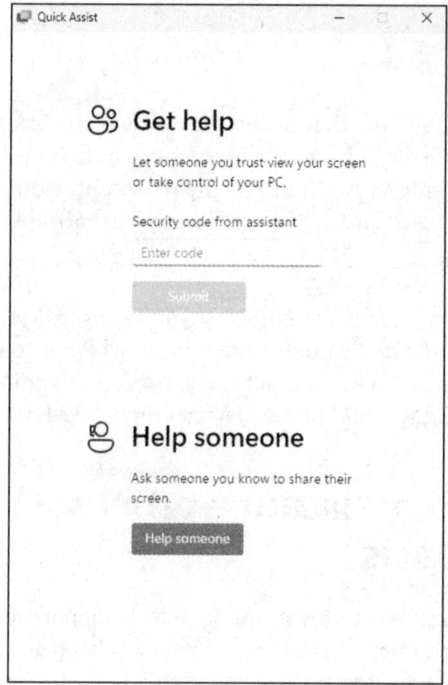

FIGURE 3-9: Quick Assist allows you to help others and receive help remotely.

5. **Wait for the other person to enter the code in the Quick Assist app.**

   After the connection is established, you see their desktop in the Quick Assist app window and a toolbar at the top with options for what you can do, as shown in Figure 3-10.

6. **Hover your mouse cursor over each icon on the toolbar to see its name and understand what it does.**

7. **When you want to start helping the other person, click or tap Request Control and wait for the other person to approve your request.**

   Once the request is approved, you can remotely control the other person's computer and help them out.

8. **When you've finished helping the other person, click or tap Leave.**

   You are informed that the screen sharing has ended.

9. **Close the Quick Assist app.**

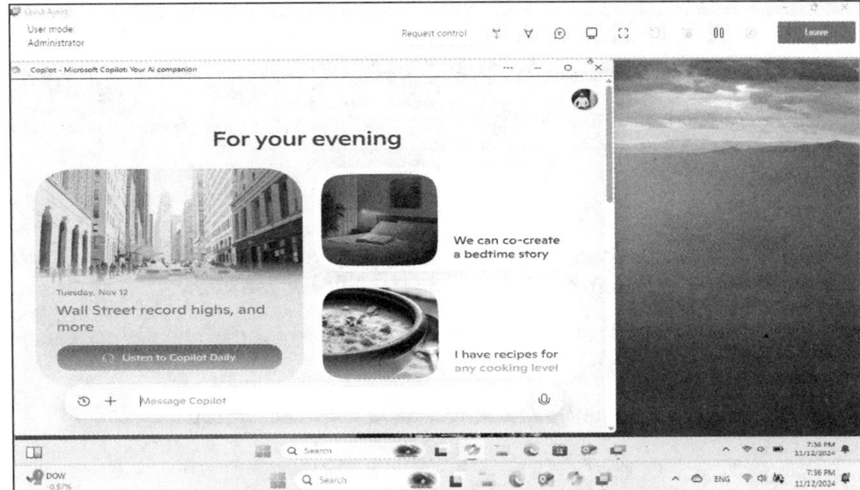

FIGURE 3-10: With Quick Assist you can remotely control another person's computer.

Receiving remote assistance through Quick Assist

If you are the person who needs remote assistance with troubleshooting or guidance in doing something, here's how to allow someone you trust to remotely access your PC with Quick Assist:

1. **Click or tap inside the Search box on the taskbar and type** assist.

   A list of search results appears.

2. **Select Quick Assist.**

   The Quick Assist app appears (refer to Figure 3-9).

3. **In the Security Code for Assistant text box, enter the code you received and then click or tap Submit.**

   The Quick Assist app establishes the connection between the two computers, and you're asked whether you want to allow screen sharing.

4. **Select the box next to I Understand the Security Implications of Sharing My Screen, and then click or tap Allow.**

   Quick Assist informs you that screen sharing is on and displays a toolbar at the top side of the screen, as shown in Figure 3-11. Your desktop also has yellow margins to signal that someone else can view it. The toolbar has a chat icon, a pause icon, and a Leave button, which do what their names imply. The other party can see everything on your screen. but can't control your computer unless they make a request for control and you approve it.

FIGURE 3-11: The toolbar you see when someone else connects to your computer.

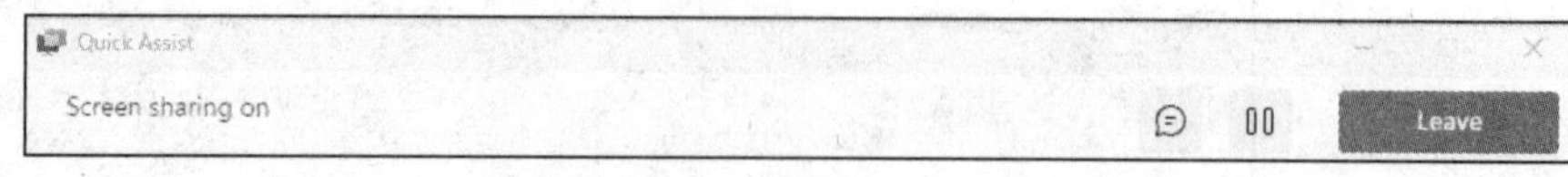

5. **When you see a message stating that the other party is requesting control of your computer, click or tap Allow.**

   The other person now has control of your computer and can help you fix your issue.

6. **When you no longer need help, click or tap Leave.**

   Quick Assist informs you that screen sharing has ended.

7. **Close the Quick Assist app.**

Experimenting with Windows Sandbox

If you run Windows 11 Pro, Education, or Enterprise, you get access to Windows Sandbox. This useful app helps you run anything you want in an isolated environment. Sandbox is a virtual machine that simulates your Windows 11 PC while being separated from the real Windows 11 environment you're using.

While Sandbox is open, what you do in Sandbox remains there. Also, when you close it, everything you've done is deleted. Suppose you receive a weird link via email, download a file from an untrusted source, or download an app with an odd name. Start Windows Sandbox, run the link or file there, and see what it does. If it's malware, it will be gone the moment you close Windows Sandbox and your machine will not be affected. Isn't that better than having your PC locked down by ransomware or fighting off the Blue Screen of Death?

Windows Sandbox is not installed by default in Windows 11. Here's how to add it:

1. **Click or tap in the Search box on the taskbar and type** features.
2. **In the list of search results, choose Turn Windows Features On or Off.**

   The Windows Features window appears, as shown in Figure 3-12.

3. **Scroll down and select the Windows Sandbox option, and then click or tap OK.**

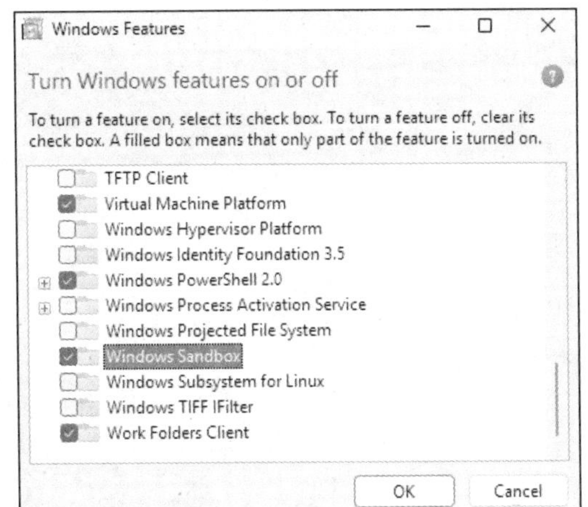

FIGURE 3-12: Adding Windows Sandbox to Windows 11.

4. **When Windows 11 completes the requested changes, click or tap Restart Now.**

   After Windows 11 restarts, it installs this feature, and you can use it after you log in.

Think of Windows Sandbox as your computer's bulletproof vest. Got a sketchy app, a fishy file, or a link that smells like trouble? Don't gamble with your PC. Instead, fire up Sandbox and test it there. This app is like a disposable playground where you can mess around without risking your real system.

In the following steps, I assume that you've received a weird link in your inbox or a chat app. Here's how to check out the link by using Windows Sandbox:

1. **Click or tap the Start icon, followed by All.**

   You see the list of apps available on your Windows 11 computer device.

2. **Scroll down to the apps that start with the letter *W* and select Windows Sandbox.**

   The Windows Sandbox opens, showing you another Windows 11 desktop, similar to Figure 3-13.

3. **Copy the link but don't paste it in your web browser.**

   Don't paste the link in an app on your desktop; instead, paste the link in Windows Sandbox.

4. **Fire up the Microsoft Edge browser inside Windows Sandbox.**

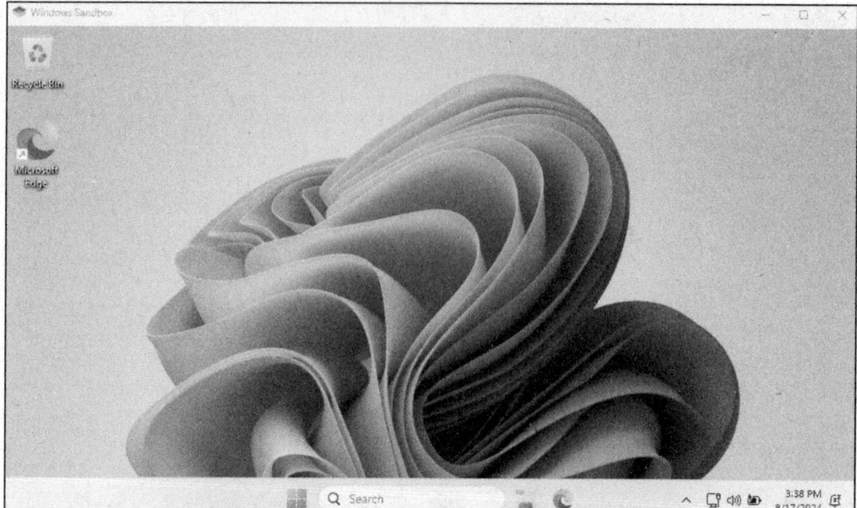

FIGURE 3-13: Using the Windows Sandbox protects you from many security headaches.

5. **Paste the link inside Windows Sandbox and see where it leads you. If the link downloads a file, let it finish, and then run the file inside Sandbox.**

   If something harmful has happened, don't worry; it will affect your current Windows Sandbox session, not your computer. If the file or link is okay, you can then access it on your computer knowing that you're safe.

6. **When you've finished experimenting, click or tap X in the top-right corner of Windows Sandbox, and confirm that you want to close it.**

   The app is closed, and all of its contents are discarded and permanently lost. Anything dangerous that happened goes away.

Getting Better Help Online

As you have seen in this chapter, Microsoft is making it easier to chat with a real, live human being when you need tech support. But you may find better answers if you hop on to the Microsoft Answers forum at `https://answers.microsoft.com`.

Lots of people join in on the forums to help (see the nearby sidebar). Many of the helpers are Microsoft MVPs (Most Valued Professionals) who work without pay just for the joy of knowing that they're helping people. Microsoft gives the MVPs recognition and thanks and some occasional benefits, such as being able to talk with people on the development teams. In exchange, the MVPs give generally good — and sometimes excellent — support to anyone who asks.

MICROSOFT ANSWERS FORUM

The Microsoft Answers forum is one of the great resources for Windows 11 customers. There are sections for just about every nook and cranny of every Microsoft product. You post questions, other people post answers, and it's free for everyone.

But it's important that you understand the limitations.

Most of the people on the Answers forum are not Microsoft employees — in fact, it's pretty rare to see Microsoft employees on the forum. (They're identified as Microsoft employees in their tagline.)

Although the typical forum user may be well-intentioned, they aren't necessarily well-informed. You must keep that in mind while wading through the questions and answers.

The Answers forum is a great place to go with immediate problems that may affect other people. It's one of the few ways that you can register a gripe and expect that, if it's a valid gripe, somebody at Microsoft will read it — and maybe respond to it.

In particular, realize that both the moderators and the Microsoft *Most Valued Professionals, or MVPs* (also identified in their taglines), are volunteers. No, the moderators are not Microsoft employees. No, Microsoft doesn't pay the MVPs either. They help on the forums out of the goodness of their hearts. Hard to believe that in this day and age, but it's true. So be kind!

IN THIS CHAPTER

» Formatting drives

» Freeing up storage space

» Checking the disk for errors

» Defragmenting drives

» Managing drives and partitions

Chapter 4

Managing Storage

In the early days of computing, maintaining your computer's performance required significant manual effort. Fortunately, Windows has evolved considerably, with Microsoft's operating system now handling most maintenance tasks automatically. However, there are occasions when you might need to format a drive or free up space. Don't worry — these tasks aren't as daunting as they might seem, and I guide you through both processes in this chapter.

I also explore defragmentation, a manual task once crucial for computer health but now largely automated by Windows. Nevertheless, if you suspect your hard drive isn't performing optimally or you're curious about its condition, I show you how to analyze and manually optimize it if necessary.

Next, I present you with Check Disk, an excellent utility for identifying and fixing storage errors. Then I move on to Disk Management, which helps you organize your storage efficiently.

By the end of this chapter, you'll be well-equipped to manage your computer's storage. Your drives will run efficiently, and you'll have plenty of space for all your important files (yes, those cat videos, too). Even though Windows 11 might occasionally misbehave, your computer will certainly appreciate your newfound storage management expertise.

Using Maintenance Tools for Your Drives

Hard drives start to malfunction at the worst possible moments, and a hard drive that's no longer working normally can display some strange symptoms: everything from long pauses when you're trying to open a file to inexplicable crashes and other errors in Windows 11 itself. Luckily, the operating system has a handful of utilities designed to help you keep your hard drives in top shape. They're split as follows:

- **Format utility:** When you format a data storage device (hard disk, solid-state drive, USB flash drive, and so on), you're preparing it for initial use. The process involves erasing the data found on the storage device and setting up a file system on it.
- **Basic utilities:** Three simple utilities stand out as effective ways to care for your hard drives. You should get to know Check Disk, Storage Sense (an improved version of the old Disk Cleanup), and Defragment and Optimize Drives. They all come in handy in the right situation.
- **Storage Spaces:** Keeps a duplicate copy of every file in case a hard drive breaks down. To use Storage Spaces effectively, you need at least three hard drives and twice as much hard drive space as you have data. Not everyone can afford that, and few people are willing to give it a try, due to its technical complexity. If you're interested, read Book 7, Chapter 5.

Formatting drives

Imagine every storage device (SSD, USB flash drive, HDD, and so on) as a big empty warehouse. Before you can use it, you must format it. And formatting is like setting up shelves and labeling systems in that warehouse so Windows 11 can store and find your files easily. When you format a drive, you're telling Windows, "Hey, get this space ready for me to use!"

WARNING

Remember that each time you format a drive, any data stored on it is deleted. Therefore, before formatting a drive, ensure that you have made a backup of the data you want to keep.

After you format it, the drive is ready to store your files. If you want to format a storage device such as a USB memory stick or an external hard disk, plug it into your PC, wait for Windows 11 to detect it, and do the following:

1. **Click or tap the File Explorer icon on the taskbar.**
2. **On the left, choose This PC.**

3. **Right-click (or press and hold) the drive that you want to format, and choose Format in the menu that appears (see Figure 4-1).**

   The Format dialog appears.

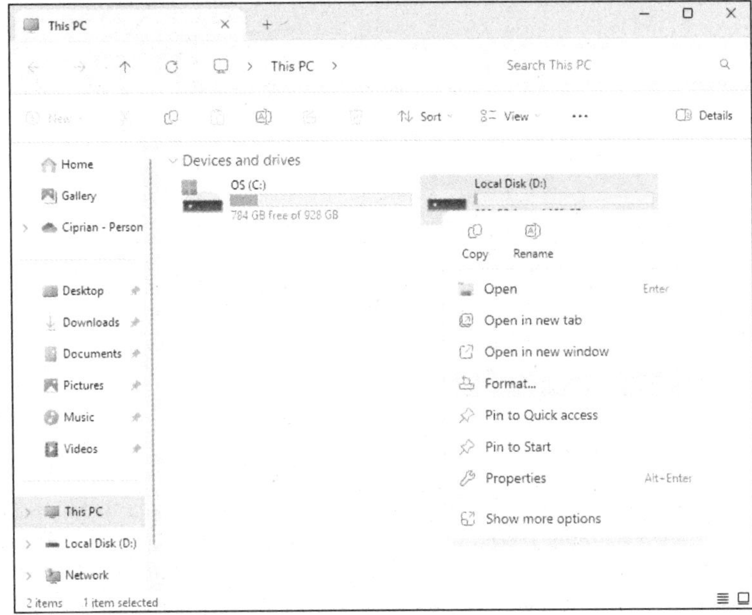

FIGURE 4-1: Format a new storage device (HDD, SSD, USB drive) before using it.

4. **Click or tap the File System drop-down list (see Figure 4-2) and choose the file system you want.**

   NTFS (New Technology File System) is the best choice because it's the file system that works best with Windows.

5. **In the Volume Label field, type the name you want for your drive.**

   The character limit for volume labels varies depending on the file system. FAT32 supports up to11 characters; NTFS and exFAT support up to 32 characters.

6. **Select the Quick Format option, so that the process is finalized in seconds instead of minutes.**

7. **Click or tap Start, and then OK when asked if you're fine with going ahead with the formatting.**

   When the formatting is finalized, a confirmation message appears.

8. **Click or tap OK and then Close.**

   You can start using the drive you just formatted and store files on it.

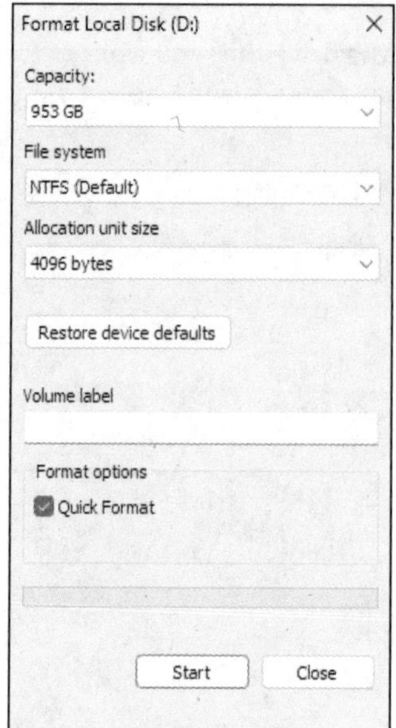

FIGURE 4-2: Choose how you want to format your drive.

TIP

You can use these steps to format or reformat any hard drive or partition other than the one that contains Windows 11. You can also format and delete all the data on rewritable DVDs, Blu-ray discs, USB flash drives, and SD or other removable memory cards. However, to reformat the drive that contains Windows, you must re-install Windows.

Freeing up storage space with Storage Sense

Storage Sense is a Windows feature that helps you free up storage space on your computer by removing things like the items in your Recycle Bin, temporary files, unused files in the Downloads folder, and unused Windows apps.

Here's how to use Storage Sense to clean up unused files from Windows 11:

1. **Click or tap the Start icon on the taskbar and then Settings.**

   Alternatively, you can press Windows+I.

2. **On the left, select System. Then on the right, click or tap Storage.**

   Storage Sense spends some time analyzing how your storage space is used, and then shows results similar to the ones in Figure 4-3.

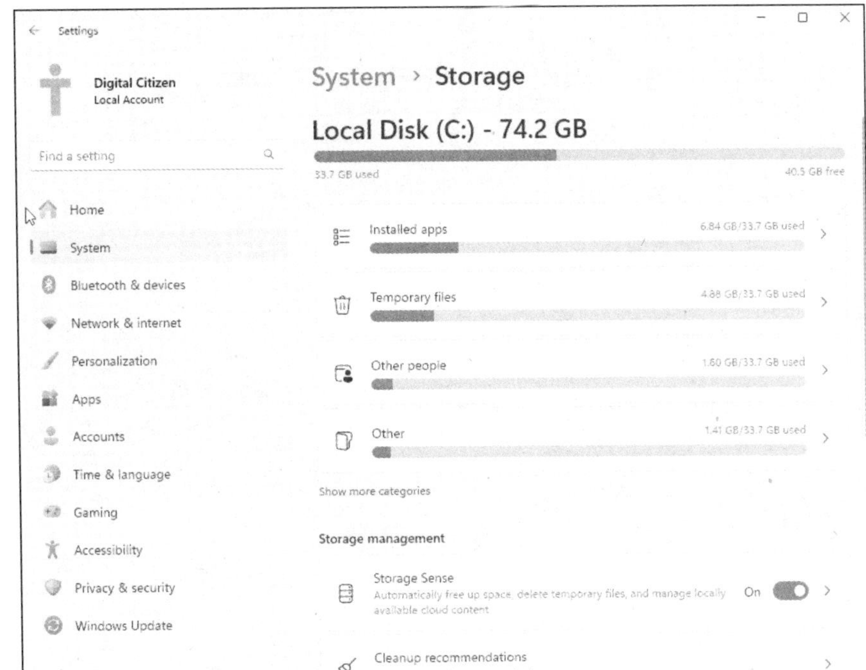

FIGURE 4-3: Storage Sense shows you how your storage space is used.

3. **Click or tap Cleanup Recommendations.**

   Storage Sense displays several recommendations for what you can delete, split into these categories: temporary files, large or unused files, files synced to the cloud, and unused apps. See Figure 4-4.

4. **Expand each category of recommendations one by one, select the items you want removed, and click or tap Clean Up followed by Continue.**

   You return to Cleanup Recommendations, where you can repeat Step 4 as many times as you want.

5. **When you've finished cleaning up unused files, close Settings.**

Running an error check on a drive

If a drive starts acting weird (for example, you see error messages when trying to open a file, or Windows 11 crashes, or a simple file copy takes hours instead of minutes), it's time to make a check for disk errors:

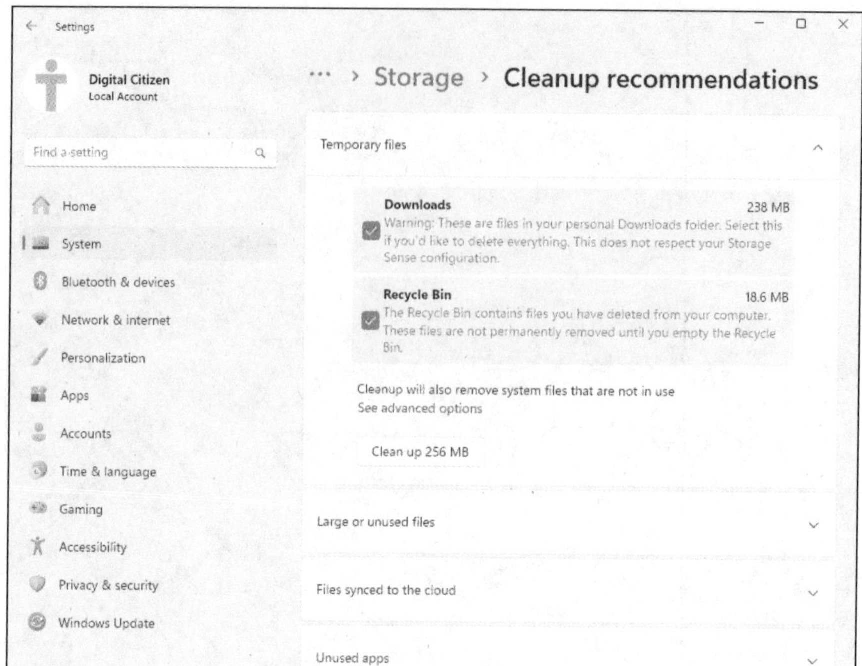

FIGURE 4-4: Choose what you want to clean from your storage.

Follow these steps to run Check Disk:

1. **Log in to an administrator account.**
2. **Bring up the drive you want to check in File Explorer:**

   (a) *Click or tap the File Explorer icon.*

   (b) *On the left, choose This PC.*

   (c) *Right-click or press and hold the drive that's giving you problems and choose Properties.*

   You see the Local Disk Properties dialog box.

3. **On the Tools tab, click or tap the Check button next to Error Checking, as shown in Figure 4-5.**

   Windows 11 may tell you that you don't need to scan the drive because it hasn't found any errors on the drive. If you're skeptical, though, go right ahead and scan it.

4. **Click or tap Scan Drive.**

   Windows 11 tells you about any problems it encounters and asks for your permission to fix them.

5. **When you're finished, click or tap Close, followed by OK.**

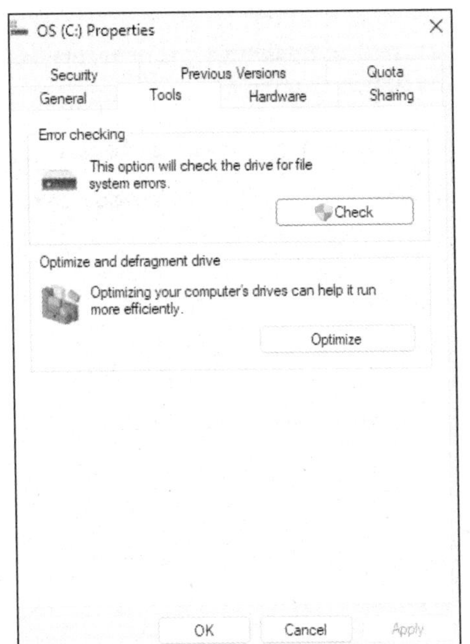

FIGURE 4-5: Run a check disk in Windows 11.

Defragmenting a drive

Defragmentation is like organizing a messy closet, but for your computer files. Back in the old days, Windows would scatter file pieces all over your hard drive, making it slow to find and use them. Defragmentation is like telling Windows, "Hey, put all these file pieces back together!" and it helps speed up old-school hard drives with moving parts. The problem? Windows didn't do this automatically, so most people forgot about it. Their hard drives ended up looking like a jumbled jigsaw puzzle! When someone finally remembered to defragment, it could take forever.

Luckily, starting with Windows 7, Microsoft got smart and made Windows tidy your drive automatically every week. Windows 11 keeps this helpful habit going. So now, you don't have to lift a finger to keep your drive neat.

TECHNICAL STUFF

Windows 11 doesn't run automatic defrags on SSDs because they're flash memory drives that don't have any moving parts. SSDs don't need defragmentation. In fact, defragmentation is bad for SSDs because it makes them wear out more quickly.

If you're curious about how your computer's doing in the defragmentation department, you can see the defragmenter report:

1. **Click or tap in the Search box on the taskbar and type** defrag.
2. **Click or tap the Defragment and Optimize Drives search result.**

   The Optimize Drives dialog appears.
3. **Choose the drive you want to look at and click or tap Analyze.**

   You see how much of the drive is fragmented or how many days have passed since the last retrim (for SSDs), as shown in Figure 4-6.

   TIP

   A *retrim* is a rerun of the trim command, which I describe in the next section.

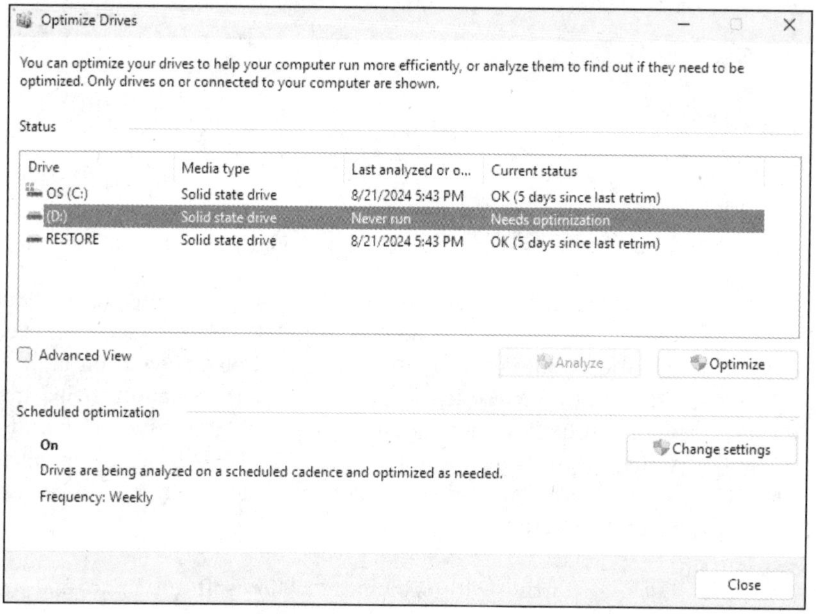

FIGURE 4-6: Windows 11's drive optimization activities.

4. **If the fragmentation is more than 20 percent or a retrim hasn't been performed for more than a week, click or tap the Optimize button.**

   Windows 11 runs the defragmentation and optimization of the selected drive and its files.

Maintaining solid-state drives

Solid-state drives (SSDs) are like the sports cars of the PC world. They're more reliable than traditional hard disk drives (HDDs) and way faster. If you need a speed boost on your computer, change your C: drive from a hard disk to an SSD. Even upgrading from an old SSD to a new one can make your computer feel snappier. Expect significantly faster file copying and loading, and a quicker Windows startup.

SSDs don't need the old-school defragmentation that HDDs do. Instead, they use something called TRIM. It's a command that tells the SSD which data blocks are no longer needed and can be deleted or marked as free for rewriting, helping Windows manage your data more efficiently.

TIP

For the best SSD performance, visit your SSD manufacturer's website and download any utilities they offer for your drive. While Windows 11 does a good job, these tools might have extra features to keep your SSD in top shape.

Managing Your Disks

Disk Management is the main Windows tool you can use to manage your disks. It gives you the lowdown on all your physical disks, volumes, partitions, and logical drives. But that's not all — it's also your go-to utility for many disk-related tasks. You can see this app in action in Figure 4-7. Disk Management utilizes a two-pane user interface. The upper pane lists system volumes, displaying essential information such as type, status, capacity, and available free space. You can execute volume-specific commands by right-clicking entries in the Volume column.

The lower pane represents physical devices, with each row showing device names (such as Disk 0, Disk 1), types, sizes, and statuses. Volume information for each device is displayed on the right. Right-clicking a disk number heading in the lower pane reveals device-wide commands while right-clicking a volume area presents volume-specific options.

With Disk Management, you can view the properties of disks and volumes, including their size, file system, and status. You can also create, format, and delete volumes, partitions, and logical drives. Last but not least, this app helps you assign drive letters to various storage devices and can extend or shrink volumes, optimizing storage space. Since I must keep the page count of this book to a reasonable amount, I can't share detailed instructions on everything you can do with Disk Management. However, I can share details about the basics to get you started.

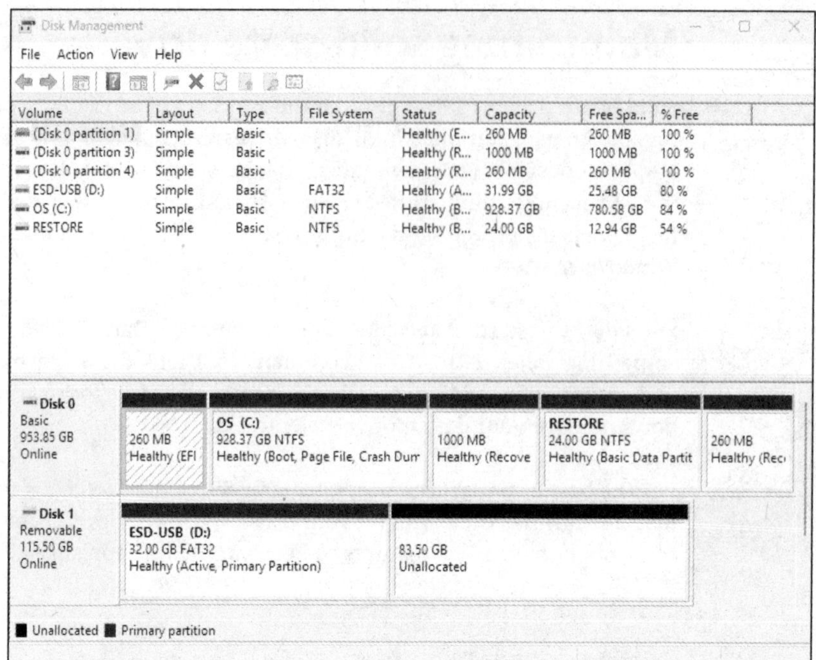

FIGURE 4-7: Disk Management helps you manage your storage.

TECHNICAL STUFF

In Disk Management, you'll see at least a system partition, which contains essential bootstrap files for the system startup and the boot menu display. This partition, known as the EFI System Partition (ESP), is at least 100 MB and is automatically managed by the operating system. The ESP is crucial for the system's boot process and is not intended for direct user modification. You'll also find a RECOVERY or RESTORE partition. It has at least 300 MB (hardware manufacturers may create a larger recovery partition to accommodate additional tools) and includes the Windows Recovery image.

Changing the drive letter

Windows assigns letters to all the drives inside your PC and those you connect externally. The partition where the operating system is installed is named C, while the others are assigned letters in alphabetical order: D, E, F, and so on. By default, letters A and B are not used unless you manually edit the letter assigned to a drive. Before you change the letter of a drive, ensure that no apps are installed on it that could start to malfunction after changing the drive letter. If everything is okay, follow these steps:

1. **Log in to an administrator account.**
2. **Right-click or press and hold the Start icon and select Disk Management.**

   The Disk Management app appears (refer to Figure 4-7). At the bottom of the app, you see all the disks on your computer and how they're partitioned. In my case, I have two disks: the SSD drive built into the laptop and a USB flash drive that I plug into the laptop. On your computer or device, things will look different.

3. **Right-click or press and hold the drive whose letter you want to change and select Change Drive Letter and Paths.**

   The dialog shown in Figure 4-8 appears.

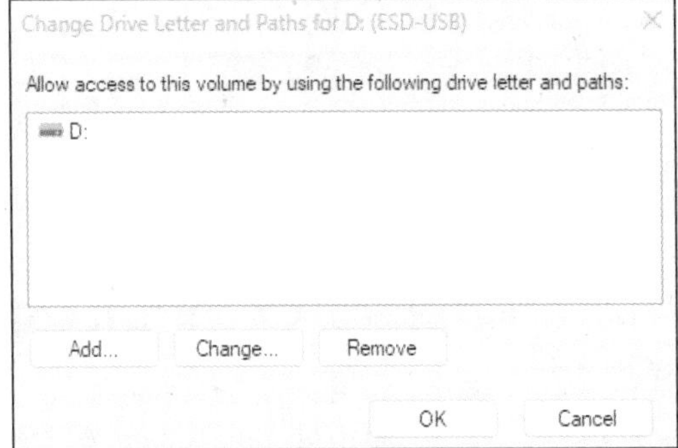

FIGURE 4-8: Changing the drive letter with Disk Management.

4. **Select the drive letter and click or tap Change.**

   You see the Change Drive Letter and Path dialog, where you can set a new drive letter.

5. **Click or tap the drop-down list next to Assign the Following Drive Letter, and select a new letter.**
6. **Click or tap OK, followed by Yes to confirm your choice.**

   The drive letter changes to match your selection.

7. **You can repeat Steps 3 to 6 for all the drives you want to change. When you've finished making changes, close Disk Management.**

   The next time you open File Explorer, you'll see your drive(s) using the new letter(s).

Deleting drives

If you no longer need a partition, you can delete it so that its space can be used for other purposes: creating a new partition with a different size, extending an existing partition, and so on. However, before deleting a partition, ensure that you back up the data from it that is useful to you, and then follow these steps:

1. **Log in to an administrator account.**
2. **Right-click or press and hold the Start icon and select Disk Management.**

   The Disk Management app appears (refer to Figure 4-7).
3. **Right-click or press and hold the partition you want to remove and select Delete Volume.**

   You are informed that deleting this volume will erase all data found on it, and you're asked to confirm that you want to continue.
4. **Click or tap Yes to go ahead.**

   The partition is deleted, its drive letter is lost, and it's labeled Unallocated.

Creating, shrinking, or extending partitions

If Disk Management reports some unallocated storage space, you can use that to create a new partition or extend an existing one. To create a new partition, do the following:

1. **Right-click or press and hold the Start icon and select Disk Management.**

   The Disk Management app appears (refer to Figure 4-7).
2. **Right-click or press and hold the unallocated space you want to use and choose New Simple Volume.**

   The New Simple Volume Wizard appears.
3. **Click or tap Next.**

   You see the minimum and maximum space you can use for the partition you are about to create, as shown in Figure 4-9.
4. **In the Simple Volume Size in MB, enter the space you want to use for the new partition (in MB), and then click or tap Next.**

   You are asked to choose a drive letter for the partition.
5. **Assign a drive letter and then click or tap Next.**

   You are asked to format the partition, choose the file system, and provide a name (or volume label).

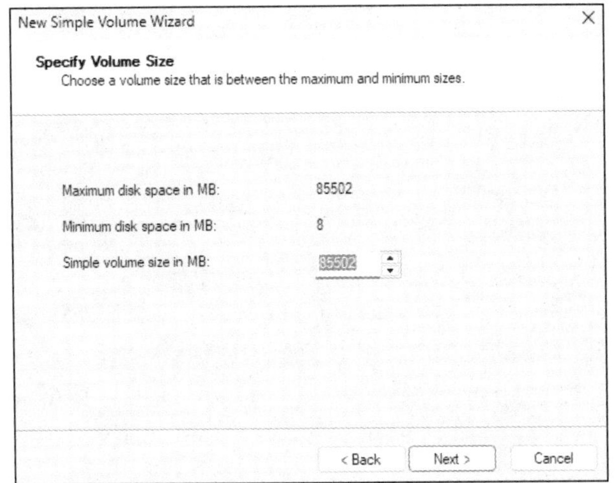

FIGURE 4-9: Creating a new partition with Disk Management.

6. **Select NTFS (or any other file system you want), type a new volume label (the name of your partition), and click or tap Next.**

   You see a summary of your selections.

7. **Click or tap Finish and wait for the partition to be created.**

   You see a notification when the process is finished, and the partition is displayed in Disk Management, where the unallocated space used to be.

TIP

To shrink a partition, right-click or press and hold the partition you want, select Shrink Volume, enter the amount of space you want to shrink in MB, and click or tap Shrink. A new unallocated space will be created using the size you've specified in MB.

TIP

To extend a partition, make sure that some unallocated space is available next to it, right-click or press and hold on that partition, and select Extend Volume. Then, follow the Extend Volume Wizard to make that partition larger.

IN THIS CHAPTER

» Understanding Storage Spaces

» Setting up Storage Spaces

» Managing and removing Storage Spaces

Chapter 5
Storing in Storage Spaces

Data loss can be a nightmare, whether it's caused by failing hard drives or backup routines that don't run as expected. Fortunately, Windows 11 offers a powerful feature called Storage Spaces that may, in and of itself, justify buying, installing, and using this operating system.

Storage Spaces is a technology that allows you to virtualize storage by grouping multiple storage drives into storage pools and creating virtual disks, known as *storage spaces*. It's important not to confuse this with Storage Sense, another feature in Windows 11 designed to clean up unnecessary files. For more on Storage Sense, refer to the Chapter 4 of this minibook.

What makes Storage Spaces valuable is its capability to treat multiple hard drives as a single entity while providing data resiliency. This means it can automatically create two or more copies of your data, ensuring that even if a hard drive fails, your information remains safe and accessible. If you don't require data resiliency, you can use it also to combine multiple drives into a huge storage pool and benefit from it as you need.

While many people prefer cloud backups using services such as OneDrive, Google Drive, or Dropbox, having a reliable local backup solution offers peace of mind. Even if you regularly back up to the cloud, knowing that your on-premises data is protected against hardware failure is reassuring. Conversely, if all your data resides in the cloud and you're not concerned about local drive failures, you might consider skipping this chapter.

The only major downside of Storage Spaces is that it can't be used on laptops unless they allow you to install multiple storage drives, and it's unusable on Ultrabooks because they tend not to be upgradable. Therefore, Storage Spaces is best used on desktop computers.

In this chapter, I introduce you to Windows 11's approach to storage virtualization and delve into the workings of Storage Spaces. You learn how to set up Storage Spaces and discover tips and tricks to maximize its benefits. Despite its technical complexity, using Storage Spaces for data backups is straightforward and user-friendly.

Understanding the Virtualization of Storage

Windows 11's Storage Spaces takes care of disk management behind the scenes, so you don't have to. You'll never know or care which hard drives on your computer hold what folders or which files go where. With Storage Spaces, volumes and folders get extended as needed, and you don't have to lift a finger.

You don't have to worry about your D: drive running out of space because you don't *have* a D: drive. Or an E: drive. Windows 11 just grabs all the hard drive real estate you give it and hands out pieces of the hard drive as needed.

REMEMBER

If you have two or more physical hard drives of sufficient capacity, any data you store in a Storage Spaces pool is automatically mirrored between two or more independent hard drives. If one of the hard drives dies, you can still work with the ones that are alive, and not one bit of data is out of place. Run out and buy a new drive, stick it inside your computer, tell Windows 11 that it can accept the new drive into Storage Spaces, wait an hour or two while Windows performs its magic, and all your data is back to normal. It's really that simple.

When your PC starts running out of disk space, Windows tells you. Install another drive — internal, external, USB, eSATA, and so on — and, with your permission, it's absorbed into the storage pool. More space becomes available, and you don't need to care about any of the details — no new drive letters, no partitions, no massive copying or moving files from one drive to another. For those accustomed to the many quirks of Windows, the Storage Spaces approach to disk management feels like a breath of fresh air.

When you add a new hard drive to the Storage Spaces pool, everything that was on that new hard drive gets obliterated. You don't have any choice. No data on the drive survives — it's all wiped out. That's the price the drive pays for being absorbed into Storage Spaces, but this choice has many benefits.

Here's a high-level overview of how you set up Storage Spaces with data mirroring:

1. Tell Windows 11 that it can use two or more drives as a storage pool.

   Your C: drive — the drive that contains Windows — cannot be part of the pool.

   TIP

   The best configuration for Storage Spaces: Get a fast solid-state drive for your system files and make that the C: drive. Then get two or more big drives for storing all your data. The big drives can be slow, but you'll hardly notice. You can use a mixture of spinning disks and solid-state disks if you like.

2. After you set up a pool of physical hard drives, you can create one or more spaces.

   In practice, most home and small business users will want only one space. But you can create more if you like.

3. Establish a maximum size for each space and choose a mirroring technology if you want the data mirrored.

   The maximum size can be bigger than the total amount of space available on all your hard drives. That's one of the advantages of virtualization: If you run out of physical hard drive space, instead of crashing, Windows 11 just asks you to feed it another drive.

   TECHNICAL STUFF

   For a discussion of the available mirroring technologies, see the sidebar "Mirroring technologies in Storage Spaces."

4. If a drive dies, keep going and put in a new drive when you can. If you want to replace a drive with a bigger (or more reliable) one, tell Windows to get rid of (*dismount*) the old drive, wait an hour or so, turn off the PC, take out the old drive, stick in a new one, and away you go.

   It's that simple.

TIP

If you've ever heard of RAID (Redundant Array of Inexpensive Disks) technology, you may think that Storage Spaces sounds familiar. The concepts are similar in some respects, but Storage Spaces doesn't use RAID. Instead of relying on specialized hardware and fancy controllers — both hallmarks of a RAID installation — all of Storage Spaces is built into Windows 11 itself, and Storage Spaces can use any kind of hard drive — internal, external, IDE, SATA, USB, eSATA, you name it — in any size, mix or match. No need for any special hardware or software other than Windows itself.

MIRRORING TECHNOLOGIES IN STORAGE SPACES

When it comes to mirroring — Microsoft calls it *resiliency* — you have several choices. You can

- Choose to *not mirror* at all, meaning the *simple (no resilience)* option. That way, you lose the automatic real-time backup, but you still get the benefits of pooled storage.
- Designate a space as a *two-way mirrored* space, thus telling Windows 11 that it should automatically keep backup copies of everything in the space on at least two separate hard drives and recover from dead hard drives automatically as well. It's important to realize that your programs don't even know that the data's being mirrored. Storage Spaces takes care of all the details behind the scenes. *Two-way mirror* spaces require at least two drives to make your files resilient to drive failure.
- Use *three-way mirroring,* which is only for the most fanatical people with acres of hard drive space to spare. As its name implies, it creates copies of everything on three separate hard drives. *Three-way mirror* spaces require at least five drives to provide you with the necessary resilience to drive failures.
- Use another form of redundancy called *parity,* which calculates checksums on your data (values calculated from your data to verify its integrity) and stores the sums in such a way that the data can be reconstructed from dead disks without having two full copies of the original file sitting around. Spaces using parity for resiliency are best for storing many file archives and streaming media, such as music and videos. This type of redundancy requires at least three drives to protect you from a single drive failure and at least seven drives to protect you from two drive failures. If you're using single parity, Storage Spaces splits data chunks into two disks and uses a third one as a parity disk. *Dual parity* is the same, but parity data gets split onto two disks.

Setting Up Storage Spaces

Even though you can set up Storage Spaces with just two hard drives — your C: system drive plus one data drive — you don't get much benefit out of it until you move up to three drives. So, in this section, I assume that you have your C: drive plus two more hard drives — internal or external— hooked up to your PC. I further assume that those two hard drives have absolutely nothing on them that you want to keep — because all the data on them will be lost.

Ready to set up a space? Here's how:

1. **Click or tap the Start icon, followed by Settings.**

   Windows opens the Settings app.

2. **On the left, choose System. On the right, click or tap Storage, followed by Advanced Storage Settings.**

   A list of options extends.

3. **Click or tap Storage Spaces.**

   You see the Storage Spaces page from the Settings app, as shown in Figure 5-1.

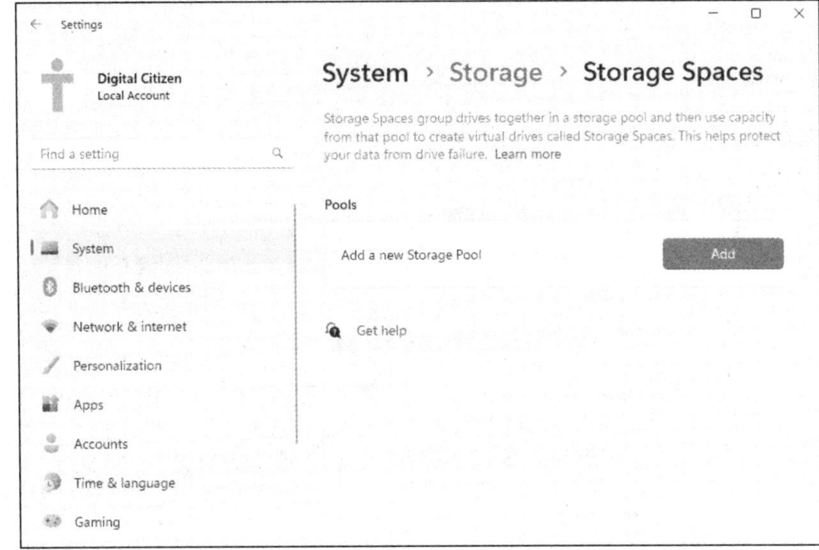

FIGURE 5-1: The Storage Spaces page in the Settings app.

4. **Click or tap Add.**

   You must create a storage pool first — that is, assign physical hard drives to the storage pool. Windows 11 offers to create a storage pool, as shown in Figure 5-2, and lists the drives it finds available.

5. **Carefully select the check boxes next to the drives that you want to include in the storage pool.**

WARNING

Be careful! If you accidentally select a drive that contains useful data, your data is going to disappear. Irretrievably. And I do mean *irretrievably.* You can't use Recuva or some other disk-scanning tool to bring back your data. After the drive is absorbed into the storage pool, the data is gone.

New storage pool

Name

Storage pool

Add disks

Select which disks you want to add to the storage pool.

Total projected pool capacity: 0 bytes

Available disks

MTFDKBA1T0QFM-1BD1AABGB 953 GB
Disk 0
SSD

TUF Gaming AS1000 953 GB
Disk 2
SSD

Create Cancel

FIGURE 5-2: Choose the drives you want to add to the storage pool.

6. **Click or tap Create.**

   Windows 11 displays the New Storage Space dialog box, as shown in Figure 5-3.

7. **Give your storage space a name.**

   You use the name as if the storage pool you are about to create is made of just one drive (like the rest you have on your computer or device), even though the storage space spans two or more hard drives. You can format the storage space drive, copy data to or from the drive, and even partition the drive as if it were a physical drive.

8. **Set a logical size for the storage space.**

   The logical size of the storage space can exceed the available hard drive space. There's no downside to having an exceptionally large logical size other than a bit of overhead in some internal tables.

9. **Choose a resiliency type.**

   For a discussion of your choices — simple (no resiliency), two-way mirror, three-way mirror, parity, and dual parity — see the sidebar "Mirroring technologies in Storage Spaces" earlier in this chapter.

New Storage Space

Storage Spaces settings page.

Name

Storage space

Size & resiliency

A Storage Space can be larger than the capacity of the storage pool. You can add more disks to the pool later to increase pool capacity.

900 GB

Resiliency is a way to protect against disk failures by making copies of files.

Simple (no resiliency)

A simple storage space writes one copy of your data and doesn't protect you from disk failure.

Maximum pool usage 900 GB

Pool capacity (Storage pool) 953 GB (953 GB free)

Create Skip

FIGURE 5-3: Give the new storage space a name, and choose the size and the resilience.

10. **Click or tap Create.**

    Windows 11 asks you to format the new volume and choose a drive letter and a file system.

11. **Use the default values, and then click or tap Format.**

    The storage pool is created, and Windows opens File Explorer to show the newly created disk.

TECHNICAL STUFF

If you try to create a new storage pool and Windows doesn't display a disk that you've attached, click or tap Cancel, and then delete any existing volumes from that disk using Disk Management. Read Chapter 4 in this minibook for details. You can also try to run the same procedure using the Control Panel version of Storage Spaces. You can access it by searching for storage spaces in the Search box on the taskbar and choosing Manage Storage Spaces. Some users report that the Control Panel version sometimes does a better job at detecting available disks than the Settings version. I once, too, encountered this bug, and it baffled me.

Managing Storage Spaces

First, realize that for all the user accounts and apps on your machine, your storage space looks just like any other hard drive. You can use the drive letter of the storage pool the same way you'd use any other drive letter. The folders inside work like any other folders. And if you have a cranky old program that requires a simple drive letter, the storage space won't do anything to spoil the illusion. That said, storage space drives can't be defragmented or run through the Check Disk utility.

Here's how to find the properties of your storage pool:

1. **Click or tap the Start icon, followed by Settings.**

   Windows opens the Settings app.

2. **Go to System, Storage, Advanced Storage Settings, and click or tap Storage Spaces.**

   You see the storage pool you've created and its status.

3. **Click or tap on the name of your storage pool.**

   Windows 11 displays the properties of your storage pool, including the physical disks that are used for it, as in Figure 5-4.

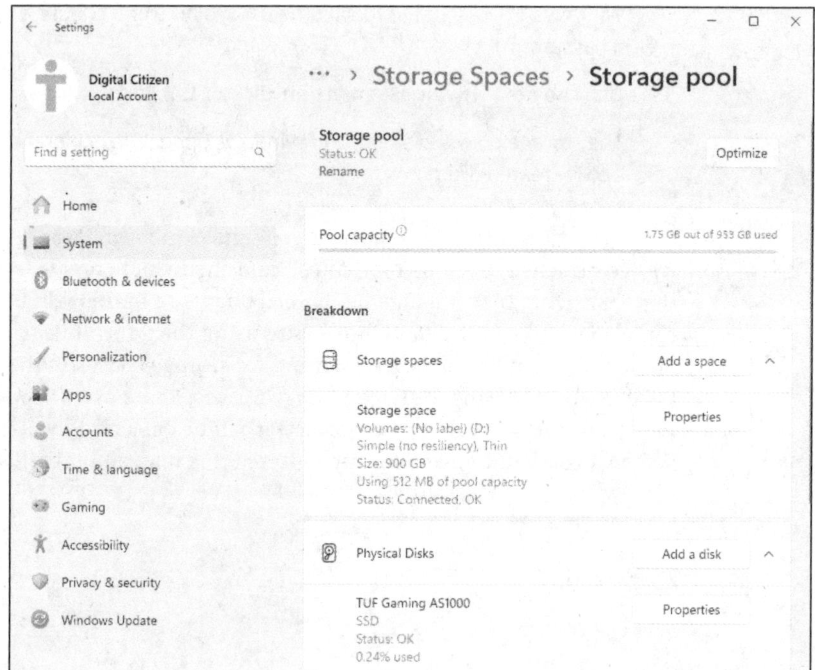

FIGURE 5-4: Here you find a breakdown of your storage pool.

This Storage Spaces report tells you how much real, physical hard drive space you're using, what the storage space looks like to your Windows 11 apps, and how your physical hard drives have been organized and set up to support your storage pool. Here, you can add a new storage space, attach more disks to the existing storage pool, rename your storage pool, optimize it, and more.

It's quite a testament to the designers of Storage Spaces that all this works so well — and invisibly to the rest of Windows. This is the way storage should've been implemented years ago!

Storage Space Strategies

You can save yourself a headache by following a few simple tricks:

- Use your fastest hard drive as your C: drive. (If you have a solid-state drive, use it for C:) Don't tie it into a storage space.
- If a hard drive starts acting up, remove it from the storage space and replace it at your earliest convenience.
- Remember that in a three-drive installation, where two drives are in the storage space, the two-way mirror option limits you to the amount of room available on the smaller storage space drive.
- When you need to add more drives, don't take out the existing drives. The more drives in storage space, the greater your flexibility.

Removing Drives and Storage Pools

If you create a storage pool with two or more drives in it, you can remove a drive from it, and the data stored on that drive gets moved to the other drives in the pool. However, depending on how much data you have stored, this process may take a long time. You can also delete the storage space you've created if you decide that you no longer need it. Before doing that, you must back up your data because it gets deleted in the process, and you won't be able to recover it. Follow these steps to remove a drive from a storage pool and then remove a storage pool altogether:

1. **Click or tap the Start icon, followed by Settings.**
2. **Go to System, Storage, Advanced Storage Settings, and then click or tap Storage Spaces.**

   You see the storage pool you've created and its status.
3. **Click or tap on the name of your storage pool.**

   You see the properties of your storage pool (refer to Figure 5-4).
4. **Under Physical Disks, click or tap Properties next to the disk you want to remove.**

   You see the properties of your disk, as shown in Figure 5-5.

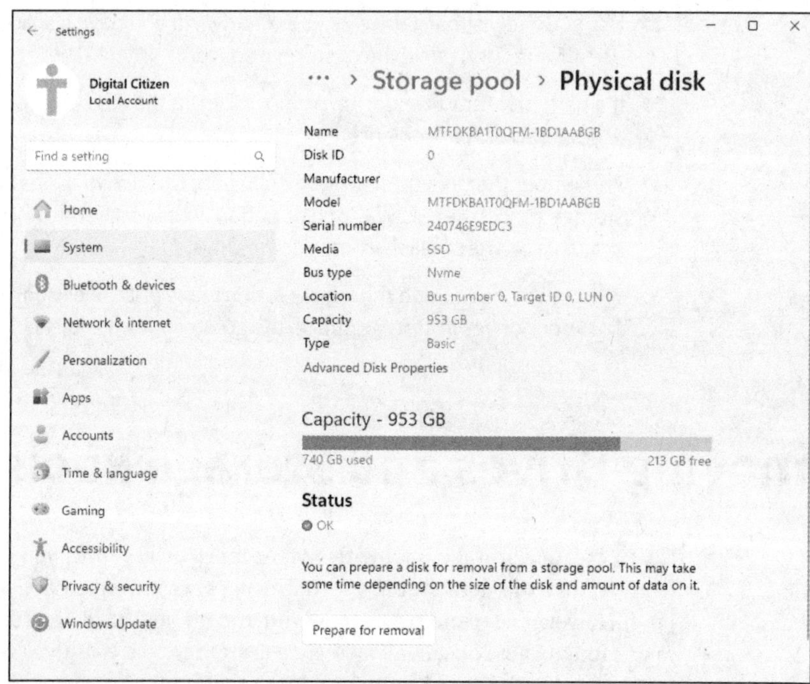

FIGURE 5-5: The status and properties of the selected disk.

5. **Click or tap Prepare for Removal.**

   Windows spends some time preparing the drive and moving all the data from it. This process can take quite a long time. When done, the status of the drive changes to Retired, OK.

6. **Under Status, click or tap Remove.**

   The drive is now removed from the storage pool. You can repeat this process for all the drives you want to remove. When Storage Spaces hits the minimum resiliency threshold, it won't allow you to remove any more drives.

7. **If you want to go ahead and remove the storage pool too, scroll down the page with the properties of your storage pool, and click or tap Delete next to Delete This Storage Pool.**

   Windows informs you about what this process entails and asks for your confirmation to continue, as shown in Figure 5-6.

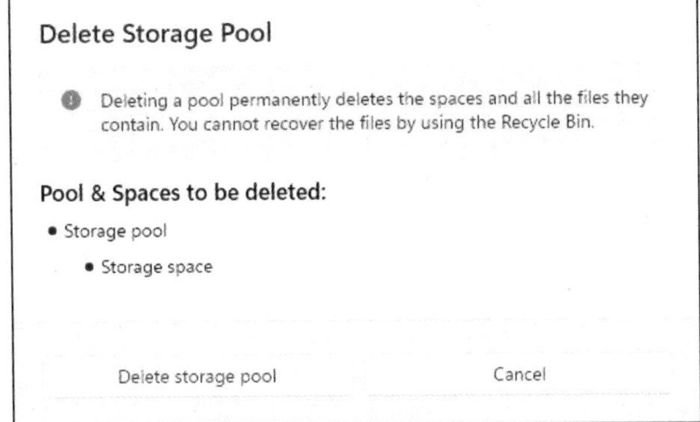

FIGURE 5-6: Confirm whether you want to delete the storage pool.

8. **Click or tap Delete Storage Pool one more time.**

   Windows removes all the data from the pool, and you can use your remaining drives like normal ones, outside of the storage pool of which they were a part.

IN THIS CHAPTER

- » Adding a new printer to your PC or network
- » Printing from Windows 11
- » Solving print queue problems
- » Troubleshooting other problems with printers
- » Removing a printer from Windows

Chapter 6
Working with Printers

Wouldn't it be amazing if we didn't need printers anymore? No more cluttered file cabinets, no more heavy boxes of paper, and no more trees sacrificed for dull paperwork. Sounds like a dream, right? But let's be real — it's about as likely as your email inbox reaching zero messages.

Experts have been promising a paperless office for decades, but we're still far from it. Printers are here to stay, just like the never-ending requests for password resets and the cookie prompts for Europeans browsing the web.

One of the biggest challenges is finding a good and affordable printer. Toner and ink are so pricey that they're starting to look like luxury items. And a $65 printer might print only a hundred pages before it starts acting like it's auditioning for a drama series. To make things worse, the refills can cost as much as the printer itself. It's like buying a car and realizing the gas costs more than the vehicle. It's a sad picture, isn't it?

On the upside, one of the best things in printing today is the network-connected printer. Such printers connect to your network router, either with a cable or through Wi-Fi, so you don't need to hook them up to a specific PC. And the best part? Many of them are relatively affordable and are easier to use in a network than printers connected to one computer on a network and shared with others.

Because you're here to learn about printers, you should know that Windows 11 has excellent printer support, which has improved since its initial release. Getting your printer to work well is easy after you grasp a few basic skills.

In this chapter, I show you how to install a printer in a home network, as well as the basics of using and troubleshooting your printer. That's because, eventually, we all run into problems, no matter how expensive and advanced the printer.

Installing a Printer

You have three ways to make a printer available to your computer:

- Attach the printer directly to the computer through a USB cable.
- If the printer can connect directly to a network, attach the printer directly to the network's router or switch, either with a network cable or via a Wi-Fi connection. Make sure that your computer is connected to the same network and that you install the printer so that you can access it and use it.
- Connect your computer to a network, attach the printer to another computer on the same network and turn both of them on, and then share the printer with the other computers on that network. This approach was the norm decades ago, but it was fraught with problems. Luckily, modern printers can connect directly to the network, making the entire experience simpler.

Having used all three attachment methods for many years, I can tell you without reservation that if you have a home network, it's worth getting a Wi-Fi-connected printer.

REMEMBER

Connecting a computer directly to a network router or switch isn't difficult if you have the right hardware. Each printer is different, though, so follow the manufacturer's instructions for installing it.

Attaching a local printer to your computer

So, you have a new printer and want to use it. Attaching it *locally* — which is to say, plugging it directly into your PC — is the simplest way to install a printer, and it's the only option if you don't have a network.

All modern printers that connect to a PC have a USB connector that plugs into your computer. (Network printers work differently; see the next section.) In theory, you plug the connector into your PC's USB port and turn on the printer, and then

Windows 11 recognizes it and installs the appropriate drivers. You're done in less than a minute!

TIP

Even though Windows 11 may have drivers for your printer, it's a good idea to go to the manufacturer's website and download the latest drivers for your specific model. Older printers don't have Windows 11 drivers bundled in their packaging, so a visit to the manufacturer's website will be mandatory. To help you with that, refer to Table 6-1. Note that these links might change as companies revamp or reorganize their sites. Can't find the right site? Bing or Google are your friends.

TABLE 6-1 Driver Sites for Major Printer Manufacturers

Manufacturer	Find Drivers at This URL
Brother	www.brother-usa.com/brother-support/driver-downloads
Canon	https://global.canon/en/support/
Dell	www.dell.com/support/home/en-us//products
Epson	https://epson.com/Support/sl/s
HP	https://support.hp.com/us-en/drivers
Samsung	www.samsung.com/us/support/downloads/
Xerox	www.support.xerox.com/

WARNING

While I recommend that you install the manufacturer's software, keep in mind not to blindly accept all the recommended apps. Some are junk or simply trialware you don't need. Be mindful and install only the printer's drivers and the apps that make it work, such as the scanning app if your printer is a multifunctional one with a built-in scanner on top.

When the printer is installed properly, you can see it in the Printers & Scanners list. To get there, click or tap the Start icon and then the Settings icon. Next, go to Bluetooth & Devices and click or tap Printers & Scanners. You see a list like the one in Figure 6-1.

Installing a wireless printer

If you have a network, you can attach a printer to (almost) any computer on the network and have it accessible to all users on (almost) all computers in the network. You can also attach different printers to different computers and let network users select the printer they want to use as the need arises. However, the best idea is to buy one Wi-Fi printer, connect it to the wireless network broadcast by your router, and then add it to all the computers that you want to have access to it.

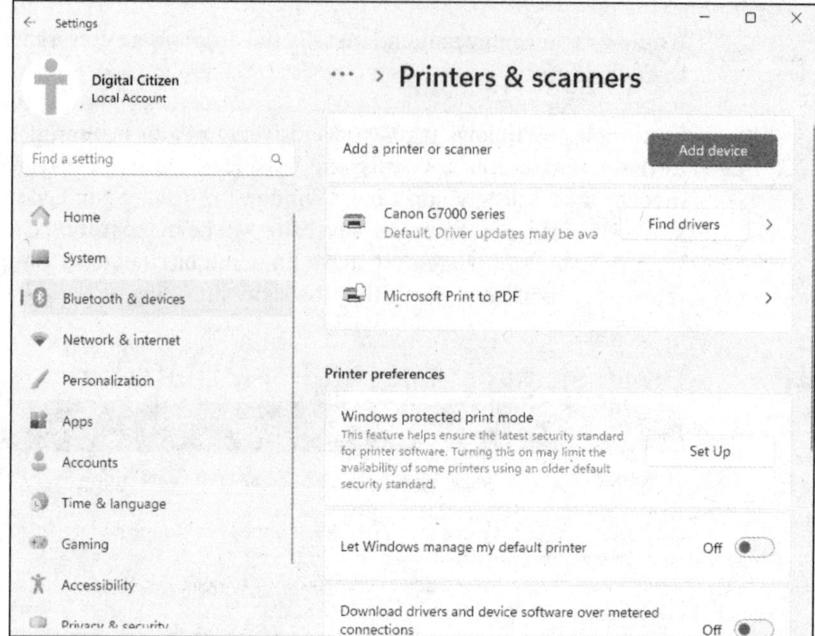

FIGURE 6-1: Your printers and scanners appear in this list.

Before you install a network printer, first download the latest drivers from the manufacturer's website and use those to guide you through the setup process. Again, refer to Table 6-1 for the list of websites with drivers for the major printer manufacturers.

The setup wizard for my Canon Pixma G7040 printer carefully guided me through the setup process based on the connection method I chose, as shown in Figure 6-2. The setup wizard for your specific printer will do the same.

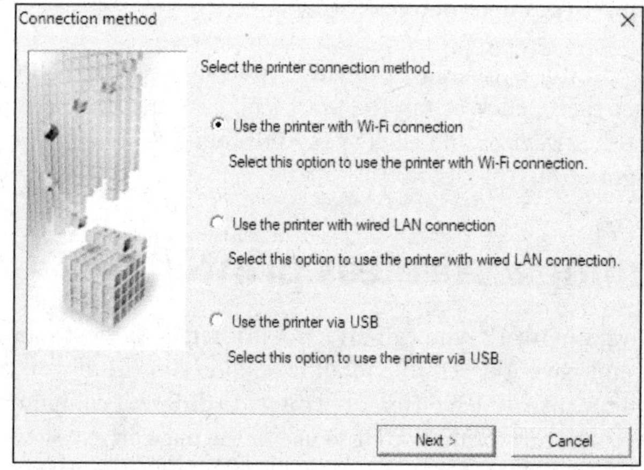

FIGURE 6-2: When installing a network printer, it's best to use the drivers from its manufacturer.

If you don't like the setup process offered by the printer's manufacturer or you can't find the printer's drivers, you can use the options offered by Windows 11 to install it. But before you opt to use them, make sure that the printer is turned on and connected to your Wi-Fi or to the network router through a cable. Then follow these steps:

1. **Click or tap the Start icon and then Settings. On the left, choose Bluetooth & Devices.**
2. **On the right, click or tap Printers & Scanners.**

   The Printer list appears (refer to Figure 6-1).
3. **At the top, click or tap the Add Device button.**

   Windows 11 looks all through your network to see whether any printers are available and displays any printers that are turned on, as shown in Figure 6-3.

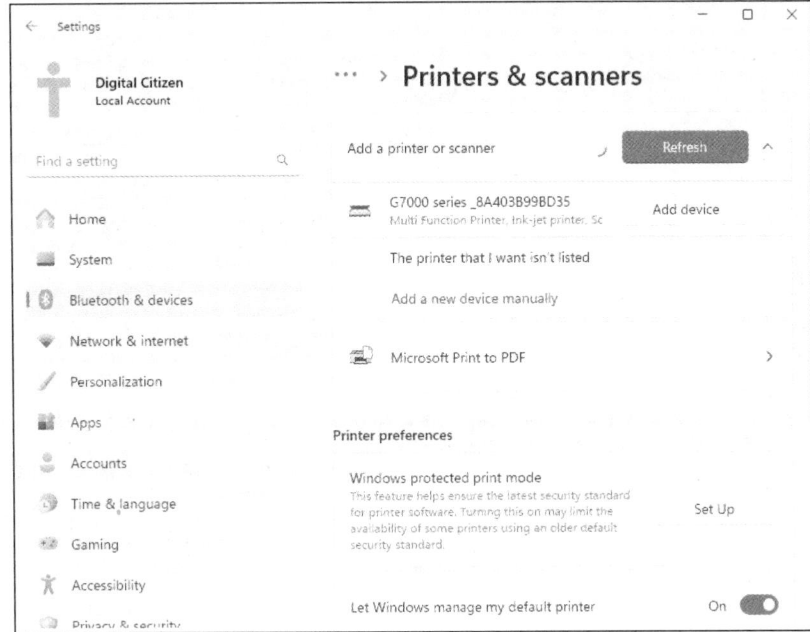

FIGURE 6-3: Windows 11 lists the printers it finds on your network.

4. **Click or tap Add Device next to the name of the printer you want to install.**

   Windows 11 looks to see whether it has a driver handy for that printer. After a bit of work, it tells you that the printer is ready. If it can't find a driver, look for drivers on the printer's support page.

5. **To set the newly added printer as your default, scroll down and set to off the Let Windows Manage My Default Printer switch, by clicking or tapping it.**

6. **Click or tap the name of your printer.**

   Windows 11 displays several links and buttons for configuring your printer, as shown in Figure 6-4.

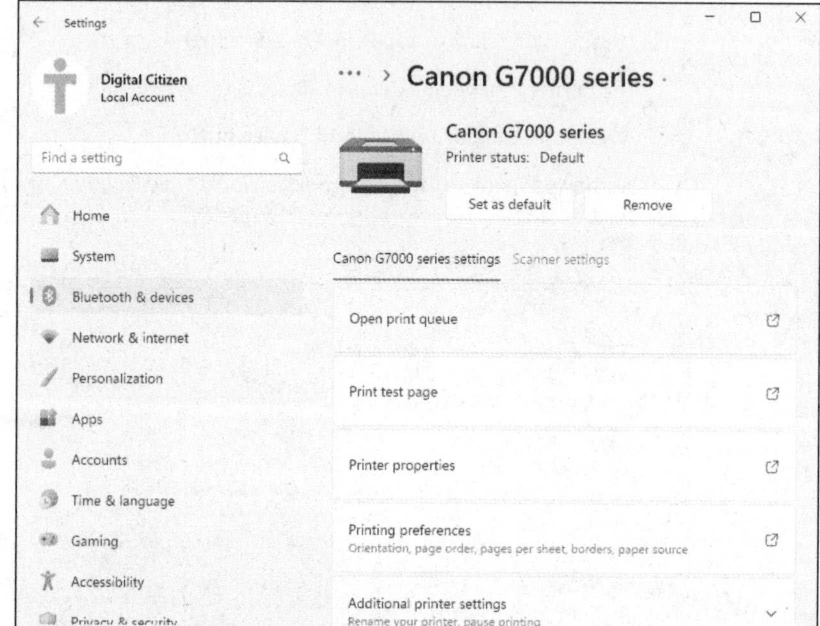

FIGURE 6-4: Setting the new printer as the default.

7. **Click or tap the Set as Default button, and then close Settings.**

   Your new printer appears in the Printers & Scanners list and is set as the default.

Printing from Windows 11

The universal keyboard shortcut for printing anything is Ctrl+P. However, before using it, make sure that the printer is turned on and has enough paper in its feed. Then follow these steps to see how the printing process works:

1. **Open any app from which you want to print, such as Microsoft Edge.**

2. **Open the content you want to print, like this web page:**

   `www.digitalcitizen.life/ways-print-any-windows-app-or-program/`

3. **Press Ctrl+P.**

   The Print dialog appears (refer to Figure 6-5).

4. **Select the printer that you want to use, enter how many copies you want printed, and set all the other available parameters.**

5. **Click or tap the Print button.**

   Windows 11 sends the printing command to the selected printer, which then starts printing your content.

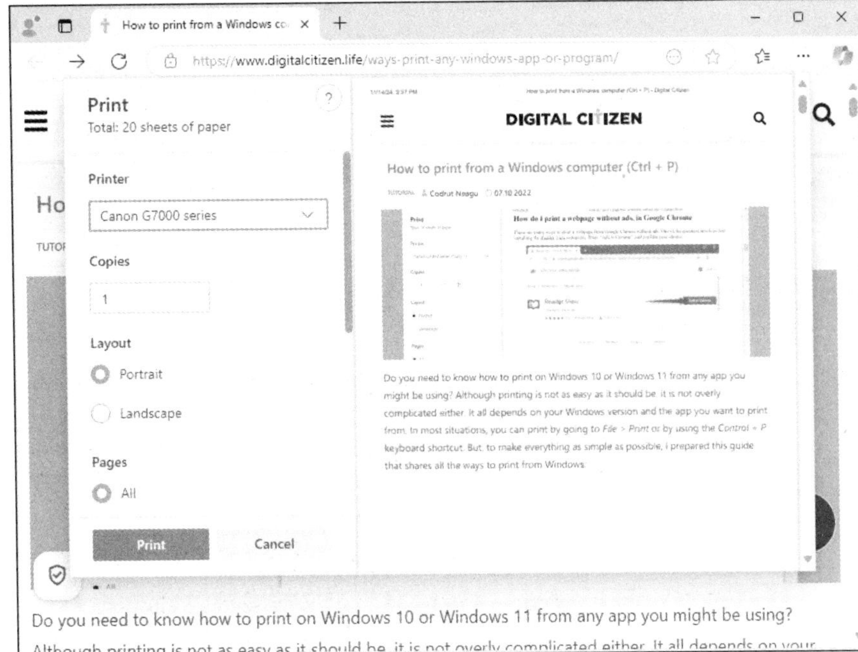

FIGURE 6-5: The Print dialogue in Microsoft Edge.

The printing process works the same in all apps that support printing: Word, Excel, PowerPoint, Acrobat Reader, Google Chrome, the Photos app, Paint, OneNote, and so on. Apps also have a Print option in their menus, but its placement varies from app to app. Their Print dialog also varies, with each app prioritizing certain options over others. Luckily, the Ctrl+P keyboard shortcut works the same in every app.

MICROSOFT PRINT TO PDF

When you start playing around with printers, you'll find a reference to a printer called Microsoft Print to PDF or Save as PDF. While it isn't exactly a printer, it's close enough, and it can be a big help.

In Windows 11, whenever you print something, Microsoft Print to PDF shows up as if it were a real printer. If you select it as your printer, you don't print anything on a physical piece of paper. Instead, Windows generates a PDF file, which you can then take or send just about anywhere: to a WhatsApp chat window, a Microsoft Teams call, attach to an email, and more.

PDF files are as close to a universal print format as you're likely to encounter. They can be sent to any kind of computer or device, and when opened, they'll look (and print) the same as they did on your computer — at least, as long as the device you're using has a decent PDF reader.

Using the Print Queue

You may have noticed that when you print a document from an application, the application reports that printing is finished before the printer finishes the printing on paper. If the document is long enough, you can print several more documents from one or more programs while the printer works on the first one. This is possible because Windows 11 saves printed documents in a *print queue* until it can print them.

If more than one printer is installed on your computer or network, each one has its own print queue. The queue is maintained on the host PC — that is, the PC to which the printer is attached. If you have a network-attached printer, the printer itself maintains the print queue.

Windows 11 uses print queues automatically, so you don't even have to know that they exist. If you know the tricks, though, you can control them in several useful ways.

Displaying the print queue

You can display information about any documents that you currently have in a printer's queue by following these steps:

1. **Click or tap the Start icon and then Settings.**
2. **On the left, choose Bluetooth & Devices. On the right, click or tap Printers & Scanners.**

   A list of printers appears (refer to Figure 6-1).
3. **Click or tap the printer's name and then Open Print Queue.**

   The print queue appears, as shown in Figure 6-6. The jobs in the print queue are listed from oldest at the top to newest at the bottom. If you have multiple printers installed, you can click or tap Printers on the top and select the printer you want to view. For each printing job, you see its name, a preview image, its status, the number of pages about to be printed, the file size, the user who initiated the print job, and when the job was initiated.

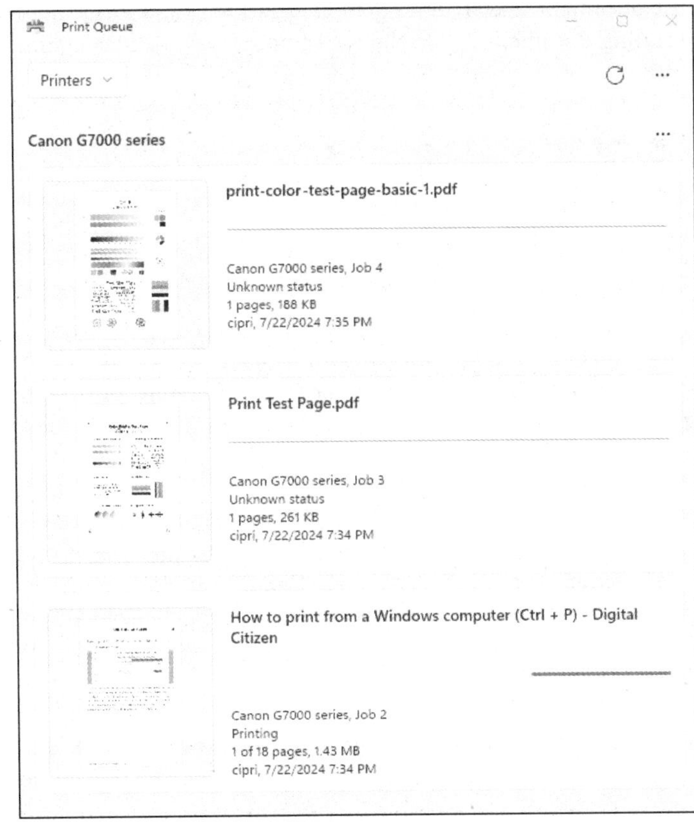

FIGURE 6-6: The documents waiting to print are displayed in the queue.

4. **To stop a document from printing, right-click (or press and hold) its name, choose Cancel, and confirm by pressing Yes.**

   In many cases, Windows 11 must notify the printer that it's canceling the document, so you may have to wait awhile for a response.

5. **Keep the print queue window open for later use or minimize the print queue window and keep it on the taskbar.**

TIP

   Keeping it open can be handy if you're running a long or complex print job.

Pausing and resuming a print queue

When you *pause* a print queue, Windows 11 stops printing documents from it. If a document is printing when you pause the queue, Windows tries to finish printing the document and then stops. When you *resume* a print queue, Windows starts printing documents from the queue again. Follow these guidelines to pause and resume a print queue:

- **To pause a print queue,** when you're looking at the print queue window (refer to Figure 6-7), click or tap the ellipsis icon (three dots) on the top right, and in the menu, select Pause All.
- **To resume the print queue,** click or tap the ellipsis icon again and select Resume All in the menu.

TIP

Why would you want to pause the print queue? Say you want to print a page for later reference, but you don't want to bother turning on your printer to print just one page. Pause the printer's queue, and then print the page. The next time you turn on the printer and resume the print queue, the remaining pages will be printed.

Sometimes, Windows 11 has a tough time finishing the document — for example, you may be dealing with print buffer overruns (see the "Troubleshooting Printing" section, later in this chapter) — and every time you clear the printer, it may try to reprint the overrun pages. If that happens to you, pause the print queue and turn off the printer. As soon as the printer comes back online, Windows 11 is smart enough to pick up where it left off.

Also, depending on how your network is set up, you may or may not be able to pause and resume a print queue on a printer attached to another user's computer or to a network.

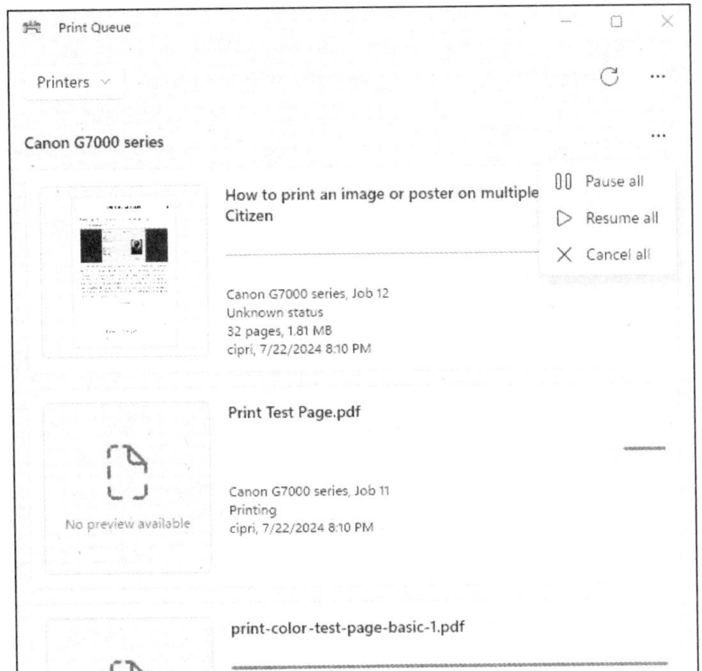

FIGURE 6-7: The menu for pausing and resuming the print queue.

Pausing, restarting, and resuming a document

Here are some reasons why you may want to pause printing a document. Consider the following:

- Suppose you're printing a web page that documents an online order you just placed, and the printer jams. You've already finished entering the order, and you have no way to display the page again to reprint it. Pause the document, clear the printer, and restart the document.
- You're printing a long document, and the phone rings. You don't want to hear the printer while you talk, so pause the document. When you're finished talking, resume printing the document.

Here's how pausing, restarting, and resuming work:

- **Pause a document:** When you pause a document, Windows 11 is prevented from printing that document. It skips the document and prints later documents in the queue. If you pause a document while Windows is printing it, Windows halts in the middle of the document and prints nothing on that printer until you take further action.

» **Restart a document:** When you restart a document, Windows 11 is again allowed to print it. If the document is at the top of the queue, Windows prints it as soon as it finishes the document that it's now printing. If the document was being printed when it was paused, Windows stops printing it and starts again at the beginning.

» **Resume a document:** Resuming a document is meaningful only if you paused it while Windows was printing it. When you resume a document, Windows resumes printing where it paused.

REMEMBER

To pause a document, right-click (or press and hold) the document in the print queue. The menu shown in Figure 6-8 opens. Choose Pause. The window displays the document's status as Paused. To resume the paused document, right-click or press and hold that same document and choose Resume. To restart a print job, right-click (or press and hold) its name and choose Restart.

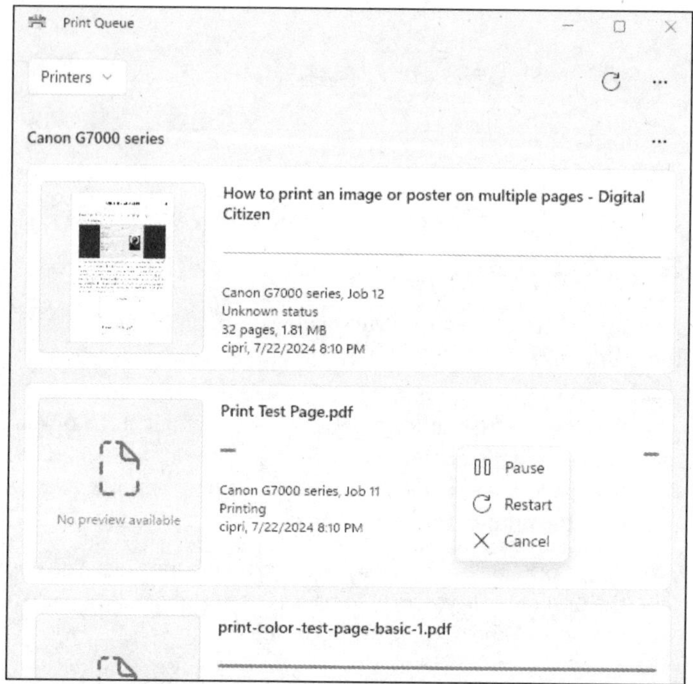

FIGURE 6-8: Pausing and resuming a print job is easy.

Canceling a document

When you cancel a document, Windows removes it from the print queue without printing it. Here's a common situation where document canceling comes in handy: You start printing a long document, and as soon as the first page comes out, you realize that you forgot to set the heading. What to do? Cancel the document, change the heading, and print the document again.

To cancel a document, right-click (or press and hold) its name in the print queue window, choose Cancel, and confirm by clicking or tapping Yes.

REMEMBER

No Recycle Bin exists for the print queue. When you delete a document from the print queue, it's gone from the printing process. However, the document remains available as a file on your computer.

Conversely, most printers have built-in memory that stores pages while they're being printed. Network printers can have sizable buffers. You may go to the print queue to look for a document, only to discover that it isn't there. If the document has already been shuffled off to the printer's internal memory, the only way to cancel it is to push the Stop or Cancel button on the printer or turn off the printer.

Troubleshooting Printing

The following list describes some typical problems with printers and the solutions to those sticky spots:

- **I'm trying to install a printer. I connected it to my computer, and Windows doesn't detect its presence.** Be sure that the printer is turned on and that the cable from the printer to your computer is properly connected at both ends. Check the printer's manual; you may have to follow a procedure (such as pushing a button) to make the printer ready for use.
- **I'm trying to install a printer that's connected to another computer on my network, and Windows doesn't detect its presence. I know that the printer is okay; it's already installed and working as a local printer on that system!** If the printer is attached to a Windows 10 or Windows 11 computer, the PC may be set to treat the network as a public network — in which case, it doesn't share anything. To rectify the problem, set the network as private. Read Book 3, Chapter 5 for details.
- **I can't use a shared printer that I've used successfully in the past. Windows 11 says that it isn't available when I try to use it, or Windows doesn't even show it as an installed printer anymore.** This situation can happen if something interferes with your connection to the network or the connection to the printer's host computer. It can also happen if something interferes with the availability of the printer — for example, if the host computer's user has turned off sharing or has set its network location to public.

If you can't find a problem or if you find and correct a problem (such as the network location set to public), but you still can't use the printer, try restarting Windows on your own machine. If that doesn't help, remove the printer from your system and re-install it.

To remove the printer from your system, follow the instructions in the next section. To re-install the printer on your system, use the same procedure you used to install it originally.

- **I printed a document, but it never came out of the printer.** Check the print queue on your PC. Is the document there? If not, investigate several possible reasons:

WARNING

  - *The printer isn't turned on or is out of paper.* Hey, don't laugh. I've done it. In some cases, Windows 11 can't distinguish a printer that's connected but not turned on from a printer that's ready, and it sends documents to a printer that isn't operating.
  - *You accidentally sent the document to some other printer*. Hey, don't laugh — I've done this when working in a large multinational company.
  - *Someone else unintentionally picked up your document and walked off with it.*
  - *The printer is turned on but not ready to print, and the printer is holding your entire document in its internal memory until it can start printing.* A printer can hold several hundred — or even several thousand — pages of output internally, depending on the size of its internal memory and the complexity of the pages. Network printers frequently have 16MB or more of dedicated buffer memory, which is enough for a hundred or more pages of lightly formatted text.

  If your document is in the print queue but isn't printing, check for these problems:

  - *The printer may not be ready to print.* See whether it's plugged in, turned on, and properly connected to your computer or its host computer.
  - *Your document may be paused.*
  - *The print queue itself may be paused.*
  - *The printer may be printing another document that's paused.*
  - *The printer may be thinking.* If it's a laser printer or another type of printer that composes an entire page in internal memory *before* it starts to print, it appears to do nothing while it processes photographs or other complex graphics. Processing may take as long as several minutes.

Look at the printer and study its manual. The printer may have a blinking light or a status display that tells you it's doing something. As you become familiar with the printer, you'll develop a feel for how long various types of jobs should take.

- *The printer is offline, out of paper, jammed, or unready to print for some other reason.*

Removing a printer

If you need to uninstall a printer from Windows 11 for troubleshooting or just because you don't use it anymore, follow these steps:

1. **Click or tap the Start icon and then Settings.**
2. **On the left, choose Bluetooth & Devices. On the right, click or tap Printers & Scanners.**

   You see a list of printers (refer to Figure 6-1).
3. **Click or tap the printer's name.**

   You see the printer's properties (refer to Figure 6-4).
4. **Click or tap the Remove button (at the top).**

   The printer is removed without any confirmation required, and you won't see its name in the list of available printers unless you re-install it.

IN THIS CHAPTER

» Connecting and removing USB devices to Windows 11

» Configuring AutoPlay for removable devices

» Connecting and disconnecting Bluetooth devices

» Setting up the RGB lighting on your accessories

Chapter 7

Managing USB, Bluetooth, and RGB Devices

Few people use CDs, DVDs, or Blu-ray discs with their computers. The world has been swept away by USB flash drives and USB hard disks instead, for several good reasons: They're cheap, small, and easy to carry around. You can write any data on them, and they work with all operating systems — even with Android if you have a USB Type C flash drive to connect to your smartphone.

Therefore, it makes sense to have a USB flash drive around. And if you're using one or more, it's a good idea to know how to get around some annoyances, like the AutoPlay dialog you see every time you plug in a USB device. To limit your frustration with it, I share how to customize AutoPlay for removal devices. Also, even if Microsoft says otherwise, it's good to know when it's safe to unplug a USB device from your computer, so I share some tips on that, too.

Bluetooth technology is built into all laptops and tablets as well as some desktop PCs. (If you need Bluetooth and you don't have it inside your PC, just buy a Bluetooth USB adapter, which is cheap and easy to find online.) As you would expect,

Windows 11 works with Bluetooth devices. But why do you need Bluetooth? One commonplace example is that you may want to connect a Bluetooth mouse and keyboard and get rid of wires, or you need to use a Bluetooth headset for conference calls. In this chapter, I show you how to do all that, as well as how to disconnect Bluetooth devices from Windows 11 when you no longer need to use them.

Another trend in the world of devices is RGB (red green blue) lighting, which has become synonymous with gaming. Most hardware manufacturers sell accessories and components with RGB lighting. They not only look good and can be personalized but also sell better, at higher prices, and help manufacturers lock you into their ecosystem. To disturb a bit of this vendor lock-in approach, Microsoft has implemented an RGB lighting management system called Dynamic Lighting, which is now part of Windows 11. Its main benefit is that it allows you to use accessories with RGB lighting from multiple vendors and personalize them from a single user interface. If this sounds useful, read this chapter until the end and learn how it's done.

Connecting USB Devices to Your PC

Attaching a USB device to a Windows 11 computer is easy. Simply plug your device into a free USB port. The operating system detects the device automatically, plays a beep sound, and displays an AutoPlay notification in the bottom-right corner of the screen, as shown in Figure 7-1. This notification informs you that a removable drive was detected, tells you its name and drive letter, and asks you to choose what happens with removable drives.

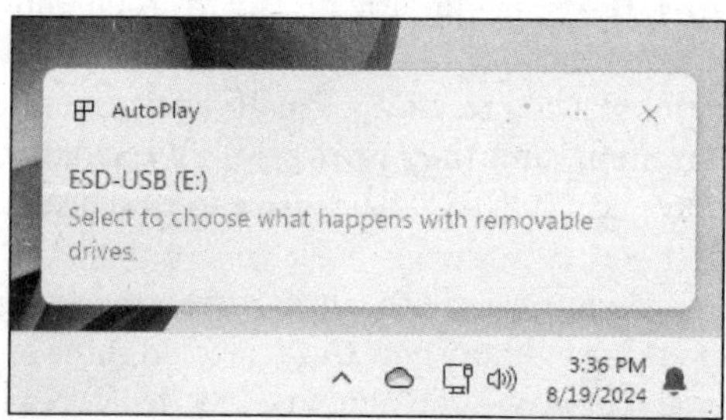

FIGURE 7-1: Each time you plug in a USB device, you see this notification.

You can ignore the notification; it will go to the notification center (see Book 2, Chapter 3 to learn more). Or you can click or tap it and choose what you want Windows to do. The options you see depend on the apps installed in Windows 11 and the specific device you plugged in. In Figure 7-2, I captured the options shown when I plugged in a USB memory stick in a computer without any third-party apps installed. A similar notification is shown when you plug a microSD card into the SD card reader slot of your laptop (if it has one). On your computer, you'd likely see one or more additional options, depending on whether you've installed third-party apps that can interact with removable devices such as USB memory sticks or microSD cards.

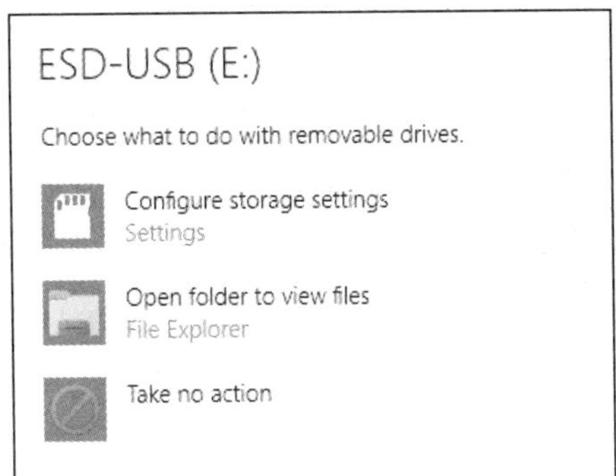

FIGURE 7-2: Options for handling removable drives.

Windows 11 remembers what you choose in this menu, and the next time you plug in a USB drive, it automatically does what you selected. It doesn't matter whether you plug in the same USB flash drive or another one. Because I tend to store files on USB flash drives, I frequently select Open Folder to View Files. Windows remembers this choice in its AutoPlay settings and repeats this action over and over. Other users select Take No Action to avoid notifications bothering them each time they plug in a new USB device or microSD card.

Configuring AutoPlay for removable devices

If you're not happy with the way you've set AutoPlay or with the fact that it always asks you what to do, simply change its behavior. You can choose a different default action, or you can set it always to ask you what you want to do. Here's how to disable or configure AutoPlay to do what you want:

1. **Click or tap the Start icon and then Settings. Or press Windows+I.**

   The Settings app starts and loads its Home page.

2. **In the column on the left, choose Bluetooth & Devices.**
3. **On the right, scroll down to AutoPlay and click or tap it.**

   The AutoPlay settings appear, as shown in Figure 7-3.

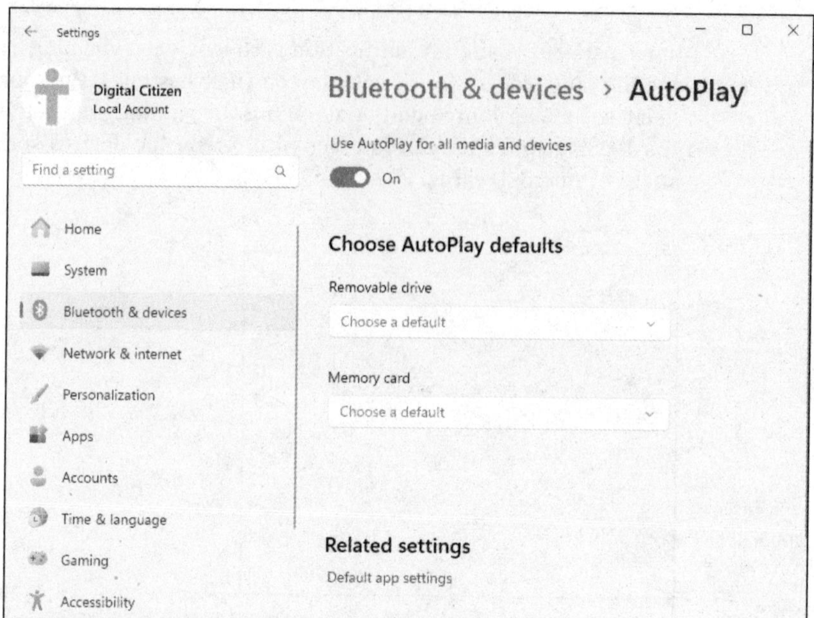

FIGURE 7-3: Setting AutoPlay in Windows 11.

4. **If you want to disable the AutoPlay dialogs completely, click or tap the Use AutoPlay for All Media And Devices switch off.**

   The feature is now disabled, and you will no longer see any prompts when you plug something into your Windows 11 computer.

5. **If you want to change what AutoPlay does for removable devices, click or tap the drop-down list for Removable Drive (under Choose AutoPlay Defaults).**

   A list of options appears, as shown in Figure 7-4.

6. **Choose an action from the list.**

   If you don't want AutoPlay to do anything, select Take No Action. If you want it to ask you what you want each time you plug in a USB device, choose Ask Me Every Time.

7. **If you use microSD cards, repeat the same choice for the Memory Card drop-down list.**

8. **Close the Settings app.**

   Your settings are applied immediately.

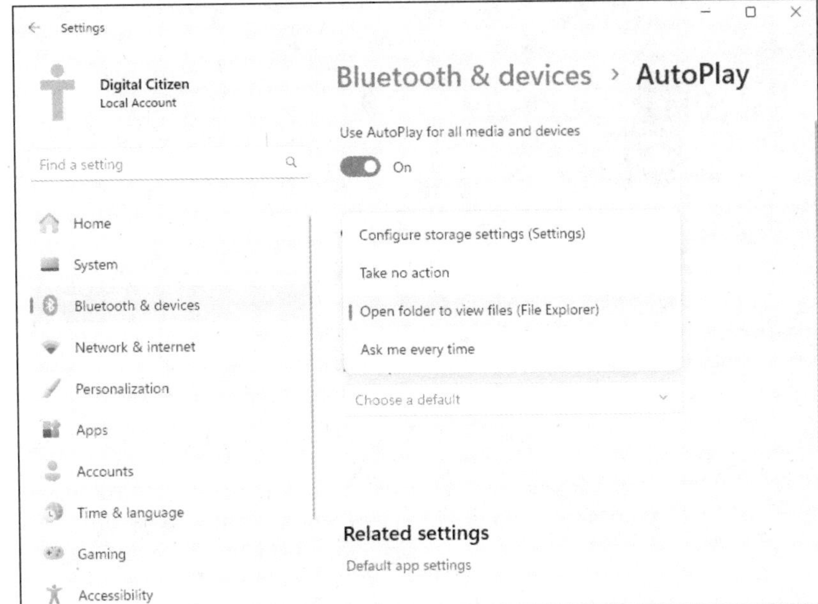

FIGURE 7-4: Choose what AutoPlay should do for removable drives.

Removing USB devices

Microsoft developed a feature called quick removal, which lets you unplug a USB drive anytime you want. This is the default setting for both Windows 10 and Windows 11, and most people will tell you that when you want to disconnect a USB flash drive or hard disk from your PC, you just unplug it and go.

However, you may not know whether an app or Windows is actively writing data on the USB drive. If this happens and you eject the drive, the data on it might get corrupted. Also, you don't get to save the latest modifications you've made. To avoid such situations, I recommend using the Safely Remove Hardware option, like you used to do back in the days of Windows 7. Here's how it works in Windows 11:

1. **With the USB drive still plugged in, click or tap the arrow pointing upwards in the bottom-right corner of the desktop.**

   The icon is named show hidden icons, and after you click it, it displays a list of, well, hidden icons.

2. **In the list of hidden icons, click or tap the icon that looks like a USB flash drive.**

   You see a list of the devices connected to your computer, as shown in Figure 7-5. The list includes removable devices such as USB flash drives, external hard drives, or microSD cards.

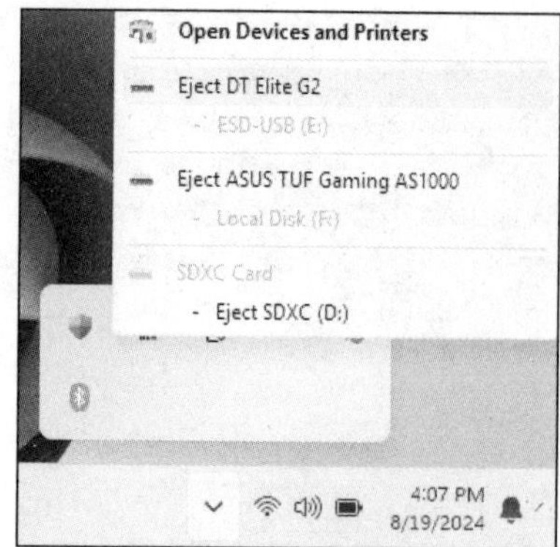

FIGURE 7-5: Choose the USB device you want to remove safely.

3. **Click or tap the Eject option for the USB device that you want to unplug.**

   After a few seconds, Windows tells you that it's Safe to Remove Hardware in a notification at the bottom-right corner of the screen.

4. **Unplug the USB device from your computer.**

WARNING

If Windows 11 tells you that the device is currently in use, don't unplug it until you close all open apps and ensure that no data is actively written on it. Once you do that, repeat the process and eject the device after you receive confirmation from Windows that it's safe to do so.

TIP

You can remove a USB flash drive from File Explorer, too: go to This PC, right-click (or press and hold) the USB drive, and select Eject.

Connecting Bluetooth Devices

Bluetooth is ubiquitous these days, and is included in all Windows 11 laptops and tablets. Think about it — you probably prefer using a Bluetooth mouse with your laptop instead of its touchpad to boost productivity. Or perhaps you need to connect a wireless headset or those fancy noise-canceling earbuds for your next work call. And let's face it, most laptop speakers are underwhelming. If you want to watch a movie on your laptop or listen to music while working from home, it's a good idea to connect a Bluetooth speaker or even your living room soundbar.

All these gadgets typically use Bluetooth, a clever technology that allows devices to communicate wirelessly over short distances. However, before your devices can start conversing with one another, they need to get acquainted through a process called *pairing*, which is a meet-and-greet for your gadgets. Once they're paired, they remember each other for future connections.

Connecting Bluetooth devices to Windows 11 is generally straightforward, but there are a few minor differences depending on what you're connecting. Keyboards, for example, require one extra step compared to mice or headsets. With that in mind, let's walk through how to connect a Bluetooth device to your Windows 11 laptop or tablet:

1. **Click or tap the Start icon, followed by Settings.**

   The Settings app opens.

2. **In the left sidebar, choose Bluetooth & Devices, and make sure that the Bluetooth switch on the right is on.**

   You see all the options and settings for handling Bluetooth and other types of devices, as shown in Figure 7-6.

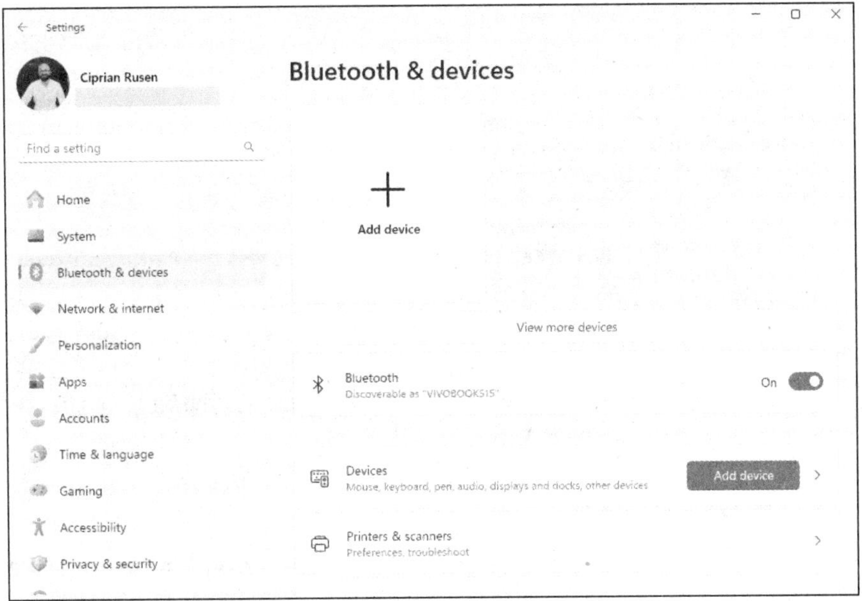

FIGURE 7-6: Add devices here.

3. **To start the connection process, click or tap the Add Device button.**

   The Add a Device window appears, as shown in Figure 7-7, with options for connecting all kinds of wireless devices.

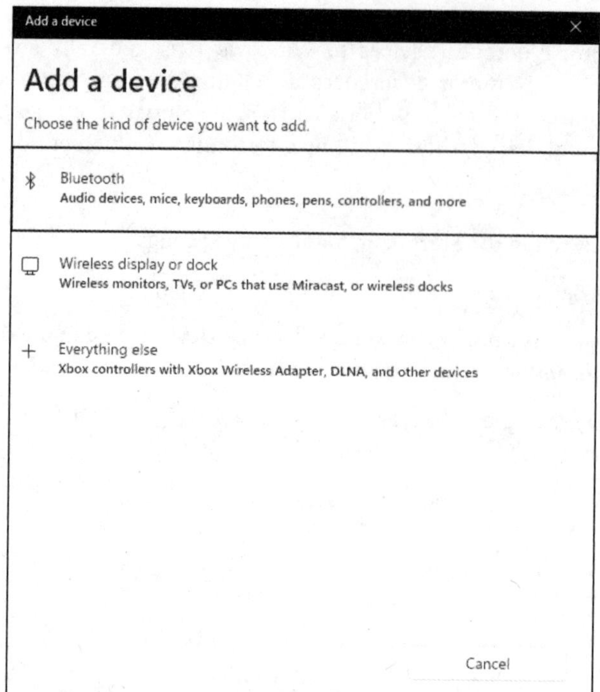

FIGURE 7-7: Choosing the type of device you want to add.

4. **Click or tap Bluetooth, and then press the Pairing button on your Bluetooth device.**

   The Pairing button usually sports the Bluetooth symbol (shown in the margin). However, some devices require you to press and hold their power button. In the Add a Device window, you should see the Bluetooth device that you want to connect to.

5. **Click or tap the name of the Bluetooth device that you want to connect to.**
6. **If you're adding a Bluetooth keyboard and are asked to type a PIN code and press Enter, do as requested on the Bluetooth device.**

   You are informed that your device is ready to go.

7. **Click or tap Done and close Settings.**

   The Bluetooth device is now connected and ready for use.

TIP

When you want to disconnect a Bluetooth device but leave it paired with your Windows 11 laptop or tablet, simply turn off the Bluetooth device. Alternatively, to stop using Bluetooth, you can click or tap the network icon or the volume icon on the right end of the taskbar to open Quick Settings and then click or tap the Bluetooth icon.

Unpairing Bluetooth Devices

If you no longer want to use a Bluetooth device, it's a good idea to remove it from Windows 11 so that your computer no longer searches for it and they stop connecting automatically when both are turned on. The process is quick and painless:

1. **Click or tap the Start icon and then Settings.**
2. **In the Settings app, go to Bluetooth & Devices.**
3. **On the right, click or tap Devices.**

   You see all the devices connected to Windows 11 (Bluetooth and others), as shown in Figure 7-8.

4. **Find the Bluetooth device that you don't want to use anymore and click or tap its name to expand the options you have for interacting with it.**
5. **Click or tap the Remove button under the device's name.**

   The Bluetooth device is removed from the list, and Windows 11 no longer connects to it.

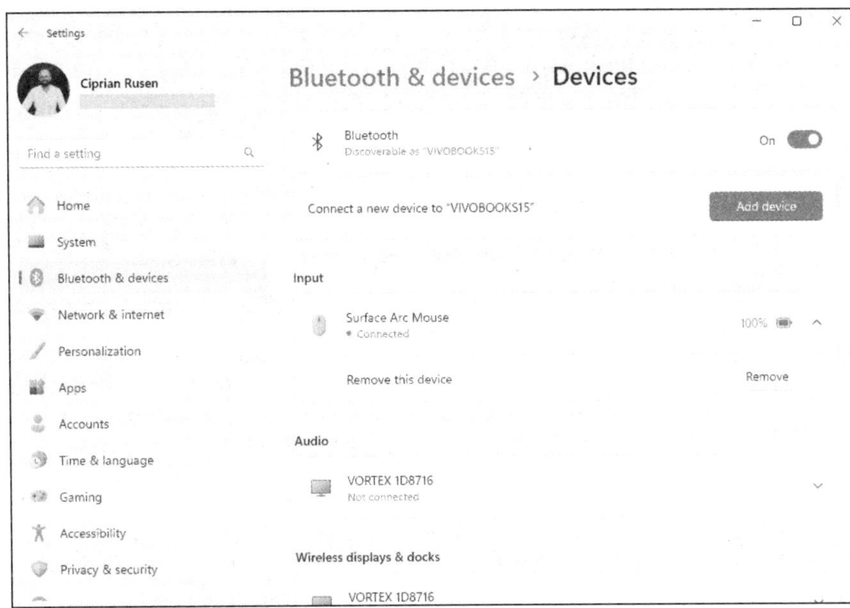

FIGURE 7-8: Removing Bluetooth devices requires a few clicks or taps.

As you can see, working with Bluetooth devices in Windows 11 is quite easy, and the process for connecting and disconnecting such devices works the same.

Setting up RGB Lighting

RGB lighting has been a staple in gaming hardware for years, allowing for detailed personalization and eye-catching aesthetics. However, this technology comes with a frustrating drawback: vendor lock-in. Accessories from different manufacturers typically don't play well together, forcing users to juggle multiple apps for a cohesive RGB lighting setup.

Luckily, Microsoft decided to intervene and introduced a feature named Dynamic Lighting. As of September 2023, this feature is embedded into Windows 11 and aims to standardize RGB lighting controls across brands, allowing users to manage all their RGB devices from a single place. This initiative is based on the HID LamArray standard which was designed for controlling RGB lighting in devices using a standardized interface. It was developed by industry leaders like Logitech, Google, Apple, Intel, NVIDIA, Synaptics, and, of course, Microsoft.

Dynamic Lighting supports a wide range of devices, from keyboards and mice to headsets and computer cases. Several major brands, including Razer, ASUS, HyperX, MSI, and Microsoft, started to support this feature in some of their more recent products. Initially, the rollout of Dynamic Lighting was off to a very slow start, but it gained momentum when Logitech announced its implementation across its entire Logitech G series line-up of gaming accessories. This shift promises to simplify RGB management for gamers and PC enthusiasts, creating a more unified and user-friendly lighting ecosystem.

If you have RGB accessories connected to your computer, here's how to access Dynamic Lighting and use it to configure the colors and lighting effects:

1. **Click or tap the Start icon, followed by Settings.**
2. **In the Settings app, go to Personalization and choose Dynamic Lighting.**

   You see the Dynamic Lighting settings. Your accessories with RGB lighting are displayed at the top, as shown in Figure 7-9. Note that I connected only a mouse to my laptop, but you can also connect a keyboard or a headset. In the future, I expect Dynamic Lighting to display other types of hardware, such as your motherboard with RGB, or your computer case.
3. **Click or tap the switch for Use Dynamic Lighting on My Devices to turn this feature on.**
4. **Use the Brightness slider to lower or increase the brightness of your RGB lighting effects.**

   Notice how the lighting brightness changes on your RGB accessories, and decide on the optimal level for you.

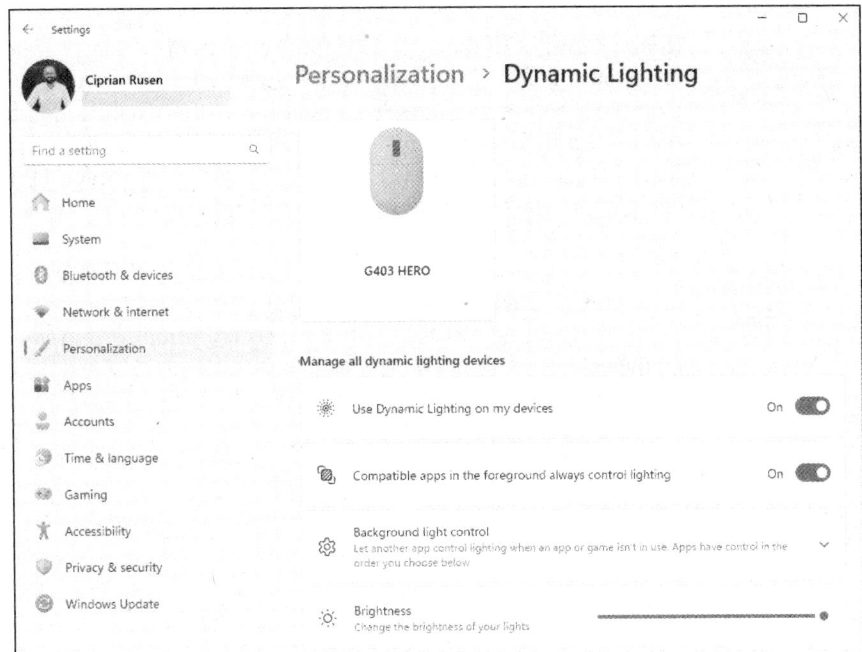

FIGURE 7-9: Setting up Dynamic Lighting for your RGB accessories and devices.

5. **Click or tap Effects to expand this section of settings and see more options.**
6. **Click or tap the drop-down list next to Effects and choose an effect from the list.**

   Depending on the effect you choose, notice how the available configuration options change. If you choose Solid Color, you get the option to choose the color you want. If you choose Rainbow, you can personalize the speed of the effect and its direction. Effects such as Wave, Wheel, and Gradient require you to set both a main color and a second color.
7. **Browse through all the effects available and their configuration options. When you've decided which to keep, close Settings.**

   Enjoy the RGB lighting on your accessories!

TIP

The settings you make in the Dynamic Lighting window shown in Figure 7-9 apply to all your accessories and hardware with RGB lighting as long as they're detected as being compatible with this feature and listed at the top of the window. If you want to personalize only an individual device with RGB lighting, simply click or tap its name in the list at the top and personalize its lighting as you want.

TECHNICAL STUFF

If your changes to Dynamic Lighting settings in Windows 11 don't seem to work, check out the top of the window in Figure 7-9. If you don't see any listed devices, your RGB accessories aren't compatible with Dynamic Lighting — or at least not yet. To fix this, try updating their drivers and software. Some even require a firmware update to a newer version that adds Dynamic Lighting support. Once compatible, your devices should appear in the Dynamic Lighting window.

TECHNICAL STUFF

If you see some devices listed under Dynamic Lighting but your settings seem to change erratically, make sure to turn off the switch for the Compatible Apps in the Foreground Always Control Lighting option so that your RGB settings are managed only by Dynamic Lighting and don't get changed by other apps you may have installed.

8 Maintaining Windows

Contents at a Glance

IN THIS CHAPTER

» Using the Windows Backup app to back up your data to the cloud

» Setting up File History for local backups to an external hard drive

» Storing your data in the cloud

Chapter 1 Backing Up Your Data

Welcome to backing up your files, apps, and Windows settings! In this chapter, I dive into the art of keeping your precious data safe and sound. Think of it as giving your files a lifejacket before they set sail on the unpredictable seas of your computer and the internet.

I explore some nifty tools built right into Windows 11, like the new Windows Backup app and the old and trusty File History. These two can be your guardians for those "Oops, I didn't mean to delete that!" moments.

I also peek into the cloud — no, not a fluffy one in the sky but the digital kind where your files can float safely and be accessible even if your computers and devices go through natural disasters. Whether you're a data hoarder or just someone who'd rather not lose those embarrassing photos from last year's holiday party, this chapter's got you covered.

So grab a cup of tea, settle in, and let's make sure your files and digital memories stick around longer than that stain on your favorite shirt.

Using Windows Backup

On August 22, 2023, Microsoft released a new Windows Backup app for users with a Microsoft account. In its initial version, this app works only on Windows 10 and Windows 11 computers and devices where people log in with a Microsoft account and use OneDrive as their cloud-storage solution. The app isn't compatible with local offline accounts, work accounts, or school accounts. For now, it's aimed only at consumer devices.

This app can back up the following types of items:

- **Folders:** Saves your personal user folders, such as Desktop, Documents, and Pictures, in your OneDrive cloud storage. However, the app won't back up any system files, and it doesn't allow you to add other folders to the backup.
- **Apps:** Creates a list of the apps available on your computer, including both apps you've installed from the Microsoft Store and those installed from elsewhere. When you restore the backup, you'll find all their shortcuts in the Start menu. Although the apps available via the Microsoft Store will be re-installed automatically, the ones from other sources will only get shortcuts with links to their websites and you have to manually re-install them.
- **Settings:** Saves some of your Windows settings, including accessibility settings, personalization settings (such as your theme and desktop wallpaper), and your language preferences.
- **Credentials:** Saves the Wi-Fi networks and passwords you've connected to and saved on your Windows computer and the accounts you've set up in apps like Outlook.

Now that you know what the Windows Backup app can do, let's start using it.

Backing up your files, apps, settings, and credentials

To begin, it's important to back up your files, apps, and settings using the Windows Backup app. If you don't have a Microsoft 365 subscription, you can still use the free OneDrive storage, but it's limited to 5 GB, which may not be enough for you. In this case, it's best to back up only your Windows 11 settings, list of apps, credentials, and important user folders that are not very large and don't go above the 5 GB limit. If you do have a Microsoft 365 subscription (refer to Book 1, Chapter 3), feel free to back up everything. Here's how it all works:

1. **Click or tap inside the Search box on the taskbar and enter** backup.

   The search results are displayed.

2. **Choose the Windows Backup search result.**

   The Windows Backup app opens, as shown in Figure 1-1.

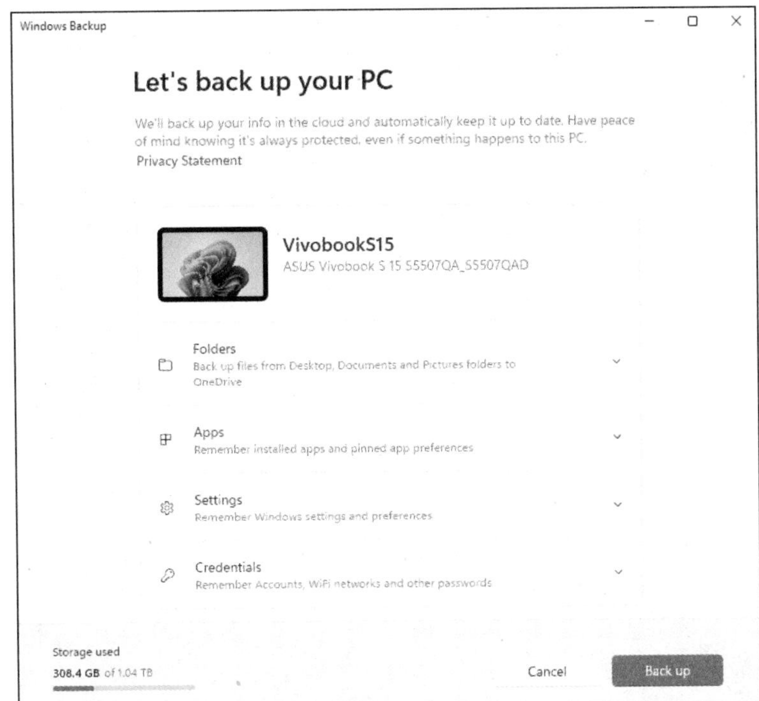

FIGURE 1-1: Windows Backup allows you to back up your user folders, apps, settings, and credentials.

3. **Click or tap Folders to expand this section.**

   You see your list of user folders shown in Figure 1-2. The list includes folders such as Desktop, Documents, Pictures, Videos, and Music. By default, all your user folders are included in the proposed backup.

4. **Click or tap to turn off the switch next to the folders you want to exclude from the backup.**

   Note how the storage estimate in the bottom-left corner of the Windows Backup app window changes to reflect your selections.

5. **Click or tap to extend the remaining sections (Apps, Setting, and Credentials) one by one and set their switches to on or off, depending on your preferences.**

   Each time you set a switch on, don't forget to take a look at your storage estimate in the bottom-left corner to ensure that you don't go over the space available in your OneDrive.

6. **When you've finished making your selections, click or tap Back Up.**

   The app displays the progress of its backup activities. You can minimize Windows Backup and go about your work while it slowly backs up everything you selected.

7. **After Windows Backup has finished its work, click or tap Close.**

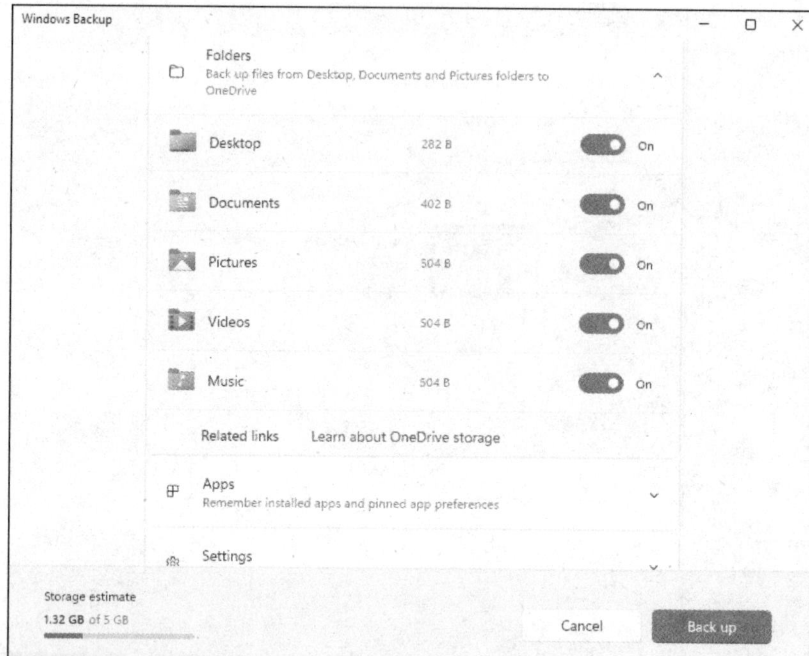

FIGURE 1-2: Choosing what to back up with Windows Backup.

Now you can rest easy, knowing that your user folders, apps, settings, and passwords are stored in the cloud and available for a quick restoration in case you get into trouble with your Windows 11 computer.

Restoring your data and settings with Windows Backup

Restoring the data that you've backed up with Windows Backup can be done only when you install Windows 11 on a new computer, when you re-install Windows or reset it to its factory defaults, and you're reconfiguring it again.

If you need some help with installing Windows, read the next chapter in this minibook, which has a dedicated section on this topic. Next, let's see how to restore your data during the Windows 11 installation process on a new computer or during its re-installation on the same computer:

1. **Install, re-install, or reset Windows 11.**

   The wizard asks to start personalizing the operating system, as shown in Figure 1-3.

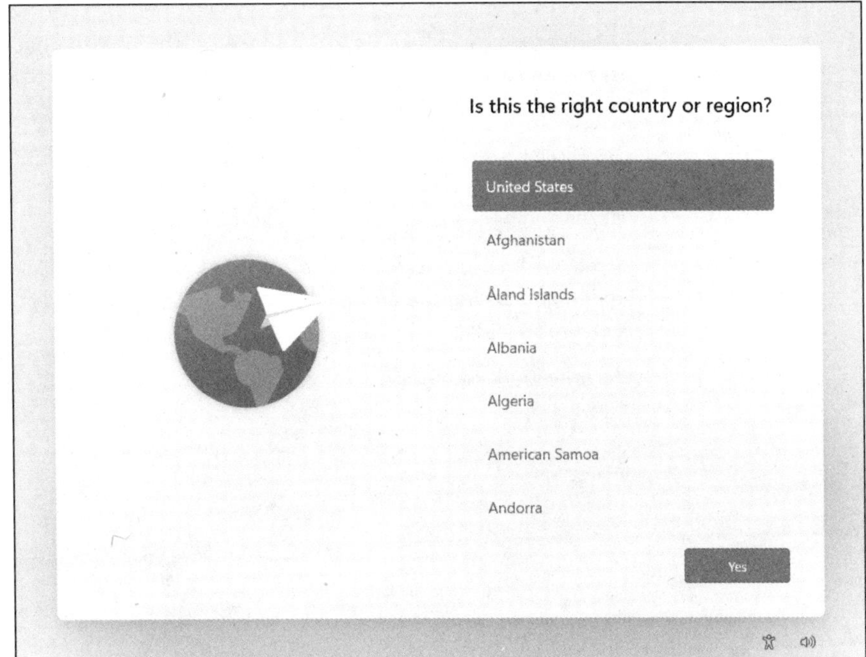

FIGURE 1-3: Personalizing Windows starts with choosing your country.

2. **Choose the country you're in and then click or tap Yes.**

   You're asked to confirm whether the suggested keyboard layout is the one you want.

3. **Choose the keyboard layout you want to use and then click or tap Yes.**

   Windows asks whether you want to add a second keyboard layout.

4. **Click or tap Skip.**

   You can add more keyboard layouts later, using the instructions from Book 7, Chapter 1.

   The Windows setup wizard checks for updates, reboots your computer and continues checking for updates. Then, it asks you to name your device.

5. **Type a name for your Windows 11 computer or device and then click or tap Next.**

   The setup wizard may reboot your computer.

6. **If you're using Windows 11 Pro, choose Set Up for Personal Use when asked how you would like to set up the device. If you're using Windows 11 Home, simply skip this step.**

   The Windows setup starts installing the updates that it has found and displays the progress of this operation. Wait patiently. It can take a while and it may involve another reboot. Then, you're asked to sign in.

7. **Sign in with your Microsoft account (see Figure 1-4) by clicking or tapping Sign In and typing the email address for your Microsoft account. Then click or tap Next.**

   You are asked to enter your account password.

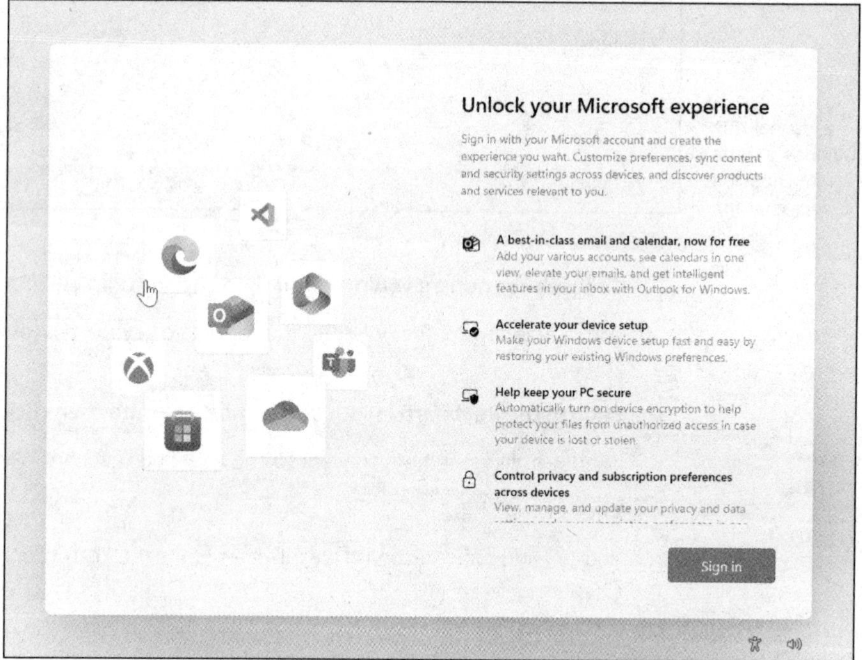

FIGURE 1-4: You must sign in with a Microsoft account.

8. **Type your password, click or tap Sign in, and then click or tap Create PIN.**

   You are asked to enter and confirm your PIN.

9. **Set up your PIN, and click or tap OK.**

10. **Choose your privacy settings by disabling the switches for the features you don't want. Then click or tap Next, followed by Accept.**

    You finally see the Welcome Back screen shown in Figure 1-5, where you can restore your PC from a backup you've made using the Windows Backup app.

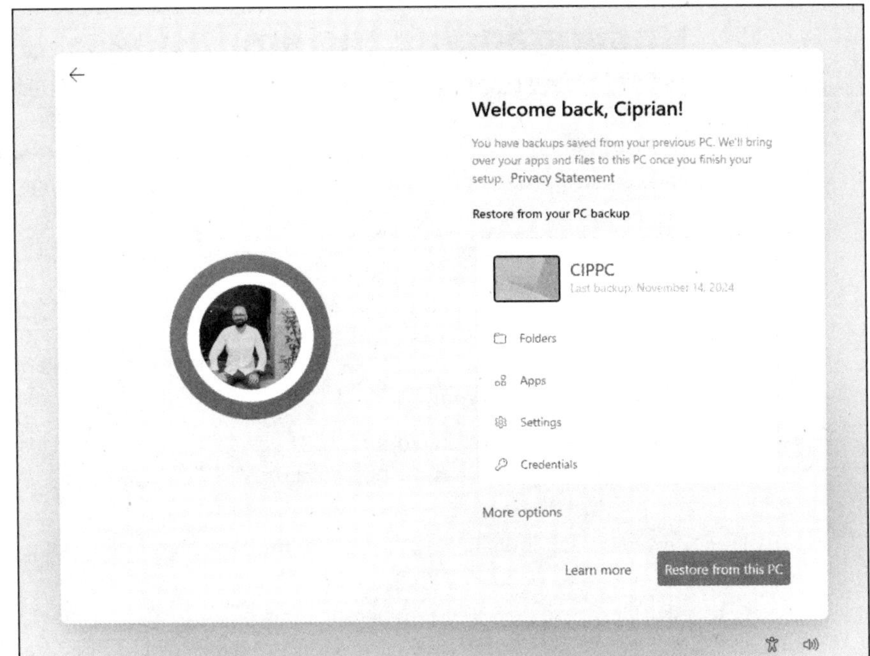

FIGURE 1-5: Choosing the backup you want to restore.

11. **If you're okay with restoring the proposed backup, simply click or tap Restore from This PC. Otherwise, click or tap More Options, choose a backup you want to restore from the list, followed by Restore from This PC.**

    The setup wizard spends some time recovering the files, apps, settings, and credentials from the selected backup. This process may take a long time if your backup is large. Once the restoration process is complete, the setup wizard will continue asking how to customize your experience.

12. **Go through the remaining questions in the setup wizard, making the choices you want.**

    At the end of this lengthy process, you'll finally see the Windows 11 desktop and can start using your computer. The data you've restored will be there, waiting for you to use it.

REMEMBER

For the restoration process to work, at Step 7, you must sign in with the same Microsoft account you have previously used to make your backup with the Windows Backup app. If you're setting up a new Microsoft account, you won't have anything to restore, and you won't see Step 11.

Understanding the limitations of Windows Backup

While Windows Backup is a simple and convenient way to back up and restore your data, it has both benefits and limitations. Let's first take a look at the good parts:

- The app is preinstalled with Windows, and you don't need to install third-party software.
- Windows Backup is easy to use and doesn't require you to configure any complex settings. You just select what you want backed up, and the app does the job for you seamlessly.
- Restoring your backup during a Windows 11 installation, re-installation, or reset is just as easy as backing it up.

However, Windows Backup has some limitations too, and they can be significant:

- It can't create full system backups. It protects only some of your personal files and folders, some apps and settings, and the credentials stored by Windows. The app can't create copies of your system files or clone your apps and their settings.
- If your computer crashes or files on it get corrupted, you have to re-install Windows or reset it to its factory defaults and restore your data from Windows Backup during the personalization process.
- You can't use Windows Backup to save backups on a portable drive such as an external hard disk or SSD. This app relies only on OneDrive cloud storage.
- The app can be used only with a Microsoft account. If you don't have a Microsoft 365 subscription, you may not have enough cloud storage space on your OneDrive to use it successfully.

If these limitations make the Windows Backup app unsuitable for you, consider using another app built into Windows 11, File History. It allows you to back up your data to an external drive without using cloud storage and with fewer limitations.

Backing Up and Restoring Files with File History

By default, File History takes snapshots of all the files in user folders (Documents, Pictures, Movies, Videos, and so on) and on your desktop. It can also take snapshots of OneDrive if you set your user folders to use OneDrive as their default location.

This app doesn't just save your files once. It keeps saving them over and over, so you end up with a bunch of different versions. This is great because if you mess something up or lose a file, you can go back in time and grab an older version. The snapshots get taken once an hour and are kept until your backup drive runs out of space or for as long as you like, if you personalize File History's settings. I explain how later in this section.

Setting up File History

To use File History, Windows 11 demands that you have an external hard drive, a second hard drive, or a network connection that leads to a hard drive. In this example, I connect to an external USB drive that is connected to my PC. You can also use a cheap external hard drive, which you can pick up at any computer store, or use a hard drive on another computer on your network.

REMEMBER

If you have lots of pictures in your Photos folder or a zillion files in the Documents folder, the first File History backup takes hours and hours. If you have lots of data and this is your first time backing up, make sure you're ready to leave the machine to do its thing for a long time.

To get File History going, attach an external drive to your Windows 11 computer and follow these steps:

1. **Click or tap inside the Search box on the taskbar and type** file history.

   The search results are displayed.

2. **Choose the File History search result.**

   The File History window pops up, displaying your external drive, as shown in Figure 1-6.

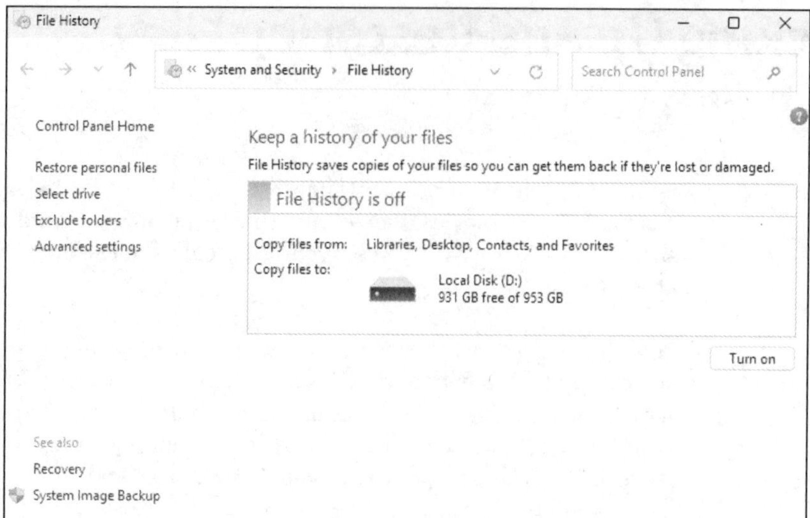

FIGURE 1-6: With an external drive connected, it's time to turn on File History.

3. **If multiple drives are connected, click or tap Select Drive, select the drive you want to use for File History, and then click or tap OK.**
4. **Click or tap the Turn On button.**

   File History is started, and it tells you that it's copying your files for the first time.
5. **If you want, close the File History window.**

   You can perform other tasks while File History works in the background.

WARNING

If you're using a Copilot+ PC device with a Qualcomm Snapdragon chip, such as the ASUS Vivobook S 15 that I'm using for this book, you might have noticed that File History is missing in Windows 11. When you search for it, you only get web results instead of the actual app. It seems that Microsoft didn't update File History for these ARM devices and simply left it out.

Checking whether File History backed up your data

Instead of relying on the File History program to tell you that the backup occurred, take matters into your own hands and look for the backup with File Explorer. To find and check your backup files, follow these steps:

1. **Click or tap the File Explorer icon on the taskbar.**

   File Explorer opens.

2. **In the left sidebar, choose This PC, and then navigate to the drive that you just used in the preceding steps for a File History backup.**

3. **Double-click or double-tap your way through the folder hierarchy:**

   - FileHistory
   - Your username
   - Your PC name
   - Data
   - The main drive you backed up (probably C:)
   - Users
   - Your username (again)
   - Desktop (assuming you had any files on your desktop that you backed up), Documents, or Pictures, or some other folder of interest

   A File Explorer screen like the one shown in Figure 1-7 appears.

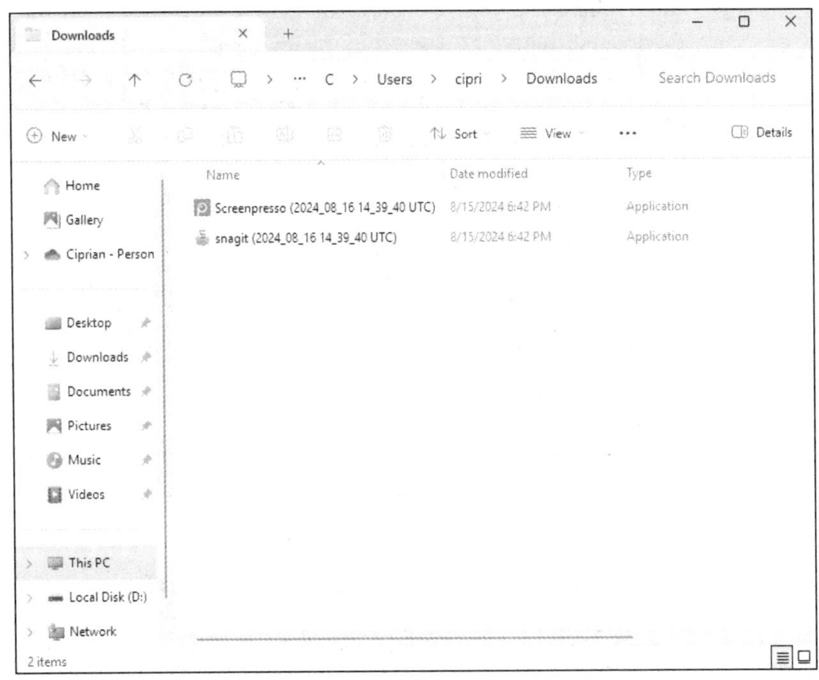

FIGURE 1-7: Your backup data appears way down in a chain of folders.

Backing Up Your Data

4. **Check whether the filenames match the files on your desktop, in your Documents folder, or in any other folder of interest, with dates and times added at the end of their name.**

5. **Do one of the following:**

   - *If the files match, close File Explorer.* Although you can restore data from this location via File Explorer, it's easier to use the File History retrieval tools. (See the next section for details.)
   - *If you don't see filenames that mimic the files on your desktop, go back to Step 1 in the preceding section and make sure File History is set up correctly.*

REMEMBER

File History doesn't run if the backup drive gets disconnected — but Windows 11 produces File History files anyway. As soon as the drive is reconnected, File History dumps all its data to the correct location, automatically.

Restoring data from File History

File History stores snapshots of your files, taken every hour unless you change the frequency. If you've been working on a spreadsheet for the past six hours and discovered that you made a big mistake sometime in the last half hour, you can retrieve a copy of the spreadsheet that's approximately an hour old. If you've been working on your résumé over the past three months and decide that you really don't like the way your design changed five weeks ago, File History can help you there too.

Here's how to bring back your files from File History:

1. **Click or tap inside the Search box on the taskbar and enter** file history**.**

   Search starts displaying a list of results.

2. **Choose File History.**

   You see the File History app window (refer to Figure 1-6).

3. **On the left, click or tap Restore Personal Files.**

   The Home — File History window appears, as shown in Figure 1-8.

4. **Navigate to the location of the file you want to restore.**

   In Figure 1-8, I went to the Downloads folder, where the file I want to resuscitate is stored.

TIP

   You can use several familiar File Explorer navigation methods in the File History program, including the up arrow to move up one level, the forward and back arrows, and the Search box in the upper-right corner.

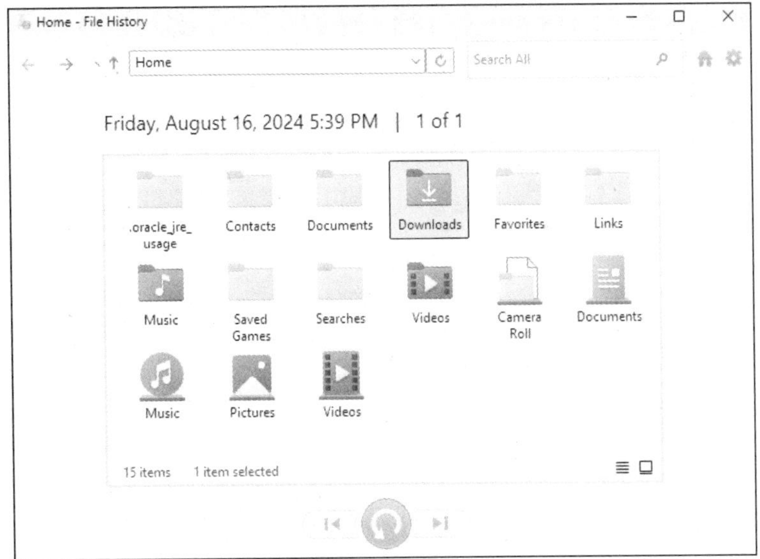

FIGURE 1-8: First, select the folder where the file you want to restore is found.

5. **Check the time and date in the upper-left corner and do one of the following:**
   - *If you see the time and date of the file you want to recover:* Click or tap the file to select it and then click or tap the arrow-in-a-circle icon (restore). You can also drag the file to whatever location you like. You can even preview the file by double-clicking it.
   - *If this isn't the right time and date:* Click or tap the left arrow at the bottom to go back to the previous snapshot. Use the left and right arrows to move to earlier and later versions of the files, respectively.
6. **If you want to restore all the files displayed in the File History window, click or tap the arrow-in-a-circle at the bottom of the screen without selecting a specific file first.**
7. **Choose to Replace the Files in the Destination (which deletes the latest version of each file) or select which files you want to replace, as shown in Figure 1-9.**

TIP

If you accidentally replace a good file, don't worry. A snapshot of that file was taken about an hour ago. You just have to find it. Kinda cool how that works, isn't it? And that old copy stays around for a long time — even years if you have enough disk space and your backup drive doesn't die.

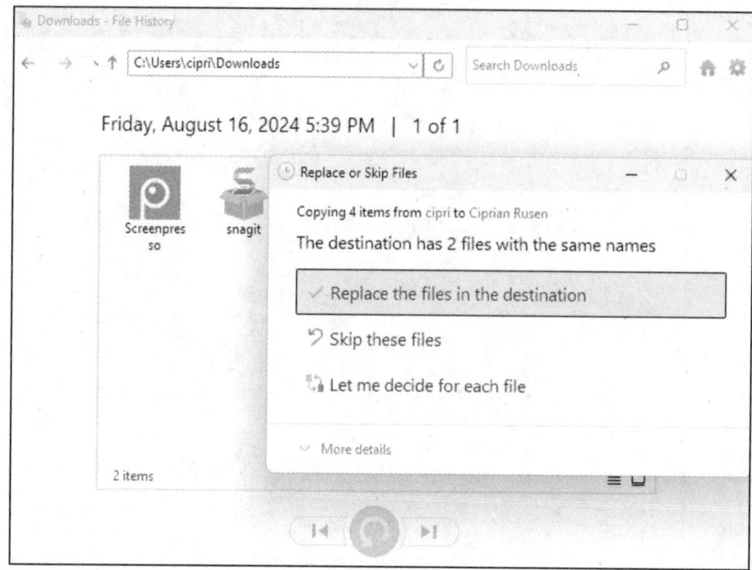

FIGURE 1-9: After finding the file, find the correct version and restore it.

Changing File History settings

File History backs up *every file in every user folder* on your computer. If you have a folder that you want to have backed up, just put it in one of the standard user folders. File History takes care of all the details.

However, if you want to change how often it backs up your data and how long it stores it, you need to access its advanced settings. Here's how:

1. **Click or tap inside the Search box on the taskbar and type** file history.

   The search results are displayed.

2. **Choose the File History search result.**

   The File History window pops up (refer to Figure 1-6).

3. **If you want to exclude some folders in your libraries so they don't get backed up:**

   (a) *Choose Exclude Folders (on the left).* File History opens a new page where you can add folders for exclusion.

   (b) *Click or tap the Add button and select a folder to put it in the exclude list.* For example, in Figure 1-10, I excluded a folder found in my Documents.

   (c) *Repeat Step 3b until you have selected all the folders you want to exclude.*

   (d) *Click or tap Save Changes to go back to the File History home page.*

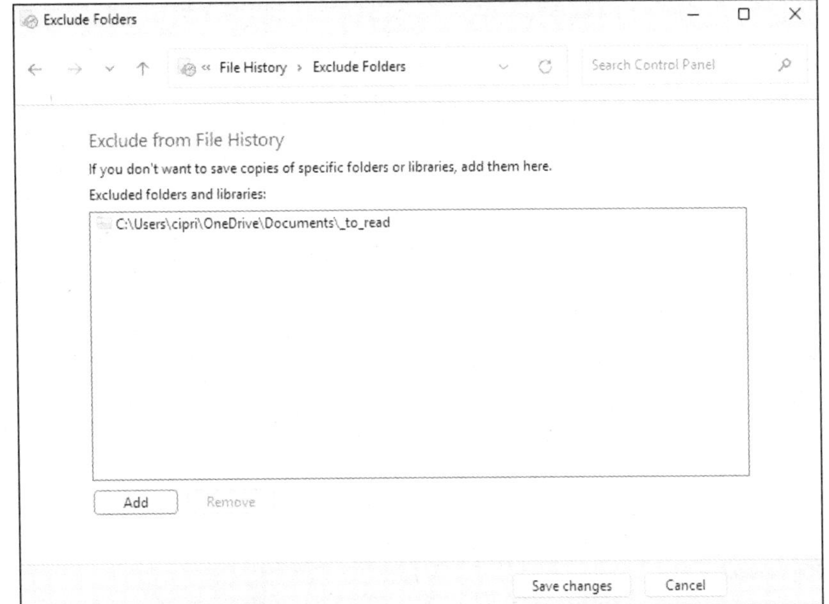

FIGURE 1-10: Exclude individual folders from File History.

4. **To change how frequently backups are made:**

   (a) *Click or tap the Advanced Settings link (on the left).* The Advanced Settings are shown like in Figure 1-11.

   (b) *Change the frequency of backups and how long versions should be kept.* See my recommendations for these settings in Table 1-1.

5. **Click or tap Save Changes.**

   Your next File History backup follows the new rules.

TIP

If you're running out of space on your backup drive, during Step 4a from Figure 1-11, click or tap Clean Up Versions, and choose how you want File History to delete older versions of your files.

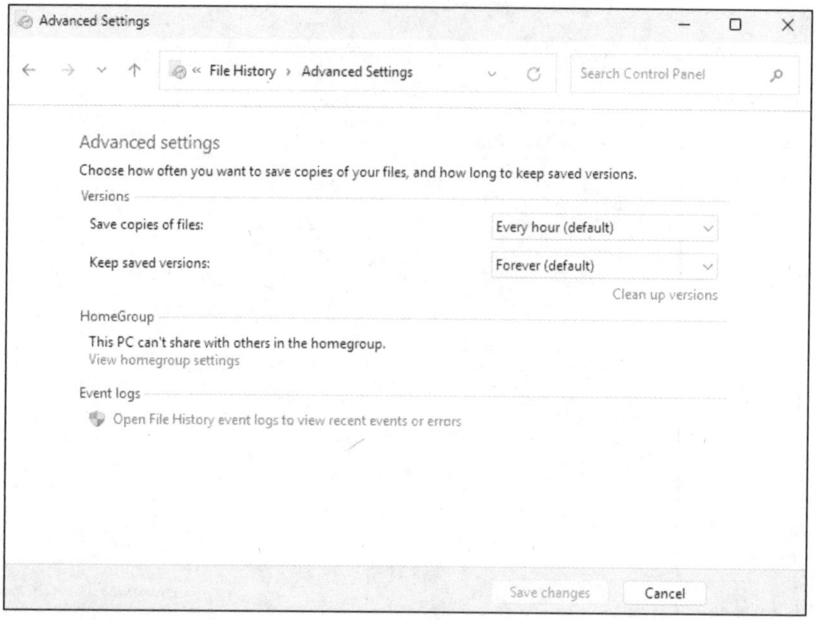

FIGURE 1-11: Choose how often backups are made and how long they're stored.

TABLE 1-1 **File History Advanced Settings**

Setting	Recommendation	Why
Save Copies of Files	Every 30 Minutes	This is mostly a tradeoff between space (more frequent backups take a tiny bit of extra space) and time — your time. If you have lots of backups, you increase the likelihood of getting back a usable version of a file, but you must wade through many more versions. I find 30 minutes strikes the right balance, but you may want to back up more frequently.
Keep Saved Versions	Forever (default)	If you choose Until Space Is Needed, File History won't help you if you run out of room on your backup drive. By leaving it at Forever, File History sends notifications when the hard drive gets close to full capacity so you can run out and buy another backup drive.

Storing Your Data in the Cloud

File History is a great product, and I use it religiously. But it isn't the be-all and end-all of backup storage. What happens if my office burns down? What if I need to get at a file when I'm away from the office?

The best solution I've found is to have File History do its thing but also keep my most important files — the ones I'm using right now — in the cloud. That's how I wrote this book, with the text files and the screenshots in Dropbox. I also used Dropbox to hand off the files to my editors and receive edited versions back.

TIP

Backing up to the internet has one additional big plus: Depending on which package you use and how you use it, the data can be accessible to you no matter where you need it — on the road, on your iPad, or even on your Android smartphone. You can set up folders to share with friends or co-workers and have them help you work on a file while you're working on it, too.

Many years ago, there was only one big player — Dropbox — in the online storage and sharing business. Now there's Dropbox, Microsoft OneDrive, Google Drive, the Apple iCloud — all from huge companies — as well as Proton, Box (formerly `Box.net`), and others from smaller companies.

What happened? People have discovered just how handy cloud storage can be. And the price of cloud storage has gone down.

REMEMBER

The cloud storage I'm talking about is designed to allow you to store data on the internet and retrieve it from anywhere, on just about any kind of device — including a smartphone or tablet. It also has varying degrees of interoperability and sharing, so, for example, you can upload a file and have a dozen people look at it simultaneously. Some cloud storage services (notably OneDrive and Google Drive) have associated programs (such as Microsoft Office and Google's Workspace, respectively) that let two or more people edit the same file simultaneously.

Considering cloud storage privacy concerns

I don't know how many times people have told me that they don't trust putting their data on some company's internet servers. But although many people are rightfully concerned about privacy issues and the specter of Big Brother, the fact is that the demand for storage in the cloud is growing every year.

The concerns I hear go something like this:

- **I must have a working internet connection to get data to or from the online storage.** Absolutely true, and there's no way around it. If you use cloud storage for only offsite backup, it's sufficient to be connected whenever you want to back up your data or restore it. Some of the cloud storage services have ways to cache data on your computer when, say, you're going to be on an airplane. But in general, you have to be online.

- **The data can be taken or copied by law enforcement and local governments.** True. The big cloud storage companies get several court orders each day. The storage company's legal staff takes a look, and if it's a valid order, your data gets sent to the cops, the feds, or some other law enforcement agency.

REMEMBER

If you're going to store data that you don't want to appear in the next issue of a certain British tabloid, it would be smart to encrypt the file before you store it. Word and Excel use remarkably effective encryption techniques, and 7-Zip (see Book 10, Chapter 4) also makes nearly unbreakable ZIPs. Couple that with a strong password, and your data isn't going anywhere soon. Unless, of course, you're required by the court to give up the password or the NSA sets one of its superpowerful password crackers on the job.

- **Programs at the cloud storage firm can scan my data.** True, once again, for most (but not all) cloud storage firms. With a few notable exceptions — `Sync.com`, Proton, Mega.io, and others — cloud storage company programs can see your data. There's been a big push in the past few years to hold cloud storage companies responsible for storing copyrighted material. For example, if you upload a pirated copy of *Barbie* to OneDrive, it's not a good idea to share it with others. It will likely get flagged by Microsoft's copyright protection systems and removed.
- **Employees at the cloud storage firm can look at my data.** True again. Certain cloud storage company employees *can* see your data — at least in the larger companies. They must be able to see your data to comply with court orders. Does that mean Billy the intern can look at your financial data or your family photos? Well, no. It's more complicated than that. Every cloud storage company has strict, logged, and monitored rules for who can view customer data and why. Am I absolutely sure that every company obeys all these rules? No, not at all. But I don't think my information is interesting enough to draw much attention.
- **Someone can break into the cloud storage site and steal my data.** Well, yes, that's true, but it probably isn't much of a concern. Each of the cloud storage services encrypts its data and uses two-step verification, so it'd be difficult for anyone to break in, steal, and then decrypt the stolen data. Can it happen? Sure. Will I lose sleep over it? Nope. That said, you should enable two-factor authentication (so the cloud storage service sends an entry code to your email address or sends you a code on your phone, requiring the entry code to access your data). And if you want to be triple-sure, you can encrypt the data before you store it — 7-Zip, among many other apps, makes it easy to encrypt files when you ZIP them.

Reaping the benefits of backup and storage in the cloud

So much for the negatives. Time to look at the positives. On the plus side, a good cloud storage setup gives you the following:

- **Offsite backups** that won't get destroyed if your house or business burns down or is affected by extreme weather events such as a hurricane.
- **Access to your data from anywhere,** using just about any imaginable kind of computer, including smartphones and tablets.
- **Controlled sharing** so you can password-protect specific files or folders. Hand the password to a friend, and they can look at the file or folder.
- **Broadcast sharing** from a public folder or file that anyone can see.
- **Direct access from apps that run in the cloud.** Both Google Workspace and the many forms of Microsoft Office are good examples. The list includes iWork (the Apple productivity apps) if you're using Apple's iCloud.
- **Free packages, up to a certain size limit,** offered by most of the cloud storage services.

Choosing an online backup and sharing service

So, which cloud storage service is best? Tough question. I use three of them: Google Drive for all my work at Digital Citizen, Dropbox when I work on book projects with my publisher, and Microsoft OneDrive for all my computers, smartphones, and tablets.

They all have programs that you run on your PC or Mac to set up folders that are shared. Drag a file into the shared folder, and it appears on all the computers and devices connected to the shared folder. Go on the web and log in to the site, and your data's available there too. Install an app on your iPhone or Android smartphone or tablet, and the data's there as well. Here's a rundown of what each cloud storage service offers:

- **Dropbox** offers 2GB of free storage, with 2TB for $11.99 per month. It's easy to use, reliable, and fast. I use it for synchronizing project files — including the files for this book. Visit `www.dropbox.com` for details.

- **OneDrive** has 5GB of free storage, with 100GB for $1.99 per month. Note that many Microsoft 365 (formerly known as Office 365) subscriptions have 1TB of OneDrive storage included, for as long as you're a subscriber. I talk about OneDrive in Book 4, Chapter 6. Also visit `www.onedrive.com` for details.
- **Google Drive (also known as Google One)** has 15GB of free storage, with 100GB for $1.99 per month and 2TB for $9.99 per month. Google Drive isn't as slick as the other two, but it works well enough for most people. Visit `https://one.google.com` for details.
- **Apple iCloud** is an Apple-centric service. The first 5GB is free, and then it's $0.99 per month for an additional 50GB. It works great with iPads, iPhones, and Macs, with extraordinarily simple backup of photos. Photo and video backup and synchronization take place automatically; you don't have to do a thing. Visit `www.icloud.com` for details.

The other services have specific strong points:

- **SugarSync** (`www.sugarsync.com`) lets you synchronize arbitrary folders on your PC. That's a big deal if you don't want to drag your synced folders into one location.
- **Box** (`www.box.com`) is designed for large companies and provides tools to control which files employees can share.
- **Proton** (`proton.me`) offers end-to-end encryption, which ensures that no one, not even the company providing this service, can access your files. Files, filenames, folder names, and more are fully encrypted at rest and in transit to your secure cloud.

IN THIS CHAPTER

» Getting back to Windows 10, if you have issues with Windows 11

» Resetting Windows 11 and keeping your files

» Resetting your PC to its factory settings

» Installing Windows 11 from scratch

Chapter 2

Downgrading, Resetting, and Installing Windows 11

If you've worked with Windows for a couple of years, you're aware that the operating system can occasionally start misbehaving. You might encounter problems generated by faulty updates, hardware components malfunctioning due to buggy drivers, or new apps causing disruptions.

These issues are even more likely to occur when upgrading from one version of Windows to the next, such as from Windows 10 to Windows 11. Microsoft is heavily promoting this upgrade, but some users may find themselves frustrated by technical issues in Windows 11 that didn't exist in Windows 10. That's why I begin this chapter by exploring how to roll back to Windows 10 if you've upgraded but find yourself unhappy with Windows 11. This option is available for a limited time, but if you follow my instructions, you should be able to downgrade back to Windows 10 quickly and easily.

Next, I delve into resetting Windows 11, a useful troubleshooting tool for when your system isn't performing as it should. I cover in detail the two reset options provided by Microsoft: one that keeps your personal files intact and another that removes everything for a clean slate. I explain what each option does and help you make an informed decision.

For those who prefer starting fresh, I guide you through the process of installing Windows 11 from scratch. I share how to create Windows 11 installation media, check its system requirements, and navigate the Installation wizard. To ensure my instructions are thorough, I also cover the often-overlooked personalization steps that follow the initial setup.

Lastly, I provide tips for installing Windows 11 with a local (offline) account, offering an alternative to Microsoft's push for online accounts during the Windows setup. There's plenty of ground to cover, so let's get started.

Rolling Back to Windows 10

Microsoft's pushing Windows 11 pretty hard, especially through Windows Update. If you're a Windows 10 user, you've seen the company's promotional messages. Some folks who upgrade are happy with the new Windows 11 look and features, while others aren't so thrilled. Then there are those who like it but run into technical issues. The good news? Microsoft gives you a 10-day window to change your mind. If you upgrade to Windows 11 and decide it's not for you, you can return to Windows 10 without losing your files or data. It's a good safety net, but still a big decision.

WARNING

If you choose to do this, keep in mind the following limitations of this downgrade process:

- The rollback to Windows 10 takes quite a bit of time, so you should keep your laptop or PC plugged in during the process.
- You might need to re-install some apps and programs after the downgrade. For example, the apps that you installed after upgrading to Windows 11 will likely be lost during the downgrade process.
- Any settings you've changed after upgrading to Windows 11 will be lost.
- If you had a password configured for your user account in Windows 10 and you've changed it while using Windows 11, you need to know the previous password. Otherwise, you won't be able to sign in after you downgrade from Windows 11 to Windows 10.

If you're okay with these limitations and can't wait to get back to Windows 10, log in with a user account that has administrator permissions and follow these steps:

1. **Click or tap the Start icon and then Settings. Or press Windows+I.**

   The Settings app opens on its Home page.

2. **On the left, choose System. On the right, choose Recovery.**

   You see the system recovery options shown in Figure 2-1.

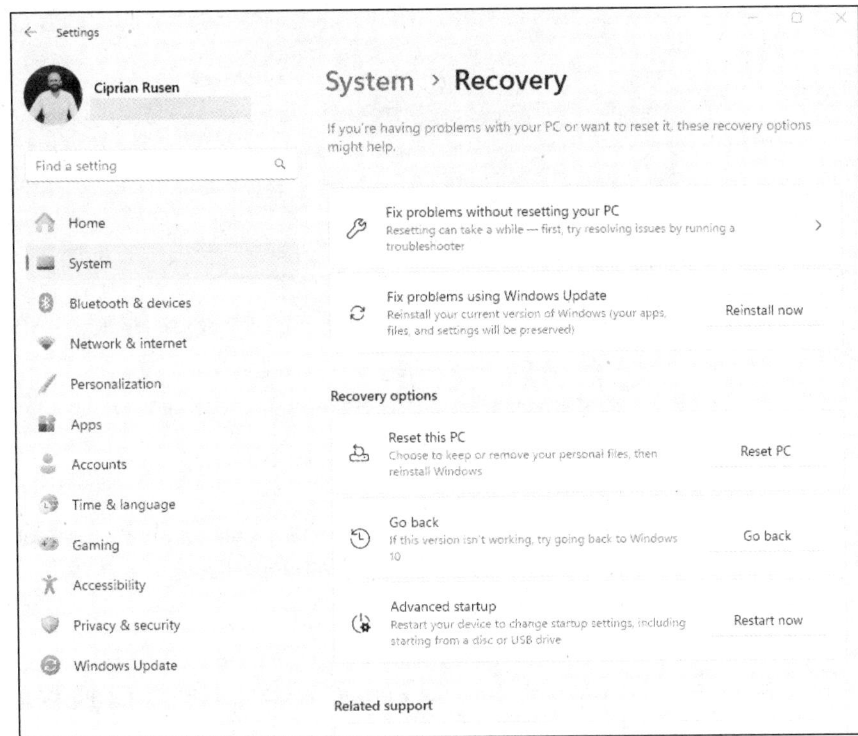

FIGURE 2-1: Your system recovery options.

3. **In the Recovery Options section, click or tap the Go Back button.**

   Windows starts the Go Back to Windows 10 wizard and asks why you're going back, as shown in Figure 2-2.

WARNING

If you don't see a Go back button, your PC may have come with Windows 11 preinstalled by its manufacturer. Or you may have upgraded from Windows 10 to Windows 11 more than ten days ago, and the Windows.old folder that was created at the end of the upgrade process was deleted. In this situation, your only solution is to manually re-install Windows 10 and delete your Windows 11 installation.

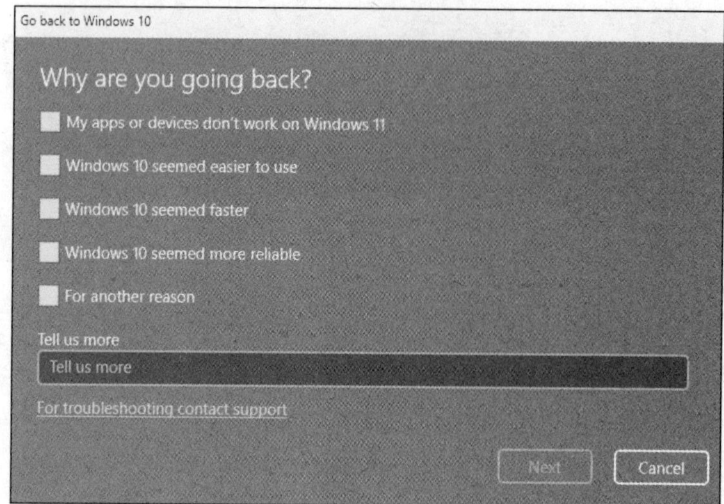

FIGURE 2-2: Going back to Windows 10.

4. **Choose a reason from the list and click or tap Next.**

   Microsoft tries to convince you to continue using Windows 11 by asking whether you'd like to check for updates because they might fix the problems you're having.

5. **Choose No, Thanks.**

   You're informed about what happens after going back to Windows 10. Read everything carefully before moving forward.

6. **Click or tap Next.**

   The wizard explains that you must know the password that you used to sign in to Windows 10 so that you don't get locked out after going back.

7. **If you know the password you used in Windows 10, click or tap Next.**

   You are finally given the option to get back to Windows 10.

8. **Click or tap Go Back to Windows 10.**

   Windows 11 reboots and then says that it's restoring your previous version of Windows. This process takes several minutes and involves several reboots. Wait patiently for the restoration process to be performed. When it's over, the Windows 10 lock screen is shown.

9. **Click or tap anywhere or press any key on your keyboard, and then sign in to Windows 10 using your user account and password.**

   You see the Windows 10 desktop.

Resuscitating Malfunctioning Windows 11 PCs

When resuscitating a Windows 11 machine that no longer works well, consider these three Rs: remove the latest update (read Book 7, Chapter 2), reset but keep your programs and data, and reset and remove everything, including your data. It's important that you're careful when you apply any of these Rs.

If you've decided that you want to go ahead and reset your Windows 11 computer, keep in mind that there are two ways to reset it, and they are as different as night and day:

- **Reset with Keep My Files** keeps some Windows settings (accounts, passwords, the desktop, Microsoft Edge favorites, wireless network settings, drive letter assignments, and BitLocker settings) and all personal data (in the Users folder). It wipes out all programs and then restores the apps available in the Microsoft Store. This option is pretty drastic, but at least it keeps the data stored in the most common locations — the Documents folder, Desktop, Downloads, Pictures, and the like. As a bonus, the Reset with Keep My Files routine keeps a list of the apps it removed and puts the list on your desktop so you can look at it when your machine's back to normal.
- **Reset with Remove Everything** removes everything on your PC and re-installs Windows. Your programs, data, and settings all get wiped out — they're irretrievably lost. This option is one of the most drastic things you can do with your computer. Most hardware manufacturers have this procedure customized to put their crapware back on your PC. If you run Reset with Remove Everything on those systems, you don't get a clean copy of Windows 11; you get the factory settings version. Yes, that means you get the original manufacturer's drivers (see the "Why would you want factory drivers?" sidebar). But it also means you get the manufacturer's bloatware.

  If you like, you can tell Reset with Remove Everything to do a *thorough* reformatting of the hard drive, in which case random patterns of data are written to the hard drive to make it almost impossible to retrieve anything you used to store on the disk. But in the end, you get the same bloatware that comes with a new computer.

WHY WOULD YOU WANT FACTORY DRIVERS?

An important downside to running a Reset with Remove Everything is that you get all the junk that manufacturers ship with their new computers. Some of the apps they ship are supposed to make managing your PC better. Others are simply advertising, for which the advertiser pays.

The one upside to running a Reset with Remove Everything? You get back the original drivers. I can't say that I've seen a situation where a clean install of Windows 11 resulted in useless drivers. In the unusual situation where you get suboptimal drivers, one trip through Windows Update should get you up to speed. But if you're worried that a truly clean install will leave you begging, Reset with Remove Everything is the way to go.

Resetting your Windows 11 PC

Now, let's see how the Windows 11 reset works when using the Keep My Files options. Running a Keep My Files reset *keeps* all these:

- **Some of your Windows 11 settings:** Your user accounts and passwords, wireless network connections and their settings, BitLocker settings and passwords, drive letter assignments, and your Windows 11 installation key are kept.
- **Files in the Users folder:** Files in every user's Documents folder, Desktop folder, Downloads folder, and so on are kept. Reset with Keep My Files keeps File History versions, and it keeps folders stored on drives and in partitions that don't contain Windows (typically, that means it doesn't touch anything outside of the C: drive).
- **Windows 11 apps from the Microsoft Store:** The app settings are saved too. So if you're up to the 16th level of Candy Crush before you run a Reset with Keep My Files, afterward you're still on the 16th level. Confusingly, if you bought a desktop app in the Microsoft Store, its settings get removed during the reset. Only your Windows 11 apps come through untouched.

WARNING

Running Reset with the Keep My Files option *destroys* the following:

- **Many of your Windows 11 settings:** Display settings, firewall customizations, and file type associations are wiped out. Windows 11 removes most of your settings because they could be the ones causing the problems you're facing.

- **Files — including data files — outside the Users folder:** If you have files tucked away in some unusual location on the C: drive, don't expect them to survive Reset. However, partitions other than C: are not touched by the reset process.
- **Desktop apps or programs:** The settings disappear too, including the activation keys you need to install them or the passwords you use to authenticate in those programs. You need to re-install them all. However, the reset routine makes a list of the programs that it removes and puts it on your desktop.

To run a Windows 11 reset with the Keep My Files option, first sign in with an account that has administrator permissions and follow these steps:

1. **Click or tap the Start icon and then Settings.**

   You see the Settings app on its Home page.

2. **Go to System and select Recovery.**

   You see the recovery options (refer to Figure 2-1).

3. **Click or tap Reset PC.**

   Windows 11 asks if you want to keep your files or remove everything, as shown in Figure 2-3.

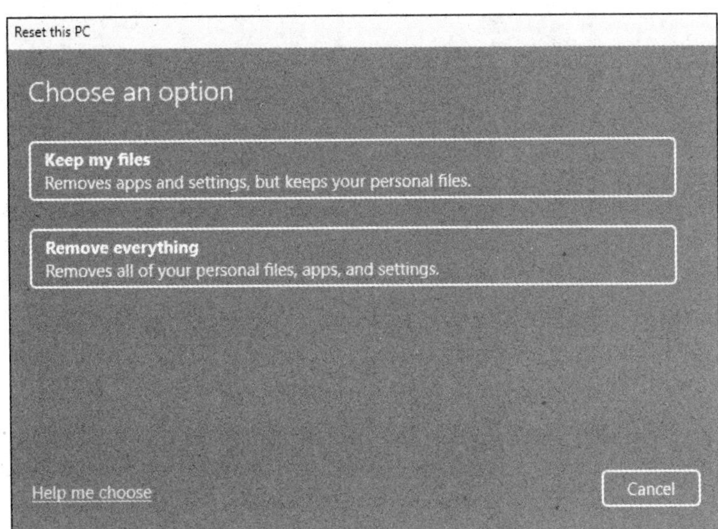

FIGURE 2-3: Choosing the kind of reset you want.

4. **Unless you're going to recycle your computer — give it to charity or the kids — try the less destructive approach by choosing Keep My Files.**

   You're asked how you want to re-install Windows: from the cloud or locally from your device. The first option takes a lot more time because it downloads the Windows 11 Setup files from Microsoft servers. However, it gives you more up-to-date Windows files. Even so, I prefer the second option because it's a lot faster.

5. **Choose whether you want a Cloud Download or Local Reinstall, and then click or tap Next.**

   After some time, you're informed about what the resetting will do to your Windows 11 computer or device.

6. **To see which apps won't make it through the reset process, click or tap View Apps that Will Be Removed.**

   A list of apps appears, similar to Figure 2-4.

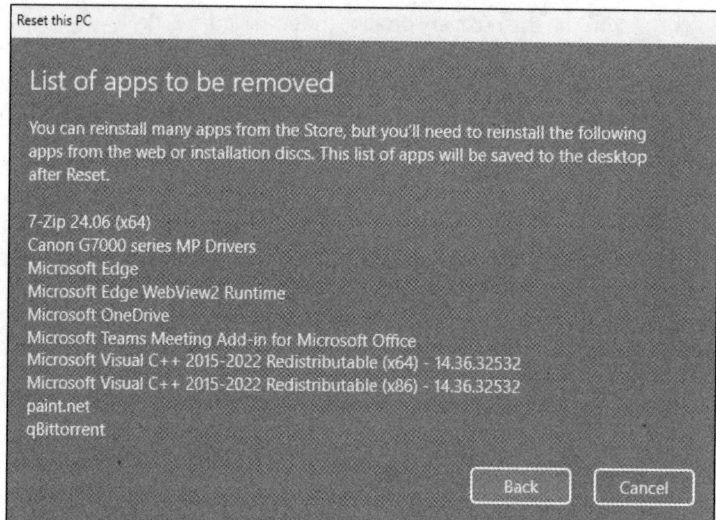

Reset this PC
List of apps to be removed
You can reinstall many apps from the Store, but you'll need to reinstall the following apps from the web or installation discs. This list of apps will be saved to the desktop after Reset.
7-Zip 24.06 (x64)
Canon G7000 series MP Drivers
Microsoft Edge
Microsoft Edge WebView2 Runtime
Microsoft OneDrive
Microsoft Teams Meeting Add-in for Microsoft Office
Microsoft Visual C++ 2015-2022 Redistributable (x64) - 14.36.32532
Microsoft Visual C++ 2015-2022 Redistributable (x86) - 14.36.32532
paint.net
qBittorrent
Back
Cancel

FIGURE 2-4: The list of apps that are going to be removed during the reset.

7. **Click or tap Back, followed by Reset.**

   Windows 11 starts preparing the reset process and displays its progress in percentages. The preparations can take many minutes, so patience is required. Next comes the actual reset, which takes several more minutes and involves a couple of reboots, after which Windows 11 installs itself again. When the procedure is finished, you end up on the Windows 11 sign-in screen.

8. **Sign in to Windows 11 and wait for the Welcome dialog to finish.**

   You see the desktop where you can find a Remove Apps file that lists the programs that didn't make it through the resetting process. If you need them, you must manually install them again.

Resetting your PC to its factory settings

WARNING

The Reset with the Remove Everything option is similar to running Reset with Save My Files except . . .

WARNING

This procedure wipes out everything and forces you to start from scratch. You must enter new account names and passwords and re-install everything, including all your apps. When you're done, you'll have a factory-fresh copy of Windows 11. However, if you're running one of the (many) Windows 11 PCs that ship with bloatware preinstalled, all of it will reappear.

If you're selling your PC, giving it away, or even sending it off to a recycling service, Reset with Remove Everything is a good idea. If you're keeping your PC, only attempt Reset with Remove Everything after you have run Reset with Keep My Files but haven't solved your problem(s). Reset with Remove Everything is similar to a clean install. You're nuking everything on your PC, although you get your factory drivers back.

With that as a preamble, sign in with a user account that has administrator permissions, and follow these steps to reset Windows 11 to its factory settings:

1. **Click or tap the Start icon, followed by Settings. Or press Windows+I.**

   The Settings app appears on the screen.

2. **Go to System and choose Recovery.**

   You see the system recovery options (refer to Figure 2-1).

3. **Click or tap Reset PC.**

   Windows 11 asks whether you want to keep your files or remove everything (refer to Figure 2-3).

4. **Click or tap Remove Everything and choose whether you want a Cloud Download of Windows 11 from Microsoft's servers or a Local Reinstall.**

   Keep in mind that the second option is faster. After you make your choice, a summary of your settings is displayed, as shown in Figure 2-5.

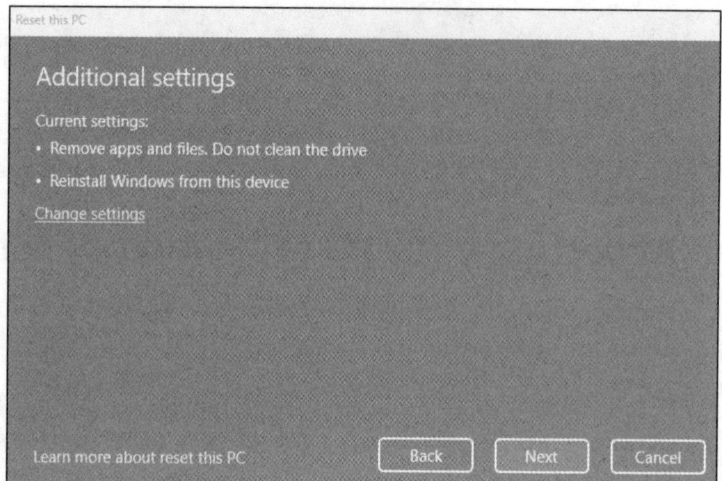

FIGURE 2-5: Reset summarizes your choices.

5. **Click or tap Next.**

   You're informed about what the resetting will do to your Windows 11 computer or device.

6. **If you're okay to go ahead, click or tap Reset. Otherwise, click or tap Cancel.**

   Windows 11 prepares the reset process. It then restarts your device and starts the factory reset, which takes a long time, especially if you're using an affordable entry-level laptop. Once the reset is over, Windows 11 installs itself again and takes you through its personalization wizard.

7. **Set up Windows 11 from scratch. You can use the instructions from the dedicated section later in the chapter.**

   Now that's a complete re-install!

Installing Windows 11 on a PC

Installing Windows 11 requires appropriate installation media, which can take several forms depending on your setup. Most people need a USB flash drive loaded with the Windows Setup files. For virtual machine installations, an ISO file is the way to go. Some users might opt for a DVD containing the Windows Setup files, though this option is less common in modern computers.

Regardless of your chosen installation media, Microsoft simplifies the process of creating it with its Windows 11 Installation Media tool. Available for download from Microsoft, this utility allows you to easily create any of these installation media types, ensuring that you have what you need to get Windows 11 up and running. Head over to this page and download the tool: www.microsoft.com/en-us/software-download/windows11/.

After creating your installation media, it's a good idea to check if the computer where you want to install Windows 11 meets its system requirements. Head over to this page and check them out: www.microsoft.com/en-us/windows/windows-11-specifications.

If your PC also meets these requirements, you can finally start installing Windows 11 like this:

1. **Connect the installation media, power on the PC, and select the option to boot from media. Then when instructed, press any key to boot from it.**

   The Windows 11 Setup wizard shown in Figure 2-6 is loaded.

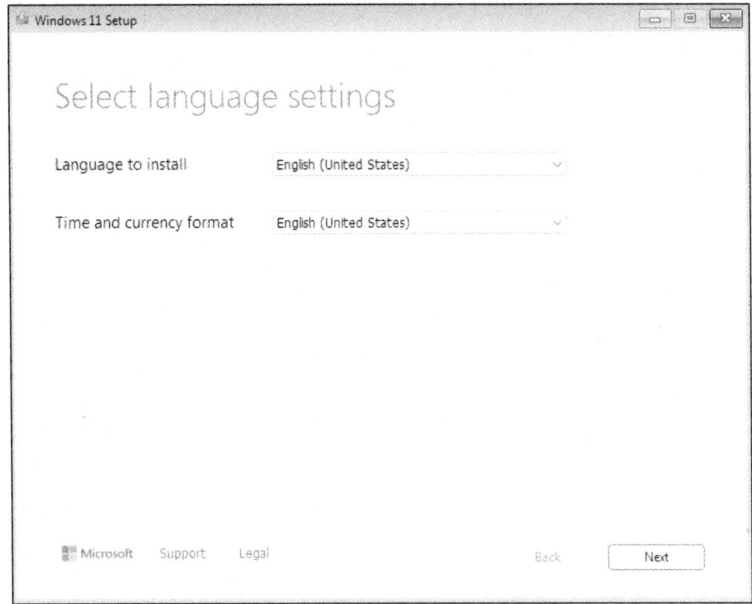

FIGURE 2-6: Windows 11 Setup starts with this step.

2. **Choose the language you want to use, the time and currency format. Then click Next.**

   You're asked to select your keyboard settings.

3. **Choose the keyboard language, and click Next.**

   You're asked to select a setup option.

4. **Select Install Windows 11 and select the box next to I Agree Everything Will Be Deleted Including Files, Apps, and Settings. Then click Next.**

   Windows 11 Setup asks you to activate Windows and enter a product key. You don't have to provide one to continue. You can also activate Windows 11 after you install it.

5. **Enter the product key or click the I Don't Have a Product Key link.**

   You're asked to choose which edition of Windows 11 you want to install, as shown in Figure 2-7. If you're feeling confused, read Book 1, Chapter 3, to learn more about all the Windows editions available.

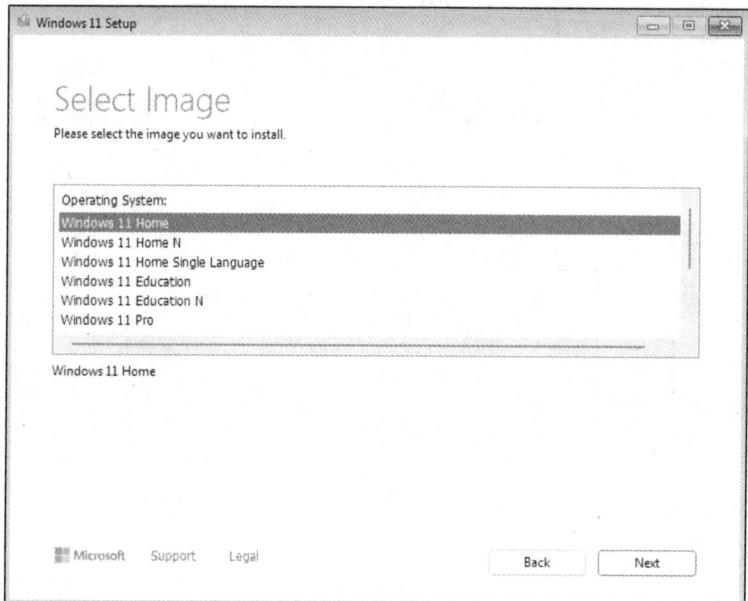

FIGURE 2-7: Choosing the Windows 11 edition you want to install.

6. **Choose the Windows 11 edition you want to install and click Next.**

   I chose Windows 11 Pro to help guide you through the process.

   It's time to read and accept the Microsoft Software License Terms.

7. **Scroll down to the bottom, and click Accept.**

   You are asked to choose where you want to install Windows 11 from the options shown in Figure 2-8.

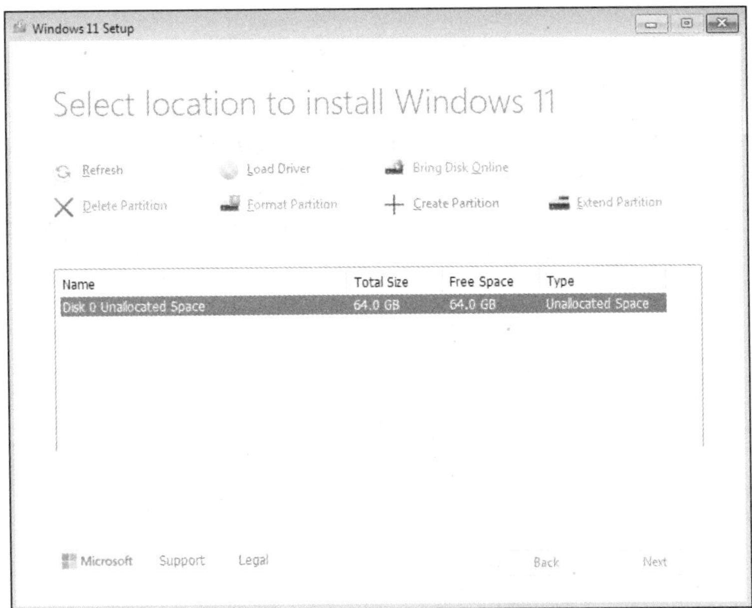

FIGURE 2-8: Selecting the drive where you want to install Windows 11.

8. **Create a new partition or choose a drive from the ones on your computer. After making your choice, click Next.**

   You see a summary of your settings.

9. **Click Install.**

   Windows 11 Setup is now installing Windows 11, a process which takes surprisingly little time. You can see its progress expressed in percentages. Wait until the installation is finished. Your computer is then rebooted, and the Personalization wizard starts, asking you to choose your country or region.

10. **Go through the Windows 11 personalization process.**

    To help you out, you can find step-by-step instructions in the next section of this chapter.

Personalizing your Windows 11 installation

Once you've completed the installation phase of Windows 11 Setup using the instructions provided in the previous section, you'll encounter a wizard designed to help personalize your Windows 11 installation. It consists of multiple steps and choices, some of which vary depending on whether you're installing Windows 11 Home or

Pro and whether your device is a desktop PC or a laptop. Here's how to navigate the Personalization wizard:

1. **When you're asked to choose your country or region, as in Figure 2-9, make your choice.**

   You're asked to select the keyboard layout you want, and you're given a suggestion based on your country.

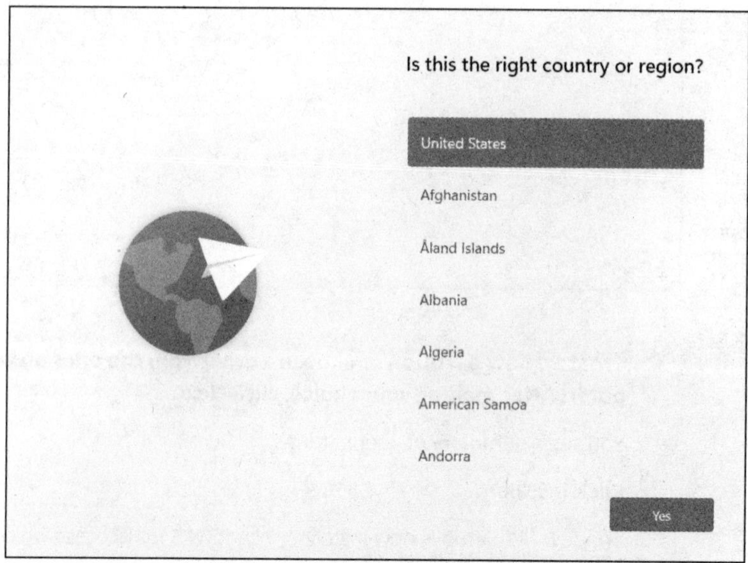

FIGURE 2-9: Personalizing Windows 11 starts with choosing your country.

2. **Choose the keyboard layout and then click or tap Yes.**

   Windows asks whether you want to add a second keyboard layout.

3. **Click or tap Skip.**

   You can add more keyboard layouts later, using the instructions in Book 7, Chapter 1. The Windows 11 Setup wizard checks for updates and it may reboot your computer. Then it asks you to name your device.

4. **Type a name for your device and click or tap Next.**

   Your computer reboots again to apply your chosen name and then asks how you would like to set up your device, as shown in Figure 2-10.

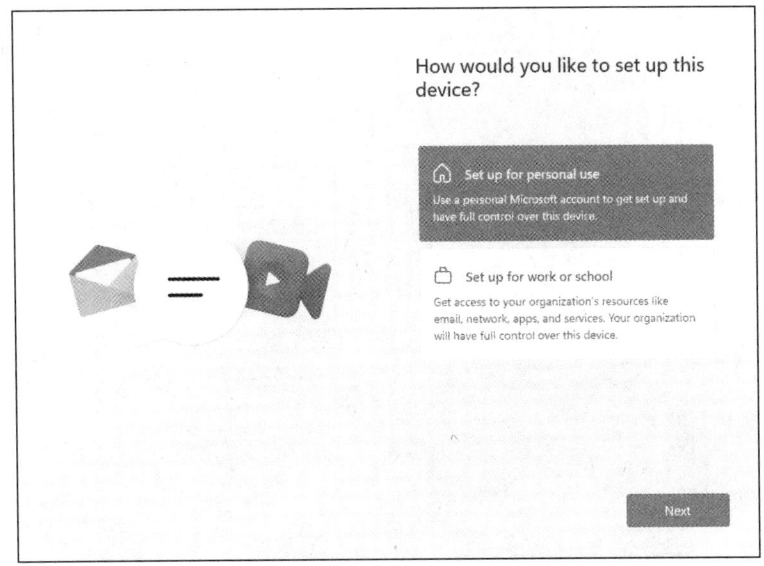

FIGURE 2-10: Choosing to install Windows 11 for personal use.

5. **Select Set Up for Personal Use and then click or tap Next.**

   The Windows 11 Setup starts installing the updates it has found and shares the progress of this operation. This process may take a lot of time and involve another reboot. When it's over, you're asked to sign in.

TIP

   If you're installing Windows 11 Home, you won't go through Step 5 and you won't see the choice shown in Figure 2-10. The Personalization wizard will simply skip this step and go to Step 6.

6. **Click or tap Sign In and enter the credentials of your Microsoft account. If you don't have one, click or tap Create One! and follow the instructions for creating one.**

   If you have enabled two-step verification, you may need to enter a code from an Authenticator app on your smartphone or a code sent via SMS or email. Then you're asked to create a PIN for your account for faster login. If you're using a laptop with Windows Hello face or fingerprint recognition, you may be asked to set up this type of authentication first, before creating a PIN.

7. **Click or tap Create PIN, enter the PIN you want, and confirm it. Then click or tap OK.**

   The wizard asks you to choose the privacy settings for your device.

8. **Go through all the available switches and turn them on or off as needed. Then click or tap Next, followed by Accept.**

   You're asked whether you want to restore your PC from an older backup, as shown in Figure 2-11.

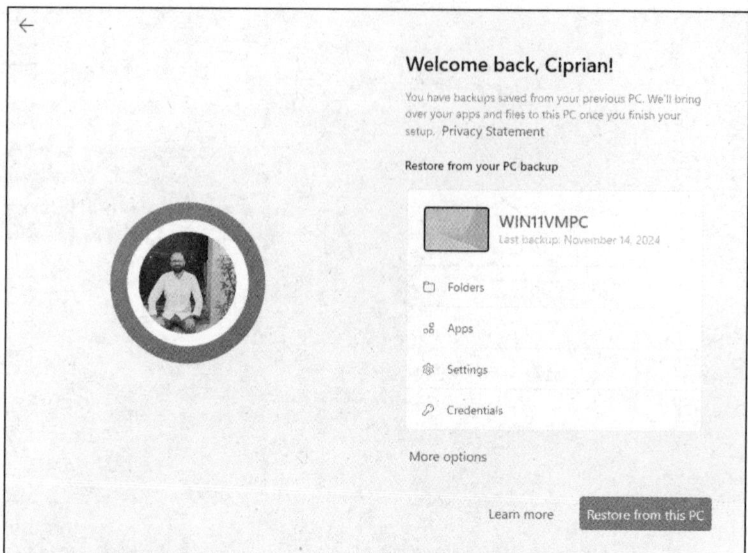

FIGURE 2-11: You can restore your PC from an older backup.

9. **If you want a fresh install, choose More Options and click or tap Set Up as a New PC twice. Otherwise, select Restore from This PC and use the suggested backup.**

   The Setup wizard spends some time recovering the files, apps, settings, and credentials from the selected backup. This process may take a long time if your backup is large. Once the restoration process is complete, the Setup wizard will continue asking how to customize your experience.

10. **For a less annoying user experience, click or tap Skip or Skip Now and keep doing that for all the things that Microsoft suggests you do.**

    You're asked to use your phone from your PC, turn on Camera Backup in the OneDrive app from your phone, and so on. When it's finally over, the wizard loads the desktop, and you can start using Windows 11.

Installing Windows 11 with an offline account

As you've seen in the preceding section, Microsoft is pushing users to sign in with a Microsoft account during their Windows 11 installations. The option to create a local offline account was hidden from Windows 11 Setup, even when installing Windows 11 Pro. Luckily, you can turn off this requirement by using an app called Rufus. Head over to the app's website at `https://rufus.ie/en/` and download the portable version of Rufus.

Also, download an ISO file with Windows 11 Setup from Microsoft at `www.microsoft.com/en-us/software-download/windows11/`.

Now that you have both pieces of the puzzle (Rufus plus the Windows 11 ISO file), you can create installation media on a USB flash drive that bypasses the requirement for a Microsoft account. To do that, first plug the USB drive into your computer, ensure that it has no data on it (because it will be formatted), and run Rufus to personalize the ISO file you've just downloaded.

In the Rufus app, select the device where you want to create the installation media, choose the ISO file for making this media, and then click or tap Start. You're asked to customize your Windows installation, and you can select the option for Remove Requirement for an Online Microsoft Account, as shown in Figure 2-12.

After you personalize and create the installation media with Rufus, you can install Windows 11 using the instructions in this chapter. The installation steps remain the same, but during the personalization stage, you can set up Windows 11 with a local offline account instead of a Microsoft one.

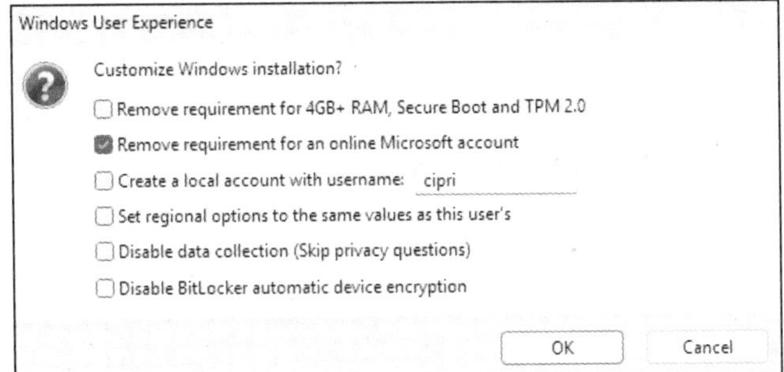

FIGURE 2-12: Rufus is great at bypassing Microsoft's restrictions.

IN THIS CHAPTER

» Understanding and accessing safe mode

» Troubleshooting in safe mode

» Introducing the Windows Recovery Environment

Chapter 3 Troubleshooting with Safe Mode

Safe mode is a useful troubleshooting tool that can help you bring your computer back to life. Windows 11 has several such modes, and in this chapter, I explain the differences between them. Luckily, most people won't need more than two types of safe modes, which makes things easier to explain and understand.

While safe mode may look intimidating, especially when choosing safe mode with command prompt, it's not complicated to use. To make your experience simpler, I show you several ways to access the different safe modes, while also giving you some tips on how they can be useful to you and what you can do while you're in safe mode.

Furthermore, Windows 11 provides a Recovery Environment that starts automatically after the operating system fails to successfully boot three times in a row. Therefore, if you find yourself in a pinch and unable to use Windows 11, the Windows Recovery Environment may save you. In this chapter, I show you how to access this environment and give you a brief description of the tools included. You may find them useful!

Working in Safe Mode

Safe mode is a special way of starting Windows in which the operating system loads only its basic user interface, essential drivers, and services. As a result, safe mode removes most of the things that can cause crashes or problems, making it easier to troubleshoot problems and repair Windows.

In safe mode, you can uninstall misbehaving apps and drivers, change important system settings, and perform maintenance tasks such as checking and repairing the drive for errors. You can also execute advanced commands using the command prompt, Windows Terminal, or PowerShell, as well as scan your computer for malware and other security threats.

You can access three safe modes:

- **Safe mode:** The standard safe mode that most people need. It doesn't load any networking drivers and services, so you can't connect to the internet. You can see it in all its minimalistic glory in Figure 3-1.
- **Safe mode with networking:** A safe mode that also loads networking drivers and services. This mode is useful when you have a working internet connection and need to download tools from the web to troubleshoot your misbehaving Windows 11 PC.
- **Safe mode with command prompt:** Automatically loads a Command Prompt window, for those times when you need quick access to the command line. You can't do anything in this mode except type commands. However, because the command prompt is also available in the standard safe mode, most people don't need to run this type of safe mode.

Accessing safe mode

Unfortunately, Windows 11 requires UEFI, a modern and more powerful type of BIOS. While it has the same role as the traditional BIOS, it does include useful features such as encryption and remote diagnostics and repair. Newer Windows versions were designed to work only with UEFI and take advantage of the additional security and features they provide.

TECHNICAL STUFF

BIOS is an acronym for basic input/output system. Think of it as the software that allows communication and facilitates data transfers between the hardware components of a computer, the software installed on it, and the users using it. UEFI stands for Unified Extensible Firmware Interface, and you can look at it as a modern BIOS.

FIGURE 3-1: Safe mode loads only the essentials.

Older people remember the good old days of using Windows 7 on their computers, when they could press F8 or Shift+F8 during the boot process to access safe mode. This keyboard shortcut can no longer be used because the modern Windows boot process can no longer be interrupted by the user pressing a specific key. However, you can get your device into Windows 11 safe mode in plenty of other ways. One of them that works well follows:

1. **Start your Windows 11 computer and click or tap anywhere when you see the lock screen.**

   If you're already logged into Windows 11, you can close all open apps and files, and click or tap the Start icon.

2. **Press and hold down the Shift key while you click or tap the Power button and select Restart.**

   Windows 11 reboots. Then it asks you to choose an option, as shown in Figure 3-2.

3. **Click or tap Troubleshoot and then Advanced Options.**

   You see several advanced options, as shown in Figure 3-3.

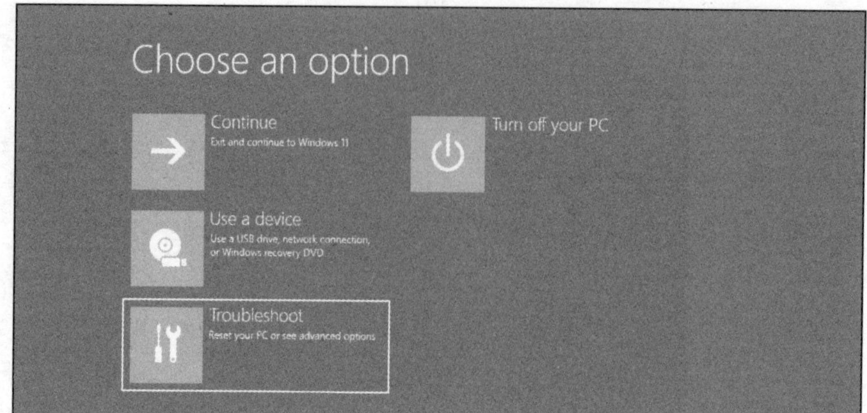

FIGURE 3-2: Choosing Troubleshoot leads you to several advanced options.

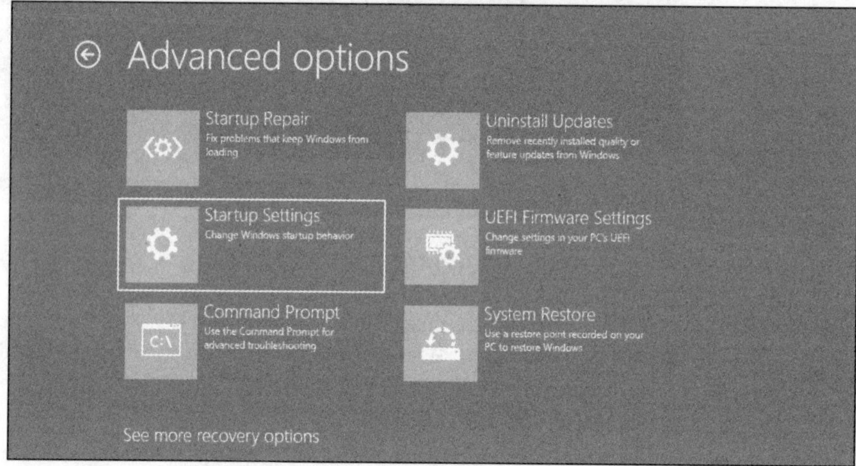

FIGURE 3-3: Changing how Windows 11 behaves at startup.

4. **Select Startup Settings. If you don't have this option, first click or tap the See More Recovery Options link.**

   Windows 11 loads a screen called Startup Settings, informing you that, after you restart your PC, you can change several Windows options. One option is enabling safe mode.

5. **Click or tap the Restart button.**

   A new Startup Settings screen appears, as shown in Figure 3-4.

6. **Press 4 or F4 on your keyboard to start Windows 11 in safe mode, or press 5 or F5 to enter safe mode with networking.**

   Windows 11 starts in Safe Mode, and you can log in using an administrator account and start troubleshooting.

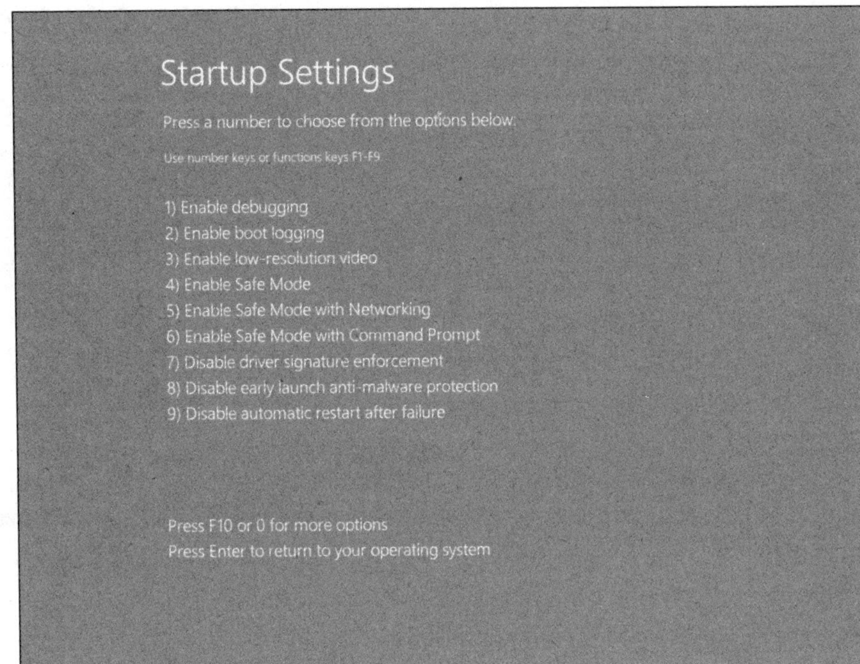

Startup Settings
Press a number to choose from the options below:
Use number keys or functions keys F1-F9.
1) Enable debugging
2) Enable boot logging
3) Enable low-resolution video
4) Enable Safe Mode
5) Enable Safe Mode with Networking
6) Enable Safe Mode with Command Prompt
7) Disable driver signature enforcement
8) Disable early launch anti-malware protection
9) Disable automatic restart after failure
Press F10 or 0 for more options
Press Enter to return to your operating system

FIGURE 3-4: Press 4 or 5 to start into safe mode or safe mode with networking.

TIP

Another way to enter safe mode is to interrupt Windows 11's normal boot process three consecutive times. Press the physical restart or power button on your computer or device while Windows 11 is loading. Then the operating system will stop trying to boot normally and load its automatic repair mode instead. On the Automatic Repair screen, click or tap the Advanced Options button and then follow Steps 3 to 6 in the preceding list.

Using safe mode for troubleshooting

The most useful of the three safe modes is safe mode with networking because it starts by giving you access to the network and the internet. It even loads Microsoft's Windows Help & Learning site automatically, as shown in Figure 3-5.

Safe mode works the same as Windows 11 normally does. You can click, tap, right-click, press and hold down, and drag and drop as usual. However, many Windows services and features don't work. You can access only the essential tools you need for troubleshooting and repairing your PC: Settings, Control Panel, Command Prompt, PowerShell, Windows Terminal, and several Windows tools such as Event Viewer, Disk Management, Task Scheduler, Computer Management, and Disk Cleanup.

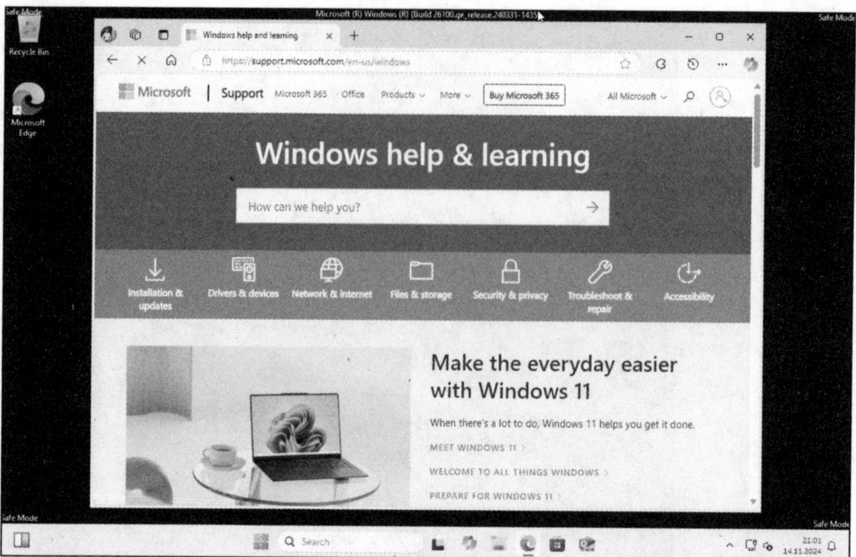

FIGURE 3-5: Safe mode with networking.

TIP

Depending on your problem, you may find the troubleshooter you need in the Settings app, by going to System ⇨ Troubleshoot. To learn more about troubleshooting Windows, read Book 7, Chapter 3.

TIP

When you want to exit safe mode, you simply restart your computer as you normally would. The next time it loads, it will try to start normally. However, exiting safe mode with command prompt is a bit more complicated and involves running the following two commands in succession:

```
bcdedit /deletevalue {current} safeboot
shutdown /r
```

Entering the Windows Recovery Environment

The Windows Recovery Environment is a sophisticated troubleshooting tool that appears when your machine fails to boot three times in a row. You can even trigger it yourself by pressing — three times in a row — the physical restart or power button on your Windows 11 computer or device to stop it during its startup process. You know you're in the Windows Recovery Environment after Windows 11 displays messages that it is Preparing Automatic Repair and then Diagnosing Your PC. You then see a blue Automatic Repair screen like the one in Figure 3-6.

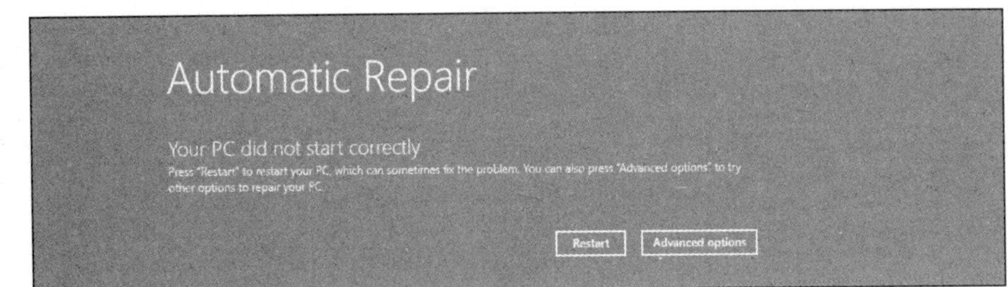

FIGURE 3-6: The Windows Recovery Environment has loaded.

In the Automatic Repair screen, click or tap Advanced Options, and then Troubleshoot. From the Troubleshoot screen, you can run Refresh or Reset directly: They behave as described in the Chapter 2 of this minibook. You can also choose Advanced Options in the Troubleshoot screen, which brings you to several interesting — if little-used — options, as shown in Figure 3-7.

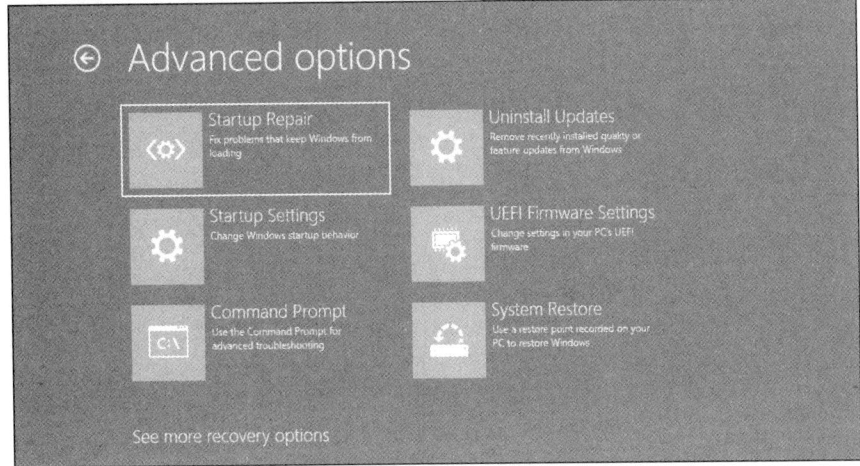

FIGURE 3-7: Advanced boot options.

Here's what the Advanced Options can do:

» **Startup Repair:** Reboots to a specific Windows Recovery Environment program and runs a diagnosis and repair routine that seeks to make your PC bootable again. I've seen this program run spontaneously when I was having hardware problems. A Start Repair log file is generated at C:\Windows\System32\Logfiles\Srt\SrtTrail.txt. While your computer is running Automatic Repair, there's nothing you can do except wait: Hold on and see whether it fixes your problem.

- **Startup Settings:** Reboots Windows and lets you go into safe mode, change the video resolution, start debugging mode or boot logging, disable driver signature checks, disable early launch antimalware protection, and disable automatic restart on system failure. All complex troubleshooting options that should be used with care.
- **Command Prompt:** Brings up an old-fashioned command prompt, just like you get if you go into safe mode with command prompt. It's useful only if you know what you're doing and you're fluent in running command-line tools to fix a malfunctioning computer.
- **Uninstall Updates:** Allows you to remove the latest quality or feature update for Windows 11. This option is useful when your problems are caused by a buggy update.
- **UEFI Firmware Settings:** Displays the UEFI for your computer, where you can set how its motherboard, processor, and other components work.
- **System Restore:** Puts your system back to a chosen restore point. It won't work unless you've turned on system protection/restore points for one or more drives on your computer.

IN THIS CHAPTER

» Working with Event Viewer

» Tracking the reliability of your Windows computer

» Viewing which services run on your Windows machine

» Checking scheduled tasks

Chapter 4
Monitoring Windows

Welcome to the thrilling world of monitoring what goes under the hood of Windows! I admit, *thrilling* is a stretch, but bear with me.

In this chapter, I discuss the tools that you can use to look at your system if something goes wrong: Event Viewer, Reliability Monitor, Services, and Task Scheduler. And believe me, something goes wrong every day, even if you don't encounter apps crashing or error messages ruining your day.

The purpose of Event Viewer is to collect all Windows logs in one place, so you can find them when you need them. Reliability Monitor gives you a visual perspective of what's wrong with your Windows 11 computer or device. Services is where you see which programs run in the background without you even knowing, while Task Scheduler shows you what tasks Windows and your apps have created to run automatically and when. Think of it like this: If your PC were a teenager, these tools would be its diary, report card, and chore list all rolled into one.

If you're a parent, you may enjoy annoying your teenager(s) now and then. So, grab a cup of tea, arm yourself with some patience, and learn about the mysteries lurking in the depths of Windows 11.

Using Event Viewer

Windows has had Event Viewer for decades, but few people know about it. At its heart, Event Viewer looks at the logs that Windows maintains on your PC. The logs are simple text files, written in a structured format called XML, which allows apps to treat them like database entries. Although you may think of Windows as having one event log file, there are administrative event logs, hardware event logs, security logs, system logs, and many other logs.

Every program that starts on your PC posts a notification in an event log, and every well-behaved app posts a notification before it stops. Every system access, security change, operating system twitch, hardware failure, and driver hiccup ends up in an event log. Event Viewer scans those text log files, aggregates them, and adds a user interface that people can use, on top of a dull, voluminous set of machine-generated data. Think of Event Viewer as a database-reporting program, where the underlying database is just a handful of text files.

REMEMBER

In theory, the event logs track significant events on your PC. In practice, the term *significant* is in the eye of the beholder. In the normal course of events, few people ever need to look at any of the event logs from Windows 11. But if your PC starts to misbehave, Event Viewer may give you important insight into the source of the problem. To use Event Viewer effectively, you must sign into Windows 11 using an administrator account. Standard user accounts barely see any useful data in Event Viewer.

Here's how to use Event Viewer:

1. **Sign in using an administrator account.**
2. **Right-click or press and hold the Start icon. Choose Event Viewer.**

   Event Viewer appears. In the middle of the window, you see a summary of the events stored in Event Viewer, organized into groups and in decreasing order of severity.

3. **On the left, expand the Custom Views section and click or tap Administrative Events.**

   It may take a while, but eventually, you see a list of notable events, as shown in Figure 4-1.

4. **Navigate through the Event Viewer logs while not freaking out.**

   For each event, you see its level, date and time, source, event identifier, and many other details. Even the best-maintained computer boasts lots of scary-looking error messages — hundreds, if not thousands of them. That's normal. See Table 4-1 for a breakdown.

5. **To see more information about an event, right-click or press and hold on it, and choose Event Properties. Or simply double-click the event.**

   You see a pop-up window split into two tabs: General and Details, where you can learn more about what went on with the selected event.

6. **Click or tap X in the top-right corner to close the pop-up window, and then close Event Viewer when you've finished browsing it.**

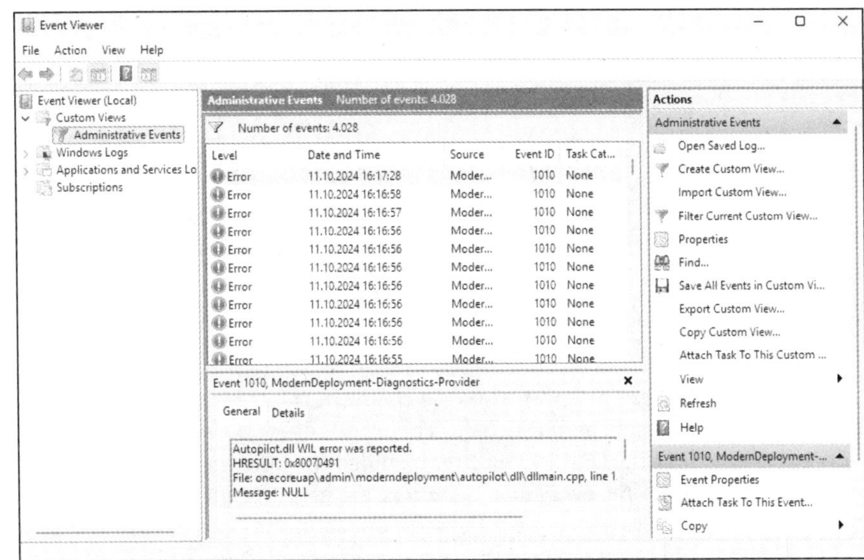

FIGURE 4-1: Events logged by Windows.

TABLE 4-1 Events and What They Mean

Event	What Caused the Event
Critical	The most severe category of events, which have the potential to cause the most damage
Error	Significant problem, including loss of data or functionality
Warning	Not necessarily significant, but might indicate a problem brewing
Information	Just a program or Windows feature calling home to say it's okay

The Administrative Events log isn't the only one you can see; it's a distillation of the other event logs, with an emphasis on the kinds of things a mere human might want to view.

TECHNICAL STUFF

Other logs include the following:

- **Application events:** Programs report on their problems. App developers decide which events are recorded by their app in the application log.
- **Security events:** They're called *audits* and show the results of a security action. Results can be successful or failed depending on the event, such as when a user attempts to log in. These events may be sign-in attempts (both failed and successful), and attempts to use and modify secured resources, such as system files.
- **Setup events:** Here you see events generated by the app installations performed on your computer or device.
- **System events:** Most errors and warnings you see in the Administrative Events log come from system events. They're reports from Windows system files about problems they've encountered, events recorded by drivers which fail to load, or reports from Windows features that you're using.
- **Forwarded events:** These are sent to your computer by other PCs in the same network.

Before you start worrying about the thousands of errors on your PC, look closely at the date and time field. Thousands of events may be listed, but they probably date back to the day you first installed the PC. Chances are good that you see a handful of items every day, and most are just repeats of the same error or warning. Most likely, they have little or no effect on the way you use Windows. An *error* to Windows should usually trigger a yawn and "Who cares?" from you.

For example, looking through my most recent event log, I see a bunch of error ID 10010 events generated by a source called DistributedCOM, which tells me that the server didn't register with DCOM within the required timeout. Really and truly, no biggie.

If you aren't experiencing problems, don't sweat what's in Event Viewer. Even if you *are* experiencing problems, Event Viewer may or may not help you.

TIP

How might Event Viewer help? In the Event ID column, note the ID number and then look it up at `www.myeventlog.com` which may point you in the right direction or at least translate the event ID into something resembling plain English. Figure 4-2 shows the results when I searched for event ID 10010 — the DCOM problem.

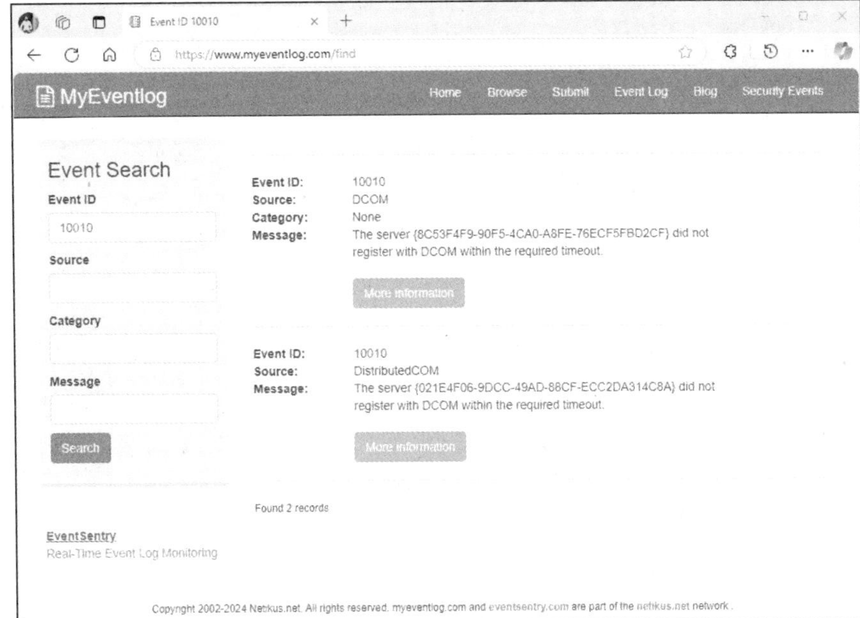

FIGURE 4-2: The result of an event lookup for error 10010.

If you are trying to track down a specific problem and notice an event that may relate to the problem, use Google or Bing to see whether you can find somebody else who's had the same problem. Event Viewer can also help you nail down network access problems because the Windows programs that control network communication spill a lot of details into the event logs. Unfortunately, translating the logs into plain English can be daunting, but at least you may be able to tell where the problem occurs — even if you haven't a clue how to solve it.

Checking System Reliability

Every Windows routine leaves traces of itself in the Windows event log. Start a program, and the event is logged. Stop it, and the log is updated. Install a security update for Windows, and a new log entry is created. Every security-related event you can imagine goes in the log. Windows services leave their traces, as do errors of many stripes: things that should've happened but didn't, as well as things that shouldn't have happened but did.

The Windows event log contains items that mere humans can understand — at least sometimes. And while Event Viewer gives you all the data that was recorded and looks like a dense, dark forest, Reliability Monitor is a complementary tool that tries to put the forest in perspective.

TIP

Reliability Monitor slices and dices the event log, pulling out information that relates to your PC's stability. It doesn't catch everything, but the stuff it does find can give you an instant insight into what ails your Windows computer or device.

Here's how to bring up Reliability Monitor:

1. **Click or tap inside the Search box on your taskbar and type** reliability.

   You see a list of search results.

2. **At the top of the list, choose View Reliability History.**

   Reliability Monitor springs to life, as shown in Figure 4-3.

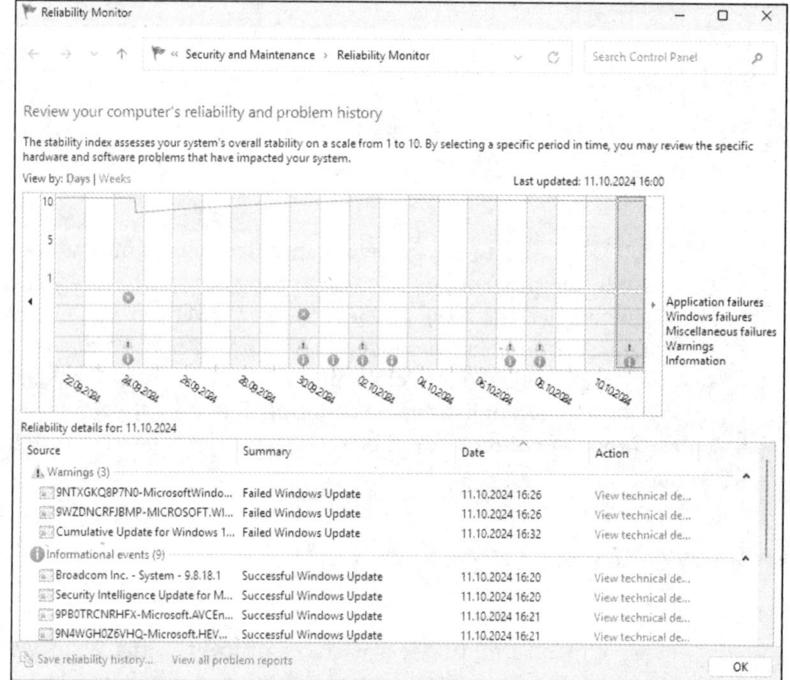

FIGURE 4-3: When something goes wrong, it leaves a trace in Reliability Monitor.

3. **Above the reliability graph, in the View By line, flip between Days and Weeks.**

   Reliability Monitor goes back and forth between a detailed daily view and a weekly overview. The box at the bottom shows you the corresponding entries in your event log.

4. **In the Reliability Details section at the bottom half of the screen, click or tap the View Technical Details link for one of the entries.**

   Reliability Monitor presents a detailed explanation of the event it logged.

5. **Click or tap OK to return to the reliability graph, and then click or tap the View Technical Details link for other entries.**

6. **Click or tap the View All Problem Reports link at the bottom of Reliability Monitor.**

   You get a summary of problem reports, as shown in Figure 4-4.

7. **Close Reliability Monitor by clicking or tapping X in the top-right corner.**

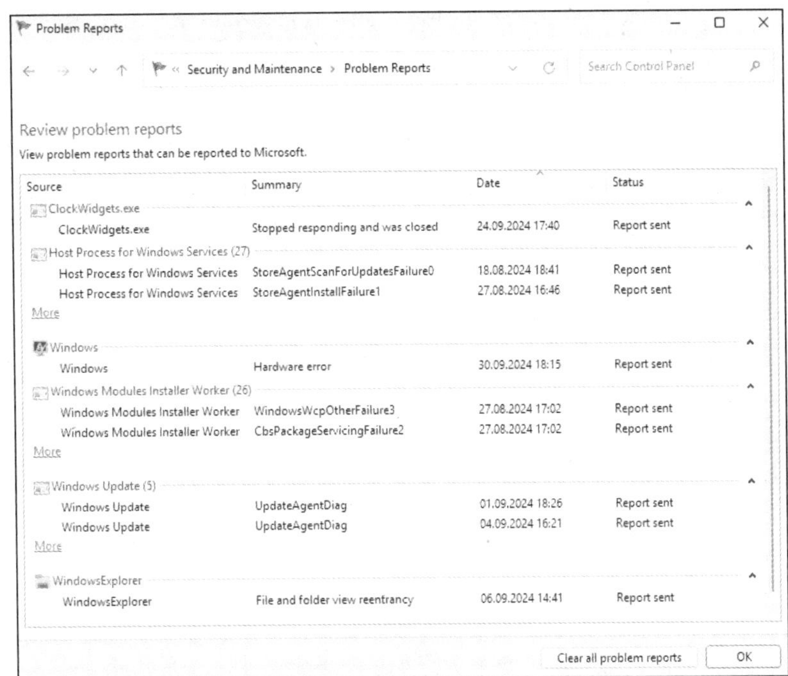

FIGURE 4-4: A more detailed view of your problem reports.

REMEMBER

Again, please don't freak out. There's a reason why Microsoft makes it hard to get to this report. It figures that if you're sophisticated enough to find it, you can bear to see the cold, hard facts.

The top line in the reliability graph is supposed to give you a rating of your system's stability, from one to ten. In fact, it doesn't do anything of the sort, but if you see the line drop, as it did in one of the days shown in Figure 4-3, something undoubtedly has gone amiss.

REMEMBER

Your rating more or less reflects the number and severity of problematic log events in four categories: application failures, Windows failures, miscellaneous failures, and warnings. The information icons (*i*-in-a-circle) generally represent an update to programs and drivers. If you installed a new printer driver, for example, there should be an information icon on the day it was installed. Microsoft has a detailed list of the types of data reported in its official documentation at `https://bit.ly/3BPMNFu`. Here's what they say:

Since you can see all of the activity on a single date in one report, you can make informed decisions about how to troubleshoot. For example, if frequent application failures are reported beginning on the same date that memory failures appear in the Hardware section, you can replace the faulty memory as a first step. If the application failures stop, they may have been a result of problems accessing the memory. If the application failures continue, repairing their installations would be the next step.

REMEMBER

Reliability Monitor isn't meant to provide a comprehensive list of all the bad things that have happened to your PC, and in that respect, it certainly meets its design goals. It's not much of a stability tracker, either. The one-to-ten rating uses a trailing average of daily scores, where more recent scores have greater weight than old ones, but in my experience, the line doesn't track reality.

The real value of Reliability Monitor is its time sequence of key events — connecting the temporal dots so you might be able to discern a cause and effect. For example, if you suddenly start seeing blue screens repeatedly, check Reliability Monitor to see whether something untoward has happened to your system. Installing a new driver, say, can make your system unstable, and Reliability Monitor can show you when the driver was installed. If you see your rating tumble on the same day a driver update got installed, something's fishy, and you may be able to identify the culprit.

The proverbial bottom line: Reliability Monitor doesn't keep track of everything and some of it is a bit deceptive, but it can provide worthwhile information when Windows 11 starts misbehaving. Reliability Monitor is worth adding to your bag of tricks.

Viewing Services

Windows services are specialized programs with unique characteristics. They operate in the background without a user interface. Services can be automatically initiated by the operating system during startup without the user signing in and may have elevated system privileges. These features distinguish services from regular apps, allowing them to perform critical system tasks and maintain continuous operation independently of user interactions.

A regular Windows service is intended to provide useful features, such as access to files, printing, error reporting, and event logging. The services built into Windows 11 are developed by Microsoft, and third-party apps installed by the user can add their own services. Antivirus products, for example, install different services to provide real-time monitoring of your system's activities, antimalware protection, firewall protection, and so on.

If you're curious to view all the services installed on your Windows 11 computer, you can use the Services app, like this:

1. **Click or tap in the Search box on your taskbar and type** services.

   You see a list of search results.

2. **In the list of results, choose Services.**

   The Services app opens, as shown in Figure 4-5, displaying a long list of services, ordered alphabetically. For each service, you see its name, description, status, startup type, and Log on As information (the account used by the service).

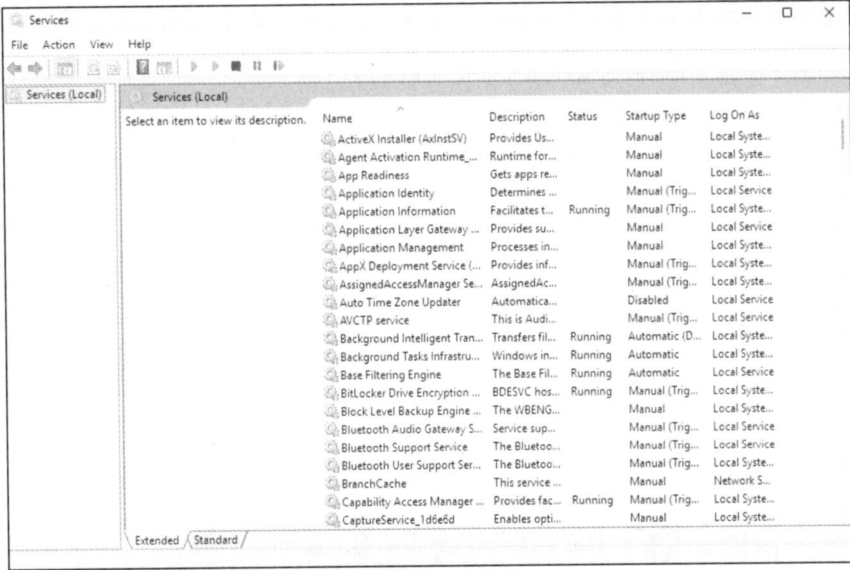

FIGURE 4-5: Checking the services that are running is easy. Understanding what they do is more difficult.

3. **In the Services list, find BitLocker Drive Encryption and double-click (or double-tap) it.**

   You see the properties of this service, which should give you more information about what it does, whether it's running on your computer, and how it's set to start. You can also interact with it, stop it from running, or disable it from starting up with Windows. However, I don't recommend you do that, especially not when it comes to BitLocker (read Book 9, Chapter 3 to learn why).

4. **Click or tap the X icon in the top-right corner of this service's properties window.**

   You return to the list of services.

5. **To view all the services currently running, click or tap the Status column heading twice.**

   Check which services are and aren't currently running.

6. **When you're finished using the Services app, click or tap X in its top-right corner.**

TIP

If you want to know which Windows services are safe to disable and when, I highly recommend an article published by my team at Digital Citizen at `www.digitalcitizen.life/which-windows-services-are-safe-disable-when/`.

Using Task Scheduler

Task Scheduler is an old but handy tool that's been part of Windows for decades. Think of it as a hidden digital assistant, setting up reminders for your PC to perform certain jobs automatically. These jobs could be running programs or scripts at set times or when certain events take place on your computer. You, Windows, and the apps that you install can set up routine operations and maintenance tasks that run automatically, without manual intervention. For example, the Microsoft Edge browser checks for updates automatically using a scheduled task. The same is true for OneDrive.

If you want to see which tasks are already scheduled on your Windows 11 PC, so you can understand what's going on behind the scenes and when these automatic jobs are happening, follow these steps:

1. **Click or tap in the Search box on your taskbar and type** scheduler.
2. **In the list of results, choose Task Scheduler.**

   The Task Scheduler app is fired up, as shown in Figure 4-6.

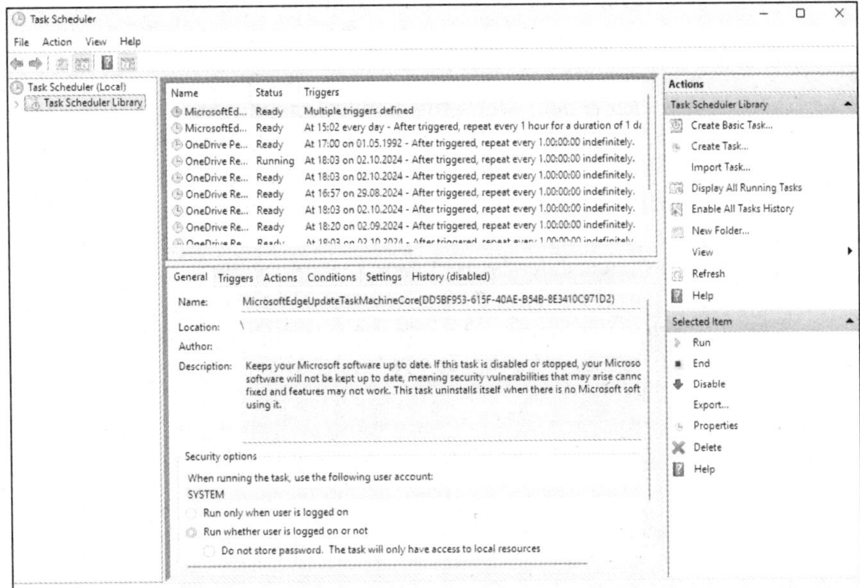

FIGURE 4-6: Checking the tasks scheduled in Windows 11.

3. **On the left side of the app, select Task Scheduler Library.**

   In the middle of the app window, you see a list of the tasks executed recently, along with their status and triggers.

4. **To learn more about a scheduled task, simply double-click (or double-tap) its name in the list.**

   You see the properties window for that task, which presents more information organized in the following tabs: General (a description of the task), Triggers (when it executes), Conditions (the conditions that, along with triggers, determine whether the task should run), Settings, and History. Unfortunately, the History tab is disabled in Windows 11.

5. **Click or tap the X icon in the top-right corner of the task's properties.**

   You return to the list of scheduled tasks.

6. **To navigate all scheduled tasks, double-click (or double-tap) Task Scheduler Library to expand it. Then do the same for all the folders you want to navigate.**

   The most interesting folder is Microsoft > Windows. It includes subfolders for all the features of Windows that have created scheduled tasks.

7. **When you've finished using the Task Scheduler app, click or tap X in its top-right corner.**

Task Scheduler offers extensive triggering and scheduling options. You can use it to create scheduled tasks that can run apps or scripts at specified times, and launch actions when the computer is idle for a specified period or when certain users sign in. Task Scheduler is also tightly integrated with Event Viewer, making it possible to use events such as an application crash or a specific error as triggers for a scheduled task.

TIP

Task Scheduler is used mostly by developers creating apps for Windows or by IT professionals. To learn more about creating software that works with Task Scheduler, check the extensive technical documentation Microsoft provides in its Learn portal at `https://learn.microsoft.com/en-us/windows/win32/taskschd/task-scheduler-start-page`.

IN THIS CHAPTER

» Unveiling Task Manager

» Viewing and ending running apps and processes

» Keeping an eye on performance

» Viewing details about running processes and services

» Managing startup apps

Chapter 5
Mastering Task Manager

Running apps in Windows 11 is easy — simply install them and click or tap their shortcut. However, sometimes apps can cause issues. For instance, your PC might slow down because too many apps automatically start when you log into Windows. Additionally, other apps might crash or become unresponsive, a common issue with web browsers such as Google Chrome, especially when too many tabs are open, consuming a lot of memory and slowing down your computer.

To help you manage these challenges, Windows 11 includes Task Manager. This powerful tool lets you see which apps and processes are running and enables you to close unresponsive ones. Task Manager also helps you monitor performance, making it easy to identify apps that are consuming excessive processor power, RAM, or network bandwidth.

In this chapter, I show you everything you need to know about using Task Manager. From starting the app to navigating it and customizing it to suit your needs, you'll gain the skills to keep your system running smoothly. With Task Manager, you can take control of your apps and startup programs, ensuring that they work for you, not against you.

Using Task Manager

Task Manager is a versatile app that can handle any of the following tasks:

- » **Stop an app or a background process from running.** It doesn't matter if you're trying to kill a Windows 11 app from the Microsoft Store, an old-fashioned desktop app, or a background process used by Windows or any of your apps. All it takes is one trip to Task Manager and *zap!*
- » **Switch to any program.** This feature is convenient if you find yourself stuck somewhere — in a game, say, that doesn't allow you to go to the desktop — and you want to jump over to a different application. You can open Task Manager and then easily go to another Windows 11 app.
- » **See which processes are slowing down your PC.** *Processes* are all the executable files run by the apps you're using, by Windows itself, by your drivers, and so on. Task Manager shows you a list of all running processes. That list is invaluable if your PC is responding like a slug and you can't figure out what is hogging the processor, eating up all your RAM, using the hard drive intensively, and so on.
- » **Get real-time performance graphs of CPU, memory, disk, GPU, or network usage.** These graphs are cool and informative and may even help you decide whether you need to buy more RAM.
- » **See which Windows apps use the most resources over a specified time period.** Did the Photos app take up the most processor time on your PC in the past month? Instagram or maybe Phone Link?
- » **Turn off autostarting programs.** This procedure used to be a headache, but now it's surprisingly easy. All Windows computers and devices have automatically starting programs that take up boot time and add to system overhead. Task Manager shows you the apps that start automatically and gives you the option to disable them.
- » **Send a message to other users on your PC.** The message shows up after the user account receiving the message signs in.
- » **Display details about processes and services.** Task Manager lists all processes and services and allows you to start them, stop them, restart them, or find out more details about them online so that you know what's what.

It's quite an impressive feature list, isn't it?

Starting Task Manager

Before you can use Task Manager, you need to know how to start it and then close it. Follow these steps:

1. **Do one of the following:**
   - Press Ctrl+Shift+Esc.
   - Press Ctrl+Alt+Delete and then click or tap the Task Manager link on the screen that appears.
   - Right-click (or press and hold) the Windows logo on the taskbar and choose Task Manager in the menu that opens.
   - Right-click (or press and hold) an empty space on the taskbar and choose Task Manager in the menu that opens.
   - Click or tap the Search box on the taskbar, type **task**, and at the top of the list of search results, click or tap Task Manager.

   The Task Manager appears with the Processes page open, showing the list of running apps and background processes (see Figure 5-1).

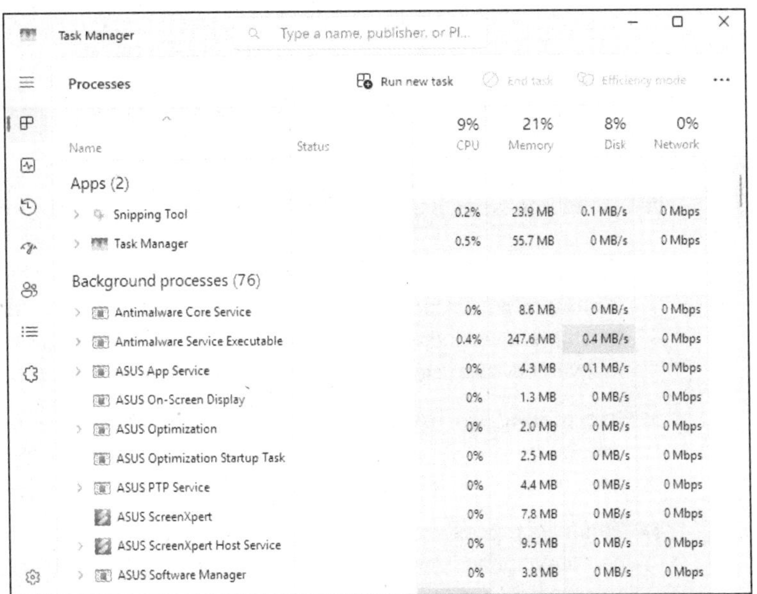

FIGURE 5-1: Task Manager is a powerful tool.

2. **Click or tap the open navigation icon (three parallel lines) in the top left.**

   The full Task Manager screen is displayed with the icons in the left navigation pane clearly labeled, as shown in Figure 5-2.

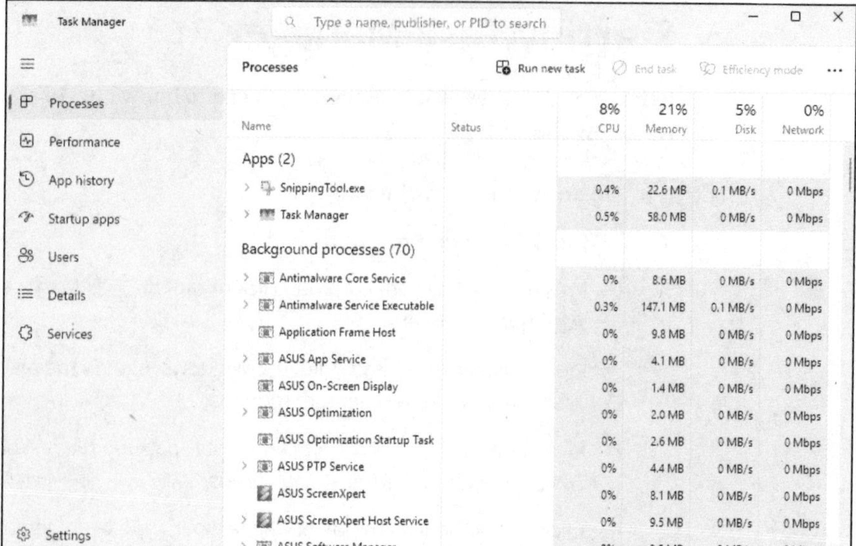

FIGURE 5-2: The expanded Task Manager in all its glory.

3. **Click or tap each icon on the left and see the data it displays.**
4. **To close Task Manager, click or tap the X in its top-right corner.**

   You're back to the desktop.

Viewing running apps and processes

When you open Task Manager, it displays the Processes page. This page organizes everything into three lists of running programs depending on their type:

- **Apps** are regular, everyday programs. They're programs you start or that are set to start automatically. You may think that *apps* mean just desktop apps or touch-friendly Windows 11 apps — but no. These are programs of any type that you have installed on your machine and are currently running.
- **Background processes** are run "hidden" from view by your installed apps, drivers, antivirus, and even Windows. Unlike apps, background processes don't have a user interface that you can see and click (or tap).
- **Windows processes** are similar to background processes, except they are part of Windows itself and are started automatically by the operating system. They're in charge of all the background work that allows Windows to run and process your commands successfully.

When your Windows 11 PC is sluggish, you can use the Processes page in Task Manager to identify which apps are eating up your CPU, memory, disk, or network bandwidth. Here's how:

1. **Start Task Manager by pressing Ctrl+Shift+Esc.**

   The Task Manager's Processes page appears (refer to Figure 5-1). If it doesn't, click or tap the Processes icon (refer to Figure 5-2).

2. **To view which apps and processes are eating up most of your processor's power, click or tap the CPU column on the right.**

   You see all the apps and processes ordered by processor utilization in decreasing order. To reverse the sort order, click or tap the heading of the current sort column.

3. **To view which apps and processes are using the most RAM, click or tap the Memory column.**

   All running apps and processes are ordered by memory use, in decreasing order, as shown in Figure 5-3. If you are using an app such as Google Chrome or Discord, it will usually show up at the top of the list.

4. **Do the same with the Disk and Network columns to view apps and processes sorted by their disk and network bandwidth utilization, respectively.**

5. **When done, click or tap X on the top-right corner to close Task Manager.**

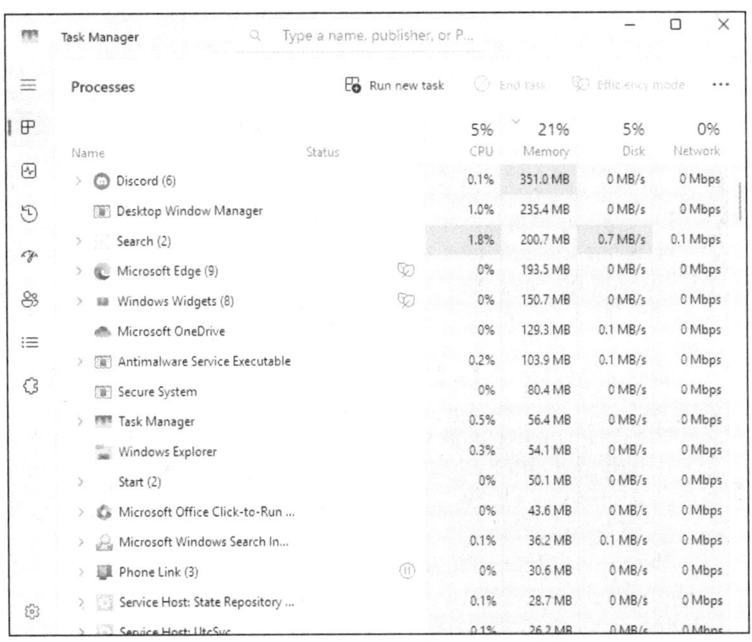

FIGURE 5-3: View all the apps that are eating up your memory.

Dealing with Misbehaving Apps

Are you using an app that is stuck and is no longer answering your commands? Or do you think some running apps are using too much RAM or eating up too much network bandwidth, but you don't know which ones? In this section, you see how to deal with both situations.

Killing apps that don't respond

When an app no longer responds to your commands, it's time to force-close it. You don't need to reboot Windows 11 — just use Task Manager. To see the steps involved, let's use Microsoft Edge as a guinea pig. I have nothing against guinea pigs — I think they're cute animals — and I like Microsoft Edge too. It's just that I must choose an app to help you understand how it all works:

1. **Start Microsoft Edge by clicking or tapping its icon on the taskbar.**
2. **Start Task Manager by pressing Ctrl+Shift+Esc.**

   You see the Processes page. If you don't, open it before moving forward.
3. **In the Task Manager window, select Microsoft Edge in the Apps list by clicking or tapping it.**

   The End Task icon (labeled in Figure 5-4) is no longer dimmed and is now usable.
4. **To force-stop Microsoft Edge, click or tap End Task.**

   Microsoft Edge closes immediately without any confirmation being requested.

WARNING

When you force-close an app in Windows, any unsaved changes you've made in the app are lost. For example, if you were working on an Excel spreadsheet and Excel stopped working, force-closing it means you would lose the latest changes between the moment the spreadsheet was last saved and when you clicked or tapped End Task.

Keeping an eye on performance

The Performance page displays live graphs of CPU usage, allocated memory, disk activity, graphics card activity, and the volume of data running into and out of your machine on an Ethernet connection, a Wi-Fi connection, or both. If Bluetooth is turned on, the Performance page also shows you the activity over your Bluetooth connection. And, if you're using a Copilot+ PC device, you also have live graphs for its NPU (Neural Processing Unit), which is used to run AI-enabled apps and services.

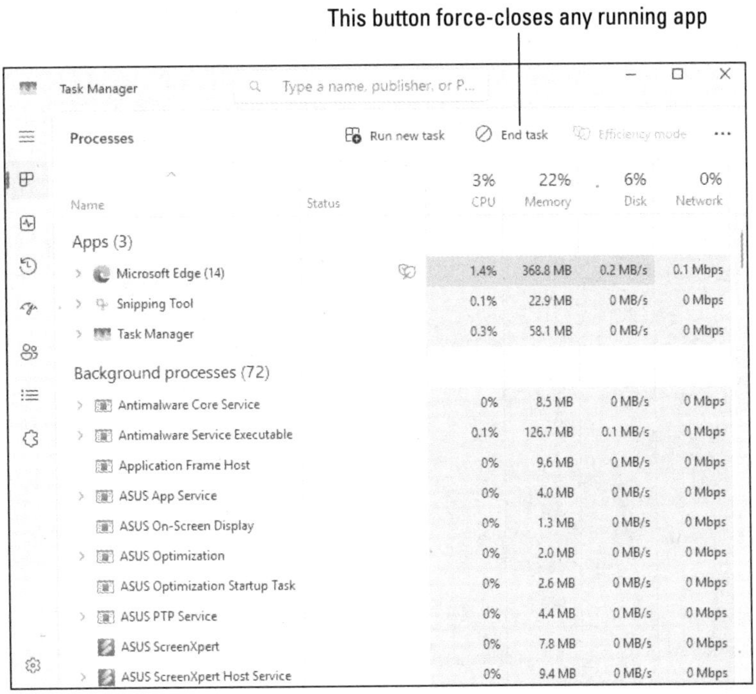

This button force-closes any running app

FIGURE 5-4: Task Manager allows you to force-close any running app.

The number of items you see in the Performance page varies based on your computer's hardware configuration. For example, if you have an SSD and a classic HDD, you see two Disk entries instead of one. If you have multiple network cards, they're all listed.

Here's how to navigate the Performance page in Task Manager:

1. **Start Task Manager by pressing Ctrl+Shift+Esc.**

   You see the Processes page (refer to Figure 5-1).

2. **On the left, click or tap the Performance icon (graph).**

   The page is split into several graphs: CPU, memory, disk, Wi-Fi, and so on.

3. **Click or tap CPU.**

   The graph and data display how much of your computer's processor is being used in real time, as shown in Figure 5-5.

4. **Click or tap the other items on the Performance page (Memory, Disk, and so on) one by one.**

   Note the graphs and information displayed about the utilization of each hardware resource in your Windows 11 computer or device.

5. **To close Task Manager, click or tap X in its top-right corner.**

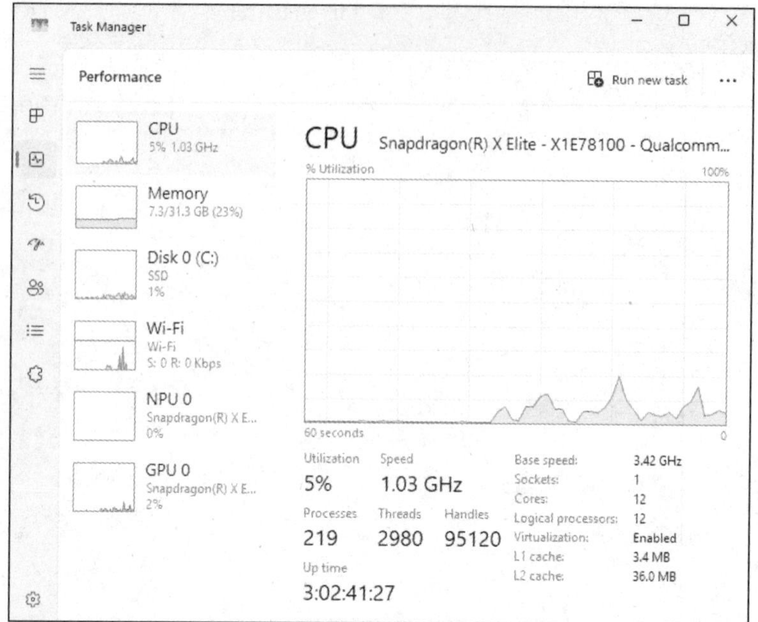

FIGURE 5-5: Keep tabs on the key components of your PC's performance.

TECHNICAL STUFF

If you want to see more detailed information on the Performance page, click or tap the see more icon (ellipsis) and choose Resource Monitor. The Resource Monitor app shown in Figure 5-6 appears.

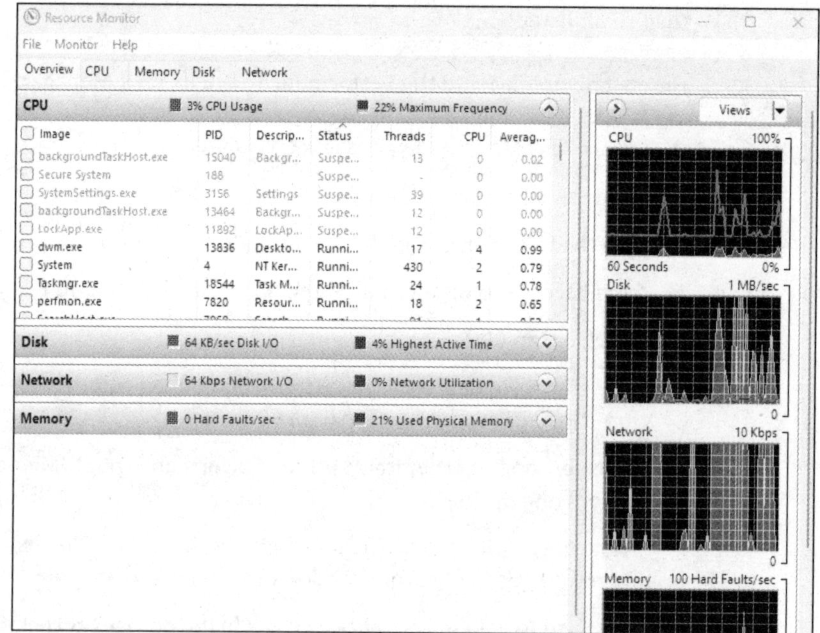

FIGURE 5-6: Resource Monitor tells you what's going wrong with your machine.

When troubleshooting performance issues, I keep Resource Monitor minimized and running on my desktop for a quick overview of my computer's current state. Resource Monitor is an excellent tool for identifying problems when something starts to misbehave, which isn't all that uncommon in Windows, is it?

Getting More Info from Task Manager

So far, I've covered the most common ways in which people use Task Manager. However, what this app can do doesn't stop here. It's time to discover some other useful features that will help you understand more about the apps you're using as well as manage the apps allowed to start with Windows.

Viewing App History

The App History page keeps a cumulative count of all the time you've spent in each of the various Windows 11 apps from the Microsoft Store. Here's how to use it:

1. **Start Task Manager by pressing Ctrl+Shift+Esc.**

   The Processes page opens in Task Manager.

2. **Click or tap the App History icon (clock rewinding time).**

   You see a list of all the Windows 11 apps you have used in the past.

3. **Click or tap the CPU Time column.**

   The list of apps is ordered based on how much they've used your computer's processor, as shown in Figure 5-7.

4. **Click or tap the Network column.**

   The apps are ordered by how much data they have transferred through your network connection.

5. **To return the App History page to its default view, click or tap the Name column.**

6. **To close Task Manager, click or tap X in its top-right corner.**

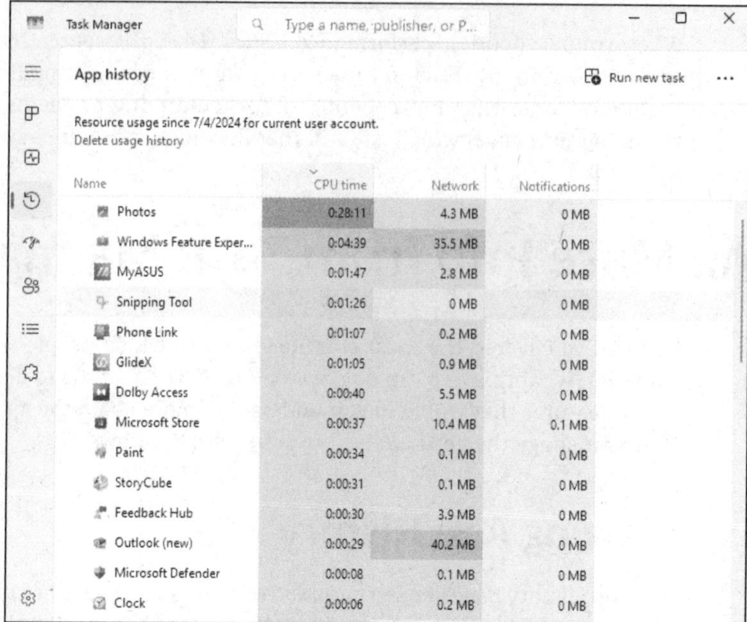

FIGURE 5-7: Check how Windows apps have used precious hardware resources.

Managing startup programs

Windows 11 automatically runs certain programs every time you start it, and those programs can slow down the boot procedure. This is especially true a couple of months after you start using your PC if you've installed many apps and games. The Startup Apps page in Task Manager displays all the programs that start automatically each time you log in and helps you disable them. For each startup program, you see its name, publisher (the company that made it), status (enabled or disabled), and startup effect (high, medium, low, and so on).

If you want to disable an autorunning program, here's what you must do:

1. **Right-click (or press and hold) an empty space on the taskbar and then choose Task Manager.**

   The Processes page opens in Task Manager.

2. **Click or tap the Startup Apps icon (speedometer).**

   All apps and programs that run during Windows 11's startup are listed, as shown in Figure 5-8.

3. **Click or tap the program that you no longer want to run when Windows 11 starts.**

   The program is selected.

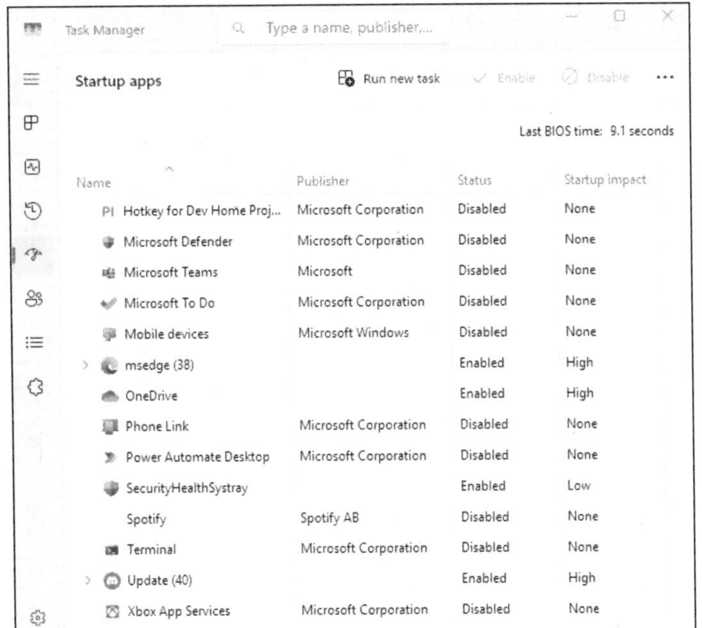

FIGURE 5-8: Task Manager displaying startup apps.

4. **Click or tap the Disable icon in the top-right corner.**

   The program is now disabled from running at Windows 11 startup.

5. **To close Task Manager, click or tap X.**

TIP

To allow an app to run at startup, simply repeat the same steps but choose Enable during Step 4.

REMEMBER

Microsoft distributes an Autoruns program that digs into every nook and cranny of Windows and lists absolutely everything running during startup, including the hidden stuff that doesn't show up in the Startup Apps page of Task Manager.

Autoruns started as a free product from the small Sysinternals company and owes its existence to Mark Russinovich and Bryce Cogswell, two of the most knowledgeable Windows folks on the planet. In July 2006, Microsoft bought Sysinternals and promised that all the free Sysinternals products would remain free. And wonder of wonders, that's exactly what happened.

To get Autoruns working, download it as a ZIP file from `https://learn.microsoft.com/en-us/sysinternals/downloads/autoruns` and extract the ZIP file. Autoruns.exe is the program you want. Double-click or double-tap to run it; no installation is required. See Figure 5-9.

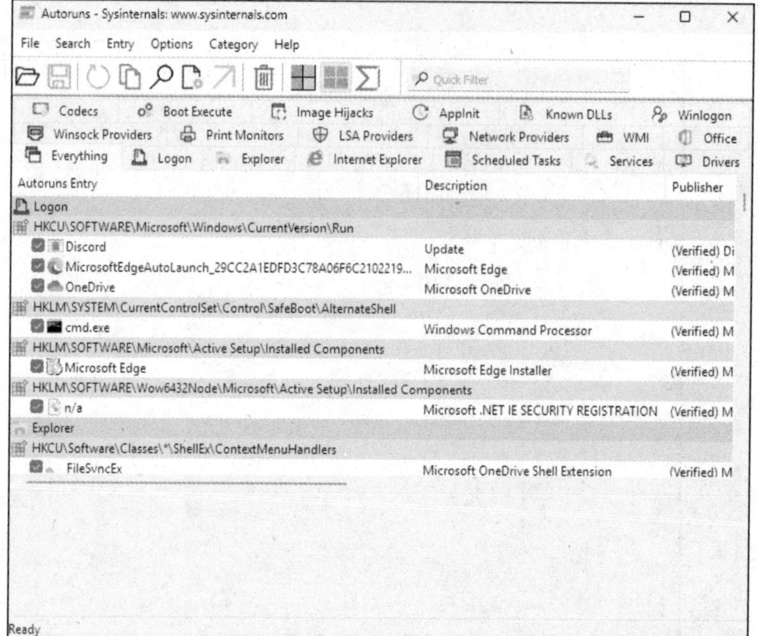

FIGURE 5-9: Autoruns finds the sneaky autorunning programs that Task Manager doesn't display.

TIP

After Autoruns is working on your computer, the following tips can help you start using the program:

- **Autoruns lists an enormous number of autostarting programs.** Some appear in the most obscure corners of Windows. The Everything list shows all programs in the order they're run during startup.
- **Autoruns has many options.** You can get a good overview on its product page at `https://learn.microsoft.com/en-us/sysinternals/downloads/autoruns`. The option I use most is the capability to hide all autostarting Microsoft programs. Choose Options, and then select Hide Microsoft Entries. The result is a clean list of all the foreign stuff being launched automatically by Windows.
- **Autoruns can suspend an autostarting program.** To suspend a program, deselect the box to the left of the program's name and reboot Windows. If you zap an autostarting program and your computer doesn't work right, run Autoruns again and select the box. Easy, isn't it?

WARNING

You shouldn't disable an autostarting program just because it looks superfluous or even because you figure it contributes to global warming or slow startups, whichever comes first. As a rule, if you don't know *exactly* what an autostarting program does, don't touch it.

On the other hand, if you concentrate on autostarting programs that don't come from Microsoft, you may find a few that you don't want or need — items that deserve to be deleted from startup.

Checking out details and services

The Details page in Task Manager shows all running processes, regardless of which user is attached to the process. See Figure 5-10. When you select a process, you can stop it from running by clicking or tapping the End Task button in the top right, or you can view its properties to learn more about what it does.

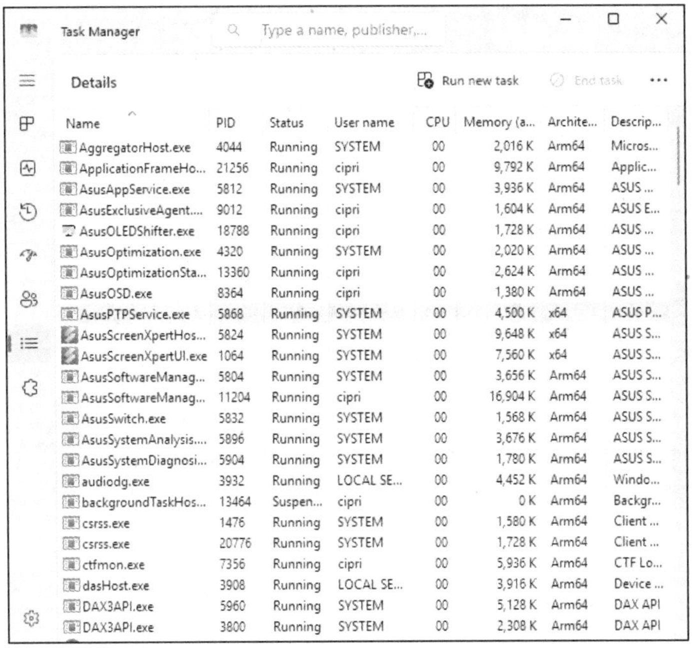

Task Manager   Type a name, publisher,...

Details   Run new task   End task   ...

Name	PID	Status	User name	CPU	Memory (a...	Archite...	Descrip...
AggregatorHost.exe	4044	Running	SYSTEM	00	2,016 K	Arm64	Micros...
ApplicationFrameHo...	21256	Running	cipri	00	9,792 K	Arm64	Applic...
AsusAppService.exe	5812	Running	SYSTEM	00	3,936 K	Arm64	ASUS ...
AsusExclusiveAgent....	9012	Running	cipri	00	1,604 K	Arm64	ASUS E...
AsusOLEDShifter.exe	18788	Running	cipri	00	1,728 K	Arm64	ASUS ...
AsusOptimization.exe	4320	Running	SYSTEM	00	2,020 K	Arm64	ASUS ...
AsusOptimizationSta...	13360	Running	cipri	00	2,624 K	Arm64	ASUS ...
AsusOSD.exe	8364	Running	cipri	00	1,380 K	Arm64	ASUS ...
AsusPTPService.exe	5868	Running	SYSTEM	00	4,500 K	x64	ASUS P...
AsusScreenXpertHos...	5824	Running	SYSTEM	00	9,648 K	x64	ASUS S...
AsusScreenXpertUI.exe	1064	Running	SYSTEM	00	7,560 K	x64	ASUS S...
AsusSoftwareManag...	5804	Running	SYSTEM	00	3,656 K	Arm64	ASUS S...
AsusSoftwareManag...	11204	Running	cipri	00	16,904 K	Arm64	ASUS S...
AsusSwitch.exe	5832	Running	SYSTEM	00	1,568 K	Arm64	ASUS S...
AsusSystemAnalysis....	5896	Running	SYSTEM	00	3,676 K	Arm64	ASUS S...
AsusSystemDiagnosi...	5904	Running	SYSTEM	00	1,780 K	Arm64	ASUS S...
audiodg.exe	3932	Running	LOCAL SE...	00	4,452 K	Arm64	Windo...
backgroundTaskHos...	13464	Suspen...	cipri	00	0 K	Arm64	Backgr...
csrss.exe	1476	Running	SYSTEM	00	1,580 K	Arm64	Client ...
csrss.exe	20776	Running	SYSTEM	00	1,728 K	Arm64	Client ...
ctfmon.exe	7356	Running	cipri	00	5,936 K	Arm64	CTF Lo...
dasHost.exe	3908	Running	LOCAL SE...	00	3,916 K	Arm64	Device ...
DAX3API.exe	5960	Running	SYSTEM	00	5,128 K	Arm64	DAX API
DAX3API.exe	3800	Running	SYSTEM	00	2,308 K	Arm64	DAX API

FIGURE 5-10: All details about every process appear here.

The Services page similarly displays all Windows services that have been started, as shown in Figure 5-11. Once in a blue moon, you may see a Windows error message telling you that some service or another (say, the printer service or a networking service) isn't running. The Services page is where you can tell whether the service is really running. From here, you can also select a service and start it, stop it, or restart it.

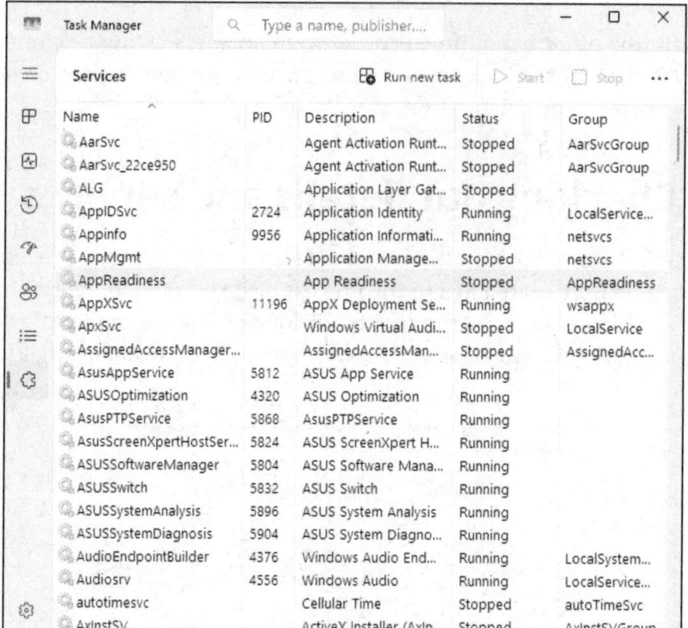

FIGURE 5-11: See details about Windows services.

Personalizing Task Manager

Task Manager has evolved a lot in Windows 11. It now offers support for Dark Mode, and it can be configured to display another start page instead of the Processes page; you can set it to remain displayed on top of other apps and increase the speed of its real-time updates. You can change all these settings and more from its Settings page, like this:

1. **Right-click (or press and hold) an empty space on the taskbar and choose Task Manager.**

   The Processes page opens in Task Manager.

2. **Click or tap the settings icon (gear) in the bottom-left corner.**

   You see the Settings page shown in Figure 5-12.

3. **Click or tap the drop-down list next to App Theme and choose whether you want to use the light theme, the dark theme, or the system setting.**

   The Task Manager app window changes, according to your setting.

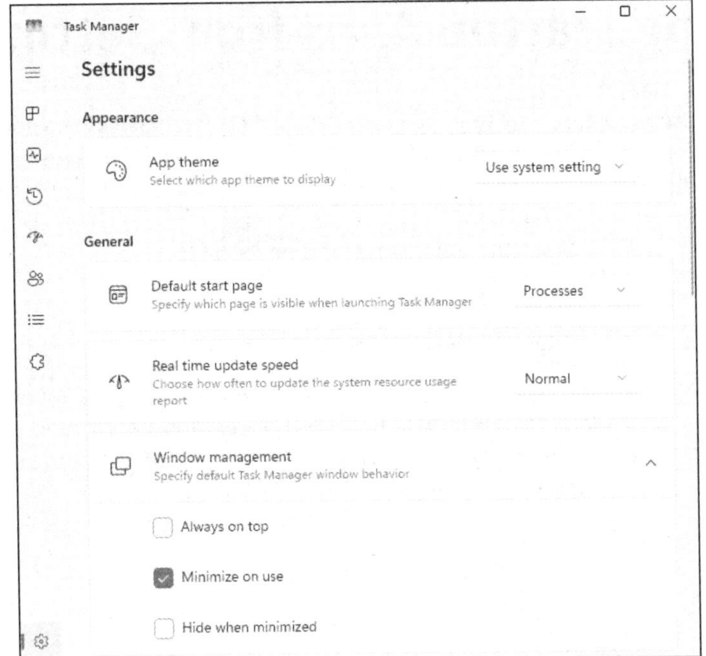

FIGURE 5-12: Task Manager allows for a great deal of customization.

4. **Click or tap the drop-down list next to Default Start Page and choose what interests you from the list.**

   Maybe you want quicker access to the Performance page, which shows detailed graphs of how your hardware resources are used. The next time you open Task Manager, it will display the page you selected.

5. **To increase the speed of updates, select High in the drop-down list next to Real Time Update Speed.**

   Task Manager speeds up its updates but also uses more hardware resources to provide you with faster real-time data.

6. **If you want Task Manager to always remain on top of other app windows, select Always on Top, which is in the Window Management section.**
7. **Scroll through the remaining settings and enable those you want.**
8. **To close Task Manager, click or tap X in the top-right corner.**

TIP

If you're not happy with your settings, you can reset Task Manager to its default behavior by repeating Steps 1 and 2, and then clicking or tapping Reset All Settings to Default, which is at the bottom of the Settings screen.

Managing Startup Apps from Settings

Another easy way to manage startup apps is from Settings, which has the advantage of working well with tablets, 2-in-1s, and other Windows 11 touchscreen devices. Just a few clicks or taps, and you're done. Here's how it works:

1. **Click or tap the Start icon and then Settings.**

   The Settings app is loaded.

2. **Go to Apps and then to Startup.**

   All apps that can be configured to start when you log into Windows 11 are displayed, as shown in Figure 5-13. For each app (or program), you see its name, the company that made it, its effect on the Windows 11 startup, and whether it's turned on or off during the Windows startup.

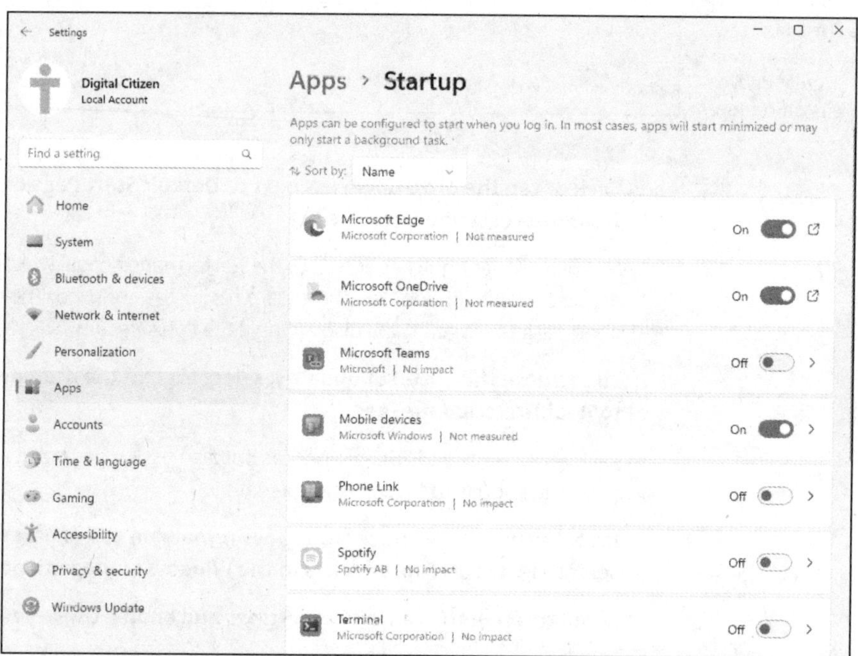

FIGURE 5-13: Managing Windows 11 startup apps from Settings.

3. **For each app that you want to stop from automatically starting with Windows, click or tap its switch to turn it off.**

   The next time you log into Windows 11, your startup settings will be applied.

9 Securing Windows

Contents at a Glance

IN THIS CHAPTER

» Understanding the many types of malware

» Reviewing a quick security checklist

» Using Windows Security to protect yourself

Chapter 1

Fighting Viruses, Ransomware, and Other Malware

Welcome to the wild world of internet security! The threats out there are real and are getting sneakier by the day. While big corporations and government agencies often make headlines because of massive data breaches that steal tons of data or take down crucial infrastructure, don't think the bad guys aren't interested in your personal computer, too.

Why would they want your data? Well, there's a whole buffet of reasons: stealing your personal information, holding your files for ransom, using your computer to attack others, or even using your PC as a steppingstone to bigger targets. Cyber-criminals are nothing if not creative and resourceful.

In this chapter, I give you an overview of the security landscape for Windows users. I start by explaining the most common threats you might face on your Windows devices, whether you're at home or in the office. Then I share a straightforward list of do's and don'ts to keep your computer and identity safe. Even if you skim the rest of this chapter, make sure you read, understand, and follow these rules.

Next, I get into how to use the Windows Security app built into Windows 11. I share how to open it, ensure that it's working properly, scan for threats, protect against ransomware, and uncover hidden nasties with an offline scan.

Finally, I introduce the Microsoft Defender app for Microsoft 365 subscribers and explain what it can (and can't) do for your security.

Remember, in today's digital age, a little knowledge, coupled with a bit of caution, goes a long way in keeping you and your data safe!

Making Sense of Malware

When it comes to security issues, most people are familiar with the term *virus*, which refers to a computer program that replicates itself and causes damage to the devices it infects. However, today's security threats are far more complex than the viruses of the past. Attackers are now more organized, often operating in criminal gangs or even acting on behalf of state-sponsored organizations. Their toolsets have become increasingly sophisticated, incorporating advanced technologies such as artificial intelligence (AI) to enhance the effectiveness and stealth of their attacks.

All unwanted software that can infiltrate our computers and devices, steal data, or perform other malicious activities is collectively known as *malware*. Various types of malware are prevalent on the internet; the most widespread follow:

- **Viruses:** Computer programs that replicate with the purpose of wreaking havoc on the devices they infect. Viruses replicate by attaching themselves to files — programs, documents, or spreadsheets — or replacing genuine operating system files with bogus ones. Once it infects a system, a virus can replicate itself and cause various problems, such as corrupting files, stealing data, or slowing down the computer. Unlike some other types of malware, a virus requires user action to spread, such as opening an infected file or running an infected program.
- **Trojans:** Malicious software that disguises itself as a legitimate program or file to trick users into installing it (inspired by the Trojan horse). Once installed, it can create a backdoor into the system, allowing its makers to gain unauthorized access, steal sensitive data, or cause damage. Unlike viruses, Trojans do not replicate themselves but rely on deception to infiltrate systems.
- **Worms:** Malicious software that can replicate itself and spread independently across networks without needing to attach to a host program. Unlike viruses, worms exploit security vulnerabilities in operating systems or applications to

propagate, often causing harm by consuming network and internet bandwidth, overloading system resources, or delivering additional malware. Their capability to spread rapidly and autonomously makes them dangerous.

- **Rootkits:** Malicious software designed to gain unauthorized access to a computer or device and hide its presence from the user and their security software. It typically grants attackers administrative privileges, allowing them to control the system, steal data, and install additional malware while remaining undetected. Rootkits are particularly insidious because they operate at a deep level within the operating system, which makes them difficult to detect and remove. They're used in target attacks against important private and public organizations to steal sensitive data or sabotage their activities.
- **Backdoors:** Programs used by attackers to bypass normal authentication and gain unauthorized access to a computer system. They allow attackers to remotely control the system, steal data, or deploy additional malware without the user's knowledge. Backdoors can be installed through other forms of malware or vulnerabilities in software, or even be created by software developers for maintenance purposes.
- **Password stealers:** Malicious programs that operate silently in the background, collecting usernames and passwords and sending them to an external attacker. The stolen credentials can then be used for making purchases, draining bank accounts, or committing identity theft.
- **Scareware:** Malicious software designed to frighten users into thinking their device is infected with a virus or other threat. Scareware typically generates alarming pop-up messages or warnings, prompting the user to purchase a fake security program or provide personal information. Scareware is often distributed through ads found on websites and apps, including mobile ones.
- **Ransomware:** Malicious software that encrypts the victim's files or locks them out of their system, rendering their data inaccessible. A ransom is demanded, typically in cryptocurrency, in exchange for restoring access to the victim's files or system. Even if the ransom is paid, there is no guarantee that the attacker will provide the decryption key or unlock the system.

Lots of money can be made with advanced malware, especially for those who figure out how to break in without being detected. To increase their success, some malware can carry bad *payloads* (programs that wreak destruction on your system), but many of the worst offenders cause the most harm by clogging networks (nearly bringing down the internet itself, at times) and by turning PCs into zombies, frequently called *bots*, which can be operated by remote control and used in other attacks against different targets.

The most successful pieces of malware these days run as *rootkits* — programs that evade detection by stealthily hooking into Windows in tricky ways. Rootkits are extremely difficult to detect and even harder to clean. Microsoft Defender Offline, discussed in this chapter, is a great choice for removing them.

All these definitions are becoming more academic and less relevant as the trend shifts to blended-threat malware. *Blended threats* incorporate elements of traditional kinds of malware — and more. Most of the most successful malware attacks you read about in the press are blended-threat malware. Cybercriminals have come a long way from the days of using old-fashioned viruses.

Basic Windows Security Do's and Don'ts

TIP

While no one can guarantee your device's complete security, not even when using the most advanced cybersecurity products in the world, there are things you can do to keep your computers, devices, and data mostly secure:

- **Check to make sure Windows Security is running.** If something's amiss, a red X appears on the Windows Security shield, which is down in the notification area near the time. If you don't see it, first click or tap the show hidden icons arrow. To check the status of Windows Security, double-click or double-tap the shield. If Windows Security is running and all's well, a check mark in a green circle appears. Problems requiring immediate attention are indicated by a red X, and less severe problems are signaled by an exclamation mark in a yellow triangle, as shown in Figure 1-1.

  Windows 11 should tell you if Windows Security stops, either via a notification or an X on the flag in the lower-right corner of the desktop. But if you want to be sure, there's no better way than to check it yourself. It takes only a few seconds.

- **Don't use old versions of web browsers.** Malicious actors can take advantage of unfixed security vulnerabilities in older versions of popular browsers. That's why it's a great idea to keep your browser up to date; when installing it, download the latest version from its official website. It doesn't matter if you prefer Microsoft Edge built into Windows, Google Chrome, Mozilla Firefox, or one of the less popular browsers such as Opera or Arc.

- **Delete chain mail.** I'm sure that you'll be bringing down the wrath of several lesser deities for the rest of your days, but do everyone a favor and don't forward junk. Please! If something you received in an email sounds too cool or way too weird, it's probably fake. Look it up at `www.snopes.com`, a website that specializes in fact-checking all kinds of online rumors.

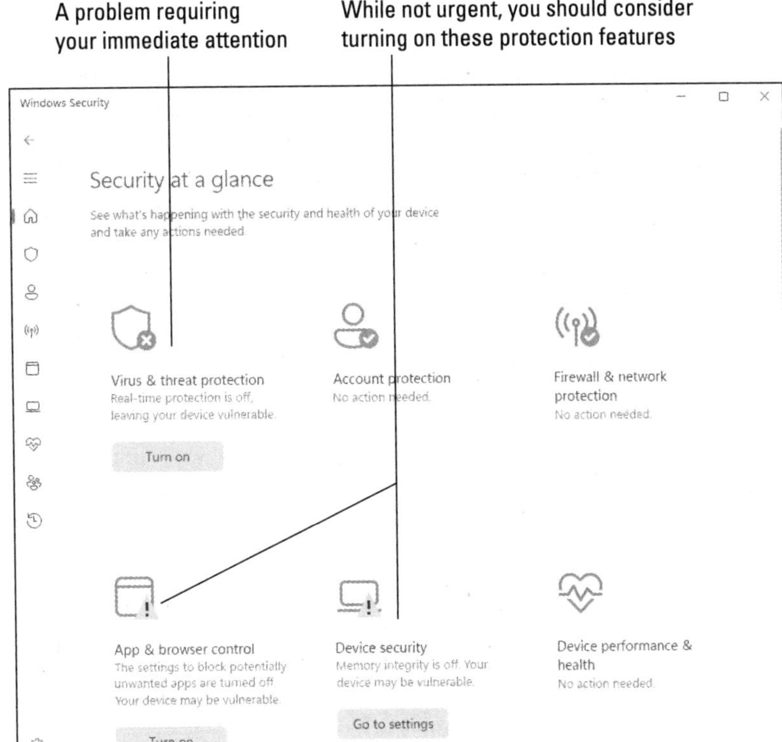

FIGURE 1-1: Windows Security gives you an overview of your computer's security.

- **Keep up to date with Windows 11 patches and (especially) updates to other programs running on your computer.** Windows should be keeping itself updated through Windows Update. Microsoft Store apps are automatically updated by the store. But desktop apps downloaded from other sources may need your supervision to get updated on a regular basis.
- **Check your credit cards and bank balances regularly.** I check my charges and balances every couple of days and suggest you do the same. Credit-monitoring services keep a constant eye on your credit report, watching for any unexpected behavior. Most companies that get hacked will offer free credit monitoring to potentially ripped-off customers. Many big banks offer the service free, too.
- **If you don't need a program anymore, get rid of it.** Use the uninstall feature in Windows 11. If the unwanted program doesn't blast away easily, use BCUninstaller (Bulk Crap Uninstaller), which I describe in Book 10, Chapter 4.
- **Change your passwords regularly.** This is another one of those things everybody recommends but almost no one does. Except you really should

because someone might see you typing your password and use it later without your consent. Or one of the computers you're using may have a hidden keylogger, recording everything you type and using it later for nefarious purposes. Check out solutions such as Bitwarden and RoboForm to help you with this task, which I describe in Chapter 3 of this minibook.

» **Every three months or so, run Microsoft Defender Antivirus (offline scan).** Such scans are useful in detecting and removing rootkits. You can find it in the scan options offered by Windows Security in its Virus & Threat Protection section.

» **Every month or so, get a second opinion from a free antivirus such as Bitdefender Antivirus Free for Windows or Malwarebytes Free.** I like both programs, and they're great at giving you a second opinion, pointing out questionable programs or files that Windows Security may not flag as suspicious. You can get Bitdefender from `www.bitdefender.com/solutions/free.html` and Malwarebytes at `www.malwarebytes.com/mwb-download`.

Here are some of the most important tips for keeping your computer, devices, and data secure:

» **Don't trust any PC unless you personally have been taking close care of it.** Even then, be skeptical. Treat every PC you encounter as if it's infected. Don't stick a USB drive into a public computer, for example, unless you're prepared to scan and disinfect the USB drive immediately when you get back to a safe computer. Don't use the business center computer in a hotel or FedEx if you must type anything sensitive. Assume that everything you type in a public PC is being logged and sent to a pimply-faced genius who wants to be a millionaire.

» **Don't install a new program unless you know what it does and you've checked to make sure you have a legitimate copy.**

WARNING

Yes, even if an online scanner told you that you have 139 viruses on your computer and need to pay just $49.99 to get rid of them.

If you install apps from the Microsoft Store, you're generally safe — although the Store has its share of crappy programs. But any programs you install from other sources should be downloaded from a reputable source (such as `https://download.cnet.com`, `www.softpedia.com`, `www.majorgeeks.com`, or `www.snapfiles.com`), and *even then* you have to be careful that the installer doesn't bring in some crappy extras.

Similarly, web browser extensions are safe as long as you stick to the well-known ones with tons of reviews or recommended by publications you trust.

» **Don't use the same password for two or more sites.** Okay, if you re-use your passwords, make sure you don't re-use the passwords on any of your email or financial accounts. Email accounts are different. If you re-use the passwords on any of your email accounts and somebody gets the password, that person may be able to break into everything, steal your money, your identity, or sensitive data you won't want to be made public. See the nearby "Don't re-use your email password" sidebar.

- **Don't use Wi-Fi in a public place unless you're running exclusively on HTTPS-encrypted sites or through a virtual private network (VPN).**

REMEMBER

If you don't know what HTTPS is and have never set up a VPN, that's okay. Just realize that anybody else who can connect to the same Wi-Fi network you're using can see *every single thing* that goes into or comes out of your computer. See Chapter 3 in this minibook to learn more about using VPN solutions in Windows 11.

- **Don't fall for Nigerian 419 scams, "I've been mugged, and I need $500," or anything else where you must send money.** There are lots of scams — and if you see the words *Western Union* or *Postal Money Order,* run for the exit. The same if you receive out-of-this-world investment proposals, you're announced that you have won a large sum of money in a lottery you didn't participate in, or you have a match on Tinder, Bumble, or some other dating platform and the other person tells you that they're in love with you but need your money to meet. Finally, don't send money through Venmo to hold an item before you receive it from a seller on eBay Marketplace.
- **Don't click or tap a link in an email message or document and expect it to take you to a financial site.** Take the time to type the address in your browser or, if you really must try the link you received, read Book 7, Chapter 3, and learn how to use Windows Sandbox. Copy and paste the link into Sandbox so that if you stumble upon something harmful, it won't negatively affect your actual Windows computer.
- **Don't open an attachment to any email message until you've contacted the person who sent it to you and verified that the person intentionally sent you the file.** Even if the person did send it, use your judgment as to whether the sender is savvy enough to refrain from sending you something infectious. For maximum safety, upload the file first to `www.virustotal.com` and have it checked for malware before you open it or execute it on your computer.
- **Don't forget to change your passwords.** Yes, another one of those things everybody recommends but few people do. Except you really should.
- **Don't trust anybody who calls you and offers to fix your computer.** The "I'm from Microsoft, and I'm here to help" scam has tricked too many people. Stay skeptical and don't let anybody else into your computer unless you know who they are.

WARNING

» **Don't forget that the biggest security vulnerability is you, the user.** Regardless of how robust your antivirus software is or how many security measures you or your company have in place, the user always remains the most vulnerable point. Acting without caution and ignoring security advice can lead to exposing sensitive information, granting attackers access to your computer, and quickly infecting your devices. Always use your judgment when dealing with suspicious emails, messages, files, links, or attachments. If something seems off, it probably is, and it's better to be overly cautious than to regret it later.

DON'T RE-USE YOUR EMAIL PASSWORD

Imagine you have a Gmail account. You also sign up for an account on a popular online shopping site. For convenience, you use the same password for both. Fast forward a day, a month, or even a year. You make a purchase on the shopping site, providing your email address and password. No big deal, right?

Then the shopping site gets hacked, and information from thousands of accounts is stolen. Unfortunately, the site stored passwords and email addresses in a way that hackers could easily crack. The stolen data gets posted online, and within minutes, people are using your Gmail address and password to try logging into various sites such as online banking, brokerage, and PayPal.

If they find a financial site that lets you reset your password with just an email address, they can use your Gmail account to reset your password and gain access. They log into your Gmail, wait for the password reset instructions, and 30 seconds later, they're into your financial account.

It doesn't stop at financial sites. Any site storing sensitive information, such as a hospital or insurance portal, can be similarly vulnerable, and this kind of breach happens every day. Literally!

To protect yourself, always turn on two-factor authentication (2FA) wherever it's available. For instance, with 2FA on your email account, any attempt to access your account from a new device will require responding to a verification code sent to your smartphone. There are many variations, but 2FA adds an essential layer of security that can prevent unauthorized access, even if someone knows your password.

Stay safe online by using unique passwords for different sites and enabling 2FA. It's a simple step that can save you a lot of trouble.

Keeping Yourself Protected with Windows Security

Windows Security in Windows 11 is a powerful and efficient antimalware program that performs exceptionally well without slowing down your computer. There's no need to spend money on other antimalware or antivirus programs because you already have one of the best protections built into Windows 11, working automatically, at no extra cost.

Windows Security is built on the reliable foundation of Microsoft Defender Antivirus, which has been trusted for years. Windows Security includes all the security features developed by Microsoft over time and adds new ones, such as exploit protection and ransomware protection, ensuring comprehensive security for your device.

Accessing Windows Security and following its recommendations

One of the most important things that you can do to ensure your security when using Windows 11 is to follow the recommendations given by Windows Security and make sure that it is turned on. Here's how to do that:

1. **Click or tap in the Search box on the taskbar and type** security. **Click or tap the Windows Security search result.**

   The Windows Security app opens, showing its status (refer to Figure 1-1).

2. **If you see an X next to an important security feature, click or tap it, and then turn on the recommended type of protection.**
3. **If you see a question mark next to a security feature, click or tap it and follow the recommendations given by Windows Security.**

   For example, in Figure 1-2, Reputation-based Protection isn't turned on, and this means my device isn't protected from potentially unwanted apps, files, and websites.

4. **Do what Windows Security recommends.**

   In my case, that's clicking or tapping the Turn On button for Reputation-based Protection.

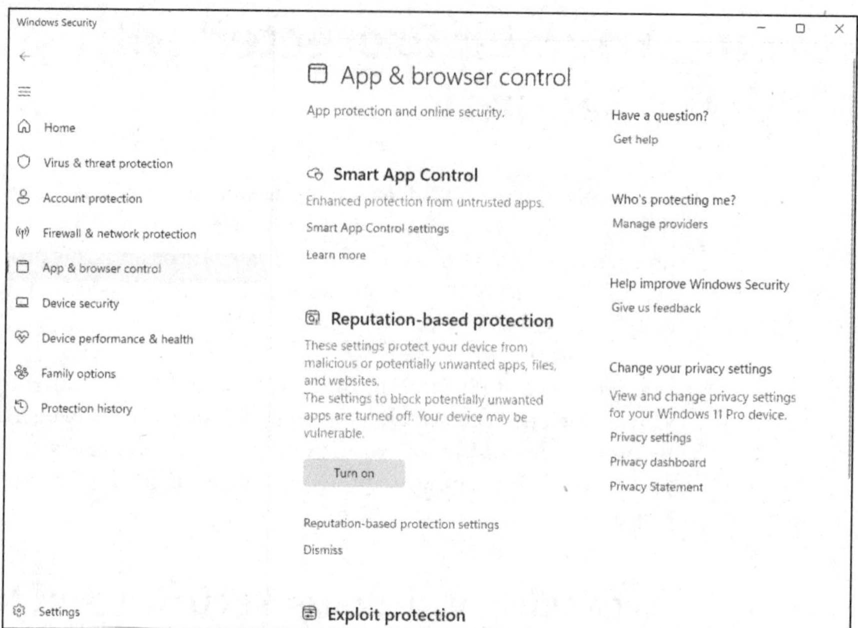

FIGURE 1-2: Checking what Windows Security recommends for more protection.

REMEMBER

When you enable some features from Windows Security, a User Account Control prompt pops up, asking whether you want to allow this app to make changes to your device. Always choose Yes when you see this prompt while configuring Windows Security.

5. **When you've finished going through all the areas that require your attention, click or tap X to close Windows Security.**

Scanning for malware

Even though your Windows 11 computer or device may run well, without any noticeable performance issues, it doesn't mean that it's clean from malware. After all, modern cybersecurity threats are particularly good at concealing themselves and remaining unnoticed while they do their nasty deeds. That's why, from time to time, it is a good idea to run a quick scan with Windows Security like this:

1. **Click or tap the Start icon, followed by All, and then Windows Security.**

   Windows Security opens, showing its status (refer to Figure 1-1).

2. **Click or tap Virus & Threat Protection.**

   You see the scanning options shown in Figure 1-3, alongside information about all the types of antimalware protection offered by Windows Security.

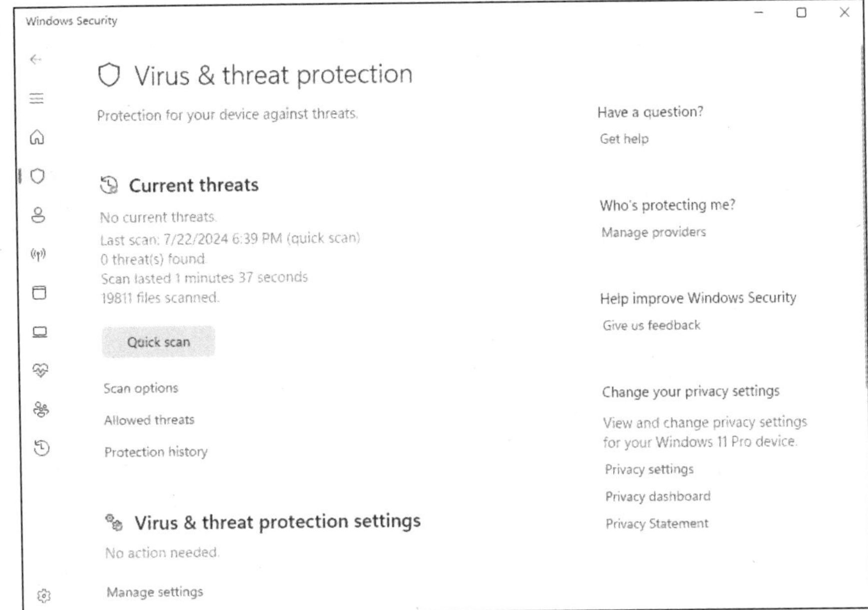

FIGURE 1-3: It's easy to perform a quick scan with Windows Security.

3. **Click or tap the Quick Scan button.**

   Windows Security starts scanning your computer and displays a progress bar, the estimated time remaining, and how many files were scanned. At the end, you receive a notification with the results. If it finds any threats, Windows Security asks how you want to deal with them.

REMEMBER

The quick scan in Windows Security checks only the folders in your system where threats are commonly found. It does this to save time and to free up computing resources, which you can then use for your work. If you want to run a full system scan, click or tap Scan Options, select Full Scan, and click or tap Scan Now.

Protecting your data from ransomware

Ransomware, a type of malicious software that encrypts your files and demands payment for their release, is a growing threat. To help users combat this, Microsoft has introduced the Controlled Folder Access (CFA) feature, which preemptively blocks many kinds of ransomware by restricting access to folders that contain your important files.

However, there's a catch: Enabling and managing CFA can be tedious. It blocks all programs from accessing protected folders unless you specifically allow them. For example, you can prevent apps from accessing your Documents folder but permit

Word and Excel to do so. This works fine until you need another app to edit a file in your Documents folder.

Because of this complexity, Microsoft doesn't enable Controlled Folder Access by default. If you want this extra layer of protection, you need to turn it on and configure it yourself. Once enabled, make sure to protect all folders containing sensitive data and whitelist any programs (set them as allowed) that need access to these folders.

Taking the time to set up CFA can significantly enhance your security and protect your files from ransomware attacks. Here's how it's done:

1. **Click or tap in the Search box on the taskbar and type** security**. Select Windows Security in the list of search results.**
2. **Click or tap the Virus & Threat Protection icon, scroll down, and then click or tap Manage Ransomware Protection.**

   The Ransomware Protection settings appear, as shown in Figure 1-4.

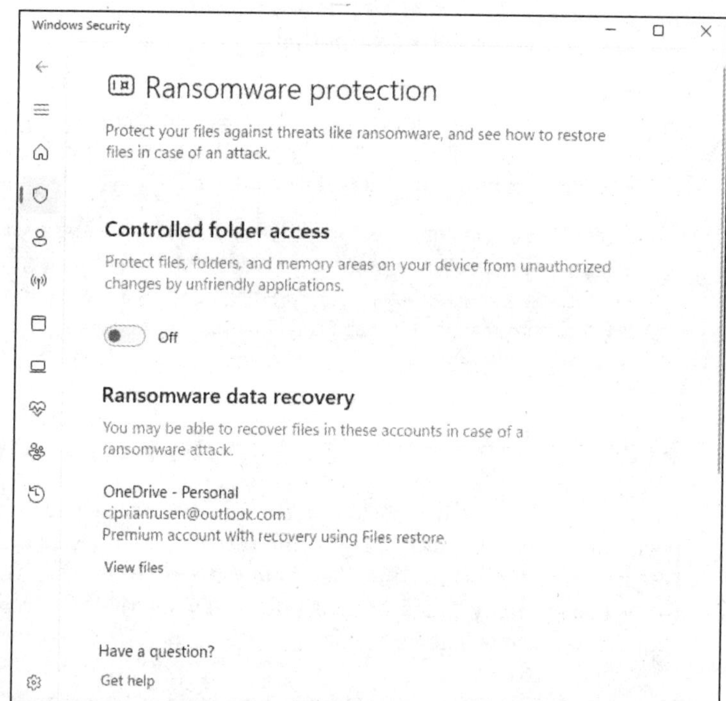

FIGURE 1-4: Setting up Controlled Folder Access is necessary to benefit from Ransomware Protection.

3. **Set the Controlled Folder Access switch on and confirm your choice when the UAC prompt shows up.**

4. **Click or tap the Protected Folders link. Click or tap Yes when asked to confirm your choice.**

   You see a list of all folders protected by CFA — Documents, Pictures, Videos, Music, Favorites, and so on. However, ransomware frequently attacks files in other locations too.

5. **If you want to add another folder to the blocked list, click or tap the Add a Protected Folder button and navigate to and select the folder. Repeat as necessary.**

   Note that Windows has automatically created (but not disclosed!) a set of programs that it deems to be friendly, which are not blocked by CFA.

6. **Click or tap the back arrow in the upper-left corner to return to the window shown in Figure 1-4.**

7. **If you have any programs that need access to those folders, and the apps aren't automatically identified as friendly:**

   a. *Click or tap the Allow an App through Controlled Folder Access link, and then click or tap Yes.*

   b. *Click or tap the Add an Allowed App button, click or tap Browse All Apps, and then navigate to the app and select it. Repeat this process to add all the apps you want.*

TIP

In 2022, Microsoft introduced an app called Microsoft Defender. At its core, this app is a user-friendly dashboard that provides an overview of the security status of your Windows 11 computer and other devices. It's compatible with Windows, Mac, Android, and iOS, offering a consolidated view for users with multiple devices. However, you need a Microsoft account and you have to sign in on all your devices. And most importantly, you need a Microsoft 365 Personal or Family subscription. For users in the United States, Microsoft Defender offers additional features such as privacy protection and identity theft monitoring. For international users, the available features are relatively basic, largely mirroring existing Windows Security functions.

Excluding files and folders from antivirus scans

If you're a software developer creating apps that work with system files on Windows, you may encounter issues with Windows Security deeming your app and its files insecure. In this situation, if you don't want your work removed from your computer, you should exclude the files and folders you're using from the scans performed by Windows Security. Here's how:

1. **Click or tap in the Search box on the taskbar and type** security. **Click or tap the Windows Security search result.**

   The Windows Security app opens (refer to Figure 1-1).

2. **Click or tap Virus & Threat Protection.**

   You see the options previously shown in Figure 1-3.

3. **Under Virus & Threat Protection Settings, click or tap the Manage Settings link.**

4. **Scroll down the Virus & Threat Protection Settings until you get to Exclusions and click or tap Add or Remove Exclusions. Click or tap Yes to confirm your choice.**

   You see the exclusion options shown in Figure 1-5.

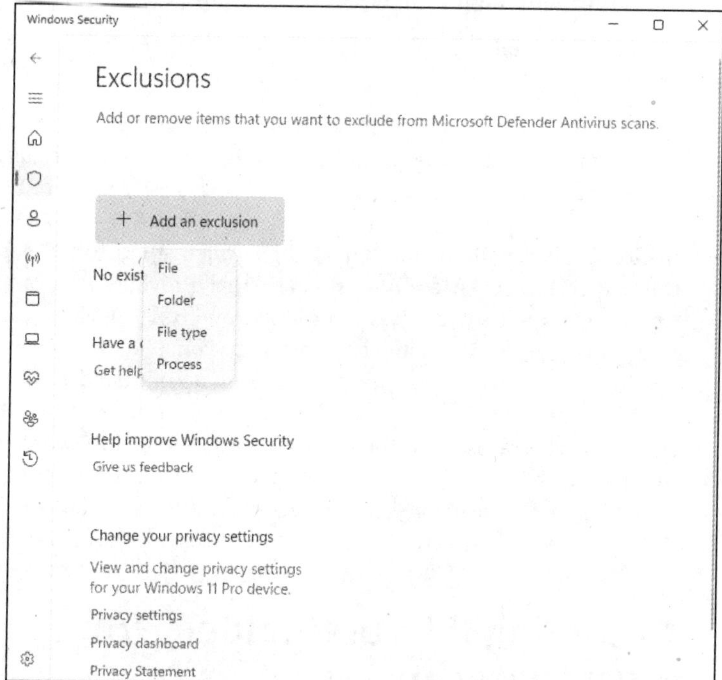

FIGURE 1-5: Adding exclusions to Windows Security.

5. **Click or tap Add an Exclusion, and select whether it is a file, a folder, or some other item. Then select the item you want.**

   You see it added to the Exclusions list, and it will no longer be scanned by Windows Security.

Running a thorough offline scan

The Microsoft Defender Antivirus offline scan in Windows 11 is like giving your PC a deep cleaning while it's "asleep." Instead of scanning while Windows is running, it checks your computer before the operating system starts up. This sneaky approach helps catch stubborn malware that might hide during normal scans like rootkits typically do. It's super thorough, checking parts of your system that are usually off-limits. Running this scan now and then, especially if your computer's acting weird, is a smart move. However, before running an offline scan, always make sure that you have closed all open apps and files so that you don't lose any work.

Here's how to use Windows Security to run a thorough offline scan:

1. **Click or tap in the Search box on the taskbar and type** security. **Select the Windows Security search result.**

   The Windows Security app appears (refer to Figure 1-1).

2. **Click or tap Virus & Threat Protection and then the Scan Options link.**

   You see the options for manually running a quick scan, full scan, custom scan, or Microsoft Defender Antivirus (offline scan), as shown in Figure 1-6.

3. **To perform a thorough scan (which can help you find rootkits), select Microsoft Defender Antivirus (Offline Scan), click or tap Scan Now, followed by Scan and Yes.**

   You're signed out of Windows 11, and your computer restarts. Then Microsoft Defender Antivirus loads and starts its offline scan in a command-line environment similar to the one in Figure 1-7. In it, you see the start time for the scan, how many items were scanned, and its completion percentage. Go have a cup of coffee. By the time you come back, you'll see a list of any dodgy stuff it found.

   If no threats are found after the scan is finished, your computer is automatically rebooted, and you are back to the Windows 11 sign-in screen. If threats are found, you see a report with more details and the options you have for dealing with them.

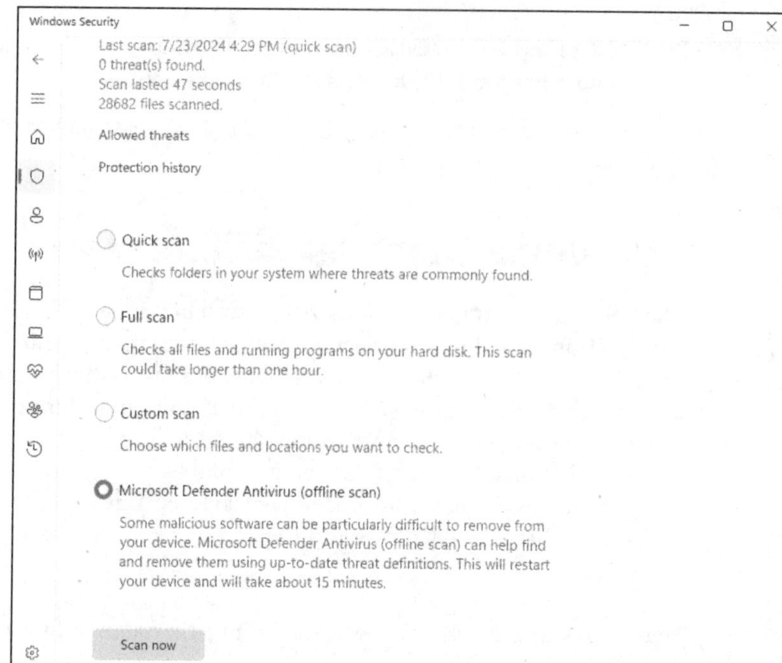

FIGURE 1-6: The scanning options available in Windows Security.

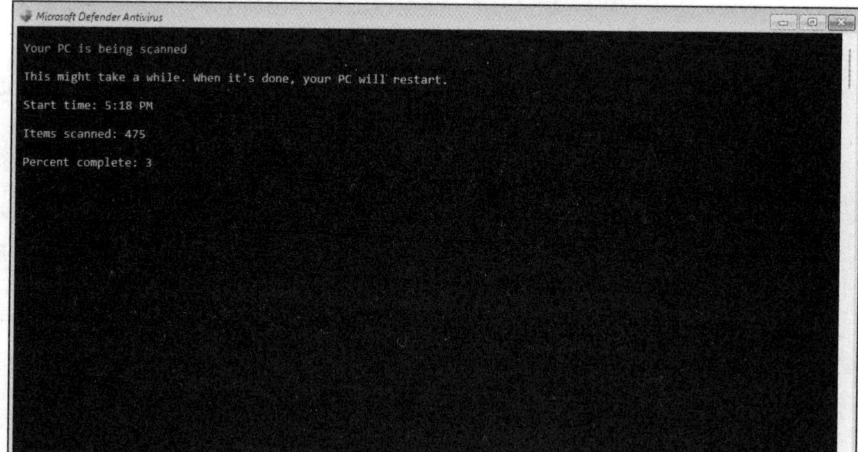

FIGURE 1-7: Regularly performing a Microsoft Defender Antivirus (Offline Scan) is a great idea.

IN THIS CHAPTER

» Dealing with User Account Control prompts

» Coping with Microsoft Defender SmartScreen warnings

» Encrypting your computer and USB devices

» Keeping your PC protected with Windows Defender Firewall

» Accessing the UEFI

Chapter 2
Enhancing Your Security

When you're using Windows 11, security is a big deal, even if you don't think about it every day. Your computer is constantly fending off potential threats from the internet and elsewhere. Luckily, Windows 11 comes packed with a variety of security features designed to keep your data safe and your system running smoothly, such as User Account Control, Microsoft Defender SmartScreen, BitLocker, and Windows Defender Firewall.

User Account Control is here to ensure that apps and users don't make changes to the system files and folders without the admin's consent, while Microsoft Defender SmartScreen protects you from dodgy websites, files, and apps you may want to access on the internet. If you don't do anything that may endanger your computer, you'll barely see prompts from these security features of Windows. However, they're there, doing their job in the background.

BitLocker is Windows 11's built-in encryption tool, designed to protect your data from unauthorized access. It works by encrypting entire drives and making their content unreadable without the correct encryption key or password. This feature is especially useful for laptop users or anyone concerned about the physical theft of their devices. BitLocker can encrypt your system drive, other internal drives, and even removable storage such as USB drives (using BitLocker To Go).

Another important security tool is Windows Defender Firewall, which monitors and controls network traffic to and from your computer. Acting like a vigilant guard helps protect your system from unauthorized access and potential threats from the internet.

Finally, I cover UEFI, the modern replacement for BIOS that Windows 11 now requires. It offers faster boot times and enhanced security features such as Secure Boot, helping prevent malware from tampering with your system's startup.

Don't worry if some of these terms sound intimidating — I break everything down into easy-to-understand concepts. By the end of this chapter, you'll have a solid grasp on how to enhance your Windows 11 security and keep those digital ne'er-do-wells at bay. So, let's roll up our sleeves and get started.

Working with User Account Control

Ever wonder why Windows keeps asking for your permission to do things? Meet User Account Control (UAC), an overzealous but well-meaning system custodian. This security feature prevents unauthorized changes to your Windows system and personal files. It was designed to put a damper on malware parties, especially those pesky self-replicating viruses. And guess what? It's been doing a good job, so malware evolved to find new ways to circumvent UAC.

In Windows, files and apps don't get an all-access pass by default. They're more like interns on their first day. They can't mess with the operating system, its files, or settings; they can't snoop around in other users' files; and they're limited to their own little workspace. When UAC is on duty (which is most of the time), apps can tinker with only their own files and settings or the current user's stuff. If an app tries to make a big system change, UAC steps in like a stern librarian, asking, "Do you want to allow this app to make changes to your device?"

If you're logged in as an administrator, UAC keeps things simple. You get a yes-or-no question, like the one in Figure 2-1. Click Yes, and the app gets its temporary backstage pass. Click No, and the app is stopped from running, preventing any changes to your system.

For standard user accounts without administrator permissions, UAC plays hardball. They need to enter an administrator's password or PIN, as shown in Figure 2-2. It's like calling the club owner to verify if someone's really on the VIP list. No PIN or password? No entry. The app is blocked from running and making system changes.

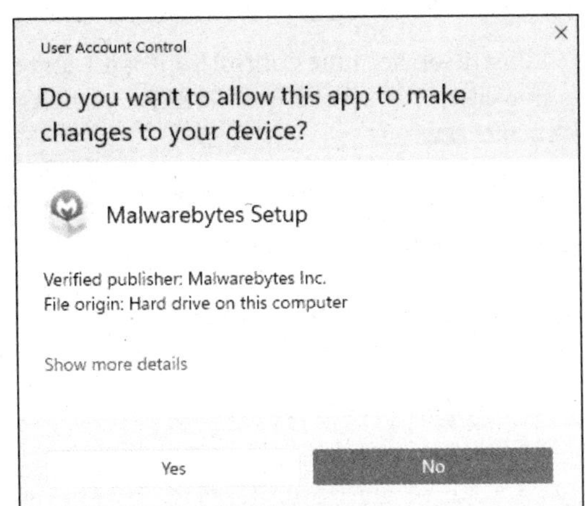

FIGURE 2-1: User Account Control tries to keep you from harming your system.

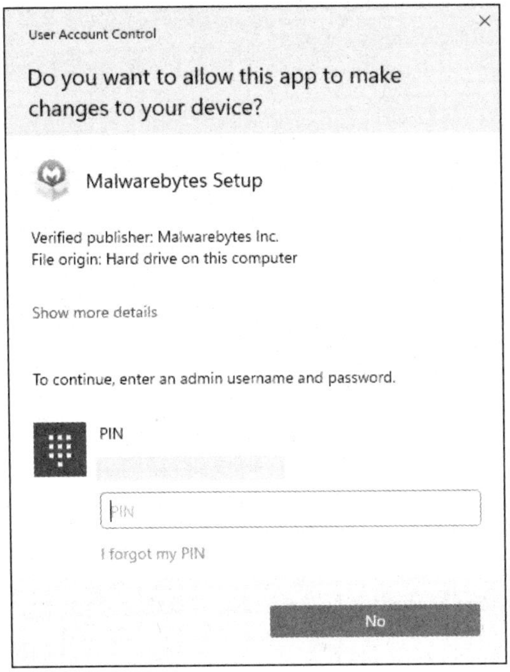

FIGURE 2-2: For standard users, UAC asks for the admin PIN or password.

UAC doesn't discriminate. Even if you, the user, are trying to change system files or settings, it'll still ask for ID. Standard users get the "To continue, enter an admin username and password" pop-up. No admin password? You're not changing anything, buddy!

Windows lets you adjust User Account Control so it isn't quite as dramatic — or you can disable it. However, that's not a good idea, because it makes your system an easier target for attackers.

To adjust your computer's UAC level, sign in to Windows 11 using an account that is set as administrator and follow these steps:

1. **Click or tap in the Search box on the taskbar and type** uac. **At the top of the ensuing list, choose Change User Account Control Settings.**

   The window shown in Figure 2-3 appears.

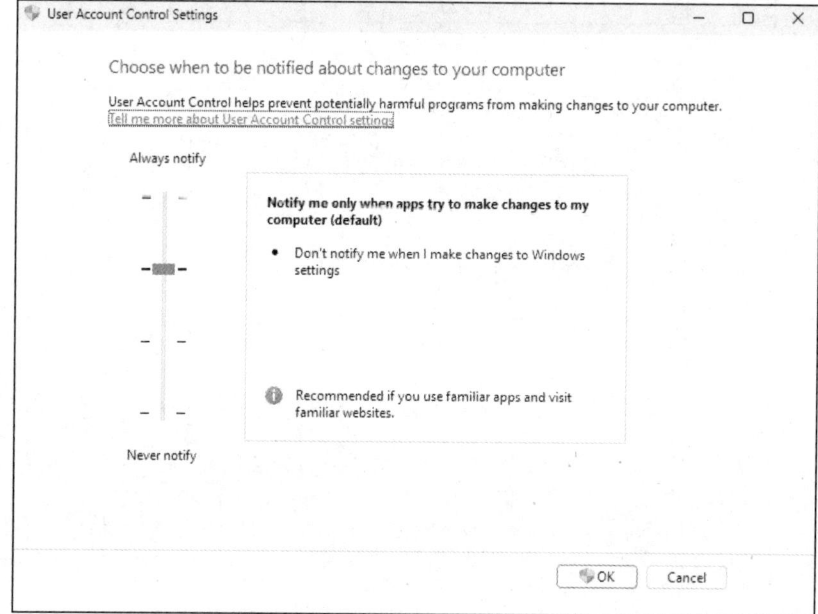

FIGURE 2-3: Windows 11 allows you to change the level of UAC intrusiveness.

2. **Adjust the slider according to Table 2-1, and then click or tap OK.**

   As soon as you try to change your UAC level, Windows 11 hits you with a User Account Control prompt. If you're using a standard account, you must provide an administrator username and password (or PIN) to make the change. If you're using an administrator account, you must confirm the change.

3. **Click or tap Yes.**

   Your changes take effect immediately.

TABLE 2-1 User Account Control Levels

Slider	What It Means	Recommendations
Level 1 (top)	Brings up the full UAC notification whenever a program tries to make changes to the computer that require an administrator account or when you try to make changes to Windows settings that require administrator permissions. You see these notifications even if you're using an administrator account. The screen blacks out, and you can't do anything until the UAC screen is answered.	Offers the highest security but also the highest hassle factor.
Level 2	Displays the UAC notification when a program tries to make changes to your computer but generally doesn't bring up a UAC notification when you make changes directly.	The default — and probably the best choice.
Level 3	The same as Level 2, except the UAC notification doesn't lock and dim your desktop.	Potentially problematic. Dimming and locking the screen present a high hurdle for malware.
Level 4 (bottom)	UAC is disabled — programs can make changes to Windows settings, and you can change anything you like, without triggering any UAC prompts. Note that this level doesn't override other security settings. For example, if you're using a standard account, you still need to provide an administrator's ID and password before you can install a program that runs for all users.	Automatically turns off all UAC warnings — not recommended.

TECHNICAL STUFF

This description sounds simple, but the details are complex. Microsoft's Help system says that if your computer is at Level 2, the default setting in Windows, "You will be notified if a program outside of Windows tries to make changes to a Windows setting." So how does Windows tell when a program is outside Windows — and thus whether actions taken by the program are worthy of a UAC prompt at Levels 2 or 3?

UAC-level rules are interpreted according to a special Windows security certificate. Programs signed with that certificate are deemed to be part of Windows. Programs that aren't signed with that certificate are outside Windows and thus trigger UAC prompts if your computer is at Level 1, 2, or 3.

Dealing with Microsoft Defender SmartScreen

Have you ever downloaded a program from the internet, clicked to install it, and then, a second later, thought, "Why did I do that?"

Microsoft came up with a technology called SmartScreen that aims to protect you before you get yourself in a nasty situation. Here's how it works:

- It checks the web content used by the apps you install from the Microsoft Store and ensures that they aren't malicious.
- It monitors the websites you visit in Microsoft Edge and blocks access to those reported as malicious.
- It examines the files and apps you download and prevents you from running them if they're known to harm other computers and devices.

SmartScreen or Microsoft Defender SmartScreen (to use its full product name) is integrated into Windows Security (read Chapter 1 in this minibook) to increase its effectiveness, and one way it manifests itself is when downloading malicious files from the web. After you click or tap Download, the malicious file isn't downloaded. Instead, you see a message that the file was blocked as unsafe by Microsoft Defender SmartScreen, as shown in Figure 2-4.

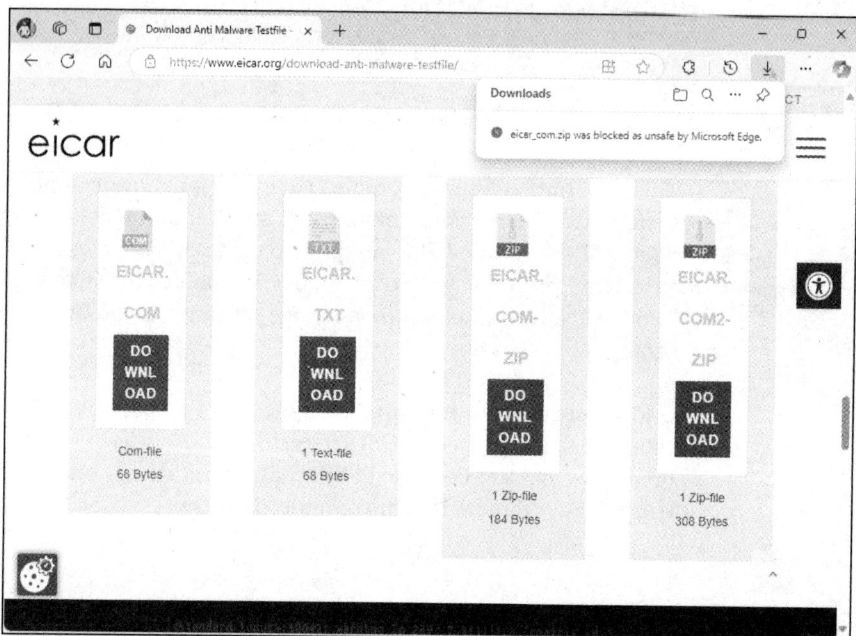

FIGURE 2-4: SmartScreen blocks you from downloading unsafe files.

Another situation where you can encounter SmartScreen is when you're browsing the web and end up on a site marked as malicious in Microsoft's security databases. You'll see a big warning sign that this website has been reported as unsafe and you are blocked access to it, as shown in Figure 2-5.

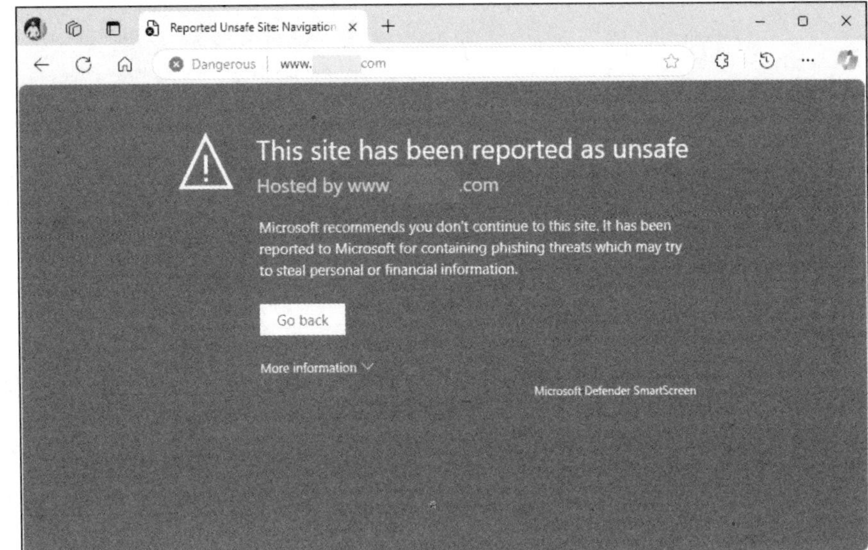

FIGURE 2-5: SmartScreen blocks access to dangerous websites too.

Enhancing Your Security

Convincing SmartScreen to unblock access to websites and files

If you know that Microsoft Defender SmartScreen wrongly blocked access to a website (this may happen once in a blue moon), you can get access to it by clicking More Information when you see the screen in Figure 2-5 and choosing Continue to the Unsafe Site (Not Recommended).

Similarly, if SmartScreen wrongly blocks you from downloading a file from the web, you can convince it to let you download it like this:

1. **Open Microsoft Edge, browse to the site you're interested in, and click or tap the Download button for the file you want.**

   The warning shown previously in Figure 2-4 appears.

2. **Click or tap the ellipsis icon next to the file.**

   The More Actions menu shown in Figure 2-6 appears.

3. **Click or tap Keep.**

   Microsoft Defender SmartScreen insists that the app or file is unsafe.

4. **Click or tap Show More to expand the dialog.**

   You reveal the options from Figure 2-7.

5. **Choose Keep Anyway.**

   The download finally starts, and you can see its progress.

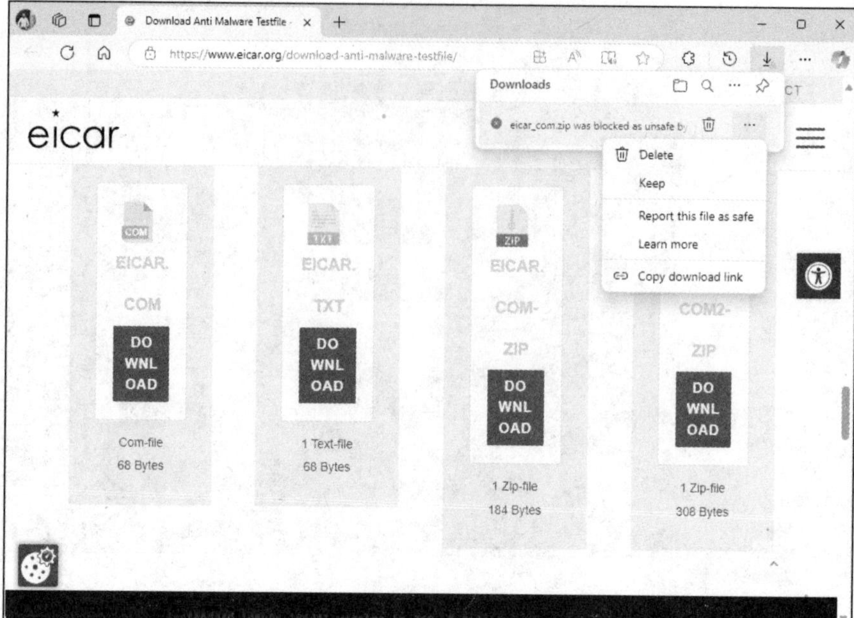

FIGURE 2-6: Telling Microsoft Defender SmartScreen that you want to keep the file.

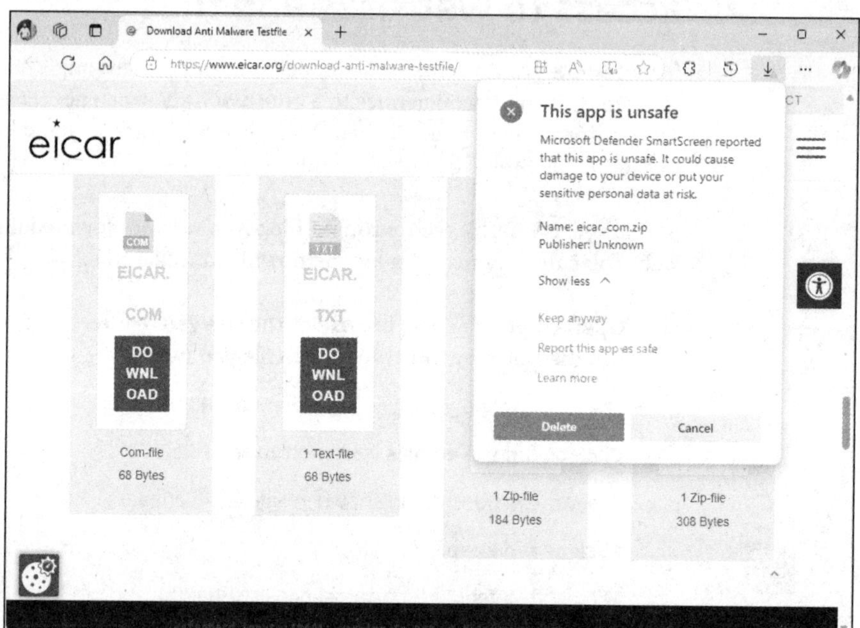

FIGURE 2-7: Insisting that you want to keep the file anyway.

WARNING

Don't ignore the warnings displayed by SmartScreen unless you're absolutely certain the file you're downloading is safe, and your certainty comes from a highly trustworthy source. However, keep in mind that this protective technology isn't perfect. Sometimes, it may block harmless files simply because they originate from less popular websites.

TIP

To create the screenshots for this section, I didn't download an actual virus. Instead, I used the EICAR test file, a harmless dummy virus that security programs use to practice catching bad guys — it helps you check if your digital security guard is awake and doing its job.

Adjusting how Microsoft Defender SmartScreen protects you

A word of caution for the tech-savvy explorer: Tinkering with Microsoft Defender SmartScreen is like adjusting the sensitivity of your home alarm system. It's best left to those who understand the nuts and bolts of digital security. That said, if SmartScreen feels a bit too overbearing, and you're willing to trade some protection for convenience, you can tweak its settings. Just remember that you need to do this from a user account set as administrator. Here's how:

1. **Click or tap in the Search box on the taskbar and type** smartscreen. **Then click or tap the Reputation-Based Protection search result.**

   The Windows Security Reputation-Based Protection window appears (see Figure 2-8).

2. **To change the behavior for SmartScreen, check the following switches one by one and set them off or on with a click or tap:**

   - **Check apps and files:** Enables or disables SmartScreen from protecting you by checking for unrecognized apps and files from the web.
   - **SmartScreen for Microsoft Edge:** Stops or allows SmartScreen to protect you while browsing the web in Microsoft Edge.
   - **Phishing protection:** Turns on or off the mechanisms for protecting your password from being stolen by malicious apps and websites.
   - **Potentially unwanted app blocking:** Stops or allows SmartScreen to protect you against low-reputation apps and downloads that may cause problems.
   - **SmartScreen for Microsoft Store apps:** Enables or disables SmartScreen from checking the web content that Microsoft Store apps use.

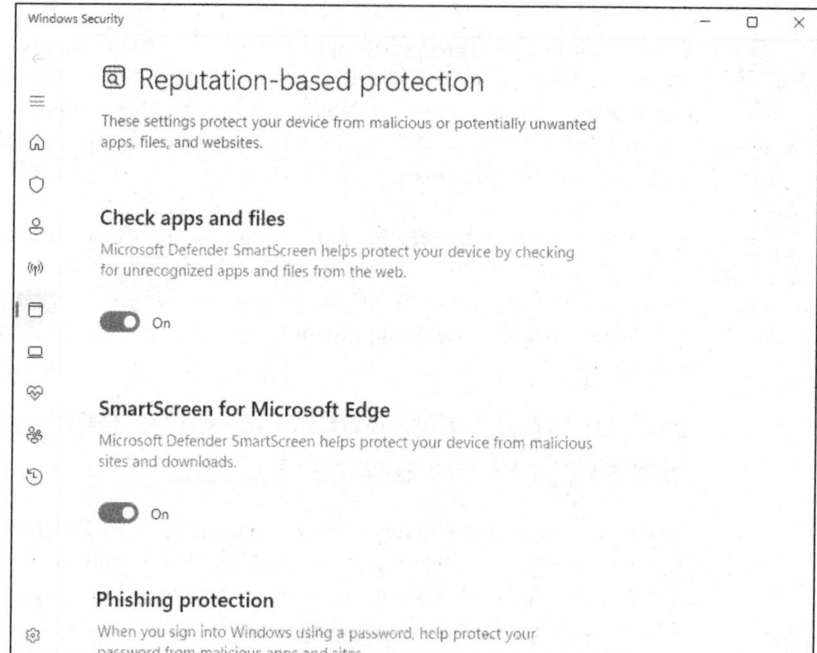

FIGURE 2-8: Think twice before turning off SmartScreen or some of its features.

3. **As soon as you make a change, a UAC prompt is shown. Click or tap Yes to confirm your choice.**
4. **Close Windows Security when you're done.**

   Its icon in the system tray area will be busy warning you that some of its protection features are disabled and recommending that you turn them on again.

Protecting Your Data with Encryption

Nowadays, Windows is primarily used on laptops, which offer great mobility but are also easier to steal or misplace than desktop PCs. And let's be honest, in today's on-the-go world, that's a real possibility. Just imagine leaving your laptop in a taxi or having it disappear from your table at a busy coffee shop — it happens more often than you'd think!

That's where tools such as BitLocker and Encrypting File System (EFS) come in handy. BitLocker is like a smart safe for your entire hard drive. If someone swipes your laptop or removes the hard disk or SSD drive from it, they can't access your files without its encryption key, which is stored in a Trusted Platform Module

(TPM) chip found on the motherboard of your laptop. BitLocker is perfect for protecting sensitive work documents or those embarrassing vacation photos you'd rather keep private.

BitLocker To Go is a complementary technology that extends this protection to your USB drives. That thumb drive with your presentation for the big client meeting? It's locked up tight with excellent encryption, even if it slips out of your pocket.

EFS, on the other hand, is an older legacy technology that can be used in a more targeted way. It lets you encrypt specific files or folders but not entire drives, as BitLocker does. Think of it as a digital lockbox for your most important documents — tax returns, financial spreadsheets, or that novel you're secretly writing.

These security features work behind the scenes, with BitLocker starting before Windows loads. They're like having a vigilant security guard who's always on duty, keeping an eye on your digital valuables.

REMEMBER

BitLocker, BitLocker To Go, and EFS are available only in the Pro, Enterprise, and Education editions of Windows 11. If you're using the Home edition, you might want to consider upgrading if data security is a priority. (For a detailed comparison of Windows 11 editions, refer to Book 1, Chapter 3.)

Although these tools sound high-tech, they're relatively easy to use once you get the hang of them. With a little setup, you can significantly boost your data security, giving you peace of mind whether you're working from home, at the office, or in your favorite local cafe.

Encrypting your PC with BitLocker

You won't find BitLocker in the shiny new Settings app. It's still hanging out in the trusty old Control Panel because Microsoft hasn't given it a modern makeover yet. Although Bitlocker hasn't been updated, encrypting your computer's drives with BitLocker is straightforward, even though it involves both a reboot and a lot of patience. Let's see how it's done:

1. **Click or tap in the Search box on the taskbar and type** bitlocker. **Select Manage BitLocker from the list of results.**

   The BitLocker Drive Encryption window appears, as shown in Figure 2-9.

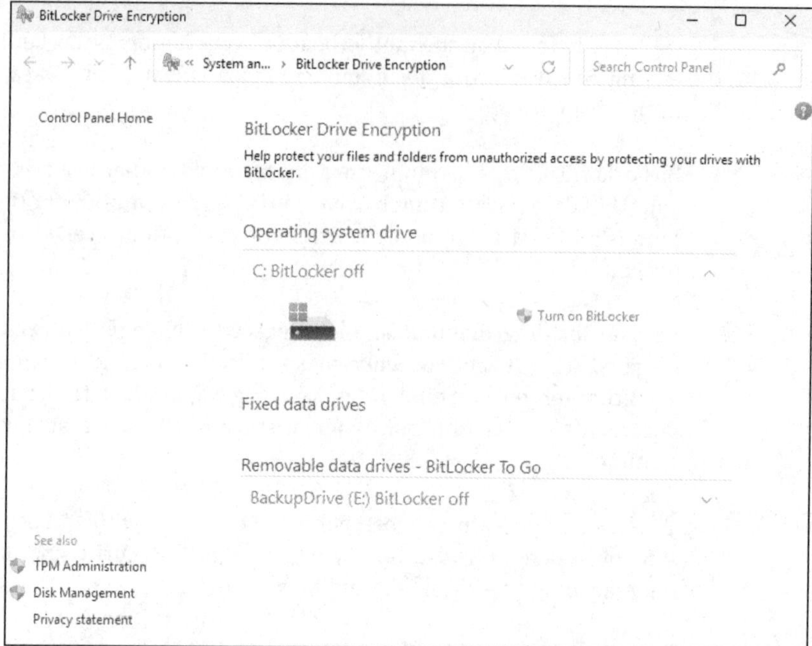

FIGURE 2-9: Manage everything from the BitLocker Drive Encryption window.

2. **Next to the drive (volume) you want to encrypt, click or tap Turn on BitLocker.**

   The BitLocker Drive Encryption setup wizard appears, and Windows 11 checks whether it meets the requirements for running BitLocker. Then, it asks where you want to back up your recovery key, as you can see in Figure 2-10.

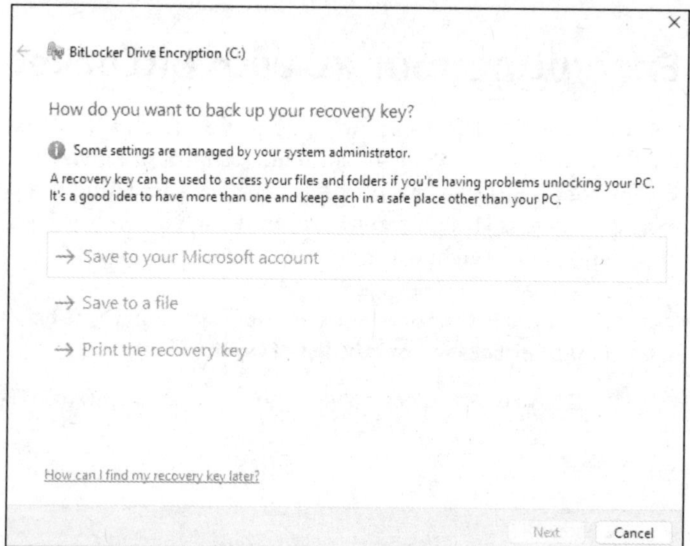

FIGURE 2-10: Choose how you want to save the BitLocker recovery key.

3. **Choose the option you prefer. When you're done, click or tap Next.**

   To ensure you don't lose the recovery key, you can opt for all three options.

4. **When asked to choose between encrypting used disk space only or the entire drive, make your choice and click or tap Next.**

   If you want the encryption to finish faster, choose to encrypt only the used disk space. Encrypting the entire drive may take many hours.

5. **Choose which encryption mode to use, and then click or tap Next.**

   The new encryption mode, which I highly recommend, uses a more secure type of encryption.

6. **Select the option to Run BitLocker System Check, and then click or tap Continue (instead of Start Encryption).**

   The system check ensures that BitLocker can read the recovery and encryption keys correctly before encrypting the drive, which is a great idea.

7. **When asked to restart your computer, close all your open apps and files, and then click or tap Restart Now.**

   When you log back into Windows 11, BitLocker encrypts your drive automatically in the background. You can continue using your PC as usual. The BitLocker icon appears on the taskbar. If you click or tap it, you see the progress of the encryption process.

8. **When the encryption process is finally over, click or tap Close in the BitLocker Drive Encryption window.**

TIP

In case you were wondering, yes, you can use BitLocker on Storage Spaces too. BitLocker encrypts the entire Storage Space.

Encrypting USB drives with BitLocker To Go

We all like our USB sticks and external hard drives, right? They're like magic pockets that can hold everything from family videos to that super-important presentation for the board meeting or even the files of a secret project that's going to revolutionize modern medicine. But here's the catch: These pocket-sized wonders are also easy to misplace. And losing one with sensitive information is a recipe for a major headache (or worse).

That's why you should consider BitLocker To Go for encrypting your data. It's like turning your USB drives into Fort Knox. Without the encryption password, smart card, or recovery key, anyone who finds (or steals) your drive won't be able to access your files.

So, grab your USB drive, buckle up, and let's enable the BitLocker To Go encryption:

1. **In the Search box on the taskbar, type** bitlocker**, and then select Manage BitLocker in the list of results.**

   The BitLocker Drive Encryption window appears (refer to Figure 2-9).

2. **Under Removable Data Drives, click or tap the letter of the drive you want to encrypt to see more options.**

3. **Next to the USB drive you want, click or tap Turn on BitLocker.**

   The BitLocker Drive Encryption setup wizard appears and takes some time to initialize the drive. Then it asks you to choose how you want to unlock the drive, as shown in Figure 2-11.

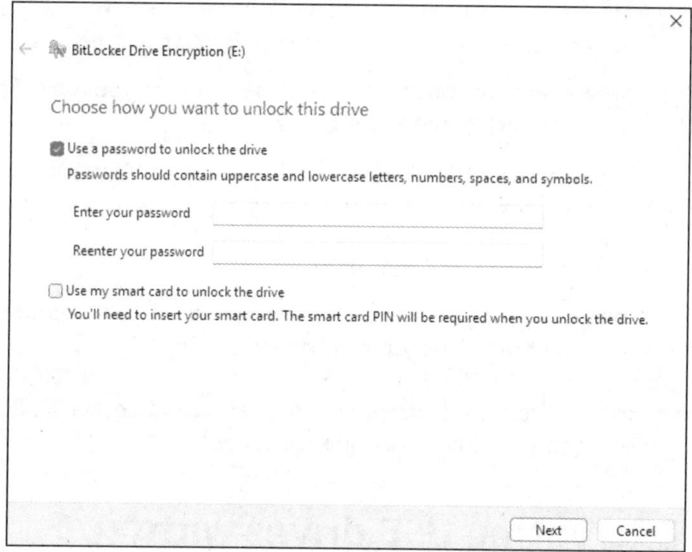

FIGURE 2-11: Setting the encryption password for the USB drive.

4. **Select Use a Password to Unlock the Drive, type the password you want to use, and confirm it. Then, click or tap Next.**

   Keep in mind that the password should contain uppercase and lowercase letters, numbers, spaces, and symbols.

5. **Choose how you want to back up your recovery key, and then click or tap Next.**

6. **Choose between encrypting used disk space only or the entire drive, and then click or tap Next.**

   If you want the encryption to finish faster, choose to encrypt only the used disk space. Encrypting the entire USB drive will take a lot longer.

7. **Choose which encryption mode to use, and then click or tap Next.**

   It's best to choose Compatible Mode for USB drives if you plan to use them on devices without Windows 11 or Windows 10. Otherwise, New Encryption Mode works fine.

8. **When asked if you're ready to encrypt your drive, choose Start Encrypting.**

   BitLocker starts encrypting the USB drive. You can continue using your PC as usual. The BitLocker icon appears on the taskbar. If you click or tap it, you see the progress of the encryption process.

9. **When the encryption process is finally over, click or tap Close in the BitLocker Drive Encryption window.**

REMEMBER

From now on, you can use your USB drive as you would normally. However, the icon of the USB drive in File Explorer now has a small lock to highlight the fact that the drive is encrypted. If you plug the USB drive into another computer, you need to type the password that you set during Step 4 to unlock the drive and access the data stored on it. Without the password, all its data is rendered inaccessible. If you forget the encryption password, you can unlock the drive only by using the recovery key.

Encrypting Folders with EFS

Even though you can use Encrypting File System (EFS) to encrypt both files and folders, it's easier to encrypt folders and place inside them all the files you want encrypted. Here's how encrypting with EFS works:

1. **Click or tap the Start icon and then File Explorer. Or press Windows+E.**

   The File Explorer app opens.

2. **Navigate to the folder you want to encrypt, right-click (or press and hold) its name, and choose Properties.**

   The Properties window for the selected folder opens on the General tab.

3. **In the General tab, click or tap Advanced.**

   The Advanced Attributes window in Figure 2-12 shows up.

4. **Select the box next to Encrypt Contents to Secure Data, and then click or tap OK twice.**

   If the folder you selected contains files or subfolders, a Confirm Attribute Changes dialog box opens, showing the attribute change to encrypt.

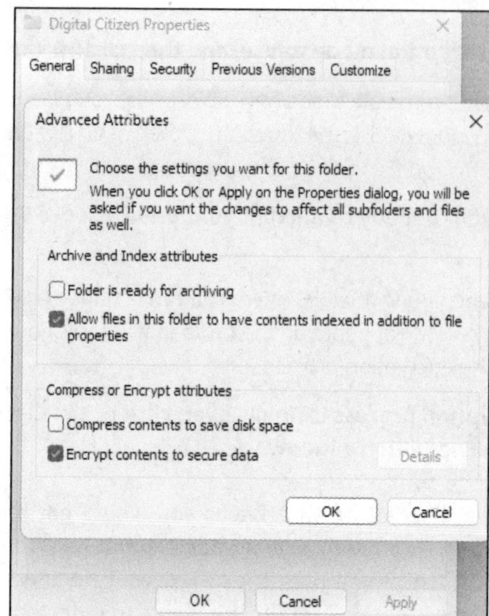

FIGURE 2-12: Encrypting a folder with EFS.

5. **Select Apply Changes to This Folder, Subfolder, and Files, and then click or tap OK.**
6. **To encrypt additional folders, follow Steps 2 through 5. When you've finished encrypting folders, close File Explorer.**

TIP

After a folder is encrypted with EFS, its icon in File Explorer includes a lock on the top right. However, the lock is visible only if you use the larger icon views, not Details or Small Icons.

WARNING

When it comes to protecting sensitive information, encrypting individual files with EFS might seem like a smart move, but it's not always the best idea. That's because when you open an encrypted document for editing, some applications create an unencrypted copy without you even realizing it. So, when you save your changes and close the file, the app you're using saves the unencrypted copy and gets rid of the original encrypted one. Encrypting individual files with EFS is a good idea only if you have files that you use for reference and never edit. However, even in this case, it's often simpler to just encrypt the entire folder where they're stored and call it a day.

Using Windows Defender Firewall

Once you connect a computer or device to the internet, it becomes a target for malicious actors and organizations that may want to access it to steal data from it, extort money from you, its user, or use it in coordinated attacks against other targets. An important line of defense is keeping outsiders away from your computer or devices, and this is where the firewall comes in.

A *firewall* is a security guard for your computer. It monitors and controls incoming and outgoing network traffic based on predetermined security rules. Firewalls act as a barrier between trusted internal networks and devices and untrusted external networks and devices, including the internet. Software firewalls are apps that act as a security guard, such as Windows Defender Firewall. Hardware firewalls are devices programmed to provide this feature, such as most modern routers and wireless access points. They tend to include significant firewalling capability as part of their firmware, providing protection for all the devices that you connect to the network.

Firewalls can be specialized guardians that can handle inbound traffic, outbound traffic, or both. Here's how they work:

- An *inbound firewall* focuses on monitoring and filtering incoming network traffic. It checks all the data packets trying to enter your network (or computer) and blocks those that don't meet the specified security criteria. This feature helps protect your network or PC from unauthorized access, malicious attacks, and other potential threats.
- An *outbound firewall*, on the other hand, monitors and controls outgoing network traffic. It keeps an eye on the data leaving your network (or computer) and blocks anything that looks suspicious or unauthorized. Outbound firewalls help prevent sensitive information from being sent out without permission and stop malware from communicating with external sources.

All versions of Windows 11 ship with a decent and capable, but not foolproof, stateful firewall named Windows Defender Firewall (WDF).

In general, a *stateful firewall* is like a super-smart security guard for your computer or network, depending on where it's used. The firewall not only checks the ID of each data packet but also keeps track of the entire conversation history between your PC or network and the outside world. By remembering the state of each connection, a stateful firewall can quickly spot and stop any suspicious activities or unauthorized communications. It's an efficient way to keep your network safe by monitoring the context of each connection, not just individual packets.

In Windows Defender Firewall, inbound protection is on by default. Unless you change something, it's turned on for all connections on your PC. For example, if you have a LAN cable, a wireless networking card, and a 5G USB modem on a specific computer, WDF is turned on for them all. The only way Windows Defender Firewall gets disabled is if you deliberately turn it off or if the network administrator on your big corporate network decides to disable it by remote control or by installing the operating system with WDF turned off.

You can change WDF settings for inbound protection relatively easily. When you make changes, they apply to all connections on your PC. On the other hand, WDF settings for outbound protection make the rules of cricket look like child's play.

WARNING

In unusual and rare circumstances, malware (viruses, Trojans, whatever) has been known to turn off Windows Defender Firewall. If your firewall kicks out, Windows lets you know loud and clear with Windows Security notifications.

Understanding Windows Defender Firewall

All right, it's time to dive into some technical jargon so you can become knowledgeable at managing Windows Defender Firewall. Don't worry; the concepts aren't as complicated as they might sound. If you find yourself feeling a bit lost while exploring the firewall's configuration options, just refer to this section for a quick refresher.

As you know, computers can send and receive varying amounts of data over a network, from tiny bits to massive files. To make this data transfer manageable, computers break it down into smaller, more digestible pieces called *packets*. These packets are like little envelopes containing a portion of the data, along with a label that tells the computer where the data came from and where it needs to go. On the internet, packets can be sent in two ways:

- **User Datagram Protocol (UDP):** UDP is fast and sloppy. The computer sending the packets doesn't keep track of which packets were sent, and the computer receiving the packets doesn't make any attempt to get the sender to resend packets that vanish mysteriously onto the internet. UDP is the kind of *protocol* (transmission method) that can work with live broadcasts, where short gaps wouldn't be nearly as disruptive as long pauses while the computers wait to resend a dropped packet.
- **Transmission Control Protocol (TCP):** TCP is methodical and complete. The sending computer keeps track of which packets it has sent. If the receiving computer doesn't get a packet, it notifies the sending computer, which resends the packet. These days, almost all communication over the internet goes by way of TCP.

TECHNICAL STUFF

Every computer on a network has an *IP address*, which is a collection of four sets of numbers, each between 0 and 255. For example, 192.168.0.2 is a common IP address for computers connected to a local network, while web servers handling sites on the internet can have addresses like 104.18.4.55. You can think of the IP address as analogous to a telephone number.

TECHNICAL STUFF

When two computers communicate, they need not only each other's IP address but also a specific entry point called a *port* — think of it as a telephone extension — to talk to each other. For example, most websites respond to requests sent to port 443 when using HTTPS (the protocol used to securely send data between a web browser and a website). Nothing is magical about the number 443; it's just the port number that people have agreed to use when trying to get to a website's server. If your web browser wants to look at any website, it sends a packet to its IP address using port 443.

Windows Defender Firewall works by handling the following duties simultaneously:

- **It keeps track of outgoing packets and allows incoming packets to go through the firewall if they can be matched with an outgoing packet.** In other words, WDF works as a stateful inbound firewall.
- **If your computer is attached to a private network, Windows Defender Firewall allows packets to come and go on ports 139 and 445, but only if they come from another computer on your local network and only if they're using TCP.** Windows Defender Firewall needs to open those ports for file and printer sharing.
- **Similarly, if your computer is attached to a private network, Windows Defender Firewall automatically opens ports 137, 138, and 5355 for UDP, but only for packets that originate on your local network.**
- **If you specifically told Windows Defender Firewall that you want it to allow packets to come in on a specific port and the Block All Incoming Connections check box isn't selected, WDF follows your orders.** You may need to open a port for online gaming, for example.
- **You can tell Windows Defender Firewall to accept packets directed at specific programs.** Usually, any company that makes a program designed to listen for incoming internet traffic (Skype is a prime example; qBittorrent is another) adds its program to the list of designated exceptions when the program is installed.
- **Unless an inbound packet meets one of the preceding criteria, it's simply ignored.** Windows Defender Firewall blocks it without a peep. Conversely, unless you've changed something, any and all outbound traffic goes through unobstructed.

Making inbound exceptions

Firewalls can sometimes be infuriating. You may have a program that has worked for years on all sorts of computers, but the minute you install it on a Windows 11 machine with Windows Defender Firewall in action, it just stops working.

You can get mad at Microsoft and scream at Windows Defender Firewall, but when you do, realize that at least part of the problem lies in the way the firewall must work. It has to block packets that are trying to get in unless you explicitly tell the firewall to allow them to get in.

Perhaps most infuriatingly, WDF blocks those packets by simply swallowing them, not by notifying the computer that sent the packet. Windows Defender Firewall has to remain stealthy because if it sends back a packet that says, "Hey, I got your packet, but I can't let it through," the bad guys get an acknowledgment that your computer exists, they can probably figure out which firewall you're using, and they may be able to combine those two pieces of information to give you a headache. It's far better for Windows Defender Firewall to act like a black hole.

Some programs need to listen to incoming traffic from the internet; they wait until they're contacted and then respond. Usually, you know whether you have this type of program because the installer tells you that you need to tell your firewall to back off.

If you have a program that doesn't add itself to the list of rules used by Windows Defender Firewall, you can tell WDF to allow packets destined for that specific program. You may want to do that for an online game that needs to accept incoming traffic, for example. Here's how:

1. **Make sure that the program you want to allow through Windows Defender Firewall is installed.**
2. **In the Search box on the taskbar, type** firewall. **Choose Allow an App through Windows Firewall.**

   Windows Defender Firewall presents you with a lengthy list of apps that you may want to allow (see Figure 2-13). If a box is selected, Windows Defender Firewall allows unsolicited incoming packets of data directed to that program and that program alone, and the column tells you whether the connection is allowed for private or public connections.

   REMEMBER

   These settings don't apply to incoming packets of data that are received in response to a request from your computer; they apply only when a packet of data appears on your firewall's doorstep without an invitation.

   In Figure 2-13, the Windows Media Player app is allowed to receive inbound packets whether you're connected to a private or a public network.

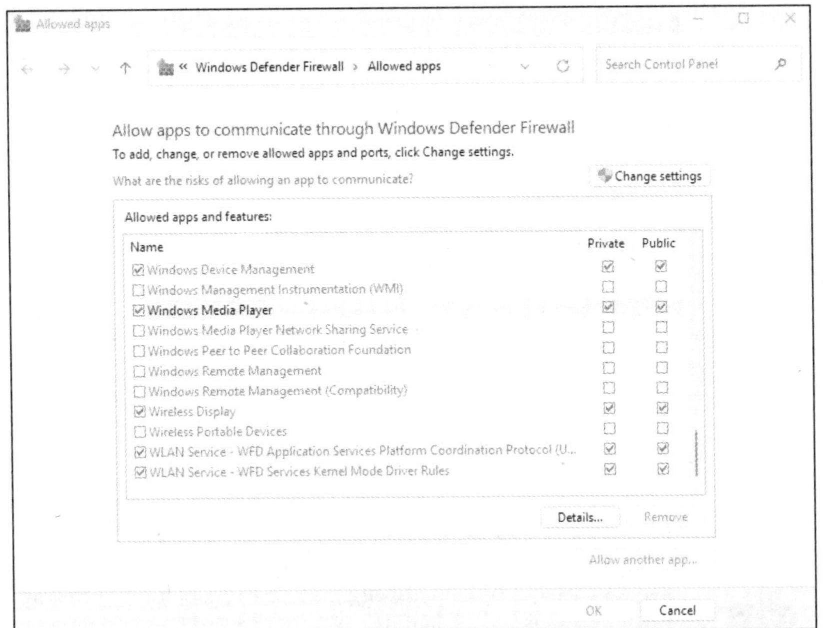

FIGURE 2-13: Allow installed programs to poke through the firewall.

3. **Click or tap Change Settings, and do one of the following:**

   - *If the program that you want to poke through the firewall is listed in the Allow Apps And Features list:* Select the check boxes that correspond to whether you want to allow the unsolicited incoming data when connected to a private network and whether you want to allow the incoming packets when connected to a public network. It's rare indeed that you'd allow access when connected to a public network but not to a private network.
   - *If you can't find the program that you want to poke through the firewall:* You need to go out and look for it. Click or tap the Allow another App button at the bottom and then click or tap Browse.

   Windows Defender Firewall goes out to all common program locations and finally presents you with the Add an App list, as shown in Figure 2-14. The process can take a while.

4. **Browse to the program's location and select it. Then click or tap Open, and then Add.**

   You return to the Windows Defender Firewall Allowed Apps list (refer to Figure 2-13), and your newly selected program is now available.

5. **Select the check boxes to allow your poked-through program to accept incoming data while you're connected to a private or public network. Then click or tap OK.**

   Your program can immediately start receiving inbound data.

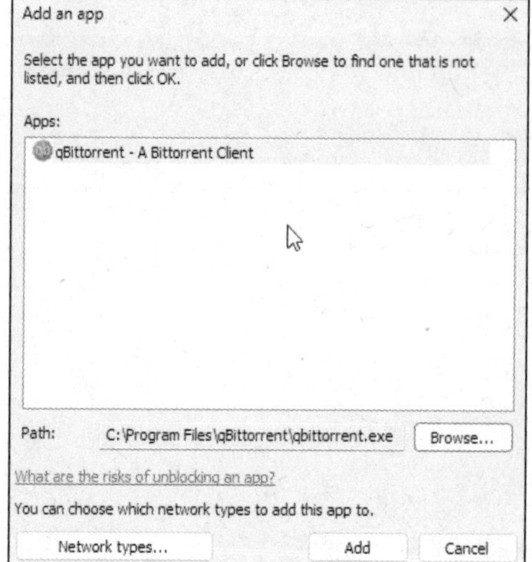

FIGURE 2-14: Allow a program (that you've thoroughly vetted!) to break through the firewall.

TECHNICAL STUFF

In many cases, poking through Windows Defender Firewall doesn't solve the entire problem. You may have to poke through your modem or router as well — unsolicited packets that arrive at the router may get kicked back according to the router's rules, even if Windows 11 would allow them in. Unfortunately, each router and the method for adding rules to the router's inbound firewall differ. Check the site `https://portforward.com/router.htm` for an enormous amount of information about poking through routers.

Booting Securely with UEFI

Starting with Windows 8, Microsoft pulled the industry kicking and screaming out of the BIOS generation of computers and into a far more capable *Unified Extensible Firmware Interface* (UEFI). Although UEFI machines in the time of Windows 7 were unusual, starting with Windows 8, every new machine with a Runs Windows sticker was required to have UEFI; it was part of the licensing requirement. Windows 11 enforces this requirement by refusing to install on non-UEFI systems.

A brief history of the BIOS

Let's take a journey through time to understand where Windows is headed by looking at where it's been. The *BIOS*, or Basic Input/Output System, has been a constant companion inside PCs for over 45 years, spanning the entire history of personal computing. Believe it or not, the first IBM PC had a BIOS that wasn't all that different from the one you might be wrestling with today.

Think of BIOS as your PC's morning routine. When you hit the power button, it springs into action, getting all your computer's hardware in order, booting up Windows, and then handing over the reins to the operating system. It's like a backstage crew that sets up everything before the main show (Windows) takes center stage.

In the early days of computing, operating systems such as DOS relied heavily on BIOS for input and output functions. But modern operating systems, including Windows, have grown up. They now use their own device drivers, making BIOS control largely obsolete once the operating system is up and running.

Every BIOS comes with its own user interface, which looks much like the one in Figure 2-15. You can access it by pressing a specific key during startup. You can then take control over your PC's hardware, select boot devices (in other words, tell BIOS where the operating system is located), overclock the processor, disable or rearrange hard drives, and the like.

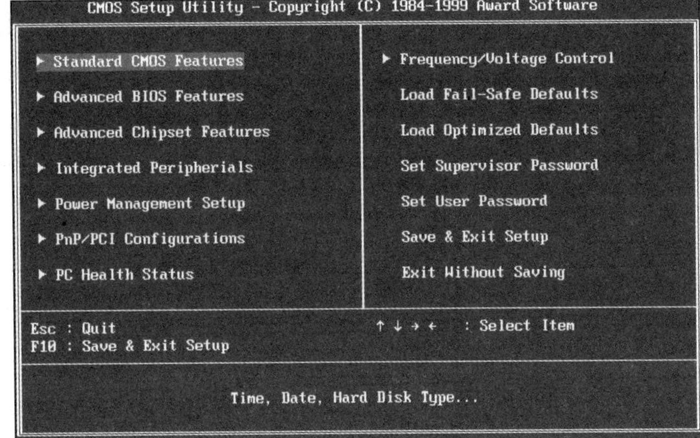

FIGURE 2-15: The classic AwardBIOS Setup Utility.

How UEFI is different from and better than BIOS

BIOS has all sorts of problems, not the least of which is its susceptibility to malware. Rootkits like to hook themselves into the earliest part of the booting process — permitting them to run underneath Windows — and BIOS has a big Kick Me sign on its back.

That's why the BIOS got a super-cool makeover, went to tech college, and became UEFI (Unified Extensible Firmware Interface). It's like BIOS on steroids, and it speaks the language of modern computers, handling bigger hard drives and fancier graphic cards with ease. Plus, it has some nifty security tricks up its sleeve, such as *Secure Boot,* which helps keep nasty malware from sneaking onto your system during startup. Unlike BIOS, which sits inside a chip on your PC's motherboard, UEFI can exist on a disk, just like any other program, or in nonvolatile memory on the motherboard or even on a network share.

In a nutshell, UEFI is very much like an operating system that runs before your final operating system kicks in. It has a slick graphical interface, as shown in Figure 2-16, so you can use your mouse instead of fumbling with keyboard commands. It can even access the internet and download updates straight from its manufacturer. If you've ever played with BIOS, you know that UEFI is in a whole new dimension. Compare Figure 2-15 with Figure 2-16, and you'll have some idea of where the technology has been and where it's heading.

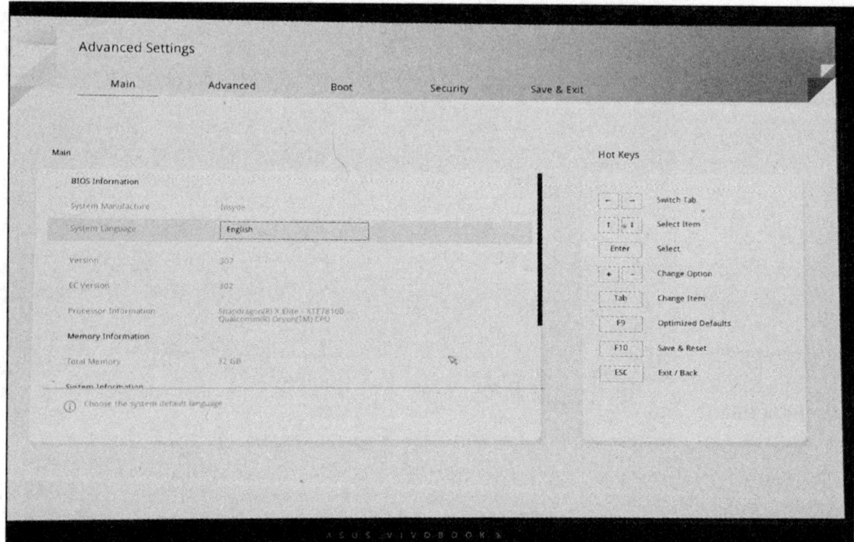

FIGURE 2-16: The UEFI interface on an ASUS Vivobook S 15 Copilot+ PC.

Unlike BIOS, UEFI boots your computer in a flash and acts like a tough bodyguard against malware. UEFI makes it easier to run multiple operating systems and even lets you use your mouse during startup. The coolest part? It can check if an operating system is safe before letting it run. This extra security is great, but it's also sparked some debates about control. Basically, UEFI is trying to make your computer safer and easier to use, but like any new technology, it comes with its own set of pros and cons.

How Windows 11 uses UEFI

I mentioned Secure Boot earlier. It's a feature of UEFI that acts as the security guard for your computer's startup process. When it's turned on, Secure Boot checks whether programs are allowed to run by looking for a special digital signature. This is new for some operating systems, such as Linux, which never needed this before. However, Windows 11 is designed to work with Secure Boot natively, as follows.

UEFI checks the digital signature and then asks Windows Security to double-check it online. This means Windows Security has a say in what operating systems can start on your computer when Secure Boot is on. This has caused some concern, especially for Linux users. They wonder why Microsoft should have any control over whether their chosen operating system can run on a computer.

If you want to use an operating system that doesn't have this special signature on a computer with UEFI Secure Boot, you have two choices:

- You can turn off Secure Boot.
- You can manually add a key to the UEFI validation routine, specifically allowing that unsigned operating system to load.

This new system aims to make computers more secure, but it also means less freedom in some ways for users who like to customize their systems.

TECHNICAL STUFF

Some PCs won't let you turn off Secure Boot. So, if you want to dual boot Windows 11 and some other operating system on a Windows 11-certified computer, you may have lots of hoops to jump through. Check with your hardware manufacturer.

Accessing UEFI from Windows 11

Even though the UEFI is the kind of place where you should rarely indulge in accessing, you may need to do that and adjust settings such as turning on the virtualization features for your processor so that you can run virtual machines or installing UEFI firmware updates for your Windows 11 computer or device. If you need to access the UEFI, close all the apps and files you have open, and follow these steps:

1. **Click or tap the Start icon and then Settings.**

   The Settings app opens.

2. **Go to System and then select Recovery.**

   You see the recovery options shown in Figure 2-17.

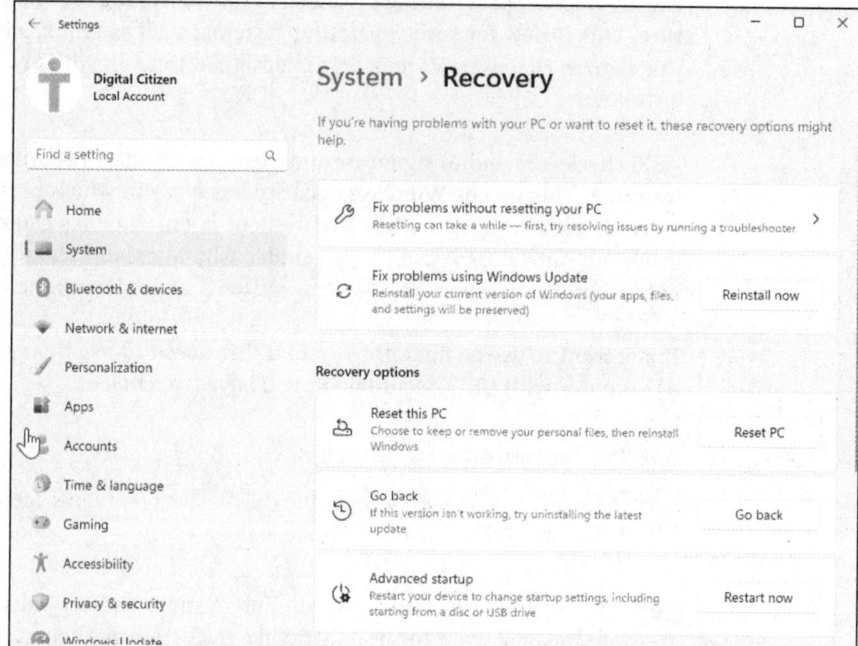

FIGURE 2-17: The Recovery options from Windows 11.

3. **Next to Advanced Startup, click or tap Restart Now twice.**

   Windows 11 reboots and loads a blue screen where it asks you to choose an option.

4. **Click or tap Troubleshoot, followed by Advanced Options.**

   You see the advanced options shown in Figure 2-18.

5. **Choose UEFI Firmware Settings, and then click or tap Restart.**

   After your Windows 11 computer or device reboots, it loads the UEFI interface.

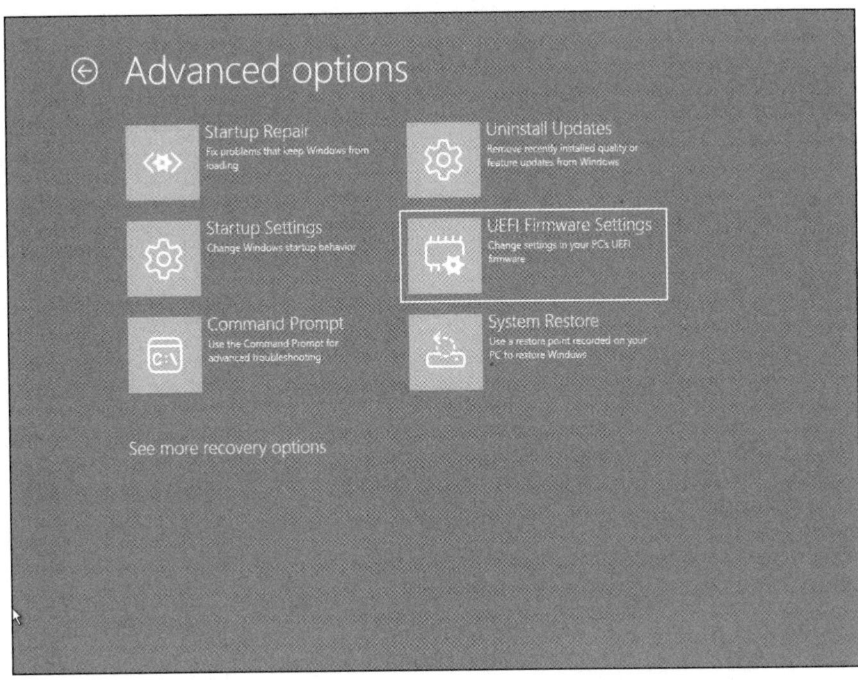

FIGURE 2-18: Accessing UEFI Firmware Settings.

TIP

The UEFI user interface is different from device to device, and it includes various settings. To get help in navigating it successfully, check the user manual for your specific device. It's usually found online in PDF format on the support website of its manufacturer.

IN THIS CHAPTER

» Managing and securing your online passwords

» Securing connections with VPN

» Setting up the use of a proxy server

» Choosing between VPN and proxy

Chapter 3

Protecting Your Passwords and Connections

With the internet touching every aspect of our lives, protecting our online presence has never been more crucial. To help you with this challenge, in this chapter I focus on two key elements of digital security: password management and securing internet connections.

First, I dive into the world of password managers. With countless online accounts to juggle, a robust system for managing passwords is mandatory. Many password managers are available, including some built into your favorite web browser, but I prefer to focus on two services that I like and give you some arguments as to why I appreciate them and why you should consider trying them.

Next, I tackle the vital issue of keeping your online activities private. Whether you're working from an airport lounge, a train, or a local cafe, protecting your data from prying eyes is paramount. That's why I introduce you to Virtual Private Networks (VPNs), explaining how Windows 11 can be set up to use one. I also present some VPN services that prioritize your privacy with strict no-logs policies, offering a shield against unauthorized surveillance.

Lastly, I demystify proxy servers. If you've worked in a corporate environment, you've likely encountered these network intermediaries. But what exactly are they, and do they have a place in your home setup?

By the end of this chapter, you'll have a clear understanding of these essential tools. You'll be equipped to set up VPNs and proxy servers in Windows 11, and you'll have the knowledge to choose the best solution for your needs. Let's get started.

Managing Your Passwords

You've probably heard lots of advice about creating strong passwords using clever tricks and memory aids. But here's a common mistake many people make: re-using passwords on websites they think aren't important. This is a big no-no!

Why is this dangerous? If someone hacks a small website and steals your password (which happens way too often these days), they can then access any other site where you've used that same password. Yikes!

WARNING

Even security experts have fallen for this trap. In recent years, hackers have broken into super-secure systems by stealing usernames and passwords from less important sites and then trying that same combo on high-security sites. This gave them access to top-secret stuff such as sensitive emails or bank account information. The lesson? If the pros can make this mistake, anyone can. Stay safe by using unique passwords for every site!

Using password managers

I don't know about you, but I have dozens of usernames and passwords that I use fairly regularly. There's just no way I can remember them all. And my computer monitor isn't big enough to handle all the yellow sticky notes they'd demand.

TIP

That's where a password manager comes in. A *password manager* keeps track of all your online passwords. It can generate truly random passwords with the click of a button. Most of all, it remembers the username and password necessary to log in to a specific website.

Every time I go to `www.ebay.com`, for example, my password manager fills in my username and password. It does the same for my banking portal, Gmail, `Outlook.com`, Facebook, my company's Google Workspace, and so on. I have to remember the one password for accessing and using the password manager, but after that, everything else gets filled in automatically. It's a huge timesaver.

A password manager won't log into Windows for you, and it won't remember the passwords on documents or spreadsheets. But it does keep track of every online password and autocompletes the passwords you need with no hassle.

My recommendations

Many password management services are available, including ones built into web browsers such as Chrome, Edge, Opera, and Firefox. However, I like and trust two password managers more than others.

The big difference between them? One was originally designed to run on a USB drive; the other has always been in the cloud, which is to say, on the internet:

- **RoboForm** initially could store passwords on your hard drive or on a USB drive. However, this capability has been retired from the free plan, and now this service is based in the cloud, works with all major web browsers, and has simple tools for synchronizing passwords. It's free to use on a single device, and it offers affordable plans for single users and families.
- **Bitwarden,** which stores passwords on its website, uses an encryption technique (AES-256) that guarantees your passwords won't get stolen or cracked. One cool aspect is that it's an open-source platform, and its source code, features, and infrastructure security are vetted and improved by a global community through regular third-party security audits. Most of its features are available for free when it comes to personal accounts, with premium features such as security reports and emergency access available for just $1 a month.

Which one is better? It depends on how you use your computer. If you always use the same computer, you may want the free plan offered by RoboForm. However, if you use many devices and want password management on all of them, a solution like Bitwarden is better. Opinions are all over the place, but I prefer Bitwarden's interface to that of RoboForm. You should feel comfortable using either one.

Rockin' RoboForm

The RoboForm app (`www.roboform.com`) has all the features you need in a password manager. It manages your passwords with excellent recognition of websites, automatically filling in your login details. But it will also generate random passwords for you, if you like, and fill in forms on the web.

RoboForm stores all its data in AES-256 encrypted format, too. If someone steals your RoboForm database, you needn't worry. Without the master key — which only you have — the entire database is unusable.

WHAT IS AES-256?

When it comes to keeping your data safe, AES-256 is the go-to encryption method. AES stands for Advanced Encryption Standard, developed by the US National Institute of Standards and Technology. The 256 refers to the encryption key size in bits, making it incredibly difficult to crack.

What makes AES-256 special is its widespread use and high-level security. It's the first publicly available encryption method trusted by the US National Security Agency for top secret information. It's used in cloud storage services, messaging apps, and even crypto-currency wallets. However, in the world of cybersecurity, nothing is without controversy. Some speculate that since the NSA recommends AES-256, they might have a secret way to decrypt it. But there's no solid evidence to support this claim.

While newer encryption methods are always in development, AES-256 remains the current standard for excellent security.

RoboForm has versions for Windows, Mac, Linux, Chromebook, iPhone, iPad, and Android smartphones and tablets. There's a free plan for one computer or device and paid plans that cover all your devices. There's even a family plan that helps save some money. You can also enjoy a 30-day trial version of RoboForm Premium, so that you can make an informed decision before buying.

RoboForm can read the passwords from any web browser and migrate them over to your RoboForm account, as shown in Figure 3-1.

Liking Bitwarden

Bitwarden (`https://bitwarden.com`) stores everything in the cloud on its company servers. Like RoboForm, Bitwarden keeps track of your user IDs, passwords, automatic form-filling information (think name, address, phone, credit card number), and other settings and offers them to you with a click.

Using Bitwarden can't be simpler. Download and install it, and it'll appear with a blue and white icon in the upper-right corner of your browser (see Figure 3-2).

You don't really need to do anything. Bitwarden will prompt you for the master password when you start using your browser. If Bitwarden is turned off, its icon turns gray. Click or tap it and provide the master password: The Bitwarden icon turns blue, and the service is ready to roll.

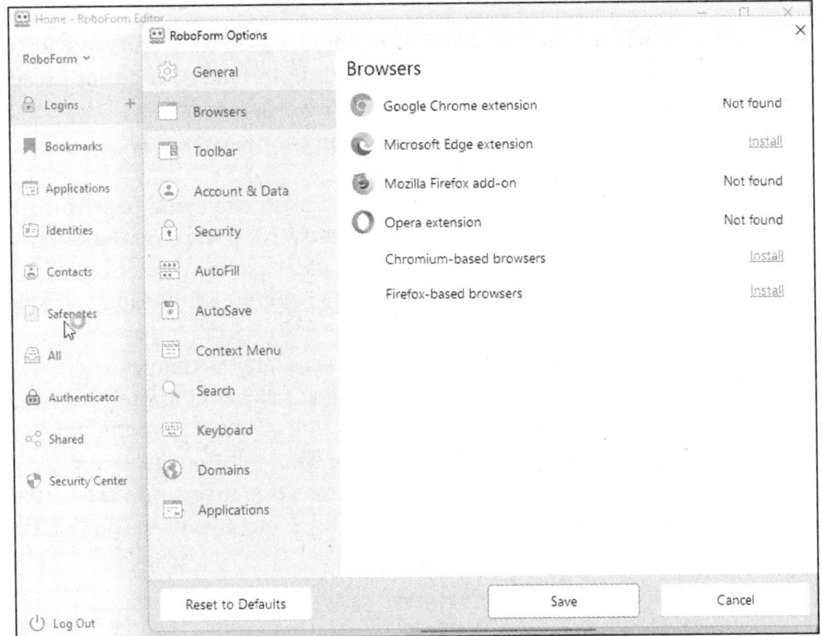

FIGURE 3-1: RoboForm is easy to use and can import passwords from all browsers.

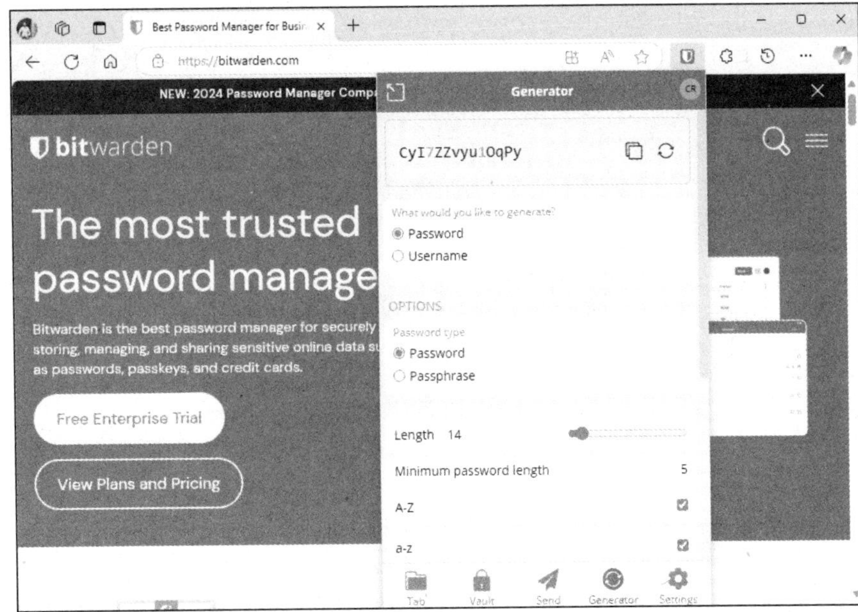

FIGURE 3-2: Bitwarden is on the job if you can see its icon in the upper-right corner.

When you go to a site that requires a username and password, if Bitwarden recognizes the site, it fills them both in for you. If it doesn't recognize the site, you fill in the blanks and click, and Bitwarden remembers the credentials for the next time you surf this way. Form filling works similarly.

Any time you want to look at the usernames and passwords that Bitwarden has squirreled away, click or tap the Bitwarden icon. You have a chance to look at your *vault* — which is your password database — or look up recently used passwords and much more. You can even keep encrypted notes to yourself.

TIP

You can maintain two (or more) separate usernames and passwords for any specific site — for example, if you log in to a banking site with two different accounts. If Bitwarden has more than one set of credentials stored for a specific site, it takes its best guess as to which one you want but then gives you the option of using one of the others. In Figure 3-3, I have several separate credentials for the site, and Bitwarden allows me to choose which one I want to use this time.

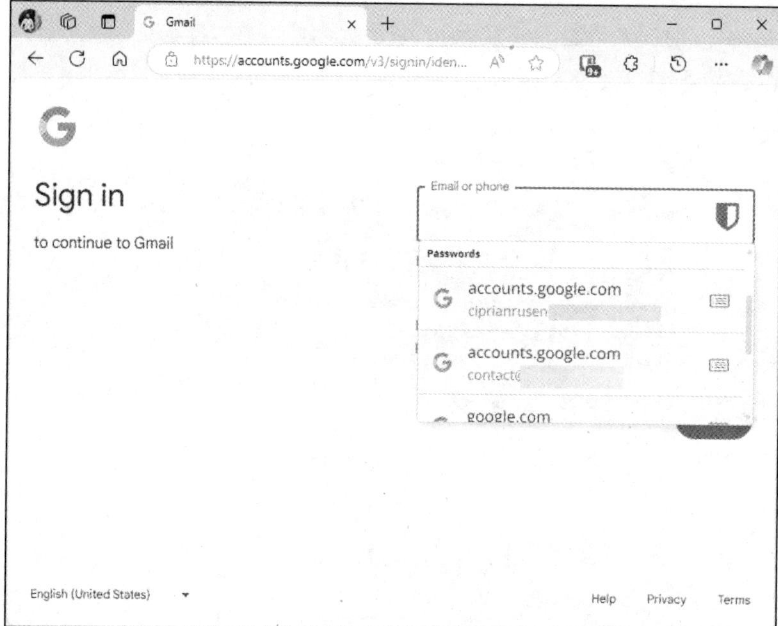

FIGURE 3-3: Bitwarden displays all the accounts you use on a website and allows you to choose.

REMEMBER

Bitwarden's approach to safeguarding your data is ingenious. It uses AES-256 encryption to protect all your passwords. But here's the clever part: The encryption and decryption happen right on your device, not on Bitwarden's servers. What does this mean for you? Your master password, the key to your digital kingdom, stays with you and you alone. Even if hackers managed to break into Bitwarden's servers, all they'd get is a jumble of encrypted data — about as useful as a pile of digital confetti.

But Bitwarden isn't just for passwords. It's a secure vault for all your sensitive information. You can store secure notes for private thoughts or important information, form-filling data to speed up online shopping, credit card details for quick and secure payments, addresses, and other personal information.

For those who like their security on the go, Bitwarden offers a portable USB app. You can download this Portable App for Flash Drives from their website, allowing you to carry your encrypted vault with you wherever you go. It's like having a high-tech secret agent briefcase, but it fits in your pocket!

Remember, while Bitwarden provides top-notch security for your passwords, the strength of your master password is crucial. Make it long, complex, and unique — it's the guardian of all your other passwords.

Bitwarden is free for individual use, and it works on all major PC and mobile platforms. If you want some advanced features such as file attachments or emergency access, you need the Premium edition, which costs $10 a year.

Securing Your Communication with VPN

Protecting your online privacy, especially when connected to public Wi-Fi like those found in cafes, airports, or train stations, is crucial in today's digital world. While networks using WPA2 or WPA3 encryption (typically password protected) offer relatively good security, public hotspots without passwords leave your data vulnerable. To defend against sniffing and other kinds of threats, consider using a Virtual Private Network (VPN). A VPN creates a secure, encrypted tunnel for your internet traffic, safeguarding your data even on unsecured networks. For Windows 11 users, setting up a VPN is a straightforward process that provides a valuable layer of protection. And, if you have a Microsoft 365 subscription and are based in the US, UK, Germany, or Canada, you get a VPN service included with your subscription straight from Microsoft.

What's a VPN?

VPN started as a way for big companies to securely connect PCs over the regular phone network. It used to take lots of specialty hardware, but if you worked for a bank and had to get into the bank's main computers from a laptop in another country, VPN was the only choice. Times have changed. Now, you can get free or low-cost VPN connections that don't require any special hardware on your end, and they work surprisingly well.

When you set up a VPN connection with a server, you create a secure tunnel between your PC and the server. The tunnel encrypts all the data flowing between your PC and the server, provides integrity checks so no data gets scrambled, and continuously looks to make sure no other computer has taken over the connection.

VPNs prevent sidejacking because the connection between your PC and the wireless access point runs inside the tunnel: A sniffer can see the data going by but can't decipher what it means. VPNs do much more than block sniffing attacks: They provide complete end-to-end security, so nobody — not even your internet service provider — can snoop on your communication or look to see if you're using a service such as BitTorrent. If you're traveling in a country subject to governmental eavesdropping, a VPN is necessary. However, keep in mind that some countries, such as Russia, China, and Turkey, have banned people from using state-unapproved VPN services.

With a VPN, data goes into the tunnel from your PC, out of the tunnel at the VPN server, to whatever location you're accessing, back into the VPN server, and out at your PC. The people running the VPN server can match you up with your data stream, but nobody else can.

Setting up a VPN in Windows 11

You can set up your wireless router to work as a VPN server and connect to it from anywhere on the internet so that you remain protected. Or maybe your workplace has set up a VPN server for you to connect to directly from Windows, so it's easier to access the company's apps and internal websites. No matter the situation you're in, all you need is the domain name or the IP address of the VPN server, a username, and a password, and you can connect to that VPN server directly from Windows.

Here's how to add a VPN to Windows 11 and how to connect to it:

1. **Click or tap the Start icon and then Settings (or press Windows+I).**

   The Settings app is shown.

2. **On the left, choose Network & Internet. Then on the right, click or tap VPN.**

   The VPN settings appear, as shown in Figure 3-4.

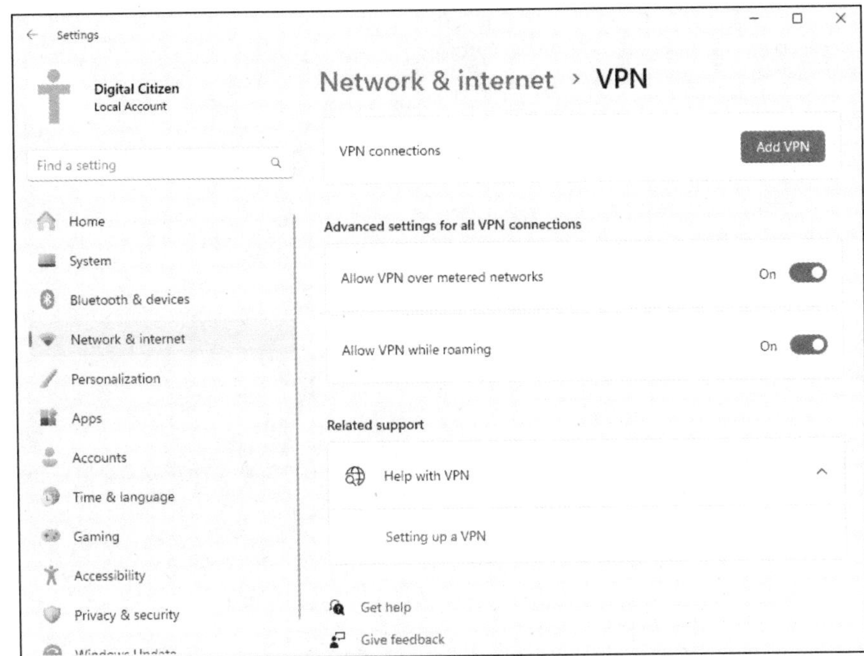

FIGURE 3-4: Windows 11 can manage VPN connections with ease.

3. **Click or tap the Add VPN button.**

   The Add a VPN Connection dialog opens, as shown in Figure 3-5.

4. **Under VPN Provider, choose Windows (Built-In).**
5. **Under Connection Name, enter a descriptive name for your VPN connection.**
6. **Type the IP address or the name of the VPN server (something like `vpnserver.dummies.com`).**
7. **Choose the VPN type, and then type the username and password.**
8. **Don't forget to select the box for Remember My Sign-In Info, and then click or tap Save.**

   The VPN connection is added under the Add VPN button.

9. **Click or tap the Connect button next to the VPN connection.**

   If your internet connection and the VPN server are working, you should be connected in a matter of seconds.

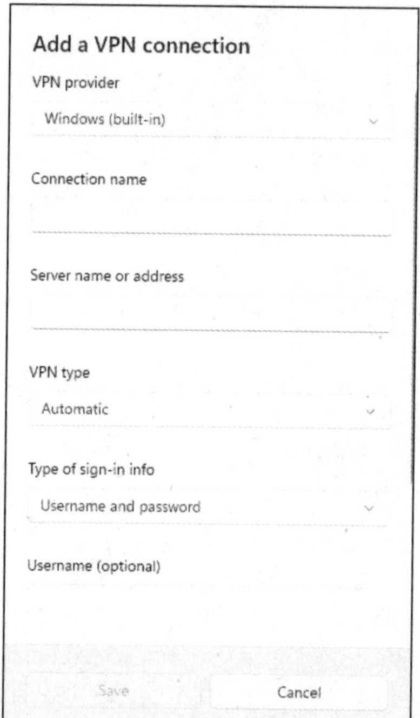

FIGURE 3-5: Add the details of your VPN connection.

Which paid VPN services should you consider?

If you want a VPN that offers useful features such as no logs of your activities, super-strong encryption, and the option to unlock services you don't normally have access to (such as watching Netflix and its entire USA portfolio, using your computer from the UK, Italy, or some other country), consider the following paid services:

- **NordVPN (`https://nordvpn.com`):** This is one of the fastest and best-rated VPN services on the internet. It offers a strict no-logs policy and easy-to-use VPN apps for all platforms, including Windows.
- **CyberGhost (`www.cyberghostvpn.com`):** Another fast service, CyberGhost also blocks ads while you browse the web. One aspect that makes it stand out from other VPN services is that it has one of the largest server networks.
- **Surfshark (`https://surfshark.com`):** Alongside its no-logs policy and easy-to-use apps, it also includes an antivirus engine that protects you while connected to its VPN servers.

TIP

All these services have free trials, so you can try them out before subscribing. Also, if you don't like the current price, subscribe to their email newsletter. In a few weeks, you're sure to receive an email with a discount offer. The competition is tough between VPN services, so discounts occur frequently.

Setting Up a Proxy Server

In the world of corporate networks, you might encounter something called a *proxy server*. Think of it as a digital middleman between your PC and the internet. When you want to visit a website, instead of your request going directly to that site, it first stops at the proxy server.

Here's how it works in practice: Let's say you're at work and want to visit `www.dummies.com`. You type the address in your browser, but instead of going straight to Dummies, your request takes a detour. It goes to the proxy server first, which then forwards the request to Dummies on your behalf. When Dummies sends back its home page, it goes to the proxy server, which then passes it along to you. If the proxy server already has the data (because another co-worker has recently visited the same website), it simply returns it to you, without forwarding the request to Dummies.

An interesting side effect of this process is that from the perspective of `www.dummies.com`, it looks like the proxy server is the one visiting the site, not your individual computer. This can add a layer of anonymity to your web browsing.

Proxy servers are common in corporate settings and can serve various purposes, from improving security to managing network traffic.

Windows 11 offers support for using proxy servers. When used on laptops inside corporate networks, it can even autodetect whether it should use a proxy server or not, depending on how the company network is configured by its administrators. However, if you need a more manual setup, you can enable Windows 11 to use a setup script for the proxy server or even use a manual proxy setup, like this:

1. **Click or tap the Start icon and then Settings. Alternatively, press Windows+I.**

   The Settings app opens.

2. **On the left, choose Network & Internet. Then on the right, choose Proxy.**

   The Proxy settings appear, as shown in Figure 3-6.

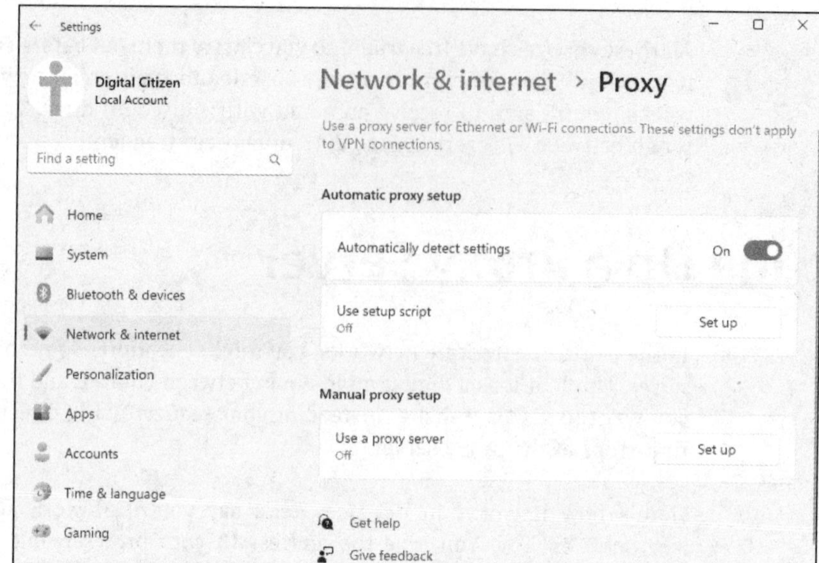

FIGURE 3-6: Windows 11 has built-in support for using proxy servers.

3. **If you're working in a large organization, it is always a good idea to click or tap the Automatically Detect Settings switch and turn it on.**

   This will enable Windows 11 to automatically read the appropriate proxy server settings and use them without you doing anything else.

4. **If you want to use a script, click or tap Set Up, next to Use Setup Script.**

   The Edit Setup Script dialog shown in Figure 3-7 appears.

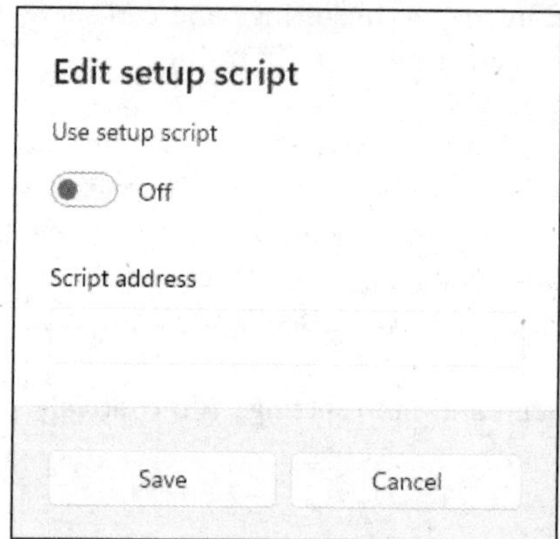

FIGURE 3-7: Adding a proxy setup script.

5. **Set the Use Setup Script switch on, enter the script address, and click or tap Save.**

6. **If you want to manually enter the proxy server details, click or tap Set Up, next to Use a Proxy Server.**

   You see the Edit Proxy Server dialog from Figure 3-8.

Edit proxy server
Use a proxy server
Off
Proxy IP address
Port
Use the proxy server except for addresses that start with the following entries. Use semicolons (;) to separate entries.
Don't use the proxy server for local (intranet) addresses
Save
Cancel

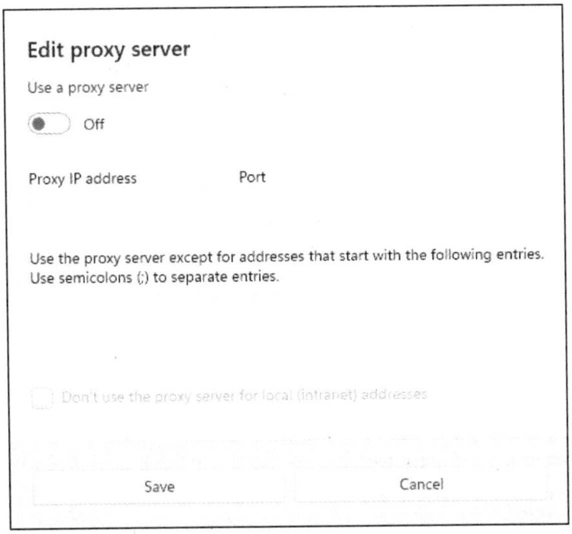

FIGURE 3-8: Manually setting up a proxy server in Windows 11.

7. **Click or tap the Use a Proxy Server switch to enable it.**

8. **Enter the IP address of the proxy server and the port required for connecting to it.**

9. **When you're done setting things up, click or tap Save.**

After you set up your proxy server in Windows 11, all the major web browsers (Microsoft Edge, Google Chrome, Opera, and so on) are usually set by default to use the proxy settings of the operating system. Therefore, they'll automatically use the proxy set by you to browse the web.

TIP

If you take your laptop from work elsewhere and the connection to the proxy server doesn't work anymore, you can disable it by repeating the same steps and setting the switches you turned on back to off.

Proxy versus VPN: Choosing Your Privacy Tool!

Some people wonder whether they should use a proxy server or a VPN. While these technologies share some similarities, they have key differences, and VPNs are the superior choice for most users.

Proxy servers can mask your computer's IP address and location, offering basic protection for web browsing. However, they don't encrypt your internet traffic, leaving you vulnerable to eavesdropping.

VPNs, on the other hand, provide stronger anonymity and security. They encrypt all your internet activity, shielding it from prying eyes. The only entity that could potentially see your online actions is your VPN provider itself.

The main drawback of VPNs is their higher cost compared to proxy servers. If you need to hide only your IP address or location from websites doing basic checks, a proxy might suffice. But for true anonymity, security, and confidentiality, a VPN is the way to go.

When choosing a VPN, ensure that it has a no-logs policy and doesn't share data with third parties. This extra step guarantees your privacy remains intact.

Finally, if you're wondering whether you can use a proxy and a VPN together, at the same time, the answer is yes. However, it's not something I recommend because the VPN already does the proxy's job while also encrypting your traffic. Furthermore, even if you might be tempted to think that a proxy server is faster than a VPN, if you use both, the internet speed you get is the one of the slower service: either that of your proxy or that of your VPN.

10

Enhancing Windows

Contents at a Glance

IN THIS CHAPTER

» Connecting your Android phone to your Windows 11 PC

» Linking your Android smartphone with Phone Link

» Using Phone Link to interact with your smartphone

» Using your phone as a webcam for your PC

Chapter 1
Linking Android to Windows

We all know the saying: If you can't beat them, join them! Well, that's exactly what Microsoft did: It lost the mobile war, stopped developing Windows Phone, and decided to integrate itself into the mobile ecosystem that beat it: Android. Microsoft partnered with Samsung, the world's biggest manufacturer of Android devices, and made a tight-knit integration with its ecosystem. As a result, owners of Samsung devices get Microsoft's OneDrive, Office, and Phone Link apps preinstalled by default. What's Phone Link, you ask? Well, it's how Microsoft wants you to link your mobile devices with your Windows ones.

Phone Link enables you to pair an Android smartphone with a Windows 11 PC and access the smartphone from your PC, with a mouse and keyboard. If that sounds cool to you, read this chapter. In it, I explore how to connect your Android smartphone to Windows 11 computers, add it to Phone Link, and interact with it from Windows 11.

Lastly, in this brave new world of hybrid work environments, not everyone has a webcam. One smart way to fix this problem is to use your smartphone as a webcam for your Windows 11 PC. In this chapter, you learn how to set it up.

If you're an iPhone user, you can skip this chapter and go straight to the next one, which shows you how to integrate your iPhone with Windows 11.

Connecting Your Android Device to a PC

If you're trying to get your Android smartphone or tablet to interact with your Windows 11 PC, you need to know several tricks.

First, take the USB charging cable you're using for your device and plug it into your computer and your device. Most Android devices can connect to a USB port. Chances are good that Windows 11 will recognize the device and install a driver for it. On your smartphone, you may be asked to choose how you want to use the USB connection you just established, as shown in Figure 1-1. Choose to use it to transfer files.

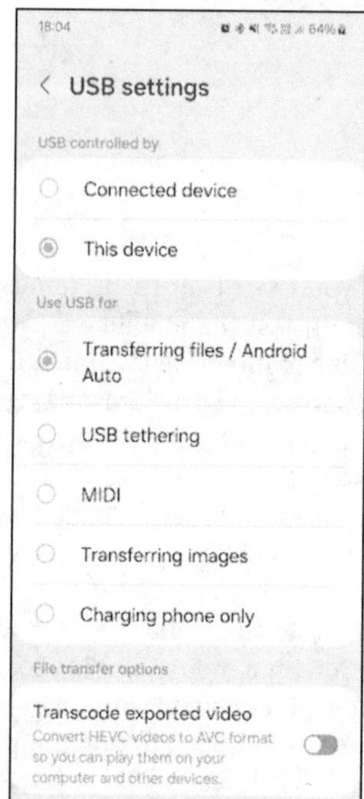

FIGURE 1-1: On your Android phone, select that you want to transfer files.

Then, Windows 11 should display an AutoPlay notification, as shown in Figure 1-2. Click or tap it, and you see several options for actions you can perform: importing photos and videos, synchronizing digital media, and opening the device to view files.

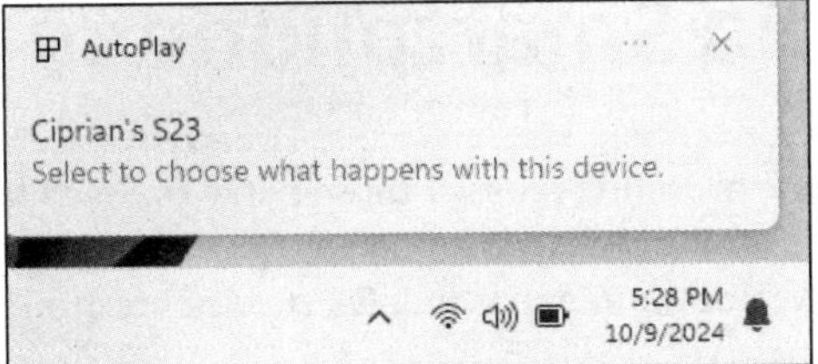

FIGURE 1-2: Windows 11 automatically detects Android devices and installs the appropriate drivers.

You can access all the files on the Android device through File Explorer. The Android device appears in File Explorer's This PC section. Depending on the device you attached, you'll see one or two folders: Internal Storage or Phone is for the phone or tablet itself, and SD Card is for any additional storage you have on the device. On my Samsung Galaxy S23 smartphone, the pictures I took with my phone are in the folder \Phone\DCIM\Camera, as shown in Figure 1-3. The path should be similar on your smartphone.

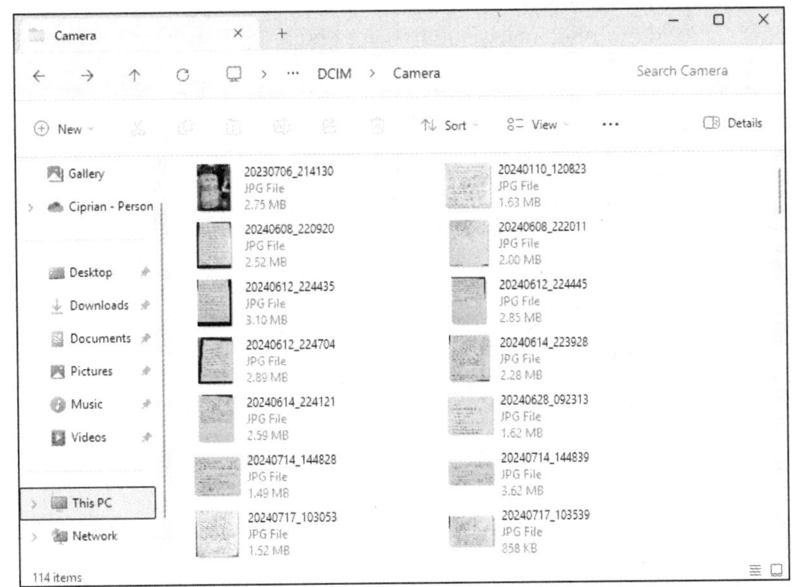

FIGURE 1-3: If the Android device installs properly, you can access the files on it through File Explorer.

From File Explorer, you can cut or copy files, moving them to your PC. Read Book 3, Chapter 4 to learn more about working with File Explorer.

Linking an Android Smartphone to a PC

Many Android devices, including most of those made by Samsung, HONOR, OPPO, ASUS, and Vivo, come with a Link to Windows app preinstalled, which allows them to easily connect to Windows 10 and Windows 11 computers and devices.

On the other hand, Windows 11 also has a Phone Link app preinstalled. When you install Windows 11, the setup wizard asks you to link your smartphone with your PC by using the Phone Link app. Most users, myself included, want to finish their Windows 11 installation sooner rather than later, so they choose to skip this step. Luckily, you can link your phone later from Settings, using the same Phone Link app.

Phone Link displays notifications from your Android device and allows you to respond to messages from your computer, make calls, and access the photos from your mobile device. You can also launch Android apps from Windows 11 and use them on your computer. If you do your work both on your Windows 11 laptop and Android smartphone, using Phone Link may be a great idea to enhance your productivity.

Before using Phone Link, you must link your Android smartphone with your Windows 11 PC, by following these steps:

1. **Click or tap the Start icon, followed by Settings.**
2. **In the Settings app, go to Bluetooth & Devices. On the right, select Mobile Devices.**

   You see the options shown in Figure 1-4.
3. **Click or tap to turn on the Phone Link switch.**

   The Phone Link window opens, asking you to choose your device to get started.
4. **Choose Android, followed by your Microsoft account, and then click or tap Continue.**

   Windows Security verifies your identity. You're asked to authenticate using your PIN, Windows Hello face, or fingerprint recognition, depending on how you set up your Windows 11 computer.
5. **Verify your identity using the options given by Windows Security.**

   You are asked to link the mobile device to your account and shown a QR code to scan on your mobile device, as shown in Figure 1-5.

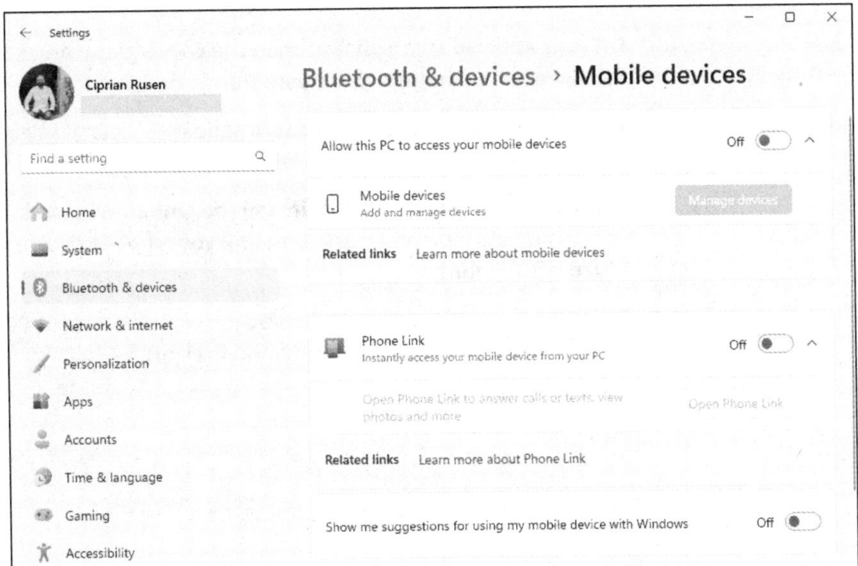

FIGURE 1-4: Starting the phone link is done from the Settings app.

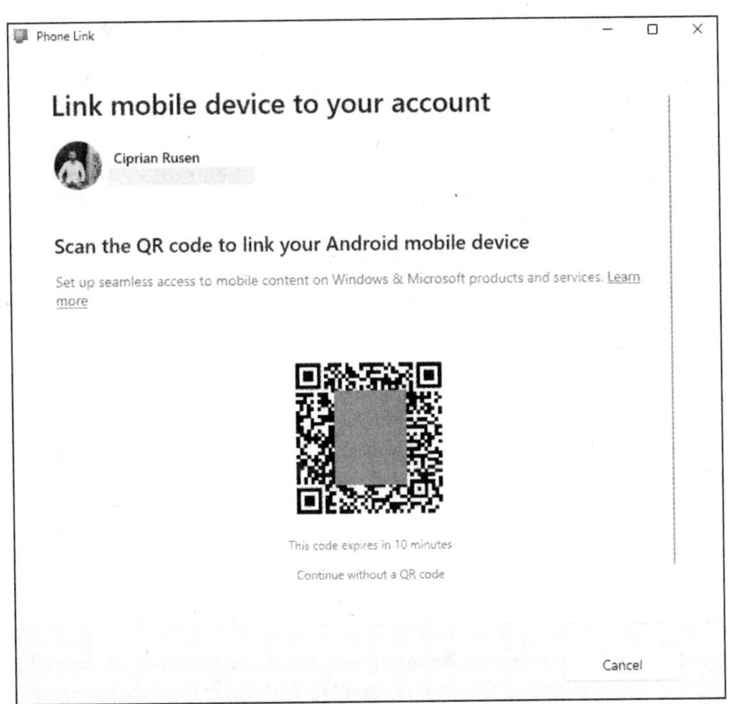

FIGURE 1-5: Scan the QR code with your phone and follow the instructions closely.

6. **On your Android smartphone, open the Camera app and scan the QR code shown by Phone Link on your PC.**

   On some smartphones, such as those made by Google or Motorola, you're asked to install the Link to Windows app.

7. **On your Android smartphone, install the Link to Windows app (if necessary). Tap Continue when asked to link your mobile device to your Microsoft account.**

   You're asked to enter the code shown by Phone Link on your PC. The code should have a format like the one shown in Figure 1-6.

FIGURE 1-6: Type the code on your Android smartphone.

8. **On your Android smartphone, type the code and tap Continue.**

   You're asked to enter the password for your Microsoft account.

9. **On your Android smartphone, type the account password and sign in. If two-step verification is enabled for your Microsoft account, perform the necessary actions to confirm your identity.**

   You're asked to allow Link to Windows to do all kinds of things, such as view your SMS messages, manage your calls, take pictures, or record videos. For this feature to work well, you must allow it to do everything it asks.

10. **On your Android smartphone, provide all the necessary permissions and tap Done.**

    On your PC, Phone Link confirms that everything is set.

11. **On your Windows 11 PC, click or tap Continue.**

    On your PC, you see the Phone Link window, displaying the welcome message shown in Figure 1-7.

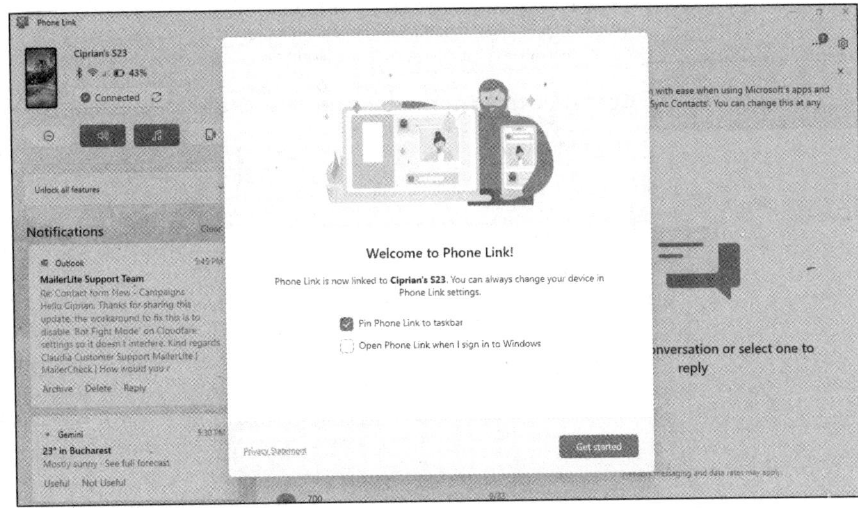

FIGURE 1-7: The Phone Link app is ready.

12. **On your Windows 11 PC, choose either Pin Phone Link to Taskbar or Open Phone Link When I Sign In to Windows.**

13. **Click or tap Get Started, and then follow the steps in the welcome dialog.**

    You can finally start using Phone Link to interact with your smartphone from your PC. At first, it may ask for more permissions before you can use it fully. Give it the necessary permissions for the features you want to have access to.

REMEMBER

To use the Phone Link app, you must use the same Microsoft account on your Windows 11 PC and Android smartphone. Also, if you want to take calls from your PC, Bluetooth discovery must be enabled on your smartphone and PC.

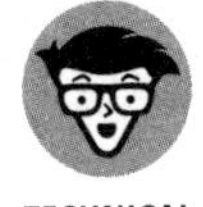

TECHNICAL STUFF

Some features, such as the capability to run apps from your smartphone on your PC, are not available on all Android devices. They work only with some smartphones made by Samsung, Microsoft, HONOR, OPPO, ASUS, and Vivo.

Using the Phone Link app

The user interface of the Phone Link app is easy to understand. On the left, you have the name of your phone and icons for activating or deactivating different phone features, like Do Not Disturb mode and the volume. Below them, you see your most recent notifications, while on the top right you have tabs for accessing your messages, calls, apps, and photos. Let's take a brief tour of the Phone Link app to get yourself acquainted with it:

1. **Click or tap the Start icon, followed by All.**

   You see the list of apps available on your Windows 11 computer or device.

2. **Scroll down to Phone Link and click or tap its shortcut.**

   The Phone Link app opens, as shown in Figure 1-8.

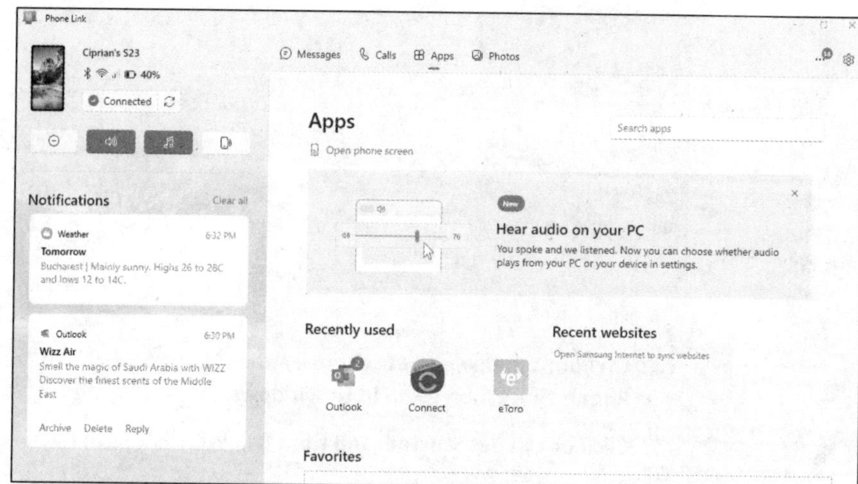

FIGURE 1-8: Phone Link is easy to use, but it may request additional permissions from you.

3. **If you see a notification on the left side of the Phone Link app, click or tap it. If necessary, unlock your Android smartphone.**

   The app that sent that notification appears on your Windows 11 PC. Now you can use the app as if you were on your smartphone, but from your PC.

4. **Close the mobile app you've just opened by clicking or tapping the X icon on its top-right corner.**

   Note how the notification is cleared from the Notifications section in Phone Link.

5. **Click or tap Messages (at the top of the screen) and check the messages you recently received on your smartphone.**

6. **Click or tap Calls and check who has called you recently.**

   If this is the first time you've accessed this section in Phone Link, you may be asked to pair your PC with your smartphone via Bluetooth.

7. **Follow the instructions given by Phone Link to use its calling capabilities.**
8. **Click or tap Apps and scroll through the apps available on your phone.**

   Remember that this option appears only if your smartphone supports Windows running its apps.

   Any app can be opened with a click or tap, and then by unlocking your smartphone. Some apps may require you to perform additional steps.

9. **Click or tap Photos and scroll down through the recent pictures you've taken with your phone.**

   You can open any picture from your smartphone, copy it, save it to your computer, share it with others, or delete it.

10. **When you're done using Phone Link, click or tap X on its top-right corner to close it.**

While you use the different features of the Phone Link app in Windows 11, you'll notice that it needs even more permissions than the ones you've given it during the initial link. If you want to use it fully, follow the instructions you get from the app and give it all the permissions it needs on your Android smartphone. These may vary depending on your phone and the specific thing you're trying to do.

REMEMBER

The features you get vary from phone to phone. For example, only owners of select Samsung, Microsoft, HONOR, OPPO, ASUS, and Vivo smartphones can run Android apps with Phone Link. If you have a smartphone from Motorola, Google, or another vendor, you're out of luck: No running Android apps for you. Furthermore, you can't run Android apps unless your smartphone is unlocked.

Disabling Phone Link

If you tried the Phone Link app but decide you dislike it, here's how to stop using it and disable its automatic link between your computer and your smartphone:

1. **On your Windows 11 PC, click or tap the Start icon and then Settings.**
2. **On the left, click or tap Bluetooth & Devices. On the right, select Mobile Devices.**

   You see the options shown previously in Figure 1-4.

3. **Click or tap the switch next to Phone Link off.**

4. **On your Android smartphone, open Settings.**
5. **Search for Link to Windows and set this feature off.**
6. **Close the Settings apps both on your Android smartphone and your Windows 11 PC.**

   The next time you open Phone Link on your PC, you must redo the link between your Android smartphone and your Windows 11 PC.

TIP

If your smartphone is not made by Samsung, Microsoft, HONOR, OPPO, ASUS, or Vivo, skip Steps 4 to 6. Instead, uninstall the Link to Windows app from your smartphone and close the Settings app on your Windows 11 PC.

TIP

On Samsung Galaxy smartphones, Link to Windows is found by going to Settings and then to Connected Devices. On phones from other brands, this feature is placed in a different location of the Settings app.

Managing Mobile Devices from Windows 11

After you add a smartphone to Phone Link, you can set Windows 11 so that you can manage your mobile device straight from your computer and enable or disable additional capabilities. Here's how it works:

1. **On your Windows 11 PC, click or tap the Start icon and then Settings.**
2. **On the left, choose Bluetooth & Devices. On the right, select Mobile Devices.**

   You see the options shown previously in Figure 1-4.
3. **Click or tap the switch next to Allow This PC to Access Your Mobile Devices to turn it on.**

   The Manage Mobile Devices window shown in Figure 1-9 opens. Here you see the smartphones you've connected to with Phone Link.
4. **Click or tap the switch next to your phone's name and set it to Enabled, so that you can manage that device from your Windows 11 PC.**

   You then see switches for enabling or disabling features such as using the phone as a connected camera for your PC and getting notifications when new pictures are found on your smartphone.

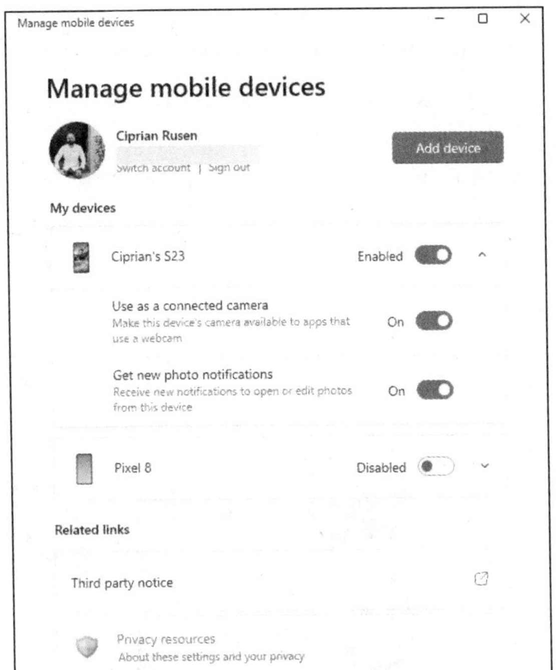

FIGURE 1-9: Enabling Windows 11 to manage your mobile devices.

5. **If you need to use your smartphone as a webcam for your PC, click or tap to enable the Use As a Connected Camera switch.**
6. **Click or tap X in the top-right corner of the Manage Mobile Devices window to close it.**

Now you can use your smartphone as a webcam for your PC. Keep reading to learn how it works.

Turning Your Android Smartphone into a PC Webcam

You can use your Android smartphone as a webcam for your PC. You can even switch between the cameras on your phone (front or back) and add visual effects to your video stream. Here's how:

1. **On your Windows 11 PC, click or tap the Start icon and then Settings.**
2. **On the left, choose Bluetooth & Devices. On the right, select Cameras.**

   You see the list of cameras connected to your computer. You should have at least one with your phone's name.

3. **Under Connected Cameras, click or tap the name of your smartphone.**

   You see the properties of your phone's camera and a new pop-up window with your phone's name.

4. **Unlock your smartphone to start the video, as shown in Figure 1-10.**

   The pop-up window presents you with options for switching between the front and back cameras on your phone and for pausing and resuming the video footage.

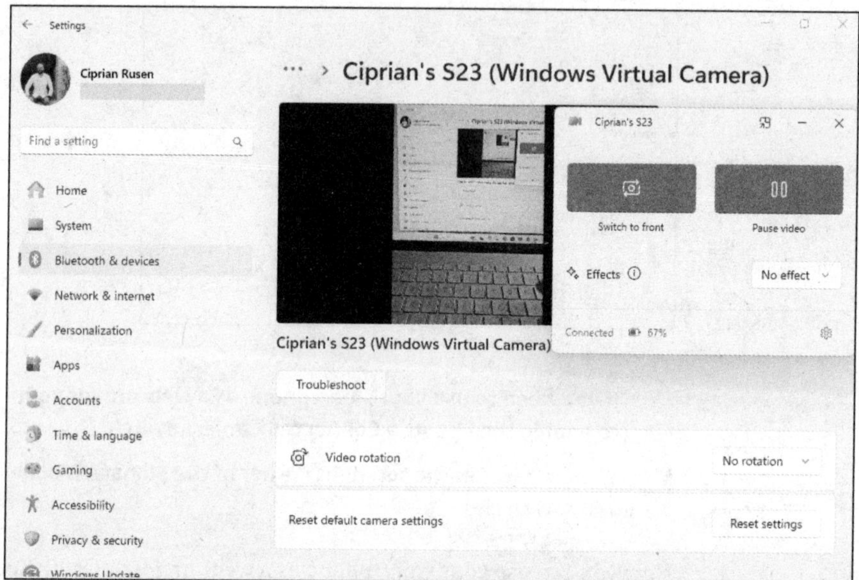

FIGURE 1-10: Setting up your phone as a webcam for your PC.

5. **Arrange your smartphone in the position you want and start the app where you want to use it as a webcam (such as Teams, Zoom, or Skype).**

   Work with the selected app as you normally would. Enjoy using your smartphone as a webcam.

IN THIS CHAPTER

» Connecting your iPhone to your PC

» Setting up Phone Link with your iPhone

» Using Phone Link

» Installing iCloud to sync your data

Chapter 2

Using Your iPhone with Windows

Many people own an iPhone, an iPad, or both, and love using them. However, they may also have a Windows laptop or PC rather than a Mac. If that's the case for you, you may be interested in making your Apple and Windows devices work together and sync pictures and videos.

Unfortunately, the integration offered by Microsoft and Apple is not nearly as good as that of Microsoft and Android, at least not when using the Phone Link app. However, you can still use it to access your messages and receive calls, but you can't run iPhone apps from Windows through Phone Link.

Another issue is that you can't access your iPhone or iPad files from File Explorer, at least not at the level you do with Android devices. To import your pictures and videos to your PC, you must use the Photos app from Windows 11 or iCloud.

In this chapter, I share the basics about connecting your iPhone to a Windows 11 PC, setting it up with Phone Link, and installing iCloud to access the stuff you want from your iPhone or iPad from Windows.

APPLE'S WALLED GARDEN VERSUS ANDROID

When you deal with iPhones and iPads (as well as the iCloud, Macs, AirPods, and all those other iThingies), you're living in a walled garden. Apple controls this garden from beginning to end. That's one of the reasons why all the different Apple devices work together so well — the hardware and software come from the same company, and they're designed to fit together. But you pay for the privilege.

On the other hand, Android devices come from a huge array of manufacturers, many with different ideas about what makes a good user experience. Although Google is in the driver's seat, hardware manufacturers are free to take Android in any direction they like. That's why your experience with Samsung differs from the one with Xiaomi, Motorola, or OnePlus.

Android is an open-source project led by Google. However, Google's services (Maps, Gmail, Google Photos, and so on) are not. They're closed, just like Apple's.

Connecting Your iPhone to a PC

While you can connect your iPhone to a Windows 11 PC using your USB-C or Lightning-to-USB cable (depending on your iPhone version), you can't do as many things as when you connect an Android phone. Even so, there's a benefit to establishing a connection between the iPhone and Windows 11 PC. First, connecting the two devices allows your iPhone to charge from your PC. Then, on your iPhone, you're asked whether you want your PC to access your photos and videos, as shown in Figure 2-1. Tap Allow if you want that.

FIGURE 2-1: On your iPhone, allow your PC to access your photos and videos.

Next, on your Windows 11 PC, you see the AutoPlay notification from Figure 2-2, which asks what you want to do with your iPhone. Click or tap this notification, and you see a list of possible actions: importing photos and videos using OneDrive or the Photos app, opening the device to view files, and doing nothing.

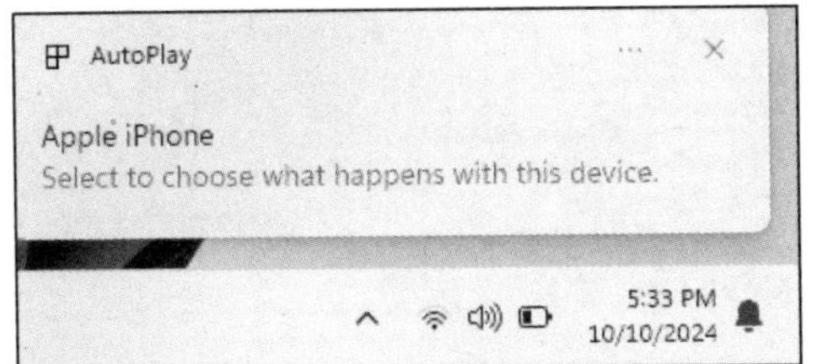

FIGURE 2-2: Windows 11 automatically detects your iPhone and installs the appropriate drivers.

After connecting the two devices, your iPhone appears in File Explorer's This PC section. You'll likely see Apple iPhone as its device name. If you open it, you can view its internal storage, where pictures and videos are organized in folders by the date when they were taken or recorded. If you browse the photos and videos on your iPhone with File Explorer, you'll likely encounter error messages like "Can't read from the source file or disk" or "Error 0x8007065D: Data supplied is of wrong type." This happens because iPhones use a proprietary high-efficiency format for storing pictures and videos, which isn't very compatible with operating systems from companies other than Apple.

REMEMBER

Don't use File Explorer to copy or move your photos and videos from your iPhone to your PC. Instead, use the Photos app in Windows 11 (read Book 4, Chapter 4) to import them, so they can be converted automatically to a format that works well with Windows. Alternatively, you can open the Microsoft Store, look for and install iCloud, and use it to synchronize your pictures and videos between your iPhone and Windows. I share how it's done at the end of this chapter.

Linking an iPhone to a PC

Phone Link works with iPhones, but it has fewer features than when using Android smartphones. However, this doesn't mean Phone Link can't be useful to some people. If you decide to use it, Phone Link displays notifications from your iPhone and allows you to respond to messages from your computer, and receive or initiate calls.

To use Phone Link, you must first link your iPhone with your Windows 11 computer, like this:

1. **Click or tap the Start icon and then Settings.**
2. **In the Settings app, go to Bluetooth & Devices. On the right, select Mobile Devices.**

   You see the options shown in Figure 2-3.

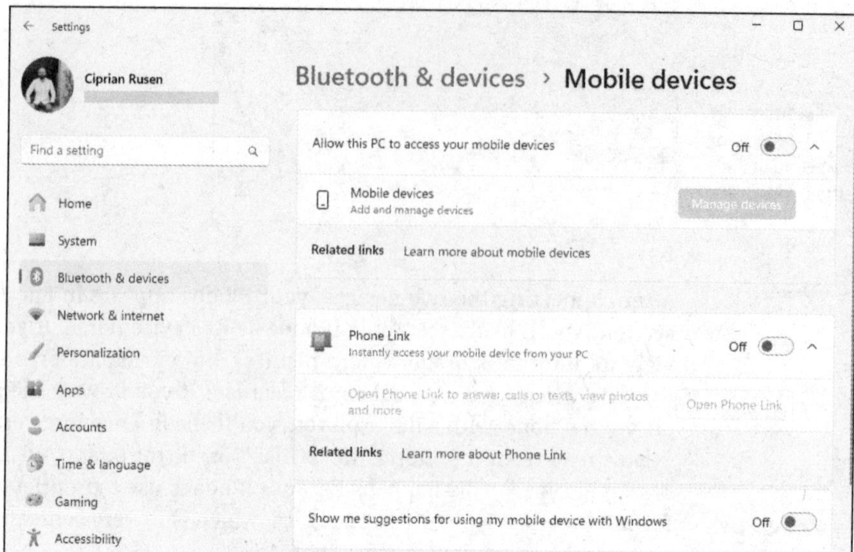

FIGURE 2-3: Starting the phone link is done from the Settings app.

3. **Click or tap to turn on the switch next to Phone Link.**

   The Phone Link window opens, asking you to choose your device.

4. **Choose iPhone, followed by your Microsoft account, and then click or tap Continue.**

   Windows Security verifies your identity. Depending on how your Windows 11 computer is set up, you're asked to authenticate using your PIN, Windows Hello face, or fingerprint recognition.

5. **Verify your identity using one of the options offered by Windows Security.**

   You're asked to open your iPhone camera and scan a QR code, as shown in Figure 2-4.

6. **On your iPhone, do the following:**

   a. **Open the Camera app and scan the QR code shown on your PC.** You're asked to pair your devices.

   b. **Tap Open, followed by Continue.** Your iPhone asks whether you want to allow Link to Windows to find Bluetooth devices.

   c. **Tap Allow.** You see a pairing code on your PC, while on your iPhone, you receive a Bluetooth Pairing Request.

7. **On your PC, Phone Link says you're almost there and shares two steps you must perform on your iPhone in its Bluetooth Settings, as shown in Figure 2-5.**

   Without these steps, you won't be able to utilize Phone Link and all its features.

FIGURE 2-4: Scan the QR code with your iPhone and follow the instructions closely.

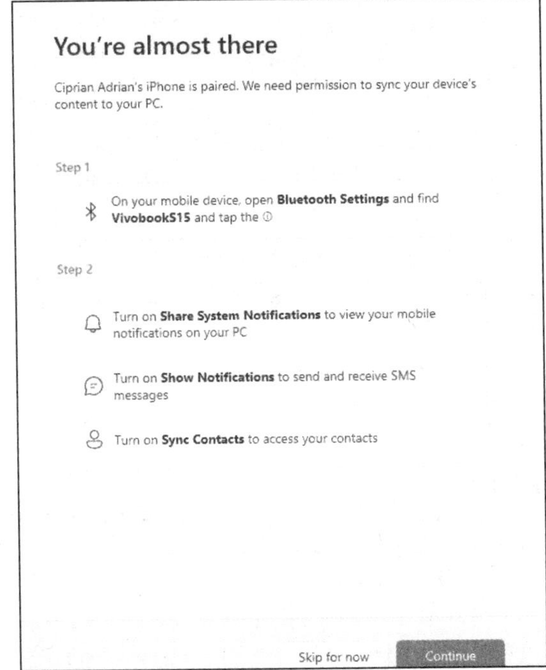

FIGURE 2-5: Phone Link shares the settings you must enable on your iPhone.

8. **On your iPhone, follow the instructions shared by Phone Link.**

9. **On your PC, click or tap Continue.**

   Phone Link informs you that you're all set.

10. **Click or tap Continue one more time.**

    On your PC, you see the Phone Link window, displaying a welcome message similar to Figure 2-6.

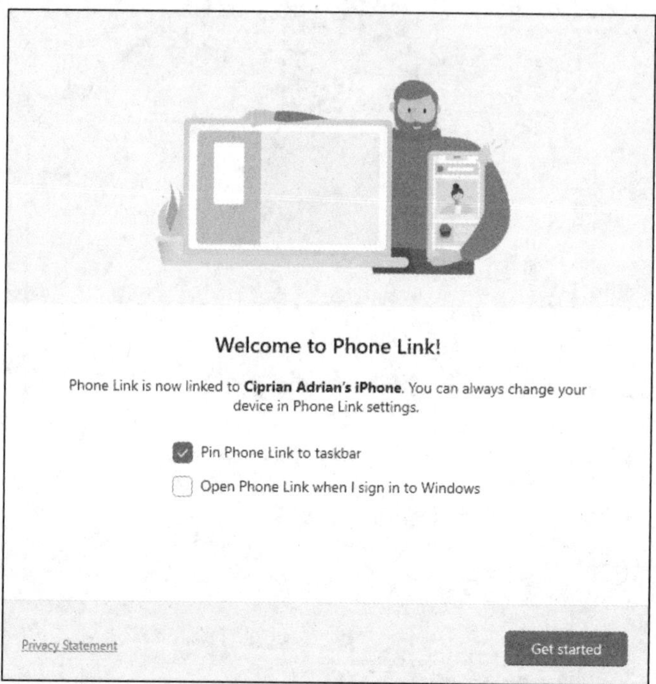

Welcome to Phone Link!
Phone Link is now linked to Ciprian Adrian's iPhone. You can always change your device in Phone Link settings.
Pin Phone Link to taskbar
Open Phone Link when I sign in to Windows
Privacy Statement
Get started

FIGURE 2-6: The Phone Link app welcomes you.

11. **On your Windows 11 PC, choose either Pin Phone Link to Taskbar or Open Phone Link When I Sign In to Windows.**

12. **Click or tap Get Started, and then follow the remaining steps in the welcome dialog.**

    You can start using Phone Link to interact with your iPhone.

TECHNICAL STUFF

If you didn't change all the settings recommended by Phone Link in Step 7, the Phone Link app will request that you grant it additional permissions when you start using it. If so, click or tap Show Me How and follow the instructions.

Using Phone Link with your iPhone

Now that you've paired your iPhone with your Windows 11 PC, it's time to use Phone Link to interact with your iPhone from your PC. You can do things like check and send messages straight from your PC, send and receive calls, check your iPhone notifications, and control music playback. Here's a brief tour to familiarize yourself with Phone Link:

1. **Click or tap the Start icon and then All.**

   You see the list of apps available on your Windows 11 computer or device.

2. **Scroll down to Phone Link and click or tap its shortcut.**

   The Phone Link app opens, as shown in Figure 2-7.

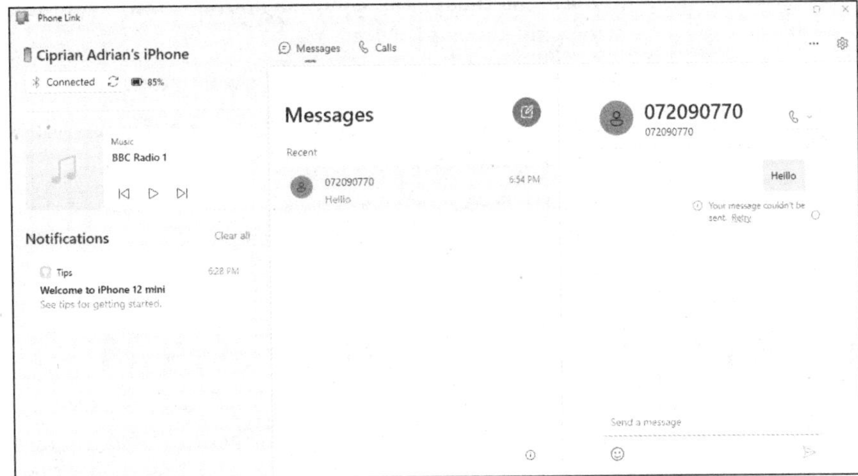

FIGURE 2-7: The options shown by Phone Link when using an iPhone.

3. **If you see a notification on the left side of the Phone Link app, read it, and then click or tap X in its top-right corner to close it.**

   The notification is cleared, making room for new ones.

4. **Click or tap Messages and check the messages you recently received on your smartphone.**
5. **Click or tap Calls and check who has called you recently.**
6. **To refresh all the content shown by Phone Link, click or tap the Refresh icon under your iPhone's name.**
7. **When you're finished using Phone Link, click or tap X in its top-right corner to close it.**

Disabling Phone Link

If you tried the Phone Link app and decided you dislike it, here's how to stop using it and disable its automatic link between your computer and your iPhone:

1. **Click or tap the Start icon and then All.**

   You see the list of apps available on your Windows 11 computer or device.

2. **Scroll down to Phone Link and click or tap its shortcut.**

   The Phone Link app opens (refer to Figure 2-7).

3. **Click or tap the Settings icon in the top-right corner of Phone Link.**
4. **Select Devices, and then click or tap the three vertical lines next to your iPhone's name.**
5. **In the menu that opens, choose Remove. Confirm your choice by clicking or tapping Remove Device.**
6. **On your iPhone, open Settings and tap Bluetooth.**
7. **Tap the *i*-in-a-circle to the right of the name of your Windows 11 PC, and then tap Forget Device.**

   The next time you open Phone Link on your PC, you must re-create the link between your iPhone and your computer.

Installing iCloud on Windows 11

Your iPhone uses iCloud to back up your photos, mail, contacts, bookmarks, and other items. Switching your iPad or iPhone over to using iCloud is simple: In the iPad or iPhone Settings app, tap your Apple Account, and then tap iCloud. Make sure you have the right account set up. (You don't want to hassle with mismatched accounts.) Tap iCloud Backup and turn on the switch to Back Up This iPhone or Back Up This iPad. Then wait.

TIP

Your initial iCloud backup may take hours and is best done when connected to fast Wi-Fi.

You can then use iCloud to synchronize your iPhone data with other devices, including those made by Apple or Microsoft. If you regularly use Windows 11, iCloud is a handy way to get access to what you want from your iPhone. However, you must install and configure iCloud to access it, like this:

1. **Open the Microsoft Store, search for and select iCloud, and then click or tap Get or Install.**

   The progress of the installation is shown under the Get/Install button.

2. **In the Microsoft Store window, click or tap Open. In the User Account Control prompt that asks for permissions, click or tap Yes.**

   You see the iCloud app window.

3. **Click or tap on Get Started, type your Apple ID and password, and then click or tap Sign In.**

   A verification code is sent to your iPhone.

4. **On your iPhone, tap Allow to see the verification code.**

5. **In the iCloud app's prompt on your Windows 11 PC, type the verification from your iPhone.**

   You're asked whether you want to sync iCloud photos to Microsoft Photos, followed by other questions about integrating iCloud with other Windows 11 apps.

6. **Make your choice for the first question and the ones that follow. When you're done, click or tap Finish Setup.**

   You see the iCloud user interface sharing a summary of your choices, as shown in Figure 2-8.

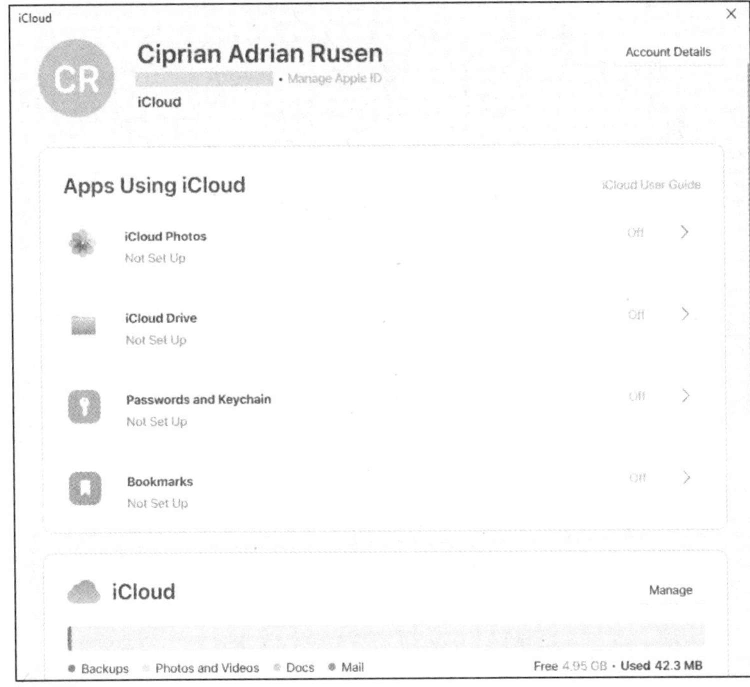

FIGURE 2-8: iCloud lets you choose what you want to sync between your iPhone and Windows 11.

IN THIS CHAPTER

» Adding Hyper-V to Windows 11

» Creating virtual machines

» Using virtual machines

Chapter 3

Working with Hyper-V

Hyper-V is like having a computer within your computer. It's a niche feature in Windows 11 Pro, Enterprise, and Education that lets you create and run virtual machines. Think of a *virtual machines* as separate, self-contained computers that exist in your host computer. They can run different operating systems, including different versions of Windows and Linux, without affecting your main computer.

Why would you want this? Hyper-V is great for testing software without risking your main system, running old programs that don't work on newer versions of Windows, or even learning about different operating systems without needing additional computers. It's especially useful to IT professionals, software developers, and tech enthusiasts who need to work with multiple operating systems.

In this chapter, I share how to add Hyper-V to your Windows 11 computer, create your first virtual machine, and start using it. I walk through the process step-by-step, from setting up Hyper-V to running your virtual machine. You'll also learn how to download premade virtual machines from Microsoft, which can save you time and effort. By the end of this chapter, you'll be comfortable creating, starting, and using virtual machines in Hyper-V. And, don't worry if it sounds complicated — I keep things simple and easy to follow, without getting too technical.

Adding Hyper-V to Windows 11

The Hyper-V platform includes the Hyper-V hypervisor and a group of services that manage virtual hardware, connect to virtual networks, and run virtual machines. In Windows 11, you interact directly with only two apps: Hyper-V Manager and Virtual Machine Connection.

As its name implies, Hyper-V Manager provides the management features. You can use it to create virtual machines, adjust the configuration of existing ones, and modify the settings of the Hyper-V platform itself. Virtual Machine Connection is the app that lets you interact with running virtual machines by using the keyboard and mouse of the host PC.

Before you can use Hyper-V, you must have Windows 11 Pro, Enterprise, or Education installed on your computer. Hyper-V isn't included by default, so you must add it to your machine from the list of optional features offered by Microsoft. Here's how:

1. **Click or tap in the Search box on the taskbar and type** features. **At the top of the ensuing list, choose Turn Windows Features On or Off.**

   The Windows Features dialog shown in Figure 3-1 appears. You see a list of optional features that can be added to your Windows 11 machine.

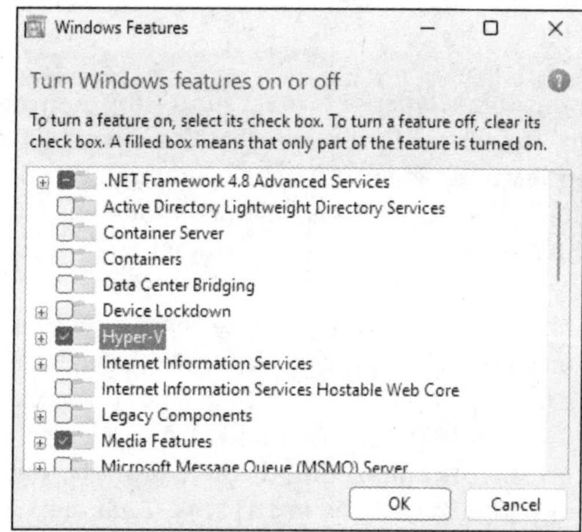

FIGURE 3-1: Adding optional features to Windows 11.

2. **Select the box next to Hyper-V, and then click or tap OK.**

   Windows spends some time searching for, downloading, and installing the required files. When the process is over, you're informed that it has completed the requested changes.

3. **Close all open apps and files, save any ongoing work you may have, and then choose Restart Now in the Windows Features dialog.**

   Windows 11 reboots your system and shows you the progress of the Hyper-V installation in percentages. When it finishes, it displays the lock screen.

4. **Click or tap anywhere on the lock screen and sign in.**

   You see the Windows 11 desktop, and Hyper-V is available for use.

TIP

The same steps can be used to add other niche features to Windows 11, including the Windows Subsystem for Linux or Internet Information Services (IIS), which may be useful to software developers and IT professionals.

Working with Hyper-V Virtual Machines

While you can use Hyper-V Manager to create your own virtual machine, the process is lengthy and involves adjusting many settings. If you need a virtual machine to test a specific app, file, or feature of Windows 11 for a while, you can download a premade virtual machine straight from Microsoft. It includes an evaluation version of Windows 11 Enterprise, which has an expiry date communicated on its download page. This virtual machine also includes tools that are useful for developers, such as Visual Studio, the Windows Subsystem for Linux, and Windows Terminal. But even if you're not a software developer, you too can download and add a virtual machine to Hyper-V Manager. You can also use Hyper-V Manager to run virtual machines with other operating systems, such as older Windows versions, and Linux.

To download a Windows 11 virtual machine, head over to `https://developer.microsoft.com/en-us/windows/downloads/virtual-machines/` and choose the Hyper-V option. The ZIP file you'll download is large, around 21 GB, so be patient until the download finishes. The download will be especially lengthy if you're using a slow internet connection. After you download the ZIP file and extract its content, you'll find a file for the virtual machine with the extension (or file type) VHDX. This is the file you're going to use in Hyper-V Manager.

REMEMBER

Another aspect to remember is that Microsoft's trial virtual machines require at least 8 GB of RAM and at least 70 GB of free storage space. At the time of this writing, these virtual machines don't work on computers with ARM processors, and Microsoft doesn't have any plans to create such virtual machines.

Creating virtual machines with Hyper-V Manager

After you've downloaded the virtual machine from Microsoft, it's time to create a virtual machine with it on your Windows 11 computer. The process is shorter than when creating other types of virtual machines, for which you don't have a VHDX file. Here's how it works:

1. **Click or tap in the Search box on the taskbar and type** hyper-v. **In the list of results, choose Hyper-V Manager. If you see a UAC prompt, click or tap Yes.**

   The Hyper-V Manager app window appears.

2. **In the column on the left, click or tap your computer's name.**

   The Hyper-V Manager app displays the options shown in Figure 3-2.

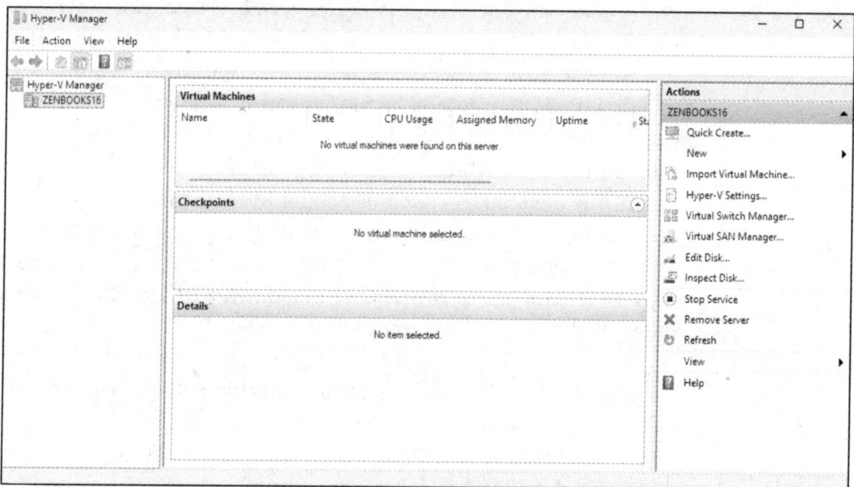

FIGURE 3-2: The Hyper-V Manager allows you to create and manage virtual machines.

3. **In the column on the right, click or tap Quick Create.**

   You see the Create Virtual Machine wizard shown in Figure 3-3.

4. **Select Windows 11 Dev Environment, and then click or tap Local Installation Source, followed by Change Installation Source.**

   The Open window appears, where you must find the VHDX file you downloaded earlier.

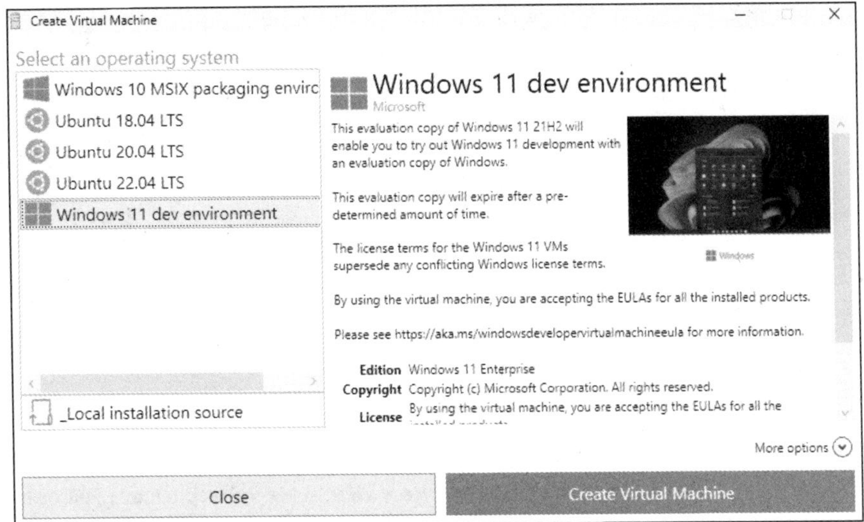

FIGURE 3-3: Creating a virtual machine in Hyper-V Manager.

5. **Browse your computer, select the VHDX file with the virtual machine, and choose Open.**

   The virtual machine you're about to create will use the data and settings from the file you've downloaded from Microsoft.

6. **Type a name for your virtual machine, and then click or tap Create Virtual Machine.**

   The Create Virtual Machine wizard creates the virtual disk necessary for the virtual machine. This process requires a bit of time, so be patient. When it's over, you're informed that the virtual machine was created successfully.

7. **Click or tap X in the top-right corner to close the Create Virtual Machine wizard.**

   You see the new virtual machine in the Virtual Machines section, in the middle section of Hyper-V Manager.

Using a Hyper-V virtual machine

Hyper-V virtual machines are opened in the Virtual Machine Connection window. While you're asked to set a specific display resolution for each virtual machine, you can change it later to any resolution you want from those supported. After you set up these virtual machines, they function like independent computers but are contained in an app window on your desktop.

Here's how to start, use, and shut down a Hyper-V virtual machine:

1. **Click or tap in the Search box on the taskbar and type** hyper-v. **In the list of results, choose Hyper-V Manager.**

   The Hyper-V Manager app window appears.

2. **In the column on the left, click or tap your computer's name.**

   The Hyper-V Manager app displays the options shown previously in Figure 3-2.

3. **In the Virtual Machines section, select the virtual machine you want to use.**

   A new set of options is shown in the column on the right side of Hyper-V Manager.

4. **On the right, under New Virtual Machine, click or tap Connect.**

   You see a new window stating that the selected virtual machine is turned off.

5. **Choose Start.**

   Hyper-V starts your virtual machine and displays the progress of this operation. When the virtual machine is started and Windows 11 is loaded, you're asked to select the size of your desktop, as shown in Figure 3-4.

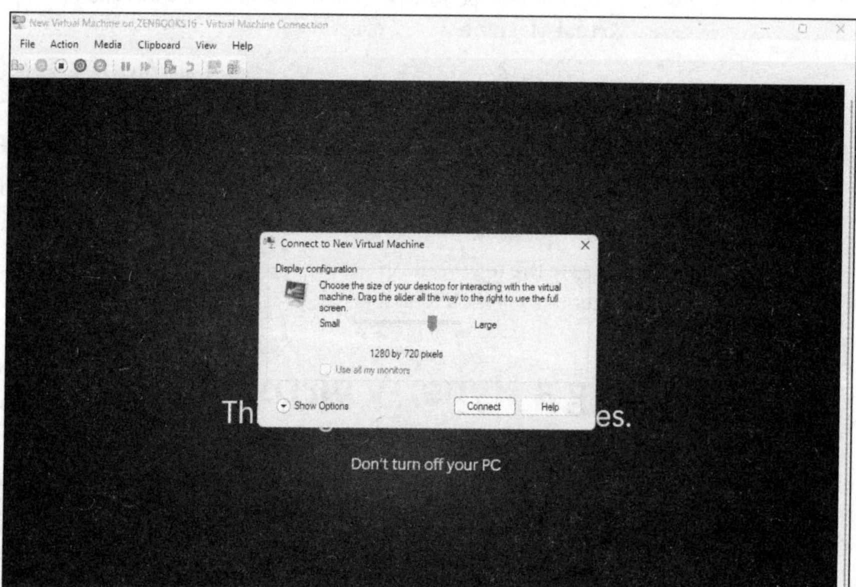

FIGURE 3-4: Choosing the size of your desktop before using the virtual machine.

6. **Select the size you want and click or tap Connect.**

   Hyper-V makes the necessary adjustments, and you can then sign in to Windows 11, in the virtual machine you're running.

7. **Click or tap Sign In, and you see the desktop of your virtual machine.**

   Use the virtual machine as needed. It accepts keyboard and mouse input, as if it were an app on your computer. Also, don't hesitate to use the toolbar at the top to operate the virtual machine.

8. **When you're finished working with the virtual machine, click or tap Action, followed by Shut Down. Confirm your choice by clicking or tapping Shut Down one more time.**

   Hyper-V shuts down the virtual machine.

9. **Click or tap X in the top-right corner to close the virtual machine.**

   Hyper-V shuts down the virtual machine.

TIP

To access the Ctrl+Alt+Del function in a Hyper-V virtual machine, use Ctrl+Alt+End or the corresponding toolbar button. Windows 11 reserves the actual Ctrl+Alt+Del combination for the host computer.

IN THIS CHAPTER

» Finding out which Windows apps you must have

» Adding Google Drive and other Google apps to Windows

» Figuring out what software you don't need

Chapter 4

Discovering the Best Free Windows Add-Ons

I really like Windows 11, but it has some limitations that can only be addressed by using non-Microsoft software. For instance, while the Media Player app works well for playing video files, it can't compare to the VLC Media Player, which is available online for free. Another example is Paint, which has received many recent upgrades, but it can't hold a candle to Paint.NET when you need to do some advanced picture editing.

In this chapter, I will guide you through two different types of software. First, there are a few programs that will help fix some of the weaknesses of Windows. Second, there is a larger group of applications that simply improve the functionality of Windows. Both collections have one thing in common: They are free for personal use.

At the end of this chapter, I turn to one of my favorite topics: software that you *don't* need and should never pay one cent to acquire.

Windows Apps You Absolutely Must Have

Depending on what kind of Windows 11 computer or device you're using, there's a short and sweet list of free software you need. Some of it is very useful, and it's going to make you more productive. Here's what I recommend you consider installing.

VLC Media Player

Although Microsoft made some improvements to its media handling in Windows 11 — adding the capability to play FLAC lossless audio, MKV video, and a handful of less interesting media formats — it remains underpowered in its capability to work with a wide variety of media files.

One issue is that the Media Player app from Windows 11 cannot play movies from DVDs or Blu-ray discs because Microsoft chose not to pay for the required codecs (programs that compress and decompress media files so they can be played back to you) starting from the days of Windows 8. While it's true that many people no longer purchase computers with DVD drives, there are still some of us who have movie collections that we value. I personally have one.

Therefore, if you're looking for a comprehensive media player that can handle all media formats, including your old-school movie collection stored on DVDs and/or Blu-rays, I highly recommend the free VLC Media Player, or VLC for short. Its versatility and wide range of supported formats make it a worthy addition to your Windows 11 experience.

Unlike other media players, VLC sports simple controls; built-in codecs for almost every file type imaginable; and a large, vocal online support community. VLC plays internet-streaming media with a click, records media played on your screen, converts between file types, and even supports individual-frame screenshots. VLC is also well-known for tolerating incomplete or damaged media files. It will even start to play downloaded media before the download is finished.

Hop over to VLC (`www.videolan.org`) and install it (see Figure 4-1). You can also look for it in the Microsoft Store, install it from there, and benefit from automated updates. Yes, it looks spartan, but it works very well.

Recuva

Being able to recover deleted files has always been important for computer users. For many years now, the most popular undeleter has been Recuva. It's fast, free (even though it has a paid Pro version), and very thorough. You can see it in action in Figure 4-2.

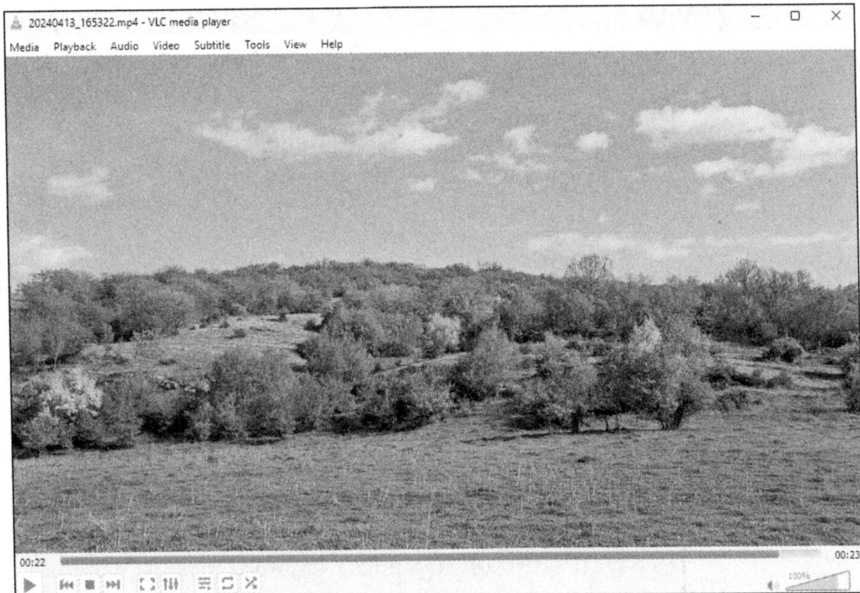

FIGURE 4-1: VLC Media Player plays every song and video type imaginable, even your video DVDs.

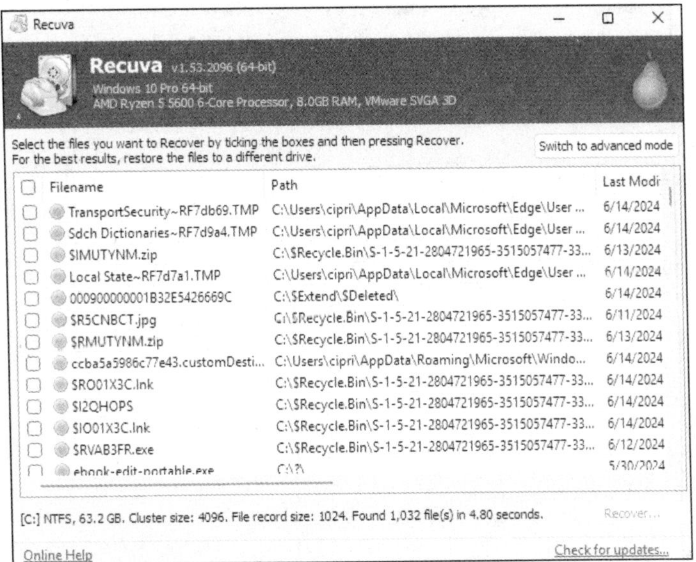

FIGURE 4-2: Recuva undeletes files from your computer.

When you empty the recycle bin, the files that are part of it aren't destroyed; rather, the space they occupy is marked as free space, available for writing new data. Undelete routines scan your hard drive or SSD and put the pieces back. As long as you haven't added new data to a drive, undelete (almost) always works. And if you've added some data, there's still a good chance that you can get most of the deleted stuff back.

Recuva can also be used to recover deleted data from a USB drive, an SD card, and many smartphones and digital cameras that can be attached to your PC.

Powerful stuff. For more advanced features, there's a Pro version for about $20. You can find more details at `www.ccleaner.com/recuva`.

The Best of the Rest — All Free

Here are my recommendations for useful programs that you may or may not want, depending on your circumstances:

Ninite

Leading the list of traditional desktop apps is one that helps you install (and update) other programs. Actually, it isn't a program — it's a website. When you start looking for desktop apps to install, your first stop should be to `https://ninite.com/` (see Figure 4-3). Select the applications you want, click or tap Get Your Ninite, and when you run the resulting file, Ninite will download the latest versions of those apps, install them free of crapware, and leave you in the driver's seat.

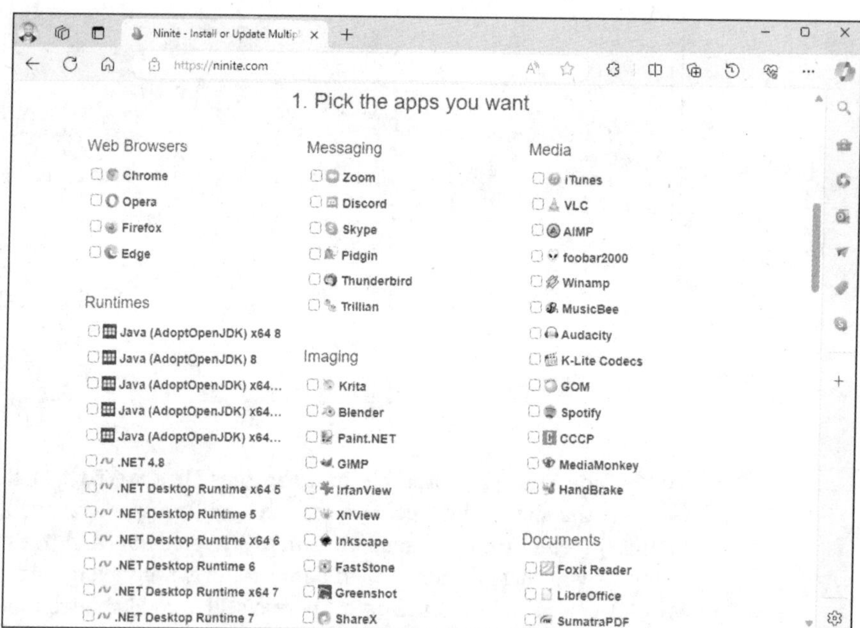

FIGURE 4-3: Install or update popular desktop apps with Ninite.

Need to update your apps? Run the same Ninite file again. Everything's brought up to date without any hassle. For the full royal treatment — where Ninite notifies you of changes to programs you've installed and allows you to deploy updates from a web browser —Ninite Pro ($1/month for one computer) works like a champ.

The beauty of the Ninite approach is that all these apps are a click away — no fuss, nags, or charge. It's the best way I know to install a bunch of good programs on a new machine in just a few minutes. The downside? Its app library is not exceptionally large and misses a few of my favorite desktop apps.

BCUninstaller (Bulk Crap Uninstaller)

Bulk Crap Uninstaller (in short BCUninstaller or BCU) is a free, open-source program that you can use to make sure that you completely remove installed programs from Windows and all the traces they leave behind. You can find it at `www.bcuninstaller.com`, download it, and install it from there.

When you use BCUninstaller, you first select the app that you want to remove from the list shown in Figure 4-4 and follow its Uninstall wizard. BCU first runs the uninstaller for the app you chose and watches while it works, looking for the location of program files and for registry keys that the uninstaller zaps. It then goes in and removes leftover pieces based on the locations and keys that the app's uninstaller took out.

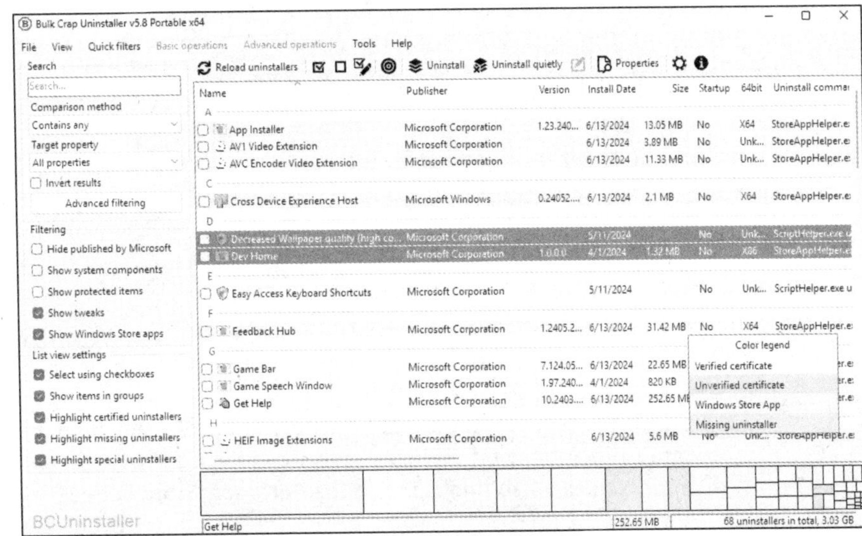

FIGURE 4-4: BCU helps you remove Windows apps completely, as well as their leftovers.

BCUninstaller gives you a great deal of flexibility in deciding just how much you want to clean and what you want to save. It also does a great job at making backups of Windows Registry keys before deleting them so that you can revert back if something was removed in by mistake.

This program can be used in both private and commercial settings for free and with no obligations as long as the conditions of its Apache 2.0 open-source license are not broken.

Paint.NET

In Book 4, Chapter 10, I talk about the Paint app from Windows 11, which can help you put together graphics in a pinch. However, for powerful, easy-to-use photo editing with layers, plugins, and all sorts of special effects, along with a compact and easily understood interface, I stick with Paint.NET (see Figure 4-5).

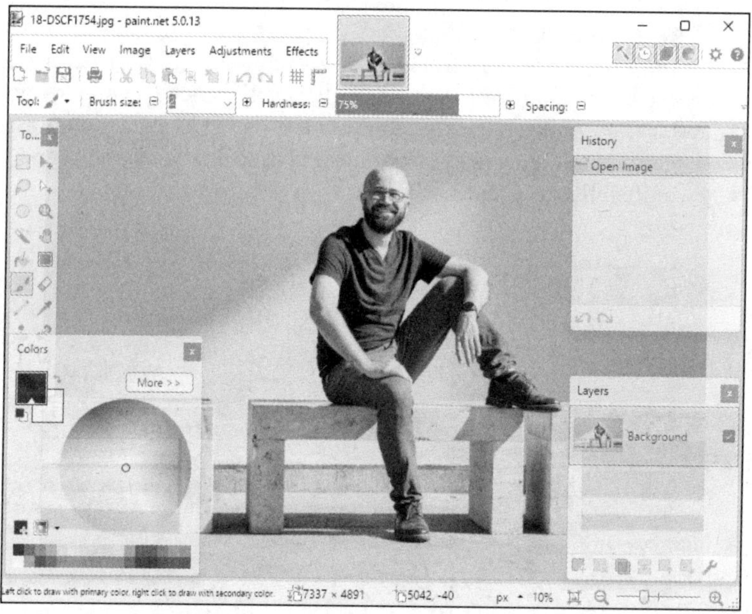

FIGURE 4-5: Paint.NET is a powerful image editor.

This program puts all the editing tools a nonprofessional might reasonably expect into a remarkably intuitive package. Download it at `www.getpaint.net` and give it a try. You can also find it inside the Microsoft Store but getting it from there will cost you $9.99.

WARNING

Pay attention when downloading Paint.NET. Unfortunately, its official site displays many intrusive ads. Make sure to close them all, and don't get tricked into downloading something else. If you want a simpler download process, try `www.techspot.com/downloads/657-paint-net.html` instead.

TIP

With dozens of good — even great — free image editors around, it's hard to choose one above the others. IrfanView, for example, has tremendous viewing, organizing, and resizing capabilities, but it is not as versatile at editing as Paint.NET.

7-Zip

Another venerable utility, 7-Zip (`www.7-zip.org`) still rates as a must-have, even though Windows 11 supports the ZIP format natively and now works with the 7z and TAR formats, too.

Why? Because some people will send you files in the RAR archive format from time to time, and 7-Zip is the fast, easy, free way to handle them. Another reason is that 7-Zip allows you to create password-protected file archives in any format you want, and Windows can't do that, at least not yet.

7-Zip also creates self-extracting EXE files, which can come in handy (although heaven help you if you ever try to email one — most email scanners won't let an EXE file through because such files are usually used to spread malware). And it supports AES-256-bit encryption. Its interface may look clunky by modern standards (see Figure 4-6), but it gets the job done with ZIP, RAR, CAB, ARJ, TAR, 7z, and many lesser-known formats. It even lets you extract files from ISO disc images.

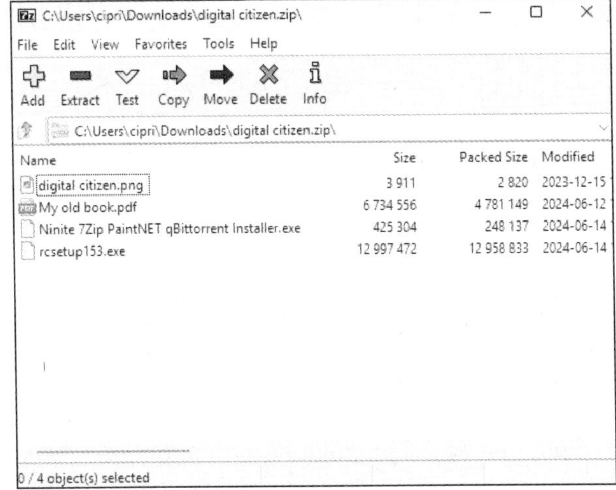

FIGURE 4-6: 7-Zip may not have the greatest interface, but it's a powerful file archiver.

This app is another poster boy for the open-source community because it does all these amazing things free of charge, without bundling unwanted browser extensions or other types of crapware, and is continuously updated and improved.

TIP

You don't need to register or pay for 7-Zip. Don't fall for a website with a similar name. To get the real, original, one-and-only free 7-Zip with a crapware-free installer, go to www.7-zip.org.

qBittorrent

If you aren't yet using torrents (a method of distributing files over the internet), you may feel tempted to start now. Torrents have gotten a bad rap for spreading illegal pirated software, music, movies, you name it. Although that reputation is entirely deserved, it's also true that many torrents are legitimate. And they are the single most efficient way to distribute files online.

For years I've used and recommended uTorrent, but the current version's installer includes crapware — and in previous versions, it has installed some obnoxious crapware.

Instead, try qBittorrent, shown in Figure 4-7. It's simple, fast, and easy to use, and it supports magnet links (which simplify downloads) with extensive bandwidth reporting and management. Download it at www.qbittorrent.org.

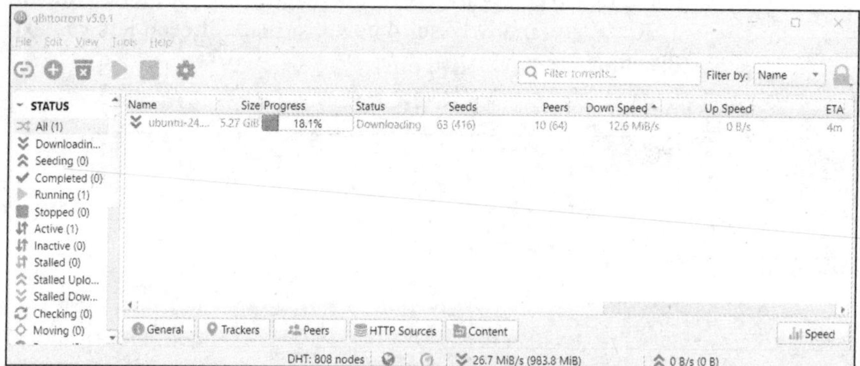

FIGURE 4-7: qBittorrent doesn't have uTorrent's baggage.

Other interesting free software

If you connect over public Wi-Fi, like the one in a coffee shop, you should use a Virtual Private Network (VPN). I talk about VPNs in Book 9, Chapter 3. Session hijacking, pioneered by the program Firesheep, can let others pose as you, even while your session is in progress. Navigating the web using only secure websites with the HTTPS protocol helps, but even that traffic can be subverted in certain circumstances. When you're connected to a network that you don't know and trust, your best bet is to stick with using VPN.

TIP

Need to rip a DVD? Forget trying to use Windows. Get the open-source, free, and junk-free HandBrake at `https://handbrake.fr`. Works like a champ on any DVD.

Wonder what programs run whenever you start Windows? Look at Microsoft's venerable and free-as-a-breeze Autoruns at `learn.microsoft.com/en-us/sysinternals/downloads/autoruns`. Autoruns finds more autostarting programs (add-ins, drivers, codecs, gadgets, shell extensions, whatever) in more obscure places than any other program anywhere. Autoruns not only lists the autorunning programs but also lets you turn off individual programs. It has many features, including the ability to filter out Microsoft-signed programs, a quick way to jump to folders holding autostarting programs, and a command-line version that lets you display file hashes. Autoruns doesn't require installation. It's a program that runs, collects information, displays it using a simple user interface, allows you to manage your system, and then you can close it and go about your day.

TIP

Want to know what hardware you have? It's a common question that's easily answered with a nifty free utility called HWiNFO, available at `www.hwinfo.com`. HWiNFO delves into every nook and cranny. From the summary to a detailed tree of information, HWiNFO can tell you everything anyone could want to know about your machine. You can also enable real-time monitoring which tells you the status of everything under the sun: temperatures, speeds, usage, clocks, voltages, wattages, hard drive SMART stats, read rates, write rates, GPU load, network throughput, and on and on.

Dropbox, Google Drive, or OneDrive?

Even if the thought of putting your data on the internet drives you nuts, sooner or later, you're going to want a way to store data away from your main computer, and you're going to want an easy way to share data with other people and other devices (desktops, laptops, tablets, and smartphones).

Choosing a cloud storage service can be tough as there's no clear winner among them. Just choose one and set it up. Having cloud storage could be a lifesaver one day. For this book, I used Dropbox to store and share all the chapters and images. I keep my personal files on OneDrive, and I use Google Drive for my blogging work at Digital Citizen.

They all have free introductory options, and some give you a good amount of storage for free or for a small fee. Some even provide a large amount of storage if you subscribe to a related service such as Microsoft 365. Simply take a look at their plans (see Figure 4-8) and choose the one you consider best.

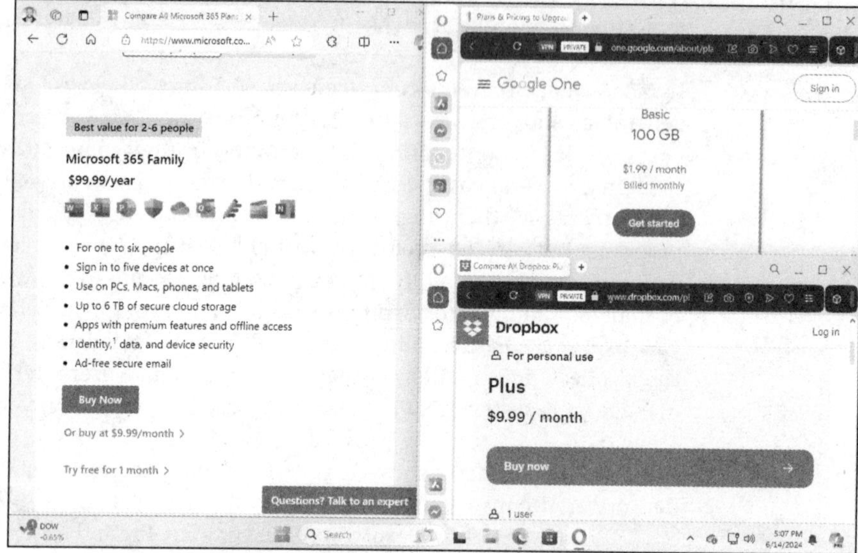

FIGURE 4-8: Check the plans available for Dropbox, OneDrive (Microsoft 365), and Google Drive (Google One).

Adding Google's Apps to Windows

If your needs are simple and you don't have to edit fancy documents created in Word, Excel, or PowerPoint, you may be able to get by with Google's web apps that are included in their Google Workspace (head to `workspace.google.com`) or LibreOffice. The web-based Microsoft 365 Online apps are also good — and free for personal use. Go to `www.microsoft365.com` and try them out.

TIP

Let's do a bit of math: LibreOffice is free. Google apps are free for personal use. Microsoft 365 Family (which includes six licenses), $99.99/year. Office 2024 Home (for personal use only, no Outlook), $149.99. Home & Business, $249.99. Microsoft 365 Online, free for personal use.

The big advantage to Microsoft 365 subscriptions: You get not only licenses for six users who get the latest versions of the Office programs — Word, Excel, PowerPoint, Outlook, OneNote, Access, and Publisher — for PCs or Macs but also licenses for five devices for each user. They can use any kind of device: a tablet, a smartphone, a PC, a MAC, and so on. In addition, you get 1TB of OneDrive online storage per user for up to six users. Unless you have a visceral reaction to renting Office — I can sympathize — Microsoft 365 at $100/year or less comes across as a bargain.

Whenever somebody asks me, "Why do you recommend Microsoft 365 when LibreOffice does everything for free?" I must cringe. It's true that Office is expensive, and with Microsoft 365, you're locked into the annual or monthly fee. It's also true that good, but not great, alternatives exist, including Google Workspace. But here are two substantial problems:

- » As much as I would love to recommend a free replacement for Word, Excel, or PowerPoint, the simple fact is that the free alternatives (other than Microsoft 365 Online) aren't 100 percent compatible. If you work with complex files with tons of data and diverse formatting, you may encounter issues. Even Microsoft's free Office web apps aren't as fully featured as the real Word, Excel, and PowerPoint. If your needs are modest, by all means, explore the alternatives. But if you must edit a document that somebody else is going to use and it has any unusual formatting, you may end up with a mess.
- » LibreOffice does a good enough job, but its user interface is rather dated, it doesn't feature any online collaboration features, and it lacks apps that can do any kind of document editing on mobile devices like iPhones, iPads, or Android smartphones and tablets.

If you can get by with Google Workspace, and you don't mind doing all your document editing in a web browser, then you'll want to add Google Drive to File Explorer so that you can access your online documents as if they were files on your computer.

Adding Google Drive to File Explorer

Unfortunately, Google doesn't love Microsoft at all, and except for their popular Google Chrome browser, they don't provide much in terms of apps for Windows. This is the reason we don't have Google apps such as Docs, Sheets, or Slides for Windows, but we do have them for Android and iOS. Luckily, we can install Google Drive for Windows and have it work in a way that is similar to OneDrive and Dropbox. Here's where to get it and how to install it:

1. **Open your favorite web browser and navigate to** `support.google.com/drive/answer/10838124?hl=en`.
2. **Click or tap Install & Set Up Drive for Desktop for Windows to expand this section.**

   You might have to scroll to find this section. You should see instructions for downloading Google Drive for desktop, as well as a download button, shown in Figure 4-9.

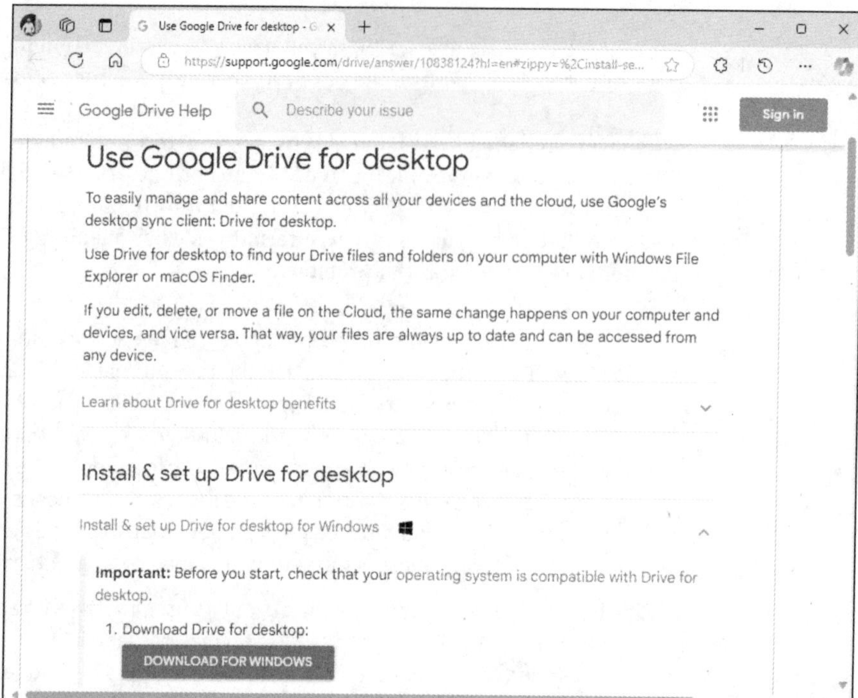

FIGURE 4-9: Download Google Drive for Windows from this page.

3. **Click or tap Download for Windows.**

   Your browser will download the GoogleDriveSetup.exe file on your computer.

4. **Open File Explorer and go to your Downloads folder.**
5. **Double-click or double-tap GoogleDriveSetup to install this app, and click or tap Yes when you see the User Account Control prompt.**

   The Google Drive installation wizard shown in Figure 4-10 appears.

6. **Choose the shortcuts you want added to your desktop and click or tap Install.**

   The wizard starts installing Google Drive on your Windows 11 computer.

7. **Click or tap Launch.**

   A wizard appears, welcoming you to Google Drive and presenting information about how it works.

8. **Click or tap Get Started, and then Sign In.**

   A web page appears in your web browser, where you're asked to enter your user account information.

9. **Enter your Google account username and password, and sign in.**

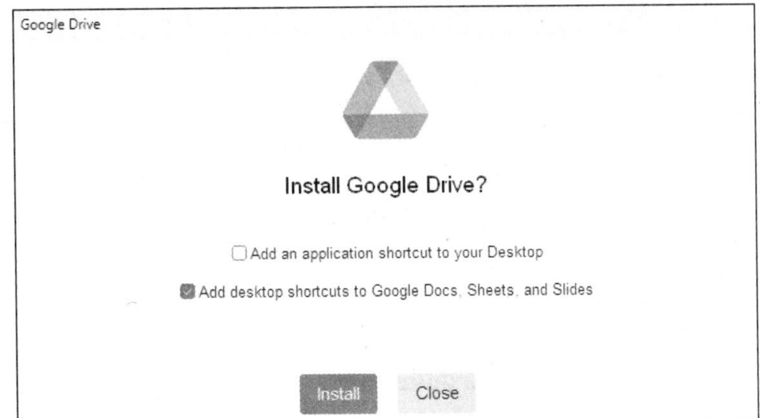

FIGURE 4-10: Installing Google Drive for Windows requires many steps.

10. **Close the web browser and return to the Google Drive wizard.**

    You are then asked to choose which folders from your computer you want to synchronize to Google Drive.

11. **Make your selections and click or tap Next until you reach the end of the wizard.**

    You are asked to choose many things, including whether you want to back up your photos and videos to Google Drive.

12. **When you've finished making your selections, click or tap Open Drive.**

    From now on, Google Drive shows up as a folder in File Explorer, just under your user folders on the left.

TIP

After Google Drive is installed on your Windows 11 machine, you can work with the files you stored there like they were local files and perform tasks like renaming them, deleting them, and moving them around. When you open a file from Google Drive, like a document or spreadsheet, it will open in your default web browser, using the appropriate Google app for it: Docs, Sheets, Slides, and so forth.

Making your own YouTube Music app

I use many Google services on a daily basis, and I'm sure most people reading this book do the same. One of those services is YouTube, and I watch videos on a variety of subjects like tech news, psychology, economics, history, world news, and local news. To make YouTube more profitable, Google has increased the number of ads viewers have to watch to access the service for free. At some point, this became very frustrating for me. So, I decided to pay for a YouTube Premium subscription to get rid of the ads. One important benefit of YouTube Premium is that it includes access to YouTube Music as well, which means you can stop paying for Spotify or any other music streaming service to save some money. It's interesting to note that YouTube Premium is separate from a Google One subscription, and they're not part of the same package.

Once I purchased this subscription, the issue for me was that Google doesn't offer a YouTube Music app for Windows. So, I found a workaround: I created one with the help of the Microsoft Edge browser. You can do the same with Google Chrome, but you have fewer personalization options. Here's how it works:

1. **Open Microsoft Edge and navigate to `music.youtube.com`.**
2. **Sign in with your Google account.**
3. **Click or tap the Settings and More button in the top-right corner.**

   The menu shown in Figure 4-11 appears.

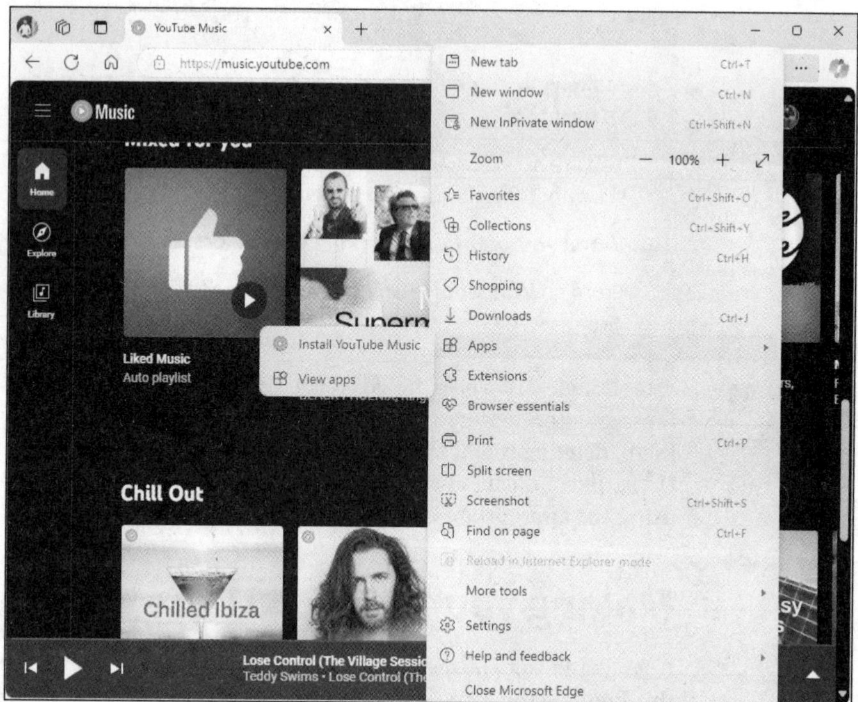

FIGURE 4-11: Installing YouTube Music from Microsoft Edge.

4. **Click or tap Apps followed by Install YouTube Music.**

   A pop-up appears, informing you on what is about to happen when you install YouTube Music.

5. **Choose Install.**

   The YouTube Music app that is created looks similar to Figure 4-12. You are asked whether you want to allow this app to pin itself to the taskbar, pin itself to the Start menu, create a desktop shortcut, and autostart on your device login.

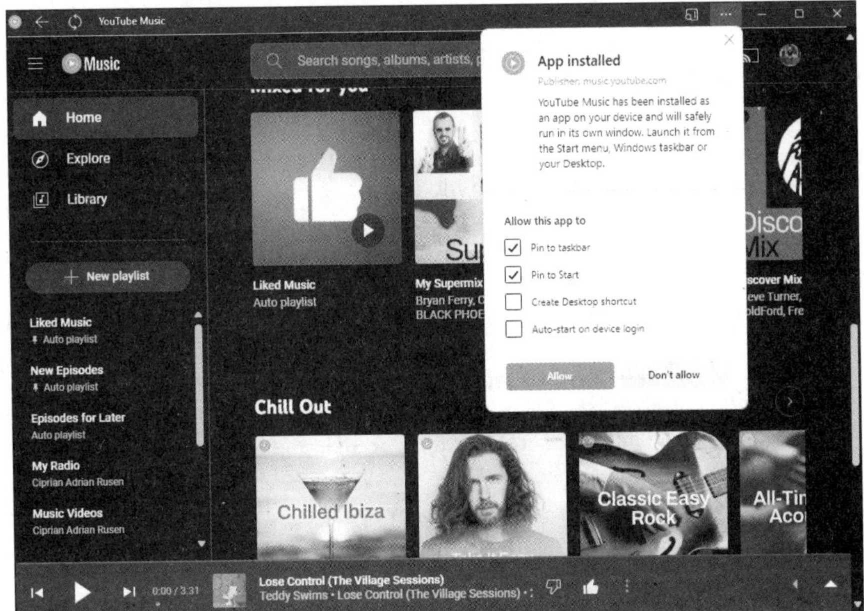

FIGURE 4-12: Choose the shortcuts you want for YouTube Music.

6. **Select the options you want and click or tap Allow.**
7. **If you see a prompt to pin the YouTube Music app to the taskbar, click or tap Yes.**

   The YouTube Music app is now added to Windows, and you can use it like any other app.

The YouTube Music app remains subscribed to your account, and it loads your playlists every time. It looks and works as if it were an individual Windows app. However, the reality is that it's running in Microsoft Edge as a browser tab. It's just not presented as such. You'll also notice that if you sign out from your Google account in Microsoft Edge, the YouTube Music app will get signed out as well, and you'll need to sign back in to continue using it.

TIP

Google doesn't offer a Gmail app for Windows, but you can add your Gmail account to the Outlook app and check your emails from it. Read Book 4, Chapter 3, to learn how to do that. If you don't like the Outlook app, you can use the same procedure to create a Gmail app for Windows. The only difference is that at Step 1, you navigate to `gmail.com`.

Don't Pay for Software You Don't Need!

If you've moved to Windows 11, there are several categories of software that you simply don't need. Why pay for any of it?

Some people write to ask me for recommendations about antivirus software, utility programs, registry cleaners, or backup programs. The simple fact is, if you've moved up to Windows 11, you don't need lots of this stuff.

In this, the last section of the final chapter in the book, I'm going to lay it on the line — point out what you don't need, in my opinion — and try to save you a bunch of money. With a bit of luck, the following handful of tips will save you the price of the book.

Windows 11 has all the antivirus software you need

Windows Security includes Microsoft Defender Antivirus, formerly known as Windows Defender. It works great and doesn't cost a cent. If you follow the recommendations in this book, you don't need to pay a penny for antivirus, antispyware, or anti-anything software. And you don't need a fancy outbound firewall either. (I talk about Windows Security and Windows Defender Firewall in Book 9, Chapter 2.)

You do need *other* kinds of security programs, however. I list those in Book 9, Chapter 3, and as you'll see for yourself, they're free of charge.

Windows 11 doesn't need a disk defragger

The way Windows stores and reclaims data on a hard drive can lead to file fragmentation, with data scattered all over the drive. Defragmentation reorganizes this data to speed up access by putting files back together.

While severely fragmented drives do run slower, the practical differences aren't significant, especially if you defrag your hard drives every month or two. It's important to note that you should never defrag a solid-state drive. Windows 11 trims them automatically once a month. What does this mean, you ask?

SSD trimming erases blocks of data that are no longer in use for storing files and marks them as free for rewriting with new data. In other words, **trim** is a command that helps Windows know precisely where the data that you want to move or delete is stored. That way, the solid-state drive can access only the blocks holding the data. Furthermore, whenever a file delete command is issued by the user or the operating system, the trim command immediately wipes the blocks where the files are stored. This means that the next time Windows tries to write new data in that area, it does not have to wait first to delete it.

The conclusion is that with Windows 11, there's no need to run a defrag. If you have a solid-state drive, defragging can wear it out and doesn't improve anything. For traditional hard drives, Windows performs a defrag by default once a week.

Windows 11 doesn't need a disk partitioner

I am not a fan of disk partitioning, but instead of getting into a technical argument (I know that dual-boot systems with a single hard drive require multiple partitions), I will focus on extolling the benefits of Windows 11's partition manager, named Disk Management.

This disk partition manager may not be a full-fledged program, but it handles everything with partitions that most people need, and it does the job without causing issues to your hard drive. This is more than I can say for some third-party disk partition managers.

To run Windows 11's built-in disk partitioner, type **partition** in the Search box on the taskbar. Click or tap Create and Format Hard Disk Partitions, which should be the first link. That displays the Disk Management program (see Figure 4-13), where it's easy to see, delete, expand, and change your partitions with a few simple clicks.

WARNING

If you're not familiar with disk management tools and concepts like partitioning, I think it's best that you don't use Disk Management without a detailed step-by-step tutorial that explains everything you need to know.

TIP

If you want to create a partition, right-click on any empty area and choose Create Volume. If you want to make a new partition on a volume that's full, right-click on the volume and choose Shrink Volume.

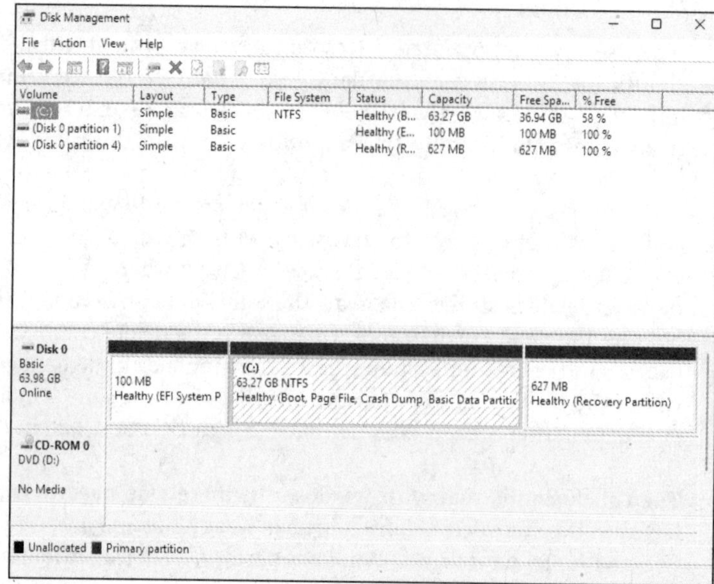

FIGURE 4-13: Disk Management helps you to manage your partitions with ease.

DON'T TURN OFF SERVICES OR HACK YOUR REGISTRY

Sometimes people write to me and are all excited because they've found a Windows service that they can turn off with no apparent ill effect. Other people tell me about a neat Windows hack they've found, in which a couple of flipped bits in the registry can speed up their computer. Before their Windows boot times were so slow. Now, with the hack enabled, it's like having a new PC again!

I refer to this phenomenon as the "Windows Registry Placebo Effect." You come across an article, book, or YouTube video that explains how to delve into the depths of Windows to make a change that the author claims will speed up your computer. When you try it, your computer actually does seem to run faster! Don't believe it? Try it and see for yourself: Your computer will perform significantly better!

Sure. Once upon a time in the early days of Windows, turning off a few *services* (little Windows background programs that run automatically every time you boot) may have added a minor performance boost to your daily Windows ME routine. Features such as Clippy could offer its helpful admonitions a fraction of a second faster. But these days, turning off Windows services is ineffective. Why? The service you turn off may be needed, oh, once every year. If the service is disabled, your PC may crash, lock up, or behave in a strange way. Services are small, low-overhead software components. Let them be. Real performance gains are made only through hardware upgrades, by removing unnecessary apps and junk files, and by other means.

Windows 11 doesn't need a registry cleaner

Windows Registry is a crucial database for the operating system, containing settings necessary for Windows and its services, apps, and background processes to run correctly. Microsoft doesn't include a built-in registry cleaner in Windows 11 because doing so would mean more trouble than it's worth.

I've never seen a real-world example of a modern Windows computer that improved in any significant way after running a registry cleaner. As with disk defraggers, registry cleaners may have served a useful purpose for Windows XP or Windows 7, but I think they're useless nowadays.

Unfortunately, many registry cleaners nowadays include "goodies" like spyware or adware you don't want on your computer. And even though they pretend to be easy to use, when used by people without the necessary technical background, they may cause system instability or even data loss, instead of improving performance.

Therefore, stay away from registry cleaners. They're not worth it. If you want more performance, it's a much better idea to remove unnecessary apps, disable startup programs you don't need, and clean up junk files.

Windows 11 doesn't need a backup program

Another type of software that used to be popular with computer users was backup programs. Fortunately for us, in Windows 11, we don't need this type of software either. That's because Microsoft offers two good options which are integrated into their operating system: the new Windows Backup app and the older File History. They're both good options, which work well, and I discuss them at length in Book 8, Chapter 1.

The only possible exception is if you're paranoid enough to want a clone backup of your entire hard drive. In that case, yes, you must buy a third-party backup program. But why bother? Windows 11's tools work just fine.

That covers the main points. I hope that this chapter alone justifies the cost of the book — the rest is just a bonus!

Index

Symbols and Numerics

A

B

C

D

E

F

G

H

I

N

O

P

Q

R

S

T

U

V

W

X

Y

Z

About the Author

Ciprian Adrian Rusen is a tech blogger and author of several titles about Windows and Office. From 2016 to 2023, Microsoft recognized him as Windows Insider MVP, an honorary title given for his public contribution and expertise in the Windows ecosystem. This book is one of the many ways he helps Windows users worldwide.

Ciprian leads the team at `www.digitalcitizen.life`, a website that provides useful how-to content for Windows, Android, and iPhone users. If you want to learn how to tame the computers, smartphones, and gadgets you use regularly, visit his blog and subscribe.

Dedication

To my partners in tech-writing crime: Codrut and Diana. Your attention to detail and thoughtful suggestions helped me improve this book. I appreciate you both.

Author's Acknowledgments

Thanks to Susan Pink, Guy Hart-Davis, Steve Hayes, and the Wiley staff for helping me put this massive tome together in record time.

Thanks to ASUS and AMD for loaning me the two Copilot+ PC devices I used to test things and write portions of this book.

A special thanks goes to the editorial team at `www.digitalcitizen.life` for being on top of all the problems — and answers — that make this book and the site tick.

Many thanks to all of you!

Publisher's Acknowledgments

Executive Editor: Steve Hayes
Project and Copy Editor: Susan Pink
Technical Editor: Guy Hart-Davis
Proofreader: Debbye Butler

Production Editor: Saikarthick Kumarasamy
Cover Image: © Alex Robinson/Getty Images